CYRIL Z. MEADOW INSTITUTE

ESSENTIAL PAPERS IN PSYCHOANALYSIS

ESSENTIAL PAPERS ON BORDERLINE DISORDERS

One Hundred Years at the Border

Michael H. Stone, M.D.
Editor

New York University Press
New York and London
1986

Library of Congress Cataloging-in-Publication Data
Main entry under title:

Essential papers on borderline disorders.

(Essential papers in psychoanalysis)
Bibliography: p.
Includes index.
1. Borderline personality disorder—Addresses,
essays, lectures. I. Stone, Michael H., 1933–
II. Series.
RC569.5.B67E87   1985   616.89   85-15384
ISBN 0-8147-7849-6
ISBN 0-8147-7850-X (pbk.)

Clothbound editions of New York University Press books are Smyth-sewn and printed
on permanent and durable acid-free paper.

Book design by Ken Venezio

For Beth

Contents

Acknowledgments

We wish to gratefully acknowledge *Alienist and Neurologist* for C. H. Hughes, "Moral (Affective) Insanity—Psychosensory Insanity," Vol. 5, pp. 296–315, 1884.

We wish to gratefully acknowledge *Journal of Nervous and Mental Disease* for Irving C. Rosse, "Clinical Evidences of Borderland Insanity," Vol. 17, pp. 669–683, 1890.

We gratefully wish to acknowledge *The Psychoanalytic Quarterly* for permission to reprint Adolph Stern, "Psychoanalytic Investigation of and Therapy in the Border Line Group of Neuroses," Vol. 7, pp. 467–489, 1938; and Helene Deutsch, "Some Forms of Emotional Disturbance and their Relationship to Schizophrenia," Vol. 11, pp. 301–321, 1942.

We gratefully wish to acknowledge *American Journal of Psychotherapy* for permission to reprint the following: Melitta Schmideberg, "The Treatment of Psychopaths and Borderline Patients," Vol. 1, pp. 45–70, 1947; and Michael H. Stone, "The Borderline Syndrome: Evolution of the Term, Genetic Aspects and Prognosis," Vol. 31, pp. 345–365, 1977.

We gratefully wish to acknowledge Human Sciences Press for permission to reprint the following from *Psychiatric Quarterly:* Paul Hoch and Phillip Polatin, "Pseudoneurotic Forms of Schizophrenia," Vol. 23, pp. 248–276; and John Frosch, "The Psychotic Character: Clinical Psychiatric Considerations," Vol. 38, pp. 1–16, 1964.

We gratefully wish to acknowledge The Menninger Foundation for permission to reprint from the *Bulletin of the Menninger Clinic,* Robert P. Knight, "Borderline States in Psychoanalytic Psychiatry and Psychology," Vol. 17, pp. 1–12, 1953.

We gratefully wish to acknowledge International Universities Press for permission to reprint the following: Edith Jacobson, ON THE PSYCHOANALYTIC THEORY OF CYCLOTHYMIC DEPRESSION, pp. 228–241, 1971; and Edith Jacobson, THE SELF AND THE OBJECT WORLD, pp. 49–69, 1964.

We gratefully wish to acknowledge International Universities Press for permission to reprint from the *Journal of the American Psychoanalytic Association* the following: Leo Stone, "The Widening Scope of Indications for Psychoanalysis," Vol. 2, pp. 567–594, 1954; Erik Homburger Erikson, "The Problem of Ego Identity," Vol. 4, pp. 66–81, 1956; Otto Kernberg, "Borderline Personality Organization," Vol. 15, pp. 641–685, 1967.

We wish to gratefully acknowledge the *American Journal of Psychiatry* for the following: Sandor Rado, "Dynamics and Classification of Disordered Behavior," Vol. 110, pp. 406–416, 1953; and John G. Gunderson and Margaret T. Singer, "Defining Borderline Patients," Vol. 132, pp. 1–10, 1975.

We wish to gratefully acknowledge Basic Books for the following: Roy Grinker, Sr., B. Werble, and R. C. Drye, THE BORDERLINE SYNDROME; A BEHAVIORAL STUDY OF EGO FUNCTIONS, pp. 23–34; 98–112; 172–181.

Reprinted with permission Seymore S. Kety, et al., "The Types and Prevalence of Mental Illness in the Biological and Adoptive Families of Adopted Schizophrenics," from THE TRANSMISSION OF SCHIZOPHRENIA, by David Rosenthal and Seymour S. Kety, © 1968, Pergamon Press.

We wish to gratefully acknowledge Associated Book Publishers (U.K.) Ltd. for permission to reprint the following: Michael Balint, THE BASIC FAULT, pp. 11–17, 18–23, 159–172.

We wish to gratefully acknowledge Yale University Press for permission to reprint from THE PSYCHOANALYTIC STUDY OF THE CHILD, edited by Ruth S. Eissler et al. "A Study of the Separation-Individuation Process" by Margaret S. Mahler, pp. 403–424, 1971.

We wish to gratefully acknowledge Jason Aronson for permission to reprint Harold F. Searles, "The Countertransference with the Borderline Patient," from LeBoit, Joseph and Capponi, Attilio, ADVANCES IN PSYCHOTHERAPY OF THE BORDERLINE PATIENT, pp. 309–346, 1979.

We wish to gratefully acknowledge the *Archives of General Psychiatry* for permission to reprint Robert L. Spitzer, Jean Endicott, and Miriam Gibbon, "Crossing the Border into Borderline Personality and Borderline Schizophrenia," Vol. 36, January 1979, pp. 17–24. Copyright 1979, American Medical Association.

We wish to acknowledge the *American Journal of Clinical Psychiatry* for Hagop S. Akiskal, et al., "Borderline: An Adjective in Search of a Noun," 1984.

Introduction

So much literature has accumulated, over so long a period, on borderline conditions in psychiatry, that the time has come for an anthology. Hence this book. It is not an altogether pleasant task preparing the collection of articles that makes up such an anthology, since one is aware at the outset of pleasing only a few—while offending many—authors, both living and dead, since many more works must be excluded than selected. I feel something of the awe and of the anxiety that must have attended those who labored to gather the "100 Greatest Books." The first few titles are easy. Shakespeare. Dante. Homer. Oh yes, and the Bible. But what then? Does one bump "Faust" for *Crime and Punishment?* Or keep them both in, at the expense of Plutarch's *Lives? Moby Dick* or (to save space) *The Old Man and The Sea? Anna Karenina* or (to save space) *Madame Bovary* or (to save even more space) *The Scarlet Letter?* And so on.

In this anthology, I soon noticed that while I chose some very prominent authors for inclusion (Kernberg, Gunderson, Jacobson, Erikson) others even more prominent I could allude to only obliquely (Freud, Kraepelin, Wilhelm Reich) because they had only a little to say that bore directly on borderline conditions. Some of the great articles do not mention the word "borderline." And some of the older articles that do use the word, are not great.

In evaluating the literature available to me—a literature composed of articles in French, German, Spanish, Norwegian, Italian and Russian besides the larger bulk in English—I kept as my guiding principle the long tradition out of which the current concepts of "borderline" were to grow. Had I instead started with the DSM-definition and worked backwards, I would have omitted certain articles oriented toward schizophrenia—key articles in their day, albeit no longer so relevant to the current definitions, which have decoupled themselves for the most part from schizophrenia, as they have taken on the coloration in recent years of an atypical affective disorder. The articles of Helene Deutsch and Robert Knight, for example, though written in the belief that "borderline" depicted an incipient or dilute variant of schizophrenia, are classics in the field, important not only in understanding how the term "borderline" has evolved but in appreciating at first hand the origins of object-relational and other "nonorthodox" psychoanalytical approaches that have come to serve as the theoretical underpinnings to contemporary notions of borderline psychology.

A survey of the important contributors to the borderline concept—particularly those who may be considered contemporary—reveals something of interest about the transfer and spread of ideas. The schools of thought, along with their ardent supporters, differ from one another, sometimes narrowly, sometimes in what seems like an unbridgeable gap. The leaders of the various schools cannot all speak to each other—but, instead, line themselves up, in what takes shape as a kind of intellectual bucket brigade, where each passes his best ideas along to the expert nearest him in theoretical or therapeutic philosophy. Meissner, for example, can communicate with Kohut or (now Kohut is dead) with his followers. I can communicate with Meissner, but only poorly with the Kohutians, who strike me as insufficiently biological in orientation. Akiskal can communicate with me but only poorly with Meissner and not at all with Kohut. Guze and Donald Klein can communicate with Akiskal, would see me as *almost* biological enough to appreciate their theoretical stance and would have increasing difficulty in talking to Kernberg, let alone to a Kleinian like Grotstein or to a Kohutian like Ornstein or Ernest Wolf. Without this "brigade" psychoanalytic controversies such as those concerning "innate anxiety" (of which Greenacre spoke) or the source of rage (innate?, from parental maltreatment?) in borderlines (i.e., the Kernberg/Kohut debate) would be condemned to spin around endlessly, like the circular squirrel-cages in the pet store, moving fast but getting nowhere. Thanks to the brigade, an idea, such as Kernberg's about innate aggression, gets passed to someone like Gunderson, who passes it down the line to someone like Siever or Pickar, in whose labs possible correlates might be studied between excessive firing in certain dopaminergic tracts and "innate aggression." Without the people in the middle, the adherents of each extreme position (it's all in the mind . . . it's all in the body) become locked in their own private worlds; their research, sterile. I used to decry this situation, as though it were a "shame" that Klein was not more sympathetic to the analysts or Kohut to the biologists, but it is clear now that this is how it has always been and will always be. It is the way the world is. What is required is not unanimity but openness to the views of your neighbors in the line. It is only in this interconnectedness that science, especially in the healing professions, zigzags toward the Truth: each investigator's brain a world unto itself; each, at the same time, a neurone in the larger brain of science.

Long-term studies of borderlines are thus far confined to hospital populations, with the exception of my anecdotal reports on approximately 50 patients seen in private practice.* Granted the greater ease with which methodical outcome studies can be carried out in hospitalized samples, one hopes for long-range results from both sectors. Such data will help answer questions concerning the fate of borderlines as they reach middle life. One has the impression, thus far, that certain characteristics (turbulent relationships, suicide gestures, impulsivity) by which borderlines are diagnosed initially become (mercifully) rarer or fainter with the advancing years; people in their forties usually have worked out a satisfying relationship with someone or else given up on intimacy altogether, leaving only a residue of this or that personality disorder. Again, by age 45, either a small minority of borderlines have actually died by suicide or else, because the biochemical/psychological flames once buffeting their souls burn more coolly now, have stopped making suicidal acts. Personality traits and a certain fragility remain where the florid borderline action proneness once dominated the clinical picture. But this is only my impression. In the future we will have the facts.

Prognostic factors that may figure more significantly in the balance, when the longer-term follow-up studies are completed, will probably include, besides motivation, psychological aptitude and intelligence, certain wild-card items like talent and money. The same borderline person whose anxieties can scarcely be quelled except through the acquisition of a new dress or a new set of cuff-links every week or through suddenly "taking off" for a weekend trip has no troubles if the money is available. But if not, there may be trouble with the law (from shoplifting) or an anxiety that reaches explosive proportions for want

* Gunderson and his colleagues have been gathering data more systematically from private practitioners, using a standardized questionnaire. Preliminary findings indicate, among other things, a drop-out rate within six months of treatment of about 50 percent in borderlines. This figure is not out of line with my own experience in private practice (a 40 percent dropout rate).

of an acceptable outlet. Artistic, musical, or other forms of talent permit some borderlines to structure and to find satisfaction enough in a life that would otherwise collapse into chaos.

The 1990s will see the drawing up of reliable criteria for diagnosing certain children and adolescents as "borderline"—borderline, that is, in relation to various already existing diagnostic categories and dimensions relevant to these age backets. This will be the first step in carrying out prospective studies of these young people, to see what becomes of them over time. How many take on, during adult life, the characteristics that would justify the borderline label by the then accepted criteria for a borderline condition in adults? How many veer off onto other paths, becoming distinctly bipolar, schizophrenic, epileptic, or whatever? We know, anecdotally and from a few brief reports such as that of Fard and Welner (1978), that some adolescent borderlines turn up as classic manic depressives (rarely, as schizophrenics) by their twenties. How many settle down into adult life as fairly calm neurotics with little damage to show for all the flamboyant psychopathology of their youth? To these questions, the answers will come more slowly, perhaps crystallizing out of the psychiatric literature of the next century.

The question whether there also exists a so-called "borderline" personality over and above the syndrome (broadly defined), which should then be placed alongside other structures of the personality is more problematical, as is also the question about causation. However seductive they may seem, psychoanalytic theories have not been able to demonstrate rigorously the influence of psychodynamic factors, and there seems no alternative but to underline the importance of constitutional and sociocultural factors.

PART I

1880s THROUGH 1920s

1880s

In the 1880s the concept of the borderline was just taking shape. This is in part a reflection of the (to our way of thinking) rather primitive state of hospital psychiatry at that time. The concepts of schizophrenia and manic depression—for us, the firm ground to which other, less well-defined diagnostic concepts are anchored—were themselves new and imprecise. Morel's *démence précoce* was not to evolve into the dementia praecox of Kraepelin for another decade. Meantime psychiatric taxonomists were busy inventing labels for every nuance of paranoid or otherwise delusory ideation. Baillarger's notion of *folie de double forme,* the forerunner of our manic-depressive illness, was just beginning to win wide acceptance. Kahlbaum and his pupil, Hecker, were just enunciating their concepts of catatonia and hebephrenia destined to become two of the four main subtypes of schizophrenia, once Bleuler's term won out in popularity over "dementia praecox."

At the time when the first article of this anthology was originally published, Freud was 28 years old and had just discovered the anesthetic properties of cocaine. Psychoanalysis was about nine years away (if we take Freud's paper with Breuer on hysteria in the 1893 Neurologisches Centralblatt as our starting point).

Absent the more sharply defined concepts of specific mental conditions, to which we have now grown accustomed, the realm of diagnosis consisted mainly of two nebulous concepts about psychosis and neurosis, (the latter as a catchall phrase for any mild nervous condition). If there were to be a borderline case, it had to be found somewhere in the amorphous territory between these two indistinct concepts. Lombroso (1870) found it useful to describe certain cases of criminality as occupying the border between madness and normality, since the idea of considering a criminal to be normal, simply because he was not delusional, was repugnant to Lombroso, as it is to us. The first *borderland* or *borderline* cases were thus nondelusional sociopaths. A little later, as we see from the articles by Hughes and by Rosse, included here, these adjectives some to denote cases of chronic mental illness that fell short of outright madness, but never approached normality either: they, too, occupied the territory between psychosis and neurosis.

1890s

Though a number of articles and books appeared during this decade, containing case descriptions of serious but nondelusional mental disorders, the terms borderline or borderland were used rarely if at all as qualifiers.

The case descriptions were often very detailed, enough so to permit the reader, even a century later, to establish with some conviction that certain patients of that era were very much like our borderline patients today. The histrionic, moody women depicted first by Donald Klein and then by Michael Liebowitz in our day, under the heading "hysteroid dysphoria" (almost all of whom are borderline simultaneously by Gunderson, Kernberg, and DSM criteria), are quite similar to the women of the 1890s with what Falret was calling *"folie hystérique"* (1890). The *folie hystérique* of Falret was at the extreme of a continuum relating to hysterical character. The latter already embraced many of the items now recognized in the DSM as intrinsic to borderline personality. Falret mentions lability of affect, impulsivity, and an extreme *contradictoriness* of attitude (such as Kernberg emphasizes in his description). This contradictoriness, along with the duplicity, absorption in fantasy, and rapid shift from one state of beliefs and values to another, that Falret also underlines, constitutes the kind of identity disturbance and "as-if" quality to the personality that later authors (Helene Deutsch, Otto Kernberg) were to hold as central to the borderline concept. When the ideas become so absurd, the actions so violent as to constitute a true mental condition, not merely a characterological aberration, Falret spoke of crossing the line into *folie hystérique*. Since many cases of folie hysterique were not chronically delusional, in our sense of the term, they would still be classified, by contemporary standards, as borderline.

To give the reader the flavor of Falret's observations I have translated here a paragraph of his comments on the hysteric.

To begin with, one notices a great lability in all their emotional dispositions, which fluctuate according to the moment one is observing them. They alternate, and at very brief intervals, from excitement to depression, in the same manner that they change abruptly, from the standpoint of physical expression, between an outbreak of laughter and an outbreak of tears. They wax enthusiastically, with ardor and with passion, for any person or object they wish to possess at all costs. They shrink before no effort or sacrifice to attain their goal. But once obtained—or even before their goal is achieved—they swing suddenly to the other extreme. Their love transforms itself into hatred; their sympathy, into disdain; their desire, into repulsion—and they bend as much effort into rejection and avoidance of the object they had just been pursuing as they had expended the moment before in winning it. They are thus, and in everything, fanciful and capricious, presenting an extreme of changeability in either ideas or feelings . . . (Falret, 1890, p. 502).

1900–1909

Whereas the clincial descriptions of Falret that resemble our borderlines were not viewed as the *formes frustes* of a neatly defined psychosis, and thus were not "borderline" in that respect, the equally detailed descriptions of Kraepelin *were* considered by their author in this light. Kraepelin's career flourished on both sides of the *fin de siècle,* so it is for reasons more arbitrary than accurate that I situate him in this first decade of our century. His magnum opus—the *Psychiatrie*—appeared in 1905. The subtlety of Kraepelin's thinking is not much appreciated in our day, perhaps because the 2372 pages of his textbook have not been translated, excerpts aside, into English. Having incorporated many cases known formerly under a variety of titles into his central concepts of dementia praecox and manic-depression, Kraepelin then set about describing milder forms of these conditions. These cases were thought of specifically as borderline to the major psychoses, though, again, Kraepelin does not use an adjective "borderline" so much as refer to a middle territory between frank psychosis and normalcy. Kraepelin's descriptions of the temperaments associated with manic depression stand up well in the light of contemporary research and nosology. He was also aware of milder, nondeteriorating instances of dementia praecox, though he was usually misunderstood in midcentury America at least, as cognizant only of unequivocal cases.

To return for the moment to the purely descriptive level, we should mention the work of Janet, whose sketches of hysterical, obsessional, anorectic, and other cases that resembled the borderlines of the next generation were even more complete than those of Falret. (See Raymond and Janet on obsessional patients, 1903; Janet on the hysteric, 1911.)

How is it, one may ask, that Janet and, to a lesser extent, Kraepelin languished in obscurity? Certainly not because of a language barrier. Any psychiatrist in that era with a pretense to breadth read French and German. German remained the lingua franca of psychiatry until World War II. But Janet and Kraepelin stood apart from psychoanalysis. The great new movement gathered adherents and rolled past them because it offered more hope of a cure or, failing that, hope of a deeper understanding than that offered by the descriptive talents, however perspicuous, of Janet or the nosologic talents, however sagacious, of Kraepelin. Psychoanalysis offered a new dimension to psychiatry: the *dynamic,* next to which the cleverest nosologist or phenomenologist seemed arid.

1910s

Little was added during the 1910s to the descriptive and phenomenologic aspects of moderately severe (and later to be called borderline) psychiatric disorders. In that regard, we can all be said to have reinvented the wheel, following the contributions of Falret, Kraepelin, and Janet. But in regard to dynamic studies, a whole new territory was opening up. Psychoanalysis was expanding into the realm of the psychoses, especially schizophrenia. Freud called them "narcissistic neuroses," felt such patients had no libido to invest in objects (being all bound up in the self), made no transference, and thus placed themselves outside the pale of psychoanalytic therapy. He expressed this opinion at one of his Wednesday evening meetings with his inner circle of colleagues at around the time Bleuler's great monograph on schizophrenia was about to appear. Some of the "pioneers" were willing to challenge Freud on this point: Alfonse Maeder in 1911 and the Swede, Poul Bjerre, in 1912, began to apply analytic principles to paranoid cases with promising results. Some of these patients were, by today's standards, borderline schizophrenics or, in the language of DSM, "schizotypal personalities."

The humanistic interventions, endlessly patient therapeutic approach, and perceptive understanding of the psychodynamics are most impressive. Maeder and Bjerre were joined later in the decade by Isador Coriat (the first president of the American Psychoanalytic Society) in their enthusiasm for the applicability of psychoanalysis to schizophrenia (or dementia praecox, as many were still calling this group of conditions). This work provided considerable stimulus to the task of establishing the limits of utility to the analytic method. The borderline case, not just with respect to nosology, but to analyzability, needed to be defined and described.

Despite the good work of Maeder and Bjerre, enthusiasm for analyzing schizophrenics was not destined to reach the heights in Europe as it did in the United States. It will be remembered that Freud established a beachhead here with his lectures at Clark University in 1909. Soon after, a growing number of American psychiatrists were to travel to Vienna in order to be analyzed by the Professor; others sought analysis here with the analysands who returned home.

A few psychiatrists who were not part of the analytic tradition also facilitated the spread of the psychoanalytic approach to more difficult cases. Adolf Meyer, emigrating from Germany, began to stress the need to look at schizophrenia as a "reaction type" rather than as merely a manifestation of irremediable constitutional warp. This new outlook created a more hopeful atmosphere for the psychoses, the presumption being that if certain psychological influences could push the vulnerable person into a schizophrenic reaction, then perhaps a more favorable milieu and therapeutic approach could restore sanity and function. This applied to cases of intermediate (i.e., borderline) severity as well.

Bleuler, though he and Freud never met, became sympathetic to psychoanalysis. He was as sensitive as Kraepelin, if not more so, to attenuated cases—and described, in the 1911 monograph, several instances of mild, recovered and compensated schizophrenics (our borderline schizophrenics).

While some practitioners who did not use the term borderline were busy expressing their optimism about the use of psychoanalysis for patients in this domain, ironically the decade closes with a cautionary note by an analyst who did speak of borderland neuroses and psychoses.

L. Pierce Clark (1919) found analytic knowledge of dynamics and dream interpretation useful in dealing with manic-depressives, even though "Their hold upon any large fundamental plan of basic contact with the realities of life . . . was very weak and uncertain" (p. 307). In the half dozen schizophrenics he worked with, however, Clark felt their mental deterioration was ". . . too far advanced . . . for one to more than use psychoanalytic teachings in helping these patients to adjust their lives," and went on to add that any attempt at pure psychoanalysis of such cases invariably does harm (p. 307).

Regarding the borderline schizophrenics mentioned above in connection with Bleuler's work, the following paragraph (transl. by the editor from the 1911 edit.) is illustrative:

I know schizophrenics, who, following their illness, have managed to conduct complicated business of a high level; I know one who, after two outbreaks of catatonic twilight-states about 7 years apart is still capable of teaching, carrying out independent scientific activity and maintaining a world reputation in his specialty. One of our catatonics had later on become well known as a poet. Schreber became president of the senate after his first attack. A heboidophrenic patient reported by Hess is a university professor. Schumann, the composer, and Scheffel (the poet) were schizophrenic. In the 13 years I have been officiating at the State Medical examinations, I must have passed quite a number of schizophrenic students, some of whom obtained very good scores. These examples should show us that we ought not close our eyes to the possibility of favorable outcomes (E. Bleuler, 1911, p. 210).

It is of special interest that Bleuler saw Schumann as a compensated schizophrenic, in light of the recent and very scholarly reappraisal of the composer's mental condition by the Boston psychoanalyst Peter Ostwald (1985). Dr. Ostwald concludes (correctly, in all likelihood) that the evidence favors a manic-depressive diagnosis. This is the "fate" of many a recovered or borderline "schizophrenic" from the earlier literature—to be reclassified, that is, as manic-depressive. Vaillant's review (1963) of some remitted dementia praecox cases from the early part of the century lead to a similar reassessment. (See below, "1920s": comments on the "Wolf Man.") These revisions presage the revision occurring in the 1970's concerning the type of psychosis to which contemporary "borderline" cases were affiliated: if they were attenuated manifestations of a psychosis at all, it was more apt to be manic-depressive than schizophrenic.

1920s

This decade might be regarded as inauspicious in the history of the borderline concept: the term makes a fleeting appearance in 1921 under the guise of an article by the psychologist T. V. Moore on the "parataxes . . . [or] certain borderline mental states." The following excerpt from this article is worth citing at some length:

> *The Etiology of the Depression,*—Whereas, any unpleasant event may produce a feeling of sadness, not every incident can call forth the tendency to remain sad. The incident must be one that affects profoundly the individual's hierarchy of desires. It renders him for the time being hopeless so that he feels sorry for himself, feels that others should pity him, has no longer anything on which to build, for the keystone in the arch of his desires has been knocked to the ground. Thus the situation in which he finds himself is impossible. If it does not change and he does not find new interests, the psychotaxis takes on abnormal features leading to incapacitation for work and becomes a parataxis, or may even deepen into a psychosis.
>
> That an abnormal reaction occurs in some men, and not in others, depends to a large extent upon their inherited constitution. Patients suffering from manic-depressive psychoses have more insane relatives than normal individuals, and these insane relatives are frequently of the manic-depressive type. It is interesting to note also that the manic-depressive cases are to a large extent recruited from those who take to the Bohemian type of society, as artists, musicians, poets, etc. There is, therefore, in every depression an hereditary organic factor which makes the patient physically disposed to this type of reaction.

After this tentative debut, the term falls inexplicably into a state of *assoupissement*—a prolonged slumber—from which it was not to reawaken for another 17 years. (Stern's article of 1938 the reader will also find reprinted here.)

Since the distribution of patients within various diagnostic categories remained, in all likelihood, the same throughout this period, how were our borderlines labeled betweentimes? For information on this topic I am indebted to Henriette Klein, who mentioned to me that the two favorite designations for these not-quite-analyzable patients were "preschizophrenic" and "schizotypal." The latter, used even before Rado made the term more popular in the 1950s and long before DSM made it official in the 1980s, connoted—having-the-perennial-character- (or personality) of the typical schizophrenic; i.e., exquisitely shy, eccentric, socially awkward, etc. The schizotype need never become frankly schizophrenic (in the sense of psychotically delusional) and presumably seldom succumbed in this fashion. The "preschizophrenic" (a phrase we encounter again in Deutsch's speculations on her "as-if" patients) need not have exhibited this schizotypal exterior—but seemed clearly on the way to a psychotic breakdown of a schizophrenic kind. One can discern from these distinctions that the supposition was very much in force throughout this period that the not-quite analyzable cases were borderline also with respect to the central concept of schizophrenia. Viewed in this light, we can understand how Freud's Wolf-Man was considered by many American analysts as a schizotypal patient, given his chronic and quasi-delusional preoccupation (his *"over-valued idea,"* to use Wernicke's term) with his nose, his social anxiety, etc. (Recently, Abrahamson (1930) has amassed evidence to show that the Wolf-Man was really borderline with respect to the affective phychoses. Probably he had mild features of both psychoses—a borderline schizoaffective, if you will—though, as Abrahamson points out, the Wolf-Man's family history was replete with examples of affective illness).

Apropos borderline affective conditions, even in the 1920s it was recognized that, besides the schizotypal, was another group of scarcely analyzable patients: those with ungovernable propensities to "act out" the transference (or, where the person in question was not in analytic treatment, just to act impulsively, irrationally, precipitously and, often enough, meanly, as a general habit). Patients of this sort were described by Wilhelm Reich in his 1925 monograph on the "impulse-ridden character." Many of his seem like the impulsive, affectively-ill DSM borderlines of our day, though Reich felt some were *formes frustes* of schizophrenia.

Perhaps the polysymptomatic, flamboyantly "neurotic" *Anna O* of Freud's patient roster was also, by our standards, a histrionic, affectively tinged borderline patient. Her excellent recovery (she became the founder of Germany's social work-movement) is in no way out of keeping with the dramatic successes that are sometimes achieved with borderline cases of this type.

Toward the close of the decade, Gustav Bychowski (1928) was to urge a more active, confrontational style of psychoanalytic treatment with certain "schizophrenics" than was typical of the constrained, rather silent analyses of the 1920s. Probably some of these barely analyzable cases would have been classified as "schizotypals," in our book. His therapeutic recommendations square well with those that

Kernberg was to suggest 40 years later, though Bychowski did not refer to his "latent psychotics" as borderline.

It is worth nothing, in our final remarks on this decade, that Moore, along with other analysts of this era, were still steeped, during their years of training in the nineteenth century, hospital-psychiatry-based, notion of hereditary taint (cf. Moore, p. 270). Analysts of this time learned psychoanalysis *after* their immersion in traditional psychiatry. The idea of a possible hereditary factor for at least some borderline cases seemed reasonable to them. It was only later, and especially in America, that psychiatric trainees were steeped in analytic thinking from day one. This generation, beginning in the 1930s and 1940s, began to lose contact with the biologic/genetic foundation of their field and began to use "borderline" in ways that had *less* to do with the classic psychoses and *more* to do with particular patterns of dynamics and defense mechanisms. These tendencies are sketched more fully in the commentary on the 1950s.

1. A Treatise on Insanity

James Cowles Prichard (1835)*

PHENOMENA OF INSANITY DESCRIBED AS THEY ARE
MANIFESTED IN THE DIFFERENT FORMS OF THE DISEASE

Section 1. Moral Insanity

This form of mental derangement has been described as consisting in a morbid perversion of the feelings, affections, and active powers, without any illusion or erroneous conviction impressed upon the understanding: it sometimes co-exists with an apparently unimpaired state of the intellectual faculties.

There are many individuals living at large, and not entirely separated from society, who are affected in a certain degree with this modification of insanity. They are reputed persons of a singular, wayward, and eccentric character. An attentive observer will often recognize something remarkable in their manners and habits, which may lead him to entertain doubts as to their entire sanity; and circumstances are sometimes discovered, on inquiry, which add strength to his suspicion. In many instances it has been found that an hereditary tendency to madness has existed in the family, or that several relatives of the person affected have laboured under other diseases of the brain. The individual himself has been discovered to have suffered, in a former period of life, an attack of madness of a decided character. His temper and dispositions are found to have undergone a change; to be not what they were previously to a certain time: he has become an altered man, and the difference has, perhaps, been noted from the period when he sustained some reverse of fortune, which deeply affected him, or the loss of some beloved relative. In other instances, an alteration in the character of the individual has ensued immediately on some severe shock which his bodily constitution has undergone. This has been either a disorder

---

* So that the reader may be better prepared for his journey through the last 100 years of papers on *the borderline*, a few pages from Prichard's classic text of 1830 have been reprinted here as a kind of prelude.

affecting the head, a slight attack of paralysis, a fit of epilepsy, or some febrile or inflammatory disorder, which has produced a perceptible change in the habitual state of the constitution. In some cases the alteration in temper and habits has been gradual and imperceptible, and it seems only to have consisted in an exaltation and increase of peculiarities, which were always more or less natural and habitual.

In a state like that above described, many persons have continued for years to be the sources of apprehension and solicitude of their friends and relatives. The latter, in many instances, cannot bring themselves to admit the real nature of the case. The individual follows the bent of his inclinations; he is continually engaging in new pursuits, and soon relinquishing them without any other inducement than mere caprice and fickleness. At length the total perversion of his affections, the dislike, and perhaps even enmity, manifested towards his dearest friends, excite greater alarm. When it happens that the head of a family labours under this ambiguous modification of insanity, it is sometimes thought necessary, from prudential motives, and to prevent absolute ruin from thoughtless and absurd extravagance, or from the results of wild projects and speculations, in the pursuit of which the individual has always a plausible reason to offer for his conduct, to make some attempt with a view to take the management of his affairs out of his hands. The laws have made inadequate provision for such contingencies, and the endeavour is often unsuccessful. If the matter is brought before a jury, and the individual gives pertinent replies to the questions that are put to him, and displays no particular mental illusion,—a feature which is commonly looked upon as essential to madness,—it is most probable that the suit will be rejected.

Persons labouring under this disorder are capable of reasoning or supporting an argument upon any subject within their sphere of knowledge that may be presented to them; and they often display great ingenuity in giving reasons for the eccentricities of their conduct, and in accounting for and justifying the state of moral feeling under which they appear to exist. In one sense, indeed, their intellectual faculties may be termed unsound; they think and act under the influence of strongly-excited feelings, and persons accounted sane are, under such circumstances, proverbially liable to error both in judgement and conduct.

I have already had occasion to observe that the existence of moral insanity as a distinct form of derangement has been recognized by Pinel; the following example recorded by that writer is a characteristic one. Pinel terms this affection "emportement maniaque sans délire."*

"An only son of a weak and indulgent mother gave himself up habitually to the gratification of every caprice and passion of which an untutored and violent temper was susceptible. The impetuosity of his disposition increased with his years. The money with which he was lavishly supplied removed every obstacle to the indulgence of his wild desires. Every instance of opposition or resistance roused him to acts of fury. He assaulted his adversary with the audacity of a savage; sought to reign by force, and was perpetually embroiled in disputes and quarrels. If a dog, a horse, or any other animal offended him, he instantly put it to death. If ever he went to a fête or any other public meeting, he was sure to excite such tumults and quarrels as terminated in actual pugilistic rencontres, and he generally left the scene with a bloody nose. This wayward youth, however, when unmoved by passion, possessed a perfectly sound judgment. When he became of age, he succeeded to the possession of an extensive domain. He proved himself fully competent to the management of his estate, as well as the discharge of his relative duties, and he ever distinguished himself by acts of beneficence and compassion. Wounds, lawsuits, and pecuniary compensations, were generally the consequences of his unhappy propensity to quarrel. But an act of notoriety put an end to his career of violence. Enraged with a women who had used offensive language to him, he threw her into a well. Prosecution was commenced against him; and on the deposition of a great many witnesses, who gave evidence to his furious deportment, he was condemned to perpetual confinement in Bicêtre."

*Traité Médico-Philosophique sur l'aliénation mentale: 2de edit. Paris, 1809, p. 156.

2. Moral (Affective) Insanity— Psychosensory Insanity

C. H. Hughes

The real question in every discussion of moral insanity, is not whether there exists in the mind of its victim, any illogical reasoning based upon a false premise of wrong and morbid feeling, but whether the feelings or impulses are so primarily and chiefly and paramountly affected as to overshadow all other evidences of mental derangement that may exist in the individual, and give the distinguishing character to his disease, as depression of feeling gives to melancholia (which Prichard regarded as a form of moral insanity) and exaltation does to general paralysis, determining the nature of delusions, if they subsequently develop; fearful, dreadful, in the one case; hopeful and grandiose in the other.[1] Some cases of moral insanity are more typically free from *appreciable* reasoning aberration than others; some appear to be entirely so, just as some cases of the general paralysis of the insane are all grandiose delusion, while others are complicated with delusions of dread and persecution, and other states of lypemania.*

Prichard's cases in illustration of what he meant by moral insanity, were not all equally free from the semblance of delusional derangement, and some alienists who have controverted the doctrine of moral insanity, have done so by seeking to show that Prichard did not understand himself and the meaning of his own definition. Blandford has analyzed this author's cases with this object, and so did Mayo,[2] before Blandford's criticism appeared. But illustrative cases speak plainer than definitions of insanity, a subject universally acknowledged to be extremely difficult, and by many psychiatrists asserted to be impossible to define.

---

[1] It is not meant here to deny that melancholia and the delirium of grandeur, may not co-exist in the same person; on the contrary they do sometimes, as clinical observation proves.

*Lypemania: a term used by Esquirol to denote morbid depression, similar to our concept of melancholia (Ed.).

[2] Croonian Lectures, 1834.

Georget, Pinel, and Esquirol, before Prichard, described *manie sans delire, manie sans lesion de l'entendement* and *folie raisonnante,* and Prichard, in illustration of what he termed moral insanity, introduced into his book their descriptions.

The vulgar idea of moral insanity (and this view has been adopted by some alienists, but without warrant from the founders of the doctrine,) is that it is always and *only* a form of immoral manifestation without disorder of the reason, which certain weak-minded and excessively sympathetic psychologists have sought to extenuate by supposing the co-existence of exculpatory mental disease, whereas Prichard said "the varieties of moral insanity are perhaps as numerous as the modifications of feeling or passion in the human mind," characterized by "excitement or the opposite state of melancholic dejection." "Propensities,"[3] he said "are so nearly allied to passions and emotions that they are generally referred to the same division of the faculties or of mental phenomena; both are included by metaphysicians in the ethical or moral department of the mind as contradistinguished from the intellectual."[4]

Prichard, referring to the cases of *manie sans delire,* or *folie raisonnante,* described by Pinel, confesses that they "failed for a long time to produce conviction" on his mind, but he became persuaded that Pinel was correct in his opinion, and states that "Esquirol had assured him that his impression on this subject was similar." M. Esquirol, though his great work, "Des Maladies Mentales," bears indubitable evidence of his conviction of the reality of this form of mental derangement, at one time entertained strong doubts of the existence of insanity without appreciable intellectual error or delusion, but when convinced, as every one must be who will open himself freely to conviction, without any mental reservation as to the necessity of co-existent intellectual aberration, he candidly confessed his error without endeavoring, as medical writers of his day did, as Prichard complains, to reconcile the phenomena of affective aberration with preconceived opinion respecting the nature of insanity, "by assuming, on conjecture, the existence of some undetected delusion," an assumption unwarranted in the ordinary nature of insanity, because the disease, even when it finally displays itself in well marked delusion, is characterized in its earlier stages by morbid

---

[3] Treatise on Insanity, p. 24, 1867.
[4] Treatise on Insanity, p. 19.

changes of feeling and conduct, not based upon delusive reasoning, but laying the foundation for the subsequently-developed delusions. But even if unappreciable, but theoretically probable, intellectual aberration exists in moral insanity, the doctrine must stand.

"There are madmen in whom it is difficult to discover any trace of hallucination, but there are none in whom the passions and moral affections are not disordered, perverted or destroyed." Esquirol records that in all his forty years of study and observation at Salpêtrière and Charenton, and in his private practice, he had seen no exceptions to this fact. The candor of Esquirol and Prichard are worthy of commendation and emulation. But it does not require, at this late day, the genius or experience of an Esquirol, to discover among the insane, those whose insanity is chiefly one of character.*

A politic, but unscientific objection to the term moral insanity, relates to the disfavor with which the plea of moral insanity as a defence for crime is received by the courts and populace.

It is considered dangerous to the moral welfare of society, and tending to defeat the ends of justice, to recognize a form of mental disease which, in some of its features, sometimes counterfeits depravity and crime. To recognize insanity under such circumstances would be, as Mayo might say, "at great expense of public good," a consideration which biased his judgment on the subject and the book he wrote, and which has likewise obscured the judgment of most of his contemporaries and followers down to the present day, who have thought fit to deny the existence of insanity of conduct without appreciable intellectual derangement.

This objection, while worthy of consideration as to the propriety of so designating this state of mental alienation under certain circumstances, without a full explanation of its real nature, lest we should jeopardize the imperiled welfare of a really insane person on trial before a prejudiced and frenzied populace, clamorous for vengence, whether the victim be mentally diseased or not, is not entitled to much weight in a scientific discussion when truth alone is sought. The same objection might be urged to any form of mental disease under the same circumstances, since the plea, under the name of "insanity dodge," of insanity in any form, has become so obnoxious, through the lax rulings of courts

---

*Cf. Frosch's *The Psychotic Character* (included here).

admitting as competent, incompetent expert testimony, that the rights of the really insane to its protection are in jeopardy whenever this defence is interposed, in many communities.

It might be profitable for us to acquaint ourselves a little more at length with Prichard's own words, to convey his understanding of the meaning of this term. In his preliminary remarks (p. 15) after referring to "affections of the understanding or rational powers," he says: "but there is likewise a form of mental derangement in which the intellectual faculties *appear* to have sustained *little or no* injury, while the disorder is manifested *principally or alone* in the state of feelings, temper or habits. In cases of this description the moral and active principles of the mind are strangely perverted or depraved; the power of self-government is lost or greatly impaired; and the individual is found to be incapable, not of talking or reasoning upon any subject proposed to him, for this he will often do with great shrewdness and volubility, but of conducting himself with decency and propriety in the business of life. His wishes, and his inclinations, his attachments, his likings and dislikings, have all undergone a morbid *change,* and this change appears to be *the originating* cause, or to lie at the foundation of any disturbance which the understanding itself may seem to have sustained, and *even in some instances to form throughout the sole manifestation of the disease."*

On page 16, he defines moral insanity to be "a morbid perversion of the natural feelings, affections, inclinations, temper, habits, moral dispositions and natural impulses, *without any remarkable disorder or defect* of the intellect or knowing and reasoning faculties, and *particularly* without any insane illusion or hallucination."

Referring to the first and third divisions of insanity adopted by Heinroth, he says his definition comprehends all the modification of feeling or affection which belong to the first division as well as the disorders of will or propensity, which constitute the third department of that writer.

Heinroth's first kind of mental disorder consists of, says Prichard, disorders of the moral dispositions.

The first division consists in disorders of passion, feeling, or affection (of the *Gemueth*), or moral disposition. This has two forms.

Heinroth's first form was: 1. Exaltation, or excessive intensity; 2.

Undue vehemence of feeling; 3. Morbid violence of passions and emotions.

Second form: Depression, simple melancholy, dejection without delusion of the understanding.

Heinroth's third division comprises disorders of the voluntary powers or of the propensities, and of will.

Heinroth's first form was: Violence of will and of propensities; *Tollheit,* or madness without lesion of the understanding.

His second form embraced weakness, or incapacity of willing, and moral imbecility. (See pp. 18 and 19, Prichard's Treatise for the verification of the quoted language.)

On page 20, beginning chapter II. of his work, Prichard again defines moral insanity with the qualification that *"it sometimes co-exists with an apparently* unimpaired state of the intellectual faculties."

"Persons laboring under this disorder are capable of reasoning," he continues (p. 22), "or supporting an argument upon any subject within their sphere of knowledge, that may be presented to them; and they often display great ingenuity in giving reasons for the eccentricities of their conduct, and in accounting for and justifying the state of moral feeling under which they appear to exist. *In one sense indeed their intellectual faculties may be termed unsound; they think and act under* the influence of strongly excited feelings, *and persons accounted sane, are, under such circumstances, proverbially liable to error, both in judgment and conduct."*

The varieties of moral insanity, he says (p. 24), "are perhaps as numerous as the modifications of feeling or passion in the human mind. The most frequent forms however, are characterized either by the kind of excitement already described" [referring to his preceding descriptions], "or the opposite state of melancholic dejection." "The faculty of reason is not manifestly impaired, but a constant feeling of gloom and sadness clouds all the prospects of life." (Ibid. p. 24)

"There are many individuals living at large, and not entirely separated from society, who are affected in a certain degree with this modification of insanity. They are reputed persons of a singular, wayward, and eccentric character. An attentive observer will often recognize something remarkable in their manners and habits, which may lead him to entertain doubts as to their entire sanity; and circumstances are sometimes discovered, on inquiry, which add strength to his suspicion. In many instances it has been found that an hereditary tendency to madness has existed in the family, or that several relatives of the person affected have labored under other diseases of the brain. The individual himself has been discovered to have suffered, in a former period of life, an attack of madness of a decided character. His temper and dispositions are found to have undergone a change; to be not what they were previously to a certain time; he has become an altered man, and the difference has, perhaps, been noted from the period when he sustained some reverse of fortune, which deeply affected him, or the loss of some beloved relative. In other instances, an alteration in the character of the individual has ensued immediately on some severe shock which his bodily constitution has undergone. This has been either a disorder affecting the head, a slight attack of paralysis, a fit of epilepsy, or some febrile or inflammatory disorder, which has produced a perceptible change in the habitual state of the constitution. In some cases the alteration in temper and habits has been gradual and imperceptible, and it seems only to have consisted in an exaltation and increase of peculiarities which were always more or less natural and habitual.

"In a state like that above described, many persons have continued for years to be the sources of apprehension and solicitude to their friends and relatives. The latter, in many instances, cannot bring themselves to admit the real nature of the case. The individual follows the bent of his inclinations; he is continually engaging in new pursuits, and soon relinquishing them without any other inducement than mere caprice and fickleness. At length the total perversion of his affections, the dislike, and perhaps even enmity, manifested towards his dearest friends, excite greater alarm. When it happens that the head of a family labors under this ambiguous modification of insanity, it is sometimes thought necessary, from prudential motives, and to prevent absolute ruin from thoughtless and absurd extravagance, or from the results of wild projects and speculations, in the pursuit of which the individual has always a plausible reason to offer for his conduct, to make some attempt with a view to take the management of his affairs out of his hands. The laws have made inadequate provision for such contingencies, and the endeavor is often unsuccessful. If the matter is brought before a jury, and the individual gives pertinent replies to the questions that are put to him, and displays no particular mental illusion—a feature which is commonly looked upon as essential to madness—it is most probable that the suit will be rejected.''

Moral Insanity is insanity of conduct, feeling or impulse, or all combined, without such appreciable intellectual derangement that it would be recognized as insanity without the display of morbid feeling, impulse or conduct. It may, as Esquirol thought, include *delire partielle,* and undoubtedly does in many cases, and still be entitled to be designated moral insanity, because of the predominance and overshadowing and overmastering character of the aberration of the moral faculties over the faculties of the understanding.

It expresses itself rather in action than in speech, though it may utter itself in both, but unlike pure intellectual mania, which is often only recognized in the patient's language, it never expresses itself alone in written or spoken words.

Before the time of Pinel or Prichard, morbid changes in the appetites, propensities and feelings were recognized by medical nosologists. The *morosities* or *morbi-pathetici* of the older nosologists embraced them. A little later, Rush, in this country, also described some of them.

Since Prichard wrote his essay on moral insanity many terms have been invented to designate varieties of affective aberration, thus contracting the morbid area over which he extended the term in his discussion of his subject.

In the discussion of his subject he refers to some that already existed, as certain forms of melancholia, satyriasis and nymphomania, nostalgia and erotomania, characterizing the two latter as disorders of sentiment. The *folie raisonnante,* or reasoning mania of Pinel, he also referred to, and justly included, under the term moral insanity.

We now have varieties of moral insanity designated as emotional insanities, and the various destructive manias, which are characterized by impulse rather than delusion, as the homicidal, suicidal, kleptomaniacal and pyromanical impulses, so-called, which, when delusion is not prominently present really belong, like some varieties of lypemania, to the class of affective aberrations, as some forms of melancholia without delusion do. Some varieties of *primaere Verruecktheit* or congenital moral aberration, might likewise be classed where Prichard placed them, among the moral insanities. Some of the limited or monomanias belong to-day where Prichard placed them, notably some of the recorded instances of motiveless morbid impulse to destroy and steal, and to do other acts at variance with the unprovoked natural impulses of the human mind, though the majority of the monomanias or limited maniacal displays, undoubtedly have delusion associated with them after they have reached that stage when we are willing to recognize them as insanities.

From the foregoing and other considerations well known to observant alienists, it is obvious that the term moral insanity is no longer so essential to designate certain forms of real affective aberration, for which there was once no other satisfactory name, except that of reasoning mania, and through usage of the best and most observant writers, even of those who recognize this form of insanity, as they of necessity must, because, since it is founded in clinical fact, they have not failed to see it, the term has become somewhat more restrictive than formerly. Some have sought, and now attempt, to erase it altogether, and in seeking to do this, think they may expunge the disease from the imperishable records of clinical psychiatry. But this is impossible. It matters not materially what becomes of the name. It may ultimately even become politic to abandon it, though the time is not yet for such abandonment. Yet the clinical fact will remain. Its indubitable features, under any and every christening, will be plainly recognized by the true clinician in psychiatry; and they should be, for the welfare of the most pitiable, but often least commiserated, because less understood, of all the pitiable victims of mental disease, may depend upon their being recognized.

As the practical student of mental disease in all of its protean forms of manifestation, asks, "What is the form and meaning of this term moral insanity?" he is compelled interrogatively to answer, as one of the earlier of Prichard's English critics did, by asking. "What insanity is not moral?" and if the earliest indications of approaching insanity are moral, as pointed out even by Mayo, in his "Elements of the Pathology of the Human Mind," where is the logic in denying the possibility of its existence without the co-existence of appreciable intellectual aberration? Its existence is confessedly recognized and conceded as the earliest indication of approaching insanity, but although the person be morbidly deranged in his moral faculties, the insanity must not be conceded till the theoretical perceptible lesion of the reason appears! How unreasonable! How inconsistent! How unscientific! How unmedical! How absurd! not to recognize mental disease, which is confessedly apparent, until certain other symptoms appear, which shall bring the disease within the pale of preconceived and ideal boundaries, on the line of which we have written or rather have permitted the law to write its criterion of responsibility! Reason and observation unite to impel the recognition of this plain clinical fact in psychiatry, while prejudice and policy, or the erroneous association of immorality as its invariable accompaniment and characteristic, are permitted to obscure perceptions of plain medical truth.

If co-existent epilepsia, delusion or congenital imbecility can be proven some will concede the existence of moral derangement, and name it something else. If they do not find these or other morbid conditions affecting the intellect they explain it away by suggestions of "innate viciousness," "defective education." or even "hysteria," though the latter is sometimes one of the gravest of neurotic disorders and an important link, often, in the chain of neuropathic descent, and a precursory condition of unmistakable delusional aberration.

Why make the recognition of one form of mental disease depend upon the co-existence of another? This is not the rule in the diagnosis of mental maladies. To do this is to confess ourselves handicapped by an unwarranted skepticism in regard to the existence of this disease which we do not permit to embarrass us in the study of any other.

Moral insanity presents two plainly recognized clinical aspects.

1. Those cases in which there is neither a perceptible hallucination, illusion or delusion of the special senses; and

2. Those in which delusions exist, but constitute a secondary and minor feature of the *tout ensemble* of morbid phenomena.

It is not denied that imperative conceptions or morbid impulsions exist in many of the morally aberrated. They are indeed quite characteristic of this form of mental disease. Nor is it denied that delusive feelings exist as well as impulses. It is in the delusive feelings as contradistinguished from delusions associated with special sense perceptions, and what Mayo called notional delusions, that the foundations of the subsequently-developed delusions of the morally aberrated are laid, which often appear as these cases progress towards universally recognized intellectual aberration, and the natural termination of progressive insanity in dementia.

Having cleared away the mists of obscurity from Prichard's definition by letting him describe, instead of others for him, the types of mental disease which he meant to include under his definition, it now only remains for us to narrate some of our own confirmatory cases.

Preliminary to their introduction it will not be amiss to select a few cases from Mayo, which, while they serve to prove at least the possible existence of moral insanity, also answer to establish the mental bias of one of Prichard's most vigorous critics, whose analysis of Prichard's cases has repeatedly been imitated but never surpassed, and whose power of analysis was only equalled by his unconscious prejudices.

SOME OF MAYO'S CASES IN ILLUSTRATION OF HIS OBJECTION TO MORAL INSANITY:

Case I.—"The Honorable Mr. Tuchet, put to death by a pistol-shot; the marker of a shooting-gallery. The act was sudden, and there was no apparent motive; but it was not performed under any semblance of delirium. Mr. Tuchet was eccentric, and he was *blasé*. He fancied that he desired to be hanged; at the gallows he would probably have thought differently; and he was reckless and brutal enough to give himself a chance of his fate at the expense of the life of a fellow-creature. I have noticed him since, in the criminal department of Bedlam, *insouciant* and indifferent enough, but certainly not insane in any sense of the word that would not entirely disintegrate its meaning.''

Case II.—''A nursery-maid, placed in Bethlehem Hospital, 1846. A trifling disappointment relative to an article of dress had produced in her a wayward state of mind. She labored at the time under diminished catamenia. An object to which she was generally much attached came in her way, namely, the infant whom she nursed; and she destroyed it, as a fanciful child breaks, in its moodiness, a favorite doll. No fact more nearly approaching to delirium than the above was stated in exculpation or excuse at the trial. But Dr. Prichard's work on ''The Different Forms of Insanity, in Relation to Jurisprudence,'' was published in 1842; and, by 1846, juries had learned to convert the uncontrolled influences of temper into what he terms Instinctive Insanity. As an instance of this class of cases, in which the judicial authorities came rightly to a very different conclusion, I will quote to you the following one from Sir Woodbine Parish's last work on Buenos Ayres. Having spoken of a certain wind occasional in that climate, which in some persons produces peculiar irritability and ill-humor, almost amounting to a disorder of their moral faculties, he proceeds as follows:

Case III.—"Some years ago, Juan Antonio Garcia, aged between thirty-five and forty, was executed for murder at Buenos Ayres. He was a person of some education, and rather remarkable for the civility and amenity of his manners; his countenance open, his disposition generous. When this *viento norte*—this peculiar north-wind—set in, he appeared to lose all command over himself; and such became his irritability, that during its continuance he was engaged in continual quarrels and acts of violence. Before his execution, he admitted that it was the third man he had killed, besides being engaged in various fights with knives. When he arose from bed in the morning, he told Sir Woodbine's informant, he was 'always aware at once of its accursed influence upon him; a dull headache first, then a feeling of impatience at everything about him. If he went abroad, his headache generally became worse; a heavy weight seemed to hang over his temples. He saw objects, as it were, through a cloud, and was hardly conscious where he went. He was fond of play; and if, in such a mood, a gambling-house was in his way, he seldom resisted the temptation. Once there, a turn of ill-luck would so irritate him, that he would probably insult some one of the by-standers; if he met with any one disposed to resent his abuse, they seldom parted without bloodshed.' The relations of Garcia corroborated this account, and added, that no sooner had the cause of the excitement passed away, than he would deplore and endeavor to repair the effects of his infirmity. 'The medical man,' says Sir Woodbine, 'who gave me this account, attended him in his last moments, and expressed great anxiety to save his life, under the impression that he was hardly to be accounted a reasonable being.' 'But,' he adds, 'to have admitted that plea would have led to the necessity of confining half the population of the city when this wind sets in.' I quite agree with the conclusion which this remark implies, as to the fate of Garcia, says Mayo. He was himself aware of the murderous instinct to which he was liable, and of its exciting causes. Surely, when such knowledge is in the possession of the delinquent, he must be made responsible for the non-avoidance of exciting causes."

Case IV.—"M. Georget gives a case, which may be usefully contrasted with the above as to its claims on the plea of insanity. Hypolite Mendic, a non-commissioned officer in the French service, had gradually become morose, capricious, and brutal in his conduct, so as to excite the disgust of all his companions. This ends in disobedience of orders, and such violence towards his commanding officer as to render him liable, on trial, to the sentence of death. The trial proceeds, with the customary anxiety of the medical witnesses to make out a plea of insanity; and the tendency of the court, observable indeed in all M. Georget's reports, to give the criminal the benefit of the most careful inquiry into extenuating circumstances, and at the same time to protect the public against that plea, when overstrained. The symptoms of this case wanted the acuteness of character which alone tended to palliate the crimes of Garcia; but, in the course of Mendic's trial, one weighty fact was made out—namely, that before his outbreaks he was subject to an epileptiform seizure, out of which he emerged into the wayward state above noticed. This might fairly justify an hypothesis of delirium, as present at those paroxysms. If judgment was overpowered in Garcia, it was suspended in Mendic.

Mayo concludes case four with the following reflection, which indicates how questions of consciousness and responsibility constitute with him pre-established criteria of mental aberration, whereas it is the duty of the physician to determine first the question of mental disease, and after that the degree of consciousness and of responsibility associated with or dependent upon it. "There are shades of distinction in the amount of man's presumed responsibility to society, which should be indicated by corresponding shades of punishment when offences come; but, in all cases, consciousness is presupposed as a condition of responsibleness; so that a disease affecting consciousness renders the agent, so far forth, unfit in kind as well as in degree, to become an object of punishment." Certain phases of irresponsible insanity undoubtedly exist in association with consciousness, while unconscious automatism may be self-induced by certain persons neuropathically endowed, while in a state of responsible sanity. But the degree of insanity should determine the responsibility, not the degree of responsibility the question of insanity.

Case I, he characterized as simply one of brutal recklessness, because the act was not performed under any semblance of delirium, though it was "sudden and without apparent motive," and the perpetrator was remorseless, perfectly indifferent to the crime of having killed without motive or provocation, an inoffending person who had done him no harm, and was "eccentric and *blasé*." Brutal recklessness explains, to the mind of Mayo all of the conduct of this man, who "without the semblance of delirium, " "fancied that he desired to be hanged." The crown thought otherwise, and confined him in Bedlam.

Case II, he regarded as one of hysteria and temper, as if there could be no insanity in hysteria or temper displayed in killing an infant to whom one is much attached, and because of a trifling disappointment which the infant could have had no hand in causing. This was a natural and rational act, as natural as for a "fanciful child to break, in its moodiness, a favorite doll!"

Case III, he would have conceded to have been one of insanity, *"but to have admitted that plea would have led to the necessity* of confining half the *population of the city when the wind set in."*

Case IV.—"One weighty fact was made out, namely, that before his outbreak he was subject to an epileptiform seizure, out of which he emerged into the wayward state above noticed. This might fairly justify *an hypothesis* of delirium as present at those paroxysms," says Mayo. Saving clause!

Thus have all subsequent objectors to moral insanity blindly reasoned under the unconscious bias of previous hypotheses or the impolicy of its recognition, even those who have not mistakenly regarded moral insanity as invariably a form of very immoral insanity, or who do not demand that before insanity shall be recognized it shall appear in its unconscious forms. If the hypothesis of delirium can be sustained the insanity will be conceded, but why not recognize the insanity without the hypothesis?

Consciously or unconsciously, they reason it is not wise to recognize forms of insanity in which there appears a degree of responsibility; hence such insanity must not be accepted as an observed fact in science.

But what has the question of responsibility to do with a question of disease? and what if science should find a form of mental disease in which responsibility does really exist?

The fear of the church once deterred men from uttering the convictions of scientific discovery. Now it is the fear of public policy.

In the present day, as in the past, society has nothing to fear from the honest discriminating disclosures of true science. Society will remain as secure from the encroachments of crime with moral insanity boldly proclaimed as distinct from voluntary viciousness, as the church is unharmed by the universal acceptance of the doctrine of the rotation of the earth on its axis. The foundations of the teachings of Pinel and Prichard are as securely laid in mental pathology as those of Galileo are in the laws of astronomy, and they will become as universal. Possibly this disease may bear some other name, but the morbid mental condition of moral insanity is a basic fact in psychiatric symptomatology which cannot be reasoned away.

Delusion is comparatively exceptional, while perverted feeling is never absent in mental disease. Some of the features of moral insanity are psychically typical of all insanity with intellectual derangement. Why then seek to exclude moral insanity from recognition because intellectual derangement is not apparent, but if present, only inferentially so in certain cases? As well might those who believe in the existence of moral insanity deny the reality of delusional insanity where derangement of the affective character might not be discernible to confirm the delusion. But psychiatric science gives us no warrant for thus seeking to reason out of existence any of her facts. On the contrary she shows by clinical confirmations unmistakable to the faithful student of mental pathology who does not suffer his perceptions to be blinded to the truth by theoretical preconception and misconception of the improbable and unproveable invariable unity and harmony of the mental operations under all circumstances of health and disease of mind, how psycho-sensory or preceptional mental aberration may precede or co-exist with psycho-reflective or conceptional insanity.

She not only shows the reason to be primarily or chiefly touched by disease, but "the wishes, inclinations, attachments, likings and dislikings" morbidly changed, *"and this change appears to be the originating cause or to lie at the foundation of any disturbance which the understanding itself may seem to have sustained, and even in some instances to form throughout the sole manifestation of the disease."*[5]

Let us then like the true artist, study and copy, not ideally fashion nature. Fancy pictures of imaginary sanity are the more fatally misleading when skillfully painted by the hand of a master in psychiatry, and have sent many an undeserving lunatic to the stake and the gallows. Victims enough have been thus executed to counterbalance in all probability, the blunders of ignorance in finding insanity where none existed.

[5] Prichard on Insanity, p. 15, Bell's Library, Philadelphia; Edition, 1837.

The unthoughtful populace may applaud when they are misled by inconsiderate or pliant pseudo-science, as they approve the counterfeit resemblances of spurious art; but if we would have our pictures of mental disease endure the test of time and our names as discriminating observers survive with them, its every phase must be faithfully painted, regardless of any theoretical notions we may entertain of the supposed nature of mind or the imaginary demands of public interests or policy, with strict fidelity to nature. It is no part of the physician's province to adjust the phenomena of mental disease before admitting its existence, to the supposed exigencies of society or state polity. No question of expediency should be permitted to obscure when the faintest feature of real disease presented to the mind of the physician, notwithstanding such questions may totally eclipse the judicial vision whenever directed to certain (to them, inexplicable and dangerous,) phases of mental aberration. The true physician will diagnose real disease in whatever form it may be presented, regardless of such irrelevant considerations.

Note to conclude fourth paragraph on p. 28—Questions of responsibility belong to Law; questions of disease, to Medicine. Law may find responsibility and testamentary capacity, where we physicians find disease, and it has found both co-existent with, sometimes much and sometimes little, disease of brain affecting the mind, but its conclusions do not change the facts of pathology. It is our duty to find out the facts, and so far as practicable in the nature of mental disease, to enlighten Law as to the bearings of our facts on the legal question of responsibility, but not to be blinded by it so that we can no longer see disease where it exists.

3. Clinical Evidences of Borderland Insanity

Irving C. Rosse

The name that I have taken to include the forms of mental degeneration about to be considered may not be the most appropriate one from a strict psychiatrical point of view. However, when we take into account the difficulty in studying the relation between sympathetic instinct and the cerebro-spinal experiences, as well as the vague line that is supposed to separate reflex action and volition, it is hardly worth while to confine one's mental perception to names, or to definitions and classifications that are purely arbitrary and comparative.

Everybody knows of positive and negative electricity: of black and white; of health and disease; of high spirits and mental depression, but our knowledge of the imperceptible difference in their intermediate conditions is extremely limited. Analagous to this is the study of the phenomena of a class of persons standing in the twilight of right reason and despair—a vast army whose units, consisting of individuals with minds trembling in the balance between reason and madness, are not so sane as to be able to control themselves, nor yet so insane as to require restraint or seclusion.

For the scientific mind the clinical observation of cases of this kind carries with it a sort of fascination; the analysis of the facts relatively thereto seems to be the order of the day, and is a subject worthy of occupying attention and exercising our sagacity. Their study being of comparatively recent date, contemporary psychiatry has created from them a special class, the so-called pseudo-monomaniacs, who not only show certain well determined psychic disturbances, but at the same time are conscious of the unusual phenomena taking place in their nerve centres, and are capable of discussing and even describing their intellectual and moral derangements.

Aside from clinical consideration patients thus affected are of forensic importance, since the study of their malady touches some special medico-legal points particularly delicate and obscure. The solution of such interlocutory questions as may arise from the latter point of view being rather juridical than medical, I shall take for granted the pathognomonic character of the malady in question, and without further generalization shall mention a few typical illustrations selected from the experience of my own practice as neurologist.

For obvious reasons the cases are shorn of many personal details, yet the omission is not such as to interfere with the material facts.

The first case that I shall mention is that of a young man, a clerk, in whom there was an aberration of the genetic instinct. He consulted me, upon the advice of Dr. N.S. Lincoln, for a morbid impulse that had troubled him for some time. The impulse was homocidal, and manifested itself in an almost uncontrollable desire to kill some member of his family, though for what reason he could not tell, as he had no idea of committing a crime, and was well aware of the difference between right and wrong. The trouble was unknown to his family, although the impulse to kill his father had come so irresistibly while sitting at breakfast, that in order not to yield to it, he suddenly quit the room and afterwards came to my office in a state of great agitation.

I found at first but little in this young man's antecedents to account for his neuropathic state. He had no marked peculiarity of look, speech or action, and a long series of questions, put with a view to lead up to a mental weak point or delusion, failed to elicit any other symptom. The great bodily functions were apparently normal, with the exception of that of the generative organs. Among other things, he informed me that for more than a year he had almost nightly visited a young woman whom he kissed and fondled in a lascivious way, but without accomplishing the act of sexual intercourse.

In this case it required but little diagnostic and pathological acumen to trace the genetic connection between the brain and testicles, and to direct the treatment accordingly.

When I last saw this patient he was fresh-colored, well nourished, and otherwise apparently well.

Subsequently to this I was consulted by a Washington lawyer with a large practice as patent attorney. This man was overworked, his system was below par; he had insomnia; absence of the patellar tendon reflex; clavus-hystericus on the right side of his head, and was myopic. He complained of pain in his right eye; of inability to use his mind for more than ten minutes at a time, and labored under the notion that he was becoming deranged and would soon wind up in an asylum. The thought of his faculties being compromised he had kept more or less in a latent state by the influence of his will, so that the trouble was unknown to any one except his medical adviser.

I had the patient carefully examined by a competent ophthalmologist, both in Washington and New York, with a view to find out the cerebroscopic indications furnished by the eye, as well as to correct any ocular defect that might account for a part of the symptoms. The treatment that followed being only partly successful, I persuaded the patient to quit work and go to Europe for a short trip. He did this with much benefit; but some months after his return the symptoms came back with renewed vigor.

I advised another long sea voyage on board a sailing vessel from Baltimore to Rio Janeiro and back. This trip was followed by highly satisfactory results to the patient, who, saved from the stigma of an asylum, regained his mental health, has since married, and is now entirely well.

In February 1884, I was consulted by a prominent business man of Washington, of middle age, who had suffered from obstinate insomnia and its train of evil consequences for eleven years, and during that time had contracted the bromide habit. He had hypochondria, morbid fear, impotency, and a suicidal impulse. In addition to treatment by local physicians, he had been under eminent neurologists in Philadelphia, New York, London and Paris, with but indifferent results. His atavistic antecedents were not entirely satisfactory, but his venereal history was fairly good; he had stopped the use of tobacco, and his habits were temperate, though he was not a teetotaler. The patient complained of general languor and debility; of a clawing pain within the head; of inability to concentrate his thoughts; of loss of will power, and a fear of insanity. He said that he had taken the bromides of potassium and sodium in enormous doses since 1873. For two years, from 1874 to 1876, he took daily 135 grains without missing a day. The quantity was gradually decreased in 1878 to 80 grains a day, and to 50 grains in 1883, during a visit to the "Healing Springs" of Virginia. He subsequently took 90 grains daily. The patient was cachectic; but there were no sensory, motor, or mental symptoms indicative of any gross organic lesion. Examination with the differential calorimeter, however, revealed the existence of a considerable degree of cerebral hyperaemia.

Under treatment my patient made but indifferent progress towards improvement. I had nearly exhausted my efforts to break up the bromide habit, when Dr. Wm. A. Hammond informed me that he had cured several cases of this habit by prescribing a solution of chloride of sodium, the dose of which is gradually increased, the bromide, at the same time being correspondingly decreased until a few minims is reached, when the patient breaks off the habit on being told that he is taking nothing but common table-salt. This plan did well for several weeks, but during my summer absence in Europe the patient accidentally learned from his druggist what he was taking, and immediately discontinued the prescription. On my return in autumn, in a fit of sheer desperation, I directed the patient to eat large quantities of grapes, the object of which was explained to him, and within a week I had the surprise and satisfaction to see a salutary change. The psychical depression was much less, and the craving for the bromides was nearly gone. The habit is now broken up, the patient sleeps fairly, has regained his virility, is rid of the morbid impulse, and is bodily and mentally reconstructed.[1]

A patient, in a state of fear and having the idea of persecution, came to me in November, 1887, in the person of a middle-aged German with a wild, uneasy, restless eye, and a suspicious manner.

He had conceived the notion that his instability was the result of his parents being much under the influence of wine at the time he was begotten; that he was sexually out of order; that he was being persecuted generally; and that he would soon be hopelessly insane.

Like many of these patients, he showed a morbid propensity to write letters, one of which details the subjective symptoms; so I will give them in his own words:

"The most foul and degrading remarks are made about me in the office I am employed in by at least one person—aside from everything else, such is the case, and simply for the purpose of annoying me. I know this. I would not mind such remarks at all, but the effect of the uttered words on my imagination is actually a terrible one; the oddest combinations are formed, and I am almost

[1] See the Medical Record, New York, October 10, 1885, p. 147.

completely subdued by them in my actions, motions, etc. All this could to some degree be avoided if I was not so morbidly sensitive; still the effect is there.

"A couple of years ago I noticed numbness in my feet. This occurred while I was walking in the street; it struck me as very peculiar. I had similar feelings on several occasions at that time, but they have since disappeared.

"Last year and the previous one I noticed that I frequently and painfully bit my tongue while eating, in an almost awkward manner. I ascribed this as a paralytic symptom. Such occurences I have not since experienced.

"After meals I feel that my stomach has to perform considerable work. I get a hot and heavy feeling in my head, which lasts for a considerable time, and which is accompanied, especially in the morning, with considerable nervousness and excitement.

"While talking with persons in the office, it seems as if I was constantly ashamed of something, which is comparatively and partly true.

"If I have to stand up when a person speaks to me, I have the desire to sit down or to take hold of something or rest my hands and elbows on something. Very often my head begins to swim; I have a feeling of falling forward and to cast my eyes down.

"I have had moments, not two months ago, when I became indescribably alarmed, as if being on the verge of losing my mind and becoming violent. This has left me since I stopped drinking coffee.

"As a fact, I have gone through all kinds of fixed ideas; I thought I had mastered them all; but now of a sudden my worst apprehensions have been excelled by persons actually expressing aloud my innermost thoughts.

"Aside from all inherited defects of mind and thought, my present trouble seems to me to be the morbid state of my sexual, mental, and physical condition. And, as remarked before, any allusion to my person in that respect makes me act almost like an hypnotic.

"Respectfully yours,

"_____ _____."

Any one familiar with such cases as the foregoing knows how few are the objective symptoms and how unsatisfactory is their treatment. Such patients, never remaining long with one physician, ultimately become the prey of quacks and charlatans, or may become hopelessly insane.

My latest knowledge of this man is that he had fallen into the hands of an itinerant quack, who mulcted him of several hundred dollars and took his notes for several hundred more.

In September, 1888, a business man, of a highly neurotic family, several members of which I had treated for nervous affections, came to me on account of his distracted mental condition. Two of his family had already died insane, and he imagined that he was going the same way. His alcoholic, venereal, and nicotinic habits were of the worst, and had left their stamp in his physiognomy, and I may even say in his speech and action. I would be too long a story to relate the numerous symptoms, subjective and objective, most of which were clearly traceable to constitutional syphilis.

I placed this patient on the twentieth of a grain of biniodide of mercury three times a day, and, being a man of means, I directed him to go to Atlantic City, to take hot baths of sea-water, and lead a quiet, sensible out-door life. Under this regimen, which the patient observed scrupulously, the cerebral symptoms soon faded away. He regained his former health, but a year subsequently relapsed into dipsomania.

Among functional intellectual troubles that may arise from morbid fear, not the least curious are those affecting the feelings or emotions in the more recently determined conditions known as moral hypochondria, agoraphobia, and the peculiar morbid condition that syphilis may sometimes give rise to. The last named I witnessed in a case of syphiliphobia in a young naval officer, who came to me on September 10, 1889. He had contracted syphilis some years previously, and had apparently been treated successfully, but having married, and his wife being pregnant, he developed a well-marked case of mental invalidism without the appearance of any distinctive syphilitic lesion. After the manner of most of these cases, he had consulted eminent medical men in various cities, both at home and abroad, who had equally failed with myself to give satisfaction. Remaining under observation but a short time, he quit me for another physician and I have since lost sight of him.

A type in which the morbid trouble is more distinct and better defined is to be found in agoraphobia, or, as it is sometimes called, kenophobia. For the last two years I have had under treatment a well-marked case that is subject to exacerbations. Two other patients that I have cannot look up to the dome of the Capitol or the summit of the Washington Monument without being seized with agoraphobic symptoms. The three cases occurred in foreigners, men of intelligence and education, who had kept the symptoms concealed from every one as long as possible, for fear of being thought insane.

I wish I could dwell longer on this interesting form of psychic insufficiency; but having written up the subject in Buck's "Reference Hand-book of the Medical Sciences," I must refer those interested to that article.

The next case to which I shall call attention is that of a priest of twenty-eight years, who was dyspeptic, emaciated, and hypochondria-cal. When a boy of seventeen he had cerebro-spinal meningitis, from which he convalesced slowly and had become deaf. What troubled him most, however, was the fact that he had lost faith in the tenets of the religion in which he had been educated. For the last two years he said that remorse had seized him, and being shrouded in spiritual darkness he fell into a lethargy of despair, cursing the sun each morning, and hoping every day would be his last.

This case convinced me that the gastro-intestinal condition and reli-gion are somewhat interdependent. I directed the treatment accord-ingly, and soon had the satisfaction to see both mental and physical improvement, after which the patient left for his home in one of the Southern States.

Another case in which religion entered as an element occurred in a boy of seventeen, whom I was called in consultation to see at a private sanitarium near Baltimore in February, 1886. Having become much preoccupied with religious matters, he developed into a case of hyster-ocatalepsy, and was in a pitiable condition when I saw him, being emaciated, motionless, and speechless. He also had the waxen flexibil-ity of limbs peculiar to the cataleptic state, and the least touch about the face caused such strong contraction of the muscles that it was necessary to give his food and medicine with a pump after forcing open the mouth with a gag in which was a round hole.

The patient made rapid improvement under treatment, and in a few weeks returned to his home near Washington, where he became strong and well under a regimen in which severe muscular exercise and suppression of the emotions were the prominent factors.

Unhappily, this young man's religious instinct was again perverted in the summer of 1889. On a chilly day in November he came home about dinner-time, refusing to speak or to eat, and showed symptoms of his former malady. These rapidly developed into acute mania, from which the patient died in the sanitarium where I first saw him.

A curious case that has puzzled me much is that of a young man of twenty-one who had partial paranoia with pseudo-aphasic ideas. He was referred to me by Dr. Godding, of the Government Asylum for the Insane, in May 1889. This man was employed in a newspaper-office, where he attended daily to his duties without having incurred suspicion as to his mental state. Being something of a student, and having lately read numerous works on psychology, he conceived the notion that he was suffering from a perversion of the ego; that he was unable to perform an act of judgment; that he had lost all his faculties save that of memory; and that all his movements were simply automatic and in no way influenced by will-power.

Having exhausted the gamut usual in examining such cases, I was unable to discern any physical reason that might account for the mental symptoms. The patient assured me that his habits were good, and he did not have that furtive, uneasy, restless look peculiar to victims of secret vice. The more noticeable features of this case were the perversity in using the pronoun "it" in reference to vague symptoms which he could not or would not explain; the ingenious manner in which he answered my questions; and the specious arguments he used in discussing his case with me—this, too, in view of the alleged fact of his inability to construct a mental process, and his belief that he was suffering from aboulimania.

An occasional aloetic aperient with a course of ergot and bromide was followed by a breaking up of the fixed idea regarding his automatism and memory; and a month later I succeeded in convincing him of his ability to perform an act of judgment to the extent of constructing a syllogism, though he could not "distribute the middle third." He also recognize the fact that he had *willed* to come and see me and to do many other acts, but he could not break up the troublesome habit of introspection, and vagueness in regard to the "it" was still as pronounced as before. In fact, there was a persistent misuse of the pronoun when he should have used a noun. In this respect he seemed to be suffering from a kind of aphasia, which showed itself in an inability to use nouns. Two months subsequently the patient still showed this phenomenon of the impairment of the function of expression. His articulate speech did not permit of its being outwardly construed or interpreted. Yet at this time the patient acknowledged that he saw an improvement in his judgment, and that he had got rid of some of the functional derangements of which he formerly complained. The latest feature of this case is the fancied loss of all emotional control, although to the observer this is no more apparent than the fabulous wealth of many general paretics.

That the brain cortex was impaired in the next observation I think will be readlily admitted. It is that of a middle-aged man who was dyspeptic, used tobacco and alcohol to excess, and suffered from obstinate insomnia. Among other peculiarities he informed me that he was a "crack-walker," and would not for any consideration knowingly step on a crack of the flag-stones when walking in the street. He had also developed the curious phenomenon known as mirror-writing. This functional agraphic condition was unaccompanied by paralysis. He wrote with the right hand, in a reverse way from right to left, anything that I could dictate. The act was done with the rapidity of ordinary writing, and the chirography was so good that when held up to a mirror it was easily read. This man is intelligent and educated, converses rationally about the peculiarities of his case, and believes that he will die insane. He is at present in business in New York.

In connection with the foregoing case it may be worth recalling Leonardo da Vinci's reversed manuscript in the Milan Library, which many neurologists think is the result of an attack of right hemiplegia, and that he had become incapable of writing otherwise.

Akin to this nervous instability of the "crack-walker" is the morbid fear arising from the neglect of something very trivial. Most of us know of the mild manifestation of morbid mental energy related of Dr. Johnson's left foot, and of his peculiarity in touching certain lamp-posts with his walking-stick. Something like this I have lately seen well illustrated in the case of a wealthy retired merchant, an American of more than average intelligence, who, while sojourning abroad at Nice, had a morbid fear of going to bed unless he has walked every day to the end of the Promenade, some distance from his hotel, and there touched with his walking-stick a certain cactus. On several occasions he went to bed without going through this little daily performance; but he had invariably to get up, dress himself, and repeat the episode before his fears had sufficiently subsided to enable him to sleep. On a subsequent visit to Washington the same alteration of the nervous level occurred. He was obliged each night to walk from Willard's Hotel to the Capitol and there touch the curbstone with his stick, or else sleep was impossible.

The mental disturbance so common about the period of the menopause may be classed in the same category as the cases just mentioned. Among other patients of this class that I have had under observation for the last year is a woman of more than usual intelligence and character. Like many of her sex, she had an unhappy love-affair in her early days, and had never married.

She was neurasthenic, had insomnia, facial paralysis, lagophthalmia of one eye, and complained of tingling and numbness in the lower extremities. Her mind had taken a decidedly erotic turn. She talked freely and with great prolixity of her sexual starvation, of the mysteries of life, of copulating with a Newfoundland dog, and of other obscene subjects. In addition to this moral obliquity, the power of attention and or memory was weakened.

Most of the bodily symptoms in this case have yielded to treatment, but mentally the patient is still hanging around the borderland. Her latest freak, shown in a propensity to write, has brought to me a correspondence that may be looked upon as a psychic autobiography. Every week or so she mails to me a letter with a special delivery-stamp. The letters are well written as far as regards grammar and choice of expression, but the ideas therein are vague and show a weakening of the logical inhibitions. One of these letters tells me of a miracle that had happened to her: that she was walking in the street, feeling so depressed as to be nearly insane with wretchedness, when suddenly she had a strange experience; the operation of natural law had stopped in her being; a beatific feeling came over her, followed by the most perfect peace and quiet, and a voice spoke to her words of consolation and good advice.

Her last letter to me was not so much wanting in the mal-assimilation of its mental components as it was in relevancy. So far as it relates to anything in my mind it is totally incomprehensible. It reads as follows:

"Now listen to a true friend, and do not imagine that any one knows, for they do not. I detected a woman watching some one's house one Sunday evening when I was starting out for church.

"That is enough for a woman who has seen such things duplicated. It is one of those cases in which a true friend can take no part except with damaging results to all and no benefit to any.

"Don't let a band of evil-doers break your friend up, and don't let him do that which men so frequently do (but women rarely).

"Running away from the effects of some one else's evildoing is neither courageous nor manly. Don't let your friend neglect his business hours or impress any one that something troubles him to the neglect of business. There is always some honorable way out of all complications in which an innocent party is a victim. Your friend will come out all right. Don't let him get the blues.

"The more hydra-headed they show themselves the better for him.

"Your friend,

"_____ _____."

In December, 1889, I was called to see a young unmarried man, a lawyer from an adjoining State, who had come to Washington for rest and recuperation from a late mental illness. From his brother and himself I learned that he had lately been engaged in an important lawsuit, the prosecution of which had incurred overwork, anxiety, and sleeplessness. Having finished his case in court, he was waiting for the train on the platform of a railway-station, where he was the subject of a visual hallucination. To his great surprise his law-partner, whom he had just left, stood beside another man at the end of the platform, and, on approaching to shake hands with him, the apparition disappeared. Turning away and walking toward the other end of the platform, the same thing occurred, to his utter terror. He subsequently suffered from obstinate insomnia and the monoideaism of paranoia, which showed itself in the belief that various persons were trying to prove him dishonest in his profession and to persecute him generally. Although conscious of the delusion, he was unable to reason himself out of it.

There was nothing that I could elicit from this patient's hereditary or atavistic antecedents to denote the existence of a vesania or a neurosis. His alcoholic and venereal history was good; but he was a great smoker, and had had a domestic trouble, the details of which it would be irrelevant to mention.

Salient features of this case were impaired general health, dilated pupils, hebetude, and a slow staccato way of talking after the manner of speech noticed in katatonia.

After a few weeks' treatment directed to restoring the general health and relieving insomnia, the symptoms gradually faded away; the patient recovered, and is now well and attends to the duties of his profession.

In studying the prodromal symptoms of psychical impairment, one seldom meets with a more curious condition than filth-dread or mania of contamination, the so-called mysophobia or rupophobia.

A case that I have came to me on May 7th. His father visited my office before I had seen the patient, and, in telling what he had noticed as peculiar in his son, unwittingly gave a very good clinical history of the affection. This boy had developed the utmost horror of becoming contaminated. The fear of defilement extended to nearly all his surroundings, both at home and in the street, and it needed constant assurances, with the exercise of much parental firmness, to relieve his mind. Aside from touching ordinary objects, after which he subjected his hands to innumerable washings, the fear of the pollution extended more particularly to greenbacks and to using the water-closet, which he did with great reluctance, after covering the seat with clean towels, and would in no circumstance touch the handle that flushed the bowl. He had a morbid fear of having his hair touched, a dread of shaking hands, of coming in contact or running against any one in the street, and an unclean or badly dressed person caused such loathing that he would cross to the opposite side.

On examination I could find no appreciable somatic cause for the condition in question. There was perfect integrity of perceptive aptitude, acoustic, tactile, and visual stimuli, and the patient talked intelligently of what he considered exaggerated peculiarities that he was unable to control by his will. At my suggestion patient has lately crossed the Atlantic in a sailing ship, and at last accounts was doing well.

Whether this morbid fear of contact be only an anomaly of the sensibility and instinct or an undeveloped paranoia, I am unable to say. The psychopathic symptoms mentioned in this case do not belong to the ful-blown variety; they occupy a sort of neutral ground that is neither Spain nor Gibraltar.

I shall not attempt to formulate any general conclusions from the neuropathic states and mental anomalies that I have endeavored to portray in the foregoing recital. But I may say that the study of cases showing rudimentary indications of insanity is of more value, from an educational point of view, than that of a fully-developed case. The early recognition of the functional derangements that precede the outset of confirmed insanity is often a matter of great difficulty. Such cases rarely come within the experience of asylum physicians, and being subjected to neglect in the incipient stage of the malady, they eventually go to make up the larger proportion of incurable lunatics.

I trust I may be pardoned for saying again that such cases are of practical importance from a juridical point of view. Who, for instance, would not question the criminal responsibility or the civil capacity of nearly all the persons just mentioned, after knowing their clinical history? In the case of a crime or a misdemeanor, who can discern clearly whether one of these has yielded to an unhealthy and irresistible incitement, and not to the suggestions of his interests or his passions? Or, in other words, whether the act would be a morbid phenomenon, and not a passional phenomenon? A question might also arise in the matter of contracts, or as to the validity of wills of such persons.

Since lawyers are dependent upon medical knowledge for enlightenment in such equivocal cases, they resolve themselves into a simple question of medical diagnosis; and the only way out of the embarrassment which will lead to a correct judgment is the rigid application of general diagnostic means and the ordinary proceedings of clinical investigation.

PART II

1930s AND 1940s

THE 1930s

By the 1930s the psychoanalytic movement had solidified, on both sides of the Atlantic, and its popularity had advanced to the point where it was becoming meaningful and increasingly important to define so-called "borderline" cases. Psychoanalysis had been branching out toward psychotic cases, hitherto off-limits, on an ever wider front. Unexpected successes, as with Ruth Mack-Brunswick's paranoid patient, described in the *Journal of Nervous and Mental Disease* in 1928, left some with the hope that only the most chronic forms of schizopherenia were beyond the border of amenability to the analytic method. Besides, the phenothiazine drugs were still a generation away, so, apart from traditional supportive technics and the kind of environmental manipulation advocated by Hinsie for schizophrenics (also in the late 1920s), psychoanalysis was, in a manner of speaking, the only game in town.

There was still a tendency in the early 1930s to speak of a border between neurosis and psychosis not so much in relation to analyzability but in relation to the original meanings of these terms, much as they might have been used by Kraepelin and other traditional alienists of the late nineteenth century. This comes through in the article of Oberndorf (1930), who, though an analyst, still was grounded in the notions of a hereditary factor in the psychoses. This notion was rapidly shucked by the next generation of analysts in America, who regarded the idea of hereditary taint as too discouraging. It could not afford to be true. It is true, all the same, but could not be accepted by psychoanalysts again until the advent of effective medications in the 1950s, at which point schizophrenia and manic depression became less frightening labels than they once were. It has, de fortiori, become easier to accept that certain milder conditions might be borderline with respect to these psychoses, in addition to being borderline with respect to analyzability.

Still, in the 1930s, Kasanin (1933) began to notice that some cases of dementia praecox had rather good outcomes, especially where the onset had been abrupt and with clear psychological precipitants. These were the so-called "schizoaffective" cases—Kasanin coined this term—borderline between neurosis (specifically schizoid personality) and (deteriorating) schizophrenic psychosis. Some of his cases were double borderlines, since they were also situated between the schizophrenic and the affective psychoses. How many would be borderline by contemporary measures is unclear, though some resembled what Hoch and Polatin called "pseudoneurotic schizophrenics," who were (in many instances) like mixtures of DMS-3 borderline and schizotypal personalities.

As the 1930s draw to a close, we see the publication of Stern's paper (included in the anthology)—the pivotal article in our history, since it put the term "borderline" on the map, at least within the analytic community, and set in motion the nosological and metapsychological trends which have crystallized into the more sharply defined concepts of the 1980s.

At the end of the 1930s and the beginning of the 1940s the borderline concept not begins to take shape as we know it today, but does so specifically in the United States. One may ask why this is so. The answer, I believe, is at least in good measure a reflection of the hasty relocation inspired, of course, by the Nazis (who, however ludicrous they appeared in the 1920s, had by 1930 to be taken quite seriously), of almost all the pioneers of psychoanalysis. Most fled to America; only a few, to France and England. Under the influence of Stern, Deutsch, Alexander, Fromm-Reichmann, Bychowski, Zilboorg, Rado, Hartmann, and many others, American psychiatry was revolutionized.

America is a young country with less firmly rooted traditions than those encountered in Europe and was correspondingly more receptive to new modes of thought. Psychoanalytic principles were welcomed and incorporated by many hospital-based psychiatrists (including those without formal analytic training), who in turn taught resident trainees to respect and to incorporate these principles into their own developing models of psychiatric nosology and treatment. Young psychiatrists here were exposed to the whole range of emotional conditions from the very worst to the very mildest; they were disposed to apply the analytic method throughout this range, taking it as far as it would go. Harry Stack Sullivan in the 1930s and John Rosen in the 1940s did not back away even from so-called "regressed schizophrenics." Hence it became important here to define borderline cases of analyzability. This need was less critical in England where a two-tier system of treatment has remained in force to this day: hospital-based, nonanalytically trained psychiatrists treating the psychotic cases; milder cases being referred by them or by other physicians to analysts, who tend to work in a classically analytic mode from the very beginning of contact with their referred patients. Given this greater split between the medically oriented psychiatrists—and the psychoanalysts, less medically oriented than their counterparts in the United States, there is less motivation for either group to concern itself with what we could consider borderline cases. The analysts' toughest cases were given other labels (narcissistic, schizoid, among others). The psychiatrists' milder cases also were assigned other labels such as "atypical depression." (See Paykel, 1982.)

It is factors of this sort—factors of language and custom—that account for the popularity of the borderline concept in some locales and for its unpopularity in others. Throughout the Western world, indeed, in almost all the world, the varieties of patients are rather the same. The proportions with which these varieties are distributed in each country are a bit different. The labels differ radically. What use the British in the 1930s did make of the term "borderline," incidentally, was not particularly illuminating. There is one comment of Melanie Klein's colleague, Edward Glover, who said, ". . . we are all larval psychotics and have been since age two." His position was that, depending on the stresses to which we are exposed, we can all slide from neurosis to borderline to psychosis and back again. This is good poetry but bad psychiatry. At all events it remains true to this day that in Britain what we call "borderline" here in the colonies are either the hospital psychiatrists' best cases or the analysts' worst cases.

THE 1940s

During the 1940s a number of the concepts associated with borderline conditions, as adumbrated in Stern's article, become defined more sharply. Although the term "borderline" became more popular as a diagnostic label among American psychoanalysts, largely through the impetus Stern's paper provided, many competing terms were still being used, or else created anew, as designations for clinical conditions that overlapped, or were coterminous altogether, with the kinds of cases others were beginning to call "borderline."

The classic paper of Helene Deutsch (1942) laid the foundation for contemporary psychoanalytic formulations of the borderline, most notably those enunciated by Kernberg. The importance of evaluating object relations, where characteristic disturbances are encountered among borderline patients, was emphasized in Deutsch's paper. She did not use the word "borderline," referring to other borderline-level (as we would now think of them) patients by the phrase, "as-if" personality. Her patients experienced a mild but bothersome kind of depersonalization of which they were not conscious, but which others could sense and comment upon. They lacked warmth, depth, "realness;" people sensed there was something definitely, but indefinably "wrong."

The lack of warmth, the excessive formality, the quality of always acting, as though on stage, but without any enthusiasm, would appear to emanate from a serious deficiency in the central feeling about the self. The as-if patient cannot state with conviction "who I am," "what do I really stand for," etc. In this regard, Deutsch clearly has in mind the type of identity problem that Erikson was later to write on, under the heading of "ego-diffusion," and that, still later, Kernberg was to situate as the cornerstone of his psychostructural model of borderline personality organization. The formality and lack of genuineness of Deutsch's "as-if" patients, if we hold these qualities up against the item lists of borderline and schizotypal personalities in DSM-3, coincide more with what is referred to as the schizotypal's "poor rapport." With respect to their mimicry of good adaptation, they characteristically show the "good superficial socialization" stressed by Gunderson in his description of the borderline personality disorder. Unlike the borderline established by Gunderson and DSM, however, Deutsch's as-if patient adapts via superficial identification with others and, at least in the beginning of a new relationship, suppresses anger. This lends an air of what Deutsch called "mild amiability," readily convertible, as she so accurately perceived, to evil. The current syndromal definitions of Gunderson, and DSM, in contrast, underline the quality of anger.

The DSM item of "emptiness" is to be found in Deutsch's description of the as-if. One of the patients she described in detail had complained, "I am so empty! . . . I have no feelings." Elsewhere in the same article Deutsch (p. 317) alludes to the impoverishment of the total personality as a characteristic distinguishing the as-if from the neurotic-level hysteric, with whom the former could at times be confused.

The other feature singled out as crucial to the concept of borderline structure or personality organization in contemporary parlance is the preservation of the capacity to assess reality accurately. (See below, Frosch, 1964; Kernberg, 1967.) This attribute is also mentioned specifically in the paper on the as-if patient: "The fact that reality-testing is fully maintained removes this condition from our concept of psychosis" (p. 318).

The difficulty in finding socially acceptable channels either for dealing with anxiety or for expressing the main interests of the self—a difficulty common in borderline patients of whatever description—is alluded to by Deutsch in her mention of a "deep disturbance in the process of sublimation." From this derives Kernberg's "non-specific" diagnostic feature: "poor sublimatory channeling." Central to this is the failure to knit together into a "single, integrated personality" the multitude of early identifications with caretakers. In such situations, as Deutsch depicts in her case examples, no one pursuit or interest emerges as special to the patient, motivating him to devote the time, practice, and dedication one ordinarily devotes to the sort of work or hobby that feels "right" for one. Without a strong inner sense of self, no line of endeavor seems more real (let alone fascinating) than any other; sublimatory activities scarcely develop. Those who do have some particular interests but who are continually buffeted by bouts of intense anxiety also, of course, fail to develop proper sublimatory outlets because the time and patience required for the perfection of such outlets keeps getting interrupted by panic, crisis, and the like. This source of disturbance, common to the borderline state, received less attention by Deutsch but is given its full due in the subsequent literature.

Impulsivity, the other "nonspecific" feature of borderline-level function, according to contemporary psychoanalytic as well as general psychiatric nosology, is not mentioned under a separate heading by Deutsch, although one of her patients clearly exhibited it (a "hypomanic" woman who "vacillated between giving in to her instincts and holding them in check" and who indulged episodically in sexual perversions).

Throughout the 1940s the tendency to suppose that schizophrenia was the psychosis that a borderline condition approximated remained very much in force. This is particularly true in America, but then it is chiefly within the United States that the borderline concept grew popular to begin with. The American habit at midcentury of labeling all but the most obviously manic psychotic patients as "schizophrenic" has been noted by many authors in the 1960s and 1970s. Even the European émigrés were caught up in this way of thinking, which is evident in the Deutsch paper itself, as well as in the works of Bychowski and Zilboorg.

While Deutsch was making advances in the so-called "metapsychological" (roughly speaking, the conceptual or theoretical) understanding of borderline conditions, similar advances in the practical realm were being made by Melitta Schmideberg.

Schmideberg, herself, constitutes an interesting chapter in the history of psychoanalysis. She was the daughter of Melanie Klein. Relations between the two appear to have been considerably less than cordial. The psychoanalytically informed reader might wish to speculate whether, in reaction to her mother (who carried theory close to the point of religious dogma, with her rather mystical pronouncements on the depressive and schizoid "positions" of infants), Schmideberg would have ended up either advocating a quite different theory or else abandoning theory altogether in favor of the down-to-earth clinical approach. However this may be, Schmideberg became renowned for her work with delinquents, was for years the head of The Association for the Psychotherapeutic Treatment of Offenders, and showed herself as tireless and inventive in the treatment of impossible and next-to-impossible cases.

As we can see from her 1947 paper, her style, both in her working-life and in her writing, was direct, firm, human, caring, flexible, and candid. We may abstract from her comments what good supportive therapy for borderlines would look like, if carried to the uttermost by someone who made himself available night and day, and will stop at nothing, within professional bounds, to get his patient better. Schmideberg's approach with borderlines was not purely "supportive," of course, but rather the shifting amalgam of analytical and supportive technics altogether appropriate to the intensive therapy of such patients.

At the end of the decade Hoch and Polatin's article on pseudoneurotic schizophrenia appeared. Their paper was in the spirit of Bleuler (who had once alluded to non-deteriorating forms of schizophrenia) and also used Bleuler's broad (and as we now consider them, imprecise) diagnostic criteria. A similar form of "good-outcome" schizophrenia was described by Kasanin, as we saw, in the 1930s. Hoch and Polatin mention "borderline" as an alternate term for the condition they were about to describe.

The symptoms and characteristics to which they drew attention include many of the items that were singled out by subsequent writers, analytic and nonanalytic alike, as crucial to the borderline case. The notion of "overvalued ideas," for example, derived from Wernicke's concept (1900), is mentioned explicitly by Hoch and Polatin as a form of thinking disorder just short of delusion. Kernberg, later on, was to emphasize overvalued ideas as central to the unrealistic thought exhibited by borderline patients, in contrast to the unshakeable and unrealistic convictions of the (deluded) psychotic patients.

Other forms of mild thought disorder in the so-called "pseudoneurotic" patient include magical thinking and depersonalization—which one notes in the current DSM description of the borderline schizophrenic (i.e., the schizotypal personality).

Proneness to rage and inappropriate anger, especially toward family members, is underlined (p. 250). In the 1970s, Gunderson also emphasized it. Following this, it became included as an item of the DSM-3 borderline. Gunderson's "brief psychotic episode" item derives in part from the description by Hoch and Polatin of psychotic episodes of short duration, followed by reintegration.

Similarly, impulsivity, now arguably the most widely accepted feature of borderline conditions, is mentioned as a feature of "pseudoneurotic schzophrenia."

Symptomatically, some of the pseudoneurotic patients were significantly depressed—enough so to lead Donald Klein (1975) to express the view that many of these patients would be seen as not being in the penumbra of schizophrenia at all, by contemporary standards, but as *formes frustes* of manic depression. This opinion has much merit. Many cases admitted to the New York State Psychiatric Institute (where Hoch and Polatin were on the staff) during the 1960s and 1970s as "pseudoneurotic schizophrenics" showed strong suicidal tendencies. The five original cases described in the 1949 article were admitted mostly for other reasons having to do chiefly with sexual guilt and gender conflicts. This may be an expression of Zeitgeist. In the 1980s it would be hard to find patients in whom guilt over masturbation had precipitated the kind of anguish and dysfunction requiring hospitalization. Hoch and Polatin allude briefly to concerns with incest, but seemed largely unaware how often the kinds of patients they were calling "pseudoneurotic" had actually experienced incestuous advances or acts in childhood or adolescence. Nowadays, at least, actual incest is a common antecedent in hospitalized female borderlines.

Of papers published in the 1940s on borderline cases, perhaps the most important of the ones not reprinted here is that of Greenacre (1941). Though she touches on many clinical phenomena now regarded as crucial to the definition of a borderline condition, Greenacre throws the spotlight onto the vicissitudes of *anxiety*. The "severe neurotic" or "borderline" states (the terms are used interchangeably) are characterized by overwhelming anxiety—most of which Greenacre considers "basic" or "elemental," attributing it to constitution, in the way that Stern did. This innate surplus of anxiety is reminiscent of Kernberg's notion of heightened "innate aggression" (in persons about to become borderline cases), though Greenacre must have felt that this disorganizingly intense anxiety was the key pathogenic element. Kernberg focuses instead on the borderline's ragefulness and irritability, to account for which the postulate of an exaggerated innate aggression appeared more convincing. (In clinical practice one encounters both varieties of borderline: the cripplingly anxious (where rage is less prominent) and the predominantly rageful). The manner in which Greenacre's "predisposition to anxiety" (cf. Kernberg's nonspecific sign "lowered anxiety-tolerance," a derivative of this concept) might engender the other signs and symptoms we have come to associate with the borderline state, is outlined in her eloquent opening remarks, which, to do them justice, I prefer to quote at length rather than paraphrase:

I believe this organic stamp of suffering to consist of a genuine physiological sensitivity, a kind of increased indelibility of reaction . . . which heightens the anxiety potential and gives greater resonance to the anxieties of later life. The increase in early tension results in . . . first an increase in narcissism, and later an insecure and easily slipping sense of reality. I referred [in an earlier paper] to the increase in the sense of omnipotence which may occur . . . to overcome or balance the preanxiety tension state of the organism, and to increased mirroring tendency arising partly . . . from the imperfectly developing sense of reality. This . . . tendency is the antecedent of the tendency toward overfacile identification of neurotic individuals . . . Libidinal attachments are urgent but shallow . . . The patient is not well-individuated . . . with the libido quickly and urgently invested and withdrawn (Greenacre, 1941, pp. 610–611).

Reading this passage written 45 years ago, one has the impression that much of what has been written since is but exegesis and commentary on Greenacre's paper.

4. Psychoanalytic Investigation of and Therapy in the Border Line Group of Neuroses

Adolph Stern

I

It is well known that a large group of patients fit frankly neither into the psychotic nor into the psychoneurotic group, and that this border line group of patients is extremely difficult to handle effectively by any psychotherapeutic method. What forced itself on my attention some three or four years ago was the increasing number of these patients who came for treatment. My custom was not to treat them analytically, except when they were suffering acutely from neurotic symptoms (i.e., anxiety, depression, etc.) and required immediate therapy. With these I tried the usual analytic therapy but in the large majority of the patients, after a more or less lengthy course of treatment, I had to stop treatment leaving them not much benefited. In the case of the 'neurotic character', which makes up a very large proportion of this border line group, much more often than not I attempted no treatment at all, for the simple reason that I had learned from experience that our knowledge of analytic therapy as employed with the psychoneurotic patients was insufficient to achieve good results with this group, especially when their suffering was not acute enough to justify immediate therapy.

In the last three to four years, these patients have increased in numbers; those that I took for treatment were in the main acutely sick and had to be treated. Repeated failure in the past taught me that the knowledge we possessed was not adequate to treat these people. The inevitable happened: it was clear to me that though I had handeled thoroughly enough the object libidinal phenomena in these patients they nevertheless remained sick, while a straightforward psychoneurotic simularly treated did well. I therefore studied my patients more closely to see what aspects of the clinical picture were unaffected by methods successful in the usual run of psychoneurotics. The results I propose to give in the following pages.

This border line group of patients shows a fairly definite clinical picture and fairly definite clinical symptoms. This has facilitated their presentation from two angles: The first avenue of approach is the historical, as given by the patients and developed in the course of the treatment. The second avenue of approach to the understanding of this border line group is by the investigation of the events in the transference situation; here we find fairly pathognomonic phenomena that enable us to see the differences between them and such phenomena as occur in the transference situations in the usual run of psychoneurotic patients.

The clinical symptoms which I enumerate and describe below come under the heading of reaction-formations or character traits. While all of them are not peculiar to the border line group, some of them are, and others are more pronounced, constant and difficult to influence by psychoanalytic therapy than is the case in the psychoneuroses. They are as follows:

1. Narcissism.
2. Psychic bleeding.
3. Inordinate hypersensitivity.
4. Psychic and body rigidity—'The rigid personality.'
5. Negative therapeutic reactions.
6. What looks like constitutionally rooted feelings of inferiority, deeply imbedded in the personality of the patient.
7. Masochism.
8. What can be described as a state of deep organic insecurity or anxiety.
9. The use of projection mechanisms.
10. Difficulties in reality testing, particularly in personal relationships.

1 Narcissism

That these patients in the border line group belong to a large extent to the narcissistic neuroses or characters, I think is generally known. My patients, as indicated above, constitute a large indefinite group between the psychoses and the transference neuroses, partaking of the characteristics of both but showing frank tendencies in the direction of the psychotic; and we are accustomed to speak of certain psychoses as the 'narcissistic neuroses.' This border line group shows the presence of narcissism to a degree not present in the usual run of neurotic patients.

It is on the basis of narcissism that the entire clinical picture is built. In the psychoneuroses we are accustomed to look for basic causes in the disturbances to which childhood sexuality was subjected. With this in mind, an investigation of the earliest narcissistic periods in very early childhood discloses factors adversely affecting their narcissistic development. In at least seventy-five percent of this group, the histories show that one or more of the following factors were present from earliest childhood. The mother was a decidedly neurotic or psychotic type, in more than one instance developing a psychosis or psychotic episodes of short duration. These mothers inflicted injuries on their children by virtue of a deficiency of spontaneous maternal affection: among them were mothers who showed much over-solicitude and over-conscientiousness; they were meticulous about the child's habits, food and behavior, but they lacked a wholesome capacity for spontaneous affection. There were in the family, extending over years, many quarrels between the parents and repeated outbursts of temper between parents or directed at the children. In some of the families, before the patients were seven years old, divorce, separation of the parents, and in one case, desertion by one of the parents, acted as added sources of great insecurity at a time when these children were already in a state of affective deprivation because of discords between the parents before the separation took place. All of my patients as children remained then with their mothers, not one of whom before the separation was really an adequate mother from the point of view of her capacity for simple, spontaneous affection for her children. Actual cruelty, neglect and brutality by the parents of many years' duration are factors found in these patients. These factors operate more or less constantly over many years from earliest childhood. They are not single experiences.

In looking over the histories of the general run of neurotic patients, such data as those above given play a decidedly less frequent rôle. Our patients suffer in the psychic field what David M. Levy has termed 'affect hunger', much the same as food deficiencies leave behind them evidence of physical hunger, that is, nutritional disturbances. Because of the above experiences this group never develops a sense of security acquired by being loved, which is the birthright of every child. These patients suffer from affective (narcissistic) malnutrition. In this connection, however, it might be advisable to raise the question, to what degree a peculiar constitution or endowment, and how much environment *per se,* or a combination of both is responsible for the clinical picture. I have no answer to this question.

On the basis of an injured, starved narcissism the clinical picture develops. Normal narcissistic gratification, normal self-preservative needs in the psychic sphere, are not adequately provided for. The roots of neurotic character traits, and in some patients also neurotic illness, are buried deep in these very early periods of psychic starvation and insecurity due to lack of parental, chiefly maternal, affection. Hence it might be inferred that a disturbance in the narcissistic development of the very young is responsible in this group for neurotic character traits or neurotic illness, just as disturbance in the sexual (object love) development is at the root of the psychoneurotic disturbances.

As Freud states, all neurotic symptom formation is an attempt on the part of the ego to minimize or eliminate the intolerable distress produced by anxiety. In the psychoneurotic group the anxiety develops on the basis of the infantile sexual impulses; in our group, in the main, on the basis of the infantile narcissistic impulses. Narcissism is present in this border line group as the basic underlying character component. It is the soil in which the phenomena to be described later take their origin, on which they depend for their form and the functions they serve. Having in mind that anxiety is the motor for defense in the formation of neurotic character traits and symptoms, I will describe in detail the above enumerated character traits as seen in the border line group.

2 Psychic Bleeding

The picture of a psychic bleeder is a familiar one. Instead of a resilient reaction to a painful or traumatic experience, the patient goes down in a heap, so to speak, and is at the point of death. There is immobility, lethargy instead of action, collapse instead of a rebound: a sort of playing 'possum. In this quiescence the patient is reflexly in a state of self-protection, necessitating a minimum of functioning, and exhibiting complete relaxation in order to counterbalance the great demands made on the organism by danger. Paralysis rather than flight or fight is the reaction. The state of collapse in a sense represents a reflex defense in the form of preparation for recuperation.

3 Inordinate Hypersensitivity

Psychic hypersensitivity is perhaps comparable to the physical hyper-sensitivity of the very young to physical sensory stimuli. That this hypersensitivity serves reflexly, automatically, as an exquisite receptive apparatus or instrument to detect danger readily and to take appropriate precautions is clear enough. That it has no reality function is as true of this as of any other neurotic symptom. But from the neurotic point of view of the patient, the hypersensitivity is a logical symptom or character trait. It is in keeping with a deeply rooted insecurity, which necessitates undue caution and awareness to danger, in this sense clearly an advantage as is any other neurotic symptom. This hypersensitivity, in many of the patients, comes close to the mechanism by means of which the paranoic develops his ideas of reference. My patients are constantly being deeply insulted and injured by trifling remarks made by people with whom they come in contact, and occasionally develop mildly paranoid ideas.

4 Psychic Rigidity: 'The Rigid Personality'

This is one of the most fascinating mechanisms to investigate, see in operation and in resolution; for one can modify 'a rigid personality' through psychoanalytic methods. If we keep in mind that anxiety is the motor stimulating action on the part of the ego for its own defense, the rigid personality becomes understandable to us. Further, as I indicated before, and shall again when discussing the transference phenomena, reactions of defense in this border line group of patients is almost of a reflex nature. The body is brought into an attitude of protective behavior because of anxiety arising from danger within or without. In the transference neuroses, on the contrary, the defense mechanisms have to a much greater extent psychological explanations and values. In evaluating the significance of the rigid personality, I have in mind by way of comparison the rigid abdomen and the rigid knee as reflex responses to inflammation in the respective areas. An extreme picture again for the sake of comparison is the rigid catatonic. With his shifting, watchful, alert eyes and the rigid picture of his body, a connection between the two, on the basis of protection against danger, becomes clear enough. In the patients under consideration, psychic rigidity and often enough physical rigidity, are constantly present phenomena, reflexly protective in nature. What I have not been able to settle in my mind is the time when such phenomena take form. In some it appears that the rigidity is present in the earliest years, before four or five, increases at important periods, as for example, puberty, and with important (to the patient anxiety-producing) experiences. Maturing for these individuals is fraught with great danger (anxiety) against which protection through psychic and physical rigidity goes forward apace. The recognition of the defensive purposes of this rigidity gives the clue to its therapeutic handling, just as it does in instances of handling defenses in the transference group.

5 Negative Therapeutic Reactions

Such phenomena are regularly observed in this group of patients. One notes depression, readily aroused anger, discouragement and anxiousness as responses to any interpretation involving injury to self-esteem. Since the handling of anxiety is attempted essentially through defensive measures, it becomes clear enough that any interpretation that impairs the neurotic defense at the same time releases the anxiety which determined the patient to resort to protective devices for a feeling of security, so that a depression ensues, or discouragement, anger, etc. The margin of security of these patients is extremely narrow, and an enlightening interpretation throws them, at least for the moment, into despondency, so that only rarely does one notice a favorable reaction to discoveries. Furthermore, in estimating the significance of the negative therapeutic reaction one must bear in mind that the marked immaturity of these patients, and their insecure, depleted narcissism impel them to react to interpretations as evidence of lack of appreciation or love on the part of the analyst. With these patients analytic therapy is like a surgical operation. The surgical operation is a therapeutic measure, in itself traumatic but necessary. Care then must be exercised that the operative technique be adapted to the particular patient at that particular time and not to the illness. Good judgment based on clinical experience, is of inestimable value here. A negative therapeutic reaction is nevertheless inevitable; in some the reaction is extremely unfavorable and, cumulatively, may become dangerous; patients may develop depression, suicidal ideas, or make suicidal attempts. In these negative therapeutic states the necessarily dependent attitudes are exaggerated, and the demands for pity, sympathy, affection and protection made on the analyst are extremely difficult to handle; the transference situation, complicated as it necessarily is, becomes even more so. Ordinarily such patients' relationship to people in authority is determined by their need of love and protection, to be obtained by them through infantile methods, especially obedience, compliance, and insistent demands for tender gentle handling. The same attitudes are operative in the transference, and the patients, though they understand the interpretations, at the same time react neurotically (i.e., through the negative therapeutic reactions) as though they were rejected. The result is an increased clinging to the analyst as a parental figure.

6 Feelings of Inferiority

In connection with these phenomena, as with the others mentioned, I attempt no explanation of their origin. My object is to show their clinical function as a logical part of the pathology of the illness (neurotic character), and to demonstrate here too that a symptom is evidence on the part of the organism, the ego, of an attempt to combat anxiety. In these patients the feelings of inferiority are pervasive, including almost the total personality. Essentially the feelings of inferiority are accepted by the patients as unpleasant but logical and inevitable for them. There is no questioning on their part as to the validity of their judgment in this respect. One gets the impression of a delusional coloring to this. The patients are convinced of their inferiority, lacking *in toto* insight in the symptomatic nature of these feelings. Not a few of my patients have become successful in their chosen fields of endeavor, have acquired excellent general and professional educations; not a few have prepossessing physical and psychological characteristics—but none of their accomplishments, nor the sum of all of their accomplishments, in the least influences them in their judgment as to their being inferior people. A close approach to this picture is the delusional self-depreciation of the melancholic.

These border line patients are cases of arrested development and patently show infantile character traits. From this point of view, as I shall try to show in some of their transference phenomena, it is quite logical from the premises of the patients that they feel inferior—immature, young, weak, timid, unworthy, never loved, etc. These feelings of inferiority are used in the service of overcoming anxiety whenever action or thinking is required of the patients that might demand of them the exercise of adult functioning. The discrepancy between adult functioning as they see it and what they feel themselves capable of doing is sufficiently great to precipitate enough anxiety to make the patients recoil and slump into inaction, acutely conscious at such time of feelings of inferiority. Assurance against recurrence of anxiety is obtained, unsatisfactory as it may be to the healthy judgment of the patient, by remaining inactive and loudly proclaiming his inferiority, with the hope that instead of being pushed to adult behavior, he will be consoled, pitied, or allowed to remain dormant. The conviction of being an inferior individual influences the patient against active behavior and is pleadingly proclaimed to the analyst (paternal figure) in order to achieve the same objectives (to bring out the parental rôle). It is among these patients that one frequently finds (the bane of the analyst's existence) those who get a thorough psychoanalytic education through being analyzed and remain quite sick people. They have the intellectual equipment to accumulate knowledge and unless the analyst is on his guard, will use this knowledge not to unravel sources of their feelings of inferiority, but neurotically to bolster up their ego, with pseduo-therapeutic results.

7 Masochism

It is not very clear how this fits in as a defensive, corrective protective phenomenon. That it is present is clear enough and easily verified. In this class of patients, self-pity and self-commiseration, the presentation of a long suffering, helpless picture of the injured one, are regularly met; also what I call wound-licking, a tendency to indulge in self-pity. All these roughly but not very clearly may be considered as agents for obtaining a compensation for what the patients, and some of them justly, regard as not being or having been sufficiently loved in their childhood, a sort of unspoken plea for help and love as a needy child seeks it. There is no doubt that such patients suffer much. Many tend in the direction of depressions and some of my patients in this group came with acute depressions; and masochism is of very frequent occurrence. The latter is demonstrated cleary enough in their dreams, their symptoms, their lives. They hurt themselves in their business, professional, social, in fact all affective relationships.

Masochism is in itself a phenomenon so malign, that it seems futile to ascribe to its constant presence in these patients a remedial or defensive purpose. In respect to the other character traits, it is comparatively easy to see such a purpose.

8 'Somatic' Insecurity or Anxiety

In a sense, the use of the word anxiety with reference to this particular clinical symptom is a misnomer, for the simple reason that anxiety as such is not a constant phenomenon, nor do these patients by any means regularly complain of its presence. On the contrary, many present to immediate observation, a placid, perhaps better put, a stolid physical and mental equanimity. They strike the observer as not enough disturbed by difficult situations. In the course of analytic investigation it becomes apparent that an inordinately adequate system of defenses had been established by means of which this pseudo-equanimity is maintained. A knowledge of this on the part of the analyst is of benefit both to him and to the patient. It should guide the procedure to undo as little of the patients' defenses at a time as possible. For these patients are capable of releasing unpleasant, at times dangerous quantities of anxiety in the course of analytic therapy, so that as the analyst pursues his efforts at investigation and therapy simultaneously, he becomes familiar with this elaborate defensive system. With treatment a clearer picture of a deep underlying insecurity is unfolded, stretching back to earliest childhood, its roots penetrating to periods beyond memory. Instead of the fairly common clinical picture of traumatic experiences in childhood, with which we are more or less familiar in our neurotic patients, it seems as though insecurity always existed or was dissipated by some device. One rarely gets an impression that these patients at any period in their lives possessed self-assurance or self-confidence, unless the environment in some form or other gave it to them for the time being through approval, or when some experience gave them a temporary feeling of being completely adequate. Self-assurance usually was an evanescent experience, rather than one gained through a process of growth, maturity, experience, reality testing. That is, in an individual of ordinary self-assurance, an unfortunate or stupid experience is regarded by him as a thing *per se,* to which he reacts as such. To an individual in our group, one such experience is interpreted to mean that he is thoroughly unfortunate or stupid and he suffers a total depreciation of his ego (self-esteem), or the reverse, an elation, or an exaggerated self-esteem from one successful experience. These individuals give an 'all or none' reaction. It is in connection with this deep insecurity that early parental love seems to play an important rôle. Those doing work with children are in a position to test directly the value of observations made in the case of these adults. I wish to say that my interest in the possible causes of these phenomena in the adult was aroused by reading material on this subject written by Dr. David M. Levy, and through talks with him. On the basis of observations, it seems of value to keep in mind that a sense of security, of self-assurance, is developed in children on the basis chiefly of spontaneous maternal affection and to a minor degree paternal. These children, deprived of something as essential to adequate psychic narcissism as food is to the body, meet experiences later in life already burdened with pathological insecurity, that is, they show a proclivity to develop anxiety. Sexual experiences or anything that is in their opinion disapproved of by authority, or which may involve danger, or put them to a test, are approached in their peculiar but to them logical way. Because of their, as they see it, already precarious state, anxiety in great quantities is ever ready to be mobilized, for disapproval or danger threatens to make an already insecure position still more so. Defense reactions are set into operation, those described above in particular. These adults in their childhood as a rule were inordinately submissive and obedient through fear and need. They clung to parents and substitutes with the desperation of the greatly endangered. In the female, penis envy and in the male, castration anxiety play considerable rôles. Anxiety because of the sexual impulse also plays a considerable rôle. The oedipus complex most assuredly does. But in connection with these facts, one thing must be kept in mind: that antedating, or coincident with the above, there is a degree of immaturity and insecurity that is not present in the ordinary transference neurosis with which we are familiar, and this deep insecurity stems from disturbances in the narcissistic needs.

9 The Use of Projection Mechanisms

We know the wide use made of projection mechanisms in the psychoses. In our patients projection mechanisms are in common use; this is one of the phenomena which links this group with the psychotics. The use

of these mechanisms implies the existence of a piece of defective judgement, which gives the patient's ego a more ready handling of his neurotic
anxiety. The causes of his anxiety are projected to the world outside;
he sets defensive behavior into operation at the cost of insight. The
immature, narcissistically needy person can thus more easily protect
himself from what he considers a hostile environment, through defensive measures (rigid personality, introversion, psychic and physical
withdrawal, mild delusional systems, etc.). He is, however, unable to
recognize that his insecurity is inwardly determined, for that would
necessitate internal psychic changes in the direction of maturity and self-
confidence which he cannot attain. The easier path is to explain his
difficulties on the basis of a hostile attitude of the environment towards
him and the inordinate difficulties that his conception of reality present,
particularly in relationship to people, chiefly people in a position of
authority.

10 Difficulties in Reality Testing

This will be described in part II, in connection with treatment of the
transference situations.

II

The development of the illness as manifested in the course of the
transference affords an intimate bedside opportunity, so to speak, for
appreciating the differences between the clinical picture of this border
line group and the picture of the frank psychoneuroses. I have attempted
to show in part I of this presentation the very important rôle that
narcissism plays as an etiological factor in the border line group: this
causative factor necessarily operates in the clinical picture both as the
patient presents it upon examination and also as he evinces it in the
unfolding of the transference relationship.

Because of the preponderant influence upon the clinical picture of
narcissism the therapeutic handling of the pathologically affected narcissistic impulse becomes a problem that is not present to an equal

degree in the transference neuroses. On this basis some modification of the psychoanalytic technique is a logical procedure.[1]

Let us keep in mind the broad picture given in part I. Just as in the transference group, so in this also, prevention of anxiety is the motor for the neurotic behavior. That the transference situation is a miniature neurosis is well enough known. The particular mechanisms used by the patients in handling anxiety that develops in the transference situation give us a clue to a diagnosis and prognosis, so that as we watch the transference phenomena develop we are in a position to estimate where we are and what we need do.

In studying the transference relationship in this group, first and foremost we see established a relationship to the analyst of extreme dependence. These affectively immature people cannot form an affective relationship on any other basis. Since the need for protection is great, we note in these patients, as evidence of dependence, a strict adherence to rules, an obedience, at times something like a compulsive application

---

[1] It is in this connection that what I called above a modification in the application of psychoanalytic therapy is indicated. Really there is no change; my experience has taught me several things in the matter of this extreme, desperately clinging and dependent transference situation. These patients need much more supportive treatment than the usual run of psychoneurotic patients. Among the border line group of patients, those who come with an acute neurosis, chiefly depression and generalized anxieties, or those who develop disturbances in the course of therapy, which is the case with most, we find to be very sick people, much sicker than those in the psychoneurotic group. This latter group regularly presents a less grave picture. So that, just as in the field of physical medicine, the very sick are coaxed along, so to speak, by all manner of supportive treatment while medical measures are concurrently applied, and radical measures put off until the patient's powers of resistance are adequate. In this field too, supportive treatment over long periods is an essential preparation for the time when psychoanalytic technique can be applied. Because these patients are gravely ill and because work on the transference relationship, acting as a frustrating agent, is borne badly by these patients, greater attention to supportive therapy marks one modification of technique. A second modification consists in a rather constant occupation with the transference relationship to the apparent neglect of the historical material and interpretations. The affectively immature attitudes, which manifest themselves for long periods and in great quantities, make intelligent work impossible, except for that which the analyst can, so to speak, force the patient's healthy ego to accomplish in the understanding of his dependent attitudes incident to his narcissistic needs. At first this, as one patient put it, cutting 'across my path' is a disturbing process, for it necessitates frustration to the patient; and this is something these patients find difficult to tolerate. However, careful handling will materially diminish the persistent impulse to cling, and a certain amount of healthy intellectual functioning becomes available for work on the historical material and interpretations.

to the analytic job, and efforts to win approval, commendation, emphasis on trouble and suffering to arouse the protective sympathy of the
analyst. So intense an affective involvement can this attachment become that attention to this aspect of the transference relationship takes
up an inordinate amount of time, much more than in the work with less
immature people.

This phase of the transference relationship gives us insight into the
degree of the patient's immaturity. It is startling at times to discover
the naïveté with which the analyst is viewed and accepted as a personal,
corporeal god and magician. Some patients, without any surprise or
sense of the unreal, accept the analyst as some vague presence without
definite form who must not even be looked at. The startling thing is not
so much the existence of these phenomena, but that the patients never
see that there is something odd and strange in their psychology to make
such attitudes possible. They accept the giant size, omnipotence and
omniscience of the analyst as children believe in fairy stories or in the
omnipotence and omniscience of the parents or God. These patients
cannot get or expect help or love or care (that is 'cure') from any but
one who reproduces in fantasy the parental figure in all the exaggerated
proportions of childhood. When these patients develop anxiety in the
analytic situation through anything that disturbs this positive protective
state, that anxiety is great, directly in proportion to the protection
destroyed or endangered.[2] Some patients state without any insight that
they feel as secure and happy in the analysis as though they were in a
Nirvana. They are just happy. One can easily picture the anxiety, the
depression and defensive anger, when the naïvely accepted love giving
object becomes hostile in the patient's eyes. When this pleasant Nirvana
state changes, there comes a fairly well marked mental confusion, and
anxiety-driven efforts to reconstruct the old situation. In these states
little can be done in the way of analytic work. The patients need soothing
and tentative attempts at explaining the change in their mood. Some of

---

[2] Among these patients one not infrequently finds those that demand and seek 'the
very best and greatest' analyst as the only one that can help them. Offhand one might
get the idea that their narcissistic love is what influences them in such ideas or quests.
The fact is that it is not at all difficult to demonstrate that they have deeply suppressed
feelings of great insecurity and inferiority, and that on this basis they need 'the best
and greatest'. The ungratified and ungratifiable narcissistic needs are responsible for
this demand.

these patients come uncomfortably near to a psychotic state in such phases of their transference. In this state as a rule the patients make violent attempts to recapture the old beatific illusion. Often through the production of analytical material (association and interpretations or through emphasis on their sufferings) they seek to soften what they think and feel is the cruel attitude of the analyst. The disturbance of the sense of reality in so far as the role of the analyst is concerned is startling, particularly in that the patients accept the unconscious implications of the relationship as though it were reality. Interestingly enough, in the mildly disturbed transference states not infrequently the patients feel thus distressed only when in the analytic session. Many say that as soon as they enter the waiting room or at times even the building itself, an acute, uncomfortable sense of anxiety takes hold of them. Not one, to my recollection, has commented on this change as something for which he could not account, but instead accepted it as something wholly in keeping with his relationship to the analyst. As one put it, 'How else can I feel but in awe of you?'

To return to the topic of neurotic character traits (the tenth on the list given in part I), disturbance of the sense of reality is a characteristic phenomenon in these patients in their relationships to the parental (imago) rôle of the analyst. Again it does not strike these patients at all strange that they attribute such gigantic proportions to this psychic and physical imago. The naïve acceptance of this is something to note; it may well warn the analyst to watch carefully for the effects upon the patient of what he says. To these people it is a god, a magician, an oracle that speaks with all the force that such beings possess for the very young; if these beings at the moment are favorably inclined to the patient as he at the moment feels, the influence upon the patient of information given by these imagos is of note. Such a process as good logical reality thinking is not to be expected under the circumstances. Sound common sense in the patient and reality testing are in abeyance, or should be expected to be. So also, when these imagos seem hostile to the patient, it is clear enough that anything savoring of criticism, as any interpretation is apt to be construed, has a most disturbing effect. Illusory improvement is a common phenomenon during the positive transference. The rise of self-esteem at what the patient interprets as approval, commendation or preference of him by the imago is marked indeed; it corresponds to the self-depreciation produced by what the patient interprets as criticism on the part of the imago. The affective immaturity of these patients precludes a transference that carries with it sufficient reality relationship to give the analyst a feeling of safety in relying to any great extent upon the patients' ability to use any but the smallest fraction of intelligence otherwise more or less competently operating in the patients' professional activities. More with these patients than with frank transference neurotics, is it necessary to watch closely the effects upon the patients of what the analyst says. For it is the imago that operates for a long time upon the psyche of the patient, rather than the analyst as a reality person. It is well known that at the outset of treatment such extreme distortions of the person of the analyst and of his functions are characteristic and expected phenomena in the transference. What looks like improvement can then be better estimated, and sad disappointment to the analyst and depressions for the patient possibly avoided.

The negative therapeutic reaction is a constant phenomenon with these patients and constitutes a far more disturbing and important clinical symptom than in ordinary run of patients. I should like to add some remarks to what has already been written about the negative therapeutic reaction based on its occurrence in and influenced by the transference. As is known, we have an expectation and assume that a patient will react favorably to some discovery made for him or by him in the course of the analytic work. Yet, are we justified in such an expectation? Certainly not when the discovery is first made. The negative therapeutic reaction in these patients is significant later, when in reference to the same piece of news or interpretation, a reaction of depression, anger, anxiety or discouragement takes place. That is to say, when some familiarity with the unpleasant material should have come about through reiteration, and some acceptance should have resulted, the patients for a long time react as though it were *de novo*. It seems to me that on the basis of the patients' premises such reactions are to be expected; for the negative therapeutic reaction means that the anxiety incident to facing a new situation of danger has been avoided at the expense of pain, i.e., depression. To admit to consciousness any painful concept is fraught with anxiety. This anxiety the patient must avoid; a successful avoidance is evidenced by a negative therapeutic reaction.

In these patients the problem of growing up is anxiety ridden. Being grown up is to these patients, especially in their relationship to people, a fantasy of perfection such as they ascribe to adults. In fantasy this can be attained, but behavior to prove it or test it out is anxiety ridden. Whenever he successfully attains adulthood, the patient has a secret idea that his performance was not real, and that he might easily be unmasked as a make-believe. To achieve a successful performance means to him a rather violent suppression of his neurotic inferiorities, and the assumption (which might be detected) of the rôle of some highly envied omnipotent imago (father, mother). The patients correctly recognize in this a certain make-believe, though far too inaccurately and inadequately to be of service to them.

The transference situation offers opportunity for study of this: at the core of this situation is the enormous over-evaluation of the imago by the patient. Except through illusion, the patient cannot identify himself with the (imago) analyst; that is, the patient never identifies himself with the analyst but with his conception of him—through a process of projection of his own ego ideal as embodied in the gigantic size of the analyst (imago). It is this figure which talks to him. Therefore, when for instance, the patient is told that what he has just said indicates some suppressed hostility from childhood to an older brother or father, the patient collapses through fear of punishment by virtue of his having been discovered. This is approximately what such an interpretation means to these patients. Frequently the patient makes a vow to get rid of the hostility as soon as possible and may return to the next session feeling fairly satisfied with himself, and tell the analyst, with the hope of being approved, that he now has mastered this hatred and rid himself of it. Usually in a short time the same material returns and the same interpretation is made. The reaction is similar to the first—chagrin, guilt, fear of punishment, dread of not being approved, all are set going again because the major portion of 'seeing' has been illusory, due to an effort to win approval from the analyst, and to enhance the patients' self-esteem and self-assurance.

Another phase of this negative therapeutic reaction is that pertaining to failure when really success should be expected on the basis of the work done and the understanding which the patient exhibits. What should not be overlooked here is the fact, really the fact, that the patients' conception of reality behavior and accomplishment is too illusory. The very immature patient feels that to be able to live in the world of reality, as he sees it, he must be as he conceives his imagos to be. Actually, the investigation of the transference phenomena informs us that as far as people go, these patients still live in a world of their own childhood—so that getting well and being adult are attained through *wishing* to be able to do what grown ups do, and this they dare not risk. In the imagination it is easy enough and while in the analysis, but independently the anxiety is too great.

Another prevalent phenomenon in the transference is the lack of contact of patients with the analyst (imago). The patients, particularly in periods of hostility and anxiety, are in a state of withdrawal. This is no light affair. One can sense that the patient has retired within his rigid protective covering and carries on his analysis from this position of security against the analyst. Most patients will talk on uninterruptedly as though oblivious of the analyst, but interruption of the flow of associations will bring about as a rule, anger or anxiety, and the information that the patient had in mind the possible influence upon the imago of the patients' effort to please or appease the anger of the imago. One notes such a tendency in other kinds of patients also but not to the degree and lengths to which our patients go. In fact, this mode of transference is typical and varies in degree with the quantity of narcissism involved (rigidity). One can ascertain that this exclusion of the analyst involves many factors, an outstanding one being the removal by the patient of himself from a hostile, critical, ridiculing parental figure. One gets the feeling about some of these patients that they crawl into their hole and pull it in after them (intrauterine state). The degree of immaturity and insecurity from which there patients suffer helps to understand the intuitive, archaic nature of this defense mechanism.

One notes readily that much of the work which these patients do is tendentious. Intellectual and superficial association, long descriptions, carefully selected words and sentences, well rounded out; a quiet, contained and constrained demeanor, the enunciation of words of anger, anxiety, love, without their emotional contents, a flatness, a monotone are what they present, regardless of the affects described. The absence of affect from the transference situation is characteristic of much of the work. Of course, these individuals have that same demeanor in their daily life outside of the analytic situation.

Those patients who come into the analysis with an overt neurosis of which anxiety is the main symptom develop at the very outset of the treatment a violent, clamoring, grasping at the analyst in their great need for protection and assurance. They almost literally attach themselves by every childhood organ or sense of prehension. In the course of the analysis in those patients who come into treatment free from much anxiety because of successful repression, the anxiety becomes overt due to study of their defense mechanisms, particularly in the field of the transference, and the same picture as above described is initiated. In fact, successful treatment is characterized by precipitation of anxiety in the case of patients who have successfully repressed it. In some patients, when the anxiety is precipitated by an unfortunate current experience outside of the analysis, we get the same clinging attachment. Those patients who do not develop any acute anxiety present a stolid, at times solid immobile exterior, though they not infrequently describe disturbing sensations of anxiety in the chest, bowels, genitals and scalp (as though it were being lifted off); only later in the analysis do these patients express affect through their voices. This last (stolid) group comprises at least fifty percent of the patients I am describing as belonging to the border line group.

One often misses, except later in the analysis, what we are familiar with as 'free associations' in the object-libido group of patients. One can gather from the trend of my presentation that the great need for these patients is protection to a degree that takes precedence over all others. One cannot therefore expect 'free associations' of a kind we get with the less immature neurotic. A difficult task for these patients is to release hostility. As one put it, 'It is bad enough as it is, how would it be if people sensed or heard my hostility?' Only as the immaturity particularly in the transference is gradually ameliorated, and the need for protection diminishes, does one get a transference picture comparable to that found in the other groups of neurosis. Only then can the patient really make appropriate, adequate use of the historical material brought into the analytic work; only then can he really understand and incorporate (digest) the significance of much of the work (interpretations) done concurrently with the almost endless work on the transference relationship. Interpretations, though not in reference to transference, are frequently made to give the patient opportunity to exercise his intellect and to derive some ego satisfaction. Interpretations are made also with a view of giving the patient knowledge. All the while the analyst knows that much of this will have to be gone over after more maturity has been attained, so as to render the effects of interpretations that are not related to transference material less tendentious. With this class of patients it is of prime importance that the analyst be fully cognizant to what extent the patient knows what he knows. Only after the transference, established on this extremely immature basis has been well worked out, can the significance of parental attachments of the oedipus period, castration threats, the sexual impulse, its pleasures and dangers and a host of other phenomena become subjects for explanation with some expectation of their being adequately understood. Only then do these phenomena take their appropriate rôle as factors in neurotic etiology in this border line group. For the anxiety which seems to be the motor for symptom of defense formation is earlier in point of time than the castration anxiety of the transference group of neuroses; the transference situation in our group then has these basic early infantile colorings. It begins in a period which appears to antedate sexual development as the factor in neurotic illness. Not that this does not later appear in this capacity, only to add difficulties to the already overburdened child in its efforts to handle an insecurity already of great magnitude.

Summary

The shortcomings of this presentation are evident enough. A certain vagueness is at present unavoidable, because the material which this group offers for study runs so clearly in two directions, namely, towards the psychotic and the psychoneurotic. Much more time and investigation are necessary to evaluate the rather obscure phenomena these patients present.

That they form a group by themselves, which one can designate as border line, is a justifiable assumption. On the basis of this assumption, one finds in this group characteristics which separate these patients from the ordinary run of psychoneurotics. These characteristics I have attempted to describe. This presentation had in mind a description from two points of view: first, the historical, as given by the patient, and then developed in the course of treatment and study, and second, study of these characteristics as they operate in the transference situation.

The latter approach offers opportunity for study of these character traits that has great advantages. One has an opportunity of seeing them mobilized by the transference situation, forming a 'miniature' neurosis, the elements of which can more easily be studied because they concern the patient and the imago (analyst); moreover, just as in the case of the transference situation of the psychoneurotics, this then tells the analyst what therapeutic measures to apply.

Since in this border line group, narcissism is the underlying material from which the symptoms (defense) originate on the basis of needs (anxiety), psychoanalytic measures are instituted just as in the case in the psychoneurotic in whom anxiety arises in connection with psychosexual impulses. However, in our group narcissism is the source of anxiety. Though we have long been familiar with narcissism, when it is present in large quantities as presenting phenomena such as our patients bring, an approach to it directly has not to any great extent been made. This presentation has as its object this aim: to show that narcissism is amenable not only to psychoanalytic investigation but to psychoanalytic therapy.

There is no doubt that these patients have not been adequately reached by methods more or less successful with the average psychoneurotic. The same psychoanalytic technique, with the variations indicated above, is applicable in cases of the border line group except that, although attention to and treatment of the disturbed psychosexual impulses is included, there must be attention to and treatment of the disturbed narcissism as well.

As is the case in the psychoneurotic, so too in this border line group, whatever there is of healthy ego functioning not involved in the sickness is utilized by the analyst in his efforts to achieve results. It is clear, however, from the description of this border line group, that a great part of ego functioning is involved in the illness, a greater part than in the transference group. This is one important feature in the border line group that makes therapy more difficult, and the prognosis more grave, than in psychoneurotics.

5. Some Forms of Emotional Disturbance and their Relationship to Schizophrenia

Helene Deutsch

Psychoanalytic observations of a few types of emotional disturbances are presented in this paper, and a series of cases reported in which the individual's emotional relationship to the outside world and to his own ego appears impoverished or absent. Such disturbances of the emotional life take various forms. For example, there are the individuals who are not aware of their lack of normal affective bonds and responses, but whose emotional disturbance is perceived either only by those around them or is first detected in analytic treatment: and there are those who complain of their emotional defect and are keenly distressed by the disturbance in their inner experiences. Among the latter, the disturbance may be transitory and fleeting; it may recur from time to time but only in connection with certain specific situations and experiences; or it may persist and form a continuous, distressing symptom. In addition, the emotional disturbance may be perceived as existing in the personality or it may be projected onto the outside world. In the one case the patient says, 'I am changed. I feel nothing. Everything seems unreal to me.' In the other, he complains that the world seems strange, objects shadowy, human beings and events theatrical and unreal. Those forms of the disturbance in which the individual himself is conscious of his defect and complains of it belong to the picture of 'depersonalization.' This disturbance has been described by many authors. In the analytic literature the reader is especially referred to the studies of Oberndorf,[1] Schilder,[2] and Bergler and Eidelberg.[3]

---

[1] Oberndorf, C. P.: *Depersonalization in Relation to Erotization of Thought*. Int. J. Psa., XV, 1934, pp. 271–295; *Genesis of Feeling of Unreality*. Int. J. Psa., XVI, 1935, pp. 296–306

[2] Schilder, P.: *Treatment of Depersonalization*. Bull, N. Y. Acad. Med., XV, 1939, pp. 258–272.

[3] Bergler, E., and Eidelberg, L.: *Der Mechanismus der Depersonalization*. Int. Ztschr. f. Psa., XXI, 1935, pp. 258–285.

Most of the psychoanalytic observations in this paper deal with conditions bearing a close relationship to depersonalization but differing from it in that they were not perceived as disturbances by the patient himself. To this special type of personality I have given the name, 'as if.' I must emphasize that this name has nothing to do with Vaihinger's system of 'fictions' and the philosophy of 'As-If.' My only reason for using so unoriginal a label for the type of person I wish to present is that every attempt to understand the way of feeling and manner of life of this type forces on the observer the inescapable impression that the individual's whole relationship to life has something about it which is lacking in genuineness and yet outwardly runs along 'as if' it were complete. Even the layman sooner or later inquires, after meeting such an 'as if' patient: what *is* wrong with him, or her? Outwardly the person seems normal. There is nothing to suggest any kind of disorder, behavior is not unusual, intellectual abilities appear unimpaired, emotional expressions are well ordered and appropriate. But despite all this, something intangible and indefinable obtrudes between the person and his fellows and invariably gives rise to the question, 'What is wrong?'

A clever and experienced man, a patient of mine, met another of my patients, a girl of the 'as if' type, at a social gathering. He spent part of his next analytic hour telling me how stimulating, amusing, attractive, and interesting she was, but ended his eulogy with, 'But something is wrong with her.' He could not explain what he meant.

When I submitted the paintings of the same girl to an authority for his criticism and evaluation, I was told that the drawings showed much skill and talent but there was also something disturbing in them which this man attributed to an inner restraint, an inhibition which he thought could surely be removed. Towards the end of the patient's not too successful analysis, she entered this critic's school for further instruction in painting and, after a time, I received a report in which her teacher spoke in glowing terms of her talent. Several months later I received a less enthusiastic report. Yes, the girl was talented, her teacher had been impressed by the speed with which she had adopted his technique and manner of artistic perception, but, he had frankly to admit, there was an intangible something about her which he had never before encountered, and he ended with the usual question, 'What is wrong?' He added that the girl had gone to another teacher, who used a quite different teaching approach, and that she had oriented herself to the new theory and technique with striking ease and speed.

The first impression these people make is of complete normality. They are intellectually intact, gifted, and bring great understanding to intellectual and emotional problems; but when they pursue their not infrequent impulses to creative work they construct, in form, a good piece of work but it is always a spasmodic, if skilled, repetition of a prototype without the slightest trace of originality. On closer observation, the same thing is seen in their affective relationships to the environment. These relationships are usually intense and bear all the earmarks of friendship, love, sympathy, and understanding; but even the layman soon perceives something strange and raises the question he cannot answer. To the analyst it is soon clear that all these relationships are devoid of any trace of warmth, that all the expressions of emotion are formal, that all inner experience is completely excluded. It is like the performance of an actor who is technically well trained but who lacks the necessary spark to make his impersonations true to life.

Thus the essential characteristic of the person I wish to describe is that outwardly he conducts his life as if he possessed a complete and sensitive emotional capacity. To him there is no difference between his empty forms and what others actually experience. Without going deeper into the matter I wish at this point to state that this condition is not identical with the coldness of repressed individuals in whom there is usually a highly differentiated emotional life hidden behind a wall, the loss of affect being either manifest or cloaked by overcompensations. In the one there is flight from reality or a defense against the realization of forbidden instinctual drives; in the other, a seeking of external reality in an effort to avoid an anxiety-laden fantasy. Psychoanalysis discloses that in the 'as if' individual it is no longer an act of repression but a real loss of object cathexis. The apparently normal relationship to the world corresponds to a child's imitativeness and is the expression of identification with the environment, a mimicry which results in an ostensibly good adaptation to the world of reality despite the absence of object cathexis.

Further consequences of such a relation to life are a completely passive attitude to the environment with a highly plastic readiness to pick up signals from the outer world and to mold oneself and one's behavior accordingly. The identification with what other people are thinking and feeling, is the expression of this passive plasticity and renders the person capable of the greatest fidelity and the basest perfidy. Any object will do as a bridge for identification. At first the love, friendship, and attachment of an 'as if' person have something very rewarding for the partner. If it is a woman, she seems to be the quintessence of feminine devotion, an impression which is particularly imparted by her passivity and readiness for identification. Soon, however, the lack of real warmth brings such an emptiness and dullness to the emotional atmosphere that the man as a rule precipitously breaks off the relationship. In spite of the adhesiveness which the 'as if' person brings to every relationship, when he is thus abandoned he displays either a rush of affective reactions which are 'as if' and thus spurious, or a frank absence of affectivity. At the very first opportunity the former object is exchanged for a new one and the process is repeated.

The same emptiness and the same lack of individuality which are so evident in the emotional life appear also in the moral structure. Completely without character, wholly unprincipled, in the literal meaning of the term, the morals of the 'as if' individuals, their ideals, their convictions are simply reflections of another person, good or bad. Attaching themselves with great ease to social, ethical, and religious groups, they seek, by adhering to a group, to give content and reality to their inner emptiness and establish the validity of their existence by identification. Overenthusiastic adherence to one philosophy can be quickly and completely replaced by another contradictory one without the slightest trace of inward transformation—simply as a result of some accidental regrouping of the circle of acquaintances of the like.

A second characteristic of such patients is their suggestibility, quite understandable from what has already been said. Like the capacity for identification, this suggestibility, too, is unlike that of the hysteric for whom object cathexis is a necessary condition; in the 'as if' individual the suggestibility must be ascribed to passivity and automaton-like identification. Many initial criminal acts, attributed to an erotic bondage, are due instead to a passive readiness to be influenced.

Another characteristic of the 'as if' personality is that aggressive tendencies are almost completely masked by passivity, lending an air of negative goodness, of mild amiability which, however, is readily convertible to evil.

One of these patients, a woman, and the only child of one of the oldest noble families in Europe, had been brought up in an unusual atmosphere. With the excuse of official duties, and quite in accordance with tradition, the parents delegated the care and training of their child to strangers. On certain specified days of the week she was brought before her parents for 'control'. At these meetings there was a formal check of her educational achievements, and the new program and other directions were given her preceptors. Then after a cool, ceremonious dismissal, the child was returned to her quarters. She received no warmth and no tenderness from her parents, nor did punishment come directly from them. This virtual separation from her parents had come soon after her birth. Perhaps the most inauspicious component of her parents' conduct, which granted the child only a very niggardly bit of warmth, was the fact—and this was reinforced by the whole program of her education—that their sheer *existence* was strongly emphasized, and the patient was drilled in love, honor, and obedience towards them without ever feeling these emotions directly and realistically.

In this atmosphere, so lacking in feeling on the part of the parents, the development of a satisfactory emotional life could scarcely be expected in the child. One would expect, however, that other persons in the environment would take the place of the parents. Her situation would then have been that of a child brought up in a foster home. In such children we find that the emotional ties to their own parents are transferred to the parent substitutes in relationship to whom the oedipus develops with greater difficulty perhaps but with no significant modifications.

This patient, in accordance with ceremonial tradition, always had three nurses, each of whom wanted to stand first in the eyes of the parents and each of whom continually sought the favor of the child. They were, moreover, frequently changed. Throughout her whole childhood there was no one person who loved her and who could have served as a significant love object for her.

As soon as she was able to conceptualize, the patient immersed herself intensively in fantasies about the parents. She attributed to them divine powers through which she was provided with things unattainable to ordinary mortals. Everything she absorbed from stories and legends she elaborated into the myth about her parents. No longing for love was ever expressed in these fantasies; they all had the aim of providing a narcissistic gain. Every meeting with the real parents separated them further from the heroes of her imagination. In this manner there was formed in the child a parental myth, a fantasmic shadow of an oedipus situation which remained an empty form so far as real persons and emotions were concerned. Not only did reality which denied her parent relationships lead to narcissistic regression into fantasy, but this process gained further impetus from the absence of any substitutive object-libidinous relationships. The frequent change of nurses and governesses and the fact that these persons were themselves subjected to strict discipline, acted on orders, and used all available measures to make the child conform to the demands of reality, measures in which a pseudo tenderness was consciously used as a means to attain didactic ends, precluded this possibility. The child was trained very early to cleanliness and strict table manners, and the violent outbreaks of anger and rage to which she was subject in early childhood were successfully brought under control, giving way to an absolutely pliant obedience. Much of this disciplinary control was attained by appeal to the parents so that everything the child did which was obedient and proper she referred to the wish or command of the mythical father and mother.

When she entered a convent school at the age of eight, she was completely fixed in the 'as if' state in which she entered analysis. Superficially, there was no difference between her life and that of the average convent pupil. She had the customary attachment to a nun in imitation of her group of girls. She had the most tender friendships which were wholly without significance to her. She went devoutly through the forms of religion without the slightest trace of belief, and underwent seduction into masturbation with quasi feelings of guilt—simply to be like her comrades.

In time, the myth of the parents faded and disappeared without new fantasies to take its place. It disappeared as her parents became clearer to her as real persons and she devaluated them. Narcissistic fantasies gave way to real experiences in which, however, she could participate only through identification.

Analysis disclosed that the success of her early training in suppressing instinctual drives was only apparent. It had something of the 'trained act' in it and, like the performance of the circus animal, was bound to the presence of a ringmaster. If denial of an instinct was demanded, the patient complied, but when an otherwise inclined object gave permission for the satisfaction of a drive, she could respond quite without inhibition, though with little gratification. The only result of the training was that the drive never came into conflict with the external world. In this respect she behaved like a child in that stage of development in which its instinctual drives are curbed only by immediate external authority. Thus it happened that for a time the patient fell into bad company, in unbelievable contrast to her home environment and early training. She got drunk in low dives, participated in all kinds of sexual perversions, and felt just as comfortable in this underworld as in the pietistic sect, the artistic group, or the political movement in which she was later successively a participant.

She never had occasion to complain of lack of affect for she was never conscious of it. The patient's relationship to her parents was strong enough to enable her to make them heroes of her fantasy, but for the creation of a warm dynamic oedipus constellation capable of shaping a healthy future psychic life in both a positive and a negative sense the necessary conditions were obviously lacking. It is not enough that the parents are simply there and provide food for fantasy. The child must *really* be seduced to a certain extent by the libidinous activity of the parents in order to develop a normal emotional life, must experience the warmth of a mother's body as well as all those unconscious seductive acts of the loving mother as she cares for its bodily needs. It must play with the father and have sufficient intimacy with him to sense the father's masculinity in order that instinctual impulses enter the stream of the oedipus constellation.

This patient's myth bore some similarity to the fantasy which Freud called the 'family romance'[4] in which, however, the libidinal relation to the parents though repressed is very powerful. By repudiating the real parents, it is possible partly to avoid strong emotional conflicts from forbidden wishes, feelings of guilt, etc. The real objects have been repressed but in analysis they can be uncovered with their full libidinal cathexis.

But for our patient there was never a living warm emotional relation-

[4] Freud designates as the 'family romance', fantasies which have in common the fact that they all relate to the ancestry of the person creating them. The typical version of the 'family romance' is 'I am not my parents' child. Whose child am I then?' The usual answer is, 'I come of a more exalted family'.

Cf. Deutsch, Helene: *Zur Genese des 'Familienromans'*. Int. Ztschr. f. Psa., XVI, 1930, pp. 249–253.

ship to the parents or to anyone else. Whether after weak attempts at object cathexis the child returned to narcissism by a process of regression or never succeeded in establishing a real object relation as the result of being unloved is, for all practical purposes, irrelevant.

The same deficiency which interfered with the development of the emotional life was also operative in the formation of the superego. The shadowy structure of the oedipus complex was gradually given up without ever having come to an integrated and unified superego formation. One gains the impression that the prerequisites for such a development also lie in strong oedipal object cathexes.

It is not to be denied that at a very early age some inner prohibitions are present which are the precursors of the superego and are intimately dependent on external objects. Identification with the parents in the resolution of the oedipus complex brings about the integration of these elements. Where this is absent, as it was in our patient, the identifications remain vacillating and transitory. The representatives which go to make up the conscience remain in the external world and instead of the development of inner morals there appears a persistent identification with external objects. In childhood, educational influences exerted an inhibitory effect on the instinctual life, particularly on the aggressions. In later life, in the absence of an adequate superego, she shifts the responsibility for her behavior to objects in the external world with whom she identifies herself. The passivity of this patient as the expression of her submission to the will of another seems to be the final transformation of her aggressive tendencies.

As the result of this weak superego structure, there is little contact between the ego and the superego, and the scene of all conflicts remains external, like the child for whom everything can proceed without friction if it but obey. Both the persistent identification and the passive submission are expressions of the patient's complete adaptation to the current environment, and impart the shadowy quality to the patient's personality. The value of this link to reality is questionable because the identification always takes place with only a part of the environment. If this part of the environment comes into conflict with the rest, naturally the patient is involved. Thus it can come about that the individual can be seduced into asocial or criminal acts by a change in his identifications, and it may well be that some of the asocial are recruited from the group of 'as if' personalities who are adapted to reality in this restricted way.

Analysis of this patient revealed a genuine infantilism, that is, an arrest at a definite stage in the development of the emotional life and character formation. In addition to particularly unfavorable environmental influences it should be noted that the patient came from a very old family overrun with psychotics and invalid psychopaths.

Another woman patient had a father who had a mental illness and a mother who was neurotic. She remembered her father only as 'a man with a black beard', and she tried to explain as something very fascinating and wonderful, his absences as he was moved to and from a sanatarium and an isolated room at home, always under nursing care. Thus she built a myth around her father, replacing him in fantasy by a mysterious man, whom she later called an 'Indian' and with whom she had all sorts of experiences, each of which served to make her a superhuman being. The prototype for the Indian was the father's male nurse, whom the little girl saw mysteriously disappearing into her father's room. The education and upbringing of the child were relegated to nurses, but despite this she succeeded in establishing a strongly libidinous attachment to the very abnormal mother. Her later relationships had elements of object-libidinous attitudes, sometimes warmer, especially in homosexual directions, but never sufficiently to change their 'as if' quality. The failure to develop an adequate object cathexis was, in this patient, related to the birth of her brother towards whom she developed an unusually aggressive envy. Comparisons of genitalia led the little girl to scrutinize her body for hours on end in a mirror. Later this narcissitic activity was gradually sublimated. At first she tried to model parts of her body in clay in order to facilitate her mirror studies. In the course of years she developed great skill in modeling and was for a brief time under the tutelage of a sculptress. Unconsciously, it was the fantasy of displaying repeatedly her body to the world. In later years she created only large, very voluptuous, matronly female figures. These proved to be weak attempts to recreate the mother she had lost in childhood to her brother. Ultimately she abandoned sculpture for music simply because she believed her teacher failed to appreciate her sufficiently.

Most conspicuous in her childhood was a monkey-like imitation of her brother with whom she was for years completely identified, not in fantasy but by acting out. Disastrously for both, the brother quite early betrayed unmistakable signs of a psychosis which culminated in a catatonic excitement. The sister imitated all her brother's bizarre activities and lived with him in a world of fantasy. Only her partial object-libidinous cathexis and a displacement of the process from the brother and identification with more normal objects saved her from being institutionalized. I was inclined at first to regard her condition as the result of an identification with her psychotic brother; only later did I recognize that the etiology of her condition lay deeper.

I believe this patient is similar to the first despite the differences in their development. In the second, it seems that a disappointment shattered the strong relationship with the mother, that the mysterious absence of the father made it impossible for the little girl to find in him a substitute when her relationship to her mother was shaken, and that further relationships to objects remained at the stage of identification. By such identification she averted her intense hatred of her brother and transformed her aggression towards him into an obedient passivity in which she submissively identified herself with hm. She developed no other object relationships. Her superego suffered the same fate as that of the first patient. The myth of the father and the very early devaluation of the mother prevented integration of her superego and left her dependent on persons in the external world.

A third patient, a pretty, temperamental woman of thirty-five with many intellectual and artistic talents, came to analysis because she was 'tired' after a long series of adventures. It soon became clear that, as the result of a certain combination of circumstances, her interest in psychonanalysis was actually an interest in the analyst, especially in her profession. While she frequently spoke of her tremendous interest in child psychology and in Freud's theory and read widely on these subjects, her understanding of them was extraordinarily superficial and her interest entirely unreal. More careful observation disclosed that this was true not only for all her intellectual interests but for everything she did or had ever done. It was surprising to recognize in this woman, who was so indefatigably active, a condition so closely related to the pseudoaffectivity of the 'as if' patient. All her experiences too were based on identifications, though her identifications were not so straightforward as were those of the other type of patient which is, one might say, more monogamous and adheres to but one person or one group at a time, while this patient had so many concurrent identifications—or symbolic representations of identifications—that her conduct appeared erratic. She was, in fact, considered 'crazy' by those who knew her. Her friends however had no notion that her apparently rich life concealed a severe lack of affect. She had come to me because of a wish to change her character, that is, to create more peace and harmony in her life by identifying herself with a 'particularly solid' professional personality.

After six months the analysis appeared to be unusually successful. The patient learned to understand many things about herself and lost her eccentricities. She determined to become an analyst and when this was denied her, she collapsed. She was completely lacking in affect and complained, 'I am so empty! My God, I am so empty! I have no feelings.' It transpired that prior to analysis she had got into serious financial difficulties by breaking off various friendships and love relationships and had realized that she would soon have to work. It was with this intention that she came to analysis. Her plan was to become an analyst by identification with her analyst. When this proved impossible, this seemingly very able and active woman changed into a completely passive person. From time to time she had extraordinarily violent fits of childish weeping or outbursts of rage, flung herself on the floor and kicked and screamed. Gradually, she developed a progressive lack of affect. She became completely negativistic and met all interpretations with, 'I don't understand what you mean by that'.

At two points in this patient's development she had suffered severe trauma. Her father was an alcoholic, and the patient often witnessed his brutal mistreatment of the mother. She sided vehemently with the latter and, when she was only seven, had fantasies in which she rescued her mother from her misery and built a little white cottage for her. She saved every penny and worked hard in school to attain this aim, only to discover that her mother was not merely a passive victim of her husband but took pleasure in being brutalized. The consequent devaluation of her mother not only deprived her of her only object of love but also arrested the development of a feminine ego ideal of an independent, adequate personality. She spent the rest of her life trying to make up for this lack by creating a whole series of identifications, in the same way as the 'as if' patients.

Deprived of tenderness and affection in her childhood, her instincts remained crudely primitive. She vacillated between giving these instincts free rein and holding them in check. She acted out prostitution fantasies, indulged in a variety of sexual perversions, often giving the impression of hypomania. She emerged from these debauches by identification with some conventional person and achieved by this means a kind of sublimation, the form dependent on the particular object. This resulted in a frequent shifting of her occupation and interests. So long as it was possible for her either to retain such a relationship or to allow herself the gratification of very primitive drives she was not aware of her lack of affect.

The following cases of emotional disturbance bear close similarity with the 'as if' group but differ in certain respects.

A seventeen-year-old boy of unusual intellectual ability, came for analysis because of manifest homosexuality and a conscious lack of feeling. This lack of emotion included his homosexual objects, about whom he created all sorts of perverse fantasies. He was obsessionally scrupulous, modest, exact, and reliable. He was passively oral and anal in his homosexuality. The analysis was extremely rich in material but progressed in an emotional vacuum. While the transference was frequently represented in his dreams and fantasies, it never became a conscious, emotional experience.

One day I gave him a ticket to a series of lectures in which I was taking part. He went to my lecture and had severe anxiety on the stairs leading to the lecture hall. By thus mobilizing his anxiety in the transference, the analysis began to progress.

An only child from a highly cultured environment, with a father who was strict and ambitious and a mother who dedicated her life to this handsome and talented son, he nevertheless suffered the fate of affective deficiency. The fact that he grew up in an atmosphere in which he never needed to seek for love, that he was overwhelmed with tenderness without having to make any effort to obtain it paralyzed his own active strivings for tenderness. He remained bound to primitive instinctual impulses, and because there were few infantile anxieties which were not warded off with scrupulous care, there was no motive in him to build up defense mechanisms.

He underwent the trauma of the depreciation of his ego-ideal when he discovered that his admired father was uncultivated and limited. This realization threatened to depreciate his own value, for he was like his father, bore his name, and heard his resemblance to him repeatedly stressed by his mother. Through rigidity and strictness, in ethical and intellectual demands, he strove to become better than the self which was identified with the father. In contrast to the previous patients, he did not identify himself with a series of objects. Instead of having emotional relationships to people, he was split into two identifications: one with his beloved mother and the other with his father. The first was feminine and sexualized; the second was overcompensatory, rigid, and narcissistic.

Unlike the 'as if' patients, he complained of lack of feeling. He completely lacked the tender emotions which would have given warmth to his emotional life. He had no relation to any woman, and his friendships with men were either purely intellectual or crudely sexual. The feelings he had were of a character he would not let himself express. These were very primitive aggressions, the wildest, most infantile sexual drives, which were rejected with the declaration, 'I feel nothing at all'. In one way he told the truth; he was really lacking in any permissible feelings, that is, in the tender, sublimated emotions.

The tendency to identification is characteristic also of this type of affective disturbance. Even though this patient did not completely sink his personality in a series of identifications, the strongest section of his ego, his intellect, lacked originality. Everything he wrote and said in scientific matters showed great formal talent but when he tried to produce something original it usually turned out to be a repetition of ideas which he had once grasped with particular clarity. The tendency to multiple identifications occurred on the intellectual level.

Another patient of this group, a thirty-year-old married woman who came from a family in which there were many psychotics, complained about lack of emotion. In spite of good intelligence and perfect reality testing, she led a sham existence and she was always just what was suggested to her by the environment. It became clear that she could experience nothing except a completely passive readiness to split into an endless number of identifications. This condition had set in acutely after an operation in her childhood for which she had been given no psychological preparation. On recovery from the anaesthesia she asked if she were really herself, and then developed a state of depersonalization which lasted a year and turned into passive suggestibility which concealed a crippling anxiety.

Common to all these cases is a deep disturbance of the process of sublimation which results both in a failure to synthesize the various infantile identifications into a single, integrated personality, and in an imperfect, one-sided, purely intellectual sublimation of the instinctual strivings. While critical judgment and the intellectual powers may be excellent, the emotional and moral part of the personality is lacking.

The etiology of such conditions is related first, to a devaluation of the object serving as a model for the development of the child's personality. This devaluation may have a firm foundation in reality or be traceable, for example, to shock at discovery of parental coitus at a period of development when the child is engaged in its last struggles against masturbation and needs support in its efforts towards sublimation. Or, as in the case of the boy described above, the successful sublimation may be interfered with by a sexualization of the relationship to an object who should serve the child as a model for its ego ideal, in this instance, a grossly sexual identification with his mother.

Another cause of this kind of emotional disturbance is insufficient stimulus for the sublimation of the emotions, as the result either of being given too little tenderness, or too much.

Infantile anxiety may suffer a similar fate. Too harsh or too indulgent treatment may contribute to failure in the economic formation of defense mechanisms resulting in remarkable passivity of the ego. It will be recalled that in the case of the boy reported, an attack of anxiety not only mobilized the transference but also opened the way to his recovery.

The question must be raised as to how the tendency of 'as if' personalities to identification with current love objects differs from the same tendency in hysteria. The great difference between the latter and the 'as if' disturbance lies in the fact that the objects with which the hysterics identify themselves are the objects of powerful libidinous cathexes. Hysterical repression of affect brings freedom from anxiety and so represents a way out of the conflict. In 'as if' patients, an early deficiency in the development of affect reduces the inner conflict, the effect of which is an impoverishment of the total personality which which does not occur in hysteria.

The patients described here might make one suspect that we are dealing with something like the blocking of affect seen especially in narcissistic individuals who have developed loss of feeling through repression. The great fundamental difference, however, is that the 'as if' personality tries to simulate affective experience, whereas the individual with a blocking of affect does not. In the analysis of the latter it can always be shown that the once developed object relationships and aggressive feelings have undergone repression and are not at the disposal of the conscious personality. The repressed, affectively toned segment of the personality is gradually uncovered during the analysis, and it is sometimes possible to make the buried part of the emotional life available to the ego.

For example, one patient had completely repressed the memory of his mother who died when he was four, and with whom, it was clear, the greater part of his emotions had been involved. Under the influence of a very weak but none the less effective transference, isolated memories gradually emerged. At first these had a negative character and denied all tenderness. During analysis this patient showed also another form of emotional disturbance, namely, depersonalization. Before analysis his self-satisfaction had been unshaken. He defended himself against the transference with all his power. In the analytic hours, when clear signs of a transference *in statu nascendi* were perceptible, the patient would complain of sudden feelings of strangeness. It was clear that in him the depersonalization corresponded to the perception of a change in cathexis. It remained a question whether this was due to a new libidinal stream emerging from repression, or to a suppression of feelings connected with transference. The inner conflict in such an instance of repression of affect has little similarity to that of an 'as if' patient. The analogy rests only on the affective impoverishment in both.

The narcissism and the poverty of object relationships so characteristic for an 'as if' person bring to consideration the relationship of this defect to a psychosis. The fact that reality testing is fully maintained removes this condition from our conception of psychosis.

Narcissistic identification as a preliminary stage to object cathexis, and introjection of the object after its loss, are among the most important discoveries of Freud and Abraham. The psychological structure of melancholia offers us the classical example of this process. In melancholia, the object of identification has been psychologically internalized, and a tyrannical superego carries on the conflict with the incorporated object in complete independence of the external world. In 'as if' patients, the objects are kept external and all conflicts are acted out in relation to them. Conflict with the superego is thus avoided because in every gesture and in every act the 'as if' ego subordinates itself through identification to the wishes and commands of an authority which has never been introjected.

From the beginning, both the personal impression given by the patients themselves and the psychotic disposition in the family, especially in the first two analytically observed cases, make one suspect a schizophrenic process. The tracing of the severe psychic disturbance directly back to the developments of early childhood seems to me completely justified, and whether this speaks against the diagnosis of a schizophrenic process must, for the time being, be left undecided. My observations of schizophrenic patients have given me the impression that the schizophrenic process goes through an 'as if' phase before it builds up the delusional form. A twenty-two-year-old schizophrenic girl came to me after a catatonic attack, oriented for time and place but full of delusional ideas. Until the onset of the confusional state she had led an existence almost indistinguishable from 'as if' patients. Her bond to objects with whom she identified herself, and who were always outstanding women, was extremely intense. As a result of rapid shifting of these relationships, she changed her place of residence, her studies, and her interests in an almost manic fashion. Her last identification had led her from the home of a well-established American family to a communistic cell in Berlin. A sudden desertion by her object led her from Berlin to Paris where she was manifestly paranoid and gradually developed a severe confusion. Treatment restored her to her original state, but despite warnings, her family decided to break off the analysis. The girl was not able to summon enough affect to protest. One day she bought a dog and told me that now everything would be all right; she would imitate the dog and then she would know how she should act. Identification was retained but was no longer limited to human objects; it included animals, inanimate objects, concepts, and symbols, and it was this lack of selectivity which gave the process its delusional character. It was the loss of the capacity for identification with human objects which made possible the erection of a new, delusional world.

Another schizophrenic patient for years had had a recurrent dream in which in great pain and torment she sought her mother but could not find her because she was always faced with an endless crowd of women, each of whom looked like her mother, and she could not tell the right one. This dream reminded me of the stereotyped, recurrent mother figures in the sculpture of the second 'as if' patient.

Freud[5] speaks of 'multiple personality' as the result of a process in which numerous identifications lead to a disruption of the ego. This may result in manifest psychopathology, or the conflicts between the different identifications can assume a form which need not necessarily be designated as pathological. Freud refers to a purely inner process of ego formation, and this does not apply to the 'as if' identifications with objects in the outer world. However, the same psychological process will also in the 'as if' personality on one occasion have a more 'normal' resolution and on another a pathological outcome which may be more or less severe.

Anna Freud[6] points out that the type of pseudoaffectivity observed in 'as if' patients is often found in puberty. I believe that the depreciation of the primary objects (also typical of puberty) who served as models for the ego ideal, plays an important rôle in both. Anna Freud describes this type of behavior in puberty as incurring the suspicion of psychosis. I believe that the reflections which I have presented here will also serve for puberty. At one time the process will lie within the bounds of the 'normal' and at another it bears the seeds of a pathological condition. The type justifies the designation 'schizoid', whether or not schizophrenia later develops.

Whether the emotional disturbances described in this paper imply a 'schizophrenic disposition' or constitute rudimentary symptoms of schizophrenia is not clear to me. These patients represent variants in the series of abnormal distorted personalities. They do not belong among the commonly accepted forms of neurosis, and they are too well adjusted to realilty to be called psychotic. While psychoanalysis seldom succeeds, the practical results of treatment can be very far-reaching, particularly if a strong identification with the analyst can be utilized as an active and constructive influence. In so far as they are accessible to analysis, one may be able to learn much in the field of ego psychology, especially with regard to disturbances of affect, and, perhaps, make contributions to the problem of the 'schizoid' which is still so obscure.

In the great delusional formations of the psychoses we see primitive

---

[5] Freud:*The Ego and the Id*. London: Institute of Psycho-Analysis and Hogarth Press, 1927.

[6] Freud, A.: *The Ego and the Mechanisms of Defence*. London: Hogarth Press, 1937.

and archaic drives returning from the depths of the unconscious in a dramatic manner. Regression takes place because the ego has failed. We speak of this as a 'weakness of the ego' and assume that the reasons for this failure are psychological, constitution, or organic. Psychoanalysis can investigate the first of these, especially in prepsychotic conditions to which these cases belong.

6. The Treatment of Psychopaths and Borderline Patients

Melitta Schmideberg

The majority of my patients suffer neither from a classical neurosis nor a definite psychosis. They are "difficult" and may or may not have circumscribed neurotic symptoms. Most of them would probably be diagnosed as "psychopaths" or "borderline cases." Personally, I am inclined to think that most of them are early cases of schizophrenia or near-schizophrenia. Some may be hysterical characters, but of a special type, closely related to psychosis. Many of them were criminals, but for the purposes of this paper I shall not deal with them. Without quibbling over diagnostic niceties, I would like to describe one group from the technical point of view, whatever their diagnosis.

Such patients are unable to stand routine and regularity. They transgress every rule; naturally they do not attend treatment regularly, are late for their appointments and, when they do appear, are unreliable about payments. They do not associate freely and often do not talk at all. They refuse to lie on the couch. They often come for analysis only under persuasion or pressure and even when they come on their own, their insight does not last nor carry them through difficulties. Even when they try to cooperate, they cannot sustain the effort. In their lives something always "happens," usually on the spur of the moment, entirely out of the blue. If they are poor, they are likely to become criminals. In general, if they belong to the upper classes they manage not to break the law too flagrantly or, at least, not to get caught. Money and background provide a greater latitude for abnormality so that people merely describe their behavior as "erratic." Yet in many cases their antisocial tendencies are only too obvious and, either by omission or commission, they hurt those who become associated with them.

As I have said, something is always "happening" to these patients and if the analyst merely adopts an expectant and detached attitude, trying slowly and conscientiously to probe their unconscious there will soon be trouble. It is difficult to establish emotional contact or, alternately, the transference is most unreliable. The patient may appear deeply attached one day and not turn up the next. The speed with which his mood changes from one extreme to another is uncanny. In one case, it was literally a question of seconds.

Such patients cannot be treated by classical analysis, and since they cannot be cured by anything short of analysis, we must modify the method. The analyst should, above all, be a therapist, and to treat the patient is more important than to adhere to certain rules. The technique should be adapted to the patient and not the patient to the technique.

I have treated well over a hundred patients of the type described, including about twenty-five definitely psychotic ones, and in almost every case I have been able to achieve at least an improvement, sometimes after only a few sessions.

The main thing is to establish immediate contact. I never aim at a sytematic anamnesis or diagnosis or try to get full information in the first interview, but try to establish contact. I talk spontaneously and appear as nonprofessional as possible. If a patient finds it difficult to talk, I ask questions or talk myself, attempting to put him at ease. If necessary, I discuss generalities or any subject he might be interested in. I never try to impress the patient, quite the contrary. An alcoholic patient called to make an appointment. I knew she was most reluctant to see me and had agreed to come only under persuasion and because she was at the end of her tether. After mentioning her name and asking me for an appointment, in an effort to make conversation, she asked how I was. I enlarged upon my difficulties in finding my way about in New York. I could sense her relief over the phone; she was immediately more at ease.

Sometimes in a tense situation I start talking about myself or my interests. A schizoid alcoholic came in to treatment in a very bad state. He was tense, inhibited, and had the greatest difficulty in saying anything. I asked question after question, getting about half a sentence in reply. Eventually I asked him about his war experiences. He told me he had been in an antiaircraft battery and had been in some raids. I burst out, "That's nothing," and went on to tell him about the London blitz. He became interested and started to speak much more fluently and spontaneously. It is not good to have too polite and soothing a manner since it is not natural.

A twelve-year-old schizoid boy came to treatment very reluctantly. His parents had to bribe, persuade and almost force him most of the time. When he was actually there, he talked quite openly but he objected to coming because the journey took so long. I agreed to his coming less and less frequently until I was seeing him only once a fortnight. At the same time I felt that he should have more opportunity to get used to me. He said, "What's the good of talking to you since I can't see you when I get upset?" So I suggested that he take my phone number and call me in such a case. He need not ask his mother and in fact she need not even know it. But I did not think he was likely to phone me, so I rang him every few days, chatting informally of what I had been doing and asking him what he had been doing. He appreciated this and as a result was much more ready to come.

The patient's difficulties are due, in the first place, to anxiety, which I try to diminish, partly by my manner and approach, partly by giving him interpretations. Some interpretations upset the patient; others re-assure him. I aim at giving only the latter type until I have established a fairly stable contact. I give interpretations in a casual conversational manner, sometimes framed as a question.

A very inhibited, schizophrenic young man came to see me. I knew that he had come only because his mother had sent him. He had seen one psychiatrist before whom he disliked. There was no means of knowing whether he thought there was anything wrong with him. When I asked him to be seated, he sat down in my chair. I said nothing and sat down on the couch. My efforts at conversation failed; he said nothing and was obviously ill at ease. So I commented on how unpleasant he must find the situation, so different from usual behavior. He had seen other doctors before, hadn't he, and I suppose he hadn't liked them. I described it as a funny situation, rather like facing a detective who suspects one of something. Since one doesn't quite know what he's suspected of nor how to behave, nor what would make him appear suspicious it is safest to say nothing. By using these analogies and "as if's," I tried to analyze the patient's paranoid fears, and after these remarks, he started to talk.

It is in the first place anxiety and often fear of masochism that makes a patient reluctant to lie down. I can by now foretell with some certainty who is likely to refuse, and in such a case I do not even suggest it. In any case, I never make an issue of it. Apart from the fact that is more convenient for the analyst if the patient lies on the couch and does not watch him, it makes little difference. I have analyzed patients while having a meal, going for a walk, or traveling in the subway with them, and in one case I analyzed a patient under the effect of luminal in the middle of the night.

If a patient's inability to associate freely is due to his inability to relax, exhortations will not help. The patient cannot relax by effort, so I just let him talk and, if necessary, I make conversation or ask questions. I am able by now to give interpretations on the basis of very little verbal material, drawing my conclusions from the patient's behavior and character, from his history, his symptoms and his general pattern, from the material he has given me in the past, from what others have told me about him, from analytic theory, and from what I know about other patients of his type and class. I put myself in his place and imagine what I would feel. I try to make the interpretations specific, avoiding symbolic interpretations. As a result of interpretations or of my talking, the patient generally becomes more communicative until a special difficulty arises which produces anxiety and hostility. It is important to discuss these issues immediately. With classical neurotics one can afford to wait and let them work out and clarify their problems. But with this type of patient, if I omit interpreting acute anxiety or the immediate disturbance of the transference situation, the chances are that I will not see him again.

I am not afraid of giving wrong interpretations since they are rarely harmful. Sometimes the right interpretation given at the wrong moment, or in the wrong manner, may upset the patient. In such a case, I analyze his reaction and try to smooth matters over. If the patient does not talk, I will. I have allowed silences to arise only on one or two occasions when the patient expressed a tremendous amount of hostility by means of his silence, but even then I interrupted after about ten minutes by saying he must find the situation uncomfortable, in order not to make him feel too badly.

It is said that one cannot analyze patients who lie. First of all, I do not think that even the ordinary patient is entirely truthful. He may not tell deliberate lies but by omissions, understatements, or sidetracking, he manages to create a false impression. I have been a patient myself and I do not think that other patients are much more sincere. There is always something that in some form or other is held back. This is an unavoidable manifestation of resistance which is not to be deprecated but valued as an important part of the analytic process. Whether his defenses take the form of verbal lies or some other form makes little difference. It is possible to analyze on the basis of very little information and I see no harm as a rule in accepting the patient's statements at face value. If I reduce his anxiety and distrust, and do not make lying a moral issue, the patient will tell me after a while that some of his previous statements were really slightly inaccurate, and I will receive this admission without any surprise or emotion. A patient once asked me whether I knew she had lied on a certain occasion. I said yes, and proceeded to tell her in a matter-of-fact way how I knew. If she had not asked me I would not have told her. It does not worry me to be fooled by a patient. I do not pretend to be omniscient, and in fact my knowing too much would arouse his paranoid fears. I would therefore tell him how I had arrived at my conclusions in order not to frighten him. If the patient does not tell me about his lies, I might, after a while, broach the subject myself, starting cautiously with such general remarks as "Of course, everybody tells a lie sometimes" of "Naturally, if one is frightened, the first impulse is to tell a lie." If I have good enough contact and we have agreed that he is prone to telling lies, then I may occasionally press him to tell me the truth on a certain matter, but I never make it an issue, or threaten, or disapprove.

I have said earlier that some interpretations reassure the patient while others upset him. This depends largely on the form of the interpretation. Most of these patients have all their lives been blamed for their bad behavior with a good deal of justification. It is essential to give my interpretations so that they are not felt as a reproach. This will depend above all on my own attitude. The patient knows if I am readly not being critical. When, or better before, interpreting antisocial impulses, it is good to draw attention to his affection or his concern for others, and to qualify the remarks about his aggression. A straightforward interpretation of his aggression may produce more guilt or anxiety than he can stand at the moment. So I mitigate my remarks by some generalization such as "It is only natural that you resented . . . ," "Anybody feels angry at times," or "I would have minded that myself." The patient is more ready to admit that he felt angry or annoyed for a brief moment in a justified situation than that he feels hostile or has sadistic

ideas. I start with situations where the patient's resentment was justifiable. If he does not tell me, I make safe guesses. It is likely that a girl
who has been in an institution has a resentment against the matron. But
the girl may insist that the matron was nice and treated her well.
"Surely," I say, "she does sound like a nice person. But you know
nobody is perfect. Sometimes something must have annoyed you."
Then she starts talking, and after fifteen minutes the matron does not
sound like a nice person at all.

In testing out my interpretations I go cautiously and watch the patient's reactions, starting on comparatively safe topics. A boy is less
likely to feel guilty about hostility towards his teacher than towards his
own father. Having discussed this without too strong a reaction, I can
proceed to talk about the father, first again in general terms, pointing
out justified resentments, and slowly becoming more pointed and later
on even insistent. The order of interpretations is important and it may
make a considerable difference whether I give a certain interpretation
five minutes earlier or later. I watch and interpret the patient's reactions
to my interpretations. If he is upset, I will either analyze it or reassure
him, or do both, or by some generality, to a certain extent, take back
my interpretation. This method, going step by step, makes it possible
for me to control the effect of my interpretations. I give my interpretations, maybe even a dozen in a session, but I give them piecemeal.
Though sometimes I put the interpretations in a generalized form I try
to make them specific. Some analysts tend to give unspecific interpretations; e.g., tell the patient that he feels guilty about something and
leave it to him to fill in the gaps. With this type of patient it is bad policy.
Unspecific interpretations stir up emotions and unless they are quickly
followed by an interpretation which relieves the tension, trouble may
arise. Ordinary neurotics can tolerate tension much better since with
them "things do not happen" so suddenly and it is enough for the
analyst to guide them a little and leave it to them to work things out.
This cannot be done safely with these patients.

I do not interpret everything indiscriminately, but only what matters
dynamically, i.e., what is likely to produce emotions. Historic interpretations alone are not likely to achieve that end. It is not enough to relate
everything to the patient's childhood. It is often useful to work out his
pattern of emotional reaction, his loves, hates, and anxieties in the

present as far as they relate to his ordinary life or the transference, and when the pattern has been established and worked through, it can be connected with what is known about his childhood.

Interpretations in order to be effective have to be specific and dynamic. To illustrate, a patient suffering from a phobia of dogs told me that his previous analyst had pointed out that the dog was a symbol of the father's penis. The interpretation did not diminish his fears. I tried to get him to remember whether as a child he used to tease dogs and how far he feared their revenge. This made some difference, and then we could proceed to analyze a similar attitude towards people in general, towards his father and his own sex life. In another case we might discover repressed interest in the dog's sex life or excretions, or sexual plays with him. Another patient suddenly developed a tendency to bite his knuckles. When I inquired into memories of thumb-sucking and nail-biting, he could only remember the story he had heard as a child of a little girl who was severely punished for it. Being acquainted with some phase of analytic theory by then, he explained to me that sucking the thumb expressed his longing for his mother. However, I was not satisfied with this explanation, and pointed out that he would not have been so upset about the story of the little girl if his own mother had not used somewhat similar methods and that his bad relation to his mother was probably due to her attempts to wean him from such habits. A patient had an obsession about straightening books to make the backs even, and various interpretations given him by his previous analysts relating to castration fear, and attacks on the protuding parts of the body such as breasts or penis, had made no difference. Once he mentioned casually the sense of inferiority he had as a child because his teeth protruded, and then I saw the connection between this and his obsessional habit. After interpreting it, the habit disappeared.

Interpretations should never be stereotyped. I always avoid technical terms and try to express myself in plain English as vividly as possible, preferably using the patient's own expressions. I sometimes use concrete examples or images as illustrations. If the analyst's interpretations appeal to the patient's imagination, they seem to achieve more effect.

Some analysts hold that with more difficult patients one should avoid interpretations of certain material for fear of upsetting them. I do not agree. I am cautious in the manner and form of interpretations and their timing, but I give a great many interpretations and analyze every aspect thoroughly. The more abnormal the patient, the greater the need to analyze, for example, pregenital material. Using the precautions I have described, I have never yet seen any ill effects.

Some analysts are cautious in giving interpretations for fear that a wrong interpretation may discredit them. This does not worry me. I do not want to impress the patient either with my omniscience or with any other virtue. One day I arrived late for a patient who was herself habitually late. I was rather apologetic about the fact that she had had to wait outside in the cold, but she beamed all over her face. Recently I had an accident and several patients saw me when I was in pain. This had a very good effect on all of them, bringing home the fact that I am human after all.

I always watch the transference closely, but this does not mean that I interpret it constantly. In fact, I sometimes do not interpret manifestations that are too obvious. Too frequent interpretations of the same type tend to become stereotyped and ineffective. By analyzing the transference, I do not mean just pointing out for example that I am a mother-substitute but I try to assess the transference situation dynamically. A schizoid patient spent a whole session discussing the relativity and reality of time in the most abstruse philosophical terms. At last I pointed out to him that he resented my being a few minutes late. Or again, if a patient is upset because somebody has "let him down," I point out that in addition to obvious factors, this has made him more dependent on me which complicates our relationship, especially as he may be afraid that I, too, will let him down.

It is essential that these patients can fall back on their relationship to me. The more so as they very often do not have anybody else. I analyze the negative transference with a view to reducing the anxiety and hostility and establishing a more stable relationship but I am careful not to do anything, at least for a considerable time, which might stir up too much anxiety or hostility in relation to me. In analyzing the positive transference, I am cautious to do it so that I do not devaluate the patient's genuine feelings. For instance, I will rarely analyze a present but simply accept it and offer thanks for it in a natural way. For a patient who has been in trouble with everybody and who has marked aggressive impulses, it is particularly important that I believe in his affection. If a patient becomes too obliging, this is likely to be an overcompensation, which I shall analyze but indicate that he has a genuine positive transference as well as an overcompensatory one. A patient wanted to give me a book which he had just received and valued greatly. He felt anxious and guilty towards me for various reasons. I pointed out to him that he wanted to bribe me and that I did not want to take from him the book which meant so much more to him than it did to me, but said that if, on another occasion, he would like to make me a present in a spirit of genuine friendliness I should be very glad to accept it.

I do not like the transference situation to become too intense, nor the position of being the only person the patient has to fall back on. I try to encourage him directly or indirectly to make other contacts and have, in one or two cases, even taken active steps to help him. However, especially in the case of poor patients, this is often difficult. It is better if the patient has more people in his life and is able to act out his ambivalence by playing one against the other than if he has to rely on me entirely. I point out to the patient in the latter part of the treatment that my helping him in reality is a drawback since it makes it more difficult for him to be hostile to me. But it is unavoidable with such patients that I advise and help them in practical difficulties.

I have mentioned that one of the main difficulties with this type of patient is his inability to be punctual. He cannot adhere to any rules; he cannot live within his income; he cannot be faithful to one person; he cannot live as other people do. This attitude is partly determined by rebellion but it is also very largely due to anxiety, to a sort of claustro-phobia, an inability to tolerate restrictions. Being punctual is for him a masochistic subjection which he can not bear—an admission of help-lessness which frightens him. I analyze every aspect of the patient's difficulties and avoid forcing him. If he is very late, I make the most of the short time left and sometimes give him extra time. But if I do this too often, he tends to regard the longer time as his regular time and he will come later still. He may also tend to come infrequently. It is more difficult to analyze a patient, especially if he is very ill, by seeing him only once a week or even once a fortnight, but it can be done. After all, time can be wasted by other methods than by failing to appear. Often a very great deal of emotion is expressed by not keeping appointments, and this may help the treatment.

If there is some improvement shown by the patient's coming infre-quently he may later on be persuaded to come more often. I regard every time I see the patient as a gain and try to make the most of it.

The same patient who comes infrequently or irregularly often wants to see me at a moment's notice or turns up without an appointment. I always try to see him if at all possible as this is a sure indication of an emergency and a good opportunity to strengthen the positive transference. I always encourage a difficult patient to telephone me when he is upset or when an emergency arises. I sometimes do a great deal of the treatment over the telephone.

The patient often tells me more over the phone than face to face, partly because it is not his routine time, and he appreciates my going to trouble for him. Sometimes he can tell me things more easily when he does not see me because he is afraid of the positive transference. In some instances, the emergency situation itself makes him talkative. I give interpretations over the telephone, reassure the patient, or simply encourage him to talk.

I need a very elastic schedule to be able to do all this. If one works twelve hours a day, there is no time to make exceptions or give extra time. Yet these exceptions are more vital for certain patients than their regular treatments. I always have some free time during the day, mainly for my own convenience, but also in order to be able to deal with emergencies. Also, I do not hesitate to change or cancel an appointment with another patient, or to interrupt a session to answer the telephone and even to speak at some length. I will analyze his resentment, but since I am elastic in my relation to him and I am ready to oblige him in turn, he is not likely to bear me a deep grudge. I once had a patient in the house who attempted suicide. I went down to the waiting room to send away patient after patient. I approached one with hestitation as he was very difficult himself and in a bad state, but, to my surprise, he acceded graciously, saying that he knew I would have done it for him too. In such a case I always talk to the patient whom I send away instead of sending him a message by another person. I express my regret and give some explanation. A patient in such a case, treated as a reasonable being, is likely to behave like one. And, of course, I see to it that it is not always the same patient who suffers. Sometimes I use an alternative. I interrupt the session to see the other patient outside. As a rule, a few minutes talk is sufficient. I once went to see a second patient in the waiting room, when a third one arrived, equally unexpectedly. So I talked to him in the hall.

It is not good trying to aim at an ideal result. Ideally speaking, naturally I want the patient to get quite well. But, in the meantime, I must achieve a workable situation. With most patients, one will encourage them to work. But sometimes the opposite is necessary. For instance, a schizoid patient came back from the army, unable to do anything but drink and do a little carpentry at home. He felt very badly about it and under great pressure to take a job. I knew that even taking the most optimistic view he would not be able to do this for a number of months and told him so. I discussed his financial situation in detail and asked him why he did not take the twenty dollars a week to which he was entitled. He said he was going to start work in a week or two so it was not worth his while. I told him he knew as well as I that he could not do that, that he had better face the fact that he was ill, and proceeded to analyze his reactions. After some weeks of analysis, he decided to apply for the twenty dollars, which meant that he accepted the fact that he was ill. In allowing himself to realize this, the pressure considerably diminished. He drank very heavily but kept his appointments however drunk he was. After he had been drinking for forty-eight hours without going home, I asked him why he was so reluctant to go home. He said he was afraid of the hangover. He knew that the longer he put it off the worse it would be, but he just had not got the courage to face it. I added that he was also afraid of meeting his father when going home and that he did not like to be seen in such a state. The hangover was like being beaten by his father—the longer he avoided it, the worse it would be, yet he did not have the courage to face it. Before he left, I asked him whether I should phone his family as they were likely to worry if he didn't go home. He said I should not; that he would go home. I said I had not meant to press him, that if he wanted to stay away longer I only thought it might help if I phoned. However, I would not do it unless he told me to. The result was that he did go home.

In this case I used implied suggestion in the way I brought up the various issues. I always use suggestion cautiously and tentatively. It has a better effect if it is put mildly so that it does not produce defiance and anxiety and also no awkward situation arises if the patient does not comply. I use suggestion only as a short-term method to cope with the practical situation or emergency or to mitigate the immediate pressure. It is necessary to reduce the pressure in a patient in order to be able to analyze him. I do not use suggestion or give advice on fundamental matters. I will advise a patient as to how to handle her husband or how to deal with some immediate difficulty, but it is for her to decide whether she wants to live with him.

I discuss practical problems with the patient both from the objective and the analytic point of view. For instance, if a patient has difficulty in getting a job, I will go into detail as to the kind of a job he wants, his possibilities of getting it, his best methods of approach, etc. I will advise or help him if possible, at the same time analyzing the aspects he is afraid of, what mistakes he has made and why, and whether his ambitions are feasible. If the patient is a writer and has difficulties in writing, I suggest that he tell me the story first. I will discuss with him the objective difficulties and perhaps advise him and then analyze the unconscious complexes connected with the form of the article or the subject matter, with the persons who are likely to read the article, with the editor, etc. In other words, I take a more active and practical personal interest, both in order to improve the practical situation—which in turn lessens the pressure on the patient—and to get material for the analysis. The only means of preventing these patients from stirring up trouble or getting themselves into difficulties or from "acting out" is to lessen the pressure on them. This I do by means of interpretations, positive transference, reassurance, advice, and trying to improve the practical situation. It is rarely possible to stop "acting out" altogether, nor is it desirable. All I want is to keep it under control for practical reasons. As soon as the inner pressure diminishes the patient becomes easier and more cooperative in the analysis and behaves more like an ordinary patient.

In analyzing adult neurotics we are for the most part in the fortunate position of being able to afford to neglect the patient's family. This is not always possible with the type of patient described here. Often we need their help in handling the patient; sometimes we must help them to bear the patient's behavior till such time as he improves. If after years of analysis a patient has worked through his difficulties and comes to the conclusion that after all he wants to live with his wife, this will be of little avail if he has treated her so badly in the meantime she has left him.

Psychiatrists sometimes do not show sufficient sympathy for the family. True, they are frequently a nuisance and add to the difficulties of the treatment, which are great enough anyhow. And it is equally true that they are often responsible for much of the patient's maldevelopment. However, blaming or lecturing them does not help. On the contrary, if their guilt becomes unbearable or their resentment is increased by the attitude of the therapist, they are sure to cause trouble.

We must understand and handle them psychologically and realize what strain the maladjustment or illness of a near relative imposes; particularly if the person under the strain has cause to feel guilty. I am at present treating a patient who has been somewhat unstable but quite well adjusted and successful until he came back from the war to find his brother in a terrible condition. He handled the situation most tactfully and sensibly, arranged treatment for his brother and advised and reassured his parents. He smoothed over the difficulties arising between his brother and his parents and was the only mainstay and confidant of his brother until the situation proved too much for him. Since childhood he had assumed a protective role toward his younger brothers and tried to give them the understanding his father had denied all of them. This was a solution for his ambivalence both towards his brothers and his father. He felt so responsible for his brother because of his guilt over some homosexual incidents in childhood and because of his violent jealousy and hostility when small. Now he had objective reason to fear his brother's suicide, which reactivated his infantile death-wishes and his guilt. Yet the more difficult the objective situation became, the more he wished the brother dead and the whole matter finished. If, in such a case, the ill patient's therapist adds further to the blame and guilt we can imagine what is likely to happen. However, this man may, instead of breaking down himself, break off his brother's treatment and deal with his own guilt by putting all the blame on the doctor, who now in turn has every reason to blame the family.

Analysis itself adds to the strain on the relatives. They usually know only vaguely that they are being discussed, yet have no right to know what is being said about them, but assume, usually with full justification, that they are being blamed. This is not only an unpleasant situation but brings back the frightening and humiliating infantile situation of being discussed by the adults behind their backs, and it arouses their paranoid anxieties as well. If these become intense, they will try to set the patient against the analyst or induce either the patient or the analyst to behave badly, in order to prove that it is not their fault.

In dealing with relatives, I try to avoid such unconscious reactions as much as possible, and I have found in almost every case that if I play fair with the relatives, they play fair with me. If I have to tell them something upsetting, I do it as unemotionally as possible. I try to reassure their sense of guilt and stress what they have done for the patient or how much they have put up with. I say that it is impossible to say why one person falls ill and another one, living in much worse conditions does not. I appear as optimistic as I reasonably can be. I advise them to handle practical situations and say which issues are not important. I encourage them to get in touch with me when they get worried and to express their worry and resentment against the patient or myself to me. This usually helps to make the situation smoother. If a mother spends twenty minutes over the phone telling me how terrible her boy is and I express my sympathy, the chances are that she will be quite pleasant to him for the rest of the day. The patient learns to appreciate this. I always give the relative the feeling that I take him into my confidence. Whether I actually do this, and to what degree, depends on the individual case.

Sometimes we must protect the relatives against the patient or at least make life bearable for them. I treated an American in London who had gone to two analysts previously. With one he spent nine months, mainly analyzing his dreams. It seems that the most important pronouncement of the analyst was the remark, "You are a complicated individual," at the conclusion of a treatment. The second analyst helped him to some degree. When he came to me, he was inhibited and depressed. His main symptom was that he broke up any relationship with a girl when it became serious. I saw him about fifty times, during which time he fell in love and married. Before he went to Germany with the Army of Occupation, he asked me to treat his wife for mild neurotic symptoms and to look after her generally. This I did, and wrote him occasionally. I had better contact with him now because what I did was not strictly "professional." I saw him again in New York when he came back from the army, discharged for neurotic difficulties. He was in a very bad state, utterly lost and lonely. He did not get on with his relatives and friends and seemed to have nobody to rely on. I was very friendly, told him I was glad to see him again, gave him a drink, etc. I hoped he would be better when his wife arrived but this only made matters worse. He always had the tendency to nag her viciously which he tried hard but unsuccessfully to control.

He also suffered from pathological jealousy, which was why he used to break off affairs. He now got his wife to confess under pressure and threats some unimportant sexual incident before marriage which may not even have taken place. He reacted most violently to the forced confession. He cried for days, lay on the floor, could not sleep or eat or do anything. Alternately he treated his wife in the most sadistic manner. His own condition improved slowly but his bad treatment of his wife lasted for over half a year and is only now beginning to improve. The sexual jealousy abated but then he found other things wrong. Yet, when she wanted to leave him, he became very upset. In addition, he was unfaithful and allowed her to find out about it.

His wife is a very young and inexperienced English girl who has never been away from home, who did not know anyone here but her husband's friends with whom she did not want to discuss the situation and with whom she had nothing in common, nor did she want to write to her parents about her husband's behavior. His constant and vicious nagging increased her sense of inferiority, and his reproaches, her sense of guilt about sex. Within a short period she lost twenty pounds and developed nightmares. I was the only person to whom she could talk. I saw her occasionally with her husband's knowledge; in fact, at his request, when things got too bad, as he naturally felt very guilty. Also he identified himself with her; she representing the naughty child—himself—whom he, the punishing parent, ill-treated, and he wanted me to undo the harm he was doing her and protect her against his sadism. Yet it was a very delicate situation as he suspected me, rightly, of being on her side. I analyzed every aspect of the situation and also pointed out his sadism towards me by putting me into an impossible situation, and tried to be as tactful as possible. Yet no intellectual insight would have enabled him with his marked paranoid attitude and anxieties and overwhelmed by guilt over his bad behavior in which he yet persisted, to tolerate this very difficult situation had it not been for the fact that he had fundamentally a good relationship with me and trusted me and that I liked him.

I saw her in a friendly way; the first time we had tea and chatted about London. Once I went to the movies with her. I introduced her to a girl with whom she became friendly and who is the only friend she has. She telephoned me or came to see me in emergencies. Once she came during her husband's session, on the verge of breaking down. I told him she was there and he suggested leaving so that I could talk to her. I let her talk and encouraged her to complain, assuring her that I was very sorry for her but that my hands were tied as her husband was my first responsibility. I suggested that she not be affected by his reproaches which are expressions of his illness which is a serious one. I reassured her that she need not fear his physical violence, a fact of which I was not so sure myself. I also advised her as to how to handle him. She had previously tried to show him that she was not affected by his attacks. Of course, he could quickly break this down by bullying her more. I told her that instead she should oblige him by appearing more upset than she actually was. He would then be more likely to desist, but she should try inwardly not to let it affect her. He always made a point that he could not leave her for her sake. When things had gone very badly over a long period I encouraged her to leave him and to consider the question of divorce seriously. She left him saying that it was for good, but came back after two days, much better for the rest and they got on better afterwards. I encouraged her to express aggression and pointed out that her anxiety was due to the resentment she was bound to feel. I admitted that, according to ordinary standards, he treated her very badly. After such a talk, she usually felt better, though on her return home she as a rule abused her husband, but he did not seem to mind this too much. In a way, it would have been easier if I had sent her to an analyst for treatment, but the chances are that he would have brought out her hostility perhaps to such a degree that it would have broken up the marriage.

In conclusion I want to quote three clinical cases:

A patient with deep depressions and strong persecutory ideas, suicidal tendencies, and depersonalization feelings came for treatment. He was very ambitious, highly intelligent, utterly irresponsible and unreliable. He had affairs with half a dozen girls at once, always had innumerable prospects of jobs and could never live within his income. Although he had great difficulties in work, he was still able to do things comparatively well, but he felt quite justifiably that he was going to have a breakdown if the analysis did not help him soon. He got on extremely badly with people. He was very distrustful of the analysis and quarreled with the consulting physician, calling all analysts robbers. In the first interview, for which he was forty minutes late, he gave me the impression that he would not turn up again. But after overcoming some initial difficulties he came. He was always late, by ten minutes, thirty minutes, or sometimes even forty-five minutes. At first he missed about one period a week, usually without letting me know. I tried every time of the day he suggested. His appointment was at 3 P.M. He would ring up at 3:30 to ask if he could come in the evening, and whenever possible I agreed. If I could not alter the time I emphasized that it was because of practical difficulties, and not on principle. I very often gave him a longer session, mainly on the days that he was very late. He paid reduced fees, although he could pay more, and he always put off paying my account. He was quite unable to use free association. He spoke in a social way, face to face, doing his best to amuse or to interest me and expected an answer after every few sentences. I very largely adapted myself to his wishes, spoke frequently, reacted to his jokes or conscious interests, and gave the interpretations in a rather easy way. I allowed him to smoke my cigarettes, to use my telephone, etc. He soon arrived at a good, personal relationship to me, but was distrustful of the analysis as such, and could not stand the idea of being "a patient." If I treated him as a patient, I was superior to him or regarded him as mad; if I were an analyst, he identified me with various persons whom he distrusted, and the doctors of whom he was afraid. The analysis must be a game. If I treated him for money, I must be a robber.

One day he invited me quite unexpectedly to the theater. He reacted to my refusal with paranoid dreams which he had not had for a long time. This showed why he needed so much reassurance. He said that he got over my refusal because some time ago I had gone to hear him lecture, and had thus shown personal interest in him. He believed that everything about him was bad except his brain. If I were not interested in his conversation and his conscious interests, I should despise the only thing which was good about him. For similar reasons he must be convinced of my intelligence; he must get relief in every session; I must be able to analyze him without effort, as a play, and as far as possible without his help, i.e., without his telling me various things. For a long time he avoided telling me about his work, because there was the risk that I might not understand him at once and thus prove a failure.

At first he found out things about me in a roundabout way; he was very much impressed when I asked him why he did not ask me simply what he wanted to know. I answered practically every question. Only thus it became clear that in spite of his intelligence and inquisitiveness he was rather inhibited in his curiosity. By answering his questions I showed him trust, soothed his persecutory ideas, and gave him a hold on reality. His greatest anxiety was of losing relationship to reality.

One day something happened outside the analysis which upset him very much. I spent the whole session discussing the situation from the reality point of view without analyzing it, and suggested that he should ring me up later in the day. He rang up and asked if he could see me. I saw him for another hour in the late evening. It was very important for him that I did not charge for this interview, that I did not regard it as professional. Afterwards he told me that he would have committed suicide if I had refused to see him that evening.

We went on for about five years in this irregular way. Though he was supposed to come twice a week, he came less often. He became more stable and balanced, managed his life better and had a successful career. For the first time since adolescence, he fell in love. His anxiety and depression had improved. He could allow himself some success and happiness. The day the Nazis marched into Vienna he broke off the analysis saying that "This is the end of all of us." From then on I did not hear from him. He did not answer my letters nor did he pay his bill. I felt very resentful but after Dunkirk I rang him up because I knew he was particularly affected. He had been politically active and was on the Nazi black-list. He was very grateful. In addition to the political situation, his private life had gone all awry. His friends had let him down; his love affair had broken up. He began coming to see me frequently and comparatively punctually. He asked me for poison. He was terrified of a Nazi invasion but wanted to see it through to the end and then, if he had a chance, escape by a small boat from Scotland. If he had poison, he could take greater risks since at the last moment he could take it to avoid falling into Nazi hands and being tortured.

I got some morphine and told him so, adding that I was very reluctant to give it to him since he was in a suicidal state, but he could have it at any moment he needed it. When he had to leave London for a few days he asked me again for the morphine "so that he would not feel so alone," and I gave it to him.

As the days passed, both the war situation and his state of mind improved. He again came less often and less punctually. He did pay his old indebtedness but raised objections over my more recent bill. He thought he was a friend and it was not a professional situation at all. I said that while I agreed, still this was my means of earning my living.

So after some fuss, with my consent he paid half of it. He later married a well-to-do girl, and I wrote him asking for the balance owed, adding that he now had more money than I. He again paid half the amount due, saying that it was very important for him "as a matter of principle" not to pay my full fees.

I saw him last shortly before I left London. He was radiantly happy, in love with his wife, who is a very nice person. He said that all that had happened was that before his marriage he didn't introduce her to his friends and lose her, as was the case with his previous girls. He still has fundamentally the same character, but he is much more stable and reliable. He still is an hour late to his apointments but he is responsible in important matters. He is unfaithful to his wife though he is in love with her, but he treats her well and they are happy. He has had no bad anxiety or depression for a considerable length of time. He is very successful in his career and gets on better with people.

In contrast to this patient with whom I had contact in a rather irregular sort of way for about ten years, I want to quote another whom I saw for only four interviews. He is the friend of a friend of mine in whose house I once spent a weekend while he was also visiting there. He is brilliant in his work but had been unable to do anything or find a job for over a year. He acquired a reputation for being erratic which injured him greatly. For instance, one morning without warning, entirely on the spur of the moment, he flew to California and did not return for several weeks. He dressed and behaved in such a manner when applying for a job that he did not get it, though he was known to be very good at his work. He had always been difficult and unbalanced and his relations with women had been unsatisfactory, but it was his last affair which "finished him.' He was in love with a girl who behaved like a prostitute until eventually he beat her up. He felt very badly about this incident and from that time was in an acute state of depression and anxiety and unable to work. He incurred debts and was on the verge of being evicted from his apartment for not paying the rent. His friend who had been helping him was no longer able to do so. The patient had some psychotherapy years before but said that it did him more harm than good and that the fees he paid were exorbitant. He therefore wanted no more of treatment and saw no way out but suicide. When I learned what turn the situation had taken I told our mutual friend to suggest that he come see me. When the patient arrived, he started by asking me for whiskey.

I told him to help himself whereupon he drank a water glass full—neat. He then started to talk, interrupting himself constantly to say that he could not talk and was unable to show his emotions. Actually, he talked all the time, cried, and continuously accused himself. I discussed with him the situations where he had been badly treated by his family and others. I then concentrated on his repressed resentment, especially his resentment against the girl who had caused his troubles and the psychotherapist who had let him down, and also said that he must feel resentment towards his friend who had done so much for him because he was under such obligation. In between, he lapsed again into self-accusation, saying that he had brought only trouble to everybody, and why should I get involved too? The best thing he could do would be to commit suicide. He tried to rush out several times but I persuaded him to remain. Then he left suddenly, rushing out very dramatically. I did not think it was serious but decided that since he enjoyed being dramatic I would oblige him, so I ran after him into the street and asked him to come back. He refused. Later I learned that he had left because he had an important assignment. He did not keep his next appointment but a day later he phoned to say that he was in a very bad way and would like to see me immediately. I agreed and cancelled another appointment. We continued our talk along similar lines. On this occasion he borrowed ten dollars from me. In the meantime, his friends had found a temporary solution for him and an arrangement was made for him to stay in the country for a time. I saw him once more at which time he was still depressed and anxious but better. He was supposed to come to New York to see me but did not do so. I occasionally kept in contact with him. Two months later he saw me again. He had done some free-lance work and was better but on seeing me again he embarked on self-acusations, telling me of the bad state he was in. I interrupted him to point out that this was no advertisement for his last doctor and asked what he thought of him. After a while he again reverted to his self-accusations, and I again brought him back to my point of view. We repeated this about six times. The last I heard from him was that he was in love with a very nice girl, was very happy, had a job and was anxious to make good. It is impossible to say how the marriage will work out, but he has been all right for the last four months although he continues to lie and to be irresponsible in minor matters.

The next patient was a girl of twenty who, before she came to see me, had made six serious suicidal attempts by poisoning. One day I came home and found a strange girl in the waiting room. (I found out later that she was the sister of a former patient.) With tears in her eyes, she begged me to see her. I took her upstairs and sent away my other patients. After a while I was struck by her manner, and she then confessed that she had taken luminal and begged me in despair not to send her to a nursing home. I put her up in my house, where she remained semi-conscious under drugs for a week before I could get in touch with her relatives. Then arrangements were made for her to live with a nurse under strict supervision. In spite of this, she made a second attempt one month later. The next difficulty was her almost complete refusal to eat for some months. When the loss of weight became dangerous I had to call in a physician, who induced her to eat by means of suggestion. Soon she relapsed again and starved herself for a year till organic complications set in. She had a phobia of most people, including her parents, and in emotional emergencies, I had to look after her a good deal, e.g., put her up for the night. She gradually became able, though with great difficulty, to carry on some work which I found for her. After about eighteen months of analysis I had to stop, owing to strong, external pressure brought to bear on her. Since then the girl has lived with her parents, led a normal and seemingly happy life, and after a time she married and has a child.

Apart from the danger of suicide, the main technical obstacle was her extreme difficulty in making contact. She suffered from emotional rigidity and severe depersonalization interrupted only occasionally by violent anxiety and despair. She had very great difficulties in speaking. These difficulties were increased by the parents' attitude, which was fundamentally very antagonistic. As it was a life and death matter I had no choice but to analyze her in the way I have described. I did so without interruption even when she was under the influence of drugs, alternating this with reassurance and comforting. Though, on the one hand, I was for her a person in authority who insisted on strict supervision and protected her against her parents, on the other, I was more motherly than to any other patient, e.g., when she was in complete despair I would put my arms around her as if she were a child.

Although this was in many respects an unusual case calling for extremely elastic handling, the interesting technical point is that I found it possible to combine the functions of a foster-mother, of a supervisor (and, on occasion, of a detective) with those of an analyst. That analysis could be carried out in such unique circumstances, was due, I believe, (a) to the fact that she felt and appreciated my attitude, (b) that I tried throughout to analyze the underlying negative transference. I want to stress that these cases are extreme examples.

There are many points with which I could not deal in this context. The danger is that by describing certain aspects these may appear overstressed at the expense of others which I have no time to discuss.

DISCUSSION

Fritz Wittels, M.D.: Dr. Schmideberg follows a method of her own in psychotherapy. My impression is that what she presented here was rather a piece of art than of an established science. Dr. Schmideberg is a champion in the treatment of psychopathy and juvenile deliquency. One is delighted but one cannot duplicate it. It is not for the first time in my life that I regret this inability. I recall Dr. Aichhorn, of Vienna, one of the greatest educators and specialists in psychopathy and delinquency whose book *Wayward Youth* may be familiar to many of you. You could realize what he did but you could not duplicate it. I often listened to his stories of how he could tame the toughest and roughest youngsters, but no one else could do what he did. Wilhelm Stekel was another great man of this class. He understood his patients in an almost miraculous way and, particularly reading their dreams, penetrated into their deepest secrets. It was always a pleasure to listen to him. One had the feeling of listening to a great artist. I am not much of an artist myself and can only try to evaluate by scientific means what we have heard to-night.

We heard that Dr. Schmideberg could establish and keep a positive transference with psychopaths and delinquents. This is indeed the first and last problem in the treatment of neurosis, and also of psychopathy. When we do not succeed with them, it is because we cannot establish and maintain a durable transference. Often we think we have done so and feel that we are making a wonderful progress. But the next day the patient may not show up and we must admit, with regret, that the transference did not carry. Dr. Schmnideberg is certainly a master in establishing transference. She can even penetrate into the darkness of psychosis and bring her patients back to our world. How does she do that?

Her patient says that she is kind, that she is nice, that she understands him, that she is sympathetic, that he did not expect approval for what he did perpetrate. In this way she can do a lot for him. I understand that often she uses the classic method of telling the patient what the causes of his anxiety are.

I believe what she says, that she helps almost all of her patients, though she cannot always completely cure them. I would have liked to hear from her a definition of psychopathy. It is almost impossible to arrive at a satisfactory one. We are told: Psychopathic people cannot stand rules and restrictions. You cannot figure them out. Again and again they do something unexpected. It would have been gratifying to hear more about the position which the psychopath occupies between the neurotic and the psychotic.

It was a pleasure to hear that at least one of us can cure a considerable percentage of psychopaths.

Emil A. Gutheil, M.D.: Listening to Dr. Schmideberg, a long row of patients marched before my mental eye whom I had the opportunity to treat and was unable to cure. These were the psychopathic personalities. Let us admit that, as a rule, we are glad when the psychopath does not return for further treatment. The job is never easy and we must admire Dr. Schmideberg's enthusiasm, spirit, and real scientific interest in selecting of all branches of psychiatry this most difficult field. I know of easier ways to make a living.

Speaking of the prognosis of psychopathic personalities, even the greatest experts agree that it is a doubtful one. Dr. Gillespie, whose textbook you know, is of the opinion that prevention is the main approach to psychopathy. What that means you can figure out by yourself. He also has another suggestion: establishing camps for those people who are not able to adjust themselves socially, to place them in an artificial society, hoping that there they might make an adjustment preliminary to their return to a normal society. I agree with Dr. Wittels that Dr. Schmideberg triumphs more by her personality than by the rules of science. But I should like to find out at least one principle in the long list of her therapeutic approaches; i.e., how she handles transference. Unquestionably, she operates with it in a way that none of us would dare operate. Judging from the results, apparently she is right and we are wrong. What happens really in her treatments? Psychopathic personalities are poorly integrated. Transference strengthens their ego, but Dr. Schmideberg goes beyond that. She does not hesitate—and I like this attitude—to engage other persons (family) and to charge them with the task of sharing the transference. She does something which experienced psychiatrists sometimes do in the treatment of psychosis; namely, establishing a multiple transference to fit the polymorphous personality of the patients.

I am sorry that I have not heard more about the dreams of these patients. In such cases I found that the dreams furnished but poor material for interpretation. They operated on the level of children and their dreams mainly expressed wish fullfillments.

J. Friedman, M.D.: Dr. Schmideberg mentioned that sometimes she came late for the appointment. I wonder if that was premeditated or accidental?

Melitta Schmideberg, M.D.: Accidental.

P. Lionel Goitein, M.D.: Dr. Schmideberg's paper recalled to my mind Freud's brilliant remark that the voice of the intellect is always soft. I cannot conceive of Dr. Schmideberg losing her temper with patients. She seems to possess that abundance of sweet reason which makes an analyst understand the patient's conflicts. Her interpretations strike me as not so much of an intellectual as a feeling operation. I think we have a lot to learn about that, at least those of us who are dogmatic and do not interpret with that emotional conviction which the job of analyzing requires. From emotionally underlined interpretations arises Dr. Schmideberg's need of positive transference in the treatment of psychopaths. I agree with the other speakers that the treatment of psychopathic personalities by the use of our accepted method is little successful. I am not afraid of negative transference, however. I believe as good a relationship can be formed on a negative basis as by trying to force a positive one at all costs. Her method is amazing but a little trying. I believe in refusing to follow the patient in all his peccadilloes. I find that the patients respond well to a touch of firmness, but I suppose the cases we heard are those exceptions that require unusual, not to say heroic, measures. In perversion cases few of us have had real success following the traditional method. I think Freud felt that the method was no longer applicable. Fenichel said that in neurosis the patient is forced to do things he does not like; in perversion he likes the things he cannot do. He is obligated in the same way as the obsessional; he wishes to do things that cannot be done and in that way he is perverse.

I also liked Dr. Schmideberg's elasticity. I think she is right in doing, in exceptional conditions, everything that relieves the patient's tension at the earliest possible moment. Anxiety is so bound up with repressed aggression that the relief obtained through a motherly analyst counts more than anything else to reduce hostility toward the negative aspects of their own nature. If the analyst permits a dramatic acting out of these hostilities, positive transference becomes possible. My impression is that Dr. Schmideberg is anxious not to allow this acting out. I encourage it.

Melitta Schmideberg, M.D.: Dr. Goitein has exaggerated my remarks slightly. I do not stop the patient from acting out but only try to control it, so that it does not cause too much trouble or endanger the patient or others. I used extreme cases for illustration. If I had to do all the things I have described for all of my patients all of the time, I could not survive it twenty-four hours. Also, I do not think I am as full of "sweet reason" as I have been described, and I have, on occasion, lost my temper.

Joseph Wilder, M.D.: May I congratulate Dr. Schmideberg on her very unorthodox approach. The question raised by Dr. Wittels is essential. It is important to master the art of establishing transference, but it is more important to know whether this art can be taught, whether it can be so formulated that we can study it. I think that this method can be taught. The future of psychotherapy lies not in the elimination of those who cannot write symphonies but in the teaching of others how to do it.

Another question is: what is the goal of the treatment? Is it cure or the maintenance of a certain level of social adjustment? The latter is the only possible result with most psychotics who often be kept out of the hospital by a lifelong contact with the analyst.

Still another question is the nature of the transference created by Dr. Schmideberg. Does it not differ from the usual transference mainly by the elimination, as far as possible, of the factor of authority from the image of the analyst? And is not the special relation to the authority as represented by father, mother, and society the most important feature of the antisocial psychopath? This method requires more courage than some would like to believe: a series of suicides or criminal acts among our patients would discourage many of us. But in psychiatry, like in other fields of medicine, when we are faced by the choice between "safety first" and maximum results, we realize that safety often can be achieved only at the expense of therapeutic possibilities. Dr. Schmideberg's method is very similar to the active and brief psychotherapeutic methods which many of us apply routinely. The question arises: why should it be limited to difficult cases? Why not apply it to easy cases in which, of course, it is also easier to use it?

Melitta Schmideberg, M.D.: I am not afraid to assume the role of authority if necessary. In the case of the suicidal girl I mentioned, I had arranged for a complicated system of supervision and one evening I was informed that she was in a bad state and possibly suicidal. I rang her and she was out—a bad sign. I went to her parents' house, and, although I knew the house to be empty, the light was burning. So I went around to the police station and asked them to break open the door and I went upstairs with the policemen. The girl had left a short while before. To avoid misunderstanding, I wish to add that this is the only case in my practice where I have ever done anything like that. I cannot foretell what I will do in a certain situation since I do not know what situation is likely to rise, but I will act according to my common sense. I do not speak my mind if I can help it, but if I do I try to hurt the patient as little as possible. I once told an objectionable patient that I did not blame him but that I just could not go on with him in this way. After that he modified his behavior to some degree. One reason for not applying such complicated methods to easy cases is that of economy. Also, my aim is to get the patient eventually to associate freely and if the patient is able to do so from the start, then all is well. I analyze dreams if they are easily understood. I cannot spend too much time on dreams that might prove inconclusive. The essential thing is to analyze the transference. I analyze the negative transference with the view of establishing a positive one. I do not want the patient to be polite; all I want is that he should be able to fall back on me when he is in trouble.

The method I have described can be taught. In London I trained a colleague who takes much worse cases than I do, treating violent criminals. I do not know enough about New York analysts to compare, but I have the impression that, on the whole, the London analysts take more difficult cases. Most of them treat perversions and Glover, Carrol, Walter Schmideberg, and others, have treated psychotics and borderline cases. Also the analytic theory held by London analysts is somewhat different and places more emphasis on pregenital contents. I had no time in my lecture to deal with the contents of interpretations but, obviously, this is a matter of paramount importance. As to the handling of the patient, sympathy is important, but sympathy alone does not cure deeply abnormal people. Some English probation officers achieve excellent results by their sympathetic methods but they send us the cases for treatment with whom they have failed.

Ernst Jolowicz, M.D.: One of the best definitions of psychopathy is that the psychopath is characterized by his inability to form an emotional tie. Dr. Schmideberg, with her vitality and special technique achieved this impossibility. That is a great feat. But I doubt whether her diagnosis of psychopathy is correct in every case. I also doubt that our system of diagnosis is properly related to the therapy we apply. So I admit that we don't need a definite diagnosis. I would like to know, though, how Dr. Schmideberg gets rid of her patients after a successful transference has been established and maintained.

Melitta Schmideberg, M.D.: I have never had any difficulties in inducing patients to stop coming for treatment. In fact, most of them have stopped too soon. I hear from some of them occasionally; sometimes years after treatment has been concluded. Often I write friendly letters to them and they reply. My method is not all based on intuition. There is underlying theory. Too little has been written about analytic methods in concrete detail; e.g., on the form and timing of interpretations, so that it is difficult to compare my method with others.

7. Pseudoneurotic Forms of Schizophrenia

Paul Hoch and
Phillip Polatin

For some time, the writers have been following a group of patients who, in their opinion, show a rather definite clinical symptomatology which, however, is little known or not sufficiently appreciated. These cases are very often diagnosed and treated as psychoneuroses. Often this error is made, not only after seeing the patient a few times, but often over a long period. Many of these patients have been analyzed for a considerable period of time; and the suspicion has never been raised that they were not psychoneurotic. Some psychiatrists concede that the clinical and psychodynamic structure of these cases differs from the neuroses—although retaining a great deal of resemblance to the neurotic disturbances—and call them "borderline cases." Again, others are struck by the similarity of the mental changes and personality structure to schizophrenia and will diagnose them as schizophrenics. The writers would like to emphasize that this group of patients is not small. They are, therefore, not advocating here a more refined classification and do not wish to indulge in diagnostic gymnastics, but do wish to emphasize that many patients in this category are admitted to mental hospitals, and that probably a much larger number are treated in the offices of private psychiatrists.

The actions of these patients, the prognoses of their cases and the therapy, as we shall see, differ markedly from those of the ordinary psychoneuroses. The writers feel justified in classifying these patients with the schizophrenic reactions because many of the basic mechanisms in these cases are very similar to those commonly known in schizophrenia. Particularly, if the disorder should show a progressive course, symptoms will often occur which will make the diagnosis of schizophrenia convincing even to the most skeptical. It is interesting that very little can be found in the psychiatric literature about the differential diagnosis between psychoneurosis and schizophrenia. Even Bleuler, who devoted a lifetime to studying this latter disease, only mentions the differentiation in a perfunctory way, calling attention to the fact that in neurasthenia, in hysteria, and in obsessive-compulsive neurosis especially, it is necessary to be alert to the problem of a schizophrenic development.

The concept of schizophrenia has undergone several evolutions. Originally dementia praecox was diagnosed only when deterioration was present, and some psychiatrists in connection with the cases to be presented here will call attention to the fact that they do not show typical schizophrenic regression and deterioration. This is true for a number of patients. In others, however, even this criterion of schizophrenia can be supplied because a fair number of the cases cited—followed up for years—showed deterioration, and certification was necessary.

Bleuler pointed out the fact that the clinical classification cannot be based solely on the final outcome of the disease and that clinical, and especially psychological, criteria of schizophrenia exist, on which the diagnosis can be based. He stressed especially his point of view that in schizophrenia there are basic symptoms and accessory symptoms. Disorder of associations, rigidity of affect, ambivalence and dereistic thinking were considered primary, whereas hallucinations and delusions, catatonic symptoms, etc., were considered secondary, and their presence for the diagnosis not a necessity. This concept was generally accepted and even applied, for instance in cases of simple schizophrenia. Nevertheless most psychiatrists felt comfortable with the diagnosis of schizophrenia only if delusions, hallucinations or gross regressive manifestations were present. It is furthermore important to emphasize that from the quantitative point of view even these symptoms had to be rather prominent before the diagnosis of schizophrenia was and is made. The final and more subtle emotional, intellectual and psychodynamic changes were rarely appraised properly—especially not in the types of cases here presented.

In establishing the diagnosis of the pseudoneurotic form of schizophrenia, it will be necessary to demonstrate the presence of the basic mechanisms of schizophrenia. These basic mechanisms differ qualitatively and quantitatively from mechanisms seen in the true psychoneuroses. None of the symptoms, which will be enumerated, is absolutely characteristic of schizophrenia. Such a symptom is significant only if manifest in a certain degree and only if several of the mentioned diagnostic criteria occur simultaneously. The diagnosis, therefore, rests on the constellative evaluation of a group of symptoms even though in any given case it is not necessary to have all the symptoms present which are now to be discussed. The basic schizophrenic mechanism, the autistic and dereistic life approach are present in a subtle way in all the cases presented; but, admittedly, it remains very much a subjective issue with each diagnostician to appraise this symptom. There is no objective way to demonstrate it clinically. The withdrawal from reality usually, however, is much more general than is seen in the neuroses, even in those with some schizoid features. Ambivalence, another basic mechanism in schizophrenia, is usually present if carefully evaluated. In contrast to the neuroses, a quantitative difference is immediately obvious. The ambivalence is not localized, but it is diffuse and widespread involving the patient's aims, his social adaptation and his sexual adjustment. From a quantitative point of view the ambivalence in these cases of schizophrenia is not so much an ambivalence as a polyvalence. Not only two contradictory impulses are present, but many constantly shifting notions in the approach to reality.

The affective behavior in these patients is often similar to that seen in the full-fledged cases of schizophrenia even though much less conspicuous and therefore often missed. This behavior is more readily observed in patients who are hospitalized than in those who are seen in office visits. Such patients very rarely show an impoverished, rigid, or inflexible affect. Some inappropriate emotional connections, however, are not rarely present, and a lack of modulation, of flexibility in emotional display is often demonstrated, especially under sodium amytal. Many of these patients show the cold, controlled, and at the same time, hypersensitive reactions to emotional situations, usually overemphasizing trivial frustrations and not responding to, or by-passing, major ones. At times lack of inhibition in displaying certain emotions is especially striking in otherwise markedly inhibited persons. For example, a shy, timid person suddenly goes into a rage directed against another person, without being able to motivate this great emotional display sufficiently. The expression of overt hatred particularly toward members of their own families is rather characteristic for these patients. The hate reaction is much more open and much less discriminating than seen in the neuroses.

From the diagnostic point of view the most important presenting symptoms is what the writers call pan-anxiety and pan-neurosis. Many of these patients show, in contrast to the usual neurotic, an all-pervading anxiety structure which does not leave any life-approach of the person free from tension. Practically everything that the patient experiences influences this anxiety. It is a polymorphous anxiety in the sense that no matter how a person tries to express himself or to side-track an issue, to break through the conflict or to avoid it, anxiety is always manifested. All these attempts, to express, side-track, break through or avoid, are present, usually simultaneously. In connection with this diffuse anxiety, a pan-neurosis is also present. The patients usually do not have one or two different neurotic manifestations, but all symptoms known in neurotic illness are often present at the same time. These patients have tensions and many conversion symptoms in connection with anxiety; gross hysterical, or often vegetative manifestations like poor sleep, anorexia, vomiting and palpitation; and at the same time they will express phobias similar to those observed in anxiety hysteria, such as fear of being killed or being in open or closed places, or riding in subways. These phobias are often combined with other obsessive-compulsive mechanisms. The patient is dominated by these neurotic manifestations which constantly shift, but are never completely absent. In a good many patients, in addition, depression is present, or a so-called anhedonic state, in which the patient does not derive any pleasure from anything. He tries, at the same time, to force pleasurable experiences but without success.

Thinking disorders in a gross way, as one sees them in outspoken cases of schizophrenia, in such forms as incoherence and irrelevancy, are not present in these patients; but condensations and concept displacements are nevertheless present in some of them. Much more conspicuous, however, is the presence of catathymic thinking, the expression of omnipotence emanating from the patient, or the feeling of an "omnipotential attitude" of the environment toward the patient. Thought magic is very often present, most commonly linked to the phobic mechanisms. Some of the more subtle schizophrenic thinking-disorders, like concreteness, the confusion between foreground and background, the stereotyped form of thinking are easier demonstrated in psychological tests like the Vigotsky, Goldstein and others, than they are observed clinically. The absurdity test is also positive in a number of these patients. On the other hand, there are a number in whom the psychological tests to do not reveal this thinking disorder.

Another important feature in these cases of schizophrenia is the manner in which the patient handles the so-called neurotic material. A neurotic patient is usually very anxious to describe his symptoms in minute detail. These detailed accounts are interspersed with explanations of the origin of the symptoms. If the neurotic individual does not know consciously the origin of these manifestations, he at least tries to rationalize them or to connect them with something which he believes is a causative factor. It is not significant whether these explanations are valid or not. What is significant is that the patient tries to explain the symptoms in a logical, coherent fashion. The pseudoneurotic schizophrenic patients, however, usually do not give a bizarre or eccentric explanation, but remain vaguely contradictory. They are unable to give details and even though in the beginning the material presented is very impressive and looks striking from a dynamic point of view, the patient does not get beyond the first presentation of additional details, but repeats in a stereotyped and rather sterile way. Repeated interviews are often fruitless except for reiteration of their symptoms, and the patient remains vague, indistinct and unclear. Free association is much more difficult in these patients than in neurotics. Early memory material is often completely blocked. This inability to associate freely is especially impressive because usually such patients have a good intelligence and an outstanding ability to verbalize.

Quite a number of the patients with the pseudoneurotic symptomatology develop psychotic episodes which are, however, often of short duration and the reintegration of the patients can be so complete that if one does not see them in the psychotic episode one does not believe that they were psychotic. This is probably also the reason why some examiners find the diagnosis of schizophrenia easy, while others insist that they are dealing with psychoneurotics, depending upon the phase of the sickness in which they see the patient. It is very important in these patients, not only to investigate the quality of the symptoms, but also the quantity. The quantitative aspect in psychiatry concerning symptom formation, and the reaction of the patient to it is markedly neglected in contrast to the qualitative investigation. In these patients we often see imperceptibly a daydream emerging into a hallucination or a vague hypochondriacal idea becoming a somatic delusion, ideas on relationship with other people, in the frame-work of social anxiety, developing into ideas of reference. To follow these gradual changes in these patients is fascinating from a psychological point of view, and would probably yield in the future a better insight into the formation of delusions and hallucinations. Many of these patients at first treat their hallucinations and delusions as overvalued ideas or perceptions. They say "it is as if I were to hear a voice," or "as if I were to be observed." When the emotional charge becomes more intense, they suddenly say, "I hear a voice," or "I am observed." Many of these patients zig-zag repeatedly over the reality line. One does not observe these changes in neurotics, not even in states of intense panic. In these short-lived psychotic attacks (micro-psychosis) usually three elements appear simultaneously which are very significant. The patient expresses hypochondriacal ideas, ideas of reference, and feelings of depersonalization. They are often interlocked.

An important aspect of these patients is their psychosexual organization. It has been pointed out by several authors that in many of these patients a mixture of all levels of libidinal development appears. Fenichel interprets this mixture as a result of restitution symptom attempts, in the sense that the patient tries to reapproach reality. It is very questionable whether this is so, because many of these patients do not develop to a genital level of sexuality and are consequently able to manipulate only the pregenital drives. Therefore, they cannot make restitution of something which wasn't there. It has also been pointed out that many of these patients show a mixture of genital and pre-genital material, and rather often disclose a pre-genital-colored Oedipus complex. In all the writers' cases, they observed that the patient usually told of a great many sexual preoccupations showing autoerotic, oral, anal, homosexual and heterosexual tendencies, and ideas which sometimes resembled a textbook of *psychopathia sexualis*. These polymorphous perverse manifestations, this chaotic organization of the patient's sexuality, the writers feel, is rather characteristic of these schizophrenic cases. Marked sadistic or sado-masochistic behavior is often linked with this sexual material. This is especially true in patients who rather overtly and without any restraint, express incestuous ideas. Many of these patients, especially under sodium amytal, verbalize these ideas freely, or they express them freely in drawings.

The psychosexual material in these pseudoneurotic schizophrenics, however, is not so openly reported as is observed in most frank schizophrenics, a fact which often leads to the assumption that these patients are neurotics. On the basis of the psychosexual material alone, however, it is not possible in many instances to make a diagnosis. The presence of narcissistic material or pregenital material is often not sufficient for the interpretation of schizophrenia. Fenichel believes that it is possible to differentiate between the anal sadistic orientation of the libido in obsessive-compulsive neurotics and in schizophrenics, saying that the destruction of the object in the schizophrenic is the more archaic phenomenon—in the compulsion neurotic the object is preserved. He, however, does not elucidate these remarks. In the writers' experiences with a good number of patients analyzed by competent therapists, the neurotic dynamics could not be distinguished from the schizophrenic ones on the basis of the psychosexual material which was offered. If such a differentiation were now possible, not so many mistakes in diagnosis would be made.

Similarly, it is not possible to make the diagnosis in these cases on symptoms of regression because regression in these patients is not so conspicuous as in the full-fledged cases of schizophrenia. The writers consider the regression theory in schizophrenia, as expressed by Freud, only partially valid. Schizophrenia is a disintegrative reaction and not a regressive reaction alone. Even though Freud and many others did not believe that schizophrenia is the same as a neurosis, nevertheless the regression theory implied that the difference would be only a regression in schizophrenia to a lower level of functioning than one sees in the neuroses, and that there would be an unbroken chain from the normals through the neurotics to the psychotics. This theory probably also implied that there is only a quantitative difference present between the transference neuroses and the narcissistic neuroses. In the symptomatology presented it is obvious that most of the deviations between the neuroses and the psychoses are quantitative. Still there are qualitative differences present which will be discussed in a later communication.

In diagnosing the pseudoneurotic case of schizophrenia, the writers found a thorough clinical examination the best first step. The Rorschach test offers a corroborative help in some cases, especially referable to the thinking disorders, like concrete thinking, the whole responses, the attention paid to insignificant details, etc.; and these are well demonstrated. Also readily observed in the Rorschach are the schizophrenic's unpredictable attitude toward various situations, the lack of constructive planfulness, the so-called passive opportunism, and the marked anxiety. The so-called contaminated whole responses, however, are not often present in these pseudoneurotic patients. The marked variability of the patient's performance, which we never see in any other disorder than schizophrenia, shows up very well in the Rorschach of many of these patients. In the writers' experience, however, the Rorschach misses quite a large number of these cases of pseudo-neurotic schizophrenia.

The most valuable aid in diagnosis is the sodium amytal interview which causes the removal of inhibitions and often releases unexpected psychotic material. In some patients, sodium amytal produces stress situations which in turn lead to psychotic manifestations, observed, as described, in micro-psychotic attacks. It is an interesting observation that recovered schizophrenic patients, in their psychic structures and organizations, show very similar symptomatology to these patients who still move on neurotic levels. The writers also observed similarities in so-called psychoneurotics who are closely related to full-blown schizophrenic patients. They believe that further study will elucidate some of the mechanisms in the so-called borderline individuals. Why some of these patients progress into typical cases of schizophrenia, while others hold on, even though in a brittle way, to reality, is quite unclear.

CASE MATERIAL

Case 1

S.S. is a girl of 21.

Family History. The parents, both of Hebrew stock, were born in Russia, but met and married in the United States. The father had had "wanderlust" and finally married at the age of 30 only at the insistence of his brother, who seemed anxious that he should have a family. The father was an inadequate provider, but was apparently attached to his children, and was said to have been faithful to his wife although she never loved him. He was very jealous of her.

The mother was a poor housekeeper, seeming never to accomplish much, even though she spent considerable time at a task. She was a chronic complainer, felt bitter over the economic difficulties the family encountered, and nagged and openly criticized her husband constantly, never indicating any love for him. She showed no affection for her daughter and openly favored her sons. The patient is the second of six siblings; the two older of her three sisters are morose, nervous girls who have few friends or interests, and the younger brother who is very thin, like the patient, is a shy "bookworm." The youngest sister (15 years old) is vivacious and apparently socially adjusted, while the other brother (18 years old) is popular and an excellent scholar, now attending a university. No mental illness is known in the direct lineage. A cousin (son of a maternal aunt) is in a mental hospital, and another cousin (daughter of another maternal aunt) has been under medical care for "nervous complaints." The patient's father died at 51 of a heart attack; he had had a cerebral hemorrhage several years before death.

Personal History. Neither available informant knew details of the patient's birth and early infancy. The baby walked and talked at the "normal ages." A sister states that the patient was the "only one that wasn't breast fed," but does not know any reason for this. Also, the patient was the only child for whom the father had a baby specialist; this was resorted to when the baby was between one and two because she didn't seem to gain any weight. The only remembered illnesses of infancy and childhood were whooping cough (age four) and measles (age six), both uncomplicated. At 10 years of age, she was bitten by a "mad dog" and had to take "20 shots."

The little girl began school at six, but from the first had an "inferiority complex" and found recitations difficult. She was always the smallest, most underweight child in her class. Enuresis persisted until she was nine; fingernail biting has continued to the present. When the parents quarreled, the patient would become upset and angry, would "scream and fuss," and attempt to interfere actively. S. S. had few friends at school, and, like her siblings, would not think of bringing acquaintances to her discordant home. The only fairly close friend was a cousin one year older, whose family was well-to-do; the patient was very jealous of her. A feeling that all the other Jewish people of the community looked down upon the whole family because they were partly dependent upon their charity concerned not only the patient but her mother and sisters as well. The patient thought this was responsible, in part at least, for her having few friends. In general, she was well behaved in school, and was a good student, though her grades fell gradually after the age of 15.

Isolated episodes of peculiar behavior which may have been harbingers of her present illness occurred at ages 12 and 15. She dates the onset of her illness from a sharply remembered experience at 15, after which obsessive-repetitions thinking of a single word has been rather constant, and phobic and compulsive reactions have been more or less prominent. However, she kept her symptoms more or less to herself and finished high school, after which she took a one-year stenographic course at a business school. She then began work at the age of 16, and had several short periods of employment in her home town. She came to New York City at 17 (in 1944) and obtained a job, working until hospitalized for an appendectomy in August 1945.

Before the time of puberty, knowledge of the broader sexual facts had been gleaned from conversation with neighborhood children and from her cousin. S. S. had discovered masturbation at 10 or 11; guilt feelings about it are still prominent, particularly because she taught her sister to masturbate. No homosexual or heterosexual experiences were described. In school, she had numerous "crushes" on boys and would talk about these boys at home, but could not talk to the boys themselves because of her "inferiority complex," and she has apparently never had a satisfactory or reciprocal friendship with a boy. Her menarche at 13 apparently was not upsetting. After coming to New York three years ago, she had few dates or social contacts of any kind. She does not drink or smoke.

The patient dates the onset of her symptoms to a night when she was 15. That night she heard what was going on between her parents, while they were having intercourse and was upset by several matters. First, her mother tried to reject her father, saying, "No, what is the matter with you—why should you want any more children when you're not even supporting the family? Sex is all you want." Second, there was personal sexual excitement, which was involuntarily experienced, and which she thought was wrong—together with the "feeling that there was something wrong with me, like I was going up in an elevator, and

I thought it would never go away; I thought maybe I couldn't experience any sexual feeling.''

The day after this experience: ''I was bitter because my father should have known better than to come to my mother's bed when he knew I could hear all that. Didn't he have any shame? The feeling of disgust was there and I thought it would never go away, and this four-letter word 'f---' was popping in my mind and kept going over and over, and not for a minute could I get it out of my thoughts. A couple of months later it was still going over in my mind and then I told myself, 'Why should you think such a word like that, that you cannot tell to anyone, if they asked you what is wrong,' so I changed it to 'worry.' Now, I don't know how I changed it. That kind of frightens me. I don't see how I could get that word out of my mind. I don't know how I ever got through school. Ever since I was 15, 'worry' kept rotating in my mind continually. I got so I couldn't swallow; I couldn't eat. Food did not agree with me because I was worried. The word 'f---' made me feel nauseated; I couldn't sleep. I would lie there with agitation, with the idea of the word going over and over.''

This change of behavior was noted by persons in the environment of the patient. After this she showed poor progress in school, barely passing many of her courses, and she had less energy and less interest in things. She began to try to figure out what had caused her sickness; and she accused her father of having made her mentally ill through his behavior. Later on, she accused her mother of having caused her illness through meanness. She also accused her sisters of being responsible, because they were mean and critical of her. She began to develop phobias, the most alarming of which, to the patient, was the fear that she would get certain specific phobias or obsessions. She developed the food phobia that she would be unable to eat, and would die that way. While living with a very orthodox Jewish woman, she became afraid that she might become concerned about the cleanliness of food and be unable to eat anything except kosher foods. Later, while living with a Catholic woman, she feared she was going to have to believe in Christ, and then she would have to tell her family, who wouldn't like it. She had an extreme fear that she might become ''insane,'' which would cause her sisters to worry. Since they were already nervous, this additional worry and guilt-feeling might make them became ''insane,'' which would make the patient in turn feel so guilty and ashamed that she would probably have to commit suicide. She also had fears that she might have delusions or hallucinations. She said the following: "I'm afraid I will have hallucinations. I know I may never have them, but I'm afraid if I keep on thinking about them, I will develop them. I'm afraid of getting a psychosis; of getting so I wouldn't be aware how much I'm suffering."

S. S. also began to develop compulsions, such as having to turn out the light about six times before going to bed, having to read things over, having to leave her shoes on a parallel line when she went to bed. Generally, she was careless, however, about her dress and personal hygiene, and was listless and indifferent. Coming to New York, the patient read a book on psychiatry. After reading it, she said, "I was a schizophrenic. The book said it's incurable. Lately I thought I'm not a schizophrenic because I have too much awareness of my surroundings." Three years ago, when she was visiting her relatives, they found her moody. She sometimes stayed in bed all day Sunday, not even dressing or going out of the house. She was afraid then, and she was very conscious of it. She believed no boy could love her because of her looks. She was rigid and particular about her eating; had to eat at exactly set times. She spoke about getting fresh food and a balanced diet, but she ate very little. She went to work regularly. About one and one-half years ago, she went home from work shaking all over and unable to talk to any one. The girl would not reveal anything about her sickness, saying, "You won't understand." She appeared to be disturbed that day and had a dazed appearance; had a fixed look in her eyes. She was taken to an endocrinologist, who found her resistive to examination, diagnosed schizophrenia, and advised psychiatric treatment.

The patient was treated in a clinic from September 1945 to 1946. The psychiatrist who treated her stated: "The diagnosis was not quite clear in the beginning. She had many symptoms of obsessive neurosis, but longer observation made it clear that she was a simple schizophrenia with obsessive ideas, with flattened affect, but a very well preserved personality."

Hospital Admission Note. The patient was admitted to the Psychiatric Institute on January 27, 1947. On admission, she stated: "I have fears of food; I have fears of something happening to my family; I cannot sleep; I get depressed; I become tense, anxious, and agitated.'' She was co-operative and pleasant during the interview and her conversation was relevant and coherent. Her affect showed tension with considerable anxiety and moderate depression. She denied hallucinations or delusions, and she was well oriented in all spheres.

Attitude and General Behavior. Asthenic, frail looking, bur reasonably active, S. S. looks younger than her 21 years. There is average neatness of dress, without peculiarities of clothes or make-up; she is reasonably clean. There is little enthusiasm for eating, her mood is generally apathetic and moderately depressed; but, at times, she is alert and even mildly excited. There is little spontaneous entry into recreational activities. S. S. indicates an interest in making friends but her choice of conversational topics is usually her own illness and details of the illness of another patient about which she is curious. She has not established any cohesive friendships on the ward. From the moment of hospital admission, she talked spontaneously and rather copiously about her illness and her own theories of its cause.

Attitude and Behavior During Interview. When being interviewed, S. S. is reasonably attentive and co-operative, and is fairly relaxed and natural in manner. Her facial expression is moderately expressive, and is appropriate to her mood. Initially, she looked mildly depressed but smiled at times when lighter topics were introduced into the discussion. She appears rather listless and shows little motor activity during interviews. No tremors, tics, etc. She looks rather hypotonic, and her posture is rather lax and ''slouchy.'' Retardation is not apparent.

Stream of Mental Activity. S. S. is rather self-absorbed, but at times is spontaneously productive, generally about her own problems. Her speech is relevant, coherent and free from gross language-deviations. Productivity is normal. She is not distractible by external stimuli but tends to wander gradually from a given topic to related matters which she feels have a bearing on the situation. Reaction time is within normal limits, but varies with topics and her related affect.

Emotional Reactions. Generally, S. S. appears mildly depressed and apathetic but is not retarded and is reasonably labile in her mood. *Mood* (as expressed in appearance and speech) is usually appropriate to thought content. At times she speaks of feeling very hopeless and of feeling that suicide is the only answer in the end; but usually she does not appear to feel this way, and more often seems rather to enjoy the uniqueness which she feels her illness possesses. Occasionally a really depressing thought will strike her; and at such times she will appear truly depressed, with ready tears and a more convincing attitude of despair. Ideas suggesting irreparable organic damage or deficits in the field of emotional experience seem most capable of provoking these markedly depressed moods which are usually short-lived. Self-pity is rather prominent and seems to be a source of satisfaction. She is emotionally responsive to situations on the ward and to ideas suggested during the interview, and usually is moved to smiling by a sympathetically humorous discussion of her tendency to derive satisfaction from her condition.

Mental Trend; Content of Thought. Grossly psychotic features are not manifest in S. S.'s mental trend. There is no persecutory trend; there are no hallucinations, no grandiose ideas, no ideas of unreality, no nihilistic ideas. She has no somatic delusions or hypochondriacal ideas, except possibly her exaggerated concern over "brain cells destroyed by shock treatments," an idea gained in her reading of popular literature and of magazines on psychiatry. Depressive trends are present, superficially attributed to her feelings that she has been emotionally and economically deprived and maltreated, with indications that deeper factors are her hostile, punitive attitudes toward her family which she cannot recognize fully because of guilt feelings. Obsessive-repetitive thinking has been prominent since the age of 15, and consists of certain ideas or words which "rotate through my mind over and over" and of phobic attitudes. Some compulsive patterns exist, but these are not elaborate or particularly important to the patient.

Sensorium, Mental Grasp and Capacity. Orientation, remote and recent memory, retention and recall, calculation, and reading—all are within normal limits. A few tests requiring close concentration and attention were handled poorly, but the capacity for these functions did not seem impaired. General knowledge is good. The Kent EGY (Kent emergency scale) score is 30. Abstraction and absurdity tests were done well, and the associative trend was good. Definition of words was only fair. Insight and judgment are fair.

In the hospital, the patient remained anxious and withdrawn, but cooperative and friendly. At times she was preoccupied, sometimes she smiled in a somewhat inappropriate way. The patient says she has many daydreams but none of a pleasurable sort. She says she has never constructed fantasies in her mind because it was always filled with "worries about the worst things which might happen." She is afraid that something will happen to her. She also is afraid that she will do harm to her people. For instance, she refused to give information about her mother and sister, and even to write out what she thought about them, fearing that, because she has hostile wishes about them, something will happen to them. She would not like to paint in the occupational therapy class because she fears that her paintings could be interpreted by people, and thus they will see how hostile she is to her mother and sister—who might die as a consequence. On the ward, the patient continually talks with a rather non-modulated affect about symptoms. The nurses have noted a certain silliness about her. She has appeared to be amused without any apparent cause. She is very apathetic; procrastinates about everything she should do. If she is reminded she should dress or eat, she says, "Never mind—I'll do it later."

S. S. gives the following information: "I used to love my father before I got sick. Maybe I tried to tell myself he had a stroke before I got sick. I'm afraid to think that maybe he got sick because I told him he had ruined my life. What happened then—I didn't want to become passionate. It wasn't a very good sexual feeling. Maybe it was partly hate. I thought the feeling would never go away. I had the feeling I was abnormal."

Under sodium amytal, the patient says, "I worried and have different fears. I keep thinking about that stuff [amytal] going up to my brain. That is one of my fears. Fears of food—just ideas that I wouldn't be able to eat. I lost my appetite. It was just painful to try to eat when you're not hungry. At first I was having these obsessive ideas, then I became depressed, then I had fears. I changed overnight. I just had one word revolving in my mind. I couldn't concentrate. I can't live a normal life. I constantly have abnormal fears and thoughts coming up and I couldn't lead a normal life or be happy. I don't know if I am a man or woman."

Summary of Salient Features. (a) *Behavior:* S. S. is careless, listless, staying in bed all day, with no initiative. No explanations are offered for staying in bed. Material is offered in a vague, stereotyped way, with no modulation of affect. (b) *Structure:* There is diffuse, all-enveloping anxiety. There is a large array of symptoms: pan-anxiety, pan-neurosis with obsessive-compulsive, phobic and hysterical complaints (anorexia, vomiting), depression, marked anhedonia, inappropriate affective response. (c) *Thought Processes:* S. S. makes use of peculiar expressions like worry as to how her brain organ is shaped. There is conscious displacement of the word "f - - -" with the word "worry." She manifests belief in thought magic and also shows a fluctuating appraisal of reality and, at times, depersonalization. Under amytal she disclosed marked ambivalence toward both parents, and overt hatred, of all members of the family, with projection tendencies. S. S. is very infantile sexually and has difficulty in deciding whether she is male or female.

Case 2

S. R. is a 29-year-old, unmarried woman of average intelligence and pleasing personality, who began, eight months before her hospital admission, to complain of fainting spells and weakness of the legs, followed by an increasing number of somatic complaints.

Family History. The family history is free of mental diseases. The father was a kind and lovable person, who died in 1929, the mother is nervous, irritable, worrisome. Four siblings are married and well.

Personal History. S. R.'s birth, development and childhood were normal. She enjoyed school and was graduated from high school with honors, then studied dress designing. For the next eight years she held different jobs in dress shops. No sex instruction was given to her, and menstruation shocked her. At 18 she had heterosexual experience. She had many girlfriends but only a moderate number of boyfriends. Masturbation and anal intercourse were practised. S. R. was always self-conscious because of her large body and plainless. She considers herself an affectionate person who has received little warmth and affection for the past 10 years. Eight months prior to her admission, she began to feel weak in both legs and had symptoms of faintness. These spells would last for a day or two, and then she would feel better for two or three weeks. In January 1945, she had seven attacks of lower abdominal pain; an appendectomy and partial ovariectomy were performed. Her symptoms, however, persisted. She became engaged; and—when she saw her fiance—the symptoms became very marked. Later, in addition to the previously-described symptoms, she began to gag and was suddenly unable to swallow. She was seen by different physicians and psychiatrists. They found that she would talk eagerly and anxiously about her symptoms; that she showed marked anxiety, hypochondriasis and hysterical features, and that the fainting attacks were typical hysterical attacks.

Soon after hospitalization, however, there was a suspicion that the patient was not a case of hysteria, but one of schizophrenia. The first examination revealed the following: S. R. complained constantly of being tired, weak and dizzy. She repeated that she was not a psychiatric case. She fainted gracefully several times. After she had complained a great deal, she apologized for talking so much and for being silly. She described her feelings in a vague way, without being able to give any detail with clarity and conciseness. She rambled, elaborated, got sidetracked and gave irrelevant details. She was anxious, depressed, fearful and preoccupied. In connection with her fainting she gave associations as follows: "My organs are all upside down. I'm all dried up inside. I'm divided. Part of me is here and part of me is floating away." After the interview, the patient walked in a stooped position, haltingly and off balance. Following a visit from her relatives, she became excited, rushed around, asked nurses and doctors to help her, said "I'm awfully worried. I had sexual relations in the posterior position and ever since I have this white stuff—this leukorrhea came out of my mouth. It also runs out of my rectum sometimes." Then she quieted down and said the following: "I'm guilty and anxious. I had a sexual relationship with a soldier to whom I was engaged." She also admitted, in a vague way, a homosexual experience. S. R. continued to complain about pain in her right ear, and of neuritis in her face and back. She said, "My organs are backside to, upside down. If only I could be turned around from back to front. I feel I'm not a woman. My body in front is just straight, my legs go straight down. I want to tell you everything now. I was afraid because I thought it wasn't nice to talk about such things but I have always enjoyed my own body. I used to masturbate a lot until I had relations with my boyfriend. I love intercourse by rectum. Is that bad?''

Under sodium amytal, this patient showed a marked emotional outburst, revealed that she was closely attached to her father and that after his death her mother became melancholy. She and her mother did not get along well because her mother was quite old, moody and sad. She disliked her brother and was very jealous as a child of the good looks of her sister. She had a repetitious dream three or four years ago in which she committed suicide. Next she said that she was very frightened when her menses began and told about two of her sister's dogs who used to "light on her chest.'' She thought they did so because they knew about her sex life. The Rorschach pictures remained her of a dog. Several times during the interview, she cried that she was ugly, unattractive and fat. She said that she has a bad odor which started immediately after her first masturbation.

In the hospital, the patient began to express sadistic thoughts toward many different people—doctors, other patients, family members. Everybody who frustrated her should be killed. She was apprehensive and fearful about almost everything. Said, "I have to analyze anything and everything which goes on, then I cannot decide. Sometimes I love, sometimes I hate. I even analyze the cleaning tissues I use.'' She says she has strong guilt feelings about perverted sex thoughts and about her past. She began to show blocking during the interview, then became confused, indecisive and agitated; expressed death wishes toward her mother; admiration and envy of her sister; marked ambivalence toward her boyfriend. This behavior was especially marked after week-end visits. Strong feelings of inferiority were maintained. Then for a short period she began to hear voices which told her how bad she was. She would see flashes of light, feel electrical impulses and think she was influenced by others. Feelings of unreality and depersonalization were also frequently reported, especially with the idea that she was becoming more like a man. Psychotherapy made very little impression upon her. She always produced the same material without being able to enlarge on details.

Summary of Salient Features. S. R. is self-conscious about her plainness. There are all-pervading anxiety, and hysterical manifestations, like fainting spells—and, in addition, abdominal pain, for which appendectomy was performed. Astasia abasia, hypochondriacal preoccupation, obsessive ideas of killing, feelings of depersonalization are manifest. There is marked ambivalence toward members of the family and toward her life-approach in general. A sexual Oedipal relationship is openly revealed. Male-female differentiation is confused. The patient also shows incipient projections and ideas of reference. Later on, she is psychotic, hearing voices, feeling electrical impulses, having paranoid delusions.

Case 3

H. McC. is a single woman of 38.

Family History. The patient's father died at the age of 55. He was a self-satisfied person, who did not get along with the patient's mother, mainly because he was in financial difficulties. The mother, a very narrow, rigid, religious woman, left her husband, lost all interest in men, and supported herself running a boarding house. The patient's older sister, aged 40, is married and well-adjusted. A brother is "nervous," otherwise adjusted. A younger sister, aged 36, is not married and not interested in men "because she saw her mother's unhappiness."

Personal History. The patient was an unwanted child. The mother's pregnancy and delivery were normal. The girl's early development was normal; she was very affectionate, obedient, a well-liked child who got along very well with other children. She attended school and did well. She was especially interested in religion. After finishing high school, she worked for a dentist in her hometown and later in New York. She was discharged because her employer felt that the patient had lost interest in her work, had become listless—her arms hung down at her sides, and she slouched along. Then she obtained a job in a hospital. She began to complain of abdominal pain. An appendectomy was performed, but this did not improve her condition. She complained of marked weakness, and of lack of strength, but was not depressed. Later, she began to complain of constipation and of a "foggy" feeling. She became very much irritated by her mother and sister, and complained that her heart hurt her. The relatives believe that the patient was magnifying her complaints and expected to be catered to, as she had had this tendency all her life.

On hospital admission she was co-operative, made a good impression; appeared, however, to be somewhat self-absorbed; showed rather meager productions during interview, but was relevant and coherent in her answers. At times she appeared to be somewhat depressed, and complained of fatigue and pain in the cardiac region. Slowly, the patient talked more freely during therapeutic interviews and related that she had had a few unhappy love affairs which were very much on her mind. She had been in love with a medical student. He had terminated the relationship, she thought, because he did not like her. She then entered into an affair with a married man, which lasted for about seven years. About four years ago, she had become pregnant and had had an abortion. In the same interview she complained of stiffness, tenseness, pains and cramps in her legs and feet, pain in the right side, and difficulty in breathing. At the same time, she expressed fear and shame whenever she had to talk with people in the course of social contacts, and a marked feeling of inferiority.

In another interview, H. McC. expressed marked hostility toward her mother and sister, saying that they were unsympathetic; they believed that she was not ill, and forced her to go out to work. She also complained about the prudishness of her mother, who tried to instill in her a hostile attitude toward men. During this interview, the patient displayed a number of hysterical mechanisms. She could not get up; and, when she walked, she tended to sink to the floor, or she walked about supporting herself by clutching the wall. Then she said, "My subconscious mind plays tricks on me. I was in a trance. I seemed to be separated from my body. My conscious mind has to pass on everything my subconscious mind does. My subconscious mind tries to do and say things that other people have in their minds. I feel what they think. The words I cannot understand are 'positive' and 'negative.' It means that I'm trying to be certain about things. I feel like I'm hypnotized. Did you hypnotize me? At times I have the feeling as if a voice was telling me to go to sleep and to act like a child and be babied. I think the girls at the hospital were making fun of me. I hear the girls there discuss subconscious mind and its effect. I double-talk. I say things that have two meanings. Anybody that does anything for me I have to follow. Now I hear a voice. I masturbated when I was five with my sister with my finger. My mother caught me and she was very angry. I did it again when my boyfriend left me, but have not done it in the last year. I have to do it. I thought I would go crazy if I didn't have a man" . . . "I love my father."

In a further interview, this patient said, "I have a male mind and a female body and I don't like women." Asked how long she had been hearing the voice, she said, "On and off for about two years." Sometimes it was a real voice, sometimes she thought it was her own ideas "which became loud." H. McC. at first expressed ideas that people about her were unsympathetic to her. When she became more fearful and anxious, she said, "They were watching me—looking at me—tried to do nasty things to me. They know I can't sleep. They know that I have desires. They know that I hate my mother. They tried to persecute me on the ward. Some patients behave toward me like my mother does. I hate her because she has destroyed my father's self-confidence. I felt that she was quarrelling with him unnecessarily and had driven him from the home, thus depriving me of his affections."

She told of the following dream: She was being pursued by the Nazis. She decided to pretend there was an escape—imagined the door and stairs and descended. The Nazis followed her, but when they got there, they also played the game and pretended they were not chasing her. They carefully ignored her. She interpreted the dream by saying that the false escape is the hospital, the Nazis inside are the patients who are really part of the dangerous outside world, but who do not seem to be persecuting her, but they only pretend to do this. When one of the patient's requests was refused, she went into a "hysterical attack," becoming immobile for a while, not responding to stimulation; suddenly, however, she reverted to normal activity. The patient called these attacks hysterical, even though they looked more like short-lived catatonic episodes. She interprets these episodes as punishment, panic, protective desires for withdrawal. She often hears a voice very clearly in such a hysterical trance. She also said the following, "I want a home and have everything nice, and peace everywhere. I want somebody to care for me and love me. I want to be good and make people happy. People make me very nervous because I don't understand them. I am very unhappy when I can't please them." She stated that she thought she loved her mother more than her father, but not after the father left. The father was much less critical than her mother. When relating this, the patient smiled inappropriately. Asked why she was smiling, she said, "I don't know. It's peculiar that I smile. I should rather cry."

Summary of Salient Features. This patient was listless, lost interest in work, had a pan-neurosis—anxiety, depression, hysterical display, abdominal pain, marked weakness, "foggy" feeling, astasia basia. There was an all-pervading feeling of inferiority. Material was presented in a self-absorbed vague way; no details were given; there was great difficulty in free association; early memories were blocked; there was open disclosure of Oedipal difficulties and marked sexual infantilism. Later, H. McC. was psychotic, with paranoid ideas, excitement, hallucinations, and inappropriate behavior.

Case 4

T. L. is a 31-year-old single man, who complains about marked tension, stammering and gritting of teeth, chronic digestive trouble, insomnia, and inability to carry on his work as a research chemist. He was treated with all kinds of psychotherapeutic approaches by different psychiatrists and psychoanalysts.

Family History. T. L.'s father is described as sympathetic, good natured, a scholar; the mother as anxious, overprotective. She had chronic indigestion all her life. When the patient was born, the parents were fairly old—the mother was 40. The father suffered from tuberculosis.

Personal History. The boy's early development was normal, except that he began to stammer when he began to talk. He developed a hernia at the age of five, which prevented him from partaking in outside activities. He usually played by himself, being an only child, and he was very much attached to his father, who studied all his lessons with him. The patient was of outstanding intelligence and was head of his class.

T. L. denies having masturbated. There was, however, some sexual pleasure connected with manipulating his hernia, which was done by himself, or whenever a physician examined him, or by his mother. At the age of 12, he began to have fantasies of kicking girls "in the shins." When he had these ideas, he manipulated his hernia. He was graduated from high school and then went to college, where he majored in chemistry. His father died in 1938. The patient then lived with his mother except for a short period when he was away from home alone, in Cleveland. In 1939 he began to have indigestion and feelings of weakness. He had an appendectomy in 1940; his symptoms cleared up temporarily. He obtained his Ph.D. in chemistry and in 1944 found a position as a research chemist. Subsequently he received a severe burn on his right arm and developed a peptic ulcer soon afterward.

He indicated that his present illness began in 1939 when he was teaching in a high school. He had been fatigued, tense and had chronic indigestion. He could not maintain discipline in his class, was very much preoccupied with himself. One of his superiors remarked that unless he learned to sell himself and had better contact with people, he would never get along in this world. In 1944, while working on his job, he believed that a superior was trying to appropriate some of his work, and he became quite suspicious of him. The fatigue became more marked and he then began to have "hissing spells," in which he would clench his hands and teeth, and making hissing noises. The patient consulted several psychiatrists who diagnosed him as psychoneurotic. A Rorschach was given the patient which indicated a deep-seated disturbance, most likely schizophrenia. He was then hospitalized for 10 months in a psychiatric institution, where a diagnosis of obsessive-compulsive neurosis was made. After discharge from this hospital, he was analyzed by two different analysts unsuccessfully, and was finally admitted to the Psychiatric Institute.

On admission, the patient was bursting with energy and appeared to be very tense. He was neat, well dressed and sociable with the other patients, displaying, however, no emotional qualms. He was relevant and coherent; polite, cheerful, pleasant; at times somewhat elated and talkative. He often laughed loudly and occasionally inappropriately. He expressed many hypochondriacal complaints about chronic indigestion, constipation, diarrhea, headaches, chronic sinusitis, and inability to have ejaculations. He had ideas that he is better than any one else, morally, socially, and intellectually, has frequent sadistic fantasies ranging from beating women to wholesale murder. These fantasies originally were associated with masturbation, but now they come on without it, and sometimes his ideas are so dominant that he cannot shut them out. The patient says he has never in his life had any sexual contact with the opposite or the same sex. He complains of being subject to outbursts

of rage—directed toward anyone who frustrates him. He also has fe-
tishistic manifestations. He likes to touch silk and women's clothes,
which produces sexual excitement in him.

During interviews the patient expressed many incestuous wishes
concerning his mother. He was usually very submissive toward the
therapist, which masked an extremely hostile attitude. Under sodium
amytal he produced the following: (What is your trouble?) "Tension
and sexual complications. My social relationship, and especially if I
want to have heterosexual relationships, fear comes up." (What difficulty do you have in approaching people?) "There is an absence of
feeling, and indifference and apathy in my relationship to people. In
professional relationships I can get on well. When the relationship
generates or becomes a social or a sexual one, a fundamental block
appears and I cannot bridge it." (What do you feel when you're with a
girl?) "I have no conception of sexual intercourse. I was successful in
avoiding it. Statements about sex came as a great surprise. I recognized
copulation in animals, in biology, but I did not face it in humans." (Do
you have any fantasies?) "Yes, I'm seeing the back of a girl and her
legs. She is being spanked or struck. I'm being an observer." (Do you
have any other fantasies?) "Yes, wholesale destruction. I want to kill
the patients, the nurses. I want to rape them. I also have the fantasies
of dropping bombs on Russia. The whole thing is a gory mess." (Do
you have ideas of destroying the world?) "I haven't yet but give me
time. It's an attractive idea."

He then says: "I have to destroy people if I meet competition in my
work. I have the feeling that I must make good, so good that I could
not be challenged. Competition mobilizes fear. I also have lack of self-
control and ability to live a quiet, placid life." (Are you more at ease
with women or men?) "Men. Physical contact with women seems dirty,
filthy and obscene. The female body is essentially weak, flabby, dirty
and does not moderate any respect at all." (Would you be better off
without sex?) "I have wondered if becoming a eunuch would be beneficial. If your right hand stinks, cut it off. These fantasies are becoming
more and more pronounced. I can't shut off the fantasy. I cannot think
of anything else. I'm very much ill at ease in social groups. It's not a
pleasurable experience to be with people." (What did you learn during
the analysis?) "Nothing. I'm bucking up a stone wall." (Do you have
any dreams?) "Rafts of them—usually violent ones and the element of

fear is in them. I have a repetitious dream—one is driving a car, another car is coming toward me. There is a head-on collision but I'm not killed. I am engaging in hunting and fishing, and there is no yield."

The patient received a small amount of "ambulatory insulin." Under the influence of insulin, he suddenly changed. He expressed weird grimaces, maniacal laughter, strutted about in the room, mumbling to himself, crying out loudly, at the same time apologizing for his conduct. Then he began to make hissing sounds, clenching and unclenching his fists, as if in a rage. Days later, with no insulin, T. L. was himself again, polite if spoken to, but appeared to be very tense, expressed aggressive ideas toward everybody around him, would like to smash the whole hospital. He denies having hallucinations, but thinks that people around him are "against him." He eats enormous amounts of food, for instance, five helpings of scrambled eggs or 10 eggs in one meal. Occasionally, he falls asleep during the day in the middle of his activity, saying that everything goes blank then.

Summary of Salient Features. T. L. is shy and seclusive, manifests pan-anxiety, and a marked feeling of social anxiety, especially in sexual situations. There are feelings of ambivalence and inferiority—and of superiority which, at times, reaches the height of omnipotence. Again, others are omnipotent and he weak. The pan-neurosis tends toward fatigue, stomach ulcer, hypertension, bulimia, sleep disturbances, diarrhea, headache, chronic sinusitis, obsessive fantasies and hypochondriasis. In addition, there are vague paranoid manifestations, psychosexual infantilism, masturbation, sado-masochistic fantasies, fetishism. Male-female differentiation is impaired. Under sodium amytal, he exhibits mass destructive fantasies. There are marked feelings of omnipotence, thought magic, autistic and dereistic formulations. Reality testing is impaired. At times. T. L. is psychotic. The Rorschach indicates: schizophrenia or epilepsy.

Case 5

P. C. is a 29-year old married woman who, following an automobile accident, in which her oldest male child was severely injured, has suffered from marked self-recriminatory ideas, a feeling that she is two persons, a desire to kill members of her family and a fear that her husband might kill her. She has been married twice; there are no children by the first union, but three by the second.

Family History. The family constellation consisted of an amalgam of, on the maternal side, Hungarian-Catholic, and, on the paternal side, Austrian-Lutheran. There is no history of mental illness on either side of the family. The mother and father came to this country just after the first world war and were almost immediately married. They had at this time and still have marked language difficulties, not only concerning English, but with each other's languages. The mother was markedly overprotective of the daughter. The father was very strict, alcoholic and somewhat improvident.

Personal History. P. C.'s birth and early development were normal. She experienced marked difficulty in speaking however, because of the general language confusion at home; and the father was very strict, not permitting the child to speak at the table. The mother was very overprotective, restricting the patient's play activities to girls; and only girls could come to the house. The mother and father were often separated because of their diverse jobs. The patient usually went with her mother from one domestic situation to another. She felt very insecure and lonely as a child, and became seclusive and moody. The father and mother constantly quarreled with each other. P. C. preferred her father even though he was abusive to the mother on many occasions. Her attitude toward the mother is now one of frank hostility, and she is rather ambivalent toward her father. The patient completed public school and then went to trade school for a year. She did some sewing and designing. Later on, however, she became a model. She received no sex education. She denies having masturbated. Her first heterosexual experience was at 19. Soon after that, she married. This marriage ended five months later by a divorce. She gave up her first husband because he was cruel, unreliable and mysterious, although she enjoyed him sexually.

P. C. was well until October 1946 when her illness was precipitated by an accident to her oldest boy. He fell out of the back seat of a car which she was driving. Similar accidents had happened to the same child twice before. On these occasions, however, she was not alone with him in the car. The patient did not mention the last accident to her husband, who was away working. She asked him to send money because the child was sick. It was established later that the patient actually did not become ill after the accident but 40 days later, when the child was practically recovered. She then began to cry, expressed self-accusatory ideas, said that she was a bad mother and an inefficient housewife. She began to feel hopeless and had no desire to live. Phobic manifestations appeared and she was afraid that she would kill her three children and be killed by her husband. She played with the idea of suicide, but made no overt attempt at it. She also complained about hearing motors roaring in her ears; began to think of herself at times very objectively; and she would smile at her own activities and reactions. She also could hear herself talk to herself as if there were two persons. At times she would laugh at her own feelings. She had a sensation of voices inside her head repeating things which she had previously thought of, or reminding her of what she had done. She realized that these voices were products of her own thinking, nevertheless she could not control them; she felt obsessed by them.

The woman was seen in a psychiatric clinic and treated unsuccessfuly for depression. Later she was sent to the Psychiatric Institute. Here she was co-operative, attentive and did not exhibit anxiety, sadness or tension. She expressed the ideas already mentioned and added that she felt two different voices inside herself. At times she stated that she would smile at herself as though she were a person looking down from a distance at her own self and her own actions. It was found that this patient had a mystical, ritualistic type of thinking.

Under sodium amytal, she talked in abstractions and in a very detached manner. She brought forth the following dream, which occurred several times. It has a definite religious, cosmic significance for her. ''I was in labor in a barn, in a cradle, part of the time I was in the cradle and part of the time I was lying in the straw, but the straw was very soft. I could see the little cradle like an old American antique. There was a gold life-like light. The baby that was born was two years old. He had little yellow ringlets. He got up and walked away and the Wise Men followed him. I sat, and the labor pains continued uneventfully. The crowds outside wanted to see him.'' This dream she did not treat as an ordinary dream. It was considered a vision and for three or four months following it, while she was 16, she considered very seriously becoming a nun. She says, ''With these dreams I used to get the feeling of being holy. It was like sunshine radiating from within. I thought it might be a feeling of ambition or a feeling to get ahead.'' She believes that all her dreams have a significance but not similar to this. She is markedly catathymic. she believes that she may attain anything by wishing. Her thoughts are, in fact, constantly wish desires, wish fulfillments. She believes that by wishing she can control, she believes in thought magic, she can kill by ideas.

P. C. related in another interview that she feels torn between two conflicting emotions concerning her husband and children. She wants to be a good wife and mother. At the same time, she resents very much that she is "tied down"; that she is not free to live her own life. She would like to become a writer. Sexually, the husband is repulsive to her, and she is frigid with him. With the first husband, she had sexual satisfaction, mainly obtained by oral activity.

The Rorschach examination revealed several "contaminated" responses which were considered pathognomonic of schizophrenia.

Summary of Salient Features. The central theme here is aggressive reaction formation around which a great deal of guilt feeling is generated. Aggression is partly outward (killing the husband and children, or the frustrating environment), partly inward (suicidal ideas, ideas of unworthiness).

Some projection is present, which is unusual; she fears being killed by her husband. The patient's mental disturbance showed three levels— neurotic, depressive and schizophrenic. On the neurotic level, P. C. displays symptoms of anxiety hysteria, phobic and obsessive manifestations. On the depressive level, there is a marked introjection; deep hostility toward the mother; marked ambivalence toward the father; a rigid conscience with a tendency to rebel; strong oral drives; the seeking of expiation of guilt. This is not an unconscious but practically on a conscious or preconscious level. On the schizophrenic level, this woman is introverted, loosely connected with the environment, replacing reality with day-dreaming, always anxious, catathymic. In her paintings, the patient shows symbolic condensations and fragmentations. She believes in thought magic, projects her ideas into utterances and performances. She animates things. Boundaries between the ego and the world are hazy. A tendency to cosmic fusion is present. Sexually, P. C. shows a strong narcissistic, exhibitionistic trend, with sado-masochistic behavior. The male-female differentiation is unclear. This patient fights disintegration vigorously and tries to hold on to reality.

SUMMARY

Attention is called to a group of patients who show a clinical symptomatology which is considered by many psychiatrists to be psychoneurotic. These patients do not deteriorate and have no delusions or hallucinations. Nevertheless, they show clinical symptomatology which is very similar to that seen in schizophrenic patients. It can be demonstrated in follow-up studies that a considerable number of these patients have short psychotic episodes or later become frankly schizophrenic. A few of these "borderline" cases are described and their symptomatology analyzed. It is suggested these patients be classified "pseudoneurotic form of schizophrenia."

BIBLIOGRAPHY

Bleuler, E.: Textbook of Psychiatry. English trans. by A. A. Brill. Macmillan Company. New York. 1924.

Fenichel, Otto: Psychoanalytic Theory of Neurosis. W. W. Norton & Company. New York. 1941.

Polatin, Phillip, and Hoch, Paul: Diagnostic evaluation of early schizophrenia. J.N.M.D., 105:3, March 1947.

PART III

1950s AND 1960s

1950s

If we paused for a moment to get a sense of how the borderline concept was evolving in the 1950s, we would note two main trends: a shift in the spotlight from descriptive to more dynamic definitions; a change of venue for its usage from traditional psychiatry (where the term all but disappears) to psychoanalysis (where its popularity is beginning to "take off"). To a man standing in 1950, schizophrenia would still have appeared as the putative father of borderline conditions: he would have seen no "evolution" here; merely a gradual loss of interest in the supposed connection. This is (in part) because hospital-based psychiatrists look at psychosis with central vision (it is part of their daily work); psychoanalysts (mostly office based), with peripheral vision. In addition, psychoanalysts were eager to understand etiology in terms of the events of childhood: it seemed a lot easier to fix the effects of environmental bad luck than of hereditary bad luck. Thus, Robert Knight focuses on the primitive defense mechanisms lurking behind the higher-level defenses, in his borderline patients, and on the relative fragility of their hold on reality. He rather assumes that a tendency to schizophrenia is in back of all this but does not dwell overly long on the point. Indeed, it is with Knight's paper that the process of decoupling the schizophrenia-concept from the borderline-concept got its major impetus. This process advanced at such a pace, in fact, that to the man perched ten years further down the time-continuum, "borderline" would have begun to look not like a mere adjective denoting less-than-classically-analyzable or as a weak brand of schizophrenia—but would have looked, for the first time, like an entity unto itself. By the end of the decade, "borderline" still had imprecise definitional borders, alas, but at least its component parts were all in place: "typical" borderline defenses, "typical" borderline abnormalities in object-relations and in reality-testing, borderline identity diffusion, even the beginnings of a separate dynamic etiology relating to disturbances in individuation.

More visible in the 1950s than in the 1940s was the struggle, within the community of orthodox Freudian analysts, to rationalize the emerging borderline concept within the framework of accepted psychoanalytic theory. Freud, it will be recalled, had died only in 1939; his "tripartite" structure—Id, Ego, Super Ego—remained the mould into which all forms of psychopathology were poured, or if need be, pounded, and few of his close associates were brave or clearsighted enough to proclaim that tripartite theory could not comfortably be stretched so far as to comprehend sicker-than-neurotic conditions. It was not so much that the house of analytic theory was shaky so much as cramped: one needed to attach a new wing along one of its sides.

Among those who had the vision to see the shortcomings of existing theory, and the courage to disagree in public, the most outstanding figure was, not surprisingly, neither German-speaking nor a direct disciple of Freud's. Rather it was Fairbairn, whom some have speculated came more easily to the required maverick role—from his relative isolation in Scotland. Even Fairbairn was cautious, out of homage to Freud, to make his object-relations appear a less radical departure from the tripartite model than he really meant it to be.

Fairbairn's theory synthesized elements of Freudian metapsychology with elements of Melanie Klein's speculations concerning her analytic work with children. Though her theorizing was at times wild to the point of caricature, and her writing opaque, Klein nevertheless paved the way for the expansion of psychoanalytic theory into the preoedipal period. Here, instead of triangular relationships and the family drama, one found dyadic relationships and the mother-child symbiosis; instead of castration-fear and sexual problems, annihilation fears and problems in separation. Whatever it was that was going on in that dark and (ontogenetically) prehistoric period, it was clearly most relevant to the understanding of borderline patients—who, though they may present themselves to us like their neurotic counterparts as disappointed lovers, either had been, or certainly behaved like, lost and cranky children.

It is something ironical that the theoreticians of the 1950s who contributed most importantly to the psychology of the borderline were the adherents of Klein, in what has come to be called The British Object-

Relations School: Fairbairn, Balint, Winnicott and Guntrip—none of whom used the word borderline except as a rare aside. They became even more divorced from the biologic underpinnings of psychosis than their American colleagues (Sullivanians excepted). Guntrip could speak of a schizoid "position" as opposed to a manic-depressive "position" during infancy—positions that were purely psychological constructs, in a psyche not moored even by a thread to the soma hovering underneath it.

One can get a sense of the contrast between this pure psychology of the Kleinians and the more so-called "psychosomatic theories" that were taking shape in the United States from the work of several prominent analysts: Jacobson, Rado, and Erikson. Jacobson was one of the first to express belief that certain depressed patients, in whom no obvious precipitants from daily life were discernible, were really in the penumbra of manic-depressive illness. These were, as we now think of them, the "borderline-affective" patients (cf. M. Stone, 1977; Akiskal, 1984, reprinted here), akin to the "borderline schizophrenics" described by analysts of the 1920s. Rado, still more biologically oriented than Jacobson, attempted to revivify the schizotypal concept and to give it clearer dimensions—as we see from the reprint of his important and long-neglected chapter on the schizotype.

Less concerned with possible constitutional factors, Leo Stone and Eric Erikson carried further the investigations into identity problems of borderline patients, outlined earlier by Stern and particularly by Helene Deutsch. It is this material on identity that becomes synthesized and refined yet again in the work of Kernberg, who, in the decade that follows, teased out the "item" of identity diffusion, along with another concerning the relationship to reality, as his necessary, and diagnostically determining attributes of the borderline's psychic organization.

Erikson was concerned not only with the issue of identity formation, as one notes from his well-known chart of the life stages, but also with the entire sequence of major life-tasks, whose proper realization is equated with ideal integrity and emotional health. Later commentators on borderline patients have found Erikson's chart useful, inasmuch as those whom we call "borderline" happen to be the same persons who have experienced serious difficulties in negotiating the first two of these major tasks. Mistrust is characteristic; so is excessive shame and self-doubt. Failure at the next two stages, as manifested by guilt and inferiority, are often glaring in borderlines as well, but these feelings (in milder degree) are less "diagnostic," since they occur regularly in neurotic persons also. The developmental stages enumerated by Erikson, which cover the whole life span, provide a neater framework within which to pinpoint key problems and "fixations" in borderlines than the developmental stages outlined by Freud. Some have tried to find a precise spot on the oral-anal-genital continuum where "narcissistic" and "borderline" patients are supposedly arrested. This has, in my opinion, proven a futile exercise, forcing into that theoretical structure more than it can conveniently contain.

1960s

The psychoanalytic concepts enjoying the widest acceptance today began to solidify in the 1960s.

A number of the trends we have alluded to in connection with the 1940s and 1950s converge in the key paper of Kernberg (included in this section); one of whose achievements was to assemble the various conceptual fragments provided by his predecessors into a coherent picture, clinically more useful and diagnostically more precise than the at times colorful (Schmideberg) but all too often amorphous descriptions of the past. The trend toward the establishment of borderline disorders as constituting a separate and discriminable entity also finds its most coherent expression in Kernberg's writing: *borderline personality organization,* as he was to call it, is now equipped with inclusion criteria and exclusion criteria. There are not as rigorous as one might hope for (such as have now been operationalized for "schizophrenia"), but, considering the multiplicity of variables that complicate the diagnosis of *milder* (as opposed to flamboyant) conditions, Kernberg's criteria are workable. In principle, for example, a good capacity to test reality distinguishes the borderline level from the psychotic; a firm sense of identity distinguishes the neurotic from the borderline. In practice, the clinician will have an easier time making the first distinction; to distinguish borderlines (especially ambulatory ones) from neurotics with respect to identity-integration is often difficult, and cannot be accomplished reliably in one or two visits.

Kernberg's indebtedness to Frosch will be clear from perusal of Frosch's paper on the psychotic character (rather equivalent to a *borderline* organization or "structure"). Frosch felt that patients of this type retained a reasonably intact capacity to grasp the reality of various problematical interpersonal situations, once the analyst has exposed to the patient a more enlightened picture of some significant but difficult "other" in the patient's life. Frosch remarked briefly on the possibility that some *psychotic characters* (Knight also used this term: 1953, p. 106) might show tendencies toward schizophrenia, others, toward manic-depression—but for the most part he focused on the psychological, not upon possible constitutional, factors in these patients. Kernberg is similarly oriented toward the psychological, but does allude to some innate aggressive impulses—which appear to be overly intense in patients with borderline organization.

A word might be in order here about the interplay between the analyst's hunch and the research psychiatrists' testable hypothesis. The dynamic equilibrium between intuition and controlled experiment is relevant to our field, of course, as well as to the natural sciences. The progress in knowledge of "borderline conditions" shares in this phenomenon. The "freefloating anxiety" of Freud may be comprehensible as the excessive firing of certain dopaminergic pathways, that Ernest Hartmann speaks of in connection with nightmares and schizophrenics (1982).

Without external validation from some chemical or neurophysiologic measure, "innate aggression" becomes an article of faith. It either sounds right to you or it does not. For years, the notion of excess innate aggression was just another untestable intuition. Currently some evidence is accumulating to the effect that, in the case of agoraphobia, the inordinate proneness to anxiety may stem in part from constitutional abnormalities of the autonomic nervous system (Mavissakalian, 1984). It is plausible to envision some similar abnormality—perhaps in the form of heightened genetic liability to bipolar illness—that may render certain individuals more "driven," more insistent that their needs be instantly gratified, and more prone to outbursts of rage when frustrated. If so, it is this kind of tendency that the psychobiologist would view in terms of neurotransmitters and genetic predisposition and which the analyst would attribute to "innate aggression." We are closer now, in the 1980s, to being able to put Kernberg's intuition of the 1960s to the test in some meaningful way.

The search for biologic correlates to psychological phenomena of borderline patients remained, throughout the 1960s, a task for the future. Further delineation of the concept was necessary, and so was the testing of reliability of the various and competing definitions. What one needed was, in fact, the optimal combination of reliability and laboratory-testability. Toward the end of the 1960s Grinker and his coworkers, in cooperation with the Chicago Psychoanalytic Institute sought to refine the loose diagnostic criteria then in use for "borderline." They carried out a detailed study of ego-functions, as well, on their sample of some 50 hospitalized borderlines. It is not possible to reprint here the book that was to emerge from their research, but a portion of it has been excerpted. Theirs was the first large-scale, methodical study of "borderline" patients, the forerunner of the many biometric, psychometric and physiologic studies of the 1970s and 1980s. For obvious reasons most of these studies are carried out on hospital populations, one result of which has been that more is know about *hospitalized* than about never-hospitalized borderlines. More is published about them, also. As a result, we witness a *drift*, beginning in the late 1960s, in the average clinician's understanding of "borderline" psychopathology, toward a definition and a prognostic expectation that is more in conformity with those types of "borderlines" who require occasional hospitalization. "Borderlines" who seldom require hospitalization (such as those whom Kohut and his largely office-based analytic colleagues were to describe during the 1970s) do *not* become the subjects of high-quality, controlled studies (with blind raters, test-retest conditions, etc.). Our knowledge of them rests on a shakier foundation, even though these ambulatory borderines are both more common than the ever-hospitalized patients and (b) more in line with the conceptual traditions of the 1940s and 1950s, as established by the predominantly office-based psychoanalysts who, after Stern, helped popularize the term in the first place.

One conclusion reached by Grinker was that the "borderline" diagnosis did not seem to reflect a homogeneous population. There appeared to be several subtypes (four were enumerated in the monograph), one of which seemed, on phenomenologic grounds at least, closer to the border with psychosis. Another seemed nearer to the neurotic level (Grinker's Type IV so-called "anaclitically depressed group"). In between were patients resembling Deutsch's description of the as-if personality, and another group—the "core borderlines," who had the depressive, angry, impulsive characteristics we now associate with the

DSM-3 "borderline." Since Grinker's book, other investigators (Gunderson, M. Stone, Andrulonis, Pope and others) have also begun to search for meaningful subtypes within the admittedly heterogeneous collection we call borderline.

At about the same time Grinker was refining the definition of "borderline" as a separate nosologic entity (he and his colleagues did not carry out a methodical assessment of family psychiatric illness, but their impression was that "borderline" was a thing apart from schizophrenia), Kety and his coworkers were reporting the results of the Danish Adoption Study of Schizophrenia. We see from the chapter included here, from their landmark monograph of 1968, that among the close relatives of certain adopted-away schizophrenics were a number of eccentric, dysfunctional persons whose condition resembled, only in an attenuated form, the fullblown illness of the probands. Kety could make a more convincing argument for genetic linkage between the two clinical states, the milder of which was called *borderline schizophrenia,* since the probands shared only genes and not the family environment with their biologic siblings and other relatives. After this study, only the most die-hard environmentalists (such as Don Jackson and Theodore Lidz) could discard heredity as accounting for at least some portion of the distal etiology of at least some psychotic conditions and their borderline variants. The reader will detect parallels between Kety's description of the borderline schizophrenic and description by Hoch and Polatin of the "pseudoneurotic" patient, and will also note how Kety's chapter served as the source whence the "schizotypal personality" of DSM-3 was derived (see below, Spitzer et al., 1979). European conceptions of the borderline during the 1960s were influenced by the Swiss, Benedetti, who suggested criteria for "borderline" similar to those outlined by Hoch and Polatin.

Not all the advances during the 1960s were confined to biometric assessments and conceptual clarification. In the more intuitive realm, we have Balint's monograph on the *Basic Fault,* in which this most eloquent member of the British Object-Relations School shares with us his psychoanalytic insights and humanistic approach to the treatment of patients who experience in a profound way the "basic fault" of which the author speaks: this eerie sense of "defect," or something being "missing"—that seems very much in keeping with persons we would characterize as borderline. There are no neat parallels between the idiosyncratic labels of Balint and the standard psychoanalytic terminology, so it is not easy to specify, say, the maximum degree of "basic fault" still compatible with the healthier, neurotic state. But Balint was one of the few (along with Sacha Nacht and Harold Searles) who could do a creditable job of capturing the ineffable in writing. Here I refer to the peculiar and strained atmosphere that soon pervades the room where therapist encounters borderline patient. This tension and strangeness seem at once too subtle ever to become an "item" in DSM-"X"— and at the same time, the very essence of what it is to be borderline. The neurotic patient immediately gets down to business, relates his difficulties in a concise and coherent fashion, respects the personhood of the therapist and comports himself in such a way as to make it easy for the therapist (especially in the opening consultation period) to retain his preferred posture of helpful and neutral observer. How great is the contrast between this mode of relatedness, this spirit of cooperation and mutual exploration—and the uncomfortable emotions engendered in us by the borderline patient, who makes us feel we have not understood him properly, that his words fail to convey his distress whilst ours fail to convey reassurance, who throws us off our professional balance momentarily (and sometimes longer) through inappropriate expressions of anger, envy, love, mistrust . . . , who walks around the room when he should be sitting down, who starts to run out before the time is up, or else stays put when the session is at an end, and so forth. All these are manifestations of Balint's "basic fault," reflecting disturbances in the preoedipal, symbiotic phase of mother-child intimacy. And because the trouble stems from this preverbal period, language fails as the vehicle of communication—which takes place instead via the borderline's peculiar behavior, instilling in his therapist the inchoate and ill-defined emotions that envelop him. As one of my borderline patients once bemoaned, "I can never get along with people because of how my mother was, but we can never get back to it: it all happened before words!" Instinctively, when a patient has this uncanny effect on us, we begin to channel our diagnostic impressions along the lines of a borderline condition. Balint's contributions greatly enhanced our ability both to understand and to treat these (usually borderline-level) patients with the *basic fault*.

A number of other important contributions were made on the clinical side of the borderline question in the 1960s. Easser and Lesser (1965) expressed their discomfort with traditional psychoanalytic character-ology, according to which the "hysterical" personality represented the healthiest form of psychoneurotic character type by virtue of its prox-imity, along the developmental continuum from orality to mature "gen-itality," to the latter pole. Some outwardly hysteric personalities seemed obviously quite ill and a long ways from having reached "gen-itality." In what conceptual frame was one to place them? Easser and Lesser drew attention to the primitivity of the dream-life (grotesque dream-imagery being common in this group—a point also made by Knight in connection with borderlines in general), their impulsivity, and chaotic interpersonal life. They were caricatures of the hysteric, and operated on a level that smacked more of primitive "orality" than of anything like mature, integrated sexuality. For these reasons Easser and Lesser saw fit to coin the term *hysteroid* (the "-oid" signifying "like, resembling") to designate this sicker group of hysterics. As it happens, this is just the sort of distinction Falret had drawn some 70 years before, in distinguishing between hysterical character and, as we saw, the *folie hystérique*. But, Falret's work lay outside analytic tradi-tion; the distinction had to be made once again and reformulated within the context of psychoanalytic theory. The usefulness of this reformu-lation was not lost upon Donald Klein, who, a few years later was to incorporate Easser's impressions into his own observations concerning certain histrionic, depression-prone, borderline-level patients (almost all of whom were women whose illness was mobilized by rejection in a love-relationship). He subsumed these cases under the rubric "hyster-oid dysphoria." Though the construct-validity of this label was later challenged by Spitzer, the clinical description of the hysteroid dysphoric does answer to one of the most common varieties of borderline condi-tion—enough so, in fact, as to make them *paradigm* cases of "border-line." Hysteroid dysphorics tend to be borderline, almost without ex-ception, in all the currently popular definitions (DSM-3, Kernberg, Gunderson) simultaneously.

An excellent clinical comment about borderlines was published to-ward the end of the 1960s by the late British analyst, Margaret Little (1969). She drew attention to something in the life drama of patients we call "borderline," which, once we catch sight of it, actually nudges us in the direction of the "sicker" diagnosis. Unlike the preoccupation with priority of place ("which of us did Mother love best?") which dominates the lives of those we are content to call "neurotic," certain patients make us aware that, for them, existence is a life-and-death struggle at every moment. The neurotic's worry about loss of love is a luxury—when viewed by someone terrified by the spectre of annihilation. Like Balint's "basic fault," Little's "annihilation fear" is, diagnostically, only a soft-sign of the borderline state. Yet to the analyst it often seems more reliable than some of the "hard signs" (like impulsivity, which, taken by itself, is seen in certain organic and psychopathic cases also). Recently a borderline (by all criteria: DSM-3, Kernberg, Gunderson, "hysteroid-dysphoria," etc.) patient of mine related to me the following dream from which she awoke in a panic.

My brother was in our house, though my parents promised me he wouldn't be coming here. I scream at my parents, "you *lied* to me! you *lied* to me!," and I stab them with knives, trying to kill them.

As with the patients Little had spoken of, this woman was clearly locked in a rivalry with her sibling so intense as to take on life-or-death meaning for her: "*if* they love him, *then* they must not love *me*, and *if* they do not love me, then I will *die*, for which the only just retribution is that *they* should die . . . " These are the kinds of all-or-none dynamics that, during the course of psychotherapy with the borderline patient, pervade and electrify the atmosphere.

8. Borderline States

Robert P. Knight

The term "borderline state" has achieved almost no official status in psychiatric nomenclature, and conveys no diagnostic illumination of a case other than the implication that the patient is quite sick but not frankly psychotic. In the few psychiatric textbooks where the term is to be found at all in the index, it is used in the text to apply to those cases in which the decision is difficult as to whether the patients in question are neurotic or psychotic, since both neurotic and psychotic phenomena are observed to be present. The reluctance to make a diagnosis of psychosis on the one hand, in such cases, is usually based on the clinical estimate that these patients have not yet "broken with reality"; on the other hand the psychiatrist feels that the severity of the maladjustment and the presence of ominous clinical signs preclude the diagnosis of a psychoneurosis. Thus the label "borderline state," when used as a diagnosis, conveys more information about the uncertainty and indecision of the psychiatrist than it does about the condition of the patient.

Indeed, the term and its equivalents have been frequently attacked in psychiatric and psychoanalytic literature. Rickman (1928) wrote: "It is not uncommon in the lax phraseology of a Mental O.P. Department to hear of a case in which a psychoneurosis 'masks' a psychosis; I have used the term myself, but with inward misgiving. There should be no talk of masks if a case is fully understood and certainly not if the case has not received a tireless examination—except, of course, as a brief descriptive term comparable to 'shut-in' or 'apprehensive' which carry our understanding of the case no further." Similarly, Edward Glover (1932) wrote: "I find the terms 'borderline' or 'pre'-psychotic, as generally used, unsatisfactory. If a psychotic mechanism is present at all, it should be given a definite label. If we merely suspect the possibility of a breakdown of repression, this can be indicated in the term 'potential' psychotic (more accurately a 'potentially clinical' psychosis). As for larval psychoses, we are all larval psychotics and have been such since the age of two.'' Again, Zilboorg (1941) wrote: ''The less advanced cases (of schizophrenia) have been noted, but not seriously considered. When of recent years such cases engaged the attention of the clinician, they were usually approached with the euphemistic labels of borderline cases, incipient schizophrenias, schizoid personalities, mixed manic-depressive psychoses, schizoid manics, or psychopathic personalities. Such an attitude is untestable either logically or clinically . . . .'' Zilboorg goes on to declare that schizophrenia should be recognized and diagnosed when its characteristic psychopathology is present, and suggests the term ''ambulatory schizophrenia'' for that type of schizophrenia in which the individual is able for the most part, to conceal his pathology from the general public.

I have no wish to defend the term ''borderline state'' as a diagnosis. I do wish, however, to discuss the clinical conditions usually connoted by this term, and especially to call attention to the diagnostic, psychopathological, and therapeutic problems involved in these conditions. I shall limit my discussion to the functional psychiatric conditions where the term is usually applied, and more particularly to those conditions which involve schizophrenic tendencies of some degree.

I believe it is the common experience of psychiatrists and psychoanalysts currently to see and treat, in open sanitaria or even in office practice, a rather high percentage of patients whom they regard, in a general sense, as borderline cases. Often these patients have been referred as cases of psychoneuroses of severe degree who have not responded to treatment according to the usual expectations associated with the supposed diagnosis. Most often, perhaps, they have been called severe obsessive-compulsive cases; sometimes an intractable phobia has been the outstanding symptom; occasionally an apparent major hysterical symptom or an anorexia nervosa dominates the clinical picture; and at times it is a question of the degree of depression, or of the extent and ominousness of paranoid trends, or of the severity of a character disorder.

The unsatisfactory state of our nosology contributes to our difficulties in classifying these patients diagnostically, and we legitimately wonder at a ''touch of schizophrenia'' is of the same order as a ''touch of syphilis or a ''touch of pregnancy.'' So we fall back on such qualifying terms as latent or incipient (or ambulatory) schizophrenia, or emphasize that it is a *severe* obsessive-compulsive neurosis or depression, adding, for full coverage, "with paranoid trends" or "with schizoid manifestations." Certainly, for the most part, we are quite familiar with the necessity of recognizing the primary symptoms of schizophrenia and not waiting for the secondary ones of hallucinations, delusions, stupor, and the like.

Freud (1913) made us alert to the possibility of psychosis underlying a psychoneurotic picture in his warning: "Often enough, when one sees a case of neurosis with hysterical or obsessional symptoms, mild in character and of short duration (just the type of case, that is, which one would regard as suitable for the treatment) a doubt which must not be overlooked arises whether the case may not be one of incipient dementia praecox, so-called (schizophrenia, according to Bleuler; paraphrenia, as I prefer to call it), and may not sooner or later develop well marked signs of this disease." Many authors in recent years, among them Hoch and Polatin (1949), Stern (1945), Miller (1940), Pious (1950), Melitta Schmideberg (1947), Fenichel (1945), H. Deutsch (1942), Stengel (1945), and others, have called attention to types of cases which belong in the borderline band of the psychopathological spectrum, and have commented on the diagnostic and psychotherapeutic problems associated with these cases.

SOME DIAGNOSTIC CONSIDERATIONS

In attempting to make the precise diagnosis in a borderline case there are three often used criteria, or frames of reference, which are apt to lead to errors if they are used exclusively or uncritically. One of these, which stems from traditional psychiatry, is the question of whether or not there has been a "break with reality"; the second is the assumption that neurosis is neurosis, psychosis is psychosis, and never the twain shall meet; a third, contributed by psychoanalysis, is the series of stages of development of the libido, with the conceptions of fixation, regression, and typical defense mechanisms for each stage.

No psychiatrist has any difficulty in diagnosing a psychosis when he finds definite evidence of falsification of reality in the form of hallucinations and delusions, or evidence of implicit loss of reality sense in the form of self-mutilation, mutism, stupor, stereotypies, flight of ideas, incoherence, homicidal mania, and the like. But these are all signs of advanced psychosis, and no present-day psychiatrist of standing would be unaware of the fact that each patient with one or more of these psychotic manifestations had carried on for some previous years as a supposedly normal individual, albeit with concealed potentialities for a psychotic outbreak, and that there must have been warning signs, various stages of development, and a gradually increasing degree of overtness of these gross expressions of psychotic illness. All science aims at the capacity to *predict,* and psychiatry will become a science the more it can detect the evidences of strain, the small premonitory signs of a psychotic process, so that it can then introduce the kinds of therapeutic measures which have the best chance of aborting the psychotic development. The break with reality, which is an ego alteration, must be thought of not as a sudden and unexpected snapping, as of a twig, but as the gradual bending as well, which preceded the snapping, and sound prognosis must inevitably take into account those ego factors which correspond to the tensile strength of the twig, as well as the kinds and degree of disruptive forces which are being applied.

A second conception which leads to misdiagnosis is that neurosis and psychosis are mutually exclusive, that neurosis never develops into psychosis, and that neurotics are "loyal to reality" while psychotics are "disloyal to reality." It is, to be sure, one of the contributions of psychoanalysis that neurotic mechanisms are different from psychotic mechanisms and that psychosis is not simply a more severe degree of neurosis. However, it is quite possible for both psychotic and neurotic mechanisms to have developed in the same individual, and this is the crux of the problem in many borderline cases. Furthermore, there is a sense in which there is a loss of reality even in neurosis. As Freud (1924) pointed out: "The difference at the beginning comes to expression at the end in this way: in neurosis a part of reality is avoided by a sort of flight, but in psychosis it is remodeled. Or one may say that in psychosis, flight at the beginning is succeeded by an active phase of reconstruction, while in neurosis obedience at the beginning is followed by a subsequent attempt at flight. Or, to express it in yet another way, neurosis does not deny the existence of reality, it merely tries to ignore it; psychosis denies it and tries to substitute something else for it. A reaction which combines features of both these is the one we call normal or 'healthy'; it denies reality as little as neurosis, but then, like a psychosis, is concerned with effecting a change in it. This expedient normal attitude leads naturally to some active achievement in the outer world and is not content, like a psychosis, with establishing the alteration within itself; it is no longer *autoplastic* but *alloplastic.*" Again, on the point of gradations in loss of reality, Freud (1922) discussed normal jealousy, projected jealousy, and delusional jealousy, pointing out their transitions from one to the other, and describing how an individual may for a time maintain his critical judgement over paranoid ideas which are already present but do not yet have the strength of conviction of delusions.

Anna Freud (1936) describes how children can use the defense of denial—denial in fantasy and denial in word and act—in ways which represent temporary breaking with reality while retaining an unimpaired faculty of reality testing. However, if adolescents and adults persist in, or resume, this kind of denial after the normal development of ego synthesis has taken place "the relation to reality has been gravely disturbed and the function of reality-testing suspended." The varieties of channeling psychotic (usually paranoid) tendencies in eccentric or fanatical ways—even to the point of developing a following of many people—and the various degrees of inappropriate emotions seen in many individuals further highlight the vagueness of the criterion of reality testing, and of the distinction between neurotic and psychotic. Also, we are well aware that in these and other borderline conditions the *movement* in the case may be toward or away from further psychotic development.

The third frame of reference, that of the levels of psychosexual development—oral sucking, oral biting, anal expulsive, anal retentive, phallic, and genital—and of the attempts to build a classification of mental disorders by linking a certain clinical condition to each level of libidinal fixation, has presented a one-sided, libidinal theory of human functioning. This psychoanalytic contribution has been of major value, but it needs to be supplemented extensively with the findings of ego psychology which have not, as yet, been sufficiently integrated with the libido theory. Reliance on the "ladder" of psychosexual development, with the line of reality testing drawn between the two anal substages, has resulted in many blunders in diagnosis—especially in the failure to perceive the psychosis underlying a hysterical, phobic, or obsessive-compulsive clinical picture.

I believe it was Freud who used the metaphor of a retreating army to illuminate the mixed clinical picture in libidinal regression. I should like to borrow the metaphor and elaborate it for the purpose of illuminating ego-defensive operations. Various segments or detachments of the retreating army may make a stand and conduct holding or delaying operations at various points where the terrain lends itself to such operations, while the main retreating forces may have retired much farther to the rear. The defensive operations of the more forward detachments would, thus, actually protect the bulk of the army from disaster; but these forward detachments may not be able to hold their positions, and may have to retreat at any time in the face of superior might. On the other hand, the main army may be able to regroup itself, receive reinforcements or gain new leadership, and recapture its morale. In that event, the forward positions may hold long enough for the main forces to move forward to, or even well beyond, the stubbornly defended outposts.

I believe this metaphor conceptualizes in an important way the psychoeconomy and the indicated therapy in the borderline cases. The superficial clinical picture—hysteria, phobia, obsessions, compulsive rituals—may represent a holding operation in a forward position, while the major portion of the ego has regressed far behind this in varying degrees of disorder. For the sake of accurate diagnosis, realistic prognosis, and appropriate therapy, therefore, the clinician must be able to locate the position, movement, and possibilities of resynthesis of the main ego forces and functions, and not be misled by all the shooting in the forward holding point. An important corollary of this conception is that the therapy should not attempt to attack and demolish the forward defensive operations when to do so would mean disaster for the main ego operations. Some forward defensive operations are a matter of life and death.

Without defending the term "borderline state" as a diagnostic label, I have thus far developed the argument to show that there is a borderline strip in psychopathology where accurate diagnosis is difficult. I have tried to show the general characteristics of such borderline conditions, and to point out why the often used diagnostic criteria of break with reality mutual exclusiveness of neurosis and psychosis, and the libido theory is insufficient and misleading in reaching accurate diagnosis, prognosis and appropriate therapeutic recommendations for such cases. What, then, are the more reliable methods of evaluating these cases so that one will not have to be content with using as a diagnosis the unspecific term "borderline state"? The attempt to answer this question will involve a discussion of certain dynamic considerations as they relate to the diagnostic techniques available to us—the psychiatric interview, the free-association interview, and the use of psychological diagnostic tests.

SOME DYNAMIC CONSIDERATIONS

We conceptualize the borderline case as one in which normal ego functions of secondary-process thinking, integration, realistic planning adaptation to the environment, maintenance of object relationships, and defenses against primitive unconscious impulses are severely weakened. As a result of various combinations of the factors of constitutional tendencies, predisposition based on traumatic events and disturbed human relationships, and more recent precipitating stress, the ego of the borderline patient is laboring badly. Some ego functions have been severely impaired—especially, in most cases, integration, concept formation, judgment, realistic planning, and defending against eruption into conscious thinking of id impulses and their fantasy elaborations. Other ego functions, such as conventional (but superficial) adaptation to the environment and superficial maintenance of object relationships may exhibit varying degrees of intactness. And still others, such as memory, calculation, and certain habitual performances, may seem unimpaired. Also, the clinical picture may be dominated by hysterical, phobic, obsessive-compulsive, or psychosomatic symptoms, to which neurotic disabilities and distress the patient attributes his inability to carry on the usual ego functions.

During the psychiatric interview the neurotic defenses and the relatively intact adaptive ego functions may enable the borderline patient to present a deceptive, superficially conventional, although neurotic, front, depending on how thoroughgoing and comprehensive the psychiatric investigation is with respect to the patient's *total* ego functioning. The face-to-face psychiatric interview provides a relatively structured situation in which the conventional protective devices of avoidance, evasion, denial, minimization, changing the subject, and other cover-up methods can be used—even by patients who are genuinely seeking help but who dare not yet communicate their awareness of lost affect, reality misinterpretations, autistic preoccupations, and the like.

Several interviews may be necessary to provide the psychiatrist with a sufficiently comprehensive appraisal of the total ego functioning, and to provide the patient with enough sense of security to permit him to verbalize his more disturbing self-observations. In spite of the patient's automatic attempts at concealment, the presence of pathology of psychotic degree will usually manifest itself to the experienced clinician. Occasional blocking, peculiarities of word usage, obliviousness to obvious implications, contaminations of idioms, arbitrary inferences, inappropriate affect and suspicion-laden behavior and questions are a few possible examples of such unwitting betrayals of ego impairment of psychotic degree.

In regard to such manifestations the appraisal of total ego functioning can be more precise if the psychiatrist takes careful note of the degree of ego-syntonicity associated with them. Momentary halting, signs of embarrassment, and attempts at correction of the peculiarity of expression are evidences of a sufficient degree of ego intactness for such psychotic intrusions to be recognized and repudiated as ego-alien; whereas unnoticed and repeated peculiarities and contaminations provide evidence that the ego has been overwhelmed or pervaded by them and has lost its power to regard them as bizarre. Likewise the expression of suspicions accompanied by embarrassed apologies or joking indicates preservation of the ego's critical function with respect to paranoid mistrust; whereas unqualified suspiciousness indicates the loss of that important ego function. Sometimes this capacity for taking distance from these psychotic productions has to be tested by questions from the psychiatrist which call attention to the production and request comments from the patient about them. Obviously such confrontations should be made sparingly and supportively.

In addition to these microscopic evidences of ego weakness in respect to id eruptions in borderline cases, there are more macroscopic manifestations which may be either frankly stated by the patient or may be implicit in his attitudes and productions. Lack of concern about the realities of his life predicament, usually associated with low voltage wishes for help or grossly inappropriate treatment proposals of his own, is one such macroscopic sign. Others are the fact that the illness developed in the absence of observable precipitating stress, or under the relatively minor stress which was inevitable for the point where this patient was in his life course; the presence of multiple symptoms and disabilities, especially if these are regarded with an acceptance that seems ego-syntonic, or are viewed as being due to malevolent external influence; lack of achievement over a relatively long period, indicating a chronic and severe failure of the ego to channelize energies constructively, especially if this lack of achievement has been accompanied by some degree of disintegration of the ordinary routines of looking after one's self; vagueness or unrealism in planning for the future with respect to education, vocation, marriage, parenthood, and the like; and the relating of bizarre dreams, or evidence of insufficient contrast between dream content and attitudes on the one hand and waking activities and attitudes on the other. All of these macroscopic manifestations will be observable, if they are present, only if the psychiatrist keeps as his frame of reference the patient's total ego functioning, with appropriate allowances for the patient's age, endowment, cultural background, previous level of achievement, and the degree of severity of the recent or current life stresses.

The question of using the free-association interview, with the patient on the couch, frequently comes up with borderline cases. The associative anamnesis has been advocated by Felix Deutsch (1949) and many analysts use free-association interviews either as a limited diagnostic tool or as a more extended trial period of analytic therapy. This technique changes the fairly well-structured situation of the face-to-face psychiatric interview into a relatively unstructured one, so that the patient cannot rely on his usual defensive and conventionally adaptive devices to maintain his front. Borderline patients are then likely to show in bolder relief the various microscopic and macroscopic signs of schizophrenic illness. They may be unable to talk at all and may block completely, with evidence of mounting anxiety; or their verbalizations may show a high degree of autistic content, with many peculiarities of expression; or their inappropriate affect may become more obvious. The diagnosis is aided by the couch—free-association technique, but the experience may be definitely antitherapeutic for the patient. Definitive evidence of psychotic thinking may be produced at the expense of humiliating and disintegrating exposure of the patient's naked pathology. Clinical judgment must be used as to how far the psychiatrist should go in breaking through the defenses in his purpose of reaching an accurate diagnosis.

In the face-to-face psychiatric diagnostic interview the patient is in a fairly well-structured situation and is reacting to the interested listening and active questioning of a visible and supportive physician; in the couch—free-association interview the patient is in a relatively unstructured situation, more or less abandoned to his own fantasies, and relatively unsupported by the shadowy and largely silent listener. Diagnostic psychological tests combine the advantages of support from a visible and interested professional listener, as in the face-to-face psychiatric interview, and the diagnostically significant unstructured situation of the couch—free-association interview.

The various test stimuli are unusual and unconventional, and there are no "correct" answers, so that the patient does not know what he is revealing or concealing. The psychological tests also have one significant advantage over either of the two kinds of diagnostic interview. The tests have been standardized by trials on thousands of cases, so that objective scoring can be done and comparisons can be made of this patient's responses to typical responses of many other patients with all kinds of psychiatric illness, whereas even the experienced psychiatric interviewer must depend on impressions and comparisons of the patient's productions with those of other remembered patients in his particular experience. The psychologist can also determine the patient's capacity to take critical distance from his more pathological responses, and thus assess the degree of ego-alienness or ego-syntonicity of the pathological material, by asking questions which elicit comments from the patient about certain of the unusual responses.

As Rapaport, et al. (1945 and 1946), Schafer (1948), and others have pointed out, the interpretation of diagnostic psychological test results is far from being a mere matter of mathematical scoring followed by comparisons with standard tables. There is also required a high degree of clinical acumen, and it is just in the field of the borderline cases that expert interpretation of the test results is essential. The Rorschach is probably the most sensitive test for autistic thinking, and the word association and sorting tests are most valuable for detecting the loosening of associations and disruption of concept formation. The Thematic Apperception Test is less sensitive to schizophrenic pathology but can give a sharply etched picture of the patient's projected image of himself and of the significant people in his life, while describing what the patient feels he and these significant people are doing to each other. The Bellevue-Wechsler intelligence test may, on the other hand, especially in borderline cases, show excellent preservation of intellectual functioning. The relatively clean and orderly responses of the Bellevue-Wechsler do not cancel out the contaminated and disorderly responses of the other tests and thus make the diagnosis doubtful. Instead, the former highlight the preservation of certain ego functions in the face of the impairment of other ego functions revealed by the latter, and thus provide a basis for critical appraisal of ego strengths in relation to threatening eruptions from the id. The Rorschach alone is often given as a test to check on possible schizophrenia, but only a balanced battery of tests can provide the range of responses which will permit accurate appraisal of total ego functioning.

In all of these diagnostic methods, then, the aim should be to take a complete inventory of ego functioning in order to discover the kind of equilibrium which exists between ego controls on the one hand and threatening impulses on the other, and to learn whether the *movement* in this patient is toward less ego control and poorer adaptation. The qualitative appraisal of ego functions is, if anything, even more important than the quantitative estimation of impulse-control balance. Even quite severely neurotic defenses may be capitalized, through therapy, and become reintegrating forces leading to a dynamic shift away, for example, from dereistic thinking to fairly well-organized compulsive striving, with marked improvement in both the defensive and adaptive aspects of ego functioning.

Some final comments are in order regarding the clinical picture in the borderline group of cases before turning to the therapeutic considerations. A useful distinction can be made between internalized or autoplastic illnesses, such as schizophrenias, depressions, and clinical psychoneuroses, and the externalized or alloplastic illnesses, such as the neurotic and psychotic characters. In the autoplastic conditions, the ego, in various stages of enfeeblement, is attempting to hold out against a barrage of ego-alien impulses and their autistic elaborations; in the alloplastic conditions, or character disorders, the ego itself has been molded and distorted by the gradual infiltration of pathogenic impulses and defenses, and the invasion of id impulses appears much more ego-syntonic. In some respects the alloplastic conditions thus represent greater integration of the ego, but just because of this integrated infiltration of pathogenic impulses into the ego these cases are more difficult to influence therapeutically. On the other hand, the autoplastic conditions may appear more severely ill than the alloplastic ones but the prognosis for therapy may be more favorable. Both the psychiatric interview and the psychological test results can aid in establishing whether the structure of the illness is primarily autoplastic or alloplastic.

SOME THERAPEUTIC CONSIDERATIONS

The ego of the borderline patient is a feeble and unreliable ally in therapy. In the incipient schizophrenias the ego is in danger of being overwhelmed by the ego-alien pathogenic forces, and in the psychotic character disorders the ego is already warped by more or less ego-syntonic pervasion by the same pathogenic forces. Yet a few adaptive functions remain, and certain psychoneurotic defense measures may still be in operation, even though the impulse-defense balance is precarious. In an environment which maintains its overtaxing demands on such patients, further regression is likely. If these patients are left to their own devices, in relative isolation, whether at home or in closed hospital, they tend toward further intensification of autistic thinking. Similarly, if they are encouraged to free-associate in the relative isolation of recumbency on the analytic couch, the autistic development is encouraged, and the necessary supportive factor of positive transference to an active, visible, responding therapist is unavailable. Thus even though a trial analysis may bring forth misleading "rich" material, and the analyst can make correspondingly rich formulations and interpretations, the patient's ego often cannot make use of them, and they may only serve the purpose of stimulating further autistic elaborations. Psychoanalysis is, thus, contraindicated for the great majority of borderline cases, at least until after some months of successful analytic psychotherapy.

Psychotherapists can take their cue from the much better front these patients are able to present and maintain in face-to-face psychiatric interviews, where the structured situation and the visible, personal, active therapist per se provides an integrating force to stimulate the patient's surviving adaptive, integrative, and reality-testing capacities. Our therapeutic objective, then, would be the strengthening of the patient's ego controls over instinctual impulses and educating him in the employment of new controls and new adaptive methods, through a kind of psychotherapeutic lend-lease. With our analytic knowledge we can see how he defends himself, and what he defends himself against, but we do not attack those defenses except as we may modify them or educatively introduce better substitutes for them. Our formulations will be in terms of his ego operations rather than of his id content, and will be calculated to improve and strengthen the ego operations.

The psychoneurotic defenses and symptoms especially are not attacked, for just these ego operations protect the patient from further psychotic disorganization. Particularly the obsessive-compulsive defense line is left untouched, except as it can be modified educatively. To return for the moment to the metaphor of the retreating army, our therapy should bypass the outposts of neurotic defenses and symptom formation, and should act as a *rescue force* for the main army of ego functions to the rear, helping to regroup them, restore their morale, and provide leadership for them. Then we might hope to bring them forward to or beyond the neurotic outpost which we by-passed. We may even take our cues for morale building and leadership from the kind of neurotic outpost we observed. If it was primarily obsessive-compulsive we might strive therapeutically for a reintegration based on strengthened compulsive trends. If it was phobic we could attempt to build counterphobic defenses.

Not only do we try to consolidate the more neurotic defenses available, but we also attempt to convert autoplastic (self-crippling) defenses into alloplastic (externally adaptive) ones. This attempt will often require considerably more therapeutic impact than can be provided in an hour a day of modified analytic psychotherapy. Both the motivation and the specific opportunities for alloplastic adaptation can be provided through group dynamics measures—group discussions, group projects, and initiative-stimulating group and individual activities. In a comprehensive attempt at providing such a setting in which to conduct the individual psychotherapy of these cases, we have discovered that many such patients can be carried on a voluntary basis and in an open hospital facility, thus avoiding the encouragement toward isolation, regression, and inertia which closed hospital care sometimes introduces.

SUMMARY

Borderline cases have been discussed in their diagnostic, dynamic, and therapeutic aspects. The term borderline case is not recommended as a diagnostic term, for a much more precise diagnosis should be made which identifies the type and degree of psychotic pathology. Far more important, however, than arriving at a diagnostic label is the achievement of a comprehensive psychodynamic appraisal of the balance in each patient between the ego's defensive and adaptive measures on the one hand, and the pathogenic instinctual and ego-disintegrating forces on the other, so that therapy can be planned and conducted for the purpose of conserving, strengthening, and improving the defensive and adaptive functions of the ego.

BIBLIOGRAPHY

Deutsh, F. (1949), *Applied Psychoanalysis; Selected Objectives of Psychotherapy*. New York: Grune & Stratton.

Deutsch, H. (1942), Some Forms of Emotional Disturbance and Their Relationship to Schizophrenia. *Psychoanalytic Quarterly, 11*:301–321.

Fenichel, O. (1945), *The Psychoanalytic Theory of Neurosis*. New York: Norton.

Freud, A. (1936), *The Ego and the Mechanisms of Defence*. New York: International Universities Press, 1946.

Freud, S., (1913), Further Recommendations in the Technique of Psycho-Analysis. On Beginning the Treatment. The Question of the First Communication. The Dynamics of the Cure. *Collected Papers, 2*:342–365. London: Hogarth Press, 1946.

—— (1922), Certain Neurotic Mechanisms in Jealousy, Paranoia and Homosexuality. *Collected Papers, 2*:232–243. London: Hogarth Press, 1946.

—— (1924), The Loss of Reality in Neurosis and Psychosis. *Collected Papers, 2*:277–282. London: Hogarth Press, 1946.

Glover, E. (1932), A Psycho-Analytical Approach to the Classification of Mental Disorders. *Journal of Mental Science, 78*:819–842.

Hoch, P. and Polatin, P. (1949), Pseudoneurotic Forms of Schizophrenia. *Psychiatric Quarterly, 23*:248–276.

Miller, W. R. (1940), The Relationship Between Early Schizophrenia and the Neuroses. *American Journal of Psychiatry, 96*:889–896.

Pious, W. L. (1950), Obsessive-Compulsive Symptoms in an Incipient Schizophrenic. *Psychoanalytic Quarterly, 19*:327–351.

Rapaport, D., Gill, M., and Schafer, R. (1945 and 1946), *Diagnostic Psychological Testing*, 2 Vols. Chicago: Yearbook Publishers.

Rickman, J. (1928), *The Development of the Psycho-Analytical Theory of the Psychoses, 1893–1926*. London: Baillière, Tindall & Cox for the Institute of Psycho-Analysis.

Schafer, R. (1948), *The Clinical Application of Psychological Tests*. New York, International Universities Press.

Schmideberg, M. (1947), The Treatment of Psychopaths and Borderline Patients. *American Journal of Psychotherapy, 1*:45–70.

Stengel, E. (1945), A Study on Some Clinical Aspects of the Relationship Between Obsessional Neurosis and Psychotic Reaction Types. *Journal of Mental Science, 91*:166–187.

Stern, A. (1945), Psychoanalytic Therapy in the Borderline Neuroses. *Psychoanalytic Quarterly, 14*:190–198.

Zilboorg. G. (1941), Ambulatory Schizophrenias, Psychiatry, 4:149–155.

9. Jacobson on the Borderline*

Edith Jacobson

ON THE PSYCHOANALYTIC THEORY OF CYCLOTHYMIC DEPRESSION

In contrast to neurotics, psychotics seek a solution to their emotional and instinctual conflicts in a regressive escape which involves not only instinctual regression but a severe regressive process in the whole personality organization. As a patient after recovery from a schizophrenic episode put it drastically: "I ran and ran, back to the womb." As a result of constitutional and environmental factors (early infantile emotional deprivations and instinctual overstimulation and/or frustration), these patients are evidently predisposed to such a profound regressive process by an arrested, defective ego and superego development.

It seems to me that the central element in this predisposition is an insufficient neutralization of libidinal and aggressive forces. We may speculate that the underlying psychosomatic processes in psychoses result in a reduction and exhaustion, or else in an insufficient reproduction, of libidinal, and possibly in an overproduction of aggressive, drives. This would change the proportion between libido and aggression in favor of the latter, and promote defusion and deneutralization of the drives. Whatever the nature of these pathogenic processes, they do not permit normal maturation to take place and thus interfere with the development of lasting libidinal cathexis of object and self representations and the maintenance of stable object relations and firm ego and superego identifications.

In the prepsychotic personality the self and object representations and the ego ideal are not sharply separated; they retain attributes of early infantile object and self images, and thus are carriers of primitive,

*This contribution is excerpted from the original published version *The Self and the Object World*, pages 49–69, and *On the Psychoanalytic Theory of Cyclothymic Depression*, pages 228–241, New York: International Universities Press.

infantile, magic values. The superego is not a firmly integrated system. It is personified, unstable in its functions, and tends either to assume excessive control over the ego or to disintegrate, dissolve, and merge with object and self representations. It is easily reprojected onto the outside world. The superego and the object and self representations are prone to regressive fragmentations, on the one hand splitting up again into primitive early images and on the other fusing with one another. There is then a tendency to react to conflicts with the object world not by ego defenses against unacceptable strivings but by withdrawals and shifts of libidinal and aggressive cathexis, not only from one object to another and from personal object to thing representations, but from the object to the self representations and the reverse.

The onset of the psychosis proper is characterized by a dangerous, irresistible defusion and deneutralization of the instinctual drives. This unleashes a furious struggle for supremacy between the libidinal and the destructive forces. Whatever sets it going, this struggle may lead eventually to a fatal libidinal impoverishment, an accumulation of sheer aggression, a destructuralization, and a dispersion of the defused drives in the whole self. I suspect that the "endogenous" psychosomatic phenomena in psychosis arise with the development of such a state.

Psychologically, the psychotic process is probably set in motion by a reactivation of infantile conflicts centered primarily around both parental love objects or their substitutes, but then spreads to the whole object world. The defective ego of the prepsychotic is unable to master these conflicts with the help of neurotic defenses. It attempts to resolve the conflicts by shifts, first of the libidinal, then of the aggressive, cathexis from the object to the self representations; by renewed efforts to recathect the objects; and finally by increasing fusions of object and self images. This goes along with a severe regressive distortion of the object and self representations, a process that leads to their breakdown and eventual dissolution and splitting into primitive images. The ego and superego identifications disintegrate and are replaced by "narcissistic identifications," i.e., by regressive fusions of superego, self and object images. The result may be a collapse of the total psychic system. These psychic events find expression in the schizophrenic's experiences of "the end of the world," his loss of identity, and feelings of having died.

In such psychotics secondary process thinking breaks down and they show severe disturbances of their sense of reality, i.e., in the perception of and the judgment regarding the object world and their own self. The ego functions and the emotional relationships with the real personal and inanimate objects deteriorate; misinterpretations of and inadequate responses to the object world abound.

The psychotic defense mechanisms aim at the maintenance and/or restitution of object and self representations. First, the real object world is used for this purpose. As I described in my Freud Anniversary Lecture (1967), the psychotic attempts to save himself by seeking support from without. He tries to buttress his ego functions by looking for emotional and ideational stimulants in the outside world. Using introjection and projection mechanisms, he borrows the ego and superego of other persons and projects parts of his own self onto certain objects in whose actions he can magically participate. If these efforts fail, he retreats from the object world. Regressively revived primitive object and self images, which have found their way to consciousness, then merge and join with remnants of realistic concepts to form new units. In this way, delusional object and self representations are built up, in disregard of reality, and are again reprojected onto the outside world.

Possibly, it is the depth and the nature of the regression that determine the development of a manic-depressive or a paranoid schizophrenic psychosis. Manic-depressives seem, at some point, to have reached a higher level in the differentiation and integration of the psychic systems. Consequently, the acute regressive process during their episodes does not go so far as in schizophrenics and is of a different type. Usually, it does not lead to a complete disintegration of the personality, but is reversible. It stops at a point that still allows a rather complete recovery. Bleuler (1911) described as a characteristic difference between the schizophrenic and the manic-depressive that the fears of the former refer to disasters occurring at the present time, those of the latter to future catastrophes. I believe that from the metapsychological point of view, this difference indicates that in the schizophrenic the object and self representations in the system ego actually break down to the point of dissolution, whereas the manic-depressive only feels threatened. His anxieties may be severe, but they are not true states of panic. The delusions in manic or melancholic states show characteristic differences from schizophrenic delusions, which, I believe, prove this point. As to the suicide of the melancholic, we recall Freud's statement (1917): that the love object is shown to be more powerful than the self. I would add that in the suicidal act the self, too, regains a feeling of power and achieves a final, though fatal, victory.

Clinical Features of the Manic-Depressive Personality

When we have an opportunity to observe cyclothymic patients before their break or during free intervals, we are often impressed by the richness of their sublimations. We are also surprised to see that as long as they are not ill, they may be delightful companions or marital partners, a feature that Bleuler mentioned especially. In their sexual life they may show full genital responsiveness, and emotionally, in contrast to schizophrenics, a touching warmth or, sometimes at least, an unusual, affectionate clinging to people they like. No doubt these persons have developed intensely vested emotional object relations and are potentially able to function extraordinarily well. Although they do not manifest a lack of inner resources, they seem to suffer from a specific ego weakness, which shows in their remarkable vulnerability, their intolerance of frustration, hurt, and disappointment.

Freud (1917) underlined the contradictory fact that these persons show simultaneously the tendency to too strong fixations to their love object and to a quick withdrawal of object cathexis. He pointed to Otto Rank's remark that the object choice of these persons must have been, to begin with, on a narcissistic basis, which permits them to regress easily to the narcissistic identification with the love object described in "Mourning and Melancholia." This is true, indeed; and we now know that it also applies to schizophrenics, although they seem to be arrested at a different narcissistic level.

Manic-depressives show a special kind of infantile narcissistic dependency on their love object. They require a constant supply of love and moral support from a highly valued love object, which need not be a person but may be represented by a powerful cause or organization of which they feel to be a part. As long as their "belief" in this object lasts, they are able to work with enthusiasm and high efficiency. Actually, however, these patients tend to make a masochistic choice of their partners or "causes" and to establish a life situation which sets the stage for their illness in that it is bound to disappoint them. Gero (1936) pointed out that manic-depressives belong to the masochistic personality type. When we have an opportunity to observe both the patient and his partner, we frequently find that they live in a peculiar "symbiotic" (Mahler, 1966) love relationship to each other. They feed on each other, but in a way that differs greatly from what we find in schizophrenics. In some instances, both partners are manic-depressives and break down alternately. In others, the partner of a manic-depressive may be an oral type of a different variety.

As a point of departure for the clinical study of the depressive conflict, the defenses, and the restitution mechanisms, I have chosen a short dream of patient N., a physician who was at the beginning of a depression. It had been precipitated by the alarming news that his mother had cancer of the uterus which required an immediate operation. During the preceding years N. had developed depressive states with a paranoid tinge, feelings of tiredness and exhaustion, and a series of psychosomatic and hypochondriacal symptoms and fears. They were initiated by his discovery that his wife had to undergo a gynecological operation which might affect her fertility.

N. dreamed that he had lost two of his "excellent" teeth. As they fell out, a fine thin silver cord that held them together went to pieces. N.'s immediate interpretation was that the two teeth represented himself and his mother, and that the connecting structure was the umbilical cord by which he was still attached to her. If his mother should die, he would feel as though he had lost his own self. The silver cord also represented his weak personality which, in the case of her death, would break down.

When this patient was not depressed, he manifested a rather conspicuous self-inflation. He expressed his feelings of being very good-looking, bright and smart, as "excellent" in his field as his teeth were. In these states he also talked incessantly of his worship of his mother, of her unending kindness and generosity, her great intelligence, her physical and mental strength. He had married his wife because she seemed to resemble his mother. Neither woman in any way corresponded to this ideal picture. They were neurotic, over-anxious, clinging women, and, as mentioned above, both suffered from gynecological conditions. The patient had managed for years to deny their weaknesses, including their physical handicaps. He himself had gone through several serious illnesses to which he had regularly responded with a depressive state and hypochondriacal complaints and fears. At other times, the patient exhibited unusual pride in his body.

His dream of the loss of his teeth referred to an experience in his adolescence when he had lost a tooth because his mother had neglected to arrange for adequate dental care for her children, in the same way as she had neglected her own present illness until it was almost too late for help. At the time of his tooth trouble, the boy had had to take matters into his own hands. He found a dentist who extracted the tooth, supposedly because it couuld not be saved. I may interject here that N. went into medicine because his mother's only brother as well as his own brother, a father substitute, were physicians; he had greatly admired these men. Hence his vocation, medicine, represented an ideal derived from both parental love objects, for his mother had told him repeatedly how she had nursed and cured him during his early childhood diseases. But an outstanding early childhood trauma had been the death of his maternal grandmother whom neither uncle nor brother had been able to cure. And both, uncle and brother, had been very gifted and promising young men who failed completely in their careers.

During the dream session the patient began to express his deep resentment of his mother's and his wife's inability to take proper care of their own health and that of their children. He blamed his mother for his severe childhood diseases, which had probably been neglected as much as his teeth. As the session proceeded, the patient started derogating the whole medical profession for its utter impotence. He talked of prominent but incompetent doctors who drew a fortune from their patients' ignorance. Finally, he indulged in severe self-reproaches. He blamed himself for being an incompetent, neglectful physician, uninterested in his patients and unable to cure them. He ended the session with an expression of deep guilt feelings toward his mother, whose sickness he had ignored and neglected, and diagnosed too late to save her. He left in a very depressed state.[1]

The dream and dream material, and the corresponding emotional reactions during this one session, show in a nutshell the prerequisites for the depressive conflict and its development.

---

[1] The patient's mother is still alive, but she suffered from a severe senile depression which required shock treatment.

The superfical symbolic interpretation offered by the patient immediately informs us about the pathogenic core of the manic-depressive personality. The thin, fragile silver cord in the dream indicates the weakness of his ego, resting on the intimate bond between himself and his mother. The two teeth are symbols of his love object and his self representations. The one tooth, representing his mother, is his own. The two teeth are connected. In other words, we see what I regard as characteristic of these patients: the insufficient separation between the representations of the love object and the self. There is a lack of distinct boundaries between them, which accounts for the patient's too strong fixation to the parental love objects. The self representations extend, so to speak, to the object representations; both show insufficient maturation and stability.

The patient gauges his love objects and himself by infantile value measures, predominantly by their omnipotent physical power and invulnerability. These standards are embedded in his high-flung ideal of a competent, in fact, omnipotent, physician who devotes his whole life to the rescue of his patients. In the patient's associations, we also observe the personification of his ego ideal, its insufficient distinction from the ideal parental image. He talks indiscriminately of the value or worthlessness of the whole medical science and profession, and of the individual physicians who represent parental images.

His example shows, furthermore, how in manic-depressives all ambitions and pursuits revolve only about representations of the overvalued parental love objects, which extend, as it were, to the whole world. This is why all their ego functions fail when the love object becomes disappointing and is depreciated. Frequently we observe that manic-depressives live on their ideals or their idealized partners rather than on their own ego. They exhibit an unusual pride in their idealizations, as though their own idealism would per se turn them into valuable human beings. I may add that the "idealism" of the manic-depressive differs greatly in type from that of the schizophrenic. The latter is more abstract, removed from personal objects; the former, as in the case of N., is mostly attached to a personal representative object. This accounts for the seeming "realism" of the manic-depressive, which clinical psychiatrists, such as Lange, have described.

The Development of the Depressive State

Clinically, this patient's depressive states were always "reactive" in nature. This time his depression was precipitated by his mother's illness, but at other times it had developed when he himself became ill or met with failure in his work, with financial difficulties or with disappointments in his love life. In other words, his depressive states would be precipitated by a failing either of his love object or of himself. But the analysis showed that, in either case, he felt hurt and blamed the love object for it. In fact, this patient expressed with unusual clarity his feeling that all his achievements or failures were due to the effectiveness or failure of his "intuition"—in German, *Eingebung;* that is, all achievements or failures were the result of what had been given to him. He regarded his ego functions not as his own productions but as reproductions of what he had received.

We understand that in disregard of his potential abilities, his self representations retained the infantile conception of a helpless self drawing its strength from a powerful, ideal love object. He tried to keep the image of this love object hypercathected, by constantly depriving the self image of its libidinal cathexis and pouring it on the object image. He then had to bolster his self image again by a reflux of libido from the image of his love object. These continuous cathectic fluctuations found expression in corresponding emotional vacillations. In his actual attitudes he would show a mixture of conceited and humble, sadomasochistic and protective behavior to the love object, and simultaneously demand continuous evidence of the latter's value, power, and devotion.

This position is inevitably unstable and facilitates easy, rapid, and cathectic changes on the slightest provocation. The manic-depressive protects himself against this danger by strong pathological safeguards, essentially by the denial mechanisms which I have discussed before and which were so beautifully described by Lewin (1950). He can maintain a lasting libidinal overcathexis of the love-object image only by constant efforts to deny both his own intrinsic value and the weaknesses of the real love object, i.e., by a continuous illusory overestimation of the love object and an equally illusory or even delusional under- or overestimation of himself. If he meets with disappointment or failure, the denial mechanisms will either break down or have to be so fortified that the patient may go into a manic state.

In contradistinction to schizophrenic feelings of grandeur, the manic state represents, I believe, a state of lasting participation of the self in the imagined omnipotence of the love object. The manic can afford to discharge his aggression fully and diffusely. Since, by his denial of the existence of unpleasure and destruction, the whole world becomes a valley of unending and indestructible pleasure, his aggression can do no damage.

To give an example: A patient in a hypomanic state, which terminated a nine-month period of depression, told me that she felt so voracious: she would like to eat up everything—food, books, pictures, persons, the whole world. When I jokingly and with deliberate provocation remarked that this seemed to be quite bad and dangerous, what would she do if everything were eaten up, she said, highly amused: "Oh no, the world is so rich, there is no end to it. Things are never finished. I cannot hurt anybody or anything."

If the denial mechanisms fail, the patient's first reaction will be to master the narcissistic injury and build up his self-esteem by disparaging the love object in a way as illusory as he had previously glorified it. He will try to repair the hurt by switching the whole aggressive cathexis to the object image and the libidinal cathexis to the self image. In adolescence this mechanism was still effective in my patient: he asserted himself by derogating his neglectful mother and by reactive identification with her ideal image. Thus he went ahead and took care of his tooth, instead of and in spite of his mother. But he indicated in his dream that unconsciously he regarded his success—for good reasons—as a failure; he actually lost his tooth, which in the dream was equated with his own self and his mother. In fact, manic-depressives may react to success in love or work in the same way as to failure: with either a hypomanic or manic state or with a depression. Their reaction depends on what the success means: an aggressive self-assertion by derogation and destruction of the love object, or a present from the powerful love object. Their inability to accept success is not always or not only an expression of their moral masochism and of their guilt conflict.

One of my depressive patients regularly responded to achievements by a struggle between feelings of tremendous pride and of rising anxiety and emptiness. He felt as though the most precious thing in life were gone; life would be empty forever. He lost his interest in his previous endeavors and finally felt that his whole work had been worthless anyhow. This response is merely more intense and pathological than the well-known attitude of narcissistic people who value an object so long as they cannot get it, and depreciate it as soon as they have got it.

The manic-depressive cannot bear a self-assertion through derogation of his love object. He tries to avoid such a situation by keeping the valued love object at a distance, as it were, which protects it from deflation. The simultaneous libidinal hypercathexis of the object clearly distinguished this attitude from the schizoid remoteness. Since the love object has to stay unattainable, he may avoid success by delaying a final achievement or the real consummation of a love relationship, for which he has desperately struggled.

Evidently, he is so afraid of a lasting self-inflation at the expense of the love object because it might lead to a complete libidinal withdrawal and unleashing of all his severe hostility on this one object. His fear of a "loss of the object" is fear of a destructive absorption of the "good, powerful" object image by the self image. Here is a situation that induces an immediate and intense need to retrieve his old position. He will be overperceptive of any flaw in his achievements, and use it to confirm his own weakness and to reinstate the strength and value of the object. This is why success afflicts the manic-depressive in the same way as failure. Both may arouse an initial hostile derogation of the love object, which cannot be tolerated, and which yields to a rapid reversal, undoing, and denial of the previous situation.

There will be an immediate, increased reflux of aggression from the love object to the self image, but by this time the pathological process may have proceeded so far that the patient is too depleted of libido to recathect the object sufficiently. All he can achieve may be an aggressive devaluation of both: of himself and of his love object. He will return to his position of participation, but in the worthlessness instead of the value of the love object. Many patients, especially those with chronic "simple" depressions, and many depressive children may represent this picture. They manifest a general pessimism, disillusionment, and lack of interest in life and in themselves. They maintain a continuous denial of the world's and their own value.

I have stated previously that I regard this as the primary depressive disturbance, which may be distinguished from the secondary attempts at defense and restitution. Some patients give evidence indeed of very intense efforts to recathect and build up the love-object image again, and to regain their original unstable equilibrium.

We will now investigate the defenses which the patient uses for this purpose. Since his libidinal resources are fading, his first line of defense will be to turn to the real object world for support. He will try to resolve the inner conflict by help from without (Jacobson, 1967). He wants to use the love of an outside person, to whom he has attached his ideal object image, as a stimulant for his failing ability to love. This is the stage when the patient, in his frantic endeavor to stop the depressive process, persistently and increasingly clings to the person he has chosen for this purpose. He gathers all his available libido and pours it on this one person, in a desperate appeal to give such convincing evidence of unending love and indestructible power and value as the evoke a libidinal response in himself, and in this way enable him to re-establish an ideal object image that cannot be deflated and destroyed.

It is a phase of acting out that we can well observe in the treatment of depressives in the transference situation. The patient exhausts himself in efforts to concentrate on the analyst whatever love is still at his disposal. He behaves in an extremely submissive, masochistic, and at the same time sadistic way: he gives himself up to the analyst, but expects the impossible in return. He desires the analyst's constant presence and tries to blackmail him into a continuous show of omnipotent love, value, and power.

Much depends, at this stage, on the analyst's handling of the transference situation. As the depressive episode develops, things may get out of hand. The analyst may no longer be able to live up to the patient's expectations. Analyst and patient will be in a trap. The patient will be less and less able to tolerate the analyst's warmth and sympathy, which, failing to elicit an adequate libinal response, will only increase the disappointment and the hostile claim for a more powerful love. In his fear of a complete breakdown of the object image, the patient regresses a step further. We realize that the deserted child prefers an aggressive, strong love object to its loss. Correspondingly, the patient may now attempt to hold on at least to the reanimated image of an omnipotent, not loving, but punitive, sadistic object. This manifests itself in the patient's increasing, masochistic provocations of the analyst's anger, to a show of aggression, which may bring temporary relief but will actually promote the pathological process.

If the outside world has failed to help the patient in the solution of this conflict, he may turn to his last line of defense: retreat from the object world. The conflict may become fully internalized and an acute, blatantly psychotic depressive syndrome may develop.

Before I turn to the problem of melancholia, I should like to interpolate that for reasons of simplification I have so far deliberately neglected the superego aspects of the depressive conflict.

The melancholic introjection mechanisms seem to represent the last failing attempt at a recovery of the lost original position. What they achieve is at least to restore the powerful object image by marking it a part of the self. What happens, is briefly, this:

The patient's final escape from the real object world, first of all, facilitates a withdrawal of cathexis from the realistic part of the object representations. Consequently, the object images are split up. During the last phase of the conflict the archaic wishful image of a powerful, but punitive, love object was built up—as against the image of a weak, bad love object. This reanimated, inflated wishful image is now dissolved as a representation in the system ego and is absorbed by the superego, whereas the deflated worthless object image merges with the self representations. A dangerous schism develops, which still reflects the patient's efforts to rescue the valued object by keeping its wishful concept protected from his destructive impulses at an unattainable distance from the denigrated self image. Accordingly, the aggressive forces accumulate within the superego and cathect the self image, while the ego gathers the reduced libidinal forces and surrenders to the assault.

Thus the patient succeeds in rescuing the powerful love object, but only by a complete deflation or even destruction of the self. The incessant complaints and self-accusations of the melancholic, his exhibition of his helplessness and his moral worthlessness, are both a denial and a confession of guilt: of the crime of having destroyed the valuable love object. Both indeed tell the truth: the powerful image has collapsed as an object representation in the ego, but it has been reconstituted in the superego.

These introjection processes differ from normal or neurotic ego and superego identifications. In normal and neurotic superego identifications, the object representations in the ego system are maintained, whereas the melancholic introjection of the idealized (powerful, but punitive) object image into the superego goes along with a giving up of the "good" object representations in the ego, and leads to their merging with and a personification of the superego. This is facilitated by an insufficient initial separation between the wishful object image and the ego ideal. The introjection mechanism in the ego, on the other hand, leads not to an identification of the ego with the love object but to a merging of the "worthless" object image with the image of the self. The ego does not assume any characteristics of the love object; the self is perceived and is treated by the superego as though it were a deflated love object.

My discussion and metapsychological description of the problem of depression have been of necessity one-sided and schematic. I have deliberately left out of consideration the corresponding instinctual processes. In the frame of this chapter it has seemed to me to be of lesser importance that the melancholic divulges cannibalistic incorporation and anal-sadistic ejection fantasies. All psychotics, schizophrenic and manic-depressive, manifest such deeply regressive id material, which corresponds to the processes I discussed: the threatening destruction of the object and self representations and their restitution by their partial merging.

The questions I have tried to explore in this chapter are: where, in psychotic depression, these fusions, i.e. introjections, take place from the structural point of view, and what they mean with regard to the pathology of the ego and superego functions. This is why I wished to concentrate on the following issues: on the importance of the concepts of self representations and of wishful, good and bad, object representations for an understanding of the depressive type of identifications; on the cathectic fluctuations and shifts from self to object representations and the reverse, and their fusions; on the struggle of the manic-depressive to maintain and recover his position of participation in the power of his love object; on the defensive function of the patient's clinging to the real, outside love object during the depressed period; and finally, on the melancholic symptom formation as an expression of his last, failing attempts at restitution of a powerful love object in the superego.

Naturally, the phases in the development of the depressive conflict and its pathological solution are interwoven and cannot be distinguished so clearly as they are in this description. Even during the free intervals we usually find that the manic-depressive shows more or less continuous vacillations in his mood and efficiency, and tries to recover his narcissistic equilibrium once by clinging to his real love objects and by claims for support from without, and then again by temporary retreats into a pseudo self-sufficiency and attempts to resort only to his own superego standards. This is why I consider it not quite sufficient to say that during his free intervals he shows compulsive attitudes. Paranoid schizophrenics, too, may develop compulsive attitudes; they are conspicuously rigid. The main difference between the attitudes of the manic-depressive and the compulsive personality, however, seems to be the former's simultaneous or alternate leaning on an idealized love object and on his own superego. He suffers from mixture of pseudo independence and dependency, which true compulsives do not show.

THE CHILD'S DISCOVERY OF HIS IDENTITY AND HIS ADVANCE TO OBJECT RELATIONS AND SELECTIVE IDENTIFICATIONS

As the child enters his second year of life, changes in the nature of his relations to the object world set in, which are indicative of his gradual transition from the early infantile symbiotic phase to the stage of individuation and of beginning secondary ego autonomy. They mark the introduction into the psychic organization of a new time category, the concept of the future. Moreover, they presuppose the ability to distinguish single physical and mental features of the love objects, to compare and to perceive differences between objects—animate and inanimate—as well as between the objects and the self. When the child has advanced to this point, his narcissistic strivings begin to take a new turn: their aims change. Expressive of the child's rapid body growth and the growth of his ego, ambitious strivings develop which no longer revolve exclusively about wishes to control magically the love objects on which he depends. In their stead, ambitious efforts for realistic achievements can be observed, which seem in part to be independent of the child's instinctual needs. But under the influence of his instinctual conflicts these strivings soon become highly charged with aggressive energy and find increasing expression in competitive struggles with admired, powerful love objects, in particular with his rivals. As these trends develop, the child's desires to remain part of his love objects, or to make them part of his own self, will slowly recede and give way to wishes for realistic likeness with them. This goal can be achieved by virtue of selective identifications, based on mechanisms of "partial introjection."

Evidently, this new and advanced type of identification represents a compromise between the child's need to retain the symbiotic situation, to depend and lean on the need-gratifying, protective, and supportive love objects, and opposing tendencies to loosen the symbiotic ties by way of aggressive narcissistic expansion and independent ego functioning. Under the influence of oedipal rivalry, this conflict will reach its first climax toward the end of the oedipal period and will then be resolved by superego formation. But it will be intensely revived during adolecence, and come to its final peak and find its definite solution in the adolescent's rupture of his oedipal ties and the establishment of ego and superego autonomy.

To return to the preoedipal child, it seems that his identifications with the mother, both as the aggressor (A. Freud, 1936, 1949) and as the person who imposes instinctual restrictions (A. Freud, 1936), pave the way to these new processes of identification. In contrast to his magic fantasies of fusion and his primitive affective identifications and merely formal imitations, they have a meaningful content and a realistic aim. Such an aim can be reached by way of deep-seated modifications of the ego, which now really assumes certain characteristics of the admired object.

This presupposes a new stage in the development of the self images: the distinction between realistic and wishful self images. In fact, the ego cannot acquire a realistic likeness to the love object unless admired traits of this object become enduringly introjected into the child's wishful self images. These wishful self images thus become expressive of both: of the child's own ambitions, of his own strivings for narcissistic expansion and ego growth, and of admired characteristics of his love objects. In so far as the realistic self representations become a mirror of the ego, they now begin to reflect the traits actually taken over from the object of identification, so that a likeness between object and self images can now be experienced on a realistic basis. This new step in the development of the self images and the growing distinction between wishful and realistic images of the self are so meaningful because they are a prerequisite for the establishment of ego ideal and ego goals, i.e., of realistic goals regarding the future. This will be discussed below.

But I may here emphasize that the growing distinction between wishful self images and realistic self representations has very significant implications regarding the development of the feelings of identity.

Whereas the child's wishful self images increasingly give him direction by pointing to potential changes in the future, his representations of the actual self point to his present state and to the past stages in his development. Thus their differentiation must strengthen the feeling of selfsameness in spite of continuous changes.

Of course, the child will be protected from relapses into the world of magic fantasies of fusions and early infantile types of identifications to the extent to which he succeeds in building up true object relations which no longer display the narcissistic qualities described above. This again presupposes the constitution of well-defined self representations separated by distinct, firm boundaries from the likewise realistic representations of his love objects.

However, I cannot follow up the fascinating interplay between these developmental processes without first trying to derive some orientation from a preliminary schematic survey. Its sole purpose is to correlate the various stages of energic and structural differentiation to the constitution and cathexis of object and self representations, and to the corresponding ideational, affective, and functional development.

We may visualize the process of structural and energic differentiation as passing through the following infantile stages:

1. The primal (embryonal) condition of diffuse dispersion of undifferentiated drive energy in the unstructured "primal" psychophysiological self; discharge occurs predominantly by silent physiological processes.

2. With birth, growing cathexis of the perception and memory systems, of the motor apparatus and of the pregenital erogenous zones sets in; pleasurable and unpleasurable sensations begin to be perceived and become attached to, though still confused with, beginning outside perceptions. Energic differentiation occurs; libidinal and aggressive cathectic gathering poles are formed around nuclei of as yet unorganized

and disconnected memory traces. Discharge to the outside begins by way of primitive, biologically prepatterned (instinctive) reactions to internal and external stimuli. Affective organ language develops.

3a. The stage of beginning structural differentiation and ego formation. Pleasure principle and "primary process" prevail. Unconscious (early preoedipal) fantasy life, pregenital sexual and affectomotor activity begin to develop, although affective organ language is still predominant. Multiple, rapidly changing and not yet clearly distinguished part images of love objects and body part images are formed and linked up with the memory traces of past pleasure-unpleasure experiences and become vested with libidinal and aggressive forces. Corresponding affect components arise; impulsive affectomotor reactions to external and internal stimuli change in quick sequence, reflecting the variability of unconscious imagery, the cathectic fluidity, and the tendency to immediate drive discharge; signal affects begin to become effective.

3b. When the child learns to walk and talk and acquires urinary and bowel control, a more organized stage sets in. Object and self awareness grows, perception and organization of memory traces expand. The object imagery gradually extends to the surrounding animate and inanimate world. Language symbols, functional motor activity, and reality testing develop. But magic animistic fantasy life, preverbal at first, predominates and remains concentrated on the mother until preoedipal and later oedipal triangle configurations shape up. Object constancy develops. Specific affect qualities and more sustained emotional states come into being, influenced by increasing formation of countercathexes.

4. Infantile sexuality reaches its climax; fusion and neutralization of sexual and aggressive drives has set in. Thought processes are organized, functional motor activity and object relations develop rapidly. Accordingly, single affects begin to merge into compound fusions. Emotional and instinctual control is being established; tension tolerance increases. Preponderance of libido and enduring libidinal object investments develop. As tender attachments grow and affects become attached to ego functions, awareness of self begins to extend to awareness of emotional and thought processes, of ego attitudes and ego functions. A concept of the self as an entity that has continuity and direction is formed. Reality principle and "secondary" process become more dominant. Signal anxiety (castration fear) exerts a drastic influence on repression and countercathectic formations.

5. Drive neutralization is greatly enhanced by superego formation; the latency period begins. Physical and mental activities make rapid progress; conceptual thinking develops and expands; maturation and structural organization of ideational and emotional processes advance with the growing ability of the ego to bind down psychic energy in enduring cathexes; increasingly realistic preconscious representations of the animate and inanimate, concrete and abstract object world are formed, and can be stabilized by their firm and lasting cathexis with libidinal, aggressive, and neutralized forces. The superego establishes a lasting and dominant control over the cathexis of the self representations. Superego fear becomes the leading affect signal. In the process of final taming, repatterning, modification, and organization of the affects under the influence of the superego, enduring feelings and feeling states develop on a large scale as an expression of the ego's state and reactivity. The subtle differentiation of the emotional qualities proceeds hand in hand with an increasing awareness of the qualities of emotional experiences. These changes and the establishment of physical, intellectual, and moral achievement standards enhance the experience of a consistent self that maintains its continuity despite changes.

We know, of course, that the most influential factor in the child's development is the child-parent relationship, whose part in the building up of the ego we may summarize briefly as follows. Parental influences stimulate the growth of the ego and support the control, partial inhibition, partial fusion, neutralization and utilization of sexual and aggressive drives in the service of the ego and of "secondary"-process functioning. Thus they contribute greatly to the psychosexual development and the maturation of feelings, thinking, acting, and the sense of reality, and promote the establishment of aim-inhibited personal and social relations and of solid identifications with the love objects in the ego and superego. In general, they promote the child's gradual individuation and his advance from the psychobiologically determined dependency situation to independent ego activity spreading out to social, cultural, and eventually ego-syntonic sexual pursuits.

Even though we are sufficiently familiar with the parental influence on infantile development, we must at least focus on certain aspects of it which are significant in the present context. To be sure, the goal of education as I outlined it above can be reached only in an atmosphere of parental love and care, with sufficient libidinal stimulation and gratification. Since it promotes the establishment of stable, enduring libidinal cathexes both of the objects and of the self, parental love is the best guarantee for the development of object and self constancy, of healthy social and love relations, and of lasting identifications, and hence for a normal ego and superego formation. However, the instinctual and emotional frustrations and prohibitions, combined with parental demands and stimulation of social and cultural pursuits, also make significant contributions to the development of an effective, independently functioning, and self-reliant ego.

They teach the child to relinquish not only his preoedipal and oedipal sexual drives but also his early infantile magic expectance of support, protection, and wish fulfillment from without. On his way to this goal, the child passes through experiences of continual deprivations, hurt, frustration, and disappointments in his parents, which arouse intense feelings of ambivalence. Although dangerous, the child's ambivalence conflicts can be utilized by the ego for very constructive purposes. We remember that at first the child wants to take in what he likes and to spit out what he dislikes; to ascribe to his self what is pleasant and to the "strange" outside object what is unpleasant. In other words, he tends to turn aggression toward the frustrating objects and libido toward the self. Hence frustrations, demands, and restrictions, within normal bounds, reinforce in principle the process of discovery and distinction of objects and self; they throw the child back upon his resources and stimulate progressive forms of identification with the parents, which open the road to realistic independent achievements. Enhancing the narcissistic endowment of his ego, they promote the eventual establishment of secondary ego and superego autonomy.

Yet overgratifications, no less than severe frustrations, tend to induce regressive fantasies of reunion between self and love object. Constant overgratification or excessive frustration may therefore delay the child in establishing firm boundaries between the objects and the self, and hence may interfere with ego and superego formation and with the normal process of individuation. However, there are other and even more dangerous parental attitudes which may arrest this process. They are connected with the child's prolonged and only gradually receding symbiosis with his parents, which we must now examine more carefully from the viewpoint of the parents.

The earliest relationship between mother and child is of a truly symbiotic nature, for not only does the helpless infant need the mother and feed on her, but the mother also needs and—emotionally—even feeds on the child. This has been beautifully described by Benedek (1959), who showed how at any developmental stage the parents identify with their child's needs by reviving their own experiences of this phase. The significance of these mutual identifications between parents and child for the development of the sense of identity had been stressed by Greenacre (1958). But Benedek also emphasized that the childhood memories which the child revives in his parents not only induce identifications with him but also fortify the parents' identifications with their own parents (his grandparents). With regard to the child's individuation, it is indeed important to visualize the interplay between these double identifications in parental attitudes, and to consider their different roles and nature. The parents' identifications with their own parents have a long history. These identifications have modeled their ego and superego and remain the stronghold of the parental position, although different aspects are revived and brought to awareness by the child's changing stages. The parental identifications with the child are of a different order. Born of memories of the infantile past, they are limited to passing and changing fantasy and feeling identifications only, which serve the empathic understanding of the child and must be kept in bounds so as not to undermine the parental position

In discussing the development of empathy, Olden (1953, 1958) has shown how a mother's empathic understanding of her child suffers when she actually steps down to his infantile level or, the reverse, when she expects the child to react or act on her own level. In either case the mother is unable to distinguish the child's need from her own and to subordinate her own identifications with the child to a loving acceptance of him as a separate individual. Even in the earliest symbiotic stage of the mother-infant relationship, the best emotional climate is indeed one in which the mother prepares the process of the child's individuation by a kind of maternal love that is aware of the differences between her own and the child's needs and roles, and tries to gratify both. In fact, parental attitudes betraying the tendency to sustain a symbiosis with the child by "merging" with him are harmful in many respects. In recent years such pathological types of prolonged symbiosis between mother and child have been the subject of many studies, especially on psychotic children (Mahler and Elkisch, 1953; Mahler, 1957; Elkisch and Mahler, 1959).

Suffice it here to emphasize that such fantasies of merging with the child can be observed in cases where parents sacrifice their own needs to those of the child to the point of self extinction, as well as in situations where they either overprotect or dominate the child and keep him passive and dependent, or treat him as but an extension of their own self, ignoring his individual needs and sacrificing them to their own narcissistic requirements. All such attitudes increase the potential dangers to the preoedipal ego and to the superego precursors—dangers arising from the symbiotic nature of the mother-child relationship and from the indistinct line of demarcation between maternal and self images in the child. The child's fear of separation and his desire to maintain or regain the original mother-child unit are so strong, even normally, that he tends to resist the acceptance of sharply defined boundaries between his self and the mother.

It is pertinent in this context to emphasize once more that the small child's fantasies of fusion with his love objects are expressive of the early infantile situation, in which he must actually borrow the mother's ego for his own need fulfillments. If this situation is maintained for an unduly long period, the child's object relations may remain fixated forever at this primitive narcissistic level. This may be caused by unfavorable parental attitudes of a narcissistic, masochistic, or hostile, neglectful, overdepriving, or overgratifying and overprotective nature. But it may also be the result of a constitutional weakness, deficiency, or retarded maturation of the infantile ego, which may compel the child to lean heavily on the mother's ego for need gratification, support or control. The normal child seems to show the first signs of awareness of a "non-I" (Spitz, 1957) around the age of three months. Precisely how the development of self imagery and of self awareness proceeds from then on is a question which is difficult to answer, at least with regard to the first year of life. At any rate, to the extent to which the child begins to cathect and employ the executive organs of his own body and to acquire the physical and mental functions that will turn him into an autonomous, independent human being in his own right, he will be ready to develop the outlines of his future identity and, concomitantly,

to build up advanced forms of personal interrelations and identifications.

In general, about the age of two or two and a half years the child's
ego maturation, his ability to walk and to talk, the ever-widening scope
of his perceptive and locomotor functions, his increasing manual accomplishments, his weaning and cleanliness training, etc., have advanced enough to bring about the startling discovery of his own identity,
the experience of "I am I." It must be understood that this discovery
does not imply that the child has already built up an enduring, consistent
concept of his self as an entity. This concept undergoes many changes,
and induces an increasing feeling of direction and continuity as the
psychic organization grows, becomes differentiated, structured, organized and reorganized, until maturity is reached.

The child's discovery of his identity occurs in the wake of important
changes in his relations to his first love objects—changes which contribute a great deal to his individuation and his awakening sense of
identity. From the observation of early infantile and psychotic imagery
we may infer that in the child's first object images—apart from their
projective features—perceptions of different objects probably become
merged into varying image composites. But, significantly, the child,
already at the age of about eight months, sometimes even earlier, begins
to distinguish different objects: his mother from his father, from the
nurse, from strangers, etc.[2] The distinction between objects can probably proceed more rapidly and consistently than the distinction between
self and objects, because perception of the external world is easier than
self perception and, besides, because the child normally has less instinctual motivation for a fusion between different objects than for a re-
merging with his mother. In fact, the child's insatiable instinctual appetites stimulate his ability to discriminate between persons who may
offer him supplementary gratifications and those who bar his way to
need fulfillment. In any case, the beginning constitution of boundaries
between images of different objects ushers in the development of specific and different relations to his various love objects. Concomitantly
the child's first envy and rivalry conflicts take shape, conflicts which
have a decisive influence on the processes under discussion.

[2] At about fifteen to eighteen months he starts using "no" (Spitz, 1957)

A this point Greenacre's (1958) statement on identity, referring to likenesses with other and to differences from them, begins to become pertinent. Of course, experiences of likeness are bound to arise from the child's close intimacy with his mother and, as Greenacre stresses, will be favored by the mutual affective identifications between mother and child, to which I referred above. But what about the experiences of differences, which are a prerequisite for the development of identity feelings?

We know that by the end of the first year, the little boy or girl begins to show definite acquisitiveness, possessiveness, and manifestations of envy. To be sure, these ambivalent acquisitive wishes and the child's oral envy, which soon induce intense feelings of rivalry toward the father, siblings, and other objects, are the strongest incentive for his first comparisons. They teach him to distinguish, first, between his needs, his gratifications, and his frustrations; then between his and others' gratifications, and between his belongings and those of others. Passing through many frustrations, disappointments, failures, and corresponding hostile experiences of envy, rivalry and competition, the child eventually learns the difference between wishful and more or less realistic self and object images. Thus, not only the loving but also the hostile components of the infantile self- and object-directed strivings furnish the fuel that enables the child to develop his feeling of identity and the testing of external and inner reality, and on this basis to build up his identifications and object relations. This again calls attention to the significant role of aggression in these developmental processes, which has been stressed by Freud and other authors.

At first the child's acquisitive strivings are of course concentrated on his mother. But as soon as he discovers that he has rivals, he begins to displace the envious hostile impulses provoked by his frustrations from the mother onto these rivals. Projecting his own instinctual desires onto them, the child now wants to acquire what they possess and apparently received from the mother. From wanting the same gratifications and possessions as the rival, there is only a short but decisive step to looking for likeness and wanting likeness with him. Increasing love and admiration for the superior and also gratifying rival will reinforce this quest. However, frustration, hostility, and envy will compel the child also to take cognizance of such differences as may be responsible for his frustrations and shortcomings.

We note above that the child's need to keep the "good," gratifying love object as part of himself, and to spit out and rid himself of the "bad", frustrating object, tends to throw him on his own resources, to increase the narcissistic endowment of his ego, and to stimulate ambitious strivings for narcissistic expansion and independent accomplishments. Now we may add that his feelings of envy and rivalry, while arousing desires for likeness, will propel him more forcefully toward delineations from his rivals than toward distinction from his main love object, the mother. Moreover, these feelings will promote his discrimination between such rival objects.

The mother-infant relationship must certainly be regarded as the matrix of identity formation, but the child's individuation which depends so greatly on separation from the object and on the discovery of differences soon gains momentum from his more ambivalent relations to his rivals than from his close intimacy with his mother.[3] Of course this simplifies matters considerably, since the child displays envy and rivalry feelings toward the mother as well, to the extent to which he develops closeness with his father and other rivals.

So far I have described how the child's finding of his identity, although dependent on the maturational growth of his ego, gains tremendous support from his beginning emotional relations to his first love objects and especially from his preoedipal envy and rivalry conflicts. I shall now focus on the influence which the child's identity feelings exercise upon his object relations and identifications. We realize that the discovery of his identity, which is so greatly promoted by aggressive forces, is a prerequisite for his gradual transition from the stage of primitive fusions and identifications with his love objects to the level of true object relations and of only partial and selective identifications with them. In fact, the child cannot establish emotional investments in other persons as objects which are different from his own self until he is able to experience his own identity; and since active strivings to acquire likenesses to others are also motivated by the discovery of differences from them, these strivings cannot develop either until the child has become aware of such differences.

Considering the infantile cathectic conditions, we realize, moreover,

[3] I believe this is confirmed by observations of children in their second year. At that time they are already quite capable of perceiving that people differ from them particularly if these persons arouse their envy and rivalry.

that enduring selective identification processes, which follow a steady course and direction and alter the structure of the ego consistently, cannot set in before the child's object-libidinal and narcissistic strivings have advanced to a certain level. The initially continuous vacillations between self- and object-directed cathexes and between the different object cathexes must have sufficiently subsided to permit comparatively lasting emotional investments in both: in objects and in the self. Such stable investments can only develop in the wake of processes of unification and consolidation of the object and self images. These processes call on the libidinal resources of the child, which are the indispensable ferment needed to forge "total" concepts from the opposing images of good and bad love objects and of a good and bad self.

I mentioned above the child's inclination to displace hostility from the mother to his rivals. Facilitating the gradual fusion of good and bad maternal images into a unified "good" but also sometimes "bad" mother, these shifts certainly assist the development of tension tolerance and of those feelings of pleasurable anticipation which introduce the category of time and secure the establishment of lasting emotional relations with the mother, i.e., of object constancy. This implies that the development of personal relations with the mother precedes the acceptance of rival figures as total ("good" and also "bad") persons. This second step is not an easy achievement for the child. It must wait until his intense ambivalence toward the rival gradually subsides under the influence of reactive libidinal strivings, and his love wins out over the hostile, envious, jealous, derogatory feelings. The increasing prevalence of libidinal over aggressive investments concomitantly builds up the libidinal endowment of the self images, which is a precondition for the achievement of normal self esteem and for the formation of a unified concept of the self. Since the latter represents a decisive step in the development of identity feelings, this again underscores the all-important role of the libidinal forces in this process, and hence of the mother's love which helps to generate them.

I have emphasized the child's earlier delineation from the hated rivals, which soon promotes the development of his sense of identity more than does his closeness to the mother. Considering the identifications, in contrast to the object relations, it appears that this factor also tends more easily to induce partial identifications with rivals than with the main love object. To be sure, from an early age on, one can also observe identifications which appear to be induced primarily and predominantly by libidinal wishes to maintain, if not union, at least the utmost closeness with the love object, by virtue of actually becoming like it. Such identifications seem to arise directly from the child's earliest fantasy and feeling identifications with the mother rather than from instinctual conflicts. For this reason they hardly bear the imprint of the child's sexual and ambivalence struggles and do not become an important tool for his defenses. Predominantly centered about the main love object, such identifications can still be observed in adults, in situations of close intimacy, such as, e.g., between marital partners who may ultimately resemble each other physically, emotionally, ideationally, and in their behavior.

In general, though, the infantile identification processes become increasingly centered about rival figures. This will be discussed more thoroughly in connection with the processes of idealization. At this point I should like to comment on Freud's assumption that identifications, being regressive in nature, tend to liberate aggression. Hartmann and Loewenstein (1962) regard this hypothesis as valid, as far as it refers to superego formation. I do not share their or Freud's opinion, which I believe is the result of inferences drawn from Freud's study of the narcissistic identifications in melancholics. I believe that it is the severe hostility of the psychotic toward his love object which, leading to inner object loss, makes him resort to regressive, primitive, narcissistic identifications, i.e., to fantasies of partial or total fusions with objects. But the selective ego and superego identifications of the normal child cannot be regarded as regressive phenomena of this type, since they do not arise in place of object relations. In fact, the child's object relations and identifications evolve hand in hand and exercise a mutually beneficial influence on each other. As I have emphasized, identifications seem actually to serve the absorption and neutralization of aggression, which can be vested increasingly in countercathectic formations and be discharged in ego functions. Regarding the beneficial influence of object relations on identifications, the latter are all the more successful, the more the child's libidinal forces predominate, and his ego, gaining strength, becomes able to tolerate frustration and to build up sublimations. For this reason, the preoedipal precursors of the superego still reflect, in part, the small child's own boundless cruelty, which cannot be toned down with the support of identifications. For the same reasons, enduring selective identifications with the predominant rival, the father, cannot be established before the child's loving feelings toward him are sufficiently strengthened to permit relations with him, too, as with a total "good and bad" person. In fact, the better the totality of other persons and of the self can be experienced, the more easily can the distinction, the preception of the differences between one's own self and others be tolerated, and likeness not only discovered but accepted, desired, and acquired.

This implies that the establishment of object and self constancy must be regarded as a very important prerequisite for both a healthy process of identification and normal superego formation. Conversely, the development of moral standards supports this merging of "good" and "bad" object and self images into concepts of total "good and also bad" persons and a total "good and also bad" self.

While this re-emphasizes the role of love in the establishment of sound identifications, they will forever reflect the inherent ambivalence to which they owe their existence. Indeed, any kind of identification implies: "I don't need you; if you don't want to do it for me, I can do it myself; and if you don't want to give it to me, I can give it to myself." While identifications thus display the child's touching dependency on his parents, they bring him closer step by step to the state of independence and to the time when the parents will become dispensable. Moreover, the selectivity of identifications increasingly expresses the child's rebellious struggle for the development and maintenance of his own independent identity, since it means: "In this respect I like you and want to be like you, but in other respects I don't like you and don't want to be like you; I want to be different, in fact myself."

The process of consolidation of self and object representations advances hand in hand with processes of increasing drive fusion and drive neutralization under the influence of ego formation. Just as discrimination between external objects precedes the distinction between them and one's own self, the experience of other persons' totality develops earlier than the concept of a unified self. In fact, the formation of such a concept depends not only on the child's libidinal investment in himself but on the general growth of the ego that leads to organization and coordination, correlation and interaction of sensory, instinctual, emotional experiences with ideational preocesses and with the perceptive and executive functions.

In this connection it is of interest that children with precocious ego formation seem to establish their identity at a very early stage and to show early signs of discriminating object relations. Displaying pride in their difference from others, they may even succeed very early in reversing roles with older siblings, not only by perceiving and aggressively exploiting their own advantages, but also by actually greater accomplishments.[4]

Of course, the interplay and interdependence of these developmental processes make it difficult to decide how far the precocious ego maturation of such a child is responsible for the early onset of his discriminating object relations, his identifications, his identity formation, or the reverse: how far his speedy object-libidinal development may influence and promote his ego formation. This was already implied in what I have said about the processes of identification. They begin to show direction and to become more enduring, more consistent and more selective, to the extent to which libidinal development makes progress and personal relations become stable and specified. This will be discussed in greater detail in connection with the child's finding of his sexual identity and his oedipal development. Here I want to stress the following point: only by becoming enduring, selective, and consistent, can identifications gradually be integrated, become part of the ego, permanently modify its structure, and support the organization and stabilization of the ego's defense system. This advances ego formation and the establishment of secondary ego autonomy and concomitantly the process of identity formation to the point where the child becomes aware of having a coherent self that has continuity and remains the same despite and in the midst of changes. Here the different influence on the feeling of identity of such enduring identifications with objects, as compared to

[4] I recently observed a precocious and rather aggressive little boy of one, who is already able to outdo his three-year-old brother by playing off his "role" as "the preferred baby." Whenever he covets the other's toys or food, he tries to snatch them away from the older child, crying righteously, "baby, baby!" His mother correctly interprets this as meaning: "*I* should get it; after all, *I* am the baby." At the same time this little boy begins to identify and compete actively, and sometimes successfully, with his more passive older brother. I would regard this behavior as evidence of the awakening feeling of his identity and of his particular role in the family group. He indeed acts, and already is regarded and treated, as the aggressive but uniquely advanced and adorable baby. His mutual interrelations with mother and grandmother appear to be affectionate but are already rather different in nature. The father and his interrelationship with his boys could not be observed.

primitive fantasy and feeling identifications, becomes apparent. Only the identifications which originate in enduring emotional object invest- ments, and which result in gradual, consistent structural changes show- ing a definite direction, can fortify the inner feeling of continuity of the self. It is the proper balance between libido and aggression on which the success or failure of these processes depends. In case of a collapse of object relations because of oversevere hostility conflicts, such as can be observed in psychotic patients, we find indeed that their identifica- tions break down simultaneously. Both may eventually be replaced by fusions with objects, which, involving fantasies of destroying them or being destroyed by them, may lead to experiences of *Weltuntergang* and loss of identity. We find in such patients fears of accepting and acquiring likenesses to others, in conjunction with an inability to per- ceive and tolerate differences from them, and to relate to them as to separate and different individuals. Likeness and difference are equally frightening, because likeness threatens to destroy the self and difference the object.

The role of libido as against that of aggression in such regressive fusions between self and objects becomes evident from a comparison between experiences of ecstasy in normal persons and fusion experi- ences in psychotics. Since normal experiences of ecstasy do not aim at destruction but are founded on a fantasy of libidinal union between self and object world, they result in a transitory sense of self expansion and the feeling that the self and the world are rich. Such experiences of merging, which may briefly retransform the images of the self and the object world into a fantasy unit vested with libidinal forces, permit an immediate re-establishment of the boundaries between them. By con- trast, pathological regressive fusions caused by severe aggression may result in an irreparable breakdown of these boundaries and hence of the self and object representations.

10. The Widening Scope of Indications for Psychoanalysis

Leo Stone

The remarkable and steadfast conservatism of Freud regarding the therapeutic application of his discovery appears in several places in his writings. We may generalize briefly to the effect that Freud believed the true indications for psychoanalysis to be the transference psychoneuroses and equivalent character disturbances. While temperately hopeful for the future treatment of psychoses, the very expression "some other plan better suited for that purpose" (10), suggests how closely linked in Freud's thinking were the psychoanalytic technique and the basically reliable ego. We know from his writings that Freud was far from rigid or static in his technical methods; however, he was apparently not much concerned with developing and systematizing new techniques, or in experimenting with remote nosological groups.

Yet it was still early in the history of psychoanalysis that Abraham (1) began to treat manic-depressive psychosis, and not too long before Simmel (14) opened a psychoanalytic sanatorium where he treated very severe neuroses, incipient psychotic conditions,and addictions. Also early came the psychoanalytic interest in character, beginning with Freud himself (9), followed by the distinguished contributions of Jones and Abraham. However, character analysis as a special technical problem was precipitated sharply into the foreground of general interest by Wilhelm Reich's brilliant and stimulating, although still controversial, book (13, 15). With Anna Freud's book on *The Ego and the Mechanisms of Defense* (7), one might say that a movement toward the broadening and mutiplication of the psychoanalytic spheres of interest in the personality, and an appropriate complication of psychoanalytic technique, found general and secure acceptance.

I trust that it is not superfluous on this occasion to mention child analysis as an early special development in theory and technique, whose implications extend far beyond the immediate clinical applications. The application of psychoanalytic knowledge in the treatment of delinquents, begun by Aichhorn, continued in our own group by the Eisslers currently, has a similar importance.

Other psychiatric syndromes were rapidly brought within the scope of psychoanalytic therapy: the perversions, including homosexuality; paranoia and the schizophrenias; a considerable and growing variety of psychosomatic disorders; and, of course, that vast, important and heterogeneous group—the "borderline" cases. One might say that in the last decade or two, at least in the United States, any illness or problem which has a significant emotional component in its etiology has become at least a possible indication for psychoanalysis. In its extreme development, this indication includes not only conditions where this etiology is quite well established, but not infrequently, as in the psychosomatic disorders, only reasonably probable.

First, I should mention that this generally expanding scope of psychoanalysis, which I should judge is now on a sort of peak plateau, has more than one facet; furthermore, my own reaction to this expansion is divided, according to these facets. One element which should not elude our attention is the enthusiasm of that section of the informed public which is devoted to psychoanalysis. Among this group, not inconsiderable in size and influence in a city like New York, scarcely any human problem admits of solution other than psychoanalysis; by the same token, there is an almost magical expectation of help from the method, which does it grave injustice. Hopeless or grave reality situations, lack of talent or ability (usually regarded as "inhibition"), lack of an adequate philosophy of life, and almost any chronic physical illness may be brought to psychoanalysis for cure. It is a matter of serious interest to us that this phenomenon exists; it is of course even more important that this type of ambivalent worship not be allowed to influence, however subtly, the judgment of the psychoanalytic practitioner. A special development of this sort has occurred in the practice of general medicine. This I would regard as a small but definite public health hazard. One cannot question the tremendous scientific importance of research in psychosomatic medicine, or its potentialities for improving preventive or therapeutic medical practice. The complete displacement of well-established medical methods by purely psychological methods, even when the psychological indications are reasonably practical and sound, is quite another matter. It is, however, in the field of diagnosis where one observes the most serious deterioration. The hospital resident who on completing a negative physical examination in a patient with bowel complaints immediately calls for psychiatric consultation, then gets an X-ray report of carcinoma of the colon, is funny to his colleagues. However, under other conditions, the same orientation may occasion tragedy. I should emphasize that this tendency exists on the side of the public and the medical practitioners, *not* on the side of analysts as a group. My occasional discussions with medical men in connection with patients whom they refer to the Treatment Center (of the New York Psychoanalytic Institute) confirm this longstanding observation and conviction. Some subtle fault in the publicization of psychoanalytic findings may contribute slightly to this phenomenon. In any case, it is important to be alertly aware of, to try to understand and, if possible, to remedy this situation; at very least, to resist any distortion of judgment in response to it.

I should also like, in passing, to mention a less immediately grave but intellectually disquieting feature of this spurious increase of psychoanalytic indications. There is sometimes a loss of sense of proportion about the human situation, a forgetting or denial of the fact that few human beings are without some troubles, and that many must be met, if at all, by "old-fashioned" methods: courage, or wisdom, or struggle, for instance; also that few people avoid altogether and forever some physical ailments, not to speak of the fact that all die of illness in the end. Even if these illnesses all represent disturbances in the total psychosomatic complex which, oddly enough, I believe to be the case), they are not all indications for psychoanalysis. The "psyche" is only half of the psychosomatic continuum, and it remains a practical empirical problem as to whether a drug or surgery or psychotherapy is most effective in a given illness. If a man is otherwise healthy, happy, and efficient, and his rare attacks of headache can be avoided by not eating lobster, for example, it would seem better that he avoid eating lobster than that he be analyzed. This takes us to another indication for psychoanalysis—not spurious—but one where delicate judgment is involved; I have in mind the very mild or incipient neurosis. Here, it seems to me, a careful general evaluation of the personality is especially imperative. For, if the personality illness were judged really slight (a matter which we know, does not necessarily parallel the severity of immediate symptoms), I would regard the indication for psychoanalysis as very seriously in doubt. For psychoanalysis represents a tremendous investment of many complicated elements by two people; it should not be invoked for trivial reasons. Aside from the fact that many people can live with mild neuroses (I am certain that a good part of the population live long lives with various subclinical phobias, mild conversion symptoms, fragmentary compulsions, etc.), a simpler, less intensive form of psychotherapy may suffice for many such illnesses.

Before considering some of the more severe problems which are now being treated psychoanalytically, it may be well to say a few words about what we mean by psychoanalysis (as differentiated from psychotherapy), since it is in relation to the severe illnesses that important technical alterations may be required. If we do not have some reasonable degree of agreement about this, there is little ground for discussion regarding indications, for few would dispute the helpfulness of some form of psychotherapy in any of these instances. Most psychotherapy practiced in the United States has been strongly influenced by psychoanalysis. Certainly, the psychotherapy practiced by psychoanalysts and candidates borrows so much from the original discipline that the boundary becomes obscure, and is sometimes defined on a rather arbitrary or ritualistic basis, which is quite unsatisfactory. Sometimes bad or slovenly or inadequate psychoanalytic tactics find both definition and privilege in being "not analysis, but psychotherapy". A few years ago, I wrote on this subject; and I do not wish to burden you with a repetition of that material (17). Furthermore, I should prefer nowadays to place greater stress on the functional elements to which the formal factors are ancillary. The relevant point which I proposed was that the several formal factors which participate in the classical psychoanalytic situation—ranging from free association through the recumbent position to such matters as the character of the analyst's technical interventions and general attitude—constitute an ensemble which has much to do with the dynamics of the analytic process, and specifically with the evolution of the transference neurosis. Most important in the ultimate dynamic meaning of this ensemble is the relative emotional vacuum which the analysand must fill with transference impulses and fantasies, and the parallel reduction of reality-testing opportunity which facilitates the same process. In a sort of paradoxical *tour de force*, the very same set of factors provides the optimum background for testing and interpretative reduction of the transference neurosis. Of the several technical instrumentalilties which may be used purposively in any psychotherapeutic procedure—for instance, those listed last year by Bibring (2)—it is interpretation which is ultimately relied on for the distinctively psychoanalytic effect. I put aside the many possible interpersonal meanings which interpretation may have for a patient, and refer to the circumscribed function of communicating to a patient something true of him in a specific reference, which he has, before the interpretation, seen in a radically different light, or of which he has been quite unaware.[1] Without entering into the basic problems discussed in The Marienbad Symposium we can state in a very general descriptive way what wholly or partially occurs in analysis. We dissolve or minimize resistances, and make the ego aware of its defensive operations, ultimately of id and superego contents and operations. Through this accurate awareness, implemented by the process of "working through," we expect the effect of abolition or reduction of id and superego qualitative distortions and pathological intensities, the resolution or reduction or at least the *awareness* of intrapsychic conflict in general, and finally the extension of the ego's positive sovereignty over the instinctual life, with the freeing or facilitation of its synthetic, adaptive and other affirmative capacities. In this process, the mobilization of the transference neurosis holds a central place. Whether one views this phenomenon theoretically as essentially a resistance to recall of the past, or an affirmatively necessary therapeutic phenomenon, toward which interpretation and recall are directed for the freeing of the patient from the analyst and thus from internal parental representations, is largely a question of emphasis, which in a pragmatic sense may vary from patient to patient. For, as Freud long ago observed, an adequate positive transference is necessary even to the *acceptance* of decisive interpretations. Furthermore, the sense of reality or vividness about the past is *largely* dependent on the therapeutic transference experience; and there are many instances where the dissolution of amnesias or of the emotional isolation of memories only follows adequate emotional experience in the transference. This is even more true of the reconstruction of very early experience, which may be quite inaccessible to adult memory, or may indeed have played little or no

[1] Bibring (2) differentiates interpretation from clarification by confining the reference of interpretation to "repressed or otherwise warded-off unconscious material and its derivatives."

part in childhood consciousness. In any case, the current dynamisms of personality (and thus, of neurosis) are to be brought effectively into relation with their origins in the past, that the adult ego must per force recognize their inappropriateness to current realities and thus free itself of the disturbances attendant on the burdening from the past. That this process includes, or is at least in part dependent on or relative to, reduction of disturbances in the id and superego, is apparently implicit, although not always explicit, in current formulations.

When Freud said that any procedure which utilized the principles of transference and resistance could be called psychoanalysis whether the findings agreed with his own or not, he offered a permission, whose current acceptance or nonacceptance should be decided on a scientific rather than a factional loyalty basis. Freud at times used the term "psychotherapy" in its historical inclusive sense, or for psychoanalysis, or—when referring to *"other"* psychotherapies—for explicitly non-analytic procedures. I do not know if he foresaw the growth of a medley of practices which are called "psychotherapy" in contradistinction to analysis, which borrow from its psychological formulations, and while often including many other formidable and uncontrolled variables, tend with varying degrees of purposive clarity and thoroughness to employ interpretation as their chief manifest technical tool. I do not believe it important to participate in power struggles, to which unfortunately the nature of our work lends itself, on the issue of definition. And I do not believe that patients should bear the burden or sometimes the trauma of our distinctions. However, I do think that the scientific progress of psychotherapy in its broadest sense, with psychoanalysis as its central science and technology, depends on an increasingly clear-cut knowledge of the conditions in which findings occur. This, of course, presupposes certain minimal basic terminological distinctions. I do not believe that the distinction between psychoanalysis and psychotherapy will remain adequate, aside from linguistic considerations, for "psychotherapy" is or should be a large and complicated field. But the reasonably clear delimitation of psychoanalysis from other psychotherapies, especially interpretative psychotherapies, is a necessary beginning. In our immediate context, some such general concept as "modified psychoanalysis" would be useful and, I believe, valid. For scientific progress, the careful study of the "modifications" and their effects will be necessary, whether we think of the given procedure as psychoanalysis, or as beyond its most elastic limits. Perhaps they will prove to be less important than some of us think. But this is a very unsound *a priori*.

I would view the idea of psychoanalysis as beginning with Freud's own basic requirement. To this most of us would add, as indispensable technical and intellectual context, certain other basic elements of psychoanalytic observation and theory: the unconscious, of course, since it seems no longer inevitably implicit in the basic requirement; the libido theory; the power of infantile sexuality, possibly additional elements in instinct theory; certainly, the genetic principle, with the connotation of psychodynamic continuity with the remote past. One cannot divorce this initial context from subsequent phenomena of a real therapeutic process. We would, while acknowledging that other psychotherapeutic agents play an important role in the psychoanalytic process, assign to interpretation the unique and distinctive place in its ultimate therapeutic effect. We would, I think, require that the interpretation achieve this effect through the communication of awareness of facts about himself to the patient, with the sense of emotional reality that comes only with technically correct preparation, rather than through certain other possible effects in the transference countertransference system, which occur so frequently in other psychotherapies. (Certainly, they occur also in psychoanalysis, but they are regarded as miscarriages of effort.) I would think that the mobilization of as full and undistorted a transference neurosis as may be possible, and its ultimate dissolution (or minimization) by interpretative means, would be regarded as essential to a genuinely analytic outcome. Both for the mobilization of the neurosis *and* for its reduction by such means the essentials of the formal and emotional milieu which we associate with the classical psychoanalytic situation would usually seem necessary; these components of the milieu are then assumed integral parts of the definition. One cannot be rigid about the details of the definition; nor can one simplify it too much; the general functional meaning, with its formal requirements, can, however, be brought to discernible outlines. Probably all analyses include certain formal and subtle emotional deviations somewhere along the line, aside from the fact that no two analysts would ever give precisely the same interpretations throughout an analysis. We are therefore dealing with principles, broad outlines, tendencies. Indeed, my own clinical experience and observation lead me to believe that *too* great approximation to the mathematical ideal in certain references is antitherapeutic (in the sense of antianalytic). For example, some patients may not be able to do their "analytic work" in relation to exaggerated and artificial efforts, or to personalities, whose "neutrality" is tantamount to complete emotional detachment. Yet I am convinced that any considerable tangible deviation from the attitude of neutrality should be motivated and handled along the general lines which Eissler (5) has described in his discussion of parameters." Where the dividing line appears is impossible to specify quantitatively. From a qualitative point of view, I would speculate that the optimum exists where the patient feels that the analyst's neutrality is a self-imposed purposive technical discipline in fact, a technique), willingly accepted for good reasons, neither enjoyed as a personality gratification, nor rigidly embraced in panicky fear of rule-breaking. We must frequently remind ourselves that the analytic situation is an artificial situation, a drama in which both participants have "roles," imposed by the technique, differing from both their everyday human behavior, and the inner primitive drama of the transference. We expect of the analysand a benign split of the ego, which enables him to experience while still observing. In the classical method, we exclude any *assumption* of a role in the transference by the analyst. However, the *complete* merging of the analyst as an individual and the analyst as technician may also be inimical to the analytic process. Is it not rational to assume that since these two aspects of the analyst's identity are in psychodynamic balance with the two phases of the patient's (technical) ego activity, a grave imbalance on one side may seriously affect the other? It might contribute, for example, to an excessive avoidance of transference fantasy on one hand, or overwhelming ego-syntonic transference reactions on the other.

If we avoid involvement in the nature of other (interpretative) psychotherapies (for lack of time, not for lack of interest), we can go directly to the question: How far can the classical analytic method be modified, and still be regarded as psychoanalysis, "modified psychoanalysis," if you wish rather than another form of interpretative psychotherapy? I believe that any number and degree of parameters can be introduced where they are genuinely necessary to meet special conditions, so long as they are all directed to bringing about the ultimate purposes and processes of the analytic end requirements, as we have just described them; so long as these purposes and processes are rationally to be expected as sequellae, and are brought about to the maximum extent which the patient's personality permits. (We must distinguish between a valid psychoanalytic effort which may be unsuccessful or only partially successful, and an effort which is essentially different.) Ordinarily, this would presuppose the transition from any postulated previous psychotherapeutic methods to the classical psychoanalytic situation, without irreversible transference distortions. In an ideal sense, I think the requirements for acceptability of parameters given by Eissler, with one exception, are excellent. The exception is one which requires that the parameter *must* terminate before the end of analysis—a requirement which, as the author states, automatically excludes the time-limitation parameter, which Freud used with the Wolf Man. While the discussion of this conflict between parameter and rule would provide technical, metapsychological, and logical interest, I must waive the disproportionate space which this would require. The practical value of retention of this maneuver as consistent with true analytic work outweighs the ideal requirement, even if it must be an exception. A patient may require this confrontation with reality, in the same sense that the phobic sometimes requires the intervention which is now a general and accepted practice. Aside from this issue, however, this rule seems altogether too severe. There are very sick personalities who, to the very end of analytic experience, may require occasional and subtle or minimal emotional or technical concessions from the analyst, in the same sense that they will carry with them into their outside lives, vestiges of ego defects or modifications, which, while not completely undone, are—let us say— vastly improved. If in such patients, the essential structure and relationship of analysis have been brought about, if a full-blown transference neurosis has emerged, if the patient has been able to achieve distance from it, if it has been brought into effective relation with the infantile situation, if favorable changes in the ego have occurred as a result of interpretation and working through, if the transference has been dissolved or reduced to the maximum possible degree. I would say that the patient has been analyzed.

With regard to the earlier deviant phases of such analyses, or atypical technical residues which may persist, I would state the broad and general opinion that most parameters can be deprived of their effects on the transference, so long as they are genuinely psychotherapeutic, i.e., maneuvers bound to the immediate reality, arising from, strictly limited by, always compatible with, the role *of therapist*—as opposed to good father, or solicitous friend, or magician, or anxious husband, etc., in a patient whose reality testing and other ego functions are largely capable of the various rigors implicit in analysis, at the point we are discussing. An excellent example of how even affirmative or constructive use of wide deviations from the classical psychoanalytic situation can be made, where these deviations are necessary and rational, may be seen in Simmel's still fascinating paper about the Tegel Sanatorium (14). I am inclined to agree with Eissler that the giving of a cigarette to certain patients, in a certain context, might create serious difficulty. In general, if this occurs as an *exception* to a general climate of deprivation, I would believe it more likely to cause trouble than, let us say, an appropriate expression of sympathy in a tragic personal bereavement— or even, circumspect competent direct advice in a real emergency which requires it—precisely because the giving of a cigarette, aside from its obvious susceptibility to unconscious symbolic countertransference interpretation—is, in ordinary practice, with nonpsychotic patients, *always* unnecessary—*never* relevant to the treatment as such. Should the previous treatment methods provide insoluble transference distortions, which may well be required by the active phases of psychosis, I would agree with Eissler that a change of therapist may be necessary, *unless* more is lost thereby than is gained by the uncontaminated transference. It may be that the person who has ministered to the acute psychotic is the only one who can elicit a strong attachment from the patient; since this is indispensable to initiate analysis, I would—to be a bit slangy—"settle" for the transference distortion, with the hope that this may in time come into better perspective. This is always possible, where even outright "mothering" may retrospectively be seen as having been dictated by actual therapeutic needs of the time. If not, we may have to accept a transference situation something like that described by Miss Freud for the child, without clear-cut transference neurosis. Where to classify this, I would not know; I would hesitate to exclude this from the modifications of adult psychoanalysis, if all other analytic purposes are maintained, if the modification is judged necessary, if the analysis of the transference is extended to its utmost possible limit.

A psychological treatment which does not seek to provide to the maximum compatible with the situation the conditions necessary for a full-blown undistorted transference neurosis and therefore does not mobilize one, or which does not dissolve this neurosis or reduce it to the greatest extent which the patient's structure and the therapist's skill permit, ultimately by genetic interpretations, should not be called analysis, even if the necessary formal aspects of the analytic situation *are* reproduced. For without these important processes, the profound reorganization of the personality which we associate with analysis, and in which the cure of illness is, in a sense, an incidental part of general economic change, can not occur. At this point, I should mention, as I have elsewhere— that, in certain well-managed psychotherapeutic situations, where many ordinary emotional needs of the patient are met, within the limits of the physician-patient relationship, significant *pathological fragments* of the transference relationship (i.e., those which cannot be met in any ordinary real relationship) may separate from integrated expression in this real professional situation, and be utilized to great and genuine interpretative advantage by a skillful therapist. Classification of such treatment situations would present problems. For the moment—since they are infrequent, since they are fragmentary rather than general and systematic, since they arise under atypical and uncontrolled auspices, and since unknown large areas of transference remain integrated and unanalyzed—we shall leave them in the broad heterogeneous field of "psychotherapy."

With some conception of what we mean by psychoanalysis in mind, we can move to an examination of the expanding scope of psychoanalysis, in so far as this originates legitimately from scientific development, or practical technical experience, as opposed to irrational enthusiasm. First a few words about those conditions which have the least part in usual analytic practice. In the psychoses, we have a tremendous range, extending from those who are not independently viable, or who require hospital restraint or protection, or who cannot or will not establish voluntary co-operative contact with a therapist, or—specifically—with his therapy. From these, regardless of the particular type of psychotic expression, there is a continuous gradation down to the incipient or very mild psychotic who *complains* of his symptoms and seeks help exactly as a neurotic does; and perhaps in the very end zone of this continuum is the "borderline" patient, who is fact neither medicolegally nor clinically psychotic. With patients who are floridly psychotic, the initial management requires extraordinary measures or techniques which, however influenced or guided by psychoanalytic understanding, are certainly removed from the scope of ordinary psychoanalytic office practice. Where patients, whether through spontaneous or therapeutically induced remission or subsidence of symptoms or the initial mildness of illness present themselves voluntarily for treatment, we may think of their problems as approximating to various degrees the problems which appear in the "borderline" cases.

In the addictions and perversions alike, the *immediate* criterion of accessibility to treatment would seem to lie in the degree to which the patient experiences the tendency as illness, plus the genuineness of this experience, i.e., the question of whether this view of the problem arises from its essential incompatibility with intrinsic elements in the patient's personality, or from the impact of the police, or a desperate wife, or a desperate employer. These two types of origin are, of course, not mutually exclusive, but they must be appraised quantitatively. A special difficulty in dealing with these illnesses derives from their special nature, i.e., they are sources of relief of painful tension, or of positive pleasure. Thus, instead of providing direct incentive for the psychoanalytic effort, as in the case of ordinary symptomatic suffering, they literally compete with it. To be sure, the moral suffering involved in these disorders, or in the highly developed patient, the realistic estimate of a life pattern, may provide incentives of great power. That is what brings them within the scope of our work. In other respects, it would seem, these disorders lend themselves largely to a discussiuon of the general problems involved in the "borderline" cases, although the less severe perversions can often be treated without appreciable technical modifications. The more severe psychosomatic disorders, apart from their special physical problems, may present psychopathology of potential severity equivalent to that of the psychoses, and must be handled accordingly; milder cases may often be treated quite conventionally.

In current private practice, at least in these parts, the usual "borderline" cases are equaled in importance, perhaps exceeded, only by the character disorders. In the latter, loosely considered, are all manner of occupational maladjustments and inhibitions, and marital problems of all types. In their more severe forms, the character disorders are indeed in the "borderline" group as to psychopathologic severity. Very frequently, the presenting neurotic or neurotic-like symptom which dominated the anamnesis quickly yields first importance in the therapist's eyes to a grave character distortion. The patient with one or more classical phobias who impressed one in an initial interview with his intelligence and sincere wish to struggle for health, quickly proves to be an irritable demanding Don Juan, megalomanic, externally submissive yet irrationally and diffusely defiant, rationalizing everything to suit his one-sided view of all personal relationships, driving everyone from him and complaining unremittingly that loneliness causes his illness, and (incidentally) taking about eight times the ordinary soporific dose of a barbiturate daily. Aside from the very severe character disorders as major complaints, or those which quickly assume this position, the tendency nowadays is to perceive sensitively the characterological aspect of every neurotic complaint. This is probably due to the recent tremendous growth of interest in ego psychology, especially in the individual nuances of character, and of defense in general. That this has enriched psychoanalytic technical resources cannot be doubted, especially in dealing with the more difficult character cases, or those in whom the defense aspects of the character have great economic importance. It is barely possible that overenthusiasm in this direction may unneccesarily complicate the management of simpler neurotic problems. One sometimes suspects this when a student, reversing the traditional pedagogical problem, still shudders after a year at the idea of interpreting anything other than a subtle and intricate ego attitude of the patient.

Cases whose principal complaints lie in the sphere of character range from those which are equivalent or nearly equivalent to neuroses—true "neurotic characters"—where awareness of the disorder is present from the beginning—up to those in whom the disorder—I agree with Knight (12)—is more malignant than in most borderline cases, because it is so thoroughly ego-syntonic. One of the most difficult patients I have treated in recent years was a talented chemist of extreme oral character—with work inhibitions, occasional excessive drinking, severe sexual disturbances, Don Juanism, general financial irresponsibility, pathological jealousy, a remarkable almost legalistic capacity for rationalizing all his behavior (alternating with masochistic self-castigation), severe depressions, and a few minor neurotic-like complaints. This patient was at times quasi-psychotic in his transference reproaches, rationalizations, and acting out. The analysis has been terminated —at least, for the time—with considerable genuine improvement. I am waiting to evaluate the ultimate effect of a nonterminated parameter—that of having allowed the patient to run up a very large debt, while he dissipated his earnings elsewhere, borrowing money, ostensibily to pay me, and then not seldom spent it on carousing— simply because it was the only alternative to putting him out of the analysis prematurely, as he proposed a few times—to what I thought would be sudden or gradual self-destruction. The patient's illness prevailed, in this sphere, over my best interpretative efforts. A condition of analysis was established, in relation to which the interpretative effort continued—and not, I believe, without important analytic effect.

I think that the most common usage of the "borderline" designation would be in relation to those patients who present largely neurotic syndromes, sometimes quite conventional, who nevertheless induce in the clinician the conviction or strong suspicion of more grave illness. This may be because of psychotic fragments, or admixtures of vague unclassified suspiciously narcissistic phenomena (bodily, emotional, or intellectual, or very severe character distortions or quasi-addictions, or the sheer massiveness and multiplicity of concurrent symptoms, or the history of severe disturbances of behavior or personal relationships, or indeed by the patient's atypical reactions in the early phases of treatment immediate primitive transference reactions, extreme rigidity, early archaic material, euphoric rapid "improvement," terror of the analytic situation, and many other more subtle considerations. The important clinical issue in these cases is that, according to the individual therapist's prognostic point of view—and according to individual severity—they may be judged unanalyzable, or possibly liable to psychosis under treatment, or liable to become generally worse under treatment, or to occasion interminable analyses, or perhaps to require very long, especially skillful analyses, with eventual minimal improvement. The broad common denominator in these patients and the common feature which allies them with the psychoses—Freud's "narcisstic neuroses"—is their narcissism, not seldom specifically oral in its tendency. One might say that the problems of their treatment are similar to those of the mild or incipient psychoses, except that the initial problem of establishing or maintaining distance beween the patient and his psychotic symptom is often liable to apear, instead, in the arduous problem of placing the "borderline" patient's severe transference reactions in perspective for him.

This brings us to the question of narcissism and transference. I think that most of us would agree that true psychoanalytic therapy could not occur without transference. It would seem that apart from the specific vitiation of the therapeutic alliance by psychotic symptoms, the assumption of incapacity for transference in the narcissistic neuroses was originally held by Freud to be the reason for their therapeutic inaccessibility. Yet we know that very early Abraham began to treat psychotics; he speaks of the increments of positive transference in reaction to interpretations. Interesting enough, Abraham mentions Freud's personal communication regarding two melancholics whom he treated with good results.) The literature regarding the psychoanalytic treatment of schizophrenia has by this time grown quite formidable. In relation to our immediate problem, I should like to mention Waelder's case published in 1925 (19). This patient might be regarded as "borderline." The case is of special interest because Waelder mentions his belief that the patient remained nonpsychotic because a union occurred between his intense narcissism and his object-libidinal sublimation, which was pure mathematics. Perhaps nowadays a great many highly intellectual and artistic "borderline" patients who present themselves for treatment are not frankly psychotic for similar reasons. Unfortunately, the problems of recognition versus frustration are unusually severe in most instances, to some extent in proportion to the degree of narcissism involved. A gifted mathematician is in an unusually favorable position, in the sense that the mechanisms are so largely "narcissistic," yet the demonstrable reality value is very great. At the same time, the influence on events and persons is, in this era very great, unlike that of certain comparable activities—for example, pure philosophy. I have seen a gifted woman composer, after several years of intermittent treatment, swing for a time from a highly personal and recondite musical idiom, which brought her little of the recognition which she so desperately needed, into a routine but secure effort, quite remote in character from her original work. Interestingly enough, this change paralleled efforts to establish a genuine relationship with her husband, which would occasionally collapse in wild outbursts of aggression, whenever something resembling love would begin to appear. These phenomena occurred in the atmosphere of a mildly friendly positive transference, experienced for the first time, instead of the medley of fear, hostility, and bizarre erotic fantasies which had usually dominated the therapeutic relationship. It would seem that the conception of narcissistic incapacity for transference rests to some extent on a terminological-historical basis. For it is true that the original transference love of the hysteric or the transference fear and aggreession of the incest complex are different from the primitive phenomena of the narcissistic transferences, although all gradations between them may occur. The psychotic's transference is liable to invade or overwhelm his personality as his psychosis does, with an equal intensity, with an equal difficulty in perceiving the inappropriateness of his attitudes. I recall an intelligent ambulatory schizophrenic nurse, treated very early in my psychoanalytic career, who had made a painful oral suicidal attempt shortly before treatment was begun; who, after a few years of analysis, following some frustrations of quite impossible demands, abandoned her frequent and characteristic suicidal threats for the impulse to kill me. At this point, she dreamed of avoiding the police while she carried a pail of vomitus, which was the remains of her mother. The patient quite naïvely protested that she saw no point in analyzing this impulse, since the wish was to *do* it, and her gratification would be in doing it. Fortunately, there was enough positive transference to carry us through a difficult period; and the patient left the analysis a few months later. Incidentally, and this is not irrelevant to our general interest, this patient often complained that she felt somehow that I was a very warm person but that she could get none of the warmth. The analysis was conducted along quite strictly conventional lines. In retrospect, as in a few related instances, I am impressed at how much *was* accomplished by these methods. This suggests to me how little more may be needed in unusual cases. A little less of the novice's fear to unbend, and a little less need to react against what I viewed as unconventional features in my own early training, *might* have produced a true and thorough analysis of a relatively mild but genuine schizophrenic. At least, that is the way I tend to think of it.

To generalize further and briefly, from personal experience, regarding narcissistic transferences: it would seem to be the sheer fear of their primitive intensity, which forces certain patients to remain detached. In some patients a subtle but discernible aloofness, reservation, or superciliousness may play a similar role, while the patients for the most part "go through the motions." In one such instance, I have discerned and interpreted grandiose fantasies; in another, they were—in time— frankly and spontaneously stated. In both, the magical expectations and demands were not less strong because of these reservations. In those many instances where the transference does break through, insatiable demands may appear; or the need to control or tyrannize over the therapist; or, failing that, the polar alternative—to be completely submissive, passive, obedient, to be told what to do, or indeed whether things can be done, whether a symptom will appear or disappear; or the transference may be literally "narcissistic," i.e., the therapist is confused with the self, or is like the self in all respects; or, as emphasized by Stern (16), the therapist must be omnipotent, omniscient, God-like; or the therapist and patient—alternatively—are, in effect, parts of one another. Extreme ambivalences of simultaneous insatiable demand and destructive nullification are frequent. In the fantasy of the analyst's omnipotence, which affords intolerable anxiety should the analyst exhibit the slightest human frailty, it has been my impression that the guilt about primitive destructive aggressions plays an important part. Weird specific phenomena may occur. A medical technician whom I treated for many very difficult years would spend hour after hour of eerie indescribable fear and mistrust in my office, eyes popping, talking frantically from an endless store of historical detail, to control her fear, then leave my office to be seized with terror that I had disappeared, that I was not real! This patient feared me and held me in contempt. Yet any suggestion that she leave me produced a superpanic which quickly settled the problem. This last attitude I should say is a not infrequent trend of "borderline" transferences. Unfortunately, I cannot go into detail about the background, symptoms, genesis and fate of specific examples. The common factors are the primitiveness, the intensity—at times, the overwhelming quality—and, one should add, the relatively small quanta of genital object love. I think—from my own experience with a few very severe cases in recent years—that one may speak with justification of a transference psychosis, in the sense of a still viable variant of transference neurosis, in the extreme forms. The thin layer of observing, reality-testing ego and the thin thread of transference love and hope for love which enabled these patients to grow up in the first place, sustain the analytic situation.

Various recommendations have been made for the special management of these patients, for example: prolonged preliminary periods of supportive therapy; deliberate fostering and maintenance of the positive transference; avoidance of analysis of defenses or the dissolution of surface neurotic symptoms (Knight), long analytic periods in which the historical material is ignored for direct work with the painful distorted narcissistic transference reactions (Stern); similarly, by-passing of the incestuous conflicts until the narcissistic disturbances are worked through (Cohn, Stern). Zilboorg in his paper on "Ambulatory Schizophrenia" (20) specifies psychoanalysis as the treatment, without suggesting technical modifications. Bychowski (3) makes several technical suggestions for protecting and strengthening the ego, and avoiding regression. Greenacre (11), discussing the treatment of borderline cases in the continuation of her work on the predisposition to anxiety, gives many detailed clinical suggestions. Outstanding are strong emphasis on increasing the immediate reality hold of the patient, and strengthening of the patient's ego through education of his narcissism (with recognition that these may continue throughout the analysis); a general emphasis (with nuances) on holding the line against—or minimizing—outright concessions to the patient's demands for activity, with calmness, firm realism, and quiet competence being the effective agents in the analyst's attitude. The ultimate importance of analyzing the "essential neurosis" (as distinguished from the basic anxiety) is also stressed. In certain patients who produce abundant archaic fantasy material and ignore the actualities of their reactions to the analyst or the persons and events of their daily lives, I have found it useful to make this phenomenon itself a focus of patient repetitive interpretation. Sometimes the fantasies themselves may be interpreted in their respective specific defensive meanings in this connection or at times of their substitutive significance for the real ego or total personal conflicts, which they seek to evade. This type of "interpretation-back-into-reality" reverses direction, yet is allied to the "direct" maneuver advised by Franz Cohn (4), wherein the patient's bizarre symptom formation is quickly reduced to its origins in narcissistic bodily tensions. Each has its application according to the immediate indications; both tend to substitute more genuine experience for defensive symptom formation or fantasy evasion. In the case of the patient who "lost me" on leaving my office, the treatment was advanced, when a dream about the African native workers who stole diamonds by swallowing them and recovering them from their stools, permitted an interpretation of her cannibalistic incorporation of me. The patient, incidentally, had had a childhood fear of a dragonfly which might fly up and attack her, from her stool in the toilet bowl. As an adult, the persistent mild phobia was dissociated

from feces. However, the effect of interpretation in this instance, was
not dramatic; I would regard its effect as dependent on other long and
patient work, including reality testing, with the content of the tortured
transference experience itself. If I were to review my general experience
with such cases broadly, I would be impelled to say that—assuming
adequate perceptiveness, knowledge, and technical skill—the decisive
factor is the ability to stand the emotional strains of the powerful
tormented and tormenting transference and potential countertransference situations which such cases are liable to present over long periods,
without giving up hope, or sometimes, alternatively the severe "acting
out" which borderline patients may exhibit as the other alternative to
intercurrent clinical psychoses. Fortunately for one's development,
unfortunately for the precise evaluation of one's work, neither one's
intellectual equipment, nor one's degree of emotional maturity—or
vulnerability—are static. In general, I am surprised at how well most
of these cases have gotten along, relative to the depth and severity of
illness, considering that they were treated in rather conventional psychoanalytic fashion. I do not speak of striking total cures. Such patients,
I think, are liable to return for occasional interviews, periods of psychotherapy, or reanalysis. My own "striking successes" have been in
young persons with transference psychoneuroses, and—occasionally—
in persons of middle age with similar illnesses. A "borderline" patient
whose recovery *apparently* remains excellent, was young and unmarried
when she came to me; the same is true of a second patient who might
also be classified in this group. In one or two instances of very severe
illness, were I to do things over again in reflection, I might consider not
beginning an analysis, or I might consider discontinuing the work
shortly after beginning, although I would probably be dissuaded from
either course, by further reflection on what would happen to these
patients *without* psychoanalytic help. In each instance, I can think only
of suicide or a sanitarium. It is possible, in a few instances, that simpler
forms of psychotherapy based on maintained transference, broad didactic interpretations, and guidance might have been adequate, although I doubt it. In most it would have been inapplicable. In all
instances which I recall, I would now institute what I regard as a
minimally psychotherapeutic attitude—with the specific limitations
which I associate with that attitude (17, 18)—to a degree and for a
duration, and with revivals as necessary, which would be determined

as sensitively as I could, by the urgent need of the patient. I should stress that this would be a controlled-planned-purposive response, which is to be distinguised from a "countertransference" attitude. This would, to some degree, correspond to what is often called building up or maintaining a positive transference. This concept, I believe, originated with Abraham and has been stated in similar terms by several distinguished analysts since then. However, I believe this usage to be inconsistent with the progressively more exact interpretation of "transference." I would rather think of it as building up security in an actual personal relationship, so that it can stand the strains of the hostile transference when it appears, as it inevitably *must* appear, if there is to be analytic effectiveness within the treatment itself. It also provides a degree and type of permissible emotional gratification, which would tend to minimize early regressive demands. I am prepared too, to understand that the real personal relationship can slant and at least quantitatively influence the true transference. We do not know all about the (dynamic) relationship between transference and reality. Resemblances have indubitable importance. To reduce this to an absurdity: except where narcissism and remembered perceptions are completely detached from objects, as in psychotic hallucinations, transference requires some degree of resemblance. One may develop a father transference to a man, perhaps a woman, but not to a rocking chair. Thus paradoxically, in relation to the question of transference and narcissism, one might say that the psychotic alone can experience *pure* "transference," entirely separated from the immediate object. The problem lies in the nature and conditions of reinvestment in the objects from whom he has fled. Franz Cohn (4) speaks of transference as a specifically narcissistic phenomenon.

We know that opinions differ within our own society regarding the analytic treatment of psychoses, and so-called "latent psychoses." This may be true to a lesser degree of the "borderline" cases. [Knight, in his recent paper (12), qualifies what at first sounds like an adverse opinion, by requiring an initial period of psychotherapy.] I have heard a respected colleague say in a seminar that he thought a patient in question was basically psychotic and that the analytic treatment would be harmful to him. I am prepared to accept the fact (indeed, I must at times!) that some patients are unanalyzable; that some (psychotic or nonpsychotic!) cannot even adapt themselves to the requirements of analytic treatment; that some have a very poor prognosis for cure or improvement; that some, if ineptly handled in a powerful dynamic situation, may be precipitated into trouble; that faulty diagnosis may lead to inept handling even in expert hands; and that, in many instances, the expectations may be so poor that the time, skill and energies should be withheld for more likely application. However, I find it very hard to believe that the procedure in itself, if well managed (i.e., employed with sensitive individual adaptations where necessary) is harmful. Certainly while I recognize the profound predisposition to psychosis, I do not believe that a fully performed psychosis exists in latent form in the adult, to appear only because it is "uncovered." The psychosis may be on its way in response to everyday life stresses; it may possibly be expedited by certain formal factors of analysis and the routine emotional "vacuum" of analysis; in a sensitively modified situation, the interaction of archaic drives and potential psychotic defenses may come to a different solution in the transference. Nevertheless, this assumption of latency and inevitability is a point of view which is held, I am sure, by more than a few experienced colleagues. Aside from this point of view, since the nuances of technical approach depend on preliminary diagnosis, the problem of recognizing these patients beforehand, or at least in the very earliest phase of treatment, is extremely important. If we agree on the central importance of diagnosis, it is probable that we would find many different methods for reaching this goal. In his paper of 1938 Stern (16) lists, and then discusses, several traits which distinguish these patients as to history, nature of their symptoms, and reactions in treatment: narcissism, "psychic bleeding," inordinate hypersensitivity, psychic and body rigidity ("rigid personality"), negative therapeutic reactions, deeply imbedded feelings of inferiority, masochism, deep organic insecurity and anxiety, projection mechanisms, and disturbed reality testing in personal relationships. Knight (12), in his recent paper, goes into some detail about objective psychiatric subtleties which may reveal the "borderline" psychotic elements. In setting aside the "free association" interview as an adjunct to the formed or controlled conversational interview, Knight gives weight to psychological testing. Bychowski (3) also values projective tests. Zilboorg stresses the subtle evidences of dereism in relatively normal-seeming personalities. With due recognition that one's own biases are not synonymous with best procedure, it is fitting to state one's own preference. I believe that we require longer (and often multiple) psychiatric examinations than we have usually employed. We need detailed histories, detailed observations of the patient's thought processes and language expression, and the opportunity to observe his postural, gait, voice, and mimetic reactions. Certainly, in these modalities, the patient may reveal to the sensitive observer psychotic fragments from a descriptive psychiatric point of view. Furthermore, in being allowed to talk spontaneously at times, in his choice of material, in his response or manner of response or nonresponse to questions, the patient may tell as much that might be expected to appear in a diagnostic "free association" interview; often more, because certain questions cannot be evaded, at least from an inferential point of view. In his longitudinal history, and in the current patterning of the patient's activities, one can learn much of the personality structure which underlies the symptoms. Most significant of all is the character and pattern of his relationships with people. Finally, as a strong personal preference, I believe that the patient's reactions to the examiner in the interview can be of great diagnostic importance. Irritability, detachment, shallowness, euphoria, pompousness may sometimes mean more than pages of symptom description. In the case of the lady who made me "disappear," a greater emphasis on her anxious pressure of speech, on her shallow, strained, and euphoric eagerness in the first interview, might have rendered me, if not prepared for it, at least less surprised by what so soon appeared. As for the psychological tests, I have no doubt that these should and can reveal data which are inaccessible to us in interviews, and that these data can in time become very valuable to us clinically. However, I do not feel that these tests, in their present state of development, can offer conclusions as to clinical diagnosis, accessibility to treatment, and prognosis, which are to be balanced *against* the results of careful clinical examination. That the data can be usefully integrated with clinical observations in the thinking of a clinician who knows these tests well, I do not doubt. But there is still much to be learned about the significance of the data themselves.

I should like to return at least briefly, before closing, to the basic question posed by our "widening scope," i.e., what *are* the true indications for analysis? If one reads the indications as given a reasonably conservative authority like Fenichel (6), it soon appears that practically every psychogenic nosological category can be treated psychoanalytically, under good conditions, although obviously—they vary extremely in availability and prognosis. None of us would doubt that a true although severe hysteria in a young individual in a good life situation, with a reasonably competent analyst, has an infinitely better prognosis than—let us say—mild but genuine schizophrenia in a similar setting, even with an analyst of extraordinary experience and skill. So we must acknowledge that, imperfect as our nosology is, it is still meaningful prognostically, at least in the sense that the "hypothetical normal ego," as recently discussed by Eissler (5), is meaningful. However, the deceptiveness of a descriptively established hysteria was recognized early by Freud. Nowadays, we are groping toward recognizing and regrouping such problems in such conceptions as the "borderline" case or the "latent psychosis." This would still be an essentially (although improved) nosological approach. However, it is my feeling that there are elements of great importance which, while they may come to play a role in nosologies of the future, remain for the moment in a different sphere. I have in mind personality traits and resources, which we may try to assess from careful historical and cross-sectional evaluation of the personality. This general type of evaluation was stated succinctly by Freud in 1904 (8). I add a few details. Has the patient talent which may serve him for emergency releases of tension, or—more importantly— to give sublimated productive expression to large elements in his fantasy life? Has the patient certain simple but important capacities, such as courage, patience, deliberate purposive tolerance for unavoidable suffering (as distinguished from masochism)? Does the patient's ego participate in the primitive magical demands and expectations for cure which characterize his infantile transference? To what extent in general is the patient capable of self-observation, self-appraisal as opposed to the tendency to rationalization, as differentiated from symptomatic self-depreciation and self-castigation? Then there are the questions of the patient's biological age, his occupational, social and family milieu, the possible rewards for cure, his goals, his degree of independence of thought and action, the relative mobility or fixity of his situation in life. It is true that some of these matters may change with treatment. But some must be reckoned with as one does with the climate or with a patient's physical diathesis. What I am trying to say is that any few or several of these considerations may reverse or overturn, or at least profoundly modify, the noslogical consideration. The "borderline" patient under certain special conditions may be a better patient in the long run, for all of the intrinsic difficulties, than the hysteric whose epinosic gains are too great.

Another consideration in our field is the analyst himself. In no other field, save surgery, to which Freud frequently compared analysis, is the personal equation so important. It is up to us to know our capacities, intellectual and emotional, if we cannot always know one another so clearly in this respect. Again, special predilections, interests, emotional textures may profoundly influence prognosis, and thus—in a tangible way—the indications. I suppose one might generalize crudely to the effect that apart from skills, a therapist must be able to love a psychotic or a delinquent and be at least warmly interested in the "borderline" patient (whether or not this feeling is *utilized* technically), for optimum results. For in a sense, their "transferences" require new objects the old ones having been destroyed or permanently repudiated, or nearly so, as they will be again and again in the transference neurosis (or psychosis). The true neurotic patient can probably get along with a reasonably reliable friendliness behind the analyst's technically assumed objectivity and neutrality, and sometimes—apparently—with much less. For his transference has remained, after all, true to its original objects, whatever the dissatisfactions which he assigns to his life with them.

Now a few words in brief conclusion: the scope of psychoanalytic therapy has widened from the transference psychoneurosis, to include practically all psychogenic nosologic categories. The transference neuroses and character disorders of equivalent degree of psychopathology remain the optimum general indications for the classical method. While the difficulties increase and the expectations of success diminish in a general way as the nosological periphery is approached, there is no absolute barrier; and it is to be borne in mind that both extranosological factors and the therapist's personal tendencies may profoundly influence the indications and prognosis. Furthermore, from my point of view, psychoanalysis remains as yet the most powerful of all psychotherapeutic instruments, the "fire and iron," as Freud called it. While it should be used only with skill, care and judgment, support by painstaking diagnosis, it is basically a greater error to use it for trivial or incipient or reactive illnesses, or in persons with feeble personality resources, than for serious chronic illnesses, when these occur in persons of current or potential strength. With this, paradoxically enough, there is some ground to believe, Freud would have agreed, although not necessarily in a nosological sense. I do not believe that it should be wasted if one is convinced of a very bad prognosis; certainly it should not be applied or persisted in if one is convinced that a personality cannot tolerate it. Some of us may be too quick to abandon efforts, some too slow; these are matters which only self-scrutiny can correct. However, psychoanalysis may legitimately be invoked, and indeed *should* be invoked, for many very ill people, of good personality resources, who are probably inaccessible to cure by other methods, who are willing to accept the long travail of analysis, without guarantees of success. There is always a possibility of helping, where all other measures fail. With the progressive understanding of the actions of psychotherapeutic admixtures of a large-scale "parameters" in the psychoanalytic method, now so largely intuitive in their application, we can hope that such successes will be more frequent.

BIBLIOGRAPHY

1. Abraham, K. Notes on the psycho-analytical investigation and treatment of manic-depressive insanity and allied conditions. *Selected Papers on Psycho-Analysis*. London: Hogarth Press, 1927, pp. 137–156.
2. Bibring, E. Presentation in panel on psychoanalysis and dynamic psychotherapy—similarities and differences. *J. Am. Psycho.*, 2:160–162, 1954.
3. Bychowski, G. The problem of latent psychosis. *J. Am. Psycho.*, 1:484–505, 1953.
4. Cohn, F. S. Principal approach to the problem of narcissistic neuroses. *Psychoanal. Quart.*, 9:64–79, 1940.
5. Eissler, K. R. The effect of the structure of the ego on psychoanalytic technique. *J. Am. Psycho.*, 1:104–141, 1953.
6. Fenichel, O. *The psychoanalytic Theory of Neurosis*. New York: W. W. Norton, 1945.
7. Freud, A. (1936) *The Ego and the Mechanisms of Defense*. New York: International Universities Press, 1946.
8. Freud, S. (1904) On psychotherapy. *Collected Papers, 1*:249–263. London: Hogarth Press, 1924.
9. Freud, S. (1908) Character and anal erotism. *Collected Papers, 2*:45–50. London Hogarth Press, 1933.
10. Freud, S. (1939) *An Outline of Psychoanalysis*. New York: W. W. Norton, 1949.
11. Greenacre, P. The Predisposition to anxiety, Part II. *Psychoanal. Quart.*, 10:610–638. 1941.
12. Knight, R. P. Borderline States. *Bull. Menninger Clin.*, 17:1–12, 1953.
13. Reich, W. *Character-Analysis*. New York: Orgone Institute Press. 1947.
14. Simmel, E. Psycho-analytic treatment in a sanatorium. *Internat. J. Psychoanal.*, 10:70–89, 1929.

15. Sterba, R. Clinical and therapeutic aspects of character resistance. *Psychoanal. Quart., 22*:1–20, 1953.
16. Stern, A. Psychoanalytic investigation of and therapy in the borderline group of neuroses. *Psychoanal. Quart., 7*:467–489, 1938.
17. Stone, L. Psychoanalysis and brief psychotherapy. *Pschoanal. Quart., 20*:215–236, 1951.
18. Stone, L. Discussion in panel on psychoanalysis and dynamic psychotherapy— similarities and differences. *J. Am. Psycho., 2*:164–166, 1954.
19. Waelder, R. The psychoses: their mechanisms and accessibility to influence. *Internat. J. Psychoanal., 6*:259–281,1925.
20. Zilboorg, G. Ambulatory schizophrenias. *Psychiatry, 4*:149, 1941.

11. The Problem of Ego Identity

Erik Homburger Erikson*

Linguistically as well as psychologically, identity and identification have common roots. Is identity, then, the mere sum of earlier identifications, or is it merely an additional set of identifications?

The limited usefulness of the *mechanism of identification* becomes at once obvious if we consider the fact that none of the identifications of childhood (which in our patients stand out in such morbid elaboration and mutual contradiction) could, if merely added up, result in a functioning personality. True, we usually believe that the task of psychotherapy is the replacement of morbid and excessive identifications by more desirable ones. But as every cure attests, "more desirable" identifications, at the same time, tend to be quietly subordinated to a new, a unique Gestalt which is more than the sum of its parts. The fact is that identification as a mechanism is of limited usefulness. Children, at different stages of their development identify with those *part aspects* of people by which they themselves are most immediately affected, whether in reality or fantasy. Their identifications with parents, for example, center in certain overvalued and ill-understood body parts, capacities, and role appearances. These part aspects, furthermore, are favored not because of their social acceptability (they often are everything but the parents' most adjusted attributes) but the nature of infantile fantasy which only gradually gives way to a more realistic anticipation of social reality. The final identity, then, as fixed at the end of adolescence is superordinated by any single identification with individuals of the past: it includes all significant identifications, but it also alters them in order to make a unique and a reasonably coherent whole of them.

If we, roughly speaking, consider introjection-projection, identification, and identity formation to be the steps by which the ego grows in

*This contribution is excerpted from the original published version in the *Journal of the American Psychoanalytic Association,* Vol. 4, pp 61–81. For bibliographic references in this article, see the original published version of the *Journal.*

ever more mature interplay with the identities of the child's models, the following psychosocial schedule suggests itself:

The mechanisms of *introjection and projection* which prepare the basis for later identifications, depend for their relative integration on the satisfactory mutuality (9) between the *mothering adult(s) and the mothered child.* Only the experience of such mutuality provides a safe pole of self-feeling from which the child can reach out for the other pole: his first love "objects."

The fate of *childhood identifications,* in turn, depends on the child's satisfactory interaction with a trustworthy and meaningful hierarchy of roles as provided by the generations living together in some form of family.

Identity formation, finally, begins where the usefulness of identification ends. It arises from the selective repudiation and mutual assimilation of childhood identifications, and their absorption in a new configuration, which, in turn, is dependent on the process by which a *society* (often through subsocieties) *identifies the young individual,* recognizing him as somebody who had to become the way he is, and who, being the way he is, is taken for granted. The community, often not without some initial mistrust gives such recognition with a (more or less institutionalized) display of surprise and pleasure in making the acquaintance of a newly emerging individual. For the community, in turn, feels "recognized" by the individual who cares to ask for recognition; it can, by the same token, feel deeply—and vengefully—rejected by the individual who does not seem to care.

While the end of adolescence thus is the stage of an overt identity *crisis,* identity *formation* neither begins nor ends with adolescence: it is a lifelong development largely unconscious to the individual and to his society. Its roots go back all the way to the first self-recognition: in the baby's earliest exchange of smiles there is something of a *self-realization coupled with a mutual recognition.*

All through childhood tentative crystallizations take place which make the individual feel and believe (to begin with the most conscious aspect of the matter) as if he approximately knew who he was—only to find that such self-certainty ever again falls prey to the discontinuities of psychosocial development (3). An example would be the discontinuity between the demands made in a given milieu on a little boy and those made on a "big boy" who, in turn, may well wonder why he was first made to believe that to be little is admirable, only to be forced to exchange this effortless status for the special obligations of one who is "big now." Such discontinuities can amount to a crisis and demand a decisive and strategic repatterning of action, and with it, to *compromises* which can be compensated for only by a consistently accruing sense of the social value of such increasing commitment. The cute or ferocious, or good small boy, who becomes a studious, or gentlemanly, or tough big boy must be able—and must be enabled—to combine both sets of values in a recognized identity which permits him, in work and play, and in official and in intimate behavior to be (and to let others be) a big boy *and* a little boy.

The community supports such development to the extent to which it permits the child, at each step, to orient himself toward a complete *"life plan"* with a hierarchical order of roles as represented by individuals of different age grades. Family, neighborhood, and school provide contact and experimental identification with younger and older children and with young and old adults. A child, in the multiplicity of successive and tentative identifications, thus begins early to build up expectations of what it will be like to be older and what it will feel like to have been younger—expectations which become part of an identity as they are, step by step, verified in decisive experiences of psychosocial "fittedness."

The *critical phases* of life have been described in psychoanalysis primarily in terms of instincts and defenses, i.e., as "typical danger situations" (23). Psychoanalysis has concerned itself more with the encroachment of psychosexual crises on psychosocial (and other) functions than with the specific crisis created by the maturation of each function. Take for example a child who is learning to speak; he is acquiring one of the prime functions supporting a sense of individual autonomy and one of the prime techniques for expanding the radius of give-and-take. The mere indication of an ability to give intentional sound-signs immediately obligates the child to *"say"* what he wants." It may force him to *achieve* by proper verbalization the attention which was afforded him previously in response to mere gestures of needfulness. Speech not only commits him to the kind of voice he has and to the mode of speech he develops; it also *defines him* as one responded to by those around him with changed diction and attention. They, in turn, expect henceforth to be understood by him with fewer explanations or gestures. Furthermore, a spoken word is a *pact:* there is an irrevocably committing aspect to an utterance remembered by others, although the child may have to learn early that certain commitments (adult ones to a child) are subject to change without notice, while others (his) are not. This intrinsic relationship of speech, not only to the world of communicable facts, but also to the social value of verbal commitment and uttered truth is strategic among the experiences which support (or fail to support) a sound ego development. It is this psychosocial aspect of the matter which we must learn to relate to the by now better known *psychosexual* aspects represented, for example, in the autoerotic enjoyment of speech; the use of speech as an erotic "contact"; or in such organ-mode emphases as eliminative or intrusive sounds or uses of speech. Thus the child may come to develop, in the use of voice and word, a particular combination of whining or singing, judging or arguing, as part of a new element of the future identity, namely, the element "one who speaks and is spoken to in such-and-such-a-way." This element, in turn, will be related to other elements of the child's developing identity (he is clever and/or good-looking and/or tough) and will be compared with other people, alive or dead, judged ideal or evil.

It is the ego's function to integrate the psychosexual and psychosocial aspects on a given level of development, and, at the same time, to integrate the relation of newly added identity elements with those already in existence. For earlier crystallizations of identity can become subject to renewed conflict, when changes in the quality and quantity of drive, expansions in mental equipment, and new and often conflicting social demands all make previous adjustments appear insufficient, and, in fact, make previous opportunities and rewards suspect. Yet, such developmental and normative crises differ from imposed, traumatic, and neurotic crises in that the process of growth provides new energy as society offers new and specific opportunities (according to its dominant conception and institutionalization of the phases of life). From a genetic point of view, then, the process of identity formation emerges as an *evolving configuration*—a configuration which is gradually established by successive ego syntheses and resyntheses throughout childhood; it is a configuration gradually integrating *constitutional givens,*

*idiosyncratic libidinal needs, favored capacities, significant identifica-
tions, effective defenses, successful sublimations, and consistent roles.*

The final assembly of all the converging identity elements at the end
of childhood (and the abandonment of the divergent ones)[1] appears to
be a formidable task: how can a stage as "abnormal" as adolescence
be trusted to accomplish it? Here it is not unnecessry to call to mind
again that in spite of the similarity of adolescent "symptoms" and
episodes to neurotic and psychotic symptoms and episodes, adolescence is not an affliction, but a *normative crisis,* i.e., a normal phase of
increased conflict characterized by a seeming fluctuation in ego
strength, and yet also by a high growth potential. Neurotic and psychotic crises are defined by a certain self-perpetuating propensity, by
an increasing waste of defensive energy, and by a deepened psychosocial isolation; while normative crises are relatively more reversible,
or, better, traversable, and are characterized by an abundance of available energy which, to be sure, revives dormant anxiety and arouses
new conflict, but also supports new and expanded ego functions in the
searching and playful engagement of new opportunities and associations. What under prejudiced scrutiny may appear to be the onset of a
neurosis, often is but an aggravated crisis which might prove to be self-
liquidating and, in fact, contributive to the process of identity formation.
  It is true, of course, that the adolescent, during the final stage of his
identity formation, is apt to suffer more deeply than he ever did before
(or ever will again) from a diffusion of roles; and it is also true that such
diffusion renders many an adolescent defenseless against the sudden
impact of previously latent malignant disturbances. In the meantime, it
is important to emphasize that the diffused and vulnerable, aloof and
uncommitted, and yet demanding and opinionated personality of the
not-too-neurotic adolescent contains many necessary elements of a
semideliberate role experimentation of the "I dare you" and "I dare
myself" variety. Much of this apparent diffusion thus must be considered *social play* and thus the true genetic successor of childhood play.
Similarly, the adolescent's ego development demands and permits play-

---

[1] Wiliam James speaks of an abandonment of "the old alternative ego," and even of
"the murdered self" (26).

ful, if daring experimentation in fantasy and *introspection*. We are apt to be alarmed by the "closeness to consciousness" in the adolescent's perception of dangerous id contents (such as the oedipus complex) and this primarily because of the obvious hazards created in psychotherapy, if and when we, in zealous pursuit of our task of "making conscious," push somebody over the precipice of the unconscious who is already leaning out a little too far. The adolescent's leaning out over any number of precipices is normally an experimentation with experiences which are thus becoming more amenable to ego control, provided they can be somehow communicated to other adolescents in one of those strange codes established for just such experiences—and provided they are not prematurely responded to with fatal seriousness by overeager or neurotic adults. The same must be said of the adolescent's "fluidity of defenses," which so often causes raised eyebrows on the part of the worried clinician. Much of this fluidity is anything but pathological; for adolescence is a crisis in which only fluid defense can overcome a sense of victimization by inner and outer demands, and in which only trial and error can lead to the most felicitous avenues of action and self-expression.

In general, one may say that in regard to the social play of adolescents prejudices similar to those which once concerned the nature of child-hood play are not easily overcome. We alternately consider such behavior irrelevant, unnecessary, or irrational, and ascribe to it purely regressive and neurotic meanings. As in the past the study of children's spontaneous games was neglected in favor of that of solitary play,[2] so now the mutual "joinedness" of adolescent clique behavior fails to be properly assessed in our concern for the individual adolescent. Children and adolescents in their pre-societies provide for one another a sanctioned moratorium and joint support for free experimentation with inner and outer dangers (including those emanating from the adult world). Whether or not a given adolescent's newly acquired capacities are drawn back into infantile conflict depends to a significant extent on the quality of the opportunities and rewards available to him in his peer clique, as well as on the more formal ways in which society at large invites a transition from social play to work experimentation, and from

---

[2] For a new approach see Anna Freud's and Sophie Dann's report on displaced children (16).

rituals of transit to final commitments: all of which must be based on an implicit mutual contract between the individual and society.

Is the sense of identity conscious? At times, of course, it seems only too conscious. For between the double prongs of vital inner need and inexorable outer demand, the as yet experimenting individual may become the victim of a transitory extreme *identity consciousness* which is the common core of the many forms of "self-consciousness" typical for youth. Where the processes of identity formation are prolonged (a factor which can bring creative gain) such preoccupation with the "self-image" also prevails. We are thus most aware of our identity when we are just about to gain it and when we (with what motion pictures call "a double take") are somewhat surprised to make its acquaintance; or, again, when we are just about to enter a crisis and feel the encroachment of identity diffusion—a syndrome to be described presently.

An increasing sense of identity, on the other hand, is experienced preconsciously as a sense of psychosocial well-being. Its most obvious concomitants are a feeling of being at home in one's body, a sense of "knowing where one is going," and an inner assuredness of anticipated recognition from those who count. Such a sense of identity, however, is never gained nor maintained once and for all. Like a "good conscience," it is constantly lost and regained, although more lasting and more economical methods of maintenance and restoration are evoked and fortified in late adolescence.

Like any aspect of well-being or for that matter, of ego synthesis, a sense of identity has a preconscious aspect which is available to awareness; it expresses itself in behavior which is observable with the naked eye; and it has unconscious concomitants which can be fathomed only by psychological tests and by the psychoanalytic procedure. I regret that, at this point, I can bring forward only a general claim which awaits detailed demonstration. The claim advanced here concerns a whole series of criteria of psychosocial health which find their specific elaboration and relative completion in stages of development preceding and following the identity crisis. This is condensed in Figure I.

Identity appears as only one concept within a wider conception of the human life cycle which envisages childhood as a *gradual unfolding of the personality through phase-specific psychosocial crises:* I have, on other occasions (9, 10), expressed this *epigenetic principle* by taking

	1	2	3	4	5	6	7	8
I. INFANCY	Trust vs. Mistrust				Unipolarity vs. Premature Self-Differentiation			
II. EARLY CHILDHOOD		Autonomy vs. Shame, Doubt			Bipolarity vs. Autism			
III. PLAY AGE			Initiative vs. Guilt		Play Identification vs. (oedipal) Fantasy Identities			
IV. SCHOOL AGE				Industry vs. Inferiority	Work Identification vs. Identity Foreclosure			
V. ADOLESCENCE	Time Perspective vs. Time Diffusion	Self-Certainty vs. Identity Consciousness	Role Experimentation vs. Negative Identity	Anticipation of Achievement vs. Work Paralysis	Identity vs. Identity Diffusion	Sexual Identity vs. Bisexual Diffusion	Leadership Polarization vs. Authority Diffusion	Ideological Polarization vs. Diffusion of Ideals
VI. YOUNG ADULT					Solidarity vs. Social Isolation	Intimacy vs. Isolation		
VII. ADULTHOOD							Generativity vs. Self-Absorption	
VIII. MATURE AGE								Integrity vs. Disgust, Despair

Figure 1. Stages of Psychosocial Development

recourse to a diagram which, with its many empty boxes, at intervals may serve as a check on our attempts at detailing psychosocial development. (Such a diagram, however, can be recommended to the serious attention only of those who can take it *and* leave it.) The diagram (Figure I), at first, contained only the double-lined boxes along the descending diagonal (I,1—II,2—III,3—IV,4—V,5—VI,6—VII,7—VIII,8) and, for the sake of initial orientation, the reader is requested to ignore all other entries for the moment. The *diagonal* shows the sequence of psychosocial crises. Each of these boxes is shared by a criterion of relative psychosocial health and the corresponding criterion of relative psychosocial ill-health: in "normal" development, the first must persistently outweigh (although it will never completely do away with) the second. The sequence of states thus represents a successive development of the component parts of the psychosocial personality. Each part exists in some form (verticals) before the time when it becomes "phase-specific," i.e., when "its" psychosocial crisis is precipitated both by the individual's readiness and by society's pressure. But each component comes to ascendance and finds its more or less lasting solution at the conclusion of "its" stage. It is thus *systematically related* to all the others, and all depend on proper development at the proper *time* of each; although individual make-up and the nature of society determine the rate of development of each of them, and thus the *ratio* of all of them. It is at the end of adolescence, then, that identity becomes phase-specific (V,5), i.e., must find a certain integration as a relatively conflict-free psychosocial arrangement—or remain defective or conflict-laden.

With this chart as a blueprint before us, let me state first which aspects of this complex matter will *not* be treated in this paper: for one, we will not be able to make more definitive the now very tentative designation (in *vertical* 5) of the precursors of identity in the infantile ego. Rather, we approach childhood in an untraditional manner, namely, from young adulthood backward—and this with the conviction that early development cannot be understood on its own terms alone, and that the earliest stages of childhood can not be accounted for without a unified theory of the whole span of pre-adulthood. For the infant (while he is not spared the chaos of needful rage) does not and cannot build anew and out of himself the course of human life, as the reconstruction of his earliest experience ever again seems to suggest. The smallest child lives in a community of life cycles which depend on him as he depends on them, and which guide his drives as well as his sublimations with consistent feedbacks. This verity necessitates a discussion of the psychoanalytic approach to "environment" to which we shall return toward the end of this paper.

A second systematic omission concerns the psychosexual stages. Those readers who have undertaken to study the diagrams of psychosexual development in *Childhood and Society* (9) know that I am attempting to lay the ground for a detailed account of the dovetailing of psychosexual and psychosocial epigenesis, i.e., the two schedules according to which component parts, present throughout development, come to fruition in successive stages. The essential inseparability of these two schedules is implied throughout this paper, although only the psychosocial schedule, and in fact only one stage of it, is brought into focus.

What traditional source of psychoanalytic insight, then, *will* we concern ourselves with? It is: first pathography; in this case the clinical description of *identity diffusion*. Hoping thus to clarify the matter of identity from a more familiar angle, we will then return to the over-all aim of beginning to "extract," as Freud put it, "from psychopathology what may be of benefit to normal psychology."

PATHOGRAPHIC: THE CLINICAL PICTURE OF IDENTITY DIFFUSION

Pathography remains the traditional source of psychoanalytic insight. In the following, I shall sketch a syndrome of disturbances in young people who can neither make use of the institutionalized moratorium provided in their society, nor create and maintain for themselves (as Shaw did) a unique moratorium all of their own. They come, instead, to psychiatrists, priests, judges, and (we must add) recruitment officers in order to be given an authorized if ever so uncomfortable place in which to wait things out.

The sources at my disposal are the case histories of a number of young patients who sought treatment following an acutely disturbed period between the ages of sixteen and twenty-four. A few were seen, and fewer treated, by me personally; a larger number were reported in supervisory interviews or seminars at the Austen Riggs Center in Stockbridge and at the Western Psychiatric Institute in Pittsburgh; the largest number are former patients now on record in the files of the Austen Riggs Center. My *composite sketch* of these case histories will remind the reader immediately of the diagnostic and technical problems encountered in adolescents in general (5) and especially in any number of those young borderline cases (28) who are customarily diagnosed as preschizophrenias, or severe character disorders with paranoid, depressive, psychopathic, or other trends. Such well-established diagnostic signposts will not be questioned here. An attempt will be made, however, to concentrate on certain common features representative of the common life crisis shared by this whole group of patients as a result of a (temporary or final) inability of their egos to establish an identity: for they all suffer from *acute identity diffusion*. Obviously, only quite detailed case presentations could convey the full necessity or advisability of such a "phase-specific" approach which emphasizes the life task shared by a group of patients as much as the diagnostic criteria which differentiate them. In the meantime, I hope that my composite sketch will convey at least a kind of impressionistic plausibility. The fact that the cases known to me were seen in a private institution in the Berkshires, and at a public clinic in industrial Pittsburgh, suggests that at least the two extremes of socioeconomic status in the United States (and thus two extreme forms of identity problems) are represented here. This could mean that the families in question, because of their extreme locations on the scale of class mobility and of Americanization, may have conveyed to these particular children a certain hopelessness regarding their chances of participating in (or of successfully defying) the dominant American manners and symbols of success. Whether, and in what way disturbances such as are outlined here also characterize those more comfortably placed somewhere near the middle of the socioeconomic ladder, remains, at this time, an open question.

1. Time of Breakdown

A state of acute identity diffusion usually becomes manifest at a time when the young individual finds himself exposed to a combination of experiences which demand his simultaneous commitment to *physical intimacy* (not by any means always overtly sexual), to decisive *occupational choice*, to energetic *competition*, and to *psychosocial self-definition*. A young college girl, previously overprotected by a conservative mother who is trying to live down a not-so-conservative past, may, on entering college, meet young people of radically different backgrounds, among whom she must choose her friends and her enemies; radically different mores especially in the relationship of the sexes which she must play along with or repudiate; and a commitment to make decisions and choices which will necessitate irreversible competitive involvement or even leadership. Often, she finds among very "different" young people, a comfortable display of values, manners, and symbols for which one or the other of her parents or grandparents is covertly nostalgic, while overtly despising them. Decisions and choices and, most of all, successes in any direction bring to the fore conflicting identifications and immediately threaten to narrow down the inventory of further tentative choices; and, at the very moment when time is of the essence, every move may establish a binding precedent in psychosocial self-definition, i.e., in the "type" one comes to represent in the types of the age-mates (who seem so terribly eager to type). On the other hand, any marked *avoidance of choices* (i.e., a moratorium by default) leads to a sense of outer *isolation* and to an *inner vacuum* which is wide open for old libidinal objects and with this for bewilderingly conscious incestuous feelings; for more primitive forms of identification; and (in some) for a renewed struggle with archaic introjects. This regressive pull often receives the greatest attention from workers in our field, partially because we are on more familiar ground wherever we can discern signs of regression to infantile psychosexuality. Yet, the disturbances under discussion here cannot be comprehended without some insight into the specific nature of transitory adolescent regression as an attempt to postpone and to avoid, as it were, a psychosocial foreclosure. A state of paralysis may ensue, the mechanisms of which appear to be devised to maintain a state of minimal actual choice and commitment with a maximum inner conviction of still being the chooser. Of the complicated presenting pathology only a few aspects can be discussed here.

2. The Problem of Intimacy

The chart which accompanied the preceding chapter shows "Intimacy vs. Isolation" as the core conflict which follows that of "Identity vs. Identity Diffusion." That many of our patients break down at an age which is properly considered more pre-adult than postadolescent, is explained by the fact that often only an attempt to engage in intimate fellowship and competition or in sexual intimacy fully reveals the latent weakness of identity.

True "engagement" with others is the result and the test of firm self-delineation. As the young individual seeks at least tentative forms of playful intimacy in friendship and competition, in sex play and love, in argument and gossip, he is apt to experience a peculiar strain, as if such tentative engagement might turn into an interpersonal fusion amounting to a loss of identity, and requiring, therefore, a tense inner reservation, a caution in commitment. Where a youth does not resolve such strain he may isolate himself and enter, at best, only stereotyped and formalized interpersonal relations; or he may, in repeated hectic attempts and repeated dismal failures, seek intimacy with the most improbable partners. For where an assured sense of identity is missing even friendships and affairs become desperate attempts at delineating the fuzzy outlines of identity by mutual narcissistic mirroring: to fall in love then often means to fall into one's mirror image, hurting oneself and damaging the mirror. During lovemaking or in sexual fantasies, a loosening of *sexual identity* threatens: it even becomes unclear whether sexual excitement is experienced by the individual or by his partner, and this in either heterosexual or homosexual encounters. The ego thus loses its flexible capacity for abandoning itself to sexual and affectual sensations, in a fusion with another individual who is both partner to the sensation and guarantor of one's continuing identity: fusion with another becomes identity loss. A sudden collapse of all capacity for mutuality threatens, and a desperate wish ensues to start all over again, with a (quasi-deliberate) regression to a stage of basic bewilderment and rage such as only the very small child knew.

It must be remembered that the counterpart of intimacy is *distantiation,* i.e., the readiness to repudiate, to ignore, or to destroy those forces and people whose essence seems dangerous to one's own. Intimacy with one set of people and ideas would not be really intimate without an efficient repudiation of another set. Thus, weakness or excess in repudiation is an intrinsic aspect of the inability to gain intimacy because of an incomplete identity: whoever is not sure of his "point of view" cannot repudiate judiciously.

Young persons often indicate in rather pathetic ways a feeling that only a merging with a "leader" could save them—an adult who is able and willing to offer himself as a safe object for experimental surrender and as a guide in the relearning of the very first steps toward an intimate mutuality, and a legitimate repudiation. To such a person the late adolescent wants to be an apprentice or a disciple, a follower, sex mate or patient. Where this fails, as it often must from its very intensity and absoluteness, the young individual recoils to a position of strenuous introspection and self-testing which, given particularly aggravating circumstances or a history of relatively strong autistic trends, can lead him into a paralyzing borderline state. Symptomatically, this state consists of a painfully heightened sense of isolation; a disintegration of the sense of inner continuity and sameness; a sense of over-all ashamedness; an inability to derive a sense of accomplishment from any kind of activity; a feeling that life is happening to the individual rather than being lived by his initiative; a radically shortened time perspective; and finally, a basic mistrust, which leaves it to the world, to society, and indeed, psychiatry to prove that the patient does exist in psychosocial sense, i.e., can count on an invitation to become himself.

12. Dynamics and Classification of Disordered Behavior

Sandor Rado

ORGANISMIC UTILITY: THE ADAPTATIONAL FRAMEWORK OF MEANING

I deeply appreciate the opportunity to address this general session. First may I define my concepts. Adaptations are improvements in the organism's pattern of interaction with its environment that increase the organism's chances for survival, cultural self-realization, and perpetuation of its type. "Autoplastic" adaptations result from changes undergone by the organism itself; "alloplastic" adaptations, from changes wrought by the organism on its environment. Phylogenetic adaptations are based on genetic mechanisms, such as *favorable* mutation—the appearance of potentially valuable new equipment. The phylogenetic accumulation of *unfavorable* mutations may lead to adaptive degradation, if not extinction of the organism and the species. In ontogenetic and situational (here and now) adaptations the psychodynamic master mechanisms are learning, creative imagination, and goal-directed activity.

Adaptational psychodynamics studies the part played in behavior by motivation and control. It deals with pleasure and pain, emotion and thought, desire and executive action, and interprets them in terms of organismic utility, that is, in an adaptational framework of meaning. Its foremost objective is to discover the mechanisms by which the psychodynamic cerebral system accomplishes its integrative task.

Adaptational psychodynamics is a development of classical psychodynamics, the theoretical system originated by Sigmund Freud, and is based on the psychoanalytic method of investigation. Looking forward to the achievement of a comprehensive, unified science of human behavior, adaptational psychodynamics places the analysis of behavior in the genetic, physiologic (biochemical, biophysical), and cultural contexts of the organism. It seeks to replace undefined and undefinable concepts by defined ones and to evolve a close-to-the-fact scientific language that will convey the most information in the fewest words. Even though the introduction of numerous new terms makes communication difficult at first, this is a crucial step toward an increasingly rigorous application of the scientific method.

Behavior disorders are disturbances of psychodynamic integration that significantly affect the organism's adaptive life performance, its attainment of utility and pleasure. They are thus marked by either (1) adaptive impairment, (2) adaptive incompetence, or (3) transgressive conduct. The term impairment indicates psychoneurosis; the term incompetence, psychosis; and the term transgressive conduct, psychopathic state.

In the analysis of behavior disorders we encounter organized sequences of events which we have come to recognize as processes of miscarried prevention and miscarried repair. They are brought into play by a disordered response of the organism which we can relate to an environmental situation and trace to comparable exposures in the past. Our analysis may thus penetrate to the point where, instead of an adaptive response, a disordered one made its first appearance. This difference cannot be explained by further psychodynamic analysis, which reaches here its terminal point. Nonetheless, we can continue the etiological inquiry. We can seek to disclose the cerebral mechanism of such a disordered psychodynamic response; we can study its broader physiologic context; and we can search for its genetic context.

The ideal etiological classification of behavior disorders will draw on their genetics and physiology as well as on their adaptational psychodynamics. Today our knowledge of the genetic and physiologic phases of etiology is too scanty to attain this goal. The best we can do is experiment with provisional classifications based mainly on the psychodynamic phase of etiology. This is what I have attempted to do in the following scheme.

SCHEME OF CLASSIFICATION

Class I. Overreactive Disorders. (1) Emergency Dyscontrol: The emotional outflow, the riddance through dreams, the phobic, the inhibitory, the repressive, and the hypochondriac patterns. (2) Descending Dyscontrol. (3) Sexual Disorders: Disorders of the standard pattern. Dependence on reparative patterns: the patterns of pain-dependence; the male-female pattern modified by replacements; the eidolic and reductive patterns. Firesetting and shoplifting as sexual equivalents. (4) Social Overdependence. (5) Common Maladaptation: A combination of sexual disorder with social overdependence. (6) The Expressive Pattern: Excessive elaboration of common maladaption: ostentatious self-presentation; dream-like interludes; rudimentary pantomimes; disease-copies and the expressive complication of incidental disease. (7) The Obsessive Pattern: Obsessive elaboration of common maladaption: broodings, rituals and overt temptations. Tic and stammering as obsessive equivalents; bedwetting, nail-biting, grinding of teeth in sleep, as precursors of the obsessive pattern. (8) The Paranoid Pattern.—Paranoid elaboration of common maladaptation: the nondisintegrative version of the Magnan sequence.

Class II. Moodcyclic Disorders. Cycles of depression; cycles of reparative elation: the pattern of alternate cycles; cycles of minor elation; cycles of depression masked by elation; cycles of preventive elation.

Class III. Schizotypal Disorders. (1) Compensated Schizo-adaptation. (2) Decompensated Schizo-adaptation. (3) Schizotypal Disintegration marked by Adaptive Incompetence.

Class IV. Extractive Disorders The ingratiating ("smile and suck") and extortive ("hit and grab") patterns of transgressive conduct.

Class V. Lesional Disorders.

Class VI: Narcotic Disorders. Patterns of Drug-dependence.

Class VII. Disorders of War Adaptation.

EXAMPLES OF ADAPTATIONAL DYNAMICS
OF BEHAVIOR DISORDERS

This classification is a by-product of studies in the adaptational psychodynamics of behavior disorders, developing from the fact that the organism's first survival concern is safety. Walter B. Cannon has shown how, by their emergency function, the peripheral systems serve the whole organism's interest in safety. Following this clue, I have attempted to outline the emergency function of the psychodynamic cerebral system, terming it "emergency control."

However, if an *overproduction* of the emergency emotions such as fear, rage, and guilty fear is the organism's response to danger, it will be unable to handle effectively the exigencies of daily life. These disordered—excessive or inappropriate—emergency responses impede rather than aid, the organism in its adaptive task. They elicit processes of miscarried prevention and miscarried repair that produce further disordering effects. These failures of emergency control lead to the simplest forms of behavior disorder, which I term "emergency dyscontrol."

With emergency dyscontrol as a point of departure, it was possible to arrange the clinically observed forms of behavior disorder according to the increasing complexity of their psychodynamic mechanisms. The resulting scheme somewhat resembles the known patterns in organic chemistry, where, starting with a simple compound, we may derive increasingly complex ones through rearrangement of the components or the addition of new components.

The various psychodynamic mechanisms of behavior disorders belong to different physiologic and genetic contexts. With advancing knowledge of these contexts the apparent inconsistencies of classification may be expected to disappear. For example, in time we should be able to characterize every behavior disorder by "lesions" of the underlying physiologic (biochemical, biophysical) functions; the separate class of Lesional Disorders will then have outlived its usefulness. Our present difficulties with classification derive from lack of etiological knowledge, not from lack of logic.

To illustrate the material listed in the above classification scheme, I shall begin with the simplest psychiatric problem, the dynamics of emergency dyscontrol and descending dyscontrol (subclasses 1 and 2 of Class I. Overreactive Disorders), and follow with perhaps the most complex psychiatric problem, the dynamics of the schizotypal disorders (Class III). The pivotal task is the same in the dynamic study of all behavior disorders: to reduce a mass of observational data to an outline of their hierarchical organization.

Class I. Overreactive Disorders

The basic emergency emotions are pain, fear, rage, and, in a wider sense, guilty fear enhanced by retroflexed rage, guilty rage. These emotions prompt the organism to emergency moves: pain elicits riddance, *i.e.,* activities aimed at getting rid of its cause; fear prompts moves of escape or submission to authority; rage evokes combat or defiance; guilty fear produces expiatory behavior aimed at recapturing loving care; guilty rage leads to violence in presumed self-defense. Retroflexed rage is defeated rage turned by the organism against itself; its self-reproach is usually assimilated with the prevailing pattern of remorse. By preparing the organism to meet emergencies, these emotions play a significant part in biologically effective emergency control.

Overproduction of these emergency emotions results in disordered—excessive or inappropriate—emergency responses which, instead of aiding the organism, threaten to damage it. The infantile organism is unable to control these disordered responses by its own psychodynamic means and enters upon a state of emergency dyscontrol. Proneness to overreaction and dyscontrol develops in childhood, presumably on a genetic basis, and is carried over into adult life.

1. Emergency Dyscontrol. Failure of the organism to control its overreaction by its own resources results in the following patterns of emergency dyscontrol: the emotional outflow, the riddance-through-dreams, the phobic, the inhibitory, the repressive, and the hypochondriac.

In the *emotional outflow* pattern the organism seeks to rid itself of its excessive emergency emotions by fits of fear or outbursts of rage.

In the *riddance-through-dreams* pattern the same result is accomplished by means of enraged dreams or terror dreams.

Phobic behavior or phobic avoidance is a pattern of miscarried prevention. It usually originates in childhood, in the child's dependency relationship to his parents. The child is terrified by a chance experience, which would not produce such an overreaction in other children. To forestall the recurrence of this crucial attack of terror, he will henceforth automatically avoid the situation—the visual context—in which the terror occurred. Sometimes the child's overreaction is the consequence of a previous parental warning and threat of punishment. Magical thinking may make this mode of prevention retroactive; the child then forgets that the parental threat and his terrifying experience ever occurred. Once the avoidance mechanism is established, the child may, by generalization, use it for the magical control of other parental threats as well. If the object of the child's phobic avoidance is a "dangerous" animal, he may have a further gain: he may actually vent his repressed rage—his resentment of the threatening parent—on this "scapegoat." Phobic avoidance in the adult retains these infantile features.

The *inhibitory* is also an infantile pattern of miscarried prevention, but with 2 different mechanisms. The first prevents the recurrence of a crucial attack of fear by the organism's automatically inhibiting the motor activity—the proprioceptive context—in which the attack occurred. The other shows an even higher degree of foresight misapplied: to play safe, the organism automatically inhibits not only the activities tabooed by the authorities, but on an ever-widening scale, also the *approaches* to those activities.

In the *repressive* pattern, while unable to stop the overproduction of emergency emotions, the organism succeeds in automatically cutting off these emotions from consciousness and outward discharge. This mechanism is of course powerless to halt an eventual overflow of the repressed emotions, which are thus bound to produce further disordering consequences.

Since fear and rage are antagonistic responses, open fear is often accompanied by repressed rage; I call this dynamic formation fear over rage. Similarly, open rage may be accompanied by repressed fear; this is called rage over fear. The battle between fear and rage is strongly influenced by the conflict between the organism's desire for security through dependence and its pride in cultural self-realization. Fear over rage shows victory of the dependency need; the resulting combination of repressed rage and hurt pride is a prolific though less conspicuous source of the patient's suffering. The contrary outcome—rage over fear—shows victory of the organism's pride in having its own way. Incomplete repression of fear and rage may produce qualitatively undifferentiated chronic tension states, marked by apprehensiveness or irascibility or both.

The *hypochondriac* pattern is marked by an excessive outflow of unrecognized guilty fear. Frantically, the patient dreads illness: in his nonreporting (unconscious) belief illness is a long overdue punishment for past disobediences (sexual self-stimulation, truculence) now catching up with him. Often the attack climaxes in an act of riddance (unnecessary surgery, precipitation of actual illness, etc.). This pattern defeats its preventive and reparative intents completely: it increases rather than decreases the overproduction of hypochondriac (that is, guilty) fear. Beneath hypochondriac (guilty) fear there is always repressed rage and hurt pride.

Following the pattern of its desires, the healthy organism seizes opportunities to attain utility and pleasure. Emergency dyscontrol interferes with these pursuits; it reduces the adaptive value of the patient's life performance and tends to make him dependent on external help. If his life situation—his relatives and friends—permits, he capitalizes on his illness; he vents his repressed rage and recaptures his pride by exploiting the privileges of the sick in the manner of a child. The same infantile and vindictive exploitation of relatives and friends may occur in every form of disordered behavior, or for that matter, in every illness. *Emergency dyscontrol enters as a basic etiological factor into the emotional dynamics of almost all behavior disorders.*

2. *Descending Dyscontrol.* The autonomic overdischarge of excessive or inappropriate emergency emotions may precipitate disease processes in the peripheral systems affected. The psychodynamic cerebral system becomes aware of the peripheral disease thus precipitated, and responds to this internal event just as it responds to events in the environment. Descending dyscontrol thus brings into play a circular operation of responses, which I call the *psychodynamic circuit of peripheral disease.* The same circuit eventuates if a peripheral disease of purely peripheral origin elicits emergency overreaction with autonomic over-discharge. Clearly, psychodynamic circuit and purely peripheral physiology are interdependent and inseparable components of the same organismic context. By including the concept of psychodynamic circuit in its body of theory, purely physiological medicine advances to comprehensive medicine.

Class III. Schizotypal Disorders

The conceptual scheme of schizotypal organization evolved from the concept of schizophrenia; we shall first briefly review this development.

In 1911, E. Bleuler defined schizophrenia as follows: "This disease is characterized by a specific type of alteration of thinking, feeling, and relation to the external world, which appears nowhere else in this particular fashion.''

The current genetic theory of schizophrenia traces its etiology to an inherited predisposition, transmitted to an offspring from both parents by a Mendelian mechanism.

In Dobzhansky's formulation genotype is the inherited cause of development, and phenotype—the organism as it appears to our senses in structure and function—the actual outcome of development. In this sense the patient suffering from an open schizophrenic psychosis is a schizophrenic phenotype, engendered by a schizophrenic genotype in its interaction with the environment. A phenotype changes continuously throughout the life span; its development is circumscribed by the genotype's "norm of reaction" to changing environmental influences.

For psychodynamic purposes I shall abbreviate the term schizophrenic phenotype to *schizotype*. Can we diagnose the patient's inherited predisposition before he develops an open psychosis or even if he never develops an open psychosis? In other words, are we prepared to view him as a schizotype from birth to death, or only during his open psychosis? Clinical observation gives us the answer.

The manifold clinical pictures—symptoms and syndromes—of the schizophrenic psychosis have been described and classified by many clinical investigators; there is substantial agreement on almost all cardinal points. But when we subject these gross manifestations of the open psychosis to minute psychodynamic analysis, we discover an underlying ensemble of psychodynamic traits which, as we shall presently see, is demonstrable in the patient during his whole life. This finding will define him as a schizotype from birth to death, and will allow us to view his life history as a sequence of schizotypal changes. The ensemble of psychodynamic traits peculiar to the schizotypes may be called *schizotypal organization*. It is this organization which is meant by the prefix *schizo-* because this organization constitutes the psychodynamic expression of the schizophrenic genotypes. Conversely, we may define a genotype as schizophrenic' if its norm of reaction is schizogenic.

Before outlining this concept of schizotypal organization I shall review some relevant propositions of adaptational psychodynamics. On evolutionary as well as clinical grounds I have suggested elsewhere that in the psychodynamic cerebral system integrative activity is spread over a hierarchy of 4 levels. In ascending order, we speak of the hedonic level, the levels of brute emotion, emotional thought, and unemotional thought.

At the hedonic level the pattern for hedonic self-regulation is established: the organism moves towards the source of pleasure and away from the cause of pain. It relies on the expectation that pleasure signals the presence of needed supplies or conditions otherwise favorable to its survival, and pain the presence of a threat to its organic integrity.

At the next 2 levels the emotions are the controlling means of integration. Emotions are central mechanisms both for the arousal of the peripheral organism, and for the peripheral disposal of superabundant central excitation. We divide them into the emergency emotions based on present pain or the expectation of pain, such as fear, rage, retroflexed rage, guilty fear, and guilty rage; and the welfare emotions based on present pleasure or the expectation of pleasure, such as pleasurable desire, joy, love, and pride.

Unemotional thought forges the tools of common sense and science. By teaching the organism to support present pain for the sake of future pleasure, foresight increases the flexibility of hedonic self-regulation.

Behavior of the whole organism may be integrated at any of these 4 levels or at any combination of them. Integrative activity may be in part nonreporting (unconscious), in part self-reporting (conscious); accordingly, the psychodynamic cerebral system falls into the nonreporting and self-reporting ranges. To advance from the nonreporting to the self-reporting range, cerebral activity must pass the pain-barrier, an organization of precautionary mechanisms upon which hedonic control rests. Communications of the organism to the environment must pass the social pain-guard, an analogous organization or precautionary mechanisms, superimposed on the pain-barrier.

The conscious range is dominated by the supreme integrative system of the entire organism, which I call its *action-self*. Of proprioceptive origin, the action-self emerges from the circular response pattern of self-awareness and willed action. It then integrates the contrasting pictures of total organism and total environment that provide the basis for the selfhood of the conscious organism. These integrations are fundamental to the organism's entire orientation and represent highly complex organizations composed of sensory, intellectual, emotional, and motor components. At first the organism attributes unlimited power to its willed actions; hence its first thought-picture of itself is one of an omnipotent being. This early thought-picture—designated as its primordial self—remains the source of its indestructible belief in magic. Recognizing the difference between attainment and aspiration, present and future, the maturing organism differentiates its thought-picture of self into a tested self and a desired self. However, under the pressure of strong desire, this forced and precarious differentiation tends to disappear.

Using this framework of meaning, I can state in simple terms the basic observation upon which the conceptual scheme of schizotypal organization rests. *In the schizotypes the machinery of psychodynamic integration is strikingly inadequate, because one of its essential components, the organizing action of pleasure—its motivational strength—is innately defective. My term for this crucial defect is "integrative pleasure deficiency."*

This formulation derives from 2 sets of data. First, the patient himself often realizes that his pleasure, his pleasurable emotions and thoughts, are inadequate if not rudimentary. "I am," said one of our clinic patients, "incapable of giving and sharing love"; and again, "I do not know how to react with people." Secondly, we can conveniently observe the motivational strength, the integrative action and scope, of the patient's emotions. We then see that the integrative action of his welfare emotions as well as of his pleasure is significantly diminished. We shall now explore the far-reaching consequences of this condition.

It is generally known that pleasurable emotions facilitate performance, keeping our zest to live at a high level. Insufficient pleasure hinders performance; the schizotype's zest for life is reduced. The welfare emotions also counterbalance the pain-connected emergency emotions. In the schizotypes, motivational weakness of the welfare emotions causes an emotional disbalance; without this adequate tempering influence the emergency emotions tend to grow excessive in motivational strength and integrative scope. The extraordinary strength of fear in the schizotypes so impressed some observers that they called it *Existentialangst* (fear of existence); the same excessive strength marks schizotypal rage, once it has free rein.

Integrative pleasure deficiency impairs the ontogenetic development of the action-self. Pleasure is the tie that really binds. An action-self deficient in connective pleasure is brittle, prone to break under stress, to lose control of the contrasting integrations, total organism, and total environment. This weakness of the action-self is the basis of the patient's oversensitivity and profound insecurity in relation to himself, to his bodily parts, and to his environment. His insecurity in human relationships is aggravated by further consequences of the patient's pleasure deficiency. Because his capacity for affection and human sympathy is reduced he cannot reciprocate when receiving them, still less elicit them. Small wonder he finds it difficult to get a firm emotional foothold in family or other groups.

The patient's limited capacity for pleasure and love renders the ontogenetic development of a healthy sexual function impossible. The resulting sexual organization is rudimentary, ill-proportioned, lacking in genuine love and tenderness, subject to fragmentation and formation of miscarried reparative patterns.

The integrative pleasure deficiency is indeed fundamental and all-pervasive: it leaves no phase of life, no area of behavior unaffected. As anticipated in Bleuler's first definition, the schizotype differ fundamentally from other human types. Often enough the patient knows this himself: he longs to be like other people. To stress the radical importance of schizotypal organization, we must describe the life performance of the patient so organized in terms not of adaptation, but of a schizotypal system of adaptation, or, briefly, schizo-adaptation.

The degree of the innate integrative pleasure deficiency and the consequent task of schizo-adaption vary widely from patient to patient. The outcome of the patient's struggle for human existence depends upon the relation of his adaptive resources to the adaptive burden of his changing life situation. To take care of its deficiencies, the organism must evolve (1) a scarcity economy of pleasure, (2) a security pattern featuring compensatory dependence, and (3) a replacement technique of integration in which the job ordinarily done by pleasurable feeling and thought is shifted to unemotional thought. It is, I suggest, the combination of these 3 reparative processes upon which the entire system of schizotypal adaptation rests.

Though we have not yet succeeded in reducing the scarcity economy of pleasure to its elementary mechanisms, its beneficial results are readily observable. Its efficacy appears to depend on the available degree of intelligence, foresight, capacity for learning, and the absence—successful avoidance or control—of emergency overreactions detrimental to pleasure. While an endowment for superior performance facilitates the task of husbanding pleasure it may introduce new complications. The schizotypes show the same variety in endowment as the rest of the population; some of them have superior intelligence, special artistic, scientific, or other gifts. The favored pursuit of a patient belonging to this elite group tends to absorb whatever capacity he has for pleasure, leaving him disastrously vulnerable to failure, actual or presumed.

The need for compensatory dependence accompanies the schizotypes throughout the life span. Often without realizing it, the patient leans heavily on external support, his relationship to others remaining that of the child to his parents. Perpetuation of this infantile need is further complicated by the fact that in a schizotype, the child's security pattern of dependence is defective from the outset. As a child a schizotype is terrified by conflict and resents the necessity of engaging in sibling rivalry or having to play one parent against the other; he would prefer to lean on everyone within his reach. He cannot give affection, the means of ingratiation; hence his response to parental demands is chiefly limited to fear or rage, obedience or defiance, yes or no; the all-important range of "between" is undeveloped or atrophied by disuse. Under stress the adult patient tends to revert to his infantile belief that an ersatz parent can and will supply his needs by magic.

The replacement technique shifts the integrative task from pleasurable to cold thought. Schizotypes lack the feel for the simple pleasures, the affectionate give-and-take of daily life. In lieu of immediate emotional grasp the baffled patient presses his intellect into service, as if trying to pick up something at a distance with lazy tongs. For the spontaneous pleasurable responses he lacks he substitutes mechanical imitations. If highly sophisticated, he may ridicule the conventional forms of affectionate behavior, dissecting and examining them as though they were the technological performance of a machine.

In favorable circumstances this system of adaptation may hold the schizotype in a compensated state. He may, in fact, go through life without ever suffering a breakdown. However, his sensitivity to loss of affection and pleasure is extreme. Because he knows only rudimentary pleasure, such warmth as he is capable of deriving from being loved has for him a unique facilitating and reassuring value. Any change in his life situation that deprives him of this help, thus undermining his pleasure, security and self-confidence, becomes a threat of decompensation. Every shred of activity he enjoys plays an important part in his equilibrium; every loss of pleasure is a tragedy which he blames on his parent or ersatz parent. He may feel harassed from without, through the fact is that it is he who drives himself too hard. Under growing pressure he develops excessive fears, guilty fears, and rages, blurred awareness and magic thought. These inordinate emergency responses signify the onset of decompensation. In a self-defeating effort to cope with these responses, to recapture his pleasure and security from dependence, he develops a scrambled form of emergency dyscontrol which is peculiar to the decompensated schizotypes. Ordinary dyscontrol seen in other types eventuates in phobic, hypochondriac, expressive, obsessive, paranoid, and other overreactive patterns which are circumscribed and intricately organized. In the decompensated schizotypes these mechanisms appear in a scramble and are much more simply organized, springing directly from the patient's obedience-defiance conflict.[1] He may feel profoundly humiliated or disgusted with himself, experiencing diffuse and strange bodily sensations or even fearing that his body undergoes a revolting decomposition. He may sense the threat of disintegration and fear that he is losing his mind. He struggles desperately to retain adaptive control; this struggle is pathognomonic of the decompensated schizotypes. When he is overcome by the impatience of a hungry infant and in addition his remorse defeats his resentment, he may develop a facade of depression or find "relief" in alcohol-dependence. Decompensation often includes endocrine or other peripheral disturbances; in the female patient a conspicuous symptom is arrest of the menses.

As distinguished from the various forms of adaptive impairment, schizotypal decompensation is a state of threatening adaptive incompetence. The decompensated patient is left with but one remedial resource, his integrative machinery of unemotional thought. This ma-

---

[1] In 1914, exploring the value of the libido theory for the interpretation of schizophrenia, Freud contrasted the neurotic (overreactive) pictures developed by schizophrenics with those developed by patients other than schizophrenic: "The difference between the transference neuroses arising in this way and the corresponding formations where the ego is normal (*i.e.*, non-schizophrenic) would afford us the deepest insight into the structure of our mental apparatus."

chinery may hold firm or it may slowly or rapidly break down. Should it collapse, the patient enters upon a process of schizotypal disintegration marked by adaptive incompetence.

The first sign of disintegration which the patient cannot hide from the environment is his thought disorder. Apparently this disorder is a direct consequence of the overburdening of the cognitive function. However, closer scrutiny reveals the presence of a less conspicuous but all the more important factor that complicates this untoward development. In actual fact the process of disintegration begins not with a thought disorder, but with an extensive *proprioceptive disorder,* a distorted awareness of bodily self. Usually its first manifestations have already appeared at the stage of decompensation.

This proprioceptive disorder eludes psychodynamic explanation. We understand neither its cause and course of development, nor its relation to the integrative pleasure deficiency. But we can see that it disorganizes the action-self with fateful consequences. The organism now ceases to have a definite selfhood, for the disorganized action-self cannot sustain the 2 basic integrations—total organism and total environment—upon which selfhood depends. Psychodynamic life is now the interaction of a *fragmented* organism with a *fragmented* environment.[2] The patient loses his grasp and control of himself as well as of the environment. I suggest that proprioceptive awareness is the deepest internal root of language and thought. By increasing the integrative burden of the already overtaxed cognitive function, proprioceptive disorder precipitates its breakdown. The patient glides into a many-faceted thought disorder that can be understood only by a comparison with normal thinking.

The healthy organism, moving from desire towards fulfillment, analyzes experience into cause and effect so that it can find the means that will lead to the ends it desires. Normal thinking is like a suspension bridge between organism and environment. Schizotypal thinking, if severely disordered, buckles this bridge and lifts it into the air; in Bleuler's terms, it is then both de-reistic and de-personalized.

Stressing the adaptive function of thinking, physicist Ernst Mach

---

[2]The term "fragmentation" was first used by William A. White; he meant by it a "molecular splitting of the psyche."

pointed out that thought organization proceeds in 2 consecutive steps: we adjust our thoughts first to the facts and then to one another, achieving a dependable degree of objectivity, logical consistency, and thought-economy. However, Mach's formulation applies only to unemotional (objective, rational, realistic) thought. In emotional thinking the adjustment of thoughts to facts is inadequate and the adjustment of thoughts to one another aims not at logical but at *emotional* consistency. Furthermore, since thought processes take place in both the nonreporting (unconscious) and the self-reporting (conscious) ranges of the psychodynamic cerebral system, simultaneous processes of emotional thought in the nonreporting range, though consistent in themselves, may be at variance with one another as well as with the facts. The characteristics of nonreporting thought-organization (Freud's "primary process") are revealed through the analysis of dreams; emotional thoughts marked by the characteristic features of primary organization and a total lack of adjustment to the world of facts may be called prime thoughts.

The raw material of conscious thinking comes in part from the sense organs, in part from the nonreporting range. On their way, as stated above, prime thoughts must pass the pain-barrier; intended communications to the environment, the social pain-guard. We also stated that pain-barrier and social pain-guard are precautionary mechanisms of hedonic control; let us now add that conscious thought-adjustment is the rational mechanism of adaptive control of both the environment and the organism itself.

These 3 mechanisms are wrecked by the disintegrative process. Prime thoughts may then enter freely the self-reporting range, escape conscious adjustment and be blurted out or acted out. There appear hallucinations and delusions which preclude the adjustment of thought to fact even if the requisite machinery is still available. Hallucinations are prime thoughts perceived as data of the senses; therefore they have the factual reality of perceptions. Delusions are prime thoughts exalted to the plane of fact-adjusted thought by the magic of the strong emotions from which they spring and by which they are controlled; for this reason they are impervious to refutation by the true facts.

Often the earliest sign of incipient thought disorder is the loss in hierarchical depth: thought organization tends to be replaced by thought aggregation, vertical meaning by horizontal irrelevance, sense by sound. As rationality dwindles to the vanishing point, infantile tonality emerges as an ordering principle.

Disintegration of the machinery of adaptive thinking renders the patient incapable of sustaining effective human relationships. He has no facilities to handle a many-sided group situation; in his fragmented field there is room for but one protagonist at a time. He seeks to operate on a child-parent dependency pattern stripped to the bone. His choice of response is now rigidly limited to yes or no (obedience or defiance); the range of "between" disappears completely. Moreover, he tends to perceive both alternatives as equally undesirable: he faces not a choice but a dilemma of yes or no. This applies to the entire gamut of his responses, intellectual, emotional, and motor.

At the same time, almost identical changes take place in the patient's relationship to himself, to his mode of handling his own impulses. To understand these changes, we shall again take a comparative view of the healthy organism.

During the period of growth the psychodynamic cerebral system builds a semiautomatic organization of self-restraining and self-prodding responses known as our conscience. The child learns to anticipate certain parental and other authoritarian demands to which he is continuously exposed, and to meet them automatically.

The same applies to the system of enforcement used by the parents. Parental reward gives rise to automatized self-reward known as self-respect and moral pride; parental punishment, to automatized self-punishment as a means of expiating one's presumed wrongdoings and reinstating oneself in the loving care of the authority thus reconciled. The adaptive gain of conscience is security through obedience; its main problem is the handling of defiant rage.

In the disintegrating schizotype, impairment of the action-self breaks up the context in which the mechanisms of conscience operate. Subsequently, it is no longer his conscience that admonishes him but once again the disciplinary authority of his present or past. Freud discovered this regressive replacement of conscience by the original child-parent relationship in paranoid behavior. Today we realize that this regression, a disintegration of the "voice of conscience", takes in all disintegrating schizotypes; the paranoid is its most conspicuous manifestation. Continuing the reparative intent of the voice of conscience, this regression seeks to reinforce the faltering mechanisms of conscience by reactivating the infantile experiences from which they originate. To the extent to which the true mechanisms of conscience fail to operate, the patient loses his ethos—his system of shared emotional values upon which cultural group membership rests. As we have seen, the disintegrating patient's human relationships are reduced to the scant residues of his infantile dependency pattern; this same pattern replaces his conscience, his human sympathy, integrity, and standards as well. As a consequence, when the patient has to act upon his own impulses, he faces the same yes-or-no dilemma as he does in his vestigial relationships to others.

The yes-or-no dilemma ushers in the yes-or-no disturbance which is peculiar to schizotypal disintegration and forms the core of what is known as the patient's activity disorder. In a challenging situation, be the stimulation external, internal, or both, the patient may be completely blocked by his dilemma and respond only with paralyzed perplexity. Or he may try to obey and defy simultaneously, presenting a picture of intellectual, emotional, or motor confusion. Or if he gets going in one direction he may be unable to stop, continuing or repeating the same response regardless of the changing situation. Whether the resulting behavior shows automatic obedience or automatic deviance, it is unrelated to the adaptive task and is as a rule terminated by a sudden and unpredictable shift.

The symptoms resulting from the yes-or-no disturbance are well-known to the clinician. They include perseveration, echolalia, echopraxy, negativism, overtalkativeness, mutism, akinesia, hyperkinesia, inappropriate emotional or motor response, stereotypes, gesturing, posturing, grimacing, extreme muscular and postural flexibility or rigidity, and finally, schizotypal excitement and stupor.

The yes-or-no disturbance, though dominated by the obedience-defiance conflict of the infantile dependency pattern, has still deeper roots in the functional design of the sensory-motor organism, notably in the contrast and persistence principle of perception and in the principle of reciprocal innervation of muscles.

The disintegrating patient may retreat into a magic universe of his own creation. Unlike the magic world of ordinary day-dreaming, the magic universe of the disintegrating schizotype is split off into irreconcilable fragments. Creative imagination disintegrates as soon as the organism loses the unity and coherence of its thought-picture of self. This is reflected in the patient's regression to archaic sources of pleasure, in his excitements, hallucinations, delusions, posturings, and other activities detached from the actual environment. Fragmentation of his magic universe may be directly represented in his dreams and artistic creations which with telling frequency feature dismemberment, isolated of dead bodily parts, and related motifs.

The patient's subjective experience, his awareness of his own disintegrating activity, eludes our comprehension. He may show signs of what Jaspers calls "double orientation": while interpreting his perceptions (thoughts, hallucinations, actions) in a disrupted context of irrationality, he simultaneously records them in the context of residual enfeebled rationality. This shadowy perpetuation of the true environmental context may enable the delusional patient suddenly to recapture realistic contact without relinquishing his delusions or, if the thought disorder subsides, to see his delusions in retrospect against the world of facts.

The remarkable phenomena of double orientation show that the disintegrating patient still struggles to maintain adaptive control. However, the disintegration of function prepares the ground for a cessation of function. This malignant turn occurs if the organism, tiring of the struggle, gives up and withdraws. There follows a process of deterioration, a progressive functional shrinkage of the psychodynamic cerebral system. The process may lead to a total retreat from the adaptive task: the patient becomes a living corpse. His withdrawal from the struggle for existence is the ultimate consequence of the disease process, not its cause.

I have shown that the characteristics of the schizotype stem from an integrative pleasure deficiency. This defect is a basic and, in my view, innate trait of schizotypal organization. However, proprioceptive disorder, with its highly disintegrative effect, cannot be traced to this pleasure deficiency. Thus one must assume that *a predisposition to proprioceptive disorder, a sort of proprioceptive diathesis, is another basic trait of schizotypal organization.* The significance of proprioceptive disorder underscores the necessity of correlating the psychodynamic mechanisms just described with the broader context of the still unknown physiologic mechanisms in which they operate. Only through such cross-interpretation can we hope to arrive at a comprehensive theory of schizotypal organization.

On psychodynamic grounds I view schizotypal disorders as developmental stages of schizotypal organization:

III. 1. Compensated Schizo-Adaptation. This is a relatively stable stage, marked by adequate operation of the schizotypal system of adaptation. Though there is a liability to decompensation, the patient may remain at this stage throughout life. The so-called schizoid is viewed here as a well-compensated schizotype.

III. 2. Decompensated Schizo-Adaptation. This stage is precipitated by emergency dyscontrol and its consequences, which overtax the security pattern of compensatory dependence and destroy the scarcity economy of pleasure. The patient develops a scramble of overreactive mechanisms (as distinguished from organized overreactive patterns seen in other types) and the first signs of proprioceptive disorder. Though he may remain at this stage for an indefinite time or recover spontaneously, he is now threatened by disintegrative breakdown. This is the stage labeled recently by P. Hoch and P. Polatin "pseudo-neurotic schizophrenia."

III. 3. Schizotypal disintegration marked by adaptive incompetence. This is the stage known as open schizophrenic psychosis. The focus of the disintegrative process is disorganization of the action-self which, brought about by a psychodynamically unexplainable proprioceptive disorder, in turn precipitates disorders of thought, activity, etc. There is a chance of spontaneous remission, and, on the other hand, a liability to progressive deterioration.

This developmental outline suggests how pressing is the need to find the criteria for the stability of the compensated stage; and the criteria for determining the patient's liabilty to decompensation, disintegration, and deterioration as against his chances for spontaneous remission.

CONCLUDING REMARKS

The adaptational theory of disordered behavior, examples of which I have just presented, has evolved gradually over a period of years and rests upon clinical data. This is also true of the adaptational psychodynamics of healthy behavior, a subject to which I could make only scanty references in this paper.

My hope is that an adaptational dynamics of disordered behavior will stimulate physiologic and genetic studies, but the main task will be to test its fruitfulness in psychodynamic and therapeutic quests.

REFERENCES

Concepts used but not fully defined in this paper are further expounded in the author's following publications:

1. Developments in the psychoanalytic conception and treatment of the neuroses. *Psychoanalyt. Quart, 8:* 427, 1939.
2. Pathodynamics and treatment of traumatic war neurosis (Traumatophobia). *Psychosom. Med., 4:* 362, 1942.
3. Psychodynamics as a basic science. *Am. J. Orthopsychiat., 16:* 405, 1946.
4. An adaptational view of sexual behavior, In *Psychosexual Development in Health and Disease,* (Hoch and Zubin, Eds.). New York, Grune & Stratton, 1949.
5. Mind, unconscious mind, and brain. *Psychosom. Med., 11:* 165, 1949.
6. Emergency behavior; with an introduction to the dynamics of conscience. In *Anxiety,* (Hoch and Zubin, Ed.,). New York, Grune & Stratton, 1950.
7. Psychodynamics of depression from the etiologic point of view. *Psychosom. Med., 13:* 51, 1951.
8. On the psychoanalytic exploration of fear and other emotions. *Trans. N.Y. Acad. Sc.II, 14:* 280, 1952.
9. Recent advances of psychoanalytic therapy. *Psychiatric Treatment,* Vol. XXI, Proceedings of the Assoc. for Research in Nervous and Mental Disease. Baltimore, Williams & Wilking, 1954.
10. Hedonic control, action-self, and the depressive spell. *Depression,* (Hoch and Zubin, Eds.). Grune & Stratton, New York, 1953.

Other publications referred to in this paper:

11. Bleuler, Eugen. *Dementia Praecox or the Group of Schizophrenias.* New York, International Universities Press, 1950.
12. Bumke, Oswald. *Handbuch der Geisteskrankheiten.* Vol. 9, Die Schizophrenie. Berlin, Julius Springer, 1932.
13. Dobzhansky, Theodosius. *Genetics and the Origin of Species.* New York, Columbia University Press, 1951.
14. Freud, Sigmund. *On Narcissism, An Introduction.* London, Hogarth, 1925.
15. Hoch, Paul and Polatin, Philip. Pseudoneurotic forms of schizophrenia. *Psychiat. Quart., 23:* 248, 1949.
16. Kallmann, Franz J. The genetic theory of schizophrenia. *Am. J. Psychiat., 103:* 309, Nov. 1946.

13. The Psychotic Character: Clinical Psychiatric Considerations

John Frosch

The purpose of this communication is to delineate a syndrome from among the so-called borderline conditions, a syndrome which I have chosen to call the psychotic character, a counterpart to the neurotic character. I propose the hypothesis that the psychotic character represents a specific and recognizable clinical entity, very much as does the neurotic character, albeit with all the limitations of the latter diagnosis. We are dealing in the psychotic character with a crystallization of features reflected in predictable modes of response to stress situations, modes which are characteristic of the psychotic just as the reactive modes of the neurotic character resemble those seen in the neurotic.

The need to establish such an entity derives from the confusion and welter of terms used to describe syndromes seen by all of us and designated by one or another term. We have all felt dissatisfied with the terms used to describe these conditions. Included among these, have been such diagnostic entities as "borderline states,"[1] "ambulatory schizophrenia,"[2] "pseudoneurotic schizophrenia,"[3-5] "pseudo-psychopathic schizophrenia,"[6] "schizophrenia without psychosis,"[7] "latent psychosis,"[8] "larval psychosis,"[9] and so on. In some instances, these conditions have been given names characterized by the main presenting features, for instances the "as-if" character[10] or "neurotic ego distortions."[11]

Kasanin,[12] in his study of thought disturbances in schizophrenia, found it necessary to delineate a group of patients who developed psychotic reactions as the culminating points in a series of attempted neurotic solutions of basic maladjustments.

The confusion among psychiatrists has also been reflected among psychologists who have been frequently nonplussed in their attempts at classifying many of these conditions. Beck[7] recently chose to designate, from among his classifications of schizophrenia, a type he called S-3, "schizophrenia without psychosis."

To propose a clinical entity such as "psychotic character" is not, in my opinion, merely to add another term to our already overloaded nosological nomenclature. But rather will it serve, in my opinion, to reduce the multiple appellations given to what I believe are clinical variations of a basically unitary syndrome.

It is my thesis that a number of these conditions have enough basic features in common to warrant their being considered as varieties of a unified clinical entity. But if we are to understand the basic thesis of my presentation, it is important not to look to the individual symptoms or symptom clusters for clarification of the over-all basic and identifiable features which these patients have in common. We may see every variety of presenting symptom in such patients; phobias, conversion phenomena, compulsive traits, paranoid features, depression, anxiety, and so forth. But as Knight[13] has pointed out, these are frequently simply the advanced defensive outposts of basic conflicts and features.

When we use the term borderline, we are obviously referring to conditions which are borderline to psychosis. Barring certain features, these people would be psychotic, as indeed they may be from time to time. If they do decompensate and become psychotic, they may reveal a recognizable clinical syndrome such as schizophrenia. On the other hand, the psychotic picture in decompensation may run the gamut of all known psychoses, paranoid, manic-depressive, and the rest. The psychosis may be difficult to categorize so that a patient may then be described as having an unclassified psychosis, or a psychosis with psychopathic personality, and so on.

What, however, is the clinical picture when these people are not psychotic? Is it sufficiently crystallized to be recognizable as a clinical entity? I believe that in many instances this is the case. This has been alluded to by some who have felt it necessary to differentiate between borderline states, borderline personalities, borderline conditions, etc.[1] It is the more crystallized borderline personality that in many instances I have chosen to designate as psychotic character. The syndrome is no more of a transitional phase on the way to or from symptom-psychosis, than the syndrome of neurotic character is a transitional phase on the way to or from symptom-neurosis. Under certain circumstances, decompensation may lead to psychosis just as neurosis may develop from decompensation in the neurotic character. But it is equally possible for such an individual to go on all his life without developing psychosis— preserving all the while the identifiable features of the psychotic character, just as the neurotic character can go on all his life without necessarily showing a symptom-neurosis and still be identified as a neurotic character.

It is the intention here to focus on some of common basic features which characterize this syndrome and to bypass any extensive examination of the multiplicity of symptoms which may derive from these basic features. For the purpose of this presentation, I shall confine myself to the clinical psychiatric features of this syndrome. In another communication, I presented a discussion of its dynamic, genetic and therapeutic considerations.[14]

To facilitate this, I have chosen to establish as the main frame of reference the state and position of the ego and its functions with regard to the external and internal environment, concentrating in the main on the position regarding reality, object relations and the other psychic structures. It is obvious, as has been repeatedly emphasized by others, that to separate these areas is a highly artificial procedure. Their interdependence and mutual influence will become increasingly evident in this discussion. It is only to scrutinize the individual features more carefully that they are separated.

Let us turn to an examination of the psychotic character, with the foregoing as a frame of reference. It must again be stressed that just as the neurotic character disorder is under the dominance of those features which characterize neurosis, the psychotic character should reveal those—in the areas which have been noted—that characterize psychosis. There are however important differences. These consist of a relative preservation of the capacity to test reality; a relatively higher level of object relations; a capacity for reversibility of regression, giving transience to the appearance of psychotic symptomatology; and the presence of a reality-syntonic adaption. Aside from these features, the psychotic character will show many of the disturbances characterizing the psychotic patient in the three areas chosen for the frame of reference.

In examining the position of the ego and its function toward reality, there are three areas which must be differentiated and scrutinized. There are the *relationship with reality,* the *feeling of reality,* and the *capacity to test reality*. It is obvious that the three are functionally very closely interwoven and should not be separated except for examination.

Each of these areas will be scrutinized separately. The relationship with reality involves a person's capacity to perceive the external and internal world and the appropriateness of his relationships to them. There should be awareness of the limits of these areas, since an important factor in a healthy relationship with reality is the existence of consistent and clearly defined ego boundaries with adequately developed differentiation of self. Object relations are certainly involved in the ego's relationship with reality, but I believe this warrants separate consideration.

In psychosis, impairment of the relationship with reality may reflect itself in perceptual distortions such as halluncinations and illusions, as well as in difficulties in separating the self from the outside world. It may reflect itself in bizarrely distorted attitudes toward the responsibilities of life within a given culture, as well as in bizarre deviations in social amenities, and so on. In the psychotic character we see that—as in psychosis—perceptual distortions ranging from the barely discernible to gross hallucinatory manifestations may be present. Such perceptual distortions may be present also for internal experiences, especially somatic sensations, which may be felt vividly and are frequently distorted.

What characterizes these perceptual disturbances, in contrast to those of psychosis, is their *relative transience and reversibility*. These characteristics are most often facilitated by the relative retention of the capacity to test reality. There may be a frightened awareness of this possibility for distortion, so that during one psychoanalytic session when the lights actually dimmed, a patient asked me with an anxious voice whether I had seen the lights dim. When I assured him that I had, he gasped with relief since he was fully aware of his propensity for distorting perception, as well as of its general significance.

A 24-year-old woman reported that while she was in the waiting room she had imagined that her boyfriend was there. He looked so real that she had begun talking aloud to him. Manifestly embarrassed at this confession, she added that she had pulled herself right back. "You'll think I'm crazy talking like this—I slip off sometimes, but I catch myself in time or else I would really go nuts."

Sometimes these patients will experience vivid distortions of reality under the influence of drugs. A 19-year-old girl, while trying a combination of dexedrine and marijuana for "kicks," began to have very disturbing sensations. She felt that she was back in her room at home and that the boy she was with was her father. This feeling would become especially vivid when she closed her eyes; then, as she was kissing the boy, she kept murmuring, "daddy, daddy." She was able to pull herself back. This happened on a number of occasions, but at other times, she said, "I wouldn't let myself relax and slip off." It was obvious that these manifestations could be reversed.

The propensity for *regressive* perceptual distortions was illustrated by this patient whenever she was in physically and psychologically stressful situations. She recognized this propensity, feared it, and yet said, "I'm afraid of it, yet I kind of like the sensation when I feel myself slipping off." She recalled that when she had infectious mononucleosis, she would let herself slip off and feel as though she were "going out of the picture." At such times incidents from her past would appear before her with unusual vividness, and she would lose contact with the present. On one occasion, she was reading an article about injuries and spinal taps. She made a quick and vividly intense identification when she looked at the picture of a spinal tap being given, since she herself had had a spinal tap in connection with a head injury a year or so before. She felt that she was back in the whole situation and was slipping off into a state in which the whole world seemed to be receding from her. She became tense, panicky, and frightened, and hurriedly "caught hold of things."

The disturbed relationship with reality is further seen in the diffusion of ego boundaries which makes it difficult at times for these people to differentiate the self from the nonhuman environment. In this respect, they are very much like psychotic patients. Yet, with it all, the psychotic character still does not lose contact with reality over a consistent period. Although showing transient episodes of fusing with the environment, he is fully aware of difference between himself and the environment.

One of my patients had a great deal of difficulty in differentiating herself from her recently vacated apartment. She felt that she had abandoned this apartment and that both shared a common loneliness and depression which made her return a number of times for mutual consolation.

Another patient, while on vacation, went into a state resembling cosmic identity. She was in a tropical country, and felt herself fused with the elements. The air, the water, the warmth of the whole place, became part of her. She was in a "state of limbo," yet, at the same time, she was aware that what was happening was unusual and different, and she was still able to maintain her identity. This peculiar difficulty in differentiating herself from the environment gave a quality of unreality to many of the objects about her. This reaction leads us to an examination of the *sensation and feeling of reality* in these patients who show many of the disturbances seen in psychosis.

One is concerned here with the feelings and sensations of outer and inner reality as *perceived by the individual*. There is ordinarily a sense that phenomena going on around and within one are real. In the psychotic, disturbances in this sphere will affect this sense of the real.

The psychotic character may, like the psychotic, show frequent disturbances in the feeling of reality—sometimes of a persistent nature. These may be reflected in mild feelings of unreality, or depersonalization, such as during the vacationing patient's fusion with the tropical environment. During an unstructured situation such as of a person in analysis or under drugs, we not infrequently encounter disturbances in the feeling of reality. In contrast to the psychotic, however, *these patients show a tendency toward rapid reversibility characteristic of the disturbances in perception described in the foregoing*. The disturbances fade into the background, constituting however, an everpresent potential.

I have emphasized the reversibility of disturbances in the relationship to reality and the feelings of reality in the psychotic character, in contrast to the case in psychosis. This, of course, is facilitated by the capacity to test reality. What we are dealing with in this ego function is an individual's capacity to evaluate appropriately the reality of phenomena going on around and within him. This may require a basis for comparison. Of course, the base line which an individual uses to test reality may be difficult to establish. It may well involve the hitherto-existing state of the individual's *relationship with and feeling of reality*. If, hypothetically, he has heard voices all his life, it may be difficult to establish the unreality of a hallucination. Testing reality involves the existing attitudes of others in a given culture, and must take into consideration conventional or socialized knowledge of reality.[15]

With these qualifications in mind, we may nonetheless say that the capacity to test reality involves the ability to arrive at a logical conclusion from a series of observable phenomena. If the individual is unable to reach such a conclusion when presented with objective data, his capacity to test reality is impaired. This, as I indicated, must make provision within a given culture for non-objective reality, as represented by conventional acceptance of such a reality without objective validation.

In studying the capacity to test reality, it is relevant to evaluate disturbances in the first two areas. One must try to delineate the boundary between the presence of such phenomena as a distortion of perception or a feeling of depersonalization, and the patient's evaluation of them. It is conceivable that a hallucination which represents a distortion in perception may, nonetheless, not be accompanied by a loss in the capacity to test reality if the patient is able to recognize the phenomenon for what it is, that is, internally derived.

A woman patient suddenly felt the floor tremble at a concert. She asked the people beside her whether they had felt this too, but they had not. "I was puzzled by this. I concluded, therefore, that this was a projection of my own vaginal orgasm." Now this certainly reveals a closeness to the id which raises suspicions of psychosis. The perception of trembling of the floor reflects some disturbance in the relationship to reality; but when two other persons did not perceive the trembling, the patient was able to realize that the experience was derived from herself.

One also sees this in hypnagogic and hypnopompic hallucinations where an individual may momentarily be carried away by what appears to him to be the vividness of an experience, only to be able to evaluate this in the face of observable facts as not having been externally derived.

In evaluating the ego's position as regards reality, all these areas have to be taken into consideration. The use of the term *break with reality* in establishing the presence of psychosis is in my opinion too broad a frame of reference. When one speaks of a break with reality one should designate the specific area involved. Is this break reflected in the *relationship with reality,* the *feeling of reality,* or the *capacity to test reality?* Obviously, all three are usually interrelated and lability in the first two, points to a rather tenuous hold on reality and affects the capacity to test reality. Yet, these may be impaired with a reasonable retention in the capacity to test reality.

In psychosis, we are generally dealing with impairment in all these areas. However, I believe that in any given condition, the existence of psychosis, insofar as the ego's position as regards reality is concerned, hinges mainly on the loss or retention of the capacity to test reality. Thus, from this viewpoint, an individual may have disturbances in the *relationship to reality* and in the *feeling of reality* and still not be psychotic.

This is what characterizes the psychotic character disorder in contrast to the psychotic, insofar as reality testing is concerned. Insofar as the ego's position concerning reality is concerned, we find, just as in psychosis, impairment in the relationship to reality, in the feeling of reality, and in the capacity to test reality. But in contrast to psychosis, the impairment is predominantly in the first two areas with relatively less involvement in the third. We are dealing of course with a *relative* preservation of the capacity to test reality in these patients. This function is still defective and may even be lost transiently. We shall generally encounter primitive modes of reality testing characteristic of the earlier stages in psychic development, so that all the senses may be actively brought into play. There is a need to touch, see, feel, hear and smell. To be real, the outer world must be vividly perceived.

A patient, shopping for clothing for her child, had a great deal of difficulty in remembering the size wanted when her child was not with her. It was as though, by not being present, the child was nonexistent. The actual physical presence and sense-stimulation was necessary for the patient to be convinced of her child's existence.

A curious anomaly in one of my patients illustrated a disturbance in relationship to reality as well as a special form of testing reality. My patient suffered from anosmia, which had been present as far back as he could remember. He could discern certain strong odors; but, in the main, his preception of strong odors was almost tactile. He could feel that the air was heavy or different. The use of this anosmia to distort and deny the reality of certain objects was illustrated by the fact that he fantasied that people did not exist and that objects were not real unless they had odors. At times, he could perceive this, as when he had sexual relations of a satisfactory nature for the first time. He himself existed because he would not bathe for weeks or months at a time—as a result of which he smelled to others and was, therefore, real to them. But since they did not smell to him, he could deny their existence.

I would say, therefore, insofar as the ego's position vis-à-vis reality is concerned, that although there are disturbances in all three areas very much as in psychosis, what differentiates the psychotic character from psychosis, is that the distortions of the psychotic character are mostly in the first two areas, and the capacity to test reality is relatively well preserved. Even if there are disturbances in these areas there is a *capacity for reversal*.

As I have indicated, although the nature and level of object relations are integral parts of the ego's *relationship to reality,* the importance of this subject warrants separate consideration. Obviously, there is a mutual relationship between the level of object relationship and all the other areas we are discussing. Furthermore, the level of object relationship achieved is considered by some to be a useful frame of reference in evaluating various clinical conditions. But the question of the level achieved in a given condition is frequently a source of confusion and dispute.

Primitivization of object relationship or nonprogression from archaic object relations is traditionally associated with psychosis. The degree or level of such primitivization in extreme instances is generally to pre-object levels of undifferentiated psychic development, that is, primary narcissism. We must bear in mind that such primitive object relations may form a spectrum from cosmic identity, on through autistic and symbiotic relationships. Furthermore, there may be progression in some aspects of object relations and not in others. But bearing these reservations in mind, one can accept as a workable hypothesis that in psychosis the nature and level of object relationships is rather primitive. This may be seen in severe identity disturbances with objects, and so forth.

In contrast to the psychotic, the psychotic character has progressed beyond objectlessness to the point of recognition of need-gratifying objects, but is still at an infantile level of object relations. At times, archaic psychotic-like manifestations of object relations appear but in contrast to psychosis these are rapidly reversed.

One of my patients who showed a propensity to de-differentiate and fuse with the environment became very disturbed when both she and her child wore a pink dress. The common color led to a fusion of herself and her child so that there was one pink object. She was very frightened by this and was able to pull herself back and to realize that she was separate from her child. She also did the same with her mother and at times could not tell the difference between herself and her mother, and when she embarked upon a buying spree, felt it was her mother who was making the selections.

It is clear, however, that episodes of de-differentiation are transient and that the actual level of object relationships is much more advanced than in the psychotic. The object relations consist of a combination of progressive and regressive attachments, with ample evidence of advanced developmental thrusts in the ego's relationship with objects.

This paves the way to a discussion of the next important area to be considered: the state of the psychic structures as well as the position of the ego and its functions in relation to the other psychic structures. Space will not permit a detailed discussion of this important area, but one might say that psychosis is characterized by a lack of harmony and equilibrium among the psychic structures that is best exemplified by a closeness of the ego to the id. Resulting from this are the invasion of derivatives from the id into consciousness in a persistent and relatively undistorted manner, a replacement of reality by fantasy, the dominant influence of the primary process on thought, feeling and behavior, the de-neutralization of instinctual drives, and so forth.

In psychosis, disturbances in the state of the ego may include the whole gamut of regressive ego alterations, expressed in disordered states of consciousness. These may be reflected in hypnoid, twilight and dream states, oceanic feelings, cosmic identification, Isakower phenomena, as well as in feelings of dissolution and disintegration, and in ego-splitting.

The id in psychosis is demanding, powerful and untamed. Insofar as the super-ego is concerned, we will frequently see evidence of regressive, archaic precursors with an alien quality, vis-à-vis ego functions and an omnipresent tendency toward externalization.

When the clinical picture is dominated by manifestations derived from disturbances in all of these areas, we are dealing with psychosis. The psychotic character may suffer from the self-same disturbances which characterize this area in psychosis. Thinking, feeling, and behavior at all levels are frequently under the influence of the primary process. Some of the patients show a frightening propensity for dipping deep into the unconscious and coming up at times with relatively undistorted id-derived material hitherto repressed. Fantasy may at times vividly invade reality, displacing it transiently. These disturbances frequently reflect themselves in oddities of manner and speech.

Primitive libidinal and aggressive impulses may *transiently* engulf and overwhelm the ego. The expression of rage and anger with paranoid outbursts may arise as a result of frustration of unrealistic demands made upon the therapist and the environment. One patient suspected that I might report him to the authorities for "illegal infringements," together with a realization that I would not do so. He was constantly tortured between his paranoid breakthrough and reality testing, which enabled him to see that his ideas were not valid.

There is also evidence of a rather primitive and archaic superego which is at the same time lacunae-riddled. Concomitant with impulsive breakthroughs, we find hypercritical and harsh reactions, so that the result might be disproportionate guilt—and depression as a reaction. At times, morbid fear exists at the possibility of such breakthroughs. This may bring inhibition in its wake, with postural and characterological rigidities.

The ego state may be characterized by *transient* regressive alterations with disturbed states of consciousness. Many bizarre acts may be carried out during these disturbed states—sometimes described as dream or twilight states. These disturbed states of consciousness may go unrecognized, as they are frequently subtle in appearance. At times, the patient feels himself caught up in a frenzy of activity carried along helplessly as in a "dream." The sense of time, place and person become vague.

One patient of the type discussed here would embark upon an alcoholic and sexual spree of a most bizarre and dangerous self-destructive nature. He would end up in some hotel, broke, disheveled and dirty. In trying to reconstruct the events preceding and during these escapades, he had difficulty in fixing exact times and the sequence of events. It was soon apparent that his escapades occurred in a disordered state of consciousness. "It's as though I were another person or in a dream state." This man was not epileptic, nor was there evidence of any other organic process to account for this state which was *not persistent*.

In the psychotic character, as in the active psychotic, anxiety may be all-pervasive. It is related to what has been designated by some as basic anxiety, closer to nonspecific tension, than to defensive anxiety, although the latter is certainly present. Frequently, when such patients are asked to describe their anxiety, they are unable to do so. "I just feel tense, I don't know what else to say." Anxiety may be accompanied by restlessness; and at times pan-anxiety expressed in phobias dominates the picture.

All the disturbances just described are those characteristic of psychosis. Yet, in the psychotic character, these disturbances are in constant conflict with a large portion of the ego that is still intact enough to function as observer and evaluator, even if it is not always in control. This facilitates the ego's capacity for *reversibility of de-differentiation and regression* which is so characteristic of the psychotic character and which is a measure of the degree of ego strength missing in the psychotic.

In connection with this, we might say that the weakness of the ego in the psychotic character, just as in the psychotic, lies in the ease of regression. However, the ego strength lies in the ability to reverse this process. I would, therefore, say the ease of regression in stress situations is to be considered one of the manifestations of the crippled ego. However, in contrast to psychosis, this *tendency to regress rather easily is coupled with a capacity for reversal.*

Growing out of all these basic disturbances are a multiplicity of symptoms, as well as of disturbances in the environmental adaptation of the individual. In psychosis one generally sees an alloplastic modification of the environment accompanied by disturbance in the capacity to test reality. There are frequently denial and replacement of reality by a new "reality," built out of autistic productions. This results in actual distortions of external material reality. One, therefore, sees in psychosis an ego-syntonic adaptation which is *dystonic* with reality.

Adaptation in the psychotic character is also alloplastic, but as in most character disorders, one finds a relative preservation of reality testing in contrast to the case in the psychotic. There are of course gaps, as described in the foregoing, with severe reality distortions, resulting in transient dystonic manifestations. We also see many evidences of autoplastic modifications.

In the psychotic character, adaptation is established at different levels and does not follow either the extreme regressive adaptations of psychosis or the more integrated higher level ones seen in neurotics, or in the normal. Evidences of regressive and progressive adaptations may be seen side by side. This can be seen in the patients' approach to life situations such as work, school, marriage, and in social amenities, where in spite of severe disturbances, they make in the main a syntonic adaptation to objective reality.

One such patient, a young man whom I first saw when he was 18 and whom I had the opportunity to follow for some time, had hair plucking as one of his outstanding symptoms. In addition, he was tall, ungainly and dis-co-ordinated in motility. In spite of excellent intelligence, he was repeatedly left back and was unable to finish school. He developed intense relationships, both positive and negative, with other people. He made insatiable demands on his parents, was considered peculiar and queer; and, with his plucked head, he certainly presented a bizarre appearance. He would frequently go into severe depressions which at times were contrasted with wild outbursts of almost manic activity. At times, he was explosive and impulsive. Although his capacity to test reality showed frequent gaps as reflected in exceedingly poor judgment, and unrealistic self-deception, he nevertheless had the capacity at other times to see himself in proper perspective. He was aware of how he appeared to others. He was ashamed and did not want to be seen because of his bizarre appearance, and similar handicaps, and would, at frequent intervals, go out only at night. He liked to be with people, would make friends very quickly but would soon lose them. After a while he did not want to go back to his school because he was so much older and bigger than the rest of the children in his class. He was subsequently able, however, to finish high school in a different school. Over a period of some 10 years, he has had no psychotic break.

Still another patient, a brilliant, 45-year-old woman, married for the third time, revealed a life pattern of disorganization in almost all areas. Her home was a model of disruption. All four children, products of three marriages, reflected this disorganization in various modes of disturbed behavior. When dressed properly, this woman was attractive but her hair was never neat, her lipstick was always on askew; a cigarette dangling from her mouth would be constantly dribbling ashes on her expensive but disarrayed dress. A not-too-clean slip could be seen from time to time extending below her dress hemline, rumpled stockings, with the inevitable run, were almost a stock piece of apparel. With all this, she did run her house after a fashion, had friends, went out socially, and was considered by many to a very likable person, if a bit queer. She was able to work at jobs rather productively, although never to her best capacity.

The anosmic patient previously described (p. 270) had many ego distortions which in some circles made him conspicuous. In dress, appearance, and behavior, this patient attracted attention. His beard, his long, disheveled and unkempt hair, his deliberate wearing of torn and dirty clothing, his rigid stance, all contributed to a bizarre appearance which commanded attention. Yet, he worked, it is true, at a level not in keeping with his brilliant intellectual endowment; he had friends, and he enjoyed transient affairs. He showed an awareness of his bizarre behavior and appearance as well as of the bizarre trend of his fantasies. In time he married and at this date seems to be adjusting, still preserving many of his bizarre qualities.

Clinically, one sometimes sees psychotic characters who have established a rigid adaptation within the framework of a highly structured situation. They are able to function as long as they remain in this overstructured situation performing useful work; and one cannot easily recognize the features described in the foregoing. But placed in an unstructured setting, such as analysis, or a psychological test situation, or under the influence of drugs, the many features described here become manifest.

SUMMARY

The psychotic character is a syndrome, delineated from among the borderline conditions. It is a counterpart of the neurotic character. In many respects, the features of the psychotic character resemble those seen characterizing the disturbances of the psychotic. These disturbances have been described, insofar as they affect the state and position of the ego and its functions in regard to reality, object relations and the other psychic structures. The psychotic character may show evidences of disturbances in all these areas, as does the psychotic. However, there are basic differences which establish that these people and generally not psychotic. Foremost among these is that the capacity to test reality, while often very defective and manifesting primitive qualities, is, nonetheless, relatively intact. Although there is a marked proclivity for regression and de-differentiation, just as in the psychotic; in contrast to the psychotic, there is a capacity for reversibility. The nature of the object relationship in the psychotic character, although at times prone to primitivization with occasional regression to archaic objectless levels, is relatively at a higher level of psychic development. These persons can establish object relations, albeit at an infantile level. In spite of severe disturbances in relation to reality, they nonetheless manage to make an adaptation, which functions reasonably well and is at a reality-syntonic level.

It is important to stress that we are dealing here with identifiable features which have become an integral part of the character structure of these individuals and that we are not dealing here with a transitional phase, on the way to or from psychosis.

I would like to point out what should be quite obvious; that what I have attempted to describe is a composite, model picture. Individual cases will show wide variations, ranging along a spectrum from relatively mild and barely discernible features to grossly evident ones. Growing out of the basic disturbance may be a multiplicity of clinical manifestations giving the impression of different clinical syndromes. What justifies their unification into a common entity are the basic characterological manifestations which I have described here, and which reflect with some differences, features characteristically seen in the psychotic. Therefore, the *psychotic character*.

REFERENCES

1. Panel Report: The borderline case. Leo Rangell, reporter. J. Am. Psychoan. Assn., 3:285–298, 1955.
2. Zilboorg, Gregory: Further observations on ambulatory schizophrenia. Am. J. Orthopsychiat., 27:677–682, 1957.
3. Hoch, Paul H., and Polatin, P.: Pseudoneurotic forms of schizophrenia. Psychiat. Quart. 23:248–276, 1949.
4. Hoch, Paul H., and Cattell, James P.: The diagnosis of pseudoneurotic schizophrenia. Psychiat. Quart. 33:17–43, 1959.
5. Hoch, Paul H., et al., The course and outcome of pseudoneurotic schizophrenia. Am. J. Psychiat. 119:108–115, 1962.
6. Dunaif, S., and Hoch, Paul H.: Pseudopsychopathic schizophrenia. In: Psychiatry and the Law. Paul H. Hoch, and Joseph Zubin, editors. Pp. 169–195. Grune and Stratton. New York. 1955.
7. Beck, Samuel J.: S-3, Schizophrenia without psychosis. Arc. Neurol. and Psychiat., 31:85, January 1959.
8. Bychowski, Gustav: The problem of latent psychosis. J. Am. Psychoan. Assn., 1:484–503, 1953.

9. Glover, Edward; A Psychoanalytic Approach to the Classification of Mental Disorders. On the early development of mind. Pp. 161–186. International Universities Press. New York. 1956.
10. Deutsch, Helene: Some forms of emotional disturbances and their relationship to schizophrenia. Psychoan. Quart., 11:301–321, 1942.
11. Gitelson, Maxwell: On ego distortion. Int. J. Psychoan., 39:1–13, 1958.
12. Kasanin, J.S.' Language and Thought in Schizophrenia. J. D. Kasanin, editor. Pp. 41–49. University of California Press. Berkeley, Calif. 1949.
13. Knight, Robert P.: Borderline states. Bull. Menninger Clin. 17:1–12, 1953.
14. Frosch, John: The psychotic character—psychoanalytic considerations. Presented before the American Psychoanalytic Association, December 1959 at panel on an examination of nosology according to psychoanalytic concepts. Synopsis in J. Am. Psychoan. Assn., 8:544–548, 1950.
15. Hartmann, Heinz: Notes on the reality principle. In: Psychoanalytic Study of The Child, XI:31–53, 1956.

14. Borderline Personality Organization

Otto Kernberg

I shall attempt a systematic description of the symptomatic, structural, and genetic-dynamic aspects of the so-called "borderline" personality disorders. In the literature this psychopathlogy is referred to by various terms: "borderline states" (36), "preschizophrenic" personality structure (44), "psychotic characters" (14), "borderline personality" (41, 45). Some authors leave it unclear whether the terms "ambulatory schizophrenia" (54) and "pseudoneurotic schizophrenia" (24) refer to borderline personality disorder or to more regressed, psychotic patients whose symptomatology resembles the borderline condition. Psychoanalytic investigations of "as if" personalities (2), schizoid personality structure (6), and patients with severe ego distortions (16) appear to deal with patients who are also related to the borderline group.

There exists an important group of psychopathological constellations which have in common a rather specific and remarkably stable form of pathological ego structure. The ego pathology differs from that found in the neuroses and the less severe characterological illnesses on the one hand, and the psychoses on the other. These patients must be considered to occupy a borderline area between neurosis and psychosis. The term *borderline personality organization,* rather than "borderline states" or other terms, more accurately describes these patients who do have a specific, stable, pathological personality organization (30); their personality organization is not a transitory state fluctuating between neurosis and psychosis.

The presenting symptoms of these patients may be similar to the presenting symptoms of the neuroses and character disorders; therefore, without a thorough diagnostic examination the particular characterological organization of these patients may be missed, with the result of a poor prognosis for treatment. Borderline personality organization requires specific therapeutic approaches which can only derive from an accurate diagnostic study.

Transient psychotic episodes may develop in patients with borderline personality organization when they are under severe stress or under the influence of alcohol or drugs. Such psychotic episodes usually remit with relatively brief but well-structured treatment approaches. When classical analytic approaches are attempted with these patients, they may experience a loss of reality testing and even develop delusional ideas which are restricted to the transference. Thus, they develop a transference psychosis rather than a transference neurosis (51). These patients usually maintain their capacity for reality testing, except under these special circumstances—severe stress, regression induced by alcohol or drugs, and a transference psychosis (14). In clinical interviews the formal organization of the thought processes of these patients appears intact. Psychological testing, particularly with the use of nonstructured projective tests, will often reveal the tendency of such patients to use primary-process functioning (44).

While it is possible to identify the main differences between borderline personality organization and psychotic states (14), it is usually more difficult to identify the differences between borderline personality organization and the neuroses. Because of this difficulty, I have attempted in this paper to clarify the complex distinctions between borderline personality organization and the neuroses.

REVIEW OF THE LITERATURE

This attempt to analyze the descriptive, structural, and genetic-dynamic aspects of borderline personality organization, with a special consideration of the characteristic pathology of object relationships, draws on the work of many authors with different theoretical positions and with different therapeutic approaches. The early literature consists largely of clinical descriptions of patients who would now be considered "borderline." Such are the descriptions by Zilboorg (54), Hoch and Polatin (24), and, from psychological testing, Rapaport, Gill, and Schafer (44). Zilboorg (55) later expanded his description, and Hoch and Cattell (23) elaborated on the diagnosis of "pseudoneurotic schizophrenia." Other aspects of the symptoms of some borderline patients were studied by Bychowski (1), who also described important structural characteristics of these patients, such as the persistence of dissociated primitive ego states and the cleavage of parental images into good and bad objects. It is to be noted that both Zilboorg and Hoch, who made fundamental contributions to the descriptive analysis of borderline conditions, believed that all such patients were schizophrenic. They seem to have been unaware that they were confronted with a different form of psychopathology.

Until recently, much confusion in the literature was caused by the fact that the term "borderline" was used to refer both to the transitory acute manifestations of patients who were rapidly regressing from neurotic symptomatology to an overt psychotic reaction, and also to patients who function chronically in a stable way at a level which was on a borderline between neurosis and psychosis (41, 45, 50). The term "borderline" should be reserved for those patients presenting a chronic characterological organization which is neither typically neurotic nor typically psychotic, and which is characterized (i) by typical symptomatic constellations; (ii) by a typical constellation of defensive operations of the ego; (iii) by a typical pathology of internalized object relationships; and (iv) by characteristic genetic-dynamic features. Frosch (14) has contributed to the differential diagnosis of borderline personality organization from psychosis. He stresses that although borderline patients have alterations in their relationship with reality and in their feelings of reality, their capacity to test reality is preserved, in contrast to patients with psychotic reactions.

The literature on the structural aspects of borderline personality organization can be divided into two groups: (i) considerations of the nonspecific manifestations of ego weakness and regression to primitive cognitive structures related to primary-process thinking; and (ii) considerations of the specific defensive operations that are characteristic of borderline personality organization. The first group was influenced by Rapaport, Gill, and Schafer (44), especially by their finding that there existed a group of "preschizophrenic" patients who revealed a predominance of primary-process thinking on psychological testing, which also reflected marked ego weakness in comparison with the typical neurotic patients. Knight (36, 37) synthesized both the general descriptive features of these patients and the implications from their ego weakness for treatment. He called attention to the severe regression in the transference, and to the need to modify accordingly the psychotherapeutic approach to these patients.

Important contributions to the second group, that is, to an understanding of the specific defensive operations which are a part of the structural organization of these patients, have come from a different theoretical orientation; particularly from the analysis of the processes of splitting, and its particular relevance to schizoid patients, as described by Fairbairn (6, 7) and Melanie Klein (35). The first reference to the mechanism of splitting was made by Freud (12, 13), but later the term was expanded by Fairbairn. He used the term to refer more to an active defensive mechanism rather that to a description of a certain lack of integration of the ego. Further contributions to the concept of splitting as a central defensive operation of the ego at regressed levels and to its relationship with other related mechanisms, were made by Rosenfeld (46, 50) and Segal (48). I have reported elsewhere a somewhat different, and certainly more restricted definition of the term "splitting" than that used by authors of the Kleinian school (30).

Edith Jacobson made additional contributions to the analysis of the specific defensive operations in borderline patients (25, 26, 27). Anna Freud (10) suggested that there existed a general need for a chronological listing of defensive operations of the ego, ranging from those characteristics of very early stages of ego development in which a clear-cut separation between ego and id had not yet taken place, to those characteristics of the more mature ego. The possibility of developing a conception of mental illness as a unitary process, and a conception of the different forms of psychopathology as related to specific orders or levels of defensive organization, has been propoosed by Karl Menninger et al. (40). Menninger's work has stimulated my efforts to improve our understanding of the specific "archaic" levels of defensive organization in patients with borderline personality organization.

The most important contribution to the understanding of borderline personality organization and to the treatment of these patients comes from the analysis of the pathology of their internalized object relationships. Helene Deutsch's (2) article on "as if" personalities was a first and fundamental contribution. The independent conclusions of Fairbairn (7, 8) and Melanie Klein (35) followed later.

A number of important contributions to the analysis of the pathology in internalized object relationships have come from ego psychology. These contributions point toward phenomena similar to those described with a different terminology by the British school of psychoanalysis influenced by Fairbairn and Klein; for example, Edith Jacobson's analysis of "the self and the object world" (28), Greenson's (17, 18) important findings, and Erik Erikson's (5) study of identity diffusion. Jacobson has contributed not only to the clarification of the pathology of the internalized object relationships of borderline patients, but also to an understanding of the relationship of that particular pathology of object relations to the vicissitudes of ego and superego formation in borderline patients. Greenson's detailed analysis of the pathology of internalized object relations of borderline patients and of its reflection on the current pathological relationships with others illustrates how a psychoanalytic understanding can be the best instrument not only for an understanding of the genetic and dynamic aspects of these patients, but also for a descriptive clarification of their chaotic behavior. Khan (31) has stressed the structural elements in regard to both specific defensive operations and the specific pathology of the object relationships of these patients.

Many of the authors referred to above also consider the genetic-dynamic aspects of borderline personality organization, and all of them stress the importance of pregenital, especially oral conflicts in these patients, and the unusual intensity of their pregenital aggression. They also stress the peculiar combination of pregenital drive derivatives and genital ones, and these issues are described in detail by Melanie Klein (34), and by Paula Heimann (22).

Because the therapeutic implications of the borderline personality organization will not be discussed in this paper, the literature relevant to treatment will not be reviewed here. However, because of the implications for diagnostic analysis Wallerstein's (51) description of psychotic transference reaction in patients who diagnostically are not psychotic, and Main's (39) illustration of the effects of the defensive operations of these patients on the immediate hospital environment must be mentioned. The diagnostic use of the countertransference reactions that borderline patients frequently evoke in the therapist was described in a previous paper (29). Two published panel discussions on borderline conditions have added to an understanding of these conditions (41, 45). Many questions that remain unanswered about the borderline personality organization are posed in an article by Gitelson (16) and the report of a panel on this subject, of which Gitelson's article was a part (50): Rosenfeld's comments during that panel discussion are pertinent. The special issues related to borderline conditions in child-hood are summarized by Ekstein and J. Wallerstein (4), and by Gelcerd (15).

I shall now attempt to analyze the descriptive, structural, and genetic-dynamic aspects of borderline personality organization.

DESCRIPTIVE ANALYSIS: THE "PRESUMPTIVE" DIAGNOSTIC ELEMENTS

Patients suffering from borderline personality organization present themselves with what superficially appear to be typical neurotic symptoms. However, the neurotic symptoms and character pathology of these patients have peculiarities which point to an underlying borderline personality organization. Only a careful diagnostic examination will reveal the particular combinations of different neurotic symptoms. No symptoms are pathognomonic, but the presence of two, and especially of three, symptoms among those which will be enumerated strongly points to the possibility of an underlying borderline personality organization. All of these descriptive elements are only presumptive diagnostic sign of borderline personality organization. The definite diagnosis depends on characteristic ego pathology and not on the descriptive symptoms. The following symptomatic categories are not an exhaustive list.

1. Anxiety

Such patients tend to present chronic, diffuse, free-floating anxiety. This symptom becomes particularly meaningful when a variety of other symptoms or pathological character traits are present. The anxiety, therefore, exceeds the binding capacity of the other symptoms and character traits. One exception is that of chronic anxiety reaction which has secondarily acquired the specific meaning of a conversion symptom, but this probably can be detected only through analytic exploration. Also, some patients in intensive psychotherapy may use anxiety itself as a resistance, a defensive operation which can become quite chronic, and this type of anxiety is to be excluded from the type of anxiety under discussion.

2. Polysymptomatic Neurosis

Many patients present several neurotic symptoms, but here I am considering only those presenting two or more of the following neurotic symptoms:

a. Multiple phobias, especially those which impose severe restrictions on the patient's daily life: also important here are phobias related to one's own body or appearance (fear of blushing, fear of talking in public, fear of being looked at), in contrast to phobias not involving one's own body but external objects (typical animal phobias, fear of storms, heights, etc.), and finally phobias involving transitional elements toward obsessive neurosis (fear of dirt, fear of contamination). Multiple phobias, especially those involving severe social inhibitions and paranoid trends, are presumptive evidence of borderline personality organization.

b. Obsessive-compulsive symptoms which have acquired secondary ego syntonicity, and therefore a quality of "overvaluated" thoughts and actions: although reality testing is maintained, and the patient wants to rid himself of his absurd thoughts or acts, he also tends to rationalize these acts. For example, a patient with compulsive hand-washing and contamination rituals had an elaborate system of "reasonable" considerations in regard to cleanliness, the dangers of dirt, etc. Also important here are patients with obsessive thoughts of a paranoid or hypochondriacal nature.

c. Multiple, elaborate, or bizarre conversion symptoms, especially if they are chronic, or even a monosymptomatic conversion reaction of a severe kind extending over many years' duration; also, the conversion symptoms of an elaborate kind, bordering on bodily hallucinations or involving complex sensations or sequence of movements of bizarre quality.

d. Dissociative reactions, especially hysterical "twilight states" and fugues, and amnesia accompanied by disturbances of consciousness.

e. Hypochondriasis: this infrequent and controversial constellation is probably more related to character pathology than to symptomatic neurosis. It is relevant here only in that excessive preoccupation with health and a chronic fear of illness, when it manifests itself in the form of chronic symptoms, health rituals, and withdrawal from social life in order to concentrate on one's health and symptoms, is often found in the borderline personality organization. This is not true of patients suffering from intense anxiety with mild hypochondriacal trends secondary to the anxiety itself.

f. Paranoid and hypochondriacal trends with any other symptomatic neurosis: this is a typical combination indicating a presumptive diagnosis of borderline personality organization. Many patients, of course, have slight paranoid traits and, as has been mentioned above, some hypochondriacal trends secondary to anxiety; but here I am talking only about patients with clear-cut, rather strong paranoid personality trends, and with clear-cut hypochondriacal trends not secondary to intense anxiety reaction.

It has to be stressed again that the presence of any of the above-mentioned symptoms is not in itself presumptive evidence of borderline personality organization. The presence of two or more of these symptomatic categories should alert one to the possibility of the underlying borderline pathology of the personality structure.

3. Polymorphous Perverse Sexual Trends

I am referring here to patients who present a manifest sexual deviation within which several perverse trends coexist. For example, a male patient of this group presented heterosexual and homosexual promiscuity with sadistic elements. Another male patient, also a homosexual, exhibited himself to women. A female patient presented homosexuality and perverse masochistic heterosexual trends. Patients whose genital life centers on a stable sexual deviation, and especially those who combine such a stable deviation with constant object relationships, are not included in this category. On the other hand, there are patients whose manifest sexual behavior is completely inhibited but whose conscious fantasies, and especially masturbatory fantasies, involve multiple perverse trends as necessary conditions for achieving sexual gratification. Such symptoms are presumptive evidence of borderline personality organization. The more chaotic and multiple the perverse fantasies and actions and the more unstable the object relationships connected with these interactions, the more strongly is the presence of borderline personality organization to be considered. Bizarre forms of perversion, especially those involving primitive aggressive manifestations or primitive replacement of genital aims by eliminatory ones (urination, defecation), are also indicative of an underlying borderline personality organization.

4. The "Classical" Prepsychotic Personality Structures

a. The paranoid personality (paranoid trends of such intensity that they themselves determine the main descriptive diagnosis);

b. The schizoid personality;

c. The hypomanic personality and the "cyclothymic" personality organization with strong hypomanic trends.

It has to be stressed that chronically depressed patients who present severe masochistic character traits, or what Laughlin (38) has called the "depressive personality," are *not* included here, in spite of the fact that depression as a syndrome can present itself with features which are borderline between neurotic and psychotic levels of depression. This category of patients will be included in a later discussion of masochistic character trends.

5. Impulse Neurosis and Addictions

I am referring here to those forms of severe character pathology in which there is chronic, repetitive eruption of an impulse which gratifies instinctual needs in a way which is ego dystonic outside of the "impulse-ridden" episodes but which is ego syntonic and actually highly pleasurable during the episode itself. Alcoholism, drug addictions, certain forms of psychogenic obesity, and kleptomania are all typical examples. This group actually merges with those forms of sexual deviation in which the perverse symptom appears in an eruptive, episodic way, while other than during specific episodes the perverse impulse is ego dystonic and even strongly rejected. This group also merges with the "acting-out" personality disorders in general (which I shall consider below), the difference with this latter group being a quantitative one. Impulse neuroses seem to center around one preferred, temporarily ego-syntonic outlet which provides direct instinctual gratification; by contrast, the "acting-out' characters present a more generalized lack of impulse control, more chaotic combinations of impulse and defense in several areas, and less clear-cut ego syntonicity and less crude, direct gratification of a determined impulse.

6. "Lower Level" Character Disorders

I am referring here to severe character pathology typically represented by the chaotic and impulse-ridden character, in contrast to the classical reaction-formation types of character structure and the milder "avoidance trait" characters. I shall try to clarify this point further when dealing with the structural analysis of borderline personality organization, and shall then refer to the suggestion made elsewhere (30) that one might classify character pathology along a continuum ("high level" to "low level") according to the degree to which repressive mechanisms or splitting mechanisms predominate. From a clinical point of view, most typical hysterical personalities are not borderline structures; the same holds true for most obsessive-compulsive personalities and the "depressive personality" (38) structures or better integrated masochistic personalities. By contrast, many infantile personalities and most typical narcissistic personalities present underlying borderline organization; the "as if" personalities also belong to this latter group. All clear-cut antisocial personality structures that I have examined have presented a typical borderline personality organization.

I shall briefly review the differential diagnosis of hysterical personalities, infantile personalities, and narcissistic personalities, which from my point of view do represent a continuum in that the hysterical personality is a typical "high level" character neurosis; the infantile personality a "middle range" one, actually reaching into the typical borderline field; and the narcissistic personality a typical "low level" character disorder, although it reaches up into the middle range of the continuum.

a. Hysterical Personality and Infantile Personality. One might group the main character constellations in hysterical personalities as related to the following headings: (i) emotional lability; (ii) "overinvolvement"; (iii) the combination of dependent and exhibitionistic traits; (iv) pseudohypersexuality and sexual inhibition; (v) selective competitiveness with men and women; and (vi) masochistic traits. Rather than giving a systematic overview of what is implied under all these headings, I would like to stress only what is relevant from the point of view of differential diagnosis with the infantile personality structure (3), with which the hysterical personality tends to become confused at times.

(i) Emotional Lability. In the hysterical personality, pseudohyper-emotionality is used as a defensive operation reinforcing repression; it is especially marked in areas of conflict (sexual involvements) and as a typical transference resistance. But these patients may appear to be quite stable emotionally and appropriate in their emotional reactions in nonconflictual areas. A hysterical patient who gets from one emotional crisis into the next in the relationship with her husband or in the transference may be remarkably stable and appropriate at her job. In contrast, the emotional lability in the infantile personality is generalized and diffuse. There are few, if any, conflict-free areas in their life, and this reflects a higher degree of social inappropriateness as compared to the hysterical personality. Hysterical personalities manifest a lack of impulse control in specific areas and only at the height of some conflict; infantile personalities manifest a lack of impulse control in a much more general way.

(ii) "Overinvolvement." The hysterical overinvolvement in relationships with others may appear quite appropriate on the surface. Nonsophisticated observers usually consider it in women as typical feminine charm. Childlike clinging, the need of constant closeness, develops only in certain selected relationships, and is especially remarkable in heterosexual relationships in which it represents a regressive defense against genital fears. The "extroversion" of hysterical personalities, the quick but superficial intuitive resonance with others, and the overidentification with the emotional implications of fantasy, art, or literature, develops within the frame of solid, secondary-process thinking and realistic evaluation of the immediate reality. In the infantile personality, by contrast, childlike overidentification is of a more desperate, inappropriate nature; there is a gross misreading of the motives, of the inner life of others, even if on the surface there is a good adaptation to them. Long-term involvements show a regressed, childlike, oral-aggressive demandingness in the infantile personality which is not typical of hysterical patients.

(iii) Dependent and Exhibitionistic Needs. The need to be loved, to be the center of attention and of attraction, has more of a sexual implication in the hysterical personality, in which oral-dependent needs are linked with direct genital exhibitionistic trends. In the infantile character the need to be the center of interest and attraction is less sexualized and it has a more helpless, mainly orally determined, inappropriately de-

manding nature, and the exhibitionism has a "cold" quality, reflecting more primitive narcissistic trends.

(iv) Pseudohypersexuality and Sexual Inhibition. The combination of sexual provocativeness on the surface and of sexual inhibition underneath, such as is reflected in frigidity, is typical of the hysterical personality structure. In the infantile personality, sexual provocativeness tends to be more direct, more crude, more inappropriate socially, and reflects when it is present a more orally determined exhibitionism and demandingness than a really sexualized approach to the opposite sex. Sexual promiscuity in hysterical women is much less frequent than that in infantile women. The hysterical personality reveals strong oedipal aspects of sexual involvements (such as chronic involvement with older or unavailable men), and there exists the capacity for a stable relationship with the sexual partner as long as certain neurotic preconditions for the relationship are fulfilled. In the infantile personality, by contrast, promiscuity is of a more "drifting" quality, with very little stability of object relationships. Also, in contrast to the general predominance of diffuse repression of sexual fantasies in the hysterical personality, there may be conscious sexual fantasies of a primitive, polymorphous perverse quality in the infantile personality.

(v) Competitiveness with Men and Women. In hysterical personalities there is usually a much clearer differentiation in the pattern of competitiveness with the same sex in contrast to that with the opposite sex. Hysterical women who tend to compete with men (in order to deny their sexual inferiority) tend to develop stable characterological patterns in this regard; in their competitiveness with other women, oedipal rivalry tends to predominate over other origins of the competitiveness. By contrast, in the infantile personality there is less differentiation in the typical behavior toward men and toward women; there is less chronic competitiveness in general, and there is rapid shifting between intense positive and negative feelings, between submission and childlike imitation of others, on the one hand and stubborn, pouting oppositionalism of short duration, on the other.

(vi) Masochism. I shall refer to this aspect in the context of the general discussion of the depressive-masochistic personality structure. In brief, what I call "high level" masochism, as reflected in character traits dynamically related to a strict, punitive superego, is frequently a part of the hysterical personality structure. By contrast, "middle range" or

"low level" masochistic character traits, with much less guilt and with direct interpenetration of sadistic and masochistic traits, are prevalent in the infantile personality.

The hysterical personality, in summary, gives evidence of a better integrated ego and superego, of a much broader range of conflict-free ego functions and structures, and of a predominance of oedipal conflicts over oral ones, although oral conflicts are also present. The sexual conflicts of the hysterical personality represent much more genital than pregenital conflicts (3). In the infantile personality, by contrast, pregenital and especially oral problems predominate. There is a reduced capacity for stable object relationships in comparison to the hysterical personality, and there is a breakdown of repression, with the emergence of primitive, polymorphous sexual fantasies. Infantile personalities show a childlike "dependency" of a more oral-demanding, aggressive kind than that seen in the hysterical personality. On a deeper level, patients with infantile personality structure really present an incapacity to depend on others, related to severe distortions in their internalized object relationships.

b. *Narcissistic Personality.* It has been said above that typical hysterical personalities do not present an underlying borderline personality organization, which many infantile personalities do, and that the same is true for most narcissistic personalities. Let us now briefly describe this last group: I would suggest that when the term "narcissistic personality structure" is strictly reserved to the patients presenting the constellation of character traits to be mentioned, most of these patients present an underlying borderline personality organization.

"Narcissistic" as a descriptive term has been both abused and overused. There does exist, however, a group of patients in whom the main problem appears to be the disturbance of their self-regard in connection with specific disturbances in their object relationships, and whom we might consider almost a "pure culture" of pathological development of narcissism (49). It is for these patients that I would reserve the term "narcissistic personalities." On the surface, these patients do not appear to be severely regressed; some of them may function socially very well, and they usually have much better impulse control than the infantile personality.

These patients present an unusual degree of self-reference in their interactions with other people, a great need to be loved and admired by others, and a curious apparent contradiction between a very inflated concept of themselves and an inordinate need for tribute from others. Their emotional life is shallow. They experience little empathy for the feelings of others, they obtain very little enjoyment from life other than from the tributes they receive from others or from their own grandiose fantasies, and they feel restless and bored when external glitter wears off and no new sources feed their self-regard. They envy others, tend to idealize some people from whom they expect narcissistic supplies, and to depreciate and treat with contempt those from whom they do not expect anything (often their former idols). In general, their relationships with other people are clearly exploitative and sometimes parasitic. It is as if they feel they have the right to control and possess others and to exploit them without guilt feelings—and behind a surface which very often is charming and engaging, one senses coldness and ruthlessness. Very often such patients are considered to be "dependent" because they need so much tribute and adoration from others, but on a deeper level they are completely unable really to depend on anybody because of their deep distrust and depreciation of others.

Analytic exploration very often demonstrates that their haughty, grandiose, and controlling behavior is a defense against paranoid traits related to the projection of oral rage, which is central in their psychopathology. On the surface these patients appear to present a remarkable absence of object relationships; on a deeper level, their interactions reflect very intense, primitive, internalized object relationships of a frightening kind and an incapacity to depend on internalized good objects (47). The antisocial personality may be considered a subgroup of the narcissistic personality. Antisocial personality structures present the same general constellation of traits that I have just mentioned, in combination with additional severe superego pathology.

The present effort to group character pathology according to the degree to which it may reflect presumptive indicators of borderline personality organization raises two questions: (i) Is it possible to make clear-cut descriptive differential diagnoses among all these character constellations? (ii) Is not a dangerous rigidity implied in attempting to pinpoint character pathology along a continuum? The fact is that within any form of character organization there tends to be much fluctuation and, for example, there are rather typical hysterical personalities who do have borderline features. To the first of these two questions I would respond affirmatively, suggesting that descriptive differential diagnosis is possible within the usual limitations of descriptive diagnosis in clinical psychiatry. Unfortunately, the development of this point would go beyond the scope of this paper. In regard to the second question my response would again be in the affirmative, recognizing the fact that an individual patient presenting any of the particular character constellations mentioned here might be placed at any point along the entire continuum of character pathology. For example, patients with typical narcissistic character may not be "borderline" at all. Nevertheless, I have gradually come to the conclusion that when the descriptive diagnosis is well founded and any particular features of the individual case which appear to go beyond that descriptive diagnosis are carefully recorded, it is indeed possible to place the patient tentatively along a continuum of severity of character pathology. His placement on the "lower level" of the continuum is presumptive evidence of borderline character pathology.

c. Depressive-Masochistic Character Structures.(i) Depressive Personality. The depressive-masochistic character structure is a very complex form of character pathology, but for this very reason it may serve to illustrate the continuum of character pathology. The "depressive personality" as described by Laughlin (38) would be a good example of the "high level" character structure, characterized mainly by reaction formations. Although pregenital pathology predominates in its genesis, structurally this form of pathology is quite close to the hysterical and obsessive-compulsive characters. A somewhat different form of masochistic personality organization is also to be considered at that same high level of our continuum. I refer here to the masochistic traits that are frequently seen in hysterical personalities, and represent dynamically an acting out of unconscious guilt over genitality (for example, a hysterical patient with a severe superego representing mainly the internalized, prohibitive oedipal mother).

(ii) Sadomasochistic Character. There is a lower level of masochistic personality organization which would probably occupy some point in the "middle range" of our continuum, typically represented by the "sadomasochistic" character. A good number of "help-rejecting com-

plainers'' (9) can probably be included here. Some infantile personalities also present these traits. Masochistic and sadistic character traits appear in some combination, the depressive perfectionism is absent, and sadistic instinctual derivatives find a more direct way into impulsive character traits. In this group we find some borderline patients, in contrast to the "higher level" group of patients with depressive personality features.

(iii) Primitive Self-Destructiveness. There exists a "low level" group of masochistic characters, in which rather primitive sexualization of masochistic needs occurs, masochistic perverse trends may be present, and aggression is discharged indiscriminately toward the outside or toward one's own body. Patients with severe self-destructiveness (but without a well-integrated superego and with a remarkable absence of the capacity to experience guilt) are members of this group. Typical examples are provided by patients who obtain nonspecific relief of anxiety by cutting themselves or by some other form of self-mutilation, or by impulsive suicidal gestures carried out with great rage and practically no depression. From a dynamic point of view, preoedipal conflicts predominate in these patients, and rather primitive fusion and defusion of aggressive and sexual impulses occur. Most, if not all, of these patients present an underlying borderline personality organization.

In the three levels of character pathology related to depressive-masochistic traits, it can be noted that patients on the higher level actually experience more depression than those on the lower one. This brings us back to the question of whether depression as a symptom may be of diagnostic value in our analysis of borderline personality organization.

(iv) Symptomatic Depression First of all, depression as a symptom has to be differentiated from depressive-masochistic character traits. Second, the quality of symptomatic depression is important, in that the more depression is combined with authentic guilt feelings, remorse, and concern about oneself, the more it is a reflection of superego integration. Depression which has more of the quality of impotent rage, or of help-lessness-hopelessness in connection with the breakdown of an idealized self concept, has much less value as an indicator of superego integration. This is important for our discussion, because the better the integration of the superego, the higher the level of character pathology. Third, the

quantity of symptomatic depression itself and the degree to which it has a disorganizing effect upon all ego functions are important. Severe depression approaching the psychotic degree of depressive reaction, which tends to produce ego disorganization in the form of "depressive depersonalization" and severe withdrawal from emotional relationships with reality, may be tentatively considered as one further presumptive indicator of borderline personality. In such instances, in spite of the fact (or rather because of the fact) of "intact" superego functioning, the ego is not able to withstand an excessively severe, sadistic superego. The combination of these three considerations (quality of the depression, quantitative factors, and level of depressive-masochistic character organization) in regard to the presence of depression makes it evident that depression as a symptom should not be used directly as an indicator of borderline personality organization. Excessive depression and its absence may both indicate "low level" character organization. The quality as well as the quantity of depression is important here.

I have detailed the analysis of the problem of depressive-masochistic character traits and of symptomatic depression in order to stress that the suggestion of a continuum of "high level" and "low level" character pathology is not meant as a simple ordering of diagnostic labels, and requires specialized descriptive, but also dynamic and structural, clinical judgments.

In summary, to focus on the descriptive aspects of psychopathology makes it possible, if present in sufficient intensity, to warrant the presumptive diagnostic conclusion of borderline personality organization. The definite conclusion in regard to this diagnosis, though, has to depend on the structural analysis of these cases, my next topic.

Structural Analysis

From a psychoanalytic viewpoint, the term "structural analysis" may have several meanings. First, it refers to the analysis of mental processes from the point of view of the three psychic structures (ego, id, superego). This is the original sense in which Freud used the term to contrast it with the older "topographic" point of view. Second, structural analysis in a broader sense refers to Hartmann's (20) and especially Rapaport and Gill's (43) viewpoints of the ego as a combination of: (a) "structures" or configurations of a slow rate of change which determine the channeling of mental processes, (b) these mental processes or "functions" themselves, and (c) "thresholds." From a clinical point of view, this second way of using the term "structural analysis" is reflected in the focus on cognitive structures (mainly primary- versus secondary-process thinking) (42), and defensive structures (constellation of defense mechanisms and the defensive aspects of character). There is a third meaning of the term "structual analysis." The term has been used more recently to describe the analysis of the structural derivatives of internalized object relationships (8, 30). The first and second meanings of structural analysis are of course intimately related, and may be unified in Hartmann's consideration of the id, ego, and superego as three overall structures of the psychic apparatus which are defined by their respective functions, overall structures within which substructures are determined by specific functions, and then in turn the substructures determine new functions. In my attempt to analyze borderline personality organization, I shall first apply the kind of structural analysis which considers the ego as an overall structure which integrates substructures and functions, and then analyze the specific structural derivatives of internalized object relationships which are relevant to this form of psychopathology.

1. Nonspecific Manisfestations of Ego Weakness

The overextension and abuse of the concept "ego weakness" have made some people abandon its use altogether. If the various aspects of "ego weakness" are individualized and differentiated, this concept remains useful. There are "specific" aspects of ego weakness, namely, the predominace of primitive mechanisms of defense characteristic of the borderline personality organization. By "nonspecific" aspects of ego weakness, I refer to three characteristics (52): (a) lack of anxiety tolerance; (b) lack of impulse control; (c) lack of developed sublimatory channels. The presence of some degree of lack of differentiation of self and object images and the concomitant blurring of ego boundaries can be considered one other "nonspecific" aspect of ego weakness in the borderline field, but this aspect is closely linked to the pathology of internalized object relationships and will be taken up in that context. The rigidity of characterological patterns is sometimes mistakenly considered to be a sign of ego strength; neither excessive rigidity of character pathology nor its "overfluidity" in itself represents ego strength or weakness, but rather both are specific modes of organization of the character pathology.

Lack of anxiety tolerance is reflected in the degree to which any additional anxiety to that habitually experienced moves the patient toward further symptom formation, alloplastic behavior, or ego regression. It has to be stressed that it is not the degree of anxiety which is important here, but how the ego reacts to any additional anxiety "load." This variable may be difficult to observe in patients who present chronic and severe anxiety. Complete absence of anxiety is not in itself an indicator of the degree of anxiety tolerance. From a practical point of view, skilled diagnostic examination over a number of weeks is perhaps the only way of adequately assessing this variable.

Inpulse-ridden character disorders are a typical example of a *lack of impulse control*. Nevertheless, nonspecific, generalized lack of impulse control has to be differentiated from highly individualized "lack of impulse control" as part of defensive characterological formation. I have noted elsewhere (30) that what appears on the surface to be simply a lack of impulse control connected with ego weakness, may reflect highly specific defensive operations and represent the emergence into consciousness of a dissociated identification system. In this case, the specificity of the "lack of impulse control" is manifested typically by the ego-syntonicity of the impulses being expressed during the time of impulsive behavior, by the repetitive nature of the kind of lack of impulse control involved, by the lack of emotional contact between that part of the patient's personality and the rest of the self experience, and finally by the bland denial which secondarily defends this dissociated "breakthrough." By contrast, nonspecific lack of impulse control can be seen typically in the infantile personality structure. Here it appears as unpredictable, erratic impulsivity, a simple reflection of an increase of anxiety or of any particular drive derivative. It is an effort at the dispersion of intrapsychic tensions rather than the re-enactment of a specific, dissociated identification system.

The *lack of developed sublimatory channels* is again difficult to evaluate; constitutional capacities such as the intelligence level and particular skills must be evaluated, and the patient's potentiality has to be compared with his achievements. The social environments of the patient also has to be considered. In a highly stimulating, culture-oriented social environment the lack of enjoyment and creativity of the borderline patient may be obscured by his surface adaptation to that optimal environment. By contrast, patients chronically submerged in a socially severely deprived environment may appear as bland, joyless, and uncreative superficially, without necessarily revealing the more severe aspects of lack of sublimatory capacity on a deeper level. Creative enjoyment and creative achievement are the main aspects of sublimatory capacity; they may be the best indicators of the extent to which a conflict-free ego sphere is available, and their absence, therefore, is an important indicator of ego weakness.

2. Shift Toward Primary-Process Thinking

Rapaport's (42) analysis of the levels of cognitive structures according to the degree to which secondary-process or primary-process thinking-predominates in them is relevant here. Actually, this may still be considered the most frequently relied upon clinical manifestation of borderline personality organization. Much of the thinking of Rapaport et al. (44) in regard to the structural differentiation between neurotic patients, "preschizophrenic" patients, and psychotic patients (the "preschizophrenic" corresponding broadly to the borderline personality organization) is linked with their analysis of levels of cognitive structures, as is also these authors' utilization of the battery of projective tests to evaluate the degree to which secondary-process or primary-process thinking predominates. Patients with borderline personality organization seldom give evidence in clinical mental-status examinations of formal disorder of their thought processes. However, on projective testing, and especially in response to unstructured stimuli, primary-process thinking tends to appear in the form of primitive fantasies, in a decrease in the capacity to adapt to the formal givens of the test material, and particularly in the use of peculiar verbalizations.

It is questionable whether this shift in the direction of primary-process functioning represents a "nonspecific" formal regression of the ego, as was thought in the past (36). It may well be that regression to primary-process thinking is the final outcome of several aspects of borderline personality organization: (a) the reactivation of pathological, early internalized object relationships connected with primitive drive derivatives of a pathological kind; (b) the reactivation of early defensive operations, especially generalized dissociative or splitting mechanisms affecting the integration of cognitive processes; (c) the partial refusion of primitive self and object images affecting the stability of ego boundaries; and (d) regression toward primitive cognitive structures of the ego because of nonspecific shifts in the cathexis-countercathexis equilibrium. Whatever its origin, the regression toward primary-process thinking is still the most important single structural indicator of borderline personality organization. Its detection through the use of projective tests makes sophisticated psychological testing an indispensable instrument for the diagnosis of borderline personality organization.

3. Specific Defensive Operations at the Level of Borderline Personality Organization

One essential task in the development and integration of the ego is the synthesis of early and later introjections and identifications into a stable ego identity. Introjections and identifications established under the influence of libidinal drive derivatives are at first built up separately from those established under the influence of aggressive drive derivatives ("good" and "bad" internal objects, or "positive' and "negative" introjections). This division of internalized object relations into "good" and "bad" happens at first simply because of the lack of integrative capacity of the early ego. Later on, what originally was a lack of integrative capacity is used defensively by the emerging ego in order to prevent the generalization of anxiety and to protect the ego core built around positive introjections (introjections and identifications established under the influence of libidinal drive derivatives). *This defensive division of the ego (in which what was at first a simple defect in integration is then used actively for other purposes) is in essence the mechanism of splitting.* This mechanism is normally used only in an early stage of ego development during the first year of life, and is rapidly replaced by higher level defensive operations of the ego which center around repression and related mechanisms such as reaction formation, isolation, and undoing, all of which protect the ego from intrapsychic conflicts by means of the rejection of a drive derivative or its ideational representation, or both, from the conscious ego. By contrast, in pathological conditions when this mechanism (and other related mechanisms to which I shall refer below) persists, splitting protects the ego from con-

flicts by means of the dissociation of active maintaining apart of introjections and identifications of strongly conflictual nature, namely, those
libidinally determined from those aggressively determined, without regard to the access to consciousness. The drive derivative in this case
attains full emotional, ideational, and motor consciousness, but is completely separated from other segments of the conscious psychic experience. Under these pathological circumstances, contradictory ego
states are alternately activated, and as long as these contradictory ego
states can be kept separate from each other, anxiety is prevented. Such
a state of affairs is, of course, very detrimental to the integrative process
which normally crystallize into a stable ego identity, and underlies the
syndrome of identity diffusion (5).

For the internalization of object relationships, there are two essential
tasks that the early ego has to accomplish in rapid succession: (i) *the
differentiation of self images from object images which form part of early
introjections and identifications; (ii) the integration of self and object
images built up under the influence of libidinal drive derivatives with their
corresponding self and object images built up under the influence of
aggressive drive derivatives.* The first task is accomplished in part under
the influence of the development of the apparatuses of primary autonomy, which are preconditions for the operation of introjection and
identification processes. Perception and memory traces, as they are
stored and integrated, help to sort out the origin of stimuli and the
differential characteristics of perception, and gradually differentiate self
from object images. Also, the gratification of instinctual needs and their
moderate frustration foster the differentiation of self images from object
images, because libidinal gratification draws attention cathexis to the
interaction between self and objects and fosters the differentiation in
that area, and because frustration brings to awareness the painful absence of the fulfilling objects and thus contributes to differentiate self
from nonself. Excessive gratification of instinctual needs may retard
the differentiation between self and objects. From a clinical point of
view, however, excessive frustration of early instinctual needs (especially oral) is probably the main cause of the lack of differentiation
between self and objects, because *excessive frustration reinforces the
normal disposition to regressive refusion of self and object images,* representing early merging fantasies between self and object in an attempt
to retain or regain absolute gratification (28). The second task is, as

mentioned above, that *self and object images built up under the influence of libidinal drive derivatives have to be integrated with their corresponding self and object images built up under the influence of aggressive drive derivatives.* Thus, idealized "all good" object images have to be integrated with "all bad" object images and the same holds true for good and bad self images. In this process of synthesis, partial images of the self and of the objects are integrated into total object and self representations, and thus self and object representations become further differentiated from each other, and also more realistic.

These two processes fail to a great extent in the case of psychosis, and to some extent in the case of borderline personality organization. In the psychoses, there is a severe defect of the differentiation between self and object images, and regressive refusion of self and object images occurs in the form of primitive merging fantasies, with the *concomitant blurring of the ego boundaries in the area of differentiation between self and nonself.* Such regressive refusion between self and object images may depend on: (i) lack of development of the apparatuses of primary autonomy; (ii) constitutionally determined lack of anxiety tolerance (even minor frustrations are intolerable, and induce regressive fusion or merging processes); (iii) excessive frustration in reality; and (iv) consequent excessive development of aggression (or constitutionally determined excessive development of aggressive drives). *Vicious circles involving projection of aggression and reintrojection of aggressively determined objects and self images* are probably a major factor in the development of both psychosis and borderline personality organization. *In the psychoses their main effect is regressive refusion of self and object images; in the case of the borderline personality organization,* what predominates is not refusion between self and object images, but *an intensification and pathological fixation of splitting processes.*

In the case of the borderline personality organization, the pathogenic factors mentioned above in regard to the development of psychosis may also be present, but regressive refusion of self and object images or lack of development and differentiation between self and object images is not predominant. The major defect in development lies here in the incapacity to synthesize positive and negative introjections and identifications; there is a lack of the capacity to bring together the aggressively determined and libidinally determined self and object images. It seems probable that in the case of the borderline personality organization, constitutional defects in the development of the apparatuses of primary autonomy are relatively unimportant. Perhaps constitutionally determined lack of anxiety tolerance interfering with the phase of synthesis of introjections of opposite quality, but especially severe intensity of aggressive drive derivatives are the main pathological factors. As mentioned above, excessive aggression may stem both from a constitutionally determined intensity of aggressive drives or from severe early frustration, and *extremely severe aggressive and self-aggressive strivings connected with early self and object images are consistently related to borderline personality organization.*

When self and object images are relatively well differentiated from each other, and when regressive refusion of these images is therefore relatively absent, then the differentiation of ego boundaries develops relatively undisturbed; consequently, the typical borderline patient maintains to a major degree intact ego boundaries, and the related capacity for reality testing. But the *lack of synthesis of contradictory self and object images* has numerous pathological consequences. Splitting is maintained as an essential mechanism preventing diffusion of anxiety within the ego and protecting the positive introjections and identifications. The need to preserve the good self, and good object images and good external objects in the presence of dangerous "all bad" self and object images leads to a number of subsidiary defensive operations. All of these subsidiary defensive operations, together with splitting itself, constitute the characteristic defense mechanisms present in the borderline personality organization. I shall describe these defensive operations, differentiating them from their later, less pathological counterparts, that is, those defense mechanisms which occur in conjunction with repression in patients with neurotic and nonborderline character pathology.

(i) Splitting. This is an essential defensive operation of the borderline personality organization which underlies all the others which follow. It has to be stressed that I am using the term "splitting" in a restricted and limited sense, referring only to the active process of keeping apart introjections and identifications of opposite quality. This narrow use of the term has to be differentiated from its broader use by some authors. I have suggested elsewhere (30) that the integration, or synthesis, of introjections and identification of opposite qualities possibly provides the most important source of neutralization of aggression (in that libi-

dinal and aggressive drive derivatives are fused and organized as part of that integration), and that therefore one consequence of pathological circumstances under which splitting is excessive is that this neutralization does not take place sufficiently, and an essential energy source for ego growth fails. Splitting, then, is a fundamental cause of ego weakness, and as splitting also requires less countercathexis than repression, a weak ego falls back easily on splitting, and a vicious circle is created by which ego weakness and splitting reinforce each other. The direct clinical manifestation of splitting may be the alternative expression of complementary sides of a conflict in certain character disorders, combined with bland denial and lack of concern over the contradiction in his behavior and internal experience by the patient. One other direct manifestation of splitting may be a *selective* "lack of impulse control" in certain areas, manifest in episodic breakthrough of primitive impulses which are ego-syntonic during the time of their expression (and splitting is prevalent in impulse neurosis and addictions). Probably the best known manifestation of splitting is the division of external objects into "all good" ones and "all bad" ones, with the concomitant possibility of complete, abrupt shifts of an object from one extreme compartment to the other; that is, sudden and complete reversals of all feelings and conceptualizations about a particular person. Extreme and repetitive oscillation between contradictory self concepts may also be the result of the mechanism of splitting. Splitting appears not as an isolated mechanism but in combination with several others. The same is true, of course, in the case of repression, which is usually combined with other mechanisms of the "higher level" type. Splitting occurs in combination with any other or several of the following:

(ii) Primitive Idealization. This refers to the tendency to see external objects as totally good, in order to make sure that they can protect one against the "bad" objects, that they cannot be contaminated, spoiled, or destroyed by one's own aggression or by that projected onto other objects. Primitive idealization creates unrealistic, all-good and powerful object images, and this also affects negatively the development of the ego ideal and the superego. "Primitive idealization" is a term I propose to contrast later forms of idealization, such as that typically present in depressive patients who idealize objects out of guilt over their own aggression toward the object. I proposed the term "predepressive idealization" for this mechanism in a previous paper (30), but "primitive

idealization'' now seems preferable. Primitive idealization implies neither the conscious or unconscious acknowledgment of aggression toward the object, nor guilt over this aggression toward the object. Thus, it is not a reaction formation, but rather is the direct manifestation of a primitive, protective fantasy structure in which there is no real regard for the ideal object, but a simple need for it as a protection against a surrounding world of dangerous objects. One other function of such an ideal object is to serve as a recipient for omnipotent identification, for sharing in the greatness of the idealized object as a protection against aggression, and as a direct gratification of narcissistic needs. Idealization thus used reflects the underlying omnipotence, another borderline defense which I shall mention below. Primitive idealization may be considered a forerunner of later forms of idealization.

   (iii) Early Forms of Projection, and Especially Projective Identification. Patients with borderline personality organization tend to present very strong projective trends, but it is not only the quantitative predominance of projection but also the qualitative aspect of it which is characteristic. The main purpose of projection here is to externalize the all-bad, aggressive self and object images, and the main consequence of this need is the development of dangerous, retaliatory objects against which the patient has to defend himself. This projection of aggression is rather unsuccessful. While these patients do have sufficient development of ego boundaries to be able to differentiate self and objects in most areas of their lives, the very intensity of the projective needs, plus the general ego weakness characterizing these patients, weakens ego boundaries in the particular area of the projection of aggression. This leads such patients to feel that they can still identify themselves with the object onto whom aggression has been projected, and their ongoing "empathy" with the now threatening object maintains and increases the fear of their own projected aggression. Therefore, they have to control the object in order to prevent it from attacking them under the influence of the (projected) aggressive impulses; they have to attack and control the object before (as they fear) they themselves are attacked and destroyed. In summary, projective identification is characterized by the lack of differentiation between self and object in that particular area, by continuing to experience the impulse as well as the fear of that impulse while the projection is active, and by the need to control the external object (30, 46). At higher levels of ego development, later forms of

projection no longer have this characteristic. In the hysterical patient, for example, a projection of sexual impulses simply reinforces repression, and the hysterical woman who despises men or is afraid of men because of their sexual interest is completely unaware of her own sexual impulses and therefore does not "empathize" fearfully with the "enemy." All of this aggressive distortion of object images also influences pathologically the develoment of the superego.

(iv) Denial. Patients with a borderline personality organization typically present much evidence of the use of this mechanism, and especially of primitive manifestations of denial in contrast to higher level forms of it. Denial here is typically exemplified "by mutual denial" of two emotionally independent areas of consciousness (in this case, we might say, denial simply reinforces splitting). The patient is aware of the fact that at this time his perceptions, thoughts and feelings about himself or other people are completely opposite to those he has had at other times; but this memory has no emotional relevance, it cannot influence the way he feels now. At a later time, he may revert to his previous ego state and then deny the present one, again with persisting memory, but with a complete incapacity for emotional linkage of these two ego states. Denial in the patients I am considering may also manifest itself only as simple disregard for a sector of their subjective experience or for a sector of the external world. When pressed, the patient acknowledges his intellectual awareness of the sector which has been denied, but again he cannot integrate it with the rest of his emotional experience. It has to be stressed that that which is denied now is something that in other areas of his consciousness the patient is aware of; that is, *emotions* are denied which he has experienced (and remembers having experienced) and awareness of the emotional relevance of a certain situation in reality is denied, of which the patient has been consciously aware or can again be made consciously aware. All of this is different from the higher level form of denial such as is implicit in the mechanism of negation (11). In negation, a mental content is present "with a negative sign"; the patient says that he knows what he himself, his therapist, or others *might* think about something, but that particular possibility is rejected as a purely intellectual speculation. In this case, the emotional relevance of what is denied has never been present in consciousness, and remains repressed. Negation in this regard is a higher form of denial linked with repression, and quite close to isolation.

An intermediate level of denial, which is also quite prevalent in patients with borderline personality organization, is the denial of emotions contrary to those which are strongly experienced at that point, especially the manic denial of depression. It is important to stress that in the denial of depression, although we talk about the denial of an emotion alone, both the manic and the depressive disposition involve the activation of specific pathogenic object relationships. In this form of denial, an extreme, opposite affect is used to reinforce the ego's stand against a threatening part of the self experience. The fact that manic denial and depression tend to be so intimately linked clinically reveals a less pathological, less "crude" dissociation within the ego than that of the "lower level" of denial. Denial, then, is a broad group of defensive operations, and probably related at its higher level to the mechanisms of isolation and other higher level defenses against affects (detachment, denial in fantasy, denial "in word and act"), and, at its lower level, of splitting.

(v) Omnipotence and Devaluation. These two mechanisms are also intimately linked to splitting, and represent at the same time direct manifestations of the defensive use of primitive introjection and identification. Patients using these two mechanisms of defense may shift between the need to establish a demanding, clinging relationship to an idealized "magic" object at some times, and fantasies and behavior betraying a deep feeling of magical omnipotence of their own at other times. Both stages represent their identification with an "all good" object, idealized and powerful as a protection against bad, "persecutory" objects. There is no real "dependency" in the sense of love for the ideal object and concern for it. On a deeper level the idealized person is treated ruthlessly, possessively, as an extension of the patient himself. In this regard, even during the time of apparent submission to an idealized external object, the deep underlying onmipotent fantasies of the patient can be detected. The need to *control* the idealized objects, to use them in attempts to manipulate and exploit the environment and to "destroy potential enemies," is linked with inordinate pride in the "possession" of these perfect objects totally dedicated to the patient. Underneath the feelings of insecurity, self-criticism, and inferiority that patients with borderline personality organization present, one can frequently find grandiose and omnipotent trends. These very often take the form of a strong unconscious conviction that they have the right to

expect gratification and homage from others, to be treated as privileged, special persons. The devaluation of eternal objects is in part a corollary of the omnipotence; if an external object can provide no further gratification or protection, it is dropped and dismissed because there was no real capacity for love of this object in the first place. But there are other sources which influence this tendency to devaluate objects. One of them is the revengeful destruction of the object which frustrated the patient's needs (especially his oral greediness); one other source is the defensive devaluation of objects in order to prevent them from becoming feared and hated "persecutors." All of these motives came together in this defensive operation against the need and the fear of others. The devaluation of significant objects of the patient's past has serious detrimental effects on the internalized object relations, and especially on the structures involved in superego formation and integration.

4. Pathology of Internalized Object Relationships

It has been noted that the mechanism of splitting separates in these patients contradictory ego states related to early pathological object relationships. We may now add that the persistence of such early internalized object relationships in a rather "nonmetabolized" condition as part of these dissociated ego states is in itself pathological, and reflects the interference of splitting with those synthesizing operations which normally bring about depersonification, abstraction, and integration of internalized object relationships. Typically, each of these dissociated ego segments contains a certain primitive object image, connected with a complementary self image and a certain affect disposition which was active at the time when that particular internalization took place. In the case of borderline personality organization, differentiation of self from object images has occurred to a sufficient degree, in contrast to what obtains in psychoses, to permit a relatively good differentiation between self and object representations and a concomitant integrity of ego boundaries in most areas. Ego boundaries fail only in those areas in which projective identification and fusion with idealized objects take place, which is the case especially in the transference developments of these patients. This appears to be a fundamental reason why these patients develop a transference psychosis rather than a transference neurosis.

Now we have to examine further the area of specific pathology of internalized object relations in the borderline personality; namely, the incapacity for synthesizing the good and bad introjections and identifications. As has been mentioned above, the main etiological factors appear to be the excessive nature of primary aggression or aggression secondary to frustration, to which probably certain deficiencies in the development of primary ego apparatuses and lack of anxiety tolerance contribute. The consequences of the persistence of split-up "all good" and "all bad" introjections are multiple. First of all, the lack of interpenetration of libidinal and aggressive drive derivatives interferes with the normal modulation and differentiation of affect dispositions of the ego, and a chronic tendency to eruption of primitive affect states remains. Also, the specific affect disposition represented by the ego's capacity to experience depression, concern, and guilt cannot be reached when positive and negative introjections are not brought together. The capacity of the ego for depressive reaction appears to depend to a large extent on the tension between different, contradictory self images, which develops when good and bad self images are integrated, so that one's own aggression can be acknowledged, and when objects are no longer seen as either totally bad or totally good, so that a combination of both love and aggression toward integrated "total" objects can be acknowledged, motivating guilt and concern for the object (32, 33, 53). Borderline patients frequently present deficiencies in the capacity for experiencing guilt feelings and feelings of concern for objects. Their depressive reactions take primitive forms of impotent rage and feelings of defeat by external forces, rather than mourning over good, lost objects and regret over their aggression toward themselves and others.

The presence of "all good" and "all bad" object images which cannot be integrated interferes seriously with superego integration. Primitive forerunners of the superego of a sadistic kind, representing internalized bad object images related to pregenital conflicts, are too overriding to be tolerated, and are reprojected in the form of external bad objects. Overidealized object images and "all good" self images can create only fantastic ideals of power, greatness, and perfection, and not the more realistic demands and goals that would be brought about by superego integration. In other words, the components of the ego ideal in these cases also interfere with superego integration. Finally, the realistic demands of the parents cannot be brought together with either the ideal self and object images and their related ego ideal or with the threatening prohibitive, sadistic forerunners of the superego because both the sadistic nature and the overidealized nature of the superego forerunners distort the perception of the parental images, preventing integration.

Because of this interference with superego integration, there is a constant projection of the demanding and prohibitive aspects of superego components. The normal ego-integrating pressures of the superego are missing, as well as the capacity of the ego to experience guilt. The tendency to devaluate objects (see above) also interferes with superego integration, especially with the normally essential internalization of realistic demands from parental images; the devaluation of significant parental images prevents these patients from internalizing a most important source of superego formation (25, 26).

In summary, primitive, unrealistic self images persist in the ego, extremely contradictory in their characteristics, and an integrated self concept cannot develop; object images cannot be integrated, either, and therefore they interfere with the more realistic evaluation of the external objects. Constant projection of "all bad" self and object images perpetuates a world of dangerous, threatening objects, against which the "all good" self images are used defensively, and megalomanic ideal-self images are built up. Sufficient delimitation between self and objects (stability or ego boundaries) is maintained to permit a practical, immediate adaption to the demands of reality, but deeper internalization of the demands of reality, especially social reality, is made impossible by the interference of these nonintegrated self and object images with superego integration. Those superego structures which do develop are under the influence of sadistic forerunners intimately linked to pregenital aggressive drive derivatives, and of other forerunners representing primitive fusion of ideal-self and ideal-object images which tend to reinforce omnipotence and megalomanic demands on the self rather than to represent a modulating ego ideal. In general, superego functions tend to remain personified, do not develop to the point of superego abstraction, and are easily reprojected onto the external world (21, 28).

All these characteristics of internalized object relationships are reflected in typical characterological traits of the borderline personality organization. These patients have little capacity for a realistic evaluation of others and for realistic empathy with others; they experience other people as distant objects, to whom they adapt "realistically" only as long as there is no emotional involvement with them. Any situation which would normally develop into a deeper interpersonal relationship reveals the incapacity of these patients to really feel or empathize with another person, the unrealistic distortion of other people and the protective shallowness of their emotional relationships. This protective shallowness has many sources. First, it reflects the emotional shallowness due to the lack of fusion between libidinal and aggressive drive derivatives, and the concomitant narrowness, rigidity, and primitiveness of their affect dispositions. The shallowness of the emotional reaction of the patients we are considering is also more directly connected with the incapacity to experience guilt, concern, and the related deepening of their awareness of and interest in others (53). An additional reason for their emotional shallowness is the defensive effort to withdraw from too close an emotional involvement, which would bring about the danger of activation of their primitive defensive operations, especially projective identification and and the arousal of fears of attack by the object which is becoming important to them. Emotional shallowness also defends them from primitive idealization of the object and the related need to submit to and merge with such idealized objects, as well as from the potential rage over frustration of the pregenital, especially orally demanding needs that are activated in the relationship with the idealized object (47). The lack of superego development, and therefore the further lack of ego integration and maturation of feelings, aims, and interests, also keeps them in ignorance of the higher, more mature and differentiated aspects of other people's personalities.

Another characteristic of these patients is the more or less subtle or more or less crude expression of their pregenital and genital aims, which are all severely infiltrated with aggression. Direct exploitiveness, unreasonable demandingness, manipulation of others without consideration or even tact are quite noticeable. In this regard, the tendency to devaluate objects, mentioned above, is also relevant. The need to manipulate others also corresponds to the defensive need to keep control over the environment in order to prevent more primitive, paranoid fears connected with the projection of aggressive self and object images from coming to the surface. Many of these patients, when their efforts to control, manipulate, devalue objects, and direct gratification of their needs through exploitation of others fail, tend to withdraw and to recreate in their fantasies relationships with others in which they can express all these needs. Some protective withdrawal and gratification in fantasy are usually present even in those borderline patients who superficially may appear as quite "sociable."

These patients may feel superficially quite insecure, uncertain, and inferior in regard to their capacities or dealings with others. These feelings of inferiority and insecurity may be in part a reflection of the more realistic aspects of their evaluation of their relationships to significant others, work, and life in general, and often also reflect a realistic awareness of some of their shortcomings and failures. Yet, on a deeper level, feelings of inferiority often reflect defensive structures. It is striking when one finds so often underneath that level of insecurity and uncertainty, omnipotent fantasies, and a kind of blind optimism based on denial, which represent the patient's identification with primitive "all good" self and object images. In this connection, there are also deep feelings of having the right to exploit and to be gratified—in short, what has been classically referred to as the "narcissism" of these patients. Their narcissism does not represent simply a turning away from external objects, but the activation of primitive object relationships in which they re-enact a primitive fusion of idealized self and object images, defensively used against the "bad" self and object images, and the "bad" external objects. Feelings of inferiority frequently represent a secondary surface layer hiding the narcissistic character traits.

The presence of contradictory introjections and identifications is what gives the "as if" quality to these patients. Although their identifications are contradictory and dissociated from each other, the superficial manifestations of these identifications persist as remnants of behavior dispositions in the ego. This permits some of these patients to "re-enact" partial identifications, which are nearly all dissociated, if this appears useful to them from the point of view of their superficial adaptation to reality. A chameleonlike quality of their adaptability may result, in which what they *pretend* to be is really the empty dressing of what at other moments they have to be in a more primitive way. This is quite confusing to the patients themselves. *All of this also represents what Erickson (5) has called identity diffusion; namely, the lack of an integrated self concept and an integrated and stable concept of total objects in relationship with the self. Actually, identity diffusion is a typical syndrome of the borderline personality organization,* which is not seen in less severe

character pathology and neurotic patients, and which is a direct consequence of active splitting of those introjections and identifications of
which the synthesis normally would bring about a stable ego identity.

In an attempt to differentiate psychotic, borderline, and neurotic
patients, one might briefly say that psychotic patients have a severe
lack of ego development, with mostly undifferentiated self and object
images and concomitant lack of development of ego boundaries (19,
28); borderline patients have a better integrated ego than psychotics,
with differentiation between self and object images to a major extent
and with the development of firm ego boundaries in all but the areas of
close interpersonal involvement; they present, typically the syndrome
of identity diffusion (5, 30); and neurotic patients present a strong ego,
with complete separation between self and object images and concomitant delimitation of ego boundaries; they do not present the syndrome
of identity diffusion. Neurotic patients have developed a stable ego
identity, with the concomitant integration, depersonification, and indi-
vidualization of the ego structures determined by object relationships,
and they present an integrated superego, within which the pregenitally
determined forerunners and the later, more realistic internalization of
parental images have been integrated. Their superego may be excessively severe or sadistic, but it is sufficiently integrated to promote ego
development and at least partially successful, conflict-free functioning.

GENETIC-DYNAMIC ANALYSIS

We can now turn from the structural analysis to an examination of the
typical instinctual content of the conflicts in the internalized object
relationships in patients with borderline personality organization. Pregenital aggression, especially oral aggression, plays a crucial role as
part of this psychopathological constellation. The dynamic aspects of
the borderline personality organization have been clarified by Melanie
Klein and her co-workers (22, 34, 48). Her description of the intimate
relationship between pregenital and especially oral conflicts, on the one
hand, and oedipal conflicts, on the other, such as occur under the
influence of excessive pregenital aggression, is relevant to the borderline personality organization.

Unfortunately, some basic assumptions of Melanie Klein, to which
she tended to adhere in a rather dogmatic way and which have rightly

been questioned by most authors in this field—the lack of consideration of structural factors in her writings; her disregard for epigenetic development; and, finally, her rather peculiar language—have made her observations difficult for most people to accept. In order to prevent misunderstandings, I would like to specify first those aspects of Melanie Klein's analysis in regard to the problems relevant here with which I strongly disagree: (i) Her assumption of a rather full development of oedipal conflicts in the first year of life: I suggest that what is characteristic of the borderline personality organization, in contrast to less severe pathological conditions, is a specific condensation between pregenital and genital conflicts, and a *premature* development of oedipal conflicts from the second or third year on. (ii) Melanie Klein assumes an innate, unconscious knowledge of the genital organs of both sexes, which I find unacceptable, and which she links with extremely early oedipal development. (iii) The entire conceptualization of internalized objects in Melanie Klein's formulation does not consider structural developments within the ego, which Fairbairn has rightly criticized; and her disregard for the findings of modern ego psychology seriously weakens her descriptions. (iv) Melanie Klein's conceptualization of the superego again disregards structural concepts; and while I would agree with her suggestion that superego functions develop much earlier than what was classically thought, the lack of consideration in her writings of different levels and different forms of internalized object relationships tends toward a serious oversimplification of the issues.

A frequent finding in patients with borderline personality organization is the history of extreme frustrations and intense aggression (secondary or primary) during the first few years of life. Excessive pregenital and particularly oral aggression tends to be projected and causes a paranoid distortion of the early parental images, especially of the mother. Through the projection of predominantly oral-sadistic but also anal-sadistic impulses, the mother is seen as potentially dangerous and hatred of the mother extends to hatred of both parents who are later experienced as a "united group" by the child. A "contamination" of the father image (by aggression primarily projected onto the mother) and lack of differentiation between mother and father (under the influence of lack of realistic differentiation of different objects because of excessive splitting operations) tend to produce, in both sexes, a combined and dangerous father-mother image, with the result that all sexual relationships are later conceived of as dangerous and aggressively infiltrated.

At the same time, in an effort to escape from oral rage and fears, premature development of genital strivings takes place; this effort often miscarries because of the intensity of pregenital aggression, which contaminates genital strivings as well, and numerous pathological developments take place which differ in both sexes.

In the case of the boy, premature development of genital strivings in order to deny oral-dependent needs tends to fail because oedipal fears and prohibitions against sexual impulses toward mother are powerfully reinforced by pregenital fears of the mother, and a typical image of a dangerous, castrating mother develops. Also, the projection of pregenital aggression reinforces oedipal fears of the father and castration anxiety in particular, further reinforcing, in turn, pregenital aggression and fear. The positive oedipus complex is seriously interfered with under these circumstances. By contrast, a frequent solution is the reinforcement of the negative oedipus complex, and specifically what Paula Heimann (22) has described as the "feminine position" in boys, which represents an effort to submit sexually to father in order to obtain from him the oral gratifications which were denied from the dangerous, frustrating mother. This is a typical constellation found in predominantly orally determined male homosexuality. It is to be stressed that on some level both father and mother are seen as dangerous; heterosexuality is seen as dangerous; and homosexuality is used as a substitute way of gratifying oral needs. The danger of the reappearance of oral frustration and aggression as a consequence of homosexual involvements is always present. One other attempted solution may be the gratification of oral-aggressive needs in a heterosexual relationship, which on a deeper level represents the effort to "rob" mother sexually of what she denied orally. This constellation is frequently found in narcissistic, promiscuous men who unconsciously seek revenge against the oral, frustrating mother through pseudogenital relationships with women. Other solutions to the danger created by a premature condensation of pregenital and genital aims can be found in the development of any of the polymorphous perverse infantile trends, especially those which permit the expression of aggression.

In the girl, severe oral pathology of the kind mentioned tends to develop the positive oedipal strivings prematurely in the girl. Genital strivings for father are used as a substitute gratification of oral-dependent needs that have been frustrated by the dangerous mother. This effort tends to be undermined by the contamination of the father image with pregenital aggression deflected from mother and projected onto him, and also because oral rage and especially oral envy powerfully reinforce penis envy in women. The denial of aggression through heterosexual love tends to fail because pathologically strong penis envy is stirred up, and also because the image of the oedipally prohibitive mother is reinforced by that of the dangerous pregenital mother. One solution frequently attempted is a flight into promiscuity in an attempt to deny penis envy and dependency upon men, and also as an expression of especially strong unconscious guilt feelings about oedipal strivings. General reinforcement of masochistic trends is another solution which attempts to gratify superego pressures stemming from both pregenital and genital mother images, internalized under the influence of the reintrojection of projected aggression. General renunciation of heterosexuality, with a search for the gratification of oral needs from an idealized mother image, which is completely split off from the dangerous, threatening mother image, is an important source of female homosexuality, quite frequent in the case of borderline personality organization. Attempts at a homosexual relationship, which implies not only a renunciation of men and the submission to the oedipal mother, but also an effort to obtain oral and other pregenital gratification from idealized, "partial" mother figures tend to fail because of the ever-present oral-aggressive needs and fears. Sadomasochistic homosexual involvements are one further consequence of this development. Other polymorphous sexual trends develop similarly to what has been described above in the case of the boys.

In summary, in both sexes *excessive development or pregenital, especially oral aggression tends to induce a premature development of oedipal strivings, and as a consequence a particular pathological condensation between pregenital and genital aims under the overriding influence of aggressive needs.* A common outcome is the presence of several of the pathological compromise solutions which give rise to a typical persistence of polymorphous perverse sexual trends in patients presenting borderline personality organization. What appears on the surface as a chaotic persistence of primitive drives and fears, the "pansexuality" of the borderline case, represents a combination of several of these pathological solutions. All of these pathological solutions are unsuccessful attempts to deal with the aggressiveness of genital trends and the general infiltration of all instinctual needs by aggression. On psychological testing, borderline patients demonstrate a lack of the normal predominance of heterosexual genital strivings over partial polymorphous drives. What appears as a chaotic combination of pre-oedipal and oedipal strivings is a reflection of the pathological condensation mentioned. The formulation often derived from psychological testing, that these patients present "a lack of sexual identity," is probably a misnomer. It is true that these patients present identity diffusion, but this identity diffusion has earlier and more complex sources than a simple lack of differentiation of any particular sexual orientation (28). Their "lack of sexual identity" does not reflect a lack of sexual definition, but a combination of several strong fixations to cope with the same conflicts.

This brings us to the conclusion of the present effort to apply psychoanalytic metapsychology to the clinical problems of the borderline personality organization.

SUMMARY

The "borderline" personality disorders are examined from the descriptive, structural, and genetic-dynamic viewpoints. It is suggested that they have in common: (i) symptomatic constellations, such as diffuse anxiety, special forms of polysymptomatic neuroses, and "prepsychotic" and "lower level" character pathology; (ii) certain defensive constellations of the ego, namely, a combination of nonspecific manifestations of ego weakness and a shift toward primary-process thinking on the one hand, and specific primitive defense mechanisms (splitting, primitive idealization, early forms of projection, denial, omnipotence), on the other; (iii) a particular pathology of internalized object relations; and (iv) characteristic instinctual vicissitudes, namely, a particular pathological condensation of pregenital and genital aims under the overriding influence of pregenital aggressive needs. These various aspects of borderline personality organization and their mutual relationships are briefly examined.

BORDERLINE PERSONALITY ORGANIZATION 317

BIBLIOGRAPHY

1. Bychowski, G. The problem of latent psychosis. *J. Am. Psycho.*, 1:484–503, 1953.
2. Deutsch, H. Some forms of emotional disturbance and their relationship to schizophrenia. *Psychoanal. Quart.*, 11:301–321, 1942.
3. Easser, B. R. & Lesser, S. R. Hysterical personality: a re-evaluation. *Psychoanal. Quart.*, 34:390–405, 1965.
4. Ekstein, R. & Wallerstein, J. Observations on the psychotherapy of borderline and psychotic children. *The Psychoanalytic Study of the Child*, 11:303–311. New York: International Universities Press, 1956.
5. Erikson, E. H. The problem of ego identity. *J. Am. Psycho.*, 4:56–121, 1956.
6. Fairbairn, W. R. D. Schizoid factors in the personality (1940). *An Object-Relations Theory of the Personality.* New York: Basic Books, 1952 pp. 3–27.
7. Fairbairn, W. R. D. Endospychic structure considered in terms of object-relationships (1944). *An Object-Relations Theory of the Personality.* New York: Basic Books, 1952, pp. 82–136.
8. Fairbairn, W. R. D. A synopsis of the development of the author's views regarding the structure of the personality (1951). *An Object-Relations Theory of the Personality.* New York: Basic Books, 1952, pp. 162–179.
9. Frank, J. D. et al. Two behavior patterns in therapeutic groups and their apparent motivation. *Hum. Rel.*, 5:289–317, 1952.
10. Freud, A. *The Ego and the Mechanisms of Defense* (1936). New York: International Universities Press, 1946, pp. 45–57.
11. Freud, S. Negation (1925). *Standard Edition*, 19:235–239. London: Hogarth Press, 1961.
12. Freud, S. Fetishism (1927). *Standard Edition*, 21:149–157. London: Hogarth Press, 1961.
13. Freud, S. Splitting of the ego in the process of defence (1938). *Standard Edition*, 23:275–278. London: Hogarth Press, 1964.
14. Frosch, J. The psychotic character: clinical psychiatric considerations. *Psychiat. Quart.*, 38:81–96, 1964.
15. Geleerd, E. R. Borderline states in childhood and adolescence. *The Psychoanalytic Study of the Child*, 13:279–295. New York: International Universities Press, 1958.
16. Gitelson, M. On ego distortion. *Int. J. Psycho-Anal.*, 39: 245–257, 1958.
17. Greenson, R. R. The struggle against identification. *J. Am. Psycho.*, 2:200–217, 1954.
18. Greenson, R. R. On screen defenses, screen hunger, and screen identity. *J. Am. Psycho.*, 6:242–262, 1958.
19. Hartmann, H. Contribution to the metapsychology of schizophrenia (1953). *Essays on Ego Psychology.* New York: International Universities Press, 1961. pp. 182–206.
20. Hartmann, H. Kris, E., & Loewenstein, R. M. Comments on the formation of psychic structure. *The Psychoanalytic Study of the Child*, 2:11–38. New York: International Universities Press, 1946.
21. Hartmann, H. & Loewenstein, R. M. Notes on the superego. *The Psychoanalytic Study of the Child*, 17:42–81. New York: International Universities Press, 1962.
22. Heimann, P. A contribution to the re-evaluation of the oedipus complex: the early stages. In: *New Directions in Psycho-Analysis*, ed. M. Klein, P. Heimann, & R. E. Money-Kyrle. New York: Basic Books. 1955, pp. 23–38.

23. Hoch, P. H. & Cattell, J. P. The diagnosis of pseudoneurotic schizophrenia. *Psychiat. Quart.*, 33:17–43, 1959.
24. Hoch, P. H. & Polatin, P. Pseudoneurotic forms of schizophrenia. *Psychiat. Quart.*, 23:248–276, 1949.
25. Jacobson, E. Contribution to the metapsychology of cyclothymic depression. In: *Affective Disorders*, ed. P. Greenacre. New York: International Universities Press, 1953. pp. 49–83.
26. Jacobson, E. Contribution to the metapsychology of psychotic identifications. *J. Am. Psycho.*, 2:239–269, 1951.
27. Jacobson, E. Denial and repression. *J. Am. Psycho.*, 5:61–92, 1957.
28. Jacobson, E. *The Self and the Object World*. New York: International Universities Press, 1964.
29. Kernberg, O. Notes on countertransference. *J. Am. Psycho.*, 13:38–56, 1965.
30. Kernberg, O. Structural derivatives of object relationships. *Int. J. Psycho-Anal.*, 47:236–253, 1966.
31. Kahn, M. M. R. Clinical aspects of the schizoid personality: affects and technique. *Int. J. Psycho-Anal.*, 41:430–437, 1960.
32. Klein, M. A contribution to the psychogenesis of manic-depressive states (1934). *Contributions to Psycho-Analysis 1921–1945*. London: Hogarth Press, 1948, pp. 282–310.
33. Klein, M. Mourning and its relation to manic-depressive states (1940). *Contributions to Psycho-Analysis 1921–1945*. London: Hogarth Press, 1948, pp. 311–338.
34. Klein, M. The oepidus complex in the light of early anxieties: general theoretical summary (1945). *Contributions to Psycho-Analysis 1921–1945*. London: Hogarth Press, 1948, pp. 377–390.
35. Klein, M. Notes on some schizoid mechanisms (1946). In: *Developments in Psycho-Analysis*, ed. J. Riviere. London: Hogarth Press, 1952. pp. 292–320.
36. Knight, R. P. Borderline states (1953). In: *Psychoanalytic Psychiatry and Psychology*, ed., R. P. Knight & C. R. Friedman. New York: International Universities Press, 1954, pp. 97–109.
37. Knight, R. P. Management and psychotherapy of the borderline schizophrenic patient (1953). In: *Psychoanalytic Psychiatry and Psychology*, ed. R. P. Knight & C. R. Friedman. New York: International Universities Press, 1954, pp. 110–122.
38. Laughlin, H. P. *The Neuroses in Clinical Practice*. Philadelphia: Saunders, 1956, pp. 394–406.
39. Main, T. F. The ailment. *Brit. J. Med. Psychol.*, 30:129–145, 1957.
40. Menninger, K. A., Mayman, M., & Pruyser, P. *The Vital Balance*. New York: Viking Press, 1963, pp. 213–249.
41. Rangell, L. Panel report: The borderline case. *J. Am. Psycho.*, 3:285–298, 1955.
42. Rapaport, D. Cognitive structures. In: *Contemporary Approaches to Cognition*. Cambridge: Harvard University Press, 1957, pp. 157–200.
43. Rapaport, D. & Gill, M. M. The points of view and assumptions of metapsychology. *Int. J. Psycho-Anal.*, 40:153–162, 1959.
44. Rapaport, D., Gill, M. M., & Schafer, R. *Diagnostic Psychological Testing*, 2 Vols. Chicago: Year Book Publishers, 1945 and 1946, 1:16–28, 2:24–31, 329–366.
45. Robbins, L. L. Panel report: The borderline case. *J. Am. Psycho.*, 4:550–562, 1956.
46. Rosenfeld, H. Notes on the psychopathology and psychoanalytic treatment of schizophrenia. In: *Psychotherapy of Schizophrenic and Manic-Depressive States*, ed.

A. Hassan & B. C. Glueck, Jr. [Psychiatric Research Report #17]. Washington, D.C.: American Psychiatric Association, 1963, pp. 61–72.
47. Rosenfeld, H. On the psychopathology of narcissism: a clinical approach. *Int. J. Psycho-Anal.*, 45:332–337, 1964.
48. Segal, H. *Introduction to the Work of Melanie Klein.* New York: Basic Books, 1964.
49. Van der Waals, H. G. Problems of narcissism. *Bull Menninger Clin.*, 29:293–311, 1965.
50. Waelder, R. et al. Ego distortion (Panel Discussion). *Int. J. Psycho-Anal.*, 39:243–275, 1958.
51. Wallerstein, R. S. Reconstruction and mastery in the transference psychosis. *J. Am. Psycho.*, pp. 551–583.
52. Wallerstein, R. S. & Robbins, L. L. The psychotherapy research project of The Menninger Foundation (Part IV: Concepts). *Bull. Menninger Clin.*, 20:239–262, 1956.
53. Winnicott, D. W. The depressive position in normal emotional development. *Brit. J. Med. Psychol.*, 28:89–100, 1955.
54. Zilboorg, G. Ambulatory schizophrenias. *Psychiatry*, 4:149–155, 1941.
55. Zilboorg, G. Further observations on ambulatory schizophrenia. *Amer. J. Orthopsychiat*, 27:677–682, 1957.

15. The Grinker Study*

Roy Grinker, Sr., B. Werble, and R.C. Drye

THE CONCEPTUAL AND OPERATIONAL THEORY OF THE RESEARCH

Hitches in Previous Clinical Research

Before undertaking the current investigation the senior author and other colleagues had completed a similar study of depressions (Grinker et al., 1961). The intent was to subject depressed patients to a detailed analysis of their *feelings and concerns* as well as their *current behavior*. In recognition that both elements were necessary to develop data from which to uncover subcategories of the depressive syndrome we utilized both depth interviews and observations of overt behavior on a nursing unit.

In our pilot study there was considerable unreliability in the descriptions of behavioral aspects made by psychiatrists in contrast with the reliability of their interpretative judgments about the patients' internal feelings and concerns. Statistical studies revealed that psychiatrists are not so adept at observing behavior as they are at eliciting feelings and concerns. Apparently, even when specifically looking for behavioral traits, psychiatrists' interest in and familiarity with the content of thoughts and feelings interfere with their observations of what goes on in front of them. Paradoxically they can communicate better about what they have to infer and interpret. Therefore, in the main study of depressions we utilized the nursing staff on the ward for observational data and happily found their reliability to be excellent.

The study report (Grinker et al., 1961) commented on the current one-sided approach to clinical psychiatry as follows:

An unfortunate by-product of focusing on the dynamics of depression has been

*This contribution is excerpted from the original published version *The Borderline Syndrome: A Behavioral Study of Ego Functions*, Chapters 3, 7, and 12, New York: Basic Books, 1968. For chapter and bibliographic references in this article, see the original published version of the book.

the underemphasis on sound clinical observations and adequate descriptions of these and other mental patients. As a matter of fact, most of American psychiatry is dynamic psychiatry, and the word descriptive has become an appellation of derogation. Descriptive psychiatry is considered to be old-fashioned and obsolete. Clinical psychiatry is incompletely taught in most of our training centers; the teachers themselves are less interested in it since they for the most part have been trained to infer and formulate rather than to describe. As a result, the details of clinical syndromes are little known, and the natural history of psychiatric diseases has been neglected.

As stated in Chapter 1, the underemphasis and derogation of clinical observations of behavior is associated with a studied neglect of diagnosis and classification without which psychiatry cannot aspire to be scientific. Such negative approaches will always obstruct sound clinical research and inevitably studies of causal relations.

Paul Meehl (1959), a distinguished psychologist, critically states: "Rather than decrying nosology, we should become masters of it, recognizing that some of our psychiatric colleagues have in recent times become careless and even unskilled in the art of formal diagnosis." The philosopher Kaplan (1964) indicates how every classification serves some purpose to disclose relationships that must be taken into account no matter what.

Sources of Evidence for Categories of Deviance

The sources of evidence concerning problems of deviance in human beings fall into several categories. Deviance, or, in medical language, disease, indicates a comparison with what is supposedly healthy and normal. Offer and Sabshin (1961) have considered normality from four perspectives: normality as health, normality as utopia, normality as average and normality as process. The concept of normality as an ontogenic process necessitates its analysis as a system maturing and developing in a specific social and cultural setting. We are faced with the problem of the frames of reference from which the processes of health or illness are to be observed.

This problem is currently seen as a conflict of approaches to all nosological classifications. In Chapter 2 the literature overview discloses that the borderline case is described or defined from behavioral observations and from inferences derived from depth or psychoanalytic interviews which probe "intrapsychic" processes. Are these ap-

322   1950s AND 1960s

proaches complementary or in opposition? To put this very crudely, can a person be sick inside and behave well, or be internally healthy and outwardly deviant? In discussing the new or revived functions of psychiatrists in resocializing patients by means of short-term hospitalization, Ruesch (1966) indicates that adequate social behavior may exist in persons with severe pathology, and temporary deviant behavior may be associated with little psychopathology. There is something radically wrong with the above question. It presupposes that inside and outside are separable, that they follow different invariants and that they require radically different methods of observation. Actually they are inseparable both in structure and function. For example, the sociologist Goffman (1966), who defines mental illness as inappropriate behavior and states that we protect our gatherings and occasions by putting those who act unsuitably into asylums, writes. "The symptomatology of the 'mentally ill' may sometimes have more to do with the structure of the public order than with the nature of disordered minds." Concentrating on behavior unsuitable for specific occasions, Goffman neglects the internal lack or adequacy of the subjects' capacities to assume these various role behaviors.

Nevertheless whenever we reach a compromise indicating unity and use such terms as holistic, process or global, we become satisfied, sense closure and flee from the operational. Empirical research requires the observation of symptoms, behaviors or functions, but these are far from fundamental causes. The sociologist looks outward to the social world of experience with his special techniques. The psychologist looks inward at processes that he terms intervening variables, and the biologist, all too frequently reductionistic, searches for genic, biochemical or physiological deficits. Yet each focus constitutes a transacting part of the larger field for which hypothetical constructs or theory may be developed and tested. Actually a nosological and classificatory focus of the interdisciplinary components of psychiatry may facilitate their articulation.

The sources of evidences pertinent for research on types of health or illness may be outlined as folows: (1) the past developmental history; (2) anecdotal episodes derived from an anamnesis concerning reactions to various life situations and stresses, for example, critical periods of growth or responses to environmental changes; (3) behavior in the family group, at school, at work or in community activities; (4) behavior on the nursing unit of a mental hospital; (5) behavior in the two-person situation of patient and interviewer or therapist, or from the transference regression in the psychoanalytic situation; (6) appropriate psychological tests; (7) artificial (experimental) stress situations such as small periods of isolation or periods of forced group activity.

The clinician uses any one or all of these sources that are available to him. His diagnostic acumen is based on his capacity to utilize the essence from all sources with which to build a gestalt, characteristic of a symptom complex currently generally recognized and labeled. Such a technique does not suffice, however, as a method for scientific studies, for example, to delineate a new category or to develop subcategories or typologies.

In general, scientific information is obtained by collecting observations and measurements under specified conditions, encoding the data in terms characteristic of the statistical model to be used, processing the data, and checking the results again against the original events. Royce (1965) exemplifies this in terms applicable to clinical research: (1) standardized conditions of observations as on a nursing unit, (2) under specified conditions even though the variables are not controlled, (3) by many persons, (4) observing specified variables, (5) repetitive observations, (6) statistical analyses leading to the determination of the contribution of each variable. To this we must add the checking of results for their logical relationship with clinical experience.

The Psychiatric-Psychoanalytic Conflict

We shall touch only lightly on this repetitive and futile conflict which has achieved no resolution over the last several decades because real conflict does not exist. However, there has been a consistent clash of ideologies which by definition are not amenable to reason. Its significance for us lies in the fact that we have attempted to utilize both positions theoretically as appropriate to the study of an organized system of clinical events, even though our operations were purely observational.

The conflict between psychoanalysis and psychiatry as "sciences" has been clearly described by Home (1966). He states that Freud took psychoanalysis out of the world of science into that of the humanities by his basic postulate that symptoms have meanings. In science including psychiatry we make observations from which we postulate explanations. In psychoanalysis we approach humans existing uniquely in time and interpret meanings inferentially. Mind is the meaning of behavior in a living subject; reification makes of mind a thing. Unfortunately, Home does not mention the proposition that even inferences and hence interpretations require the basic data of behaviors.

Among psychoanalysts there are differences in opinion which range from the complete negation of anything but "meaning" derived from introspection and imaginative empathy as, for example, Meissner (1966). He denies the significance of verbal reports and states that psychoanalytic concepts cannot be reduced to a behavioral or operational basis, thereby denying the operations of science as at the same time he speaks of scientific theory. This is what another psychoanalyst Glover (1966) calls the sophistry of modern psychoanalytic theory. On the other hand Anna Freud (1966b) advocates the use of methods other than psychoanalytic, indicating that relationships between surface behaviors as derivatives of the unconscious can signify id contents. As a matter of fact, child analysis is almost entirely dependent upon observations of *play behavior* in children.

Derivatives of the unconscious in behavior are observable diagnostic clues. From these the psychiatrist can assess genetic or dynamic processes but not as "confidently" as the psychoanalyst; however, he can adequately delineate ego-functions. In the psychoanalytic situation the transference neurosis presumably enables the analyst to observe in the regression so-called genetic processes, previous conflicts and the range of solutions. Although more indirectly, the behaviors of a subject expose not only present deficits but also past scars, ego-distortions and on-going conflicts.

Psychoanalytic techniques have been used to describe current ego-functions in terms of verbal and nonverbal behavior within the psychoanalytic situation which in itself is conducive to a weakening of ego-functioning and to regression to an earlier level of organization. Under these conditions the adequacy of ego-functioning in real-life situations cannot be determined except by the often distorted reports of the subject in retrospect. The special psychoanalytic techniques utilizing verbal behavior may reveal ego-functions in the living transference recapitulation but not always their relationship to current liabilities or assets.

In the light of this we can state the difficulties in utilizing the psychoanalytic method in clinical research: (1) transference behaviors are private; (2) they are limited in universality by differences in subjects and analytic investigators; (3) they are limited in numbers of subjects available; (4) behaviors are not replicable, because the situations are not replicable; (5) there is a single observer; (6) within the analytic transference, the individual inferences and interpretations do not always have external referrents, they often relate only to internal processes relatively independent of external events; (7) interpretations are selective.

Intrapsychic processes can be communicated to the self and others only through behaviors—verbal or nonverbal. Psychoanalysis as a process of introspection or as behavior verbally communicated exists in a setting conducive to transference regression. Since this setting, in which verbal, sometimes visceral and sometimes bodily behaviors are expressed, occurs in a constant dyadic relationship, the observations are private, nonreplicable and subject to biases and distortions of interpretations.

Despite these difficulties and the unreliability of inferences, observations of a large enough sample of subjects by a variety of observers may disclose patterns that cannot be discerned by observations in an open field with a multitude of transactions calling for many social roles. The scientific dilemma is the contamination by an initial reporter influencing all subsequent observers who can easily "confirm" in the "material" what they expect. There are few controls, no tests for reliability and great semantic vagueness.

Finally we should like to allay the conflict of dynamic vs. descriptive or more bluntly psychoanalytic vs. observational techniques. There should be no controversy because both are necessary and each method furnishes similar and different data. This is clearly indicated in the literature on the borderline, and as Glover (1933) states there is room for new syndromes achieved by "openness" for which a combination of descriptive words with genetic understanding is necessary to aid differential diagnosis and refine prognosis. In a more positive sense we should view the observable physical behaviors and the verbal introspective products as parts of one system. Mentation and behavior constitute a psychosomatic unity. It is a system composed of parts with allocated functions but integrated and organized.

Psychoanalytic Ego-Psychology

The theoretical framework utilized in this study is called in technical terms "ego-psychology." Without utilizing this name academic psychologists are constantly dealing with ego-functions in their experiments on cognition, learning and perception. Psychoanalytic theory from the very beginning utilized the concept of an ego as antithetical and in conflict with an id. Hartmann systematized and stimulated the development of what is called psychoanalytical ego-psychology when he postulated a conflict-free sphere of the ego or an autonomous ego. His contributions specified the many functions allocated to the ego which now enable us to link them to visible and measurable behaviors. Hartmann (1958, 1964) states, "Ego is the centralized functional control which integrates different parts of the personality with each other and with outer reality." However, he also calls ego a "sub-structure of the personality which is defined by its function." Forces acting on the ego include the impact of reality, the impact of the drives and autonomous factors (the hereditary core). This latter or the conflict-free structure of the ego furnishes the ground plan for maturation which is constantly sensitive to the environment.

The ego in psychological language is that allocated function of the psychic apparatus which lies at the border between internal psychological processes and the external environment. As a border process it filters perceptions of stimuli from the environment and screens action derived from internal motivation. Ego-functions have been described as strong or weak, brittle or flexible, rather than with reference to particular aspects of its several functions. Thus, for example, the latent or overt psychotic is supposedly characterized by a weak ego which succumbs to stress and then freely exposes internal archaic forms of thinking such as delusions, hallucinations or bizarre associations. On the other hand, the neurotic is characterized by a break or weakening of ego-functions in a limited sector.

The various functions attributed to the concept of ego may be arbitrarily considered under seven headings (Beres, 1965):

1. *Relation to Reality*
   a. Adaptation to reality depends upon the external demands or obstacles to need-satisfactions. The individual in action requires a repertoire of internalized social roles that he can play spontaneously and actions which on

necessity he can devise (creativity) toward people, things and tasks. This means the capacity to grow, differentiate and integrate.

   b. Reality-testing requires an accuracy of perception, capacity to orient self in time and place, tolerance for ambiguity and judgment as to the differentiation of figure and ground (focusing).

   c. Sense of reality is manifested by unobtrusive ordinary functions which differentiate self from others based on effective automatic recognition of the boundaries of self (identity). According to Federn (1952) this involves an "ego feeling" which constitutes an effective awareness of self maintained over time (stability) which also resists diffusion or depletion.

2. *Regulation and Control of Drives*
   This function concerns effective control of inner pressures which demands tolerance of frustration, anxiety and ambiguity. It depends on such tactics as detour-behavior, delay and sublimation.

3. *Object-Relations*
   The ability to form such relations and to maintain their consistency not withstanding ambivalences, rejections or frustrations.

4. *Cognitive Functions*
   These include concentration, selective scanning, memory, abstraction and ability to avoid contamination by drive expressions.

5. *Defensive Functions*
   Included are the various types of defenses appropriate to both inner and outer pressures, such as repression, reaction-formation, denial, withdrawal, and adaptive or coping mechanisms.

6. *Autonomous Functions*
   These cognitive functions are considered to be the "givens" of the conflict-free ego and include perception, intention (energy or will), intelligence, and language capacity.

7. *Synthetic Functions*
   An important capacity includes the ability to organize, to form gestalts and to compromise.

The Ego in Behavior

Lately there has been increasing awareness that clinical psychiatry as one of the behavioral sciences requires new and more refined techniques of observation, description and analysis to become progressive. For this reason it is necessary to be explicit about our concepts of behavior.

We agree with Kantor (1963) that "behaviorism" means many things. It describes an objective nonintrospective approach to psychological processes; as Skinner (1957) states, psychology is the science of behavior and mental life. But for him meaning is a property of conditions under which behavior occurs and includes inferred variables of which response or behavior is usually a function. Behaviorism is a theory and a philosophy or according to Kantor all of science itself. It excludes the invisible and intangible, including introspection or self-observation, and maintains the physical as the object of its interest, rejecting the psychological.

Nagel (1961) explains in a discussion of the methodological problems in the social sciences that the term "behaviorism" does not today have a precise doctrinal connotation, as it did in the 1920's and 1930's, and students of human conduct who today designate themselves as behaviorists do so chiefly because of their adherence to a method that places a premium on objective data; behaviorism is a methodological orientation.

Elkes (1963) states that basic to a study of the pharmacology of behavior is its description. Behavior is not an epiphenomenon but the major phenomenon of life and also a method of study from which one can demand more precision. But the varieties and subtleties of behavior challenge established techniques. In the two-person or dyadic relationship the moment-to-moment behaviors are enormous. In larger groups transactions seem too varied for recording and miss the subjective component. According to Elkes rating scales of any precision are effective only when clinical judgments are possible.

A more controversial stance was adopted by Helen Sargent (1961) who criticizes the "behavior-observation-inference" model which can only be developed by our perceptive senses. Although direct observation of the inner state of another is impossible, common sense permits us to attribute sense to what goes on in a person's mind and know what it means. She implies that including reportable affects, dreams, conflicts and memories as behaviors are escape hatches, but since they are reportable only verbally with more or less indices of affect we believe that they must be included under behaviors. Sargent states that to predict behavior we must know attitudes, intents or motives rather than acts. We contend that knowing the acts and their circumstances we can in reverse identify attitudes or motives. Unfortunately Sargent has set up a dichotomy between content and method.

There are others who take a broader view of behavioral analysis. Kanfer and Saslow (1966) utilize five approaches which include self-descriptions obtained through interviews, transactions with significant others, informants from among family and friends, work behavior and psychological tests. Kantor again includes both physical acts and psychological sets of "interbehavioralism" (transactionalism), a symmetrical field composed of acts and sets, as component parts of a behavioral system and investigated by techniques which vary with the focus on parts of the field.

We cannot conceive of a fracture of behavior into acts and mentation; they both comprise a system characterized by internal and external boundaries. They only seem to be separated in the face of disintegrations or regressions. Strauss (1967) from the sociological point of view writes about deviance as such or deviant acts. They can only be so defined if compared with standards or values held by the group or challenged by another group. Some abnormal or eccentric behavior in the larger group may not become deviant as long as the persons remain within a special and consistent line of culture and conflict is avoided. Usually, however, people belong to many groups in which they adapt successfully because they have acquired an internalized role repertoire sufficiently extensive (Grinker, 1957). In fact there are no total deviants. The question is in what way and to what extent is behavior deviant and in what setting. Thus in planning for mental health facilities the *demands* for help from the public are sometimes based on internal discomfort but more often on behavioral deviance from accepted standards of others. On the other hand *needs* are what the authoritative mental health disciplines decide and they "case-find" just those problems.

In their study of "milieu therapy" the J. and E. Cummings (1962) view the fundamental principles as the practical management and control of the executive functions of the ego leading to an increase in the number of differentiated sets. An ego is a coherent system of ideas, events and values of which the greater the variety, the more flexible, adaptive and healthy the personality. Growth occurs through the resolution of crises which the milieu controls. Professional staffs are "for the deviant but against his deviance." Finally social improvement is *followed by* ego growth.

Behavior as Ego in Action

Our study is oriented toward the observation, description and ratings of behaviors of a subclass of psychiatric patients in a particular setting. In this sense we are attempting to improve on the deficiency exposed in our research on depression. The study of depressions, however, was an attempt to deal with a wide range of symptoms in an effort to place them in subcategories or syndromes. Here we are not dealing with symptoms but functions of a specified psychic structure, the ego, as evidenced in behaviors.

Obviously we could include observations of everything the subjects did or said as grist for our qualitative and quantitative scientific rating methods. This would be a waste of time, however, in that all that is known about psychopathology would have been discarded and mountains of detail would have been accumulated only to be discarded on the basis of a post-hoc theory. We, therefore, started with both conceptual and operational theories (Grinker, 1964).

Because a study of the whole range of ego-functions is important for the proper diagnosis and prediction of outcome in spontaneous growth, development and the prediction of psychosis and/or recovery under appropriate methods of treatment, we believe that it is important to describe, classify and quantify the various ego-functions as they are expressed in behavior.

Our position utilizes the psychoanalytic theory of ego-psychology in that the several allocated functions of the ego are employed in our design for the purpose of placing observations in appropriate frames. We are enabled to obtain a sufficient quantity of raw data from a large number of observations made by many observers over time. Tests of reliability and validity as well as replication are thus possible. We can be comfortable in seeing assets as well as liabilities and directly observe problems in social living. Based on the raw data we may develop hypotheses and make excursions into speculation specifically labelled as such and attached to external referents. Whatever we lose from lack of depth interviews or psychoanalytic techniques can be overcome by bringing the results of both methods into juxtaposition. Indeed in Chapter 7 we report some patients studied carefully over time by depth interviews. Our hypotheses may enrich psychoanalysis and in turn be modified by it.

We affirm again that behavior—verbal and nonverbal—is the basic data of scientific psychiatry. Behavior represents in actuality functions allocated to a hypothetical ego which filters perceptions, on the one hand, and actions, on the other, expresses reportable motivations, affects, defenses and compromises, employs symptoms and sublimations and demonstrates integrative capacities and disintegrative trends.

We espouse a form of behavioral study that acknowledges the existence of unconscious mental processes and accepts introspection reported by verbal responses that subjects make under given conditions.

In sum, we can state that the conceptual theory under which we operate involves ego-psychology in the sense that ego-functions are the final common pathway for the expression of mentation at any level no matter what technical means are adopted for their observation or in what situation—psychoanalytic (Rapaport, 1959) or in a mental hospital nursing unit—they occur. Ego-functions are expressed in behaviors which are observable and describable. The research task in defining a clinical syndrome is to observe well-defined aspects of behavior, the raw data of which can be rated and analyzed according to sound statistical methods. Furthermore the basic date may then be used for inferences and interpretations as to their meanings.

Operationally we may observe behaviors under various headings and subheadings and then utilize well-defined scales with which to rate them numerically. These headings correspond to the allocated functions of the ego translated into operational terms. These are discussed in Chapter 4 where our design is demonstrated. For now it is sufficient to indicate the close connection between ego-functions and behaviors by referring to such large categories as *outward behavior* (to people, environment, and tasks), *perception* (awareness, differentiation, assessment), *messages* (verbal, nonverbal, reception), *affects and defenses* (relations with people, control of affect and behavior, defense mechanisms and situational mastery) and *synthesis* (integration, capacity to resist disintegrating and to carry on usual life processes).

INDIVIDUAL PATIENTS

Behavioral items which we observed in our research delineated disturbances of ego-functions of the borderline and were statistically analyzed into groups and factors. The resultant scientific skeleton requires the flesh and blood of recognizable symptoms to become useful for clinicians.

The syndrome or borderline class of patients has difficulty in achieving and maintaining affectional relations; they have trouble in controlling aggressive impulses and rarely achieve a consistent reliable and satisfying identity. Ego-alien, short-lived confusional or paranoid-like psychoses may occur, as well as temporary states of loneliness, appearing as depression without guilt, and depression of the anaclitic clinging type. Absent are evidences of cognitive disturbances, looseness of associations, or hallucinations or delusions.

In this chapter we present vignettes of borderline patients who are members of the four large groups obtained by means of clustering analysis. Our protocols contained descriptions of behaviors from a large number of observers suitable for the rating of items derived from an ego-functions framework. Hence it is not possible to utilize all these transcribed data to delineate typical clinical "cases." We have therefore chosen to fill out the clinical gap with descriptions of each of our four large groups, condensed from the protocols of several patients, other individual case reports and a previous experimental study.

It should be kept in mind that statistical analyses are procedures for the study of numbers of subjects, traits or symptoms. The identified individual patient will naturally not have all the traits or symptoms characteristic of the group. A syndrome or a subsyndrome is an idealized category, stereotype of diagnostic entity into which a patient's symptoms or behaviors make the best fit.

In this chapter we amplify the general clinical characteristics of each group already outlined in Chapter 6, to which the reader should refer.

Group I: The Border with Psychoses

Case 1 (Dr. Wolpert). At the time of admission to Psychosomatic and Psychiatric Institute (P & PI) the patient was a 30-year-old mother of two who was separated and who had been living with her parents in Chicago while her children were in the custody of her husband in California. On admission she was confused as to the reasons for admission, saying, "I don't know whether I should be here or not. My father wanted me to come." In this way she disclaimed responsibility for her treatment but would accept the facilities of the hospital, ultimately taking advantage of the hospital for room, board and social life.

Anamnesis revealed that her difficulties had begun some four years previously. On the surface she had been doing well with her husband and two children. However, she resented his seeming lack of interest in her sexually; he had taken a job as a traveling salesman, which kept him away from her a good deal of the time. As her resentment increased she accepted, without understanding why, a dinner invitation from friends she knew her husband would resent. For the entire day before the dinner and while at the dinner she felt an aimless dread but had no insight as to why she should feel so upset. Nothing unusual occurred, however, and she returned home, going to bed without incident. Early the next morning, however, she was awakened by pain in her left shoulder radiating down the arm to the fingers, associated with difficulty in breathing. She feared she would die, awakened her husband and was rushed to an emergency room where she told that she only had "nerve trouble" and needed some counseling.

For the next two years the patient received intensive psychotherapy from a younger male psychiatrist who saw her three times a week, ultimately decreasing to once a week. At one point during her therapy she became "suicidal," and although she had made no suicidal attempt she was hospitalized for three months, being allowed to sign out then against medical advice. Toward the end of the therapy she developed strong erotic feelings for her psychiatrist, characterized by sexual day-dreams, dressing in a seductive way for her sessions and beginning an affair with a neighbor. At about this time her husband became more attentive to her. She felt things were going well and terminated the treatment although the psychiatrist felt she needed more. For four months she felt relatively well, but when her lover moved to another part of the state, depression set in and she sought further psychiatric care from a second but older male psychiatrist who concurred with her own desire for electric shock treatment.

Following the second course of treatment, she told her husband of her recent affair, and the marital relationship deteriorated. He began to drink, she began to drink and use drugs, and soon they separated. From time to time she would be visited by her lover, and during such periods she would feel well, but at other times she was quite depressed. Her ability to take care of the home and children deteriorated. One year before admission to a hospital her elder child was hit by a car and suffered a brain concussion. Following the child's recovery she granted her husband a divorce, took a second lover and became depressed after he asked her to marry him. Six months before admission she took an overdose of sleeping pills, planned so that her lover found her uncon-scious, and she was hospitalized for a second time. While in the hospital the court granted custody of the children to her husband, and upon discharge the patient moved in with a girl friend. At that time she was unable to do more than drink and be isolated in the house.

The patient's family then persuaded her to return to Chicago where she saw a psychiatrist once a week but remained isolated in her parents' apartment. Because of increasingly severe depression and drinking, her parents forced her psychiatrist to place her in a hospital where she stayed for one month. Almost immediately upon admission the depression dissipated and she began to function with the patient group as if she had been a long-standing member. She had two affairs while in the hospital—one with an attendant and one with a nurse from another hospital. All in all, she felt more relaxed and more comfortable in the hospital than ever before. Because of her improvement she was discharged; once home with her parents interminable arguments and drinking began. After an argument she took some pills, slashed her wrists superficially and was readmitted to the hospital.

The patient was born and raised in Chicago. She is the elder of two children, having a brother six years younger. When asked about her early life she remembered that when she was about three or four her parents lived near her grandmother's home but she was always left out of the communication between mother, father and grandparents. While her parents were always "terribly devoted to each other," she felt, "I never belonged. Maybe that is why I felt a wall around me. I can't feel." Although she said she was always "mother's and daddy's little girl who never wanted for anything because of the type of family I lived in," in the next breath she would say she was always unsure of herself.

In high school when she was elected secretary of the senior class she noticed that the other girls who were elected officers seemed to be experiencing strong emotions, including crying and exuberance, while she herself could feel nothing. In fact, she reported that she could not feel anything except when she took drugs.

The patient is aware of how angry she sometimes becomes and how her angry outbursts often jeopardize her relationships. One such example occurred in elementary school. Mother said to her one day that if it was 40 degrees outside the next day the patient wouldn't have to wear leggings. The patient was pleased because that meant she might not have to wear the hated clothes. The next morning mother said that the patient had to wear her leggings. The patient became angry and decided to leave home to go to her grandmother's house. She remembered walking very slowly because she was frightened, and she kept looking back over her shoulder, hoping that someone would come after her.

"This is kind of what I do when I make suicidal attempts, hoping someone will save me. Finally my father did overtake me and took me home. I was glad. I was really quite relieved. When I was in California recently I told my folks over the phone that I felt like killing myself, that they do this to me. I also called my mother to tell her that I'd kill myself but what could she do about it. I guess I just wanted to hurt her. And I told my husband about the affair to shock and hurt him, and tell him how bad I really was. I guess I've always done things to be cruel, to hurt other people."

The patient dated a neighbor's son, T., for a couple of years while in high school. Finally she broke up with T. and started dating W. and D. Subsequently T. asked her out again, and instead of refusing as her other girl friends had encouraged her to do she went out with him immediately. For a period of several years she dated T. W. and D. interchangeably. She didn't particularly have a preference except for the boy that she was with at the moment.

Comment. This patient represents a prototype of Group I of the borderline. In her own statement she has never considered that she "belonged" and says very clearly that she cannot feel. Her early role assignment was that of an object of mother's narcissism; mother's concerns were of appearance and behavior, not of feelings. Having no help with her feelings, they were taken as signs of her badness and she developed a self-image of worthlessness. When she attempted independence and self-reliance, she was inhibited by mother's controls.

Now she shows she is unsure of herself; her self-image is that of an inferior person who must anxiously attempt to meet standards of others. She has difficulty in feeling anything except when she is comfortable in the hospital where there are relatively well-defined roles, or when she is under the influence of alcohol or of drugs. In order to get a feeling of belonging and identity, the patient must attach herself to someone, living an almost parasitic relationship. Information regarding her high school boy friends indicates that she didn't have a preference except for "the boy I was with at the moment." Her elopement was an impulsive desire to hang on to someone. Inward attachments, in order to be of significance to her, in view of her lack of ability to experience feelings, take the form of violent feelings, either hurting herself or hurting others. Thus, her relation with others may be quite intense but is very unstable. In this sense she is like a tabetic who has to stamp the ground to feel; to feel, the relationship must be violent.

In a vain attempt to resolve her loneliness and need for attention, the patient gradually acquires the role of the sick person; her conversion symptoms, alcoholism, drug abuse and hospitalization being the signs of this newly developed role.

Thus we see a patient unable to form stable affectionate relationships, to control aggressive feelings, or to develop a coherent self-identity, vainly trying to escape from depression by promiscuity, drugs, alcohol and hospitalization.

Case 2. A 32-year-old female entered the ISPI unit, expressing anger at the entire environment. She was so outspoken that negative reactions were evoked from everyone. Nevertheless, she had to have things her own way—right or wrong. At times she was so loud that she had to be controlled from inappropriate gales of laughter. When her husband called and left a message that her sick daughter was feeling better, she evidenced no response and acted as if she had not heard. Her appearance was that of a dishevelled person who did not care about the environment, nor was she insulted when criticized. The patient was well aware of the time schedules of various activities yet always shuffled in late. She monopolized group meetings with loud talk. She broke the rules concerned with proper dress and frequented the male section which was off-limits. When intensely angry she seemed to get further and further away from reality. There were no evidences of positive relations to anyone.

Summary. Patients in Group I in general do not achieve a sense of consistent identity and have great difficulty in establishing positive relations with others. They apparently have given up actively trying to develop object-relations and withdraw more or less from the scene. Yet they are lonely, depressed and enraged at the environment and other human beings. It is this rage that has many behavioral outlets, but these are not sufficient to protect the ego from transient and mild dissolution of the function of reality adaptation. Hence the transient psychoses superimposed on inappropriate, nonadaptive and negative behaviors (cf. Appendix III for an additional case from Group I).

Group II: The Core Borderline Syndrome

Case 3 (Therapist's Report). This 22-year-old female was a school drop-out, sometimes alcoholic, occasionally a drug-user, promiscuous and had one illegitimate pregnancy and abortion. Her psychotherapeutic sessions have been filled with accounts of vacillation between Joe and Larry, always breaking up with one or the other. No evidence of any affectionate relationship was ever found, not even to a dog she bought and permitted to die, and there were no transference manifestations in the therapy. However, the subject is stable enough to hold a job and live alone in an apartment through her own earnings. The partial contents of the 28th psychotherapeutic session reveal in the subject's own words an intellectual understanding of her hate and lack of affectional consistency.

She seemed to have a great deal of difficulty in beginning the session. She looked up at me, smiled, and in a warm, clear voice expressed that she was having difficulty starting. She said, "I don't know what to say, but I guess there's enough that happened to me that I should." She smiled. After about three or four minutes I asked her why she felt that she was having such difficulty today and she said, she didn't know. After another several minutes she said that she was going with Joe again. "I saw Joe on Friday night; he called me. We went out on Saturday and then again yesterday we went to a movie. He didn't take me to the usual bar and I asked him thinking that I was right, if he didn't want to be seen with me. Joe agreed. Not out loud, but I could tell it was true." She began talking about Friday night—Larry and Sally seeing her, and how they came up to see her; I was somewhat confused and told her that I didn't understand whether Larry and Sally had come up to her apartment to visit. She said no, that Larry came up alone and seemed to want to talk to her about what had happened. The word had gotten around that if Joe catches Larry he's going to really beat him up. Larry said that Joe could do this if he wanted to but he wasn't going to stop talking to her. She said, "Larry actually came up to explain and apologize to me that all this trouble had come about because of me. Then on Sunday I gave Joe a call and he said, let's go to the show, so we went to the show." I said, "All these things are events, things. What about your feelings, and thoughts and fantasies?" She gave a short laugh and said, "Well, I was mad all weekend. I just seemed to have so much hate. I don't know what the hate was about but it was there. I seem to hate everybody. I certainly hate Joe and Larry and yet, I need them too." I asked what she needed them for. She said, "Well, I don't want to be alone. I'm just disgusted with the whole thing. I don't really want to go back and yet I find that I am. It's like watching, waiting to see what I'm going to do next. It's almost like a play and I have a certain role and I look to see what's going to happen in the next act." I asked her if she felt like a director or a spectator, and she laughed and said, "I wish I were the director but I sort of feel like it's all happening to me and I don't have too much of a say."

She said, "I'm so disgusted, I just feel that nobody cares." I asked if that includes Joe and Larry. She said, "Yes." I said, "It seems that you would like to have closeness and concern and yet, when it's within your grasp there's something about it that seems to make you flee from it." After a long silence she said, "Yeah, I know that's true. I can see that now. But what do I do about it?" I asked her what there was about the closeness that forced her to break it off. She said, "Well, I don't know." She thought for a while, and then said, "Well, when you get into a relationship like that you get trapped. At first it's fine. But then you start getting in a pattern. You have to do what the other one wants you to do." I said "You mean you feel obligated?" She said, "Yeah, obligated. And you've got to do whatever the other person wants. Then I'm just completing a pattern. It's like when I sleep with a boy for a few months. At first it's exciting and fun. And then after a while, I just have to keep going. Not 'cause I want to any more. Then I want to be free. I want to get out of the relationship, and I don't know how to do it. So then I have to start creating little incidents so that the other one will have to break up with me. I want my freedom then, but then, when I have my freedom I just feel lonely again." I said to her that a close relationship entails, to her, meeting the other person's needs. I wondered if she was saying that when she starts meeting the other person's needs that she kind of loses herself. She said, "Yeah, and then I don't know how to break it off." There was a prolonged silence and I asked what she was reflecting about and she didn't answer. I waited a little while longer and then finally said to her, "You seem to see a close relationship as resulting in your total submission to it. I'm wondering why you should feel that that's the only way?" She said, "The ideal relationship to me would be a two month relationship. That way there'd be no commitment. At the end of the two months I could just break it off. The relationship would just evaporate and I'd be fine. But the only criterion for this would be that there would have to be someone else around so that I wouldn't get lonely." She said she seemed to see these relationships as just transient episodes which protected against loneliness. And she added, "It would be fine as long as that's the way it was. But then again," she said, "I wouldn't mind totally submitting to a relationship or losing myself or meeting someone else's needs if it was someone that I liked. But it never is." Then she thought for a while and then finally said, "I guess the ones that I could totally submit to, like Larry, would be the ones who would never permit it."

Comment. In capsule form this sector of a therapeutic session reveals all the characteristics of Group II: vacillating involvement with others, overt or acted-out expressions of anger, varying degrees of lonely depressiveness and failure in achieving her own identity.

Case 4. A 22-year-old, single male clerk complained of many problems, one of which was the suddenness with which his feelings of well-being would disappear. For example, when his girl friend seems to accept him and tells him she wants him to take care of her, all the world appears good; when she is impatient with him, all the world is bad. However, he is very unsure of his feelings toward her. At times he feels he loved her and needed her, at other times not. When she would tell him she loved him, he would have no feeling or response whatsoever. However, when he would return to his room, he would develop a strong longing for her which would disappear when he was in her presence. This patient reveals difficulty in achieving and maintaining affectionate relationships.

Summary. Patients in Group II still actively search for companionship and affection from others. They are involved but in a vacillating fashion. They move toward an object but soon become anxious and angry and retreat only to become lonely and depressed. The resultant confused picture is often labeled as "ambivalent," but in reality there is little real affection, only anger and loneliness. They do not become psychotic although the to and fro movements in relationships to objects are confusing to the observer.

Group III: The Adaptive, Affectless, Defended— "As if"

Case 5 (Nurse's Report). I got in touch with him about two or three weeks ago about coming to patient activity meeting. He was sitting at the desk in his room reading. He was very pleasant, but didn't say much. He said that he couldn't consider coming down and that he wasn't ready to do anything yet. There was really no affect at all, including no sign of annoyance. At the end of the week I contacted him about getting started with some activity and about the activity meeting. He said that he wasn't able to tolerate this group, there were too many people. I mentioned several programs such as morning recreation. O. T., and men's recreation. He was aware of these things going on. I asked him about the morning recreation program and he found cheer in the fact that he could come and observe, but he wouldn't participate. I invited him in to sit on the sidelines in the gym; he refused. He watched the entire period, leaving a short time before the group. I also talked to him about coming to O. T., and he let me know that he was assigned to work with the group and knew what it was. He said that he didn't know yet if he would be able to come, but he promised me that he would try; however, he did not appear. I asked him about any particular interests he had had before coming into the hosital. He said that he had particularly enjoyed bowling. He knew that we did go bowling, but he wasn't ready to do this. He didn't look directly at me, but he did turn somewhat toward me. This he doesn't always do. I had the feeling that the information that he volunteered, which was more than I really expected, was an effort to get things over with so that he wouldn't have to tolerate the contact any more than possible. He didn't look really depressed; he was more withdrawn. There was no real affect. I have gone in his room to talk with his roommate Mr. S. and they are both there, but there doesn't seem to be any communication. He does leave the ward quite a bit. But he's always by himself. He seems to plan his trips to the canteen when it isn't crowded, because he is always alone. He seems to have some expectation that this is just a period that he had to go through and at some point it will be over and he'll feel better and that's it.

He will come out and watch one TV program, then he will go back in his room and read. Then he might come out and watch another one later. Then he'll go back again. He was having a pretty hard time making an adjustment to having a roommate. Whenever his roommate was in the room, he was out. When the roommate was out, he was in. Now he is able to sit with his roommate in there. How much they talk I don't know, but at least he is in there with him now. Once he told me that he was sleeping during the day because his roommate snored at night and he couldn't sleep. Most of the time he reads in his room.

His father visited with him Saturday evening. They went to the canteen. His father came in and went straight to his room. I was in the dayroom. When they were ready to go to the canteen his father was with him and the patient asked: "is it all right if we go to the canteen?" I told him sure. I have never seen his expression change. It's like someone who just doesn't care about anything. He has this sort of vagueness. It's always the same. I have never seen him smile. He and Mr. S. had a date to play pool. Mr. S. went in his room and reminded him. He told him, "When I get ready, I'll let you know." Mr. S. was under the impression that he was going to be ready that evening. The pitch of his voice never changes. He just says what he wants to say and that's it.

Comment. This patient is a quite withdrawn person who attempts to maintain isolation from other human beings. He conforms very well to the ordinary rituals and seems to have a desire to please. He eats well, he shaves himself every day, and he dresses appropriately, but he avoids people. His isolated attitude becomes somewhat grotesque in that he will pretend to read without sufficient light or with the book upside down in order to avoid conversing with others. With some of the personnel his conversation is in a jocular form but without any real feeling. There's a certain teasing element in the relationship. He has a hunched-over posture as if he's trying to crawl into a shell. He doesn't smile or laugh or become angry, and his eyes remain cast down. His conversation is about sports and he does follow the sports page in the newspaper and knows a great deal about the details of baseball affairs.

Apparently large groups of people, conversation within the group, and noise create a confusion in him. He gradually was able to assert himself to some degree in that he admitted his dislike for the hospital food and began to eat downstairs in the canteen, and he has a choice of television programs. He is shy and doesn't make friends easily. Overt violence and aggressivity aparently disturb him a great deal.

This is a patient whose relationships and behavior outwardly toward people are quite bland, and he does not appear to be either anxious or depressed nor does he overtly express anger or annoyance. He simply isolates himself and has a kind of bland communication but mostly withdraws from contact with people. One could hardly ascribe any affect to him. There are no apparent hallucinations or delusions, and one can only consider him as having a defect in his total affective system in that he is unable to relate himself meaningfully to any other human being, except father.

Summary. Patients in Group III are isolated and withdrawn without even negative affect or behavior. They await cues from others and attempt to relate by assuming complementary roles. In this maneuver they constitute "as if" characters who behave as expected and often appear to be involved. Yet their role vacillations depend on the other person to whom they facilely adapt. This is how they live in a world in which they feel no personal identity.

Group IV: The Border with the Neuroses

In our laboratory we have studied a group of adult male patients who were hospitalized on a state hospital ward for chronic patients. They were erroneously considered to be suffering from chronic depressions (Oken et al., 1960).

The depression which constituted the major symptomatic complaint of these subjects had a characteristic quality. Little deep sadness was evident. In place of a sense of heartfelt sorrow and misery of the sort which stirs an empathic response, these men communicated a dull dejection and bland loneliness and hopelessness; they seemed defeated, discouraged, and cowed, apathetically accepting their state. There was little in the way of spontaneous self-remonstrance or abnegation. Rather, they were free in blaming their manifest failure or lack of "breaks," maltreatment, and misfortune; they "never had a chance."

Their own part in their difficulties was minimized, rationalized away, or blandly glossed over in a very facile manner. Only when pressed in this particular area did they show any sign of tension or anxiety, losing some of their composed resignation and becoming irritable and whining. Here, too, their response took the form of evasion and denial. They took no firm stand in their own defense; mobilized aggression was weak and diffuse. Shifts of mood occurred readily in response to changes about them. They were quite responsive to a display of interest or concern. But this, too, was devoid of force or enthusiasm. The general picture was one of resignation, *lack of involvement,* and marked passivity.

The anamnestic data were very much in keeping with these findings. All these men gave evidence of long-standing markedly limited adjustment, frequently traceable back to early childhood. The typical pattern was of a moderately stable adjustment with restricted function in a relatively protected environment, usually involving a relationship with an older woman. The relationship then broke up (or the situation somehow changed), leading to the necessity for a new adjustment. Of the six men who had married, only one was living with his wife at this time, and he gave a history of a previous divorce. In six of the group the precipitating factor was clearly the loss of the key relationship. Rarely was this break initiated by the man himself. When it was, it followed upon his becoming unable finally to bear remarkably intense and long-standing abuse and exploitation. Whatever the precipitant, the new adjustment called for never could be made. A passive deterioration of function ensued. Jobs became less frequent and less skilled, and finances deteriorated. Alcohol was used as periodic balm but there were few true binges. Overt homosexual activity sporadically occurred in many, but without enthusiasm or the development of any continuing relationship. Often this was used as a device for obtaining money.

During the latter period some symptoms appeared, chiefly in the form of depression with suicidal thoughts (but uncommon attempts), feelings of hopelessness and confusion. Any frustration called for a response of avoidance, denial, withdrawal, and flight, or when these were impossible, passive-aggressive acceptance. Solace was obtained by mutual sympathy from those similarly afflicted. Daydream fantasy was frequently used. This was of a simple wish-fulfillment type, in which they saw themselves with their troubles at an end without any intermediate steps or efforts on their part. Exacerbations, associated with periods of diminished gratification, led to deepened depression, irritability, more-or-less developed ideas of reference and also some anxiety which at times was represented as fears of going crazy or "something terrible happening to me." During such periods hospitalization was readily sought and usually resulted in rapid improvement. But there was no great urge for discharge; they had "found a home." When release was arranged they "dragged their feet" but then accepted it passively, adding it to their list of injustices. It was difficult to make a diagnosis in almost every one of these cases.

Case 6 (Nurse's Report). This female patient spends most of her time with Mrs. S. She may be sitting with someone else at dinner, or watching TV with someone else; but she does spend the majority of her time with Mrs S. I was curious as to how she was going to handle this after the patient meeting. Was she still going to stick with Mrs. S. or seek other patients? Today I noticed she is still spending the same amount of time with Mrs. S. that she did before. This morning she and Mrs. S. were laughing outside the office. Mrs. S. was laughing, scolding her for not stealing some bacon off the breakfast tray for her. Mrs. S. didn't come out for breakfast because she had her robe on and didn't want to get dressed. All the patient could say was, "I forgot. I forgot." The patient's reaction was one of real passiveness. She did seem angry and dis-gusted—she looked at me and rolled her eyes, like, "Oh, me . . . ," but she couldn't express it. She doesn't seem to object to anything that I can recall on the ward. I noticed they were watching TV. She was watching a story or something Sunday afternoon. She got up to go to her room, and when she came back the fellows had changed it to the baseball game. One of them said, "Oh, I didn't realize you were watch-ing the story you left. We could turn it back on. I just wanted to see how the game is going." She said, "No. You watch it. That's all right. I'll watch anything." I thought she would have been interested in the story because she had been watching if for about a half-hour. I know in the evenings when they vote on the programs they are going to watch she doesn't want anything special—whatever the group wants. When she eats lunch she always eats with Mrs. S. They sit at the same table across from each other in almost the same chairs every day. She looks depressed to me sometimes, but not when you are talking to her and when she's with somebody. If you happen to find her by herself, maybe watching television, she isn't really watching all the time. She does look depressed then. On the outside someone might just think she's being thoughtful. I can't think of any incident where she has initiated something. She sits there with the group and she will talk, but nothing really spontaneous occurs. I think she is well accepted by the group. She's very nice to everybody. If someone is out of cigarettes and she's going downstairs, she will offer to get them for you. From how I've seen her act with the group, I think she adapts to the situation. When she's questioned she'll voice what she has to say. She isn't aggressive to the point of initiating anything though. She spends time mostly in the dayroom. She isn't in her room too much. Her affect is always appropriate. I've never really seen her upset. When you approach her she quite readily becomes very friendly. She goes to the gym and plays well. She goes on the patio.

I feel that I don't get through to her because she just won't let me. I sense a definite need for dependency relationships, not in her relationship to me necessarily but in her relationship to this other female patient. This need for dependency still seems pretty evident perhaps because if you push her—make her feel that she's needed or wanted at a certain time—she will come. When she didn't attend the baking group last Thursday, for instance, I'm sure if I'd waited until she'd combed her hair, she would have come.

"There are a lot of people that I like, but I can't say that I love them." She was also trying to point out to Mrs. S. that everybody isn't alike. They seem to seek each other out, but they can't stand each other for long.

Comment. The outstanding characteristic in the behavior of this patient is her clinging, and need for a dependent relationship. This is demonstrated in her relations with another female patient. Otherwise the patient is adaptive and unobtrusive. Outstanding, in contrast with her needs, is her inability to love any other person or to maintain interpersonal contact for long.

Summary. Group IV patients are frequently misdiagnosed as depressives because they attach themselves to others and react with whining, crying sadness when their dependent needs are not satisfied. Thus they reveal more overt seemingly positive affect than any other borderline patients. Yet they still lack a consistent identity and have no capacity to give to others. Their clinging is not object-focused but satisfaction-oriented because they have little capacity to love.

The six patients presented in this chapter, observed and described in different settings, clearly belong within the borderline syndrome as derived from our investigations. More than that, the vignettes demonstrate the fact that between-group differences are clear enough so that the clinician can diagnose the subcategories of the borderline. The sharpness of these differences permits a specific diagnosis from history and anamnesis without the necessity of long periods of observation or depth interviews. The recognition of a patient's membership in a particular group of the borderline may in the future have practical value even if now not apparent. At any rate, the classification opens a vast area of research for possible biological, psychological and sociological correlations.

GENERAL SUMMARY AND CONCLUSIONS

Summary

The original goal of our research was to define the psychiatric entity frequently referred to as borderline. This term in itself has many historical and contemporary meanings. Although attempts have been made by a number of individual therapists to allocate the diagnosis to a specific syndrome, in general it has been used as a depository for clinical uncertainty. Even this usage is not specific because the same uncertainty existing in many clinics is hidden by the use of at least a dozen terms, ranging from chronic undifferentiated schizophrenia to anhedonism and character neuroses. These special terms seem to designate commonalities of visible symptoms rather than patterns of functions or dysfunctions.

The diagnosis of borderline has been in use for several decades, or even longer, without clear definition. The term has both technical and general implications which are difficult to separate. Our attempt to define what it denotes as a clinical psychiatric syndrome is confusing to those who literally expect the definition to include what borders on what. We have given much consideration to developing a new diagnostic appellation, which is difficult after the long usage of the old even though it is semantically unclear. We wanted to use a new word for the syndrome and other terms for the subcategories, but we have not succeeded in our efforts. This may be accomplished by others in the future.

Our primary goal, then, was to determine whether a borderline syndrome exists and if so what are its attributes (Chapter 1). Secondarily we hoped to ascertain if subcategories could be delineated and to define them if possible. Thus the goal at the onset of the research was to answer the question, *"What is the borderline?"*

We began our investigations in an era when clinical diagnoses and classifications are derogated, diagnostic skills atrophying and the life-history of psychiatric entities of not great concern. These tendencies are self-perpetuating because students are being taught to focus, sometimes to exclusion, on the internal dynamics of individual patients.

Our overview of an extensive professional literature (Chapter 2), although selective, disclosed that no systematic study of the borderline has ever been made. The same deficiency applies to other diagnostic terms, serving the purpose of labeling vague syndromes. The bulk of published reports are based on one or a few patients for whom treatment represents the only method of observation. Conclusions are couched in the form of psychoanalytic interpretations. The raw data are skimpy, "metapsychological" theory is directly applied and conclusions are inferences as to meanings rather than definitions of processes. These reports are carried through the literature as "findings" monotonously confirmed in continuity.

Despite these criticisms which are more general than specific and applicable to a whole specialty, "dynamic" studies disclose patterns that can be translated into hypotheses. The positive contributions suggest that the borderline is a specific syndrome with considerable degree of internal consistency and stability, and not a regression as a response to internal or external conditions of stress. It represents a syndrome characteristic of arrested development of ego-functions. Clinicians recognized that the borderline syndrome is a confusing combination of psychotic, neurotic and character disturbances with many normal or healthy elements. Although these symptoms are unstable, the syndrome itself as a process is recognizably stable, giving rise to the peculiar term "stable instability."

We concluded that despite the value of studies of the internal dynamics of borderline patients and the usefulness of our previous research which classified depressions into syndromes or categories on the basis of symptoms, neither was useful for the study of the borderline. Instead we decided to study the ego-functions of borderline patients in so far as they are exposed by ongoing behaviors thereby revealing what were normal healthy or adaptive functions, and what were unhealthy nonadaptive functions. Utilizing a framework of ego-psychology based on psychoanalytic theory promised a better understanding of the syndrome and its subcategories (Chapter 3).

Our research design was derived, therefore, from a different approach: instead of using the data of dyadic introspection from interviews, or various forms of psychotherapy or tapping historical or anamnestic data, we described observable behaviors (Chapter 4). In essence we observed and described behaviors and *then* rated traits extracted from an ego-psychology framework. This extraction required the redefinition of ego-functions into behavioral variables as exactly as possible and the development of quantitative coding system sufficiently clear and practiced so that rater-reliability could be achieved.

Our assumptions can be summarized as follows:

1. Behavior can be observed, described and quantified.
2. Behavior assessed in terms of ego-functions is an index of mentation that the psychotherapist does not typically observe; hence the study of such behavior adds to the therapist's store of knowledge of the patient's assets and liabilities and capacities for adaption.
3. Behavioral evidences have validity in terms of estimating the quality and quantity of internal psychological functions.
4. A large enough time-sample of the behavior of an individual patient is an adequate index of his ego-functions.
5. A finer analysis of ego-functions in a large enough sample of patients designated by a specified diagnostic term can result in a sharper definition of that specific syndrome.

Patients were selected on the basis of the known positive and negative attributes of the borderline described in the extensive literature and corresponding to our clinical experiences (Chapter 4). They were young adults from upper lower or lower middle socio-economic classes. An older age group from a previous study was also available for study. Actually we had anticipated that our selection would include a sufficient number of non-borderline patients, but most of these dropped out

(Chapter 9) so that comparison groups of schizophrenics and neurotics were utilized on the basis of information derived from the literature and our own clinical experiences.

In our design we could not include all hypothesized ego-functions since many are not expressed in behavior; others which were included had to be dropped because of insufficient evidence. Some qualities of the borderline could not be evoked and in fact may have been inhibited because of the non-stressful characteristics of the nursing unit. In fact, the behaviors that we observed must be linked to the specificity of the environment within which they occurred—far less stressful than the real world. Even the decision for discharge which we planned for our second period of "observation-description-rating" was not stressful probably because the borderline does not become committed to the institution. Their reluctance to leave was based on a distaste for living away from their families (as advised) or taking a job amidst people.

At least two independent professionals rated the protocols in juxta-position with the observational evidence for their ratings. The descriptions suitable for each rating were developed by the investigators, the raters were trained by one of us and another reviewed the ratings and reconciled them (in the relatively few cases when they were discrepant) on the basis of the recorded evidence and his clinical judgment. We believe that we achieved reliability which is always the result of well-defined scale points, common language, adequate training of raters and clinical judgments reconciling differences.

The next step was difficult because of the nature of our ratings, the large number of variables remaining viable (93) and the limited sample of patients. Factoring did not appear to be the primary method of choice for our statistical analyses. We were indeed fortunate in our search for a method to join forces with Friedman and Rubin, who utilized our data for their own investigation on clustering (Chapter 5).

They utilized a clustering procedure, the results of which were subjected to a multiple discriminant-function analysis. Ten components accurately identified membership in one of four groups for 49 of 51 patients. In addition 20 variables accurately predicted group membership for all patients. Each of these four groups was separately factor analyzed to develop internal descriptions of each group and make possible between-group comparisons.

The four groups elicited from the statistical analysis when translated into clinical syndromes coincide with clinical experience (Chapter 6). However, using our data which are fully documented, other clinicians may make other interpretations. In general Group I is closest to the psychotic border, Group IV is closest to the neurotic border, Group II represents the core process of the borderline and Group III is the most adaptive, compliant and lacking in identity ("as if").

In defining the overall characteristics of the borderline syndrome we include *anger* as the main or only affect, defect in *affectional* relationships, absence of indications of *self-identity* and *depressive loneliness*.

Within this gestalt the various groups represent different positions. Members of Group I give up attempts at relationship but at the same time overtly, in behavior and affect, react negatively and angrily toward other people and to their environments. Persons in Group II are inconsistent, moving toward others for relations which is then followed by acted-out repulsion, moving away into isolation where they are lonely and depressed. This back-and-forth movement is characteristic and corresponds with the fact that these people are both angry and depressed but at different times. Patients in Group III seem to have given up their search for identity and defend against their reactions to an empty world. They do not have the angry reactions characteristic of Group I. Instead they passively await cues from others and behave in complementarity—"as if." In no other group were the defenses observable as clearly or as consistently as in Group III. Subjects in Group IV search for a lost symbiotic relation with a mother figure which they do not achieve, and then reveal what may be called an anaclitic depression.

In the cluster analysis Group I and III were shown to be relatively close together and Groups II and IV were likewise close. This makes clinical sense because patients in both Groups I and III have given up hope of meaningful relationships and those in Groups II and IV are still searching. Patients in Group I are angry at the world and their ego integrations are endangered by this strong affect; we hypothesize that they often become temporarily psychotic as a result. Those in Group III have given up even their reactions to frustration and are compliant, passive and relate as others wish, or it may be that they successfully defend themselves against angry behavior and eruptions.

Group II includes patients who are buffeted by virtue of their own ego-dysfunctions as they attempt to relate to others, become stimulated to anger, and then withdraw and suffer loneliness. Group IV, on the other hand, is characterized by abandonment of any but dependent clinging relationships, and when this is not gratified, develop the characteristics of an anaclitic depression, weeping and feeling neglected and sorry for themselves.

The next step after the characteristic behavioral traits of the borderline category, its subgroups and factors had been put together was to check them against total case reports of individual patients. We could utilize published case histories, the protocols of our 51 patients, an indepth study of 16 traditional patients, an experimental group previously studied and one patient in treatment. This was the final pay-off because, by utilizing the behavioral characteristics designating each of the four groups isolated by statistical methods, we were able to place all of the patients in appropriate groups. Thus the statistical differentiation of the whole syndrome and of the four groups made logical clinical sense. This was not true of the finer subdivisions of each group into two factors each because too much overlapping was apparent in them to discriminate clinical entities. The within-group variance was not sharp enough. We demonstrated the way individual patients fall into one of the four groups (Chapter 7).

Interest has shifted from specific mother-child relations as primary causations in the development of neuroses and psychoses to the family of origin. Viewed as a system in its own right and not simply as a collection of individuals, investigators have searched for the families' methods of interaction, problem-solving and especially their methods of communication. The literature contains significant references to disturbed communication systems in families of schizophrenics, but none for the borderline.

Since the study of the family was an after-thought and not included in our original design, we were forced to use routine social service data rated according to specific criteria by an independent rater. Although the families of the borderline showed the usual range of concern about the illness, no specific type of family was correlated with any of the borderline groups. Nevertheless a by-product of this study was a technique for family analysis which discriminated family types. As for the borderline patient in his nuclear family, he marries infrequently and is an inadequate spouse and a poor parent (Chapter 8).

To obtain a perspective on the borderline over time we did a follow-up study (Chapter 9). We were highly successful in interviewing the majority of our residual patient sample (86 per cent) and about 40 per cent of the dropouts. Essentially we found that the borderline in the time-span of 1 to 3.5 years (we designed no set time for the follow-up) after hositalization did not become schizophrenic except for two patients in Group I. Despite therapy in the hospital oriented toward improving the social aptitudes of the patients, they remained for the most part socially isolated. Yet most of them with some psychiatric contacts returned to school or employment and maintained their instrumental roles successfully. Thirteen patients had to be rehospitalized, five of whom had been hospitalized before entering ISPI. Of the dropouts only one turned out to be a borderline.

In an attempt to answer the question—*"How does a human become a borderline?"*—in other words to determine the etiology of the syndrome we realized that we and others had little information. It has been easy, but of little value, for many writers to discuss deficiencies in early child-mother relations, or neglectful mothering or even infantile traumata. Like these genetic factors, genic, familial, and general environmental aspects of etiology are not specific. Only mother-and peer-deprived experimental monkeys suggest an analogy. In brief, no specific etiological agents or conditions are known to produce the borderline syndrome.

To emphasize that search for a single etiological agent or that emphasis on a specific psychodynamic formulation is futile, we have sketched out the value of approaching the borderline or, for that matter, any disease process, within the framework of general systems theory. Within this large field there are appropriate places for many processes, from genic to culture, all of which transact to create the borderline system. The etiology of this syndrome as for any, will come about from knowing the many parts of the system transacting, in its ontogenesis and in its life-cycle (Chapter 10). The questions what, how and why applied to the borderline require different subtheories and hypotheses leading to different techniques of investigation all of which are important. Basic to further research on the borderline is the question, "What is the borderline?" This has been the essential goal of our research which we have reported in detail.

Next we attempted to view society and culture at large in our rapidly changing Western civilization (Chapter 11). We could observe and infer the vast changes occuring but could not articulate these with genetic processes involved in etiology. The question *"Why is the borderline?"* remains unanswered except by vague philosophical approaches to the relationships between modern urban civilization and culture. The "why" becomes a humanistic rather than a scientific question. The essence of the borderline is determined by scientific data that deal with verbal and nonverbal behaviors as processes. The existential aspect is teleological, ideational and abstract, and unrelated to the content of behaviors.

Conclusions

We should like to make explicit what has been accomplished by our investigations through some generalizations over and above the summary of each chapter. In essence we have taken a psychological theory, that of psychoanalytic ego-psychology, and made of it an operational theory which served as our strategy. As tactics we developed a research design applying methods of observing, describing and rating behaviors in a specific setting.

Essentially our conclusions consist of several *hypotheses* which are now available for replication and retesting. The first hypothesis encompasses the delineation of the dimensions of the class of ego-dysfunctions by which we characterize the borderline syndrome as differentiated from all other psychiatric entities. Second, we hypothesize four groups, divisions or subcategories of the borderline.

At this time the results of our statistical analysis developed four groups which have the best fit with contemporary clinical experience. The dimensions of the syndrome are logical and clinically consistent, as are the divisions into four groups. As clinicians we can easily recognize the general characteristics of the borderline syndrome as well as the subsyndromes, matching them with cases reported in the literature, with our own clinical experiences and with the clinical study of our current sample of patients.

Our statistical analyses constituted in themselves a research program carried out by independent investigators using our data (Friedman and Rubin). They were able to develop several sets of groupings and probably could have furnished more. Indeed, in the future newer and/or better mathematical and statistical methods may produce other groupings. As clinicians we have the responsibility of choosing which are logically compatible with clinical experience and which have the optimum degree of discrimination for clinical practice.

The latter is exemplified by the fact that our statisticians at first found groupings which were too coarse in that they discriminated only between activity and passivity in overall behavior. The last attempt was too fine that it resulted in groupings that in essence were fine divisions of what is our final Group II excluding all the others. The results which we accepted resonated immediately with clinical experience.

This last statement requires some explanation because it involves the use of our human internal computers, a process which sometimes is called intuition. Before we began the research and continually during its process we become familiar with the literature on the borderline, diffuse and unsystematic as it is. Yet undoubtedly clinical patterns were taking shape within our mental processes. Second, as we read the descriptions of behavior in our protocols the dimensions of the borderline and its several varieties vaguely developed shape as input of information became programmed. Yet we could not have defined the borderline and its groups in a conscious, logical statement. Then the statistical analysis produced results that clustered items or traits which when retranslated into ego-dysfunctions elicited in us: "That's it— certainly that is what we have been observing." A fit had been accomplished which could not have been possible by clinical scanning or statistical analysis alone.

The clinician should now be able to diagnose the borderline syndrome in general with considerable accuracy and each of the four groups in detail. The investigator can use these for correlations with causes, course, natural history of the disturbance and the efectiveness of various therapies. Eventually such impersonal causal factors as the genic and socio-cultural may be discovered, but as of now our best expectations rest with elucidating what personal experiences contribute most to the development of the borderline in general and its subcategories in particular.

Within the large class or syndrome of the borderline its subcategories must show some commonalities in their manifestations in order to be members of the larger class. Therefore we would expect some overlapping in the deficits of their ego-functions. We cannot as yet apply the factors of each group for clinical discriminations, which is in keeping with the fact that although fine differences among small groups and factors may be statistically feasible, the use of the finer elements of the factors is not yet clinically practical.

We believe that psychoanalytic theory of ego-functions has been useful in deriving meanings from psychoanalytic data. We can now add that from our experience we believe that translating this theory into operational strategy is useful in discriminating ego-functions and their disturbances in behavior. From a study of the psychoanalytic literature as well as from our own research there appears to be a good fit between the results of the two techniques. The theory of ego-psychology, furthermore, when translated into operational terms, can serve as the basis of tactics applicable to a wide range of other unclear behavioral deviances or clinical syndromes.

It is far from our intention to separate artificially internal dynamics from external behavior. We have not fractured the field of "mentation-behavior." In our research we have viewed behavior as the final common pathway of a wide variety of internal processes. We have clearly defined our position as observers and our corresponding operational techniques. We could have also taken other positions, but not simultaneously. At any rate it is reassuring that data derived from introspection and that derived from overt behavior are congruent since they deal with the same processes and both reveal in the "adaptation-maladaptation" or "function-dysfunction" axes similar characteristics.

It must be clear, however, that the operational theory applied to ego-functions requires great pains in its translation into an effective research design. If the design is carefully worked out, the resulting observations and descriptions can be utilized for adequate ratings, properly scaled and tested. Raters must be trained and checked, the traits or items to be rated must be specifically defined and the quantities explicated in a useful code. The ratings cannot represent the skill of only one person and results must be fed back to insure refinement of definitions of scale-points.

The many ratings derived from multiple observers are all used for each variable and a summary rating made for each. We utilized the numerical ratings of our 93 variables for clustering and factor analysis. The results then had to be translated back into traits of behaviors which were then checked against the data of clinical experience. In simple terms the essence of this type of research is a double translation.

Theory-dependent traits are used for ratings. The resulting numbers are then subjected to statistical analysis. These are then reconverted into behavioral language in clusters or groups. Traits which were fed into the statistical analysis via numbers are recovered in combinations that must make sense and reverberate with clinical experience.

In sum, the question *"What is the border?"* as the primary and essential reason for the research was answered by a tentative structure. In addition three by-products accrued representing theoretical, methodological and statistical advances. We utilized a *theory* of functions for classification, a *method* of behavioral observations, descriptions and ratings as our tactics, and a *statistical method* based on a clustering technique.

Questions such as *how* people become borderline characters, or even worse, become ill with the borderline syndrome, and *why* in our current culture both have been appearing in our experience more frequently have not been answered. However, there are many more current questions, and even more will arise to attract investigators' interest in the subject. We hope that our researches have at least established some hypotheses for such future work, that our methods may prove useful for investigations on other unclear clinical syndromes and that we have made a beginning in operational research on ego-functions.

16. The Types and Prevalence of Mental Illness in the Biological and Adoptive Families of Adopted Schizophrenics

Seymour S. Kety, David Rosenthal, Paul H. Wender and Fini Schulsinger

Two types of evidence have been the main support of hypotheses which implicate hereditary factors in the etiology of schizophrenia—the significantly higher incidence of schizophrenia in the close relatives of schizophrenic patients[1] and an increasing incidence in such relatives which is correlated with degree of consanguinity, finding its ultimate expression in the high concordance rate for schizophrenia in monozygotic twins.[2–8] Such evidence is inconclusive, however, in that it fails to remove the influence of certain environmental factors. The higher incidence of schizophrenia in the families of schizophrenics does not permit an evaluation of the respective weights of the genetic and environmental factors both of which the family members share with the schizophrenic, while environmental as well as genetic similarity is highly correlated with consanguinity in most circumstances. In the case of monozygotic twins it has been pointed out that such individuals usually share a disproportionate segment of environmental and interpersonal factors in addition to their genetic identity.[9]

In addition, not all of the previous studies have been able to avoid certain methodological and design problems which limit the generalizability of the findings. The question of subjective bias in the diagnosis of schizophrenia or of zygosity[9] has been ruled out in only a few of the studies, while selective bias has undoubtedly affected the sampling in some of the most extensive of the twin studies.[10, 11] Tienari's finding[12] of a low concordance for schizophrenia in a series of monozygotic twins in contrast to studies reporting concordance rates of 60% or more raises the possibility which is supported by the clinical material published in some of the studies, that the concordance rate found was strongly affected by the latitude permitted in the definition of schizophrenia in the co-twin. Much of the discrepancy could be explained if Tienari had chosen too narrow a definition and studies resulting in the highest concordance rates had been too inclusive. It is interesting to note in this connection that Inouye,[6] who employed a spectrum of categories in the diagnosis of mental illness, found a variety of schizophrenic-like illnesses in the co-twins of schizophrenics.

One of us had previously pointed out the possible value of using adopted individuals who developed schizophrenia as a means of separating the hereditary from the environmental contributions to its etiology.[9] Although adopted probands had been employed in evaluating nature and nurture contributions to intelligence and mental retardation,[13] the peculiar advantages of this approach had not previously been exploited in the psychoses. The present study, the first of three in which we use adoption as a means of disentangling hereditary and genetic influences in schizophrenia,[14, 15] examines the prevalence and nature of mental illness in the biological and adoptive parents, siblings, and half-siblings of adopted individuals who had minimal contact with their biological families and who later became schizophrenic. A number of special precautions were taken to avoid the operation of subjective or selective bias. A diagnostic scheme was adopted with sufficient latitude to allow for a number of possibilities regarding the nature of the transmitted characteristics. For reasons which will become obvious later, the study was carried out in Denmark. By April 1967 practically all of the data originally contemplated had been collected, diagnoses had been made on the relatives who had been identified with evidence of mental illness, the codes broken, and the first analyses begun. The present communication is a first report. Additional data, more detailed analyses and the clinical abstracts upon which the diagnoses were based will be published in a full report at the termination of the study.

METHODS

The study as originally conceived was to be based entirely upon epidemiological information with no resort to personal contact with any of the probands or their families, and that is the nature of the present data. Interviews made by appropriate professional personnel of all probands and family members, if they can be conducted without introducing bias, may considerably increase the richness of the information and are being planned for the future.

The epidemiological study depended upon and was made possible by the existence in Denmark of three registers of remarkable quality and coverage:

Adoption Register of the State Department of Justice[1]

These archives maintained in Copenhagen contain the official records for every adoption granted in Denmark going back well before the period relevant to this study. They are filed separately for the city of Copenhagen and for the rest of Denmark, and chronologically by the date on which the adoption was granted. They contain the name, birth date, and address of the biological mother and the putative biological father. The reliability of the latter information is probably greater than is usually the case since the law requires that the putative father acknowledge paternity and contribute to the costs. In the case of the adopting parents, in addition to names, birth dates and address, they record the income of the adoptive father and his total fortune, his occupation, a description of the adoptive home and of the character of the adoptive parents. They give the name and birth date of the child and the date on which he was introduced to the adoptive home. Relationship between the adoptive and biological parents is noted as are noteworthy features of the child's medical history.

Folkeregister

This is a population register maintained for many years by every community in Denmark and established by law in 1924, giving for each individual (identified by name and birth date) the address and household in which he has lived from birth to death or emigration. By means of these registers throughout the country it is possible to trace an individual through all changes of address and changes in marital status, deriving information on his parents, children and sibships. Since there are fines for failing to report each change of address shortly after it occurs, these

---

[1] The authors are grateful to the State Department of Justice for permission to use these files with appropriate safeguards regarding their confidentiality.

records are remarkably complete. One possible loss, of relevance to the siblings recovered in this study, would be a child born in a hospital and not returned to the mother's household with her.

Psychiatric Register of the Institute of Human Genetics

This Institute of the University of Copenhagen has maintained a register going back to World War I of patients in most of the hospitals in Denmark diagnosed as having certain disorders. All nervous and mental diseases are reportable to the Institute and constitute the Psychiatric Register, which has recently been moved to the Risskov Hospital in Aarhus. Except for the Bispebjerg Hospital in Copenhagen, some departments of child psychiatry, and occasional short periods in the case of some other hospitals, all of the psychiatric hospitals and the psychiatric departments of general hospitals have been reporting all of their admissions quite faithfully. In order to test the completeness of the Psychiatric Register which is crucial to the search for mental illness in the adoptees and family members, a sample of several thousand names has been searched both in this Register and in the individual files of the 14 major psychiatric facilities in Denmark. There is an indication thus far that a search of the Psychiatric Register plus the files of psychiatric admissions to the Bispebjerg Hospital would recover about 95% of the admissions to all psychiatric facilities in the periods covered in the study.

In addition to these major sources of information we made use of the following additional sources, especially in the case of the relatives of the probands, to assure that we had obtained the maximum of recorded information on mental illness or disturbance in the sample:

Records of the Mother's Aid Organization

These contain information on the mental state and socio-economic problems of mothers or prospective mothers and pertinent information on the biological father, the child and other members of the family in applications for abortion, social or financial assistance, or the placing out of a child for adoption. These records were also a valuable source of information on the preadoption history of our probands.

Police and Court Records

The Psychiatric Register contains some information relevant to delinquency and imprisonment. Prison records and court psychiatric consultations have been used to supplement this information. Although our information regarding simple imprisonment is incomplete, it is likely that most cases in which a psychiatric question has been raised have come to our attention.

Military Records

These contain records of discharge from military service for medical or psychiatric reasons and psychiatric evaluation where that has been indicated.

By virtue of the centralization of functions to single organizations and the national scope of the Folke- and Psychiatric Registers, it was felt that there was a unique opportunity for obtaining the maximum of recorded information relevant to our sample of adoptees and their relatives.

SELECTION OF INDEX CASES

In order to take advantage of the more complete registers existing after 1920, to assure a substantial number of living parents, and to maximize the yield of index cases by selecting from a pool of adoptees who were within or beyond the period of maximum risk for schizophrenia, it was decided to include all adoptions granted in the City and County of Copenhagen (which at that time comprised 20–25% of the population of Denmark) from the beginning of 1924 to the end of 1947. Thus, the youngest of the adoptees would be more than 17 and the oldest more than 40 years of age at the beginning of the study. From these were excluded those adoptions in which one or both of the adoptive parents was a biological relative of the child. For each of the remaining 5483 adoptees the following information was recorded on a sequentially numbered special "A Form": name, sex, birth date of the adoptee; age in days, weeks or months of first transfer to the adopting parents; age at and date of adoption; name, birth date and address of the biological mother and the putative biological father; name, birth date and address of the adopting mother and father, his occupation and the stated income and fortune. The names of the adoptees were then checked in the Folkeregister to obtain all names acquired by each through life.

The Psychiatric Registers of the Institute of Human Genetics and of the Bispebjerg Hospital were then searched for the names of each of these adoptees, confirmation of identification being made by birth date and, where doubt existed, by ancillary information such as address or names of relatives. When any record was found of admission of an adoptee to a psychiatric facility, regardless of the nature of the illness, a numbered "B Form" was prepared with the following information: adoptee's name, birth date, and A Form number; for each admission to a psychiatric facility: the name of the hospital, the dates of admission and discharge, and the discharge diagnoses. This yielded a total of 507 adoptees who had been admitted to a psychiatric facility for any reason, and it was from this group that the index cases were selected.

The psychiatric hospital records for each of these 507 adoptees were then obtained and examined independently by two Danish psychiatrists. One of these was Dr. Schulsinger, who prepared a brief abstract from the record and classified the individual as definitely schizophrenic, definitely not schizophrenic, or possibly schizophrenic. The other psychiatrist was Dr. Jytte Willadsen who had not been informed of the over-all design of the study and was told simply that the study had as one of its objectives the determination of schizophrenia and other mental illnesses in a group of adoptees. On each B Form she completed a check list which included age at onset of illness, marital status, major clinical features such as: organic signs and symptoms, thought disorder, inappropriateness of mood and affect, delusional thinking, hallucinations, bizarreness, withdrawal, work performance, sexual adjustment, intellectual ability and therapy. She was asked also to record her designation of the most probable diagnosis and also to indicate the likelihood that the patient had schizophrenia. One copy of the B Form, including Dr. Willadsen's entries but not Dr. Schulsinger's, was sent to Bethesda where, on the basis of the information thus transmitted Drs. Wender and Kety independently rated each of the adoptees with a history of admission to a psychiatric facility as definitely schizophrenic, definitely not schizophrenic or possibly schizophrenic. After that process Dr. Schulsinger's ratings were received and tabulated and the three ratings compared. Where all three had rated an adoptee as definitely schizophrenic, the individual became an index case. Where all three agreed that the adoptee on the basis of the records was definitely not schizophrenic (absence of suggestive symptoms and the ability to form a clear diagnosis of another type of illness), the adoptee was dropped from further consideration as an index case. Where a question of schizophrenia had been raised by one or more of the raters, Dr. Schulsinger was asked to prepare an English summary of the case history as obtained from the hospital records but omitting his own impression. These summaries were then sent to the American authors, and where a concensus on schizophrenia by them and Dr. Schulsinger was reached, these also became schizophrenic index cases. In this way, 34 schizophrenic index cases were selected from the adoptees with a history of admission to a psychiatric facility. Two of these were found to be monozygotic twins but, since they were adopted by the same parents, have been treated as a single case, thus reducing the number of schizophrenic index cases to 33.

SELECTION OF CONTROLS

In order to arrive at an estimate of the prevalence of mental illness which would result from our search techniques and diagnostic criteria in the populations of biological and adoptive relatives of adopted children who did not become schizophrenic, a matched control for each index case was selected from the pool of 4976 adoptees without B forms (for whom no admission to a psychiatric facility had been recorded). These were selected as follows:

The file containing the A Forms in sequential order was searched systematically in equal batches before and after the A Form of each index case until at least four other adoptees were found without a history of a psychiatric admission and corresponding to the index case in sex, age, age at transfer to the adoptive parents and socio-economic status of the adoptive family. The latter was determined by occupation of the adoptive father, income, fortune and address, using criteria previously employed for Denmark. [16] Considerably more information was then obtained in Copenhagen relative to the pretransfer history of each of these adoptees. This included: time spent with biological mother, father or other biological relatives, time spent in a children's institution and the nature of the institution, time spent with a foster family other than

Table 1. Some Characteristics of the Schizophrenic Index Cases and Their Matched Controls

	Index Cases	Controls
Number	33	33
Males:Females	18:15	18:15
With biological parent(s) for:		
less than 1 month	19	20
1 month to 3 months	6	4
3+ months to 6 months	2	2
6+ months to 12 months	5	4
1+ to 2 years	0	2
more than 2 years	1	1
Months spent with biological parent(s)	3.5	4.1
Months spent in children's institution	10.2	8.0
Months spent in foster home	3.6	3.7
Age (months) at transfer to adoptive parents	18.3	16.0
Age (months) at legal adoption	38.0	33.5
Socio-economic class of adoptive parents	3.0	3.0
Mean age, 1 January 1967 (years)	36.1	35.9
Mean year of birth:		
Probands	1931	1931
Biological mother	1906	1909
Biological father	1907	1906
Adoptive mother	1896	1900
Adoptive father	1895	1895

the adoptive parents. When this information had been returned, Drs. Wender and Kety selected from the tentative controls for each index case one which best approximated the index case in the characteristics noted above and which are summarized for the index cases and the controls in Table 1.

IDENTIFICATION OF BIOLOGICAL AND ADOPTIVE RELATIVES

After the probands (index cases and control adoptees) had been selected, their A numbers were mixed together into a single group of probands which was then handled indiscriminately through all the succeeding operations. None of those who made the subsequent searches and diagnoses were given information that would have indicated which were the index cases and which were the controls. From the names and birth dates of the biological and adoptive parents, the subsequent name changes, marital and parental history of each individual was traced through the Folkeregister,[2] thus permitting the identification by name and birth date of parents, siblings and half-siblings of the proband in both his biological and adoptive families. The dates of death, emigration, or disappearance of any of these family members were also noted, and when this occurred before the age of 15 the individual was not tabulated. Individuals who moved from one part of Denmark to another could readily be followed through the respective Folkeregisters. The number of each type of relative thus identified and remaining beyond age 15 for each of the proband groups is indicated in Table 2. For the 33 schizophrenic probands and their controls, 98% of the biological mothers, 92% of the biological fathers and 98% of the adoptive parents were identified. We cannot with equal certainly establish the percentage of siblings and half-siblings identified. The loss by death, emigration or disappearance of the tabulated identified relatives represented about 6% of the total subject years under examination.

DETECTION AND CHARACTERIZATION OF MENTAL ABERRATION IN THE RELATIVES OF THE PROBANDS

The Psychiatric Register of the Institute of Human Genetics and of the Bispebjerg Hospital, the psychiatric admissions of the 14 major psychiatric hospitals, records of the Mother's Aid Organization, police records and military records were now searched for the names of any of the 463 identified relatives of the probands. If check of the birth date and ancillary information confirmed the identity, the individual was placed in a new group of relatives with a history of some mental abnormality. These were described on sequentially numbered forms with admission, discharge and diagnostic information from the Psychiatric Register or other source.

Since the diagnosis of mental illness in the biological and adoptive families of the probands was the crucial determination of the study, every effort was made to insure that this diagnosis was made independently by each of the four raters and in the absence of knowledge which

---

[2] Additional information for relatives born before 1924 was obtained from old census lists.

Table 2. Distribution of Identified Relatives

	Biological Family					Adoptive Family				
	Mothers	Fathers	Sibs	Half-sibs	Total	Mothers	Fathers	Sibs	Half-sibs	Total
For 33 index cases:										
Total identified	33	30	2	85	150	33	30	8	3	74
Lost through:										
death	9	8	0	3	20	11	13	0	0	24
emigrtion	1	2	0	1	4	0	0	1	1	2
disappearance	0	0	0	0	0	0	0	0	0	0
Total lost	10	10	0	4	24	11	13	1	1	26
Average age at loss	37	45	—	19	37	56	63	19	22	57
For 33 controls:										
Total identified	32	31	5	88	156	33	33	17	0	83
Lost through:										
death	3	6	0	0	9	13	13	0	0	26
emigration	3	2	1	4	10	2	1	0	0	3
disappearance	2	1	0	0	3	0	0	0	0	0
Total lost	8	9	1	4	22	15	14	0	0	29
Average age at loss	38	44	22	30	38	60	53	—	—	57

might bias his evaluation. For each of these relatives, the case records were obtained from the respective institutions and an English summary on each was prepared by a Danish psychiatrist, Dr. Erik Glud, who was not aware of the research design or the specific hypotheses being tested (Dr. Schulsinger prepared a few summaries before Dr. Glud joined the project). These summaries were transcribed and the transcriptions edited to delete all personal names, diagnostic opinions by the summarizing psychiatrist, adjectives such as adoptive, biological, etc., and other information which might indicate whether the subject in question was a biological or an adoptive relative and any reference which might indicate whether the subject was the relative of an index case or control. The summaries themselves varied considerably with regard to the amount of information they contained because in some cases we could find only brief notes in the files of the Mother's Aid Organization or the police; but most summaries were sufficiently ample to permit diagnostic assessment with a reasonable degree of confidence.

Four copies of the edited summary were prepared and distributed to the four authors who served as raters and who independently characterized each subject according to the classification described below. The individual ratings were then tabulated and those cases in which there was disagreement among the raters were discussed at a conference of all four authors where an effort was made to review additional edited information which it was possible to obtain and to arrive at a concensus iagnosis acceptable to all. In 4 cases there remained an evenly split opinion regarding the presence of schizophrenia or doubtful schizophrenia, and these were not included in those categories. After the concensus diagnosis was established and recorded for the 67 relatives to whom some mental or behavioral aberration could be attributed, the relationship of each relative to his proband was decoded and the data analyzed.

DIAGNOSTIC CLASSIFICATION SYSTEM FOR THE RELATIVES

Before we began to make diagnostic evaluations of the relatives, it had become clear that a system of classification with finer gradations than had been found useful in the selection of index cases would be needed. Whereas we could select only those adoptees as index cases who fulfilled particular criteria, the design of the study required that every relative with a record of mental illness or behavioral aberration be classified without the option of rejecting those who did not fit a particular label. In the diagnosis of the index cases we had found it possible to classify those we would accept as schizophrenia into three subgroups representing chronic schizophrenia, acute schizophrenic reaction, and border-line or pseudoneurotic schizophrenia. The same three categories could be applied to the probable but not definite schizophrenics. Our experience with possible index cases who were eventually rejected because they did not meet the criteria for classification as schizophrenic caused us to recognize the existence of a group similar in quality to the border-line schizophrenic but of considerably less intensity. This group is best described as inadequate personality in the standard nomenclarure. The classification scheme used in making the individual ratings was worked out largely by Dr. Wender and appears as Table 3.

RESULTS

The 66 probands (33 index cases and their controls) on search through the Folkeregister yielded 463 identified relatives who were distributed as indicated in Table 2. Although there is no significant difference in the number or distribution of identified relatives between index cases and controls, there are considerable differences in both characteristics between the biological and adoptive relatives. There are more biological than adoptive half-siblings, and few full biological siblings. This is due in part to many biological parents not being married to one another and having children with other partners. When the adoptive parents acquired additional children, which they did infrequently, they did so usually as a couple. In addition, the biological and adoptive parents differ in age, socio-economic class and in the particular selective processes inherent in their having become biological or adoptive parents, making comparisons difficult between them with respect to the prevalence of mental illness.

On the other hand, none of these differences exist between the families of index cases and controls, whether biological or adoptive. Thus, the prevalence of particular types of mental illness in each group of relatives of the index cases can appropriately be compared with that in the corresponding relatives of the controls, permitting the separate

Table 3. Diagnostic Classification System Employed

A. Definitely not schizophrenia (specify diagnosis—see note to Table 4 for diagnoses used).

B. Chronic schizophrenia ("chronic undifferentiated schizophrenia," "true schizophrenia," "process schizophrenia").
Characteristics: (1) Poor pre-psychotic adjustment; introverted; schizoid; shut-in; few peer contacts; few heterosexual contacts; usually unmarried; poor occupational adjustment. (2) Onset— gradual and without clear-cut psychological precipitant. (3) Presenting picture: presence of primary Bleulerian characteristics; presence of clear rather than confused sensorium. (4) Post-hospital course—failure to reach previous level of adjustment. (5) Tendency to chronicity.

B2. Acute schizophrenic reaction (acute undifferentiated schizophrenic reaction, schizo-affective psychosis, possible schizophreniform psychosis, [acute] paranoid reaction, homosexual panic).
Characteristics: (1) Relatively good premorbid adjustment. (2) Relatively rapid onset of illness with clear-cut psychological precipitant. (3) Presenting picture: presence of secondary symptoms and comparatively lesser evidence of primary ones; presence of affect (manic-depressive symptoms, feelings of guilt); cloudy rather than clear sensorium. (4) Post-hospital course good, (5) Tendency to relatively brief episode(s) responding to drugs, EST, etc.

B3. Border-line state (pseudoneurotic schizophrenia, border-line, ambulatory schizophrenia questionable simple schizophrenia, "psychotic character," severe schizoid individual).
Characteristics: (1) Thinking: strange or atypical mentation; thought shows tendency to ignore reality, logic and experience (to an excessive degree) resulting in poor adaptation to life experience (despite the presence of a normal IQ); fuzzy, murky, vague speech. (2) Experience: brief episodes of cognitive distortion (the patient can, and does, snap back but during the episode the idea has more the character of a delusion than an ego-alien obsessive thought); feelings of depersonalization, of strangeness or unfamiliarity with or toward the familiar; micropsychosis. (3) Affective: anhedonia— never experiences intense pleasure—never happy; no deep or intense involvement with anyone or anybody. (4) Interpersonal behavior: may appear poised, but lacking in depth ("as if" personality); sexual adjustment: chaotic fluctuation, mixture of hetero- and homosexuality. (5) Psychopathology: multiple neurotic manifestations which shift frequently (obsessive concerns, phobias, conversion, psychosomatic symptoms, etc.); severe widespread anxiety.

Table 3. Diagnostic Classification System Employed (Cont.)

C.   Inadequate personality.
Characteristics: A somewhat heterogenous group consisting of individuals who would be classified as either inadequate or schizoid by the *APA Diagnostic Manual.* Persons so classified often had many of the characteristics of the B3 category, but to a considerably milder degree.

D1, 2 or 3.   Uncertain B1, 2 or 3 either because information is lacking or because even if enough information is available, the case does not fit clearly into an appropriate B category.

---

testing of hypotheses based on genetic or environmental factors in the transmission of schizophrenia.

Psychiatric Disorders in the Biological Relatives

Table 4 presents the identified relatives and the consensus diagnosis of mental disorder in them for individual probands. We had recognized certain qualitative similarities in the features that characterized the diagnoses of schizophrenia, uncertain schizophrenia, and inadequate personality, which suggested that these syndromes formed a continuum; this we called the schizophrenia spectrum of disorders. If schizophrenia were to some extent genetically transmitted, there should be a higher prevalence of disorders in the schizophrenia spectrum among the biological relatives of the index cases than in those of their controls. Table 5 presents the data which test that hypothesis. Of 150 biological relatives of index cases 13, or 8.7%, had a diagnosis of schizophrenia, uncertain schizophrenia or inadequate personality compared to 3 of 156, or 1.9%, with such diagnoses among the biological relatives of the controls. The difference is highly significant (p, one sided probability from exact distribution = 0.0072).

One troublesome problem was the presence among the 33 index cases of a number who had lived with their biological families for various periods from one month to one year or even more. Although these made the hoped-for separation of hereditary from environmental factors less rigorous, we had decided not to exclude such cases because of the small size of our index group. There are, however, 19 index cases and 20 controls who left their biological families within one month of birth, in most cases within a few days. The prevalence of schizophrenia spectrum disorders is at least as high in the biological relatives of this subsample of index cases (9/93 or 9.7%) as it was in the biological relatives of all 33 index cases, and the difference between them and the biological relatives of the nearly separated controls (where there were no cases of such disorder in 92 relatives) reaches a higher level of significance (p = 0.002). The differences for schizophrenia alone and for schizophrenia or uncertain schizophrenia are also significant (p = 0.03 and 0.01 respectively). In fact, the difference in prevalence of schizophrenia spectrum disorders noted between the biological relatives of the total sample of index cases and controls derives from the subsample with early separation. The reason for this is a relatively high prevalence of these disorders (4.6%) in the biological families of the controls who were not transferred until late. It is possible that the presence of such illness in the biological family may have been a reason for giving the child for adoption in some cases.

By examining the distribution of schizophrenia spectrum disorders in the biological families and taking family size into consideration, no evidence is found to support the thesis that the high prevalence in the relatives of index cases derives from a few deviant families. The 13 such relatives of the total index sample come from 9 families, the 9 relatives with schizophrenia spectrum disorders among the early transferred cases represent 6 families, and the frequency of affected biological families in each sample of index cases (9/33 or 6/19) is significantly higher (p = 0.028 or 0.012) than the frequency of affected families for the corresponding control groups (2/32 or 0/19).[3]

An examination of the prevalence of schizophrenia spectrum disorders among the different relationships indicates that the prevalence is high (10-11%) among the biological half-siblings of both groups of index cases (early and late separated) while these disorders are absent among the control half-siblings. The prevalence of these disorders among the parents and the few full siblings of the index cases is not low but is not significantly different from the controls, largely because of their higher prevalence in the parents of late separated controls. The possibility has previously been raised that such illness may have been the basis for delayed adoption. A lower prevalence of schizophrenia is also found in the parents than in the siblings or progeny of schizophrenics reared in their natural families[17] and the same factors may be operating in these

---

[3] In the case of one of the 20 controls, no biological relatives were identified.

Table 4A. Diagnosed Mental Illness in the Biological and Adoptive Families of Index Cases*

Proband	Diagnosis	Months with Biological Family	Biological Family — Identified Relatives: Parents	Siblings	Half-sibs	Total	Schizophrenia Spectrum Disorders: Parents	Sibs	Half-sibs	Other Psychiatric Diagnoses: Parents	Sibs	Half-sibs	Adoptive Family — Identified Relatives: Parents	Siblings	Half-sibs	Total	Schizophrenia Spectrum Disorders: Parents	Sibs	Half-sibs	Other Psychiatric Diagnoses: Parents	Sibs	Half-sibs
S1	B1	0	2	0	0	2							2	0	0	2						
S2	B2	1	2	0	4	6							2	0	0	2				cd+ts		
S3	B3	0	2	0	3	5	B3		D1	p			2	0	0	2						
S4	B3	8	2	0	1	3			B3	dr			2	0	0	2						
S5	B1	0	2	1	3	6		C					2	1	1	4						
S6	B1	9	2	1	6	9	D3					pp dr	2	0	0	2				ca		
S7	B1	0	2	0	0	2							2	0	0	2						
S8	B1	1	2	0	2	4							2	0	0	2						
S9	B1	28	2	0	1	3				su			2	0	0	2						
S10	B2	38	2	0	0	2						dr	2	0	0	2						
S11	B3	0	2	0	3	5	C						2	0	0	2					mr	
S12	B1	0	2	0	0	2							2	2	0	4						
S13	B3	10	1	0	1	2							1	0	0	1						
S14	B2	0	2	0	5	7							2	0	0	2						
S15	B1	0	2	0	0	2							2	0	0	2						

Sample	Type																				
S16	B1	0	2	0	1	3							2	0	0	2					
S17	B2	0	1	0	0	1							2	0	0	2					
S18	B1	0	2	0	9	11				*su su*			2	0	0	2					
S19	B2	0	2	0	2	4		*B3 B3 B3*					2	0	0	2					
S20	B3	0	2	0	3	5							2	0	0	2					
S21	B3	0	2	0	0	2							2	0	0	2		*lp*			
S22	B1	0	2	0	4	6				dr + su *dl*			2	0	0	2					
S23	B3	0	2	0	3	5		B1					2	0	0	2					
S24	B2	4	2	0	2	4							2	0	0	2		hc + dr			
S25	B1	0	2	0	2	4							2	1	0	3		en + dr			
S26	B3	2	2	0	0	2		D3		*pp*			1	0	0	1		cv			
S27	B2	5	2	0	4	6															
S28	B2	1	1	0	2	3							2	1	0	3					
S29	B3	0	2	0	15	17							2	3	0	5					
S30	B1	0	2	0	2	4							2	0	0	2					
S31	B1	1	2	0	2	4							2	0	0	2					
S32	B1	0	2	0	2	4				cd *da*			2	0	2	4	*D3*				amp/B2
S33	B1	1?	2	0	1	3		*B3 D3*		cd + ca + su	ppp/B2		2	0	0	2		p			
S34	B3	10	2	0	4	6							1	0	0	1		sp/md?			
Totals		63	2	85	150	3	1	9	12	0	5	63	8	3	74	2	0	0	2	8	2	0

* For note to table 4A, see p. 000.

Table 4B. Diagnosed Mental Illness in the Biological and Adoptive Families of Controls*

Proband	Months with Biological Family	Biological Family Identified Relatives — Parents	Siblings	Half-sibs	Total	Schizophrenia Spectrum Disorders — Parents	Sibs	Half-sibs	Other Psychiatric Diagnosis — Parents	Sibs	Half-sibs	Adoptive Family Identified Relatives — Parents	Siblings	Half-sibs	Total	Schizophrenia Spectrum Disorders — Parents	Sibs	Half-sibs	Other Psychiatric Diagnoses — Parents	Sibs	Half-sibs
C1	0	2	0	1	3				cd + ca			2	0	0	2						
C2	0	2	1	5	8		B3					2	0	0	2						
C3	0	2	0	1	3				ar		cd	2	0	0	3		B3				
C4	4	2	0	8	10				dl			2	0	0	2				sp/B2		
C5	5	2	0	1	3							2	1	0	3						
C6	48	2	0	2	4				dr			2	1	0	3		D3				
C7	0	2	0	2	4							2	0	0	2						
C8	0	2	0	3	5							2	0	0	2						
C9	24	2	1	0	3	B1						2	0	0	2						
C10	0	2	0	3	5							2	0	0	2						
C11	0	2	0	5	7							2	0	0	2						
C12	0	2	0	4	6							2	2	0	4						
C13	0	2	1	1	4							2	0	0	2						

C14	2	0	3	5				*sp*		*dr*	11	1	0	3						
C15	2	0	2	4							0	1	0	2						
C16	2	0	2	4							1	0	0	2				hn *dl*		
C17	2	0	6	8							0	0	0	3						
C18	1	0	8	10							0	1	0	2						
C19	2	0	0	1				*mr*		*mr*	14	0	0	5						
C20	2	0	0	2				md?			1	3	0	2						
C21	2	0	4	6				*dr*			0	0	0	3						
C22	2	0	4	6							0	1	0	2		B1				
C23	2	0	3	5							0	0	0	4						
C24	2	0	1	3							2	2	0	3						
C25	2	0	5	6							0	1	0	2						
C26	2	0	1	3		D3					10	0	0	2						
C28	2	0	2	4					ar	o/D3	0	0	0	3						
C29	0	0	0	0							0	0	0	2						
C30	2	2	1	5							12	1	0	2				*su*		
C31	2	0	3	5						pp/D3	0	0	0	4						
C32	2	0	6	8							3?	2	0	2				*dr*		
C33	2	0	0	2							0	0	0	2						
C34	2	0	1	3							8?	0	0	2						
Totals	63	5	88	156	2	1	0	8	1	5	66	17	0	83	0	3	0	5	0	0

Note to Tables 4A and 4B

*Monozygotic twins concordant for schizophrenia and treated as one case.
Diagnoses in italic type pertain to a father or a parental half-sibling.
Diagnoses connected by + are diagnoses in the same individual.
Diagnoses separated by a / (as in amp/B2) represent failure to reach a consensus on one or the other diagnosis.

Diagnostic Symbols:

Schizophrenia spectrum disorders:

B1	Chronic schizophrenia
D1	chronic schizophrenia (uncertain)
B2	acute schizophrenic reaction
D2	acute schizophrenic reaction (uncertain)
B3	border-line schizophrenia
D3	border-line schizophrenia (uncertain)
C	inadequate personality

Other psychiatric diagnoses:

amp	amphetamine psychosis	dl	delinquency	o	organic psychosis
ar	affective reaction	dr	depressive reaction	p	imprisonment
ca	chronic alcoholism	hc	hysterical character	pp	psychopath
cd	character disorder	hn	hysterical neurosis	ppp	*post partum* psychosis
cn	character neurosis	lp	luetic psychosis	sp	senile psychosis
cv	cerebrovascular disease	md	manic depressive psychosis	su	suicide
da	drug addiction	mr	mental retardation	ts	toxic state

and in our series to explain it, i.e. incomplete diagnostic information on older relatives and the decreased rates of marriage and fertility among schizophrenics, so that among an equally genetically vulnerable population those who become parents are less likely to be overtly schizophrenic.

When the index cases are divided according to the type of schizophrenia they displayed, the frequency and type of schizophrenia spectrum disorder in the respective biological families is revealing. In the 82 biological relatives of the 16 probands diagnosed as chronic schizophrenia were found: 1 chronic schizophrenia, 3 border-line schizophrenia, 2 uncertain border-line, and 1 inadequate personality. In the 38 biological relatives of 10 probands diagnosed as border-line schizophrenia were found: 3 border-line schizophrenics, 1 uncertain chronic schizophrenia, 1 uncertain border-line, and 1 inadequate personality. Thus, these families do not differ from each other significantly in type or frequency of disorder in the schizophrenia spectrum. On the other hand, in the 30 biological relatives of 7 probands diagnosed as acute schizophrenia reaction, no instance of schizophrenia spectrum disorder was found. This raises a serious question regarding the validity of classifying that syndrome as a type of schizophrenia, and supports the tendency of European and British psychiatrists to regard it as a disorder *sui generis*. The concept of border-line schizophrenia as a milder variant of schizophrenia is, however, reinforced.

Other mental or behavioral disturbances are, in general, randomly distributed between the biological relatives of index and control probands, 17 and 14 of such disorders being represented in the two populations, respectively. Although the numbers are small and none of the differences significant, it may be interesting to note the diagnoses (other than those previously postulated as constituting the schizophrenia spectrum) which are relatively more and less frequent in the biological families of index cases than in those of the controls. Less frequent are the affective disorders, organic psychoses, senile psychoses and mental retardation. More frequent in the biological relatives of index cases are suicide, psychopathy or delinquency and character disorder. The five discovered cases of suicide among biological relatives all occurred in the index case families, involving both biological parents in the case of one proband.

Some independent considerations suggest a possible relationship between schizophrenia and suicide, psychopathy or character disorder. A relatively high rate of suicide has been found among schizophrenics;[18] Heston[19] has reported a significantly higher incidence of psychopathy and neurotic personality disorders among offspring separated shortly after birth from their schizophrenic mothers; the character disorders in this study exhibit some of the features of border-line schizophrenia or inadequate personality, but in attenuated form. One or another of these three diagnoses occurred 12 times in the biological relatives of index cases as compared with 4 instances in the biological relatives of controls. The difference, though significant ($p = 0.034$), emerged retrospectively and permits only the formulation of a hypothesis that character disorder, psychopathy and suicide may represent extensions of the spectrum of schizophrenia-related disorders.

Psychiatric Disorders in the Adoptive Relatives

In contrast to the significant concentration of schizophrenia and related disorders in the biological relatives of index cases, the adoptive families show fewer cases of such illness and these are randomly distributed between the families of index cases and controls (Table 5). Although other psychiatric diagnoses (Table 4) are somewhat more common among the adoptive families of index cases than of controls (10 *vs.* 5)

Table 5. Distribution of Schizophrenia Spectrum Disorders Among the Biological and Adoptive Relatives of Schizophrenic Index Cases and Controls

	Biological Relatives	Adoptive Relatives
Total sample of 33 index cases and 33 controls		
Index cases	$\dfrac{13}{150}$	$\dfrac{2}{74}$
Controls	$\dfrac{3}{156}$	$\dfrac{3}{83}$
p (one-sided, from exact distribution)	0.0072	N.S.
Subsample of 19 index cases and 20 controls separated from biological family within 1 month of birth		
Index cases	$\dfrac{9}{93}$	$\dfrac{2}{45}$
Controls	$\dfrac{0}{92}$	$\dfrac{1}{51}$
p	0.0018	N.S.

Numerator = number with schizophrenia, undertain schizophrenia or inadequate personality.
Denominators = number of identified relatives.

the difference is not significant and no particular pattern is discernible in the distribution of particular types of illness. The index families compared with control families showed: schizophrenia spectrum disorders (2 *vs*. 3), character disorder (1 *vs*. 0), delinquency (1 *vs*. 1), suicide (0 *vs*. 1), chronic alcoholism (1 *vs*. 0), affective disorders (2 *vs*. 1), neurosis (0 *vs*. 1), mental retardation (1 *vs*. 0), senile psychosis (1 *vs*. 1), and various types of organic psychoses (3 *vs*. 0). It is possible that the experience of these families with the psychiatric hospitalization of the proband made them more likely to receive psychiatric diagnosis and hospitalization in the case of other members.

DISCUSSION

The relatively high incidence of schizophrenia which is consistently found in the close relatives of naturally reared schizophrenics is compatible with explanations based on either genetic or environmental transmission of these disorders since such families share both types of factors. In the present study, which used adoption to disentangle these variables, 19 of the 33 schizophrenic index cases had been removed from their biological families during the first month and in most cases within a few days after birth and raised by families not biologically related to them. Whereas schizophrenia and related disorders were randomly distributed between the adoptive families of the index cases and their controls, the biological families of the index cases showed a 10% prevalence of such disorders, which is significantly higher than the prevalence in the control biological families. Furthermore, more than half of the schizophrenia spectrum disorders were found in their paternally related half siblings with whom the index cases should have had in common not even an *in utero* environment but only some genetic overlap.

The conclusion appears warranted that the roughly 10% prevalence of schizophrenia found in the families of naturally reared schizophrenics is a manifestation of genetically transmitted factors.

Although this study found little to support the importance of environmental transmission of schizophrenia between family members, it was not designed to evaluate the importance of a large number of environmental factors which may possibly operate in the etiology or pathogenesis of schizophrenic disorders. Besides the presence in the household of an individual seriously enough disturbed to have been admitted to a psychiatric facility and thus registered in our tabulations, there are many more aspects of life experience including subtle personality defects in parents or siblings, deviations in child rearing practices, nutritional peculiarities, and even exposure to toxic or infectious agents, which may serve to evoke and elaborate one or another type of schizophrenia spectrum disorder in a genetically vulnerable individual. If such environmental factors played a significant role in the etiology of schizophrenia they should have tended to make the prevalence of schizophrenia and related disorders in the adoptive siblings of our index cases somewhat higher than in those of the controls, but the number of these relatives in our sample may have been too small to constitute an appropriate test. It is possible that extensions of the present study from Greater Copenhagen to all of Denmark coupled with psychiatric interviews with identified relatives may sufficiently increase the size of the sample and the richness of information on personality and social characteristics of the families to permit a more exhaustive evaluation of possible environmental etiological factors.

The evidence obtained in this study, although strongly supporting the operation of genetic factors in the transmission of schizophrenia, is not readily compatible with any simple genetic model. It is not only schizophrenia which is found in higher prevalence in the biological relatives of schizophrenic index cases, but to an even greater extent, a spectrum of disorders having some features in common with schizophrenia but varying considerably in intensity. Furthermore, the nature and extent of these disorders in the biological families of the clearly schizophrenic and of the border-line index cases are quite indistinguishable.

The 16 index cases with fairly typical chronic schizophrenia (B1) had 82 identified biological relatives of whom 7 were classified in the schizophrenia spectrum (1 chronic schizophrenia, 3 border-line, 2 uncertain border-line, 1 inadequate personality). The 10 probands with border-line schizophrenia (B3) differed considerably from the chronic schizophrenic index cases with respect to type and severity of symptoms and would perhaps not have been called schizophrenic in some places. Yet, of their 38 identified biological relatives, 6 were classified in the schizophrenia spectrum (3 border-line, 1 uncertain chronic, 1 uncertain border-line, 1 inadequate personality). There is nothing to suggest that the biological relatives of the two types of probands are not members of the same population, a finding which is more compatible with the thesis that the schizophrenia in the probands represents some polygenic inadequacy[20] transmitted through heredity but receiving its ultimate expression and differentiation on the basis of a complex interaction among genetic factors or between them and the environment.[21] Intelligence seems more likely to be an appropriate model for the transmission of schizophrenia than does phenylketonuria.

Possible Sources of Error or Bias

It is pertinent to enumerate and discuss the possible errors in selection or diagnosis which might have come into this study despite efforts to avoid them. Some of these possibilities would have operated to decrease the preponderance of schizophrenia spectrum disorders in the biological relatives of the index cases. The enlightened social system in Denmark makes it possible for a pregnant woman to obtain a legal abortion on the basis of a history of schizophrenia in herself or in the father. This, in addition to the relative infertility of overt schizophrenics, could have resulted in the removal from our sample of adoptees of a disproportionate fraction of those with schizophrenia in the biological parents. If, in a similar manner, the adoption process screens out children born of parents with known schizophrenia, this would further have contributed to the possible impoverishment in our adoptee sample of potential index cases with an established incidence in their biological families.

On the other hand, there are biases that could have operated to exaggerate the prevalence of diagnosed schizophrenia spectrum disorder in the biological families of the index cases as compared to the other populations. Possible knowledge of the relationship existing between an index case and a member of his biological family could have affected the tendency to notice, to record, to institutionalize, or to diagnose schizophrenia spectrum disorder in one or the other individual on the part of professional or nonprofessional observers, especially if there were a prevalent belief that schizophrenia was inherited. We believe that this leakage of information was small but are at the present time engaged in determining how often such information appears in the hospital or other records.

The evaluation of mental illness in the relatives was a crucial judgment upon which the results rested, and, being to a large extent subjective, could have been affected by subjective bias in spite of the precautions which were taken to avoid it. Access to and the possibility of retention of salient information varied considerably among the raters. One author (D.R.) was not involved in making the original selection of index cases; another (F.S.) had, one or two years before, read the hospital records of the index cases which may have contained references to affected relatives. He also read and abstracted a few of the relatives' records. The three authors in the United States had available to them only coded abstracts which had been edited to remove any basis for a surmise as to where in the four populations the individual belonged. Analyses of the findings based upon the independent classifications of each of the four authors show little deviation from the analyses based upon their consensus. There is no evidence of bias and the findings of the study would have remained essentially the same if based upon the independent diagnoses of any one of the raters.

SUMMARY

Adoption has been used as a means of separating genetic from environmental factors in the transmission of schizophrenia. Among the 5483 adoptions granted in the City and County of Copenhagen from the beginning of 1924 through 1947 to adoptive parents not biologically related to the child, 507 adoptees were found who had been admitted to a psychiatric facility. In 33 of these a diagnosis of chronic schizophrenia, border-line schizophrenia, or acute schizophrenic reaction could be agreed upon by independent reviewers of the abstracted case histories. These and an equal number of matched control adoptees with no history of mental hospitalization yielded, by search of the Danish population registers, 306 identified biological parents, siblings or half-siblings and 157 adoptive relatives in similar relationships. Of these 463 relatives, 67 had at some time been admitted to a psychiatric facility. These records were abstracted, edited to remove prejudicial information, and independent and consensus diagnoses made by the four authors.

For the 33 schizophrenic index cases and for a subgroup of 19 who had left their biological families within the first month (usually within the first week) of life, there was a highly significant increased prevalence of schizophrenia and related disorders in the biological families as compared with those of the controls. The prevalence of these disorders in the adoptive families was lower and randomly distributed between the relatives of index cases and controls.

The pattern of schizophrenia-related disorders in the biological families was the same for 16 index cases diagnosed chronic schizophrenia as for 10 probands diagnosed border-line schizophrenia, supporting the inclusion of this syndrome among the schizophrenias. On the other hand, 7 index cases diagnosed acute schizophrenic reaction had no schizophrenia related disorder in the biological relatives, raising some question regarding the relationship of that state to schizophrenia.

The conclusion seems warranted that genetic factors are important in the transmission of schizophrenia; the mode of transmission seems to be polygenic rather than monogenic. The findings are compatible with diathesis-stress hypotheses of the pathogenesis of schizophrenia, although no evidence was found for the operation of one particular environmental influence, i.e. the presence of schizophrenia or related illness in the rearing family.

ACKNOWLEDGMENTS

The authors wish to acknowledge the valuable assistance given by a substantial number of individuals. Dr. Sarnoff Mednick suggested the collaboration with Dr. Schulsinger, offered the facilities of their joint research program in Copenhagen and gave valuable advice in a number of areas, especially with regard to the socio-economic ratings. The Danish psychiatrists who prepared English abstracts of the Danish case histories were Dr. Jytte Willadsen and Dr. Erik Glud. Social workers who abstracted the Danish adoption records and gathered the data relevant to the pretransfer histories of the probands were Birgit Jacobsen and Grete Skat Andersen. Clerical assistance was given by Ida Bech, Agnete Beck, Susanne Rasmussen and Tove Meier. Kitty Scharf, Copenhagen, and Alice Muth, Bethesda, assisted in the tabulation and analysis of the data.

The authors are especially grateful to Dr. Samuel Greenhouse, Chief of the Epidemiology and Biometry Branch of the National Institute of Child Health and Human Development, for invaluable advice regarding statistical treatment and interpretation of the data.

REFERENCES

1. Kallmann, F. J., *The Genetics of Schizophrenia*, Augustin, New York, 1938.
2. Luxenburger, H., Vorläufiger Bericht über psychiatrische Serienuntersuchungen an Zwillingen, *Z. ges. Neurol, Psychiat.* **116**, 297 (1928).
3. Rosanoff, A. J., Handy, L. M., Plesset, I. R. and Brush, S., The etiology of so-called schizophrenic psychoses with special reference to their occurrence in twins, *Am. J. Psychiat.* **91**, 247 (1934).
4. Kallmann, F. J., The genetic theory of schizophrenia: an analysis of 691 schizophrenic twin index families, *Am. J. Psychiat.* **103** 309 (1946).
5. Slater, E., *Psychotic and Neurotic Illnesses in Twins*, Her Majesty's Stationery Office, London, 1953.
6. Inouye, E., Similarity and dissimilarity of schizophrenia in twins, in *Proceedings of the Third World Congress of Psychiatry*, Vol. 1, p. 524, Univ. Toronto Press, Montreal, 1961.
7. Kringlen, E., Schizophrenia in twins: an epidemiological-clinical study, *Psychiatry* **29**, 172 (1966).

8. Gottesman, I. I and Shields, J., Schizophrenia in twins: 16 years' consecutive admissions to a psychiatric clinic, *Brit. J. Psychiat.* **112**, 809 (1966).
9. Kety, S. S., Biochemical theories of schizophrenia, *Science* **129**, 1528 and 1590 (1959).
10. Rosenthal, D., Sex distribution and severity of illness among samples of schizophrenic twins, *J. Psychiat. Res.* **1**, 26 (1961).
11. Rosenthal, D., Problems of sampling and diagnosis in the major twin studies of schizophrenia, *J. Psychiat. Res.* **1**, 116 (1962).
12. Tienari, P., Psychiatric illness in identical twins, *Acta psychiat. scand.* **39**, Suppl. 171, 1 (1963).
13. Skeels, H. M. and Dye, H. B., A study of the effects of differential stimulation on mentally retarded children, *Proc. Am. Ass. Ment. Def.* **63**, 114 (1939).
14. Rosenthal, D., Wender, P., Kety, S. S., Schulsinger, F., Welner, J. and Ostergaard, L., Schizophrenics' offspring reared in adoptive homes, in "The Transmission of Schizophrenia," Pergamon Press, 1968, p. 377.
15. Wender, P., Rosenthal, D. and Kety, S. S., A psychiatric assessment of the adoptive parents of schizophrenics, in "The Transmission of Schizophrenia," Pergamon Press, 1968, p. 235.
16. Mednick, S. A. and Schulsinger, F., Some premorbid characteristics related to breakdown in children with schizophrenic mothers, in "The Transmission of Schizophrenia," Pergamon Press, 1968, p. 267.
17. Slater, E., A review of earlier evidence on genetic factors in schizophrenia, in "The Transmission of Schizophrenia," Pergamon Press, 1968, p. 15.
18. Hermansen, L., Schizophrenic patients on a psychiatric ward in a provincial general hospital. A followup of schizophrenic first admissions 1956–1966, *Ugeskr. Laeq.* **129**, 1445 (1967) (in Danish).
19. Heston, L. L., Psychiatric disorders in foster home reared children of schizophrenic mothers, *Brit. J. Psychiat,* **112**, 819 (1966).
20. Gottesman, I. I. and Shields, J., A polygenic theory of schizophrenia, *Proc. Nat. Acad. Sci. USA* **58**, 199 (1967).
21. Rosenthal, D., Theoretical overview: a suggested conceptual framework, In *The Genain Quadruplets: A Case Study and Theoretical Analysis of Heredity and Environment in Schizophrenia,* Rosenthal, D. (Ed.), p. 505, Basic Books, Inc., New York, 1963.

17. The Basic Fault*

Michael Balint

THE TWO LEVELS OF ANALYTIC WORK

In order to describe the characteristic atmosphere of the level of classical therapeutic work, psychoanalytic literature habitually uses the terms 'Oedipal or genital level', contrasted with the 'pre-Oedipal, pregenital, or pre-verbal level'. In my opinion these latter terms already have a loaded meaning, and I shall presently propose a new unequivocal term which, I hope, will free us from some latent bias; but before doing so, let us examine the real meaning of these common terms.

The Oedipus complex was one of Freud's greatest discoveries, which he justly described as the nuclear complex of all human development—of health and illness, of religion and art, civilization and law, and so on. Though the Oedius complex characterizes a fairly early stage of development, Freud had no hesitation in describing the child's mental experiences, emotions, and feelings at this stage in the language of adults. (As I want to keep clear of the vexed problem of chronology, I deliberately leave open the definition of this early age. It suffices for my purpose to state that it is a very early age.) In fact, Freud's assumption was a bold projection, a daring extrapolation. He made the tacit assumption, without further proof, that the emotions, feelings, desires, fears, instinctual urges, satisfactions, and frustrations of the very young are not only closely similar to those of adults, but also that they have about the same reciprocal relation to one another. Without these two assumptions the use of adult language for describing these events would be totally unjustifiable.

I repeat, this assumption was a very bold step, but its results were subsequently fully validated, both by observations of normal children and by clinical experiences during the analysis of neurotic children. Further, it should be emphasized that, although it had started with the analysis of Little Hans (1909), all this validation took place during the same period as Freud's last revision of our theoretical concepts about the mental apparatus, namely in the twenties.

*For chapter and part references in this article, see the original published version of the book *The Basic Fault*.

To avoid a possible misunderstanding, I would add that while working on this Oedipal level, pre-genital material is not, of course, disregarded or neglected by the analyst, but is worked with in adult language, i.e. is raised for the Oedipal or 'verbal' level. This is an important point for our technique as it immediately raises the problem of what an analyst should do in a case in which the expression of pre-genital material in adult words is either unintelligible or unacceptable to the patient, i.e. in a case in which there is apparently no simple road for the patient, direct from the pre-verbal to the Oedipal.

Since the twenties our technique has progressed greatly and it is fair to say that today we can treat patients who were then considered untreatable, and we can certainly better understand the average patient, at greater depth and more reliably, than our colleagues of forty years ago. In the course of this development we have collected a rich harvest of clinical observations and of puzzling problems. All of them pertain to events happening, and observed, in the psycho-analytic situation. In the first approximation these events may be described in terms of the Oedipus conflict, and using adult language. However, *pari passu* with our growing experience and our improving powers of observation, we have got hold of events that cause considerable difficulties both for our theoretical descriptions and for our technical skill.

For instance, we have learned that there are some patients who have great difficulty in 'taking in' anything that increases the strain upon them, and there are others who can 'take in' everything in the world because, apparently, their innermost self remains largely uninfluenced by it. As I have just said, these two types create serious theoretical and technical difficulties, perhaps because their relationship to the analyst differs considerably from that which we are accustomed to meet at the Oedipal level.

The two types just mentioned are only a small sample of the many patients who are described usually as 'deeply disturbed', 'profoundly split', 'seriously schizoid', 'having as much too weak or immature ego', 'highly narcissistic', or suffering from a 'deep narcissistic wound', and so on, thereby implying that the root of their illness goes further and deeper than the Oedipus conflict. In this respect, in terms of the oft-discussed theoretical problem, it is immaterial whether they had originally arrived at their Oedipus period already ill, or whether only later traumatic events rendered the defensive mechanisms belonging to this period ineffective, thus forcing them to a regression or deviation beyond the Oedipal level. What is important in the present context is the recognition of the two different levels of analytical work.

To illustrate the kind of problem encountered on this other level, I wish to quote an eternal example from outside our fields. At our research seminars on general medical practice (Balint, M., 1964) doctors often used to report that they had explained to a patient very clearly what certain implications of an illness were; then, when the actual results of the explanation were compared with those intended, surprisingly often it emerged that the explanation was clear only to the doctor; to the patient it was not clear, often it constituted no explanation at all. So now, whenever a doctor reports that he explained something very clearly, the habitual question follows: 'clearly, but to whom?'. The reason for this discrepancy between intention and result is that the same words have a totally different meaning for the sympathetic but uninvolved doctor and his deeply involved patient.

We analysts are often faced with the same experience. We give our patient an interpretation, clear, concise, well-founded, well-timed, and to the point, which—often to our surprise, dismay, irritation and disappointment—either has no effect on the patient or has an effect quite different from that intended. In other words, our interpretation was not clear at all, or was not even experienced as an interpretation. As a rule analysts try to explain away these disappointments, using three self-reassuring trains of thought. The analyst may criticize himself for not succeeding in interpreting the most important anxiety of the situation— that is, being misled to something of secondary importance only; this self-criticism will usually be followed by frantic efforts to divine what in the patient's fantasies had barred the way to his understanding the analyst's interpretations. Or the analyst may revive in himself the eternal controversy about the relative merits and disadvantages of content, defence, or transference interpretations, which can then be continued endlessly. And, last, he might reassure himself that the patient's resistance at the operative moment was too strong, and that consequently he would need considerable time for 'working-through' it. This last formula is the more reassuring as it was used before by Freud.

Unfortunately these reassuring formulas and trains of thought are without relevance here, since all of them belong to the Oedipal level, i.e. they presuppose that the analyst's interpretations are experienced as interpretations by the patient. It was for this situation only that Freud coined the term 'working-through'. Obviously working-through is possible only if, and in so far as, the patient is capable of taking the interpretation in, experiencing it as an interpretation, and allowing it to influence his mind. With the class of 'deeply disturbed' patients this may or may not be the case. But, if the patient does not experience the analyst's interpretation as an interpretation, i.e. a sentence consisting of words with agreed meaning, no working-through can take place. Working-through can come into operation only if our words have approximately the same meaning for our patients as for ourselves.

No such problem exists at the Oedipal level. The patient and his analyst confidently speak the same language; the same words mean about the same for both. True, the patient may reject an interpretation, may be annoyed, frightened, or hurt by it, but there is no question that it *was* an interpretation.

The establishment of the two different levels gives us a third answer to our original question while, at the same time, it points to further interesting problems. But before embarking on these latter, let us survey our route up to the present point. We started with the finding—or truism—that even the most experienced among us have occasionally some difficult or even very difficult patients. We then asked ourselves what the therapeutic processes were, in which part of the mind they took place, what in them was responsible for the difficulties and, last but not least, what technical means we had to influence them. Then we surveyed our present theory of technique but found that the topological approach did not offer us much help. Going further, we realized that all our descriptions of what happens in the patient's mind during our therapy are based on the close study of patients—initiated by Freud himself in the early twenties—who can accept and 'take in' the analyst's interpretations as interpretations and who are capable of 'working-through'. And last, we found that there are at least two levels of analytic work; consequently it is very likely that there are two levels of therapeutic processes, and, further, that one aspect of this difference is the different usefulness of adult language at the two levels.

This important difference with regard to language, which may create a gulf between patient and analyst and obstruct the progress of treatment, was first described by Ferenczi, in particular in his last Congress paper (1932) and his posthumously published 'Notes and Fragments'.

He called it 'The Confusion of Tongues between the Child [singular!] and the Adults [plural!].' Since then—though usually without mentioning his pioneer work—several attempts have been made by various research workers to describe the same phenomenon. Thus, the conclusion arrived at in the previous chapter is only a reformulation of something well known, namely, that the analytical work proceeds on at least two different levels, one familiar and less problematic, called the Oedipal level, and the other, for the description of which terms like pre-Oedipal, pre-genital, and pre-verbal are in use.

I propose to retain the terms Oedipal level, period, conflict, complex, as they denote the most important features of the level to which they relate. There are several characteristics that differentiate clinically the phenomena belonging to this level from those of the other. The first is that everything at the Oedipal level—whether it relates to genital or pre-genital experiences—happens in a triangular relationship, which means that in addition to the subject, there are always at least two parallel objects involved. These two might be two persons, as in the Oedipus situation, or one person and some object, as in the sphere of anal, and almost certainly also of oral, eroticism. In the former the second object is represented by the faeces and their manifold derivatives, while in the latter, at any rate in its later stages, apart from the source of provider or the food there is always the food itself as a further object present. Although these two spheres are pre-genital by definition, the structure of the relevant relationship—certainly at the anal and the later stages of the oral phase—consisting of the subject and at least two parallel objects, brings them into the Oedipal area and raises them to the Oedipal level.

The second important characteristic of the Oedipal area is that it is inseparable from conflict. Apart from a few instances, not well studied, the conflict is caused by ambivalence arising in the complexities of the relationship between the individual and his two parallel objects. Though this conflict is inherent in the situation it can be solved or, at any rate, considerably adjusted. Perhaps the best-studied example of conflict is that in which an authority—external or internal—prescribes, or forbids, a particular form of gratification. Such a conflict leads eventually to a fixation whereby a certain amount of libido is pinned down in a fruitless struggle creating a continuous tension. Analytic treatment then has the task of mobilizing and freeing such amounts of libido either by interpretation or by offering opportunities to the patient in the transference to regress in order to find a better solution. Though no solution is ideal, in that each of them leaves some tension to be borne, it is almost always possible to find one which considerably reduces the tension.

The third important characteristic of this level is that in it adult language is an adequate and reliable means of communication—as we all know, Oedipus was an adult man. Should there ever arise a need to coin a new term for this level, I would propose to call it the level of agreed, conventional, or adult language.

It often happens in science that an unhappy choice of name leads to misunderstandings, or prejudices the unbiased study of the problem. In order to avoid these risks the two mental levels should be called by terms that are independent of each other. Just as the Oedipal level possesses its own name derived from one of its main characteristics, so the other level should have its own, and should not be called pre-something else—certainly not pre-Oedipal, because it may co-exist with Oedipal level, at any rate as far as our clinical experiences go. For the moment I wish to leave open the question whether or not there are periods when the mind knows only the one level and not the other. On the other hand it must be emphasized that this other level is definitely simpler, more primitive, than the Oedipal level. I propose to call it the level of the *basic fault,* and I wish to stress that it is described as a fault, not as a situation, position, conflict, or complex. I will later explain why.

The chief characteristics of the level of the basic fault are (a) all the events that happen in it belong to an exclusively two-person relationship—there is no third person present: (b) this two-person relationship is of a particular nature, entirely different from the well-known human relationships of the Oedipal level; (c) the nature of the dynamic force operating at this level is not that of a conflict, and (d) adult language is often useless or misleading in describing events at this level, because words have not always an agreed conventional meaning.

Though some of these characteristics will become meaningful only during the discussion in the later chapters, I can state something about the others now. First about the nature of the primitive two-person relationship at this level. In the first approach this can be considered as an instance of primary object relationship or of primary love, which I have described on several occasions (Balint, M., 1932, 1934, 1937, 1959) and in Chapter 12 of this book. Any third party interfering with this relationship is experienced as a heavy burden or as an intolerable strain. A further important quality of this relationship is the immense difference of intensity between the phenomena of satisfaction and frustration. Whereas satisfaction—the 'fitting in' of the object with the subject—brings about a feeling of quiet tranquil well-being which can be observed only with difficulty as it is so natural and soft, frustration—the lack of 'fitting in' of the object—evokes highly vehement and loud symptoms (see also Chapter 16).

Later, in Chapter 4, I shall come back to discuss the nature of the forces operating at the level of the basic fault, but I wish to illustrate here the curious vagueness of language obtaining at this level. This is brought about by the *cluster of associations* which still surrounds each word in adult usage. On the level of the basic fault, however, practically each member of the cluster may have an equal right to the possession of the word. That this is not restricted to the level of the basic fault is shown by the practical impossibility of finding exact definitions, especially in our science of psychology. In order to devise an exact definition one must strip the word of all its unwanted or undesirable associations. Experience shows that this is only very rarely possible, as people obstinately think, or even prove, that the words used imply other meanings than the one intended by the inventor of the definition. (This problem will be discussed further in Chapter 20.)

THE AREA OF THE BASIC FAULT

Accepting theoretically the existence of the level of the basic fault, we have to ask what kind of events in the course of analytic treatment have to be considered as signals that this level has been reached. Taking a fairly normal case, let us suppose that the treatment has been proceeding smoothly for some time, patient and analyst have understood each other, while the strains and demands on either of them, but especially on the analyst, were only reasonable and in particular, at all times intelligible. Then at some point, suddenly or insidiously, the atmosphere of the analytic situation changes profoundly. With some patients this might happen after a very short period, or even right from the start.

There are several aspects of what I will call the profound change of atmosphere. Foremost among them is, as discussed in the previous chapter, that interpretations given by the analyst are not experienced any longer by the patient as interpretations. Instead he may feel them as an attack, a demand, a base insinuation, an uncalled-for rudeness or insult, unfair treatment, injustice, or at least as a complete lack of consideration, and so on; on the other hand, it is equally possible that the analyst's interpretations may be experienced as something highly pleasing and gratifying, exciting or soothing, or as a seduction; in general as an irrefutable sign of consideration, affection, and love. It may also happen that common words which until then have had an agreed conventional 'adult' meaning and could be used without any great consequence, become immensely important and powerful, either in a good or a bad sense. At such times, in fact, the analyst's every casual remark, every gesture or movement, may matter enormously and may assume an importance far beyond anything that could be realistically intended.

Moreover—and this is not so easy to admit—the patient somehow seems able to get under the analyst's skin. He begins to know much too much about his analyst. This increase in knowledge does not originate from any outside source of information but apparently from an uncanny talent that enables the patient to 'understand' the analyst's motives and to 'interpret' his behaviour. This uncanny talent may occasionally give the impression of, or perhaps even amount to, telepathy or clairvoyance. (See Balint, M., 'Notes on Parapsychology and Parapsychological Healing', 1955.) The analyst experiences this phenomenon as if the patient could see inside him, could find out things about him. The things thus found out are always highly personal, in some ways always concerned with the patient, and are in a way absolutely correct and true, and at the same time utterly out of proportion, and thus untrue—at least this is how the analyst feels them.

If now the analyst fails to 'click in', that is, to respond as the patient expects him to do, no reaction of anger, rage, contempt, or criticism will appear in the transference as one would expect it at the Oedipal level. The only thing that can be observed is a feeling of emptiness, being lost, deadness, futility, and so on, coupled with an apparently lifeless acceptance of everything that has been offered. In fact everything is accepted without much resistance but nothing makes any sense. Another reaction to the analyst's failure to 'click in' might have the appearance of persecutory anxieties. Leaving on one side that in these states anxiety—in its common-sense clinical form—is usually very slight, hardly existent, the fact remains that at any frustration these patients feel that it was intentionally inflicted upon them. They cannot accept that there exists any other cause for a frustration of their desires than malice, evil intention, or at least, criminal negligence. Good things may happen by chance, but frustrations are unchallengeable proofs of evil and hostile sentiments in their environment.

Remarkably, all this is simply accepted as a painful fact and it is most surprising how little anger, still less a willingness to fight, is mobilized by it. It is still more surprising that a feeling of hopelessness hardly ever develops; it seems that despair and hopelessness belong to the Oedipal level; they are probably post-depressive. Though feelings of emptiness and deadness (cf. Balint, Enid, 1963) may be very strong, behind them there is usually an earnest, quiet determination to see things through. This queer mixture of profound suffering, absence of cheap pugnacity, and an unshakeable determination to get on makes these patients truly appealing—an important diagnostic sign that the work has reached the level of the basic fault.

The analyst's reaction also is characteristic, and is utterly different from his reaction to a resistance at the Oedipal level. I shall return to this in Parts III, IV, and V of this book; here it will suffice to say that everything touches him much more closely; he finds it rather difficult to maintain his usual attitude of sympathetic, objective passivity; in fact, he is in constant danger of subjective emotional involvment. Some analysts allow, or even elect, to be carried away by this forceful current and must then change their techniques accordingly. Others carefully and cautiously stick to their well-proven guns and consistently avoid any risk of becoming involved. There are also those who, in face of this threat, adopt—perhaps as a reaction formation against it—a somewhat omnipotent confidence, constantly reassuring themselves that their technique of interpretation is capable of dealing with any situation.

Another important group of phenomena is centered upon what may be called appreciation of, and gratitude for, the analyst's work. On the Oedipal level, provided the analyst's work has been up to professional standards, these two sentiments—appreciation and gratitude—are powerful allies and, especially during bleak periods, may help considerably. At the level of the basic fault one cannot be certain at all that the patient will bear in mind, still less that he will appreciate, that his analyst was skilful and understanding in the past, whether remote or recent. One reason for this profound change is that at that level patients feel that it is their due to receive what they need. I shall return presently to this important feature.

Thus, if the analyst provides what is needed, this fact is taken for granted and loses all its value as proof of professional skill, of exceptional gift, or of favour, and in due course more and more demands will be produced. In present-day analytical literature this syndrome is called greediness, or even oral greed. I have no objection to calling it greed, but strong objection to calling it 'oral' because this is misleading. It is not the relationship to the oral component instinct that is relevant for the understanding of this syndrome but the fact that it originates in a primitive two-person relationship which may or may not be 'oral'. To cite the range of addictions in which 'greediness' is a most important feature, there are very numerous and unquestionably 'oral' addictions, foremost among them nicotine and alchohol; but there are many that are non-oral such as morphinism, sniffing cocaine, and not forgetting the various forms of scratching as in pruritus.

At the Oedipal level the analyst is hardly ever tempted out of his sympathetic passivity; if he abandons his passivity at the level of the basic fault, he may start on a dangerous spiral of addiction—because of the peculiar lack of gratitude, or presence of greed; if he remains adamant either the treatment will be broken off by the patient as hopeless, or after a long forlorn struggle the patient will be forced to identify himself with the aggressor, as the analyst is felt to be, i.e. as I heard it described in one of my seminars—the patient is made to acquire an everlasting internal long-playing record. In Chapter 17 I shall have to return to this important technical problem.

All these events belong essentially to the field of two-person psychology and are more elementary than those belonging to the three-person Oedipal level. Moreover, they lack the structure of a conflict. This was one of the reasons why I proposed to call them 'basic.' But why fault? First, because this is exactly the word used by many patients to describe it. The patient says that he feels there is a fault within him, a fault that must be put right. And it is felt to be a fault, not a complex, not a conflict, not a situation. Second, there is a feeling that the cause of this fault is that someone has either failed the patient or defaulted on him; and third, a great anxiety invariably surrounds this area, usually expressed as a desperate demand that this time the analyst should not—in fact must not—fail him.

The term fault has been in use in some exact sciences to denote conditions that are reminiscent of that which we are discussing. Thus, for instance, in geology and in crystallography the word fault is used to describe a sudden irregularity in the overall structure, an irregularity which in normal circumstances might lie hidden but, if strains and stresses occur, may lead to a break, profoundly disrupting the overall structure.

We are accustomed to think of every dynamic force operating in the mind as having the form either of a biological drive or of a conflict. Although highly dynamic, the force originating from the basic fault has the form neither of an instinct nor of a conflict. It is a fault, something wrong in the mind, a kind of deficiency which must be put right. It is not something dammed up for which a better outlet must be found, but something missing either now, or perhaps for almost the whole of the patient's life. An instinctual need can be satisfied, a conflict can be solved, a basic fault can perhaps be merely healed provided the deficient ingredients can be found; and even then it may amount only to a healing with defect, like a simple, painless scar.

The adjective 'basic' in my new term not only means that it relates to simpler conditions than those characterizing the Oedipus complex, but also that its influence extends widely, probably over the whole psychobiological structure of the individual, involving in varying degrees both his mind and his body. In this way the concept of the basic fault allows us to understand not only the various neuroses (perhaps also pyschoses), character disorders, psychosomatic illnesses, etc., as symptoms of the same etiological entity, but also—as the experiences of our research into general medical practice have shown—a great number of ordinary 'clinical' illnesses as well (Balint, M., 1957; Balint, M., & Balint, Enid, 1961; Lask, 1966; Greco and Pittenger, 1966). By this I mean that under the influence of various emotional experiences, among them medical treatment, a 'clinical' illness may disappear to give way to a specific psychological disorder and vice versa.

In my view the origin of the basic fault may be traced back to a considerable discrepancy in the early formative phases of the individual between his bio-psychological needs and the material and psychological care, attention, and affection available during the relevant times. This creates a state of deficiency whose consequences and after-effects appear to be only partly reversible. The cause of this early discrepancy may be congenital, i.e. the infant's bio-psychological needs may have been too exacting (there are non-viable infants and progressive congenital conditions, like Friedreich's ataxia or cystic kidneys), or may be environmental, such as care that is insufficient, deficient, haphazard, over-anxious, over-protective, harsh, rigid, grossly inconsistent, incorrectly timed, over-stimulating, or merely un-understanding or indifferent.

As may be seen from my description, I put the emphasis on the lack of 'fit' between the child and *the people* who represent his environment. Incidentally, we started with a similar lack of 'fit'—between the analyst's otherwise correct technique and a particular patient's needs; this is very likely to be an important cause of difficulties, and even failures, experienced by analysts in their practice. This will be discussed in more detail in Part V.

Returning now to our main theme, I wish the reader to be aware of my personal bias, under the influence of which my description of the processes, which eventually may result in some basic fault, will be couched in terms of object-relationship. In my view, all these processes happen within a very primitive and peculiar object-relationship, fundamentally different from those commonly observed between adults. It is definitely a two-person relationship in which, however, only one of the partners matters; his wishes and needs are the only ones that count and must be attended to; the other partner, though felt to be immensely powerful, matters only in so far as he is willing to gratify the first partner's needs and desires or decides to frustrate them; beyond this his personal interests, needs, desires, wishes, etc., simply do not exist. In Chapter 21 I propose to discuss in more detail this essentially two-person relationship and to differentiate it from what I have called primary object love, or primary object relationship.

THERAPEUTIC REGRESSION, PRIMARY LOVE, AND THE BASIC FAULT

In the previous Part we have found that regression, as observed in the analytic situation, may have at least two aims: gratification of an instinct or drive and recognition by an object; in other words, it is both an intrapsychic and an interpersonal phenomenon. We also found strong indications that for the analytic therapy of regressed states its interpersonal aspects were more important.

The problem at which we have arrived here may be termed 'the healing power of relationship.' Although, as a rule, it is not stated quite so explicitly, we are compelled to recognize that the two most important factors in psychoanalytic therapy are interpretations and object relationship. It should be borne in mind, however, that with the latter we are on comparatively unsafe grounds because psychoanalytic theory knows much less about it.

We have some systematic knowledge about the instincts or drives and their vicissitudes, about the structure of the mind and the various defensive mechanisms working in it, and also about the role of conflict in psychopathology. It was on these three pillars—the theory of the instincts, of the structure of the mind, and of the pathogenic effects of conflicts—that Freud based his technical recommendations. The aim of his techniques was to make the unconscious conscious—or in a later version: where id was, ego shall be—and the tool for achieving this aim was almost exclusively interpretation. Although as early as 1912 and 1915 in his two papers on Transference, he stated in so many words that transference, that is an object relationship, may have considerable healing powers, he evidently mistrusted them, and never considered them worthy of a proper study. In consequence, interpretation became accepted as far the most important technical measure.

As I tried to show in Part IV, putting all the emphasis on the analyst's interpretative work amounted, perhaps, to an oversimplification. This worked as long as we were able to select from all the people, who asked for analytic help, those who without much difficulty could adapt themselves to the analytic setting created by us according to Freud's early papers on technique (1911–15). As long as this setting was accepted as obligatory for all of us, the analyst's work could be considered as consisting almost solely of interpretations.

However, if we recognize that the setting recommended by Freud represents only one of the many possible settings—that is, it is a sort of *primus inter pares*—a new task emerges for us which is to find other settings in which analytical work with less strictly selected patients can profitably be carried out. This task has a special importance for patients in regression.

To repeat what we have found in the previous chapters, in certain periods of the treatment, creating and maintaining a workable relationship, particularly with a patient in regression, is perhaps a more important therapeutic task than giving correct interpretations. Possibly something like this was in Freud's mind when he wrote about the therapeutic effects of transference. However, as just mentioned, his interest was centered chiefly on the intrapsychic processes that may have therapeutic effects, and he did not pay much attention to the interpersonal phenomena and their possible effects on therapy.

But, whatever the case may be, interpretations are, of necessity, always verbal. Although one of their principal aims is to help the patient to have feelings, emotions, and experiences that he was incapable of having before, they demand intellectual understanding, thinking, or a new 'insight.' All of these descriptions have close connections either with 'seeing' or 'standing,' that is with philobatic activities, which can be performed alone. In contrast, object relationship is always an interaction between at least two people and, more often than not, is created and maintained also by non-verbal means. It is difficult to find words to describe what it is that is created. We talk about behaviour, climate, atmosphere, etc., all of which are vague and hazy words, referring to something with no firm boundaries and thus reminiscent of those describing primary substances. In spite of the fact that the various forms of object relationship cannot be described by concise and unequivocal words, that is, the translation of the various object relationships into words must always be subjective, arbitrary, and inexact, the 'atmosphere,' the 'climate,' is there, it is felt to be there, and more often than not there is even no need to express it in words—although words may be an important contributory factor both to its creation and its maintenance. In contrast to 'insight,' which is the result to a correct interpretation, the creation of a proper relationship results in a 'feeling'; while 'insight' correlates with seeing, 'feeling' correlates with touching, that is, either primary relationship or ocnophilia.

Returning now to our main topic, regression, it was its intrapsychic aspects that remained in the focus of Freud's interest throughout his life. One reason, perhaps, for this comparative neglect might be that at the time when he described the regressive forms of transference, his instinct theory was practically finished; the third edition of his *Three Essays on Sexuality* appeared in 1915, that is the same year in which he published his paper 'On Transference-Love'. On the other hand, a developmental theory of object relationship was at that time in its earliest beginnings.

It was on his instinct theory that Freud based his often-quoted therapeutic recommendations that the analyst should not respond positively to a regressed patient's 'cravings', in particular, should not satisfy them. The analytic therapy must be carried out in the state of 'abstinence', 'frustration', or 'privation'. In many ways this recommendation is correct. If the analyst does not do anything else apart from gratifying his regressed patient's cravings, his action cannot but produce temporary results. Since the source of the cravings has not even been touched, after a while new cravings will appear demanding, equally strongly, new gratifications. If then the analyst, influenced by the blissful peace immediately following his action, is induced to experiment with further gratifications, a never-ending vicious spiral may develop which is not uncommon in regressed states.

Thus, responding positively to a regressed patient's longings and cravings by gratifying them, will be very likely to prove a technical error. On the other hand, responding to a patient's needs for a particular form of object relationship, more primitive than that obtaining between adults, may be a legitimate technical measure which possibly has nothing to do with the rule of 'frustration' or 'privation'.

But, if we accept this idea, we leave the boundaries of instinct or drive theory, which belongs to the sphere of one-person psychology, and enter the realm of two-person psychology. Whereas, on the basis of the former, we could maintain that both the form and the depth of regression are determined solely by the patient, his childhood, his character, the severity of his illness, etc., etc., in the latter we must consider them as the result of an interaction between the particular patient and his particular analyst. Concentrating for a moment on the analyst's contributions, that is, on his technique, we may say that the clinical appearance of a regression will depend also on the way the regression is recognized, is accepted, and is responded to by the analyst.

Perhaps the most important form of the analyst's response is interpretation; it may have a crucial influence on the treatment, whether the analyst interprets any particular phenomenon as a demand for gratification or as a need for a particular form of object relationship.

Supposing the analyst is prepared to consider regression as a request, demand, or need, for a particular form of object relationship, the next question will be how far should he go or, in other words, what sort of object relationship he should consider offering to, or accepting from, his regressed patient. This is an important technical problem and, as with almost every problem in psychoanalytic technique, it has several aspects.

The first aspect belongs to the borderland between one-person and two-person psychologies; it may be described as a problem of differential diagnosis. The analyst must be able to recognize which forms of object relationship will be adequate, or even therapeutic at this moment for his regressed patient. In order to do so, he must not only accept that these relationships exist and may have therapeutic effects but must also know enough of them to be able to choose the one with the best therapeutic possibilities.

With this we enter a controversial field. Some analysts firmly believe that only those forms of object relationship are compatible with a proper running of analytic therapy that allow the analyst to retain his role of passive, sympathetic objectivity described by Freud. I have the impression that they still feel that this is an absolute parameter, and if the analyst, for any reason whatsoever, abandons it, the treatment should no longer be called psychoanalysis. If this impression is correct, it follows that these analysts will probably maintain that this differential diagnosis is unnecessary, or even conducive to faulty, harmful technique. In Part III, in particular in Chapters 14 and 16, I discussed some of the consequences of this general policy.

In order to avoid a possible misunderstanding, it is important to realize that interpreting to the patient that he has always tried to establish a particular genital, or even pre-genital, relationship, is something utterly different from accepting, and working with, the fact that the patient at this particular stage needs a certain form of object relationship, and allowing him to create and maintain it in the analytic situation. However, in the cases of the better-known, later, object relationships, interpretations, as a rule, have enough power to start and to maintain a therapeutic readjustment to reality; in some cases there may come to be some 'acting-out' but this, too, can be dealt with by interpretations. Most of this class belong to what I called the Oedipal area, and thus the events occurring during them can be expressed fairly adequately in conventional adult language. The most important of them are—in reverse chronological order: the phallic-narcissistic form with its many variants, such as egotistic-self-assertive, aggressive-castrating, submissive, masochistic, etc.; the many anal-sadistic forms with all the over-compensations and reaction-formations belonging to them, and so on.

For the sake of completeness I must mention here the various oral forms of object relationship, summed up nowadays as 'oral dependence' which many analysts would include here as a matter of course. Since, in my opinion, 'oral dependence' is a misleading concept, may I sum up briefly my arguments against it.

The relationship that 'oral dependence' tries to describe is *not* a one-sided dependence, but an 'inter-dependence'; libidinally, the mother is almost to the same extent dependent on her baby as the baby is on her; neither of them may have this particular form of relationship and the particular satisfaction independently from the other. Though oral aspects constitute an important part of the whole phenomenon, there are various other factors present, and it is difficult to assess with certainty which is the most important. Furthermore, the mother's breast, the counterpart of the child's mouth, is about as often as not excluded by present-day nursing fashion—in most cases without seriously interfering with the mutual interdependence which, in my opinion, is the decisive factor in this relationship.

The interdependence should remind us that any attempt at describing this relationship using terms of one-person psychology will necessarily be misleading. Although this is true up to a point for all relationships, the effect of interdependence diminishes at the same rate as the importance of the partner's cooperation. An instructive example is anal domination, the theory of which is perhaps the best developed in psychoanalysis. Here the cooperation of the partner is minimal, in consequence the relationship can be described adequately by terms belonging to one-person psychology. On the other hand, in genital love it is essential that an indifferent object whom we love should be changed by us into a cooperative partner. The relationship between an individual and his indifferent object can be described fairly well with our terminology, whereas the relationship between cooperating partners needs a new terminology belonging to two-person psychology.

A further important difficulty is that all primitive relationships belong, as a rule, to the pre-verbal period of development. As we have seen in Part I, phenomena belonging to this area do not lend themselves easily to verbal description. In what follows we have to bear these two difficulties constantly in our minds: the one caused by the intense interdependence of two individuals, and the second caused by the primitive nature of the developing relationship which is hard to render in adult conventional words.[1]

After removing this obstacle, and the confusion created by it, we may return to our main problem: what sort of primitive, possibly preverbal, object relationships should the analyst consider accepting from, or even offering to, his regressed patient?

In the preceding chapters, in particular in 4, 12, 15, and 22, I described in detail the characteristics of the three chief forms observed in my analytic practice. These were: (a) the most primitive, which I called *primary love,* or primary relationship, a sort of harmonious interpenetrating mix-up between the developing individual and his primary substances or his primary object; (b) and (c) *ocnophilia* and *philobatism* which form a kind of counterpart with one another; they already presuppose the discovery of fairly stable part and/or whole objects. For the predominantly ocnophilic individual, life is safe only in close proximity to objects, while the intervening periods or spaces between objects are felt as horrid and dangerous. These phenomena have been known for some considerable time; recently under the influence of ethology they are referred to as 'attachment behaviour' (e.g. Bowlby, 1958). In contrast, the predominantly philobatic individual experiences the objects as unreliable and hazardous, is inclined to dispense with them, and seeks out the friendly expanses separating the treacherous objects in time and space.

---

[1] 'Oral dependence' is a relatively new concept. I could not discover any reference to it in Freud's writings, so it seems to be a post-Freudian, and most probably American, creation. I think it would be an interesting study to find out the exact history of its development. Here are a few data for it. 'Dependence' without the adjective 'oral' occurs a few times in Fenichel's textbook (1945). The first use of 'oral dependence' that I found was by F. Alexander in 1950. To my surprise I could not find it in Melanie Klein's writings; the first reference to it by her school seems to occur in *New Directions in Psycho-Analysis* (1955), a collection of papers written for Melanie Klein on the occasion of her seventieth birthday in 1952. Here too the adjective 'oral' was missing but the term 'dependence' referred to what today would be called oral dependence, the dependence of the child on his mother; the two authors using it were Paula Heimann and Joan Rivière. From about 1952, dependence, and even oral dependence, occurs with ever-increasing frequency in Winnicott's papers, but apparently not before that date.

The next question is, of course, what can a patient gain from regression? Why is it so important to him? As I have mentioned several times, not all patients go necessarily through a regressive period. That means that some patients can do without it, perhaps they do not even need it. However, it is difficult to get any indication about the distribution of those people who do, and those who do not, need a regressive period. The reason for this is that patients who go through an analytic treatment do not constitute a representative sample, because they have been selected according to their analyst's ideas about analysability. Still, there is perhaps some truth in the impression that in our present patient material the number of those who need regression is greater than in the past and is perhaps still increasing.

The answer to our question lies in the idea of the basic fault and in the observations that led me to the discovery of the 'new beginning'. My train of thought runs as follows: all of us have certain character traits or, expressed in modern terminology, compulsive patterns of object relationship. Some of these are the outcome of a conflict or complex in us; if the analyst with his interpretations can help his patient to solve these conflicts and complexes, the compulsive nature of these patterns will be reduced to a level flexible enough to permit adaptation to reality. In a number of cases in which, according to my ideas, the patterns originate in a reaction to the basic fault, interpretations will have incomparably less power, since there is no conflict or complex in the strict sense to solve and in the area of the basic fault, words are not quite reliable tools anyhow.

In some cases in which words, that is associations followed by interpretations, do not seem to be able to induce or maintain the necessary changes, additional therapeutic agents should be considered. In my opinion, the most important of these is to help the patient to develop a primitive relationship in the analytic situation corresponding to his compulsive pattern and maintain it in undisturbed peace till he can discover the possibility of new forms of object relationship, experience them, and experiment with them. Since the basic fault, as long as it is active, determines the forms of object relationship available to any individual, a necessary task of the treatment is to inactivate the basic fault by creating conditions in which it can heal off. To achieve this, the patient must be allowed to regress either to the setting, that is, to the particular form of object relationship which caused the original deficiency state, or even to some stage before it. This is a precondition which must be fulfilled before the patient can give up, very tentatively at first, his compulsive pattern. Only after that can the patient 'begin anew', that is develop new patterns of object relationship to replace those given up. These new patterns will be less defensive and thus more flexible, offering him more possibility to adapt himself to reality under less tension and friction than hitherto.

The next and last question in this chapter will be: what can the analyst do to foster this process? The greater part of the answer will follow in the next chapter; here I would like to stress only three highly important *negative* aspects, that is, what the analyst must try to avoid doing. Our present fashion in technique—which recommends that, if at all possible, everything should be interpreted first as transference—tempts us to turn into mighty and knowledgeable objects for our patients, thus help-ing—or forcing—them to regress into an ocnophilic world. In this world there are ample opportunities for dependence but very meagre ones for making independent discoveries. I hope it will be generally agreed that the latter is at least as important therapeutically as the former. Con-versely, this means that the analyst must not stick rigidly to one form of object relationship that he found useful in other cases or during the preceding phases of this treatment but must all the time be prepared to alternate with his patient between the ocnophilic and the philobatic primitive worlds, and even go beyond them towards primary relation-ship. This can be done only if the analyst is capable of the differential diagnosis described above.

The other important negative aspect is that at times the analyst must do everything in his power not to become, or to behave as, a separate, sharply-contoured object. In other words, he must allow his patients to relate to, or exist with, him as if he were one of the primary substances. This means that he should be willing to carry the patient, not actively but like water carries the swimmer or the earth carries the walker, that is, to be there for the patient, to be used without too much resistance against being used. True, some resistance is not only permissible but essential. However, the analyst must be careful that his resistance should create only as much friction as is needed for progress but defi-nitely not much more, otherwise progress may become too difficult owing to the resistance of the medium. Over and above all this, he must be there, must always be there, and must be indestructible—as are water and earth. We discussed some of these aspects in Chapter 22, and we shall continue with them in those following.

A corollary to the previous negative aspect is our last one, also negative, that the analyst must avoid becoming, or even appearing in the eyes of his patient, 'omnipotent'. This is one of the most difficult tasks in this period of the treatment. The regressed patient expects his analyst to know more, and to be more powerful; if nothing else, the analyst is expected to promise, either explicitly or by his behaviour, that he will help his patient out of the regression, or see the patient through it. Any such promise, even the slightest appearance of a tacit agreement towards it, will create very great difficulties, almost insurmountable obstacles, for the analytic work. Here too, the only thing that the analyst can do is to accept the role of a true primary substance, which is there, which cannot be destroyed, which *eo ipso* is there to carry the patient, which feels the patient's importance and weight but still carries him, which is unconcerned about keeping up proper boundaries between the patient and itself, etc., but which is not an object in the true sense, is not concerned about its independent existence.

Several other authors tried to describe this sort of object relationship or, more correctly, environment-patient relationship, using other terms. Anna Freud (war years) used 'the need-satisfying object'; Hartmann (1939) 'the average expectable environment'; Bion in a paper to the British Psycho-Analytical Society (1966) contrasted the 'container' with the 'contained'. The most versatile inventor of such terms seems to be Winnicott, who used (1941) the 'good enough environment', then talked about the 'medium' in which the patient can revolve like an engine in oil, then (1949) came his 'ordinary devoted mother', in 1956 the 'primary maternal preoccupation', then (1960) the 'holding function' of the mother, while in 1963 he borrowed the term 'facilitating environment' from the American literature and used it as part of the title of his last book (1967). Margaret Little called it the 'basic unit' (1961), while M. Khan proposed (1963) the 'protective shield' and R. Spitz 'mediator of the environment' (1965), while M. Mahler preferred (1952) 'extra-uterine matrix'. Any one of these terms is correct. Each describes one or the other aspect of this non-omnipotent relationship that I have in mind. Of course I am biased in favour of my term, among many others, for the one reason that mine is more general and can accommodate all the others as its particular aspects.

If we accept these ideas, then the problem of whether or not to gratify a regressed patient's cravings appears in a different light, so different that doubt arises whether we have not been struggling with a false problem which can never be solved because it is wrongly formulated. The real problem is not about gratifying or frustrating the regressed patient but about how the analyst's response to the regression will influence the patient-analyst relationship and by it the further course of the treatment. If the analyst's response, e.g. satisfying the patient's expectations, creates an impression in the patient that his analyst is knowledgeable and capable, bordering on being omniscient and omnipotent, this response should be considered as risky and inadvisable; it is likely to increase the inequality between patient and analyst, which may lead to the creation of addiction-like states by exacerbating the patient's basic fault.

On the other hand, if the satisfaction can be done in a fashion that does not increase the inequality but creates an object relationship according to the pattern of what I call primary love, then it should be seriously considered as a method of choice.

At this point I propose to digress briefly to discuss what I call *the ocnophilic bias of our modern technique* and its consequences. Psychoanalytic technique—and theory—were so impressed by the intensity of ocnophilic phenomena met in the analytic situation that they concentrated their interest on them, neglecting almost entirely the equally important primary and philobatic relationships. Thus developed the theory of object-seeking, clinging, 'attachment behaviour', and ambivalent dependence. As I pointed out in *Thrills and Regressions* (1959), especially in Chapter 12, our modern technical procedure recommends that everything that happens or is produced by the patient in the analytic situation should be understood and interpreted first and foremost as a phenomenon of transference. Conversely this means that the principal frame of reference used for formulating practically every interpretation is a relationship between a highly important, omnipresent object, the analyst, and an unequal subject who at present apparently cannot feel, think, or experience anything unrelated to his analyst.

It is easy to see that this modern technique of interpreting transference first must lead to a picture of the world consisting of a rather insignificant subject confronted with mighty, knowledgeable, and omnipresent objects who have the power of expressing everything correctly in words, an impressive example of whom is the analyst. If one accepts this picture as a true and representative sample of the early stages of human development, one gets easily to the theory of 'oral dependence'. The dependence is obvious, and the adjective 'oral' is speedily added to it under the influence of our theory of instincts, which has only this one word for the description of anything primitive or early. The fact that during the treatment conducted in this way nearly all transactions between patient and analyst happen through the medium of words, reinforces the 'oral' aspects, and analysts, patients, and our theory associate to it that interpretations—that is, words—may stand for 'milk' and the analyst for 'the breast'.

A circular argument develops in this way; everything that happens in the analytic situation is understood and interpreted in this fashion, which in turn 'teaches' the patient—as described in Chapter 15—to express, and to some extent even to feel, all his pre-verbal experiences according to this language, thus convincing the analyst that both his theory and his interpretations were absolutely right. This is another instance of an event that has happened on many occasions in practically every science, and especially in our psychoanalysis, that parts of the truth have been used to repress the whole truth. In our present instance the parts are: that 'oral' and 'dependent' phenomena occur in every primitive human relationship. What is repressed is that they are far from being able to explain the whole picture; the only thing that happened was that by our present technique their importance has been magnified out of proportion.

A very good proof for this view is Freud's example. As the study of his case histories proves, he paid due attention to transference but did not interpret it before anything else. In consequence, although he was a very important object to his patients, his technique did not force them to build up a picture of the world according to the oppressive inequality between an ocnophilic subject and his all-important object described above. As I have just mentioned, in the indexes of the twenty-three volumes of the Standard Edition the catchword 'dependence' occurs very rarely, while 'oral dependence' does not occur at all.

To illustrate a number of problems raised in this chapter, may I quote an episode from a long treatment. After an unsatisfactory session on a Friday in which the patient accepted, rather reluctantly, that no real contact could be established between himself and his analyst because during the whole session the patient had to make his analyst useless, he had great difficulties in leaving the room. Just before the door was opened he said that he felt awful and asked for an extra session, any time during the week-end, to help him to recover.

The problem of course, is how to respond to this request which, undoubtedly, is a request for gratification. I would add that this patient occasionally got extra sessions during the week-end; these always brought him very great satisfaction and, true to type, eased the tension in him considerably each time; however, it was only very rarely that in these extra sessions real analytical work was possible.

Let us suppose that the request is interpreted as another 'craving' of his, and refused on this account; even if the patient accepts this interpretation, he will feel still more wretched for having unnecessarily pestered his kind and patient analyst, and his misery will get worse. If the patient disagrees with the interpretation, he will experience the analyst as unkind and cruel, increasing thereby the tension in the therapy; it is doubtful whether the situation will be made more tolerable if the analyst interprets it as a resistance or as a transference of some aggressiveness and hatred from childhood.

On the other hand if he satisfies the request for an extra session, no matter whether he interprets it as a repetition of some early frustration prompted by, or leading to, greediness or envy, he turns himself into an omnipotent object and forces his patient into an ocnophilic relationship.

What I tried to do in this case was first to recognize and accept his distress so that he should feel that I was with him, and then to admit that I did not feel that an extra session granted by me would be powerful enough to give him what he expected and perhaps even needed at this moment; in addition this would make him small and weak while his analyst would become great and powerful, which was not desirable. For all these reasons the request was not agreed to. The patient then departed dissatisfied.

I had two aims in mind when choosing my response. On the one hand, I tried to prevent the development of undesirable relationships, such as that between someone let down or frustrated by a harsh or superior person in authority who knows better what is right, or that between someone weak and in need of kind support, and a benign and generous authority—all leading to a reinforcement of the inequality between the subject and his mighty object. On the other hand, I tried to establish a relationship in which neither of us would be all-powerful, in which both of us admitted our limitations in the hope that in this way a fruitful collaboration could be established between two people who were not fundamentally different in importance, weight, and power.

I have to add here that it was a very rare event indeed that my patient rang me up, perhaps not even as much as once per year in an emergency. This time he telephoned me the same evening after 8 p.m. He could hardly speak on the telephone, dithered to and fro for a long time, but at the end he was able to say that he had to ring me up . . . to tell me that he was very near crying . . . nothing else . . . he did not want anything from me, no extra session, . . . but he had to ring me up, to let me know how he felt.

This episode shows how the analyst's response turned a process that started in the direction of a 'craving' for satisfaction—i.e. a possibly malignant form—into a benign one—i.e. a regression for recognition. It was done by the analyst avoiding even a semblance of being omniscient and over-powerful; on the other hand he demonstrated his willingness to accept the role of a primary object whose chief function is recognizing, and being with, his patient.

The immediate effect of this incident was a considerable lessening of the tension, the patient had a comparatively good week-end, and for quite some time afterwards he was capable of contact and cooperation. I would even say that it initiated—or reinforced—a change for a better atmosphere in the analytic situation, in which it was possible to make some considerable progress.

PART IV

1970s AND 1980s

1970s

Under the influence of Kernberg, the term "borderline" became more widely used than ever before not only among American psychoanalysts grappling with their most challenging office patients but also among psychiatrists, whether analytically trained or not, working with hospitalized patients. Older terms, like "pseudoneurotic schizophrenia," "latent schizophrenia" (Bleuler; Bychowski) and " ambulatory schizophrenia" (Zilboorg), fall into desuetude. Kernberg's definition tends, by virtue of its insistence upon adequate reality-testing capacity, to exclude all but the highest-functioning schizotypals, not to mention all (psychotic) schizophrenics. This further weakened any conceptual, let alone genetic, linkage to schizophrenia. "Borderline" begins to fill in the space between existing and more sharply discriminable entities like schizophrenia and manic depression. Since Kernberg's definition operates as a level of overall function as well as a clinical syndrome, it engulfed alcoholism and sociopathy as well (most patients with these disorders function at the borderline level, even though category-oriented purists rebel against so broad a usage of the term "borderline."

The widening popularity of the term stimulated research and reformulations on a broad front, so much so that it now becomes necessary to discuss these recent developments according to some coherent outline, if the reader is not to become confused. The topic headings that follow represent my attempt to present this material in some more orderly fashion.

1. Psychodynamic Formulations

Margaret Mahler's work, an example of which is included here, centered on analysis of children. This provided her, as it had provided Melanie Klein before her, a special opportunity to develop an in-depth awareness of the subtleties of early development. Most analytic investigators acknowledge their indebtedness to her for delineating with such persuasiveness certain phases of early childhood, several of which seem particularly relevant to borderline patients. The serious problems in handling separation and in achieving an adequate sense of autonomy and self-definition (exhibited routinely by those whom we call borderline) appear to harken back to disturbances, often enough profound disturbances, in the separation-individuation phase of children (chiefly during the second and third years of life). Many have indeed attributed primary etiological significance to such disturbances in the causation of borderline psychopathology. Rinsley expresses this view; Masterson acknowledges almost nothing else in the way of prominent pathogenic factors, claiming that the mothers of borderline cases are themselves borderline. Others have inclined toward the view that, while correlations of this sort exist in many cases, other factors may at times overshadow separation problems and unfavorable mothering. Collum (1972), for example, cites instances of sexual overstimulation during childhood as an important contributing factor—a point with which I am in agreement. Despite the pitfalls that beset the retrospective analysis of family life, one does get the impression that a variety of environmental calamities (parental cruelty, neglect, sexual victimization) can engender what we later identify as borderline function, even where the separation/individuation phase proceded with no more than minor misadventures. Meantime, we await some possible classic study in the 1990s, prospective in design, to allow us to assign more realistic weights to the dynamic factors deemed critical to borderline development.

With respect to defensive patterns and characterology pertinent to borderline conditions, the Lyonnaise psychoanalyst, Bergeret, has amplified traditional analytic theory. Bergeret (1975) has also given excellent clinical examples of how the various personality types (depressive, obsessive . . .) appear, when found in borderline, rather than in neurotic, persons. In keeping with psychostructurally oriented French psychology (which, in turn, influenced Kernberg), Bergeret envisions the borderline state as reflecting a stable abnormality in the pattern of defense. Instead of repression, the chief mechanism in neurotics, one sees disavowal and denial. As the structuralist school emphasizes, these defenses function, in borderlines, to keep contradictory attitudes separated (the "splitting" mechanism) in logic-tight compartments. The same primitive defenses, as Kernberg also underlines, serve in the psychotic to ward off the terror of psychic fragmentation.

These metapsychological formulations become *diagnostic* points for analysts of the structural school. There is a danger, however, in making diagnostic distinctions in this way. To avoid circularity (splitting indicates borderline pathology; borderlines show splitting . . .), it is important to base diagnosis on signs and symptoms—observable in the consulting room, and *external* to any consideration of defenses. A correlation between a borderline diagnosis and certain defenses becomes the more convincing if, for example, borderlines diagnosed according to observable signs showed projective identification, splitting and disavowal, but patients with other standardized diagnoses, did so only rarely or not at all.

2. Phenomenology

The issue outlined in the last paragraph is precisely the one addressed in the paper (reprinted here) by John Gunderson and the psychologist, Margaret Singer, in the mid-1970s, probably the most important article devoted to the borderline question in that decade. From their careful review, and from analysis of psychlogical test data, they proposed a new definition for diagnosing borderline cases, similar in its emphasis on clinical phenomenology to that of Grinker, but more precise, and equipped with criteria of inclusion and exclusion. The diagnostic items are based on direct observation and upon anamnestic material: lowered work achievement, impulsivity, brief psychotic episodes, manipulative suicide gestures, good socialization superficially, but disturbances intimate relationships, where rageful instead of warm emotionality predominates. Psychological tests, in line with Knight's observations, tend to show good performance on the structured portions, but with breakdown on the unstructured portions (especially, on the Rorschach).

The work of Gunderson and his collaborators has facilitated the expansion in usage of the borderline concept into the wider arena of clinicians who have not been trained in analysis. The Gunderson definition delineates a clinical syndrome (rather than a level of general adaptation), distinguishable with reasonable reliability from certain neighboring concepts of psychoneurosis and schizophrenia. Gunderson's work is notable for the precision of his statistical analysis and for his methodological carefulness. Theoretically conservative, Gundersonhas had a salutary influence on investigators in this clinical realm, all of whom now feel compelled to marshall as solid a base of data in support of their contentions as one finds in Gunderson's research.

Phenomenological descriptions of the rejection-sensitive dysphoric ("hysteroid dysphoric") first were given by Donald Klein in the late 1960s and refined in the mid 1970s. He and his colleague, Michael Liebowitz, published several papers on the responsiveness of patients with this syndrome to antidepressants (particularly, to MAO inhibitors). Hysteroid-dysphoria patients are almost invariably (1) female and (2) borderline according to the other currently popular diagnostic systems. Whereas psychoanalytic formulations tend to explain the impulsivity of these patients as manifestations of acting-out various conflicts (especially if they occur in the transference situation) and to explain their moodiness in terms of the supposedly relevant vicissitudes of intercurrent relationships, etc., Klein feels that many of these patients are being buffeted by innate biological forces that would, episodically, push them toward irritability, sensation seeking, mood changes, and other forms of what Klein calls "peculiar repetitious behavior" (1977, p.381). The description Klein offers (with more accuracy than charity) resembles closely that of Falret's *folie hystérique*. That is, ". . . hysteroid dysphoric patients are fickle, emotionally labile, irresponsible, shallow, love-intoxicated, giddy and short sighted. They tend to be egocentric, narcissistic, exhibitionistic, vain and clothes-crazy. In addition, they are seductive, manipulative, exploitative, sexually provocative, and . . . illogical in their thinking. . . . when frustrated . . . they often become reproachful, tearful, abusive and vindictive, and often resort to alcohol." (p. 373).

Spitzer has recently taken issue with the validity of Klein's term, merits of which cannot (for reasons of space) be discussed here. A fair proportion of borderline patients do, at all events, demonstrate these qualities, often showing, in addition, signs of severe premenstrual tension, proneness to serious (especially bipolar-II) affective illness and a family history positive for recurrent depressive of bipolar-II conditions, or else for alcoholism.

3. Genetics

Impressed by the large number of borderline cases who had one or more emotionally ill relatives, M. Stone conducted a study of family pedigrees both of hospitalized and ambulatory borderline patients. In the article reprinted here, a high incidence of illness was reported, for both groups. Patients were diagnosed borderline by broad (Kernberg-) criteria. Two unexpected findings that emerged from this study were (1) that the incidence of severe illness in the families of borderlines was not much different than in the families of psychotic patients and (2) that the diagnostic profile of illness in the relatives was slanted toward affective conditions (especially, recurrent depressive or else bipolar illness), and away from the schizophrenic disorders to which the borderline state was, according to the older literature, supposedly affiliated. Stone was inclined to reevaluate borderline conditions as often (though by no means always) representing attenuated forms of manic depression. Subsequent studies, including a number that were methodologically more refined, pointed, for the most part, in the same direction (see pp. 549–568); toward the end of the decade, a number of biological markers of depression and other conditions were being investigated, in an effort to assess, through these external measures, the validity of Stone's hypothesis (that borderline symptoms often were a *forme fruste* or else a harbinger of a primary affective disorder).

4. Clinical Applications

Several important contributions were made throughout the 1970s to the psychotherapy of borderline patients—some in the form of new recommendations arising at the time; others, in the form of books expanding on formulations already enunciated during the 1960s and before.

In the mid-1970s Kernberg and his coworkers at the Menninger Clinic published the results of their study of borderline- and psychotic-level psychotherapy patients. The recommendation of this report, echoed shortly thereafter in Kernberg's first book (1975), was that borderlines did best with an expressive, analytically oriented technic that utilized meticulous attention to transference issues, along with appropriate limit setting and use of confrontation. Schizophrenic patients, in contrast, generally did better with a consistently supportive technic. For border-

line patients, supportive interventions (reassurances, recommendations, prohibitions, etc) were justified more often than they were for
neurotic analysands, but less often than with psychotic patients. The
proper balance between expressive and supportive interventions (e.g.,
interpretation or clarification as opposed to reassurance or advice, etc.)
shifts from time to time in accordance with the life events of the patient
and the clinical *Gefühl* of the therapist.

Toward the end of the decade, Searles' third book (on countertransference) appeared. It contained ample material on borderline patients,
over and above that relating to the analysis of schizophrenics (for which
Searles had been better known). Searles' intuitive gifts and his devotion
to the analytic treatment of severely ill patients were rarities even 20
years ago. These qualities are rarer still today among recent graduates
of psychiatric training who tend to be more biologically oriented. Diagnostically, Searles does not draw sharp distinctions between borderline
and frankly schizophrenic patients (1979, p.583). For this reason it is
hard to compare Kernberg's recommendations about supportive therapy for schizophrenics with Searles' criticism of this approach, as
expressed in the following passage (p.591).

(Some) analysts tend . . . to place these persons beyond the pale of psychoanalytic endeavors, thus relegating them to . . . phenothiazines and so-called
maintenance psychotherapy, which inevitably is consigning most of these patients to far less than half a life with regard to any fulfillment of their human
potentialities. I regard these patients as being highly capable of forming inherently analyzable transference responses . . . and I find that the limitation tends
rather to be in the analyst.

But some of "these persons" would probably be borderline by contemporary criteria, such that Kernberg would agree with Searles' position. But others are surely schizophrenic by any measure. For the
latter, candor would probably compel us to admit that, exceptional
schizophrenics and exceptional therapists aside, the nearer a patient
exemplifies unequivocal schizophrenia the grimmer the long-term prognosis, with respect to a transference-oriented therapy. This does not
detract, however, from the value of Searles' trenchant and often surprising observations for all those who conduct intensive therapy with
severely disturbed patients.

For sound practical advice about the intensive psychotherapy of
borderline cases, one may turn to the Vanggaard's *Borderlands of San-*

ity, published in 1979. A psychoanalyst who has integrated hereditary predisposition into his theoretical framework, Vanggaard speaks of cases in the spectrum of manic-depression (*borderline* affective disorders) as well as of so-called "spectrum cases" of schizophrenia. His text is widely used throughout Scandinavia as a guide to analytic therapy.

5. Diagnostic Systems; Biometrics

The popularity of "borderline" as a diagnostic label was given an immense boost by its inclusion in DSM-3. This brought it from the analytic community (1970 US pop. = 2,500) to the psychiatric community (pop. = 25,000). The efforts of Spitzer and his colleagues to objectify and standardize the diagnosis of borderline are expressed in their 1979 article (reprinted here). Two borderline subtypes were identified as a "schizotypal" (answering to the "borderline schizophrenics" described by Kety) and an "unstable" (whose characteristics were a blend of Kernberg's and Gunderson's descriptions). From this point forward the paths of these subtypes are to diverge; "borderline" no longer conveys to most practitioners the complicated mixture of meanings and overtones we have outlined in our summaries of the previous decades, but more and more the term came to signify the angry, depressed, and unreasonable sort of patient, who may or may not carry genetic predisposition to a manic-depressive disorder, such as described, under a different title, by Donald Klein.

The areas of overlap and disjunction among the more popular systems for diagnosing borderlines, established by Grinker, Kernberg, and Gunderson, were analyzed by Perry and Klerman (1978). These authors noted surprisingly little unanimity of criteria, apart from the item of impulsivity.

6. Validation from External Frames of Reference

The search for biologic markers that might prove useful in discriminating between borderline conditions and other diagnostic categories was just getting underway as the decade ended.

Attempts to refine psychological testing as a means of facilitating this distinction had already been made by Margaret Singer; attempts to improve these refinements yet again were also being made on a wider front. The diagnosis of "borderline" was to be made by those who wished to revise diagnostic criteria so as to be more in line with the changes in definitional boundaries ushered in by the newer neurophysiological and biochemical research.

1980s

Though as of this writing the decade of the 1980s is only half over, there is already such a number of articles and books on the borderline clamoring for our attention that we can scarcely do justice in a small space even to enumerate the conceptual compartments they belong in. Similarly, it is too soon to say which will have proved the most influential. Reverting to the schema followed in discussing the 1970s, I take up the same topics again, and add two other sections relating to Prognostic issues and to Overviews.

1. Psychoanalytic Theory

Kernberg has amplified his theoretical formulations concerning the borderline in his newest book on the severely disturbed patient. Kohut in *How Does Analysis Cure?* speaks of borderline cases in a quite different, not to say wholly idiosyncratic way, spelling out even more clearly than in his previous two books published in the 1970s that for him difficult analytic cases that eventually work out are narcissistic disorders, while difficult narcissistic patients with whom one fails are considered to be borderline. As Kohut stated (1984),

. . . the concept of "borderline" pathology (which I define as analyzable cryptopsychosis . . .) is a relative one, depending, at least in a substantial number of cases, on the analyst's ability or inability (a) to retain his attitude of "empathic intention" . . . and (b) to enable the patient . . . to reassemble his self sufficiently . . . to make possible the . . . exploration of the dynamic and genetic causes of the underlying vulnerability (p.184).

These sentiments are comparable to those expressed by Searles (see above, The 1970s), and do reflect a truism having to do with the fact that not every analyst can tolerate every severely disturbed patient. Where the fit is poor, the patient will appear sicker to his therapist than he would, once ensconced in a less mismatched treatment setting, to some new and more tolerant therapist. But this has nothing whatever to do with diagnosis. Kohut's contributions are valuable in that they broaden our view (as did the work of the British Object-Relations School) of the preoedipal period, especially as the events of the first few years of life help shape—or deform—the evolving sense of self. Kohut's language wants simplification. (The primary "selfobject" is usually mother. Why not call her that?) However, his chief drawback lies in his bland disregard for the canons of psychiatric diagnosis. There being no way to tell whether his borderlines and severe narcissistic cases are also our borderline cases (DSM, Kernberg, Gunderson), there is no reliable way to build bridges between his theoretical framework and the rest of the modern literature on this subject.

2. Phenomenology

In Europe "borderline" is still often used to denote schizophrenia in attenuated form. This is especially noticeable in the school of thought led by the spiritual descendant of Kurt Schneider, Professor Huber, whose colleagues, Sass and Koehler, have commented extensively on *Grenzezustaende* (borderline conditions) and have studied both the schizotypal and DSM varieties with respect to their phenomenological differences, their varying degrees of participation in Huber's "Basissymptome" (akin to our "negative symptoms of schizophrenia"), etc. The notion of a constitutional abnormality, predisposing to the emergence, later on, of a borderline condition, is, of course, congenial to most European investigators, especially to whose with a Kraepelinian orientation.

Interest in possible correspondences between Kraepelin's temperaments (allied to manic depression) and certain clinical states that might be borderline manifestations of manic depression served as the motivation for Stone's analysis of various temperament factors (such personality attributes as intensity, pessimism, irascibility and traits like compulsive gambling, pathological jealousy, scrupulousness, etc.). Many borderlines (by Kernberg or Gunderson criteria) exhibited a temperament Kraepelin considered affiliated with manic depression. Several other investigators reported parallel findings: borderline cases who had, on follow up, become bipolar; cyclothymics with bipolar relatives (Cadoret), etc.

Suggestions were made by several authors simultaneously for division of the borderline domain (as defined by broad criteria) into various subtypes that might turn out to be more homeogeneous with respect to certain biologic markers.

Andrulonis showed how the borderline syndrome could be engendered by subtle organic disorders of the central nervous system, including temporal lobe epilepsy. Stone viewed borderline conditions as representing a final common pathway for a variety of, at times, isolated, more often interacting pathogenic factors: genetic liability for affective illness, chaotic and destructive early environment (including but in no way limited to disturbances in separation), and (to a lesser extent) organic or schizophrenic factors. Certain clinical syndromes seemed to appear together: borderline syndrome, affective illness, severe premenstrual tension. How these conditions are interrelated is as yet unclear.

3. Genetics

Family-pedigree studies of borderline patients have now been carried out by a number of investigators and in several countries. Evidence has begun to accumulate that the close relatives of DSM-, Gunderson- and Kernberg- borderlines show an excess of afffective illnesses, though many (half or more) borderlines have no such relatives. Those with negative family histories tend to have fewer affective symptoms themselves (Pope, 1983). Schizophrenia is rare in the pedigrees of these borderlines, though not rare if one directs one's attention to schizotypals (i.e., to borderline schizophrenics). Originally, Kety found nuclear schizophrenics with borderline-schizophrenic relatives, but no nuclear schizophrenics in the families of borderline-schizophrenic index cases. Larger studies over the past five years have unearthed the missing link. Some borderline schizophrenic probands have a schizophrenic sibling or parent, thus strengthening the hypothesis that the conditions are, indeed, severe and dilute forms of the same hereditary predisposition.

Akiskal (in the study reprinted here) has found that borderlines were more apt to have bipolar (as well as depressive) relatives than were patients with recurrent depressions. This observatioin lent credence to the hypothesis that an important subset of borderlines exists, in which predisposition to some form of manic depression is a significant etiologic factor. It is not surprising that bipolar illness should figure so prominently in the families of borderlines, since both borderlines and bipolars (as opposed to unipolars) are prone to *irascibility* in addition to bouts of depression. Without some indications of irascibility, in fact, a depressive patient would not get labeled borderline to begin with (certainly not by DSM or Gunderson criteria). Hysteroid dysphorics are often (or sometimes become) bipolar-II patients, simultaneously. The correlation then: bipolar relatives in the families of affectively ill borderlines (themselves *formes frustres* of a bipolar condition, in many instances) makes clinical sense.

In the interactional models of causation, now favored by sophisticated clinicians and researchers alike, one envisions a schema, comparable to the model promulgated by Matthysse for schizophrenia, where high genetic loading may push certain persons toward a borderline condition, no matter how protective the rearing, while the most destructive families can produce borderlines without any help from genetic liability. The average case may reflect an interaction of more modest degrees of risk from either source. The differences among various samples of borderlines from one setting or country to another may be explainable largely as the result of differing mixtures of these etiological ingredients. Gunderson, in a recent paper, has expressed a similar conclusion.

. . . the observed concurrence of affective and borderline symptoms results from . . . heterogeneity. For either disorder, individuals may start with a biophysiological vulnerability that increases their risk of being psychologically impaired in early development.

Such early traumas may create vulnerability to either or both disorders, but the actual presentation varies as a function of later physiological and psychological reactions to environment and temperament. The key to the overlap and dissimilarities between these two disorders may be a constellation of innate and external factors that are inconsequential individually but combine to shape depression, chronic dysphoria or borderline behavior—alone or in any possible combination (Gunderson, 1985, p. 286).

4. Clinical Applications

Several monographs and anthologies have appeared in the last few years dealing with analytically oriented psychotherapy of borderline patients. The more cautiously titled book of Giovacchini and Bryce Boyer (1982) contains some important observations on the need for soothing, over and above the more widely discussed nurturing aspects of early maternal care. Many borderlines behave, as Giovacchini points out, as though they did not get enough of this aspect of optimal mothering. Viewed simplistically, mother soothes when she holds her infant; she nourishes when she feeds the baby. It is not always clear whether the adult borderline cases who seek treatment were truly shortchanged in one or both of these functions (perhaps the majority were); some may have had, despite adequate mothering, constitutionally driven needs of so overwhelming a nature as to leave them with the impression of not having been given enough. However this may be, such persons have intense cravings throughout life and are prone to abuse of alcohol and other substances. Rado (1956) was aware of this and named the tendency "pharmacothymia." One also sees promiscuity, shoplifting, compulsive gambling, sensation seeking; in a word, the impulsiveness that all authors agree is central to the core concept of the unstable borderline case; schizotypals are much less impulsive. Recognizing and dealing effectively (by means of limit-setting technics of various kinds) with this ofter innately excessive *craving* become important facets of any therapy destined to be effective with borderline patients. There is a wealth of material bearing on such matters in Giovacchini's book, as there was in the compendium edited by LeBoit and Capponi a few years earlier.

Barbara Brooks and, later, M. Stone (1981) were struck by the frequency of histories of incest (authentic, not fanciful) in the early lives of female (and even of some male) borderline patients. Among hospitalized cases, more than half of those in some institutions had had such experiences. Women who have been victimized in this manner, particularly by older male relatives, often develop sharply polarized and ambivalent attitudes toward men, an image of themselves as both angel and prostitute, a reckless and impulsive lifestyle, and chaotic, turbulent relationships with men, oscillating between adoration and jealous mistrustfulness. The borderline syndrome may develop, in other words, out of this destructive environmental factor, and in the absence of genetic predisposition to affective illness. The first few articles mentioning this correlation were directed toward consciousness raising within the mental-health community. The incest rate seems to be higher among borderline women than among schizophrenic women, suggesting that traumatization of this sort may have a certain specificity for the borderline syndrome and may help account for the female excess (2:1 to 3:1) in most populations of borderline patients. How best for clinicians to help correct the abnormal behavior patterns and distorted images of self and other in borderline incest victims remains to be delineated.

Advances in the psychopharmacology of borderline patients have been made during this half-decade. Often, one has the option of using no medication at all, especially with schizotypal patients. This is the route preferred by those most dedicated to an insight-oriented approach (Searles, Bryce Boyer, and, less vehemently, Kernberg). Some (DSM-3) borderline and schizotypals respond favorably, during certain phases and episodes of their illness, to neuroleptics (Serban and Siegel, 1984). Liebowitz has written extensively on the use of antidepressants, especially the MAO inhibitors, in (DSM-) borderlines (cf. Liebowitz and D. Klein, 1981). Not all agree with the proposed specificity of MAOI drugs and the borderline syndrome, but many clinicians now advocate the use of some antidepressant medication, during the initial phases especially, of any psychotherapeutic venture involving the more affectively-ill type of borderline patient.

The use of carbamazepine in cases of episodic dyscontrol, a borderline equivalent seen especially in young males with histories suggestive of organicity, has been described by Andrulonis (1981).

5. Diagnosis

Incorporation of "borderline" into DSM-3 (1980) has heightened the popularity of the definition offered there, such that it has, by the mid-1980s, come to overshadow the definitions from which it was derived; namely, those of Kernberg and Gunderson. This is both good news and bad news. The good news concerns improvement in reliability, compared with what can be achieved by clinicians who are not psychoanalytically trained who attempt to conduct structural interviews as outlined by Kernberg. The Gunderson instrument is reliable but more time consuming than the eight-item DSM checklist. The bad news concerns the unavoidable loss of depth compared to the sophistication of earlier concepts and a certain measure of confusion stemming from the simplistic guidelines of the DSM definition. Since only five of eight items are necessary for the diagnosis, one can construct a clinical situation where a patient satisfies all the criteria *except* identity disturbance, impulsiveness, and inappropriate anger. This patient could, depending upon the remainder of the clinical picture, be a DSM borderline but would be excluded by Kernberg and Gunderson. Such patients exist, and they point up the shortcomings of cookbook diagnosis. Perhaps in the 1990s the DSM (IV?, V?) will *insist* upon identity disturbance, impulsiveness, and anger as "necessary-but-not-sufficient" items, so that the "standard" definition will coincide, finally, with the 50 years of tradition that preceded it.

Another modification that should be introduced into future editions of DSM concern the label itself; in DSM-III one finds the phrase "borderline personality disorder." Borderline patients exhibit abnormalities of personality. Most are pouty and irritable; many are manipulative and demanding; some are uncommunicative, and so forth. But certain key items (identity disturbance, intolerance of being alone, unstable relationships) are not features of personality in the same, strict sense as are such true personality traits as seductiveness, generosity, pessimism, orderliness, fearfulness, etc. This is not a niggling point. As it happens, borderlines can manifest *any* of the true personality types (histrionic, narcissistic, paranoid, and avoidant, among others). Their prognosis is in large part a function of which personality dimension is predominant. For example, those with antisocial personality have abysmal outcomes; those with depressive/masochistic traits do rather well. The concept of borderline is best viewed as a syndrome or level of function. This makes the additional, and important, diagnosis of the personality profile peculiar to each borderline patient a less confusing exercise for the clinician.

Some specialists in child and adolescent psychiatry have adopted the term "borderline" for use in their clinical domains. Notable among them are Tove Aarkrog, in Copenhagen; Paulina Kernberg, Ricardo Vela, Fred Pine, Donald Cohen and Clarice Kestehbaum. Aarkrog's usage of the term corresponds mostly to a schizotypal or else to an organically damaged type of borderline patient. She is in the processs of developing a standardized questionnaire for objectifying this diagnosis, which cannot, in youngsters, rest upon the same criteria as for adults. Children have not reached the age of intimacy with a sexual partner, which can be either harmonious or, as in the Gunderson schema, disturbed; children seldom make manipulative suicide gestures. The other authors mentioned, contributors to Robson's recent book, have been concerned with this issue also. Vela and Gottlieb have proposed a set of criteria, commensurate with the developmental stages reached by a child of ten or 15, that may succeed in bringing the diagnosis of "borderline child" into a similar state of reliability as that enjoyed by the phrase "borderline adult."

6. Validation from External Frames of Reference

As diagnostic systems become more reliable, one hopes to fortify them through discovery of solid correlations with test results external to the narrow, and all too often solipsistic, realm of clinical diagnosis. Efforts made to validate the "borderline" concept have centerd on psychological tests (Kwawer, 1980). Andrulonis (1981) and Snyder (1982) find a rather characteristic pattern on the MMPI, not unlike that reported by Bliss in his multiple-personality cases. High scores are usually noted on the psychasthenia and schizophrenia scales. There does not appear as yet to be a psychological test profile unique to any one of the more narrowly definied borderline syndromes.

It was hoped that the dexamethasone-suppression test might help distinguish borderlines with serious depressive vulnerability from the non-depressive group. Carroll (1981) had already demonstrated that a significant proportion of borderlines (selected by DSM criteria) show abnormal suppression, suggesting that, at least in these patients, there is concomitant major affective illness. But the results have not yielded the neat cleavage one hoped for. Some non-depressed borderlines have a positive test; some depressed borderlines do not. The DST has proved an interesting but not a highly specific marker of depressive tendency.

The use of the sleep laboratory to study REM latency time (the interval between the onset of sleep and the first REM period) has shown more promise in ascertaining the high frequency with which vulnerability to affective illness occurs in a DSM-3 borderline population and also discriminating between manic-depression-prone borderlines (and their relatives) from borderlines that are not prone to manic depression (cf. Akiskal's article, in this anthology). Diminished latency has been noted in a high percentage of the borderlines and their first degree relatives even when the latter are not ill. If these studies are confirmed, one would have a reasonably reliable state marker (rather than merely a trait marker), capable, perhaps, of detecting in advance of symptom-outbreak—the "at risk" borderline-to-be (or MDP-prone) relatives from these not so at risk.

Grotesque dreams in which the dreamer sees himself as actually dead (and awakens surprised to be still living), or else as mutilated ("my penis is lying on the ground, and I see blood pouring out from my groin;" "I look in the ice-box and see my eyes floating in a water glass") are quite rare in neurotic patients. They are quite common in borderline cases (Stone, 1979/80) and in psychotic patients. Sometimes, during the opening phases of psychotherapy with a patient whose functional level is not easily diagnosed, a dream of this sort will be reported in advance of any clinical deterioration and may alert the therapist to the likelihood of a borderline condition, where fragility and proneness to decompensation are part of the clinical picture.

The heterogeneity, etiologically speaking, of borderline conditions as they are currently diagnosed, makes it unlikely any surefire method will be developed that can discriminate, by means of a biologic assay, borderline conditions from various other conditions in our nomenclature. Even in the attenuated forms of manic depression and schizophrenia, simple markers are not likely to emerge. The markers may assay only one enzyme system, whereas the underlying condition may be polygenic. It is possible, however, that, by the 1990s, certain results embodying a complex psychological and neurophysiological test battery may prove reliable indices of a borderline condition.

7. Prognosis

Meaningful studies of outcome in borderline patients could only come after the various diagnostic systems had achieved adequate reliability. Before the mid-1970s the few reports of follow-up were methodologically weak, diagnostically unclear, and, with respect to sample size, numerically small (the study of Gidro-Frank, Peretz and Spitzer, 1967). In the mid-1970s a study was carried out by Carpenter and his colleagues, comparing borderlines with schizophrenics. This is the first such study where methodological design and diagnostic criteria were of high quality and where outcome was evaluated systematically in relation to several variables (nine were selected, including "quality of social contacts," "quality of useful work," and "fullness of life"). The Carpenter study showed surprisingly little difference in outcome at five years between the two patient groups, apart from the "quality of social contacts," where the borderlines did better. There was also a trend toward more continuous useful employment in the borderlines. Two weaknesses of this study concern the small sample size and the relatively short follow-up period.

The sample size was impressive (N = 446) and the average interval equally so (15 years) that were followed in the study of McGlashan (1984). His work will almost surely be included among the "classic" papers by the time another anthology on the Borderline is drawn together in the future. Though the patients were evaluated with respect to contemporary diagnostic criteria for borderline, the focus of the study was on schizophrenia. The chart-abstract and follow-up sample consisted of 163 schizophrenics and 81 borderlines, along with 44 unipolar and 19 bipolar affective cases. As would be expected, the schizophrenics scored higher in the schizotypal realm of DSM3/Axis II; the affectively ill, higher in the DSM-borderline realm. Part II of McGlashan's report compares the outcome in the schizophrenics with that noted in the affective group (containing but not coextensive with the borderline cases). Space does not permit a detailed presentation of his findings, but, of particular interest, it was noted that " . . . roughly two-thirds of the schizophrenics were functioning marginally or worse . . . compared with one-third of the unipolar cohort. The reverse held for better outcomes" (p. 586). McGlashan found that the outcome varied little in relation to the time interval, for all diagnostic categories. That is, if one were doing well at seven years, one was apt to be doing well at 15, etc. When global outcome was assessed according to the Menninger Health Sickness Rating Scale (100 = optimal; 0 = worst), the mean follow-up score for the 163 schizophrenics was 37; for the 44 unipolar (a proportion of whom were also "borderline"), 60.

Just underway at the time of this writing is the editor's follow-up study of all the patients admitted for long-term intensive psychotherapy to New York State Psychiatric Institute between 1963 and 1976. This sample of 564 patients is composed chiefly (about two-thirds) of (Kernberg-) borderlines, many of whom also fulfill DSM and Gunderson criteria. The remainder consists of schizophrenics, schizoaffective and schizophreniform patients, and a small number of unipolar and psy-chotic-level recurrent or atypical depressives. The latter all were classed as "psychotic" from a psychostructural viewpoint. Thus far 240 patients have been traced. The Global Assessment Scale ratings (the scale is a derivative of the Menninger ratings and also uses 100 points) show a mean of 65 for the borderlines; 46 for the psychotic group. The latter group showed two peaks: the taller one in the 30's (signifying marginal function); the other in the 50's (signifying adequate function but with noticeable symptoms or difficulties in several key areas). The suicides (GAS Score = 0) were not averaged in with the other patients' scores, so as not to make the still-living psychotic patients appear worse, on average, than they were. Among the initially psychotic patients 21 suicides have been detected; in the larger border-line group, only ten. The peak in the 30's represented classic schizophrenia.

My observations concerning time-interval of assessment is mostly in accord with McGlashan's, but I note some important exceptions. Schiz-ophrenics (who formed the bulk of the Chestnut Lodge study) tend to reach a low plateau of function soon after discharge from a hospital and to remain over the years approximately at that level. Many borderlines reach a higher plateau, and remain stably at that level. But some bor-derlines, especially those who were markedly impulsive and prone to suicide gestures on admission, show a less smooth course after dis-charge. Several, for example, became, for a time, confirmed alcoholics, led chaotic lives, all but disappearing from conventional society. At a certain point, which might be as long as ten years after hospitalization, they stumbled onto Alcoholics Anonymous, met someone who cared a great deal for them, and not only achieved sobriety but turned their lives around dramatically. One such patient completed an advanced degree, married, started a family and lives a life indistinguishable from his neighbors and colleagues. There is an element of luck here, but it is the kind of luck that is more apt to visit an attractive, socially comfort-able, intelligent though recklessly impulsive borderline person than an attractive, intelligent, not particularly impulsive, but socially eccentric and inordinately reclusive schizophrenic person. Among the border-lines, it appears, intensive therapy sometimes triumphed and sometimes failed miserably. Where it failed, life would occasionally rush in to rescue what had once looked like an unsalvageable case. The greater frequency with which therapy seemed beneficial and the greater frequency with which rescuers external to the treatment situation eventually saved the day are conducive, it would appear, to the superior outcome in the borderlines. If one had conducted only a five-year follow-up, as in the Carpenter study, some of the borderlines in my series would still have been mired in social chaos and occupational doldrums, not as yet having either met their potential rescuer or found their true calling.

One might have hoped that the follow-up studies would answer such crucial questions as "Does therapy help?" in borderline patients, and if so, "What kind?" The Menninger study led by Kernberg in the 1970s, comparing ambulatory borderlines with schizophrenics, submitted credible evidence that borderlines did better with an expressive, transference-focused psychotherapy, whereas schizophrenics tended to become more disorganized when exposed to this approach. They did better when a supportive technic was used. But this study does not indicate whether some other approach would offer still better results in the borderlines. Randomized, controlled studies, using two or more technics, are hard to carry out because patients who suffer intensely (as do most borderline and psychotic persons at the height of their illness) resist being randomized or "wait-listed." Brief follow-ups are less confusing (as to what factors contributed to outcome) but less informative (some borderlines who were about to show a spurt of improvement will not have reached their turning-point). Long follow-up studies are more informative as to outcome, but, of course, harder to interpret, thanks to all the intervening variables over the years, the effects of which may overshadow the effects, if any, of the initial therapy (such as meeting a special person, referral to the "right" therapist, inheriting a lot of money, the death of an important figure in one's life, having a disastrous love affair, suffering a physical injury—to mention but a few).

For these reasons, the long-term studies are more valuable for their commentary upon the natural history of the various conditions than for any power to unlock the secrets of whether and how psychotherapy works. Knowing the natural history is in itself of great value since it provides the clinician with prognostic clues that are apt to be more accurate than the customary hunches. For instance, in the "P.I." sample, the suicide-rate among the first 113 borderlines traced (in a ten- to

20-year follow up) was 8.9 percent—higher than I had imagined before beginning this inquiry, but still considerably lower that the rate observed among the initially psychotic patients.

As to the efficacy of long-term, intensive, analytically oriented therapy for borderlines, I have the impression (as do some of the former patients) that it turned their life around for the better in a certain percentage of the cases, while in others it accomplished little. Considering the gravity of the symptoms in these patients, most of whom were in their late teens or early twenties, it was well worth the effort, and occasionally seemed to work miracles. Many who have devoted their professional lives to this effort feel the same way, and have anecdotes by the dozens to support our claim. I believe there is something more at work here than mere loyalty to a cherished system or a revered teacher. But I know that, scientifically, I cannot prove this claim to any skeptical audience (the faithful, of course, require no proof . . .). Here is a work for the 90's or the . . . (whatever it is that one calls the years 00 to 09!)

8. Overviews

Review articles on borderline states (whether DSM- defined, schizotypal, etc.) and overview chapters in monographs and books have proliferated at about the same rapid pace as the burgeoning borderline literature has itself grown. From the 1970s, one has Mack's historical perspective (1975); later, my reviews (1980;1981) as introductory chapters in two books on the borderline.

In French, there is an outstanding article by Bourgeois (1980) outlining the systems of Kernberg, Gunderson, Wolberg, Masterson, and Bergeret. The proximity of Bergeret's conception to that of Grinker's "anaclitic depressed" borderline (Type IV or the "border with neurosis" is spelled out very clearly here. Bourgeois discusses all aspects of treatment: psychotherapy, chemotherapy, hospitalization, and comments on sociocultural factors as well. Several of the reviewers touch on the question whether borderline conditions are, like anorexia nervosa, becoming truly more common or are merely becoming diagnosed more often because of shifts in terminological popularity.

In German, there is the handy volume by the Swiss, Battegay (1981), who offers brief clinical vignettes of every imaginable subtype of borderline: the paranoid borderline, the drug-craving borderline, the suicidal borderline, the narcissistic borderline, the schizoid, the phobic, and so forth. The review of Sass and Koehler, "Grenzgebiet oder Niemansland?" ("Borderline Region of No Mans Land?") focuses on important nosological issues. The theory of psychoanalytic psychotherapy of borderlines is summarized well by Kernberg (1982).

The last word has not been said on borderline conditions, either in the realm of diagnoses or of treatment, although Buie and Adler recently published an article which, in a burst of modesty, they entitled "Definitive Treatment of the Borderline Personality" (1982). Theirs is a useful, though perhaps, less than definitive, exposition of analytic therapy from a Kohutian point of view. A more definitive statement has been made by Meissner (1984) in his thoughtful and richly documented text on the current state of analytic therapy for borderlines.

Despite the best efforts of Kernberg, Kohut, Meissner, Chessick, Giovacchini, and others to keep borderlines corraled, as it were, within psychoanalytic boundaries (as a group of patients best treated by a modified analytic approach), the borderline concept has gotten away from them. DSM's definition has led the unaware into applying the label to all manner of patients who bear not the remotest resemblance to the original cases of the analytic literature. Juvenile delinquents are suddenly borderline. Any nondelusional person in a hospital is borderline. For all this, there remains an important subgroup within this new and overpopulated realm where the recommendations of the above-mentioned analytic writers are altogether appropriate. I would hope that by the 1990s, the characteristics not just of borderline cases but of those amenable to analytically oriented psychotherapy will have been further defined, refined, and widely publicized, so that there would be less in the way of inappropriate referrals for such treatment and less in the way of such treatment being applied on behalf of borderline patients who do not fit its mould. Borderline patients, to take but one example, who have been traumatized repeatedly during childhood via parental physical brutality or incestuous overtures or acts, may start out in expressive therapy, only later to fade away from continuation of the work, under various pretexts, because they find the opening up of the old wounds too searingly painful. Very few such patients have the courage, the perseverance, and the personality "assets" requisite to the task. I mention "assets" because, without marketable skills, a stable and intimate relationship to fall back on etc., there would not be enough gratifications in the patient's life to offset the pain of reexperiencing the old horrors, on the way to a healthier integration. A patient must be (or soon get to be) more than half well to tolerate depth-therapy. When morbidity is to health as the desert is to one of its small oases, the terrain is not likely to become green. It is to Meissner's credit that in his new book on the borderline spectrum (1984), he is not only aware of this issue, but offers concrete guidelines as to which borderline patients are potentially analyzable, and which, not. Meissner's conclusions are summarized in the following extract.

1. Some borderline patients are potentially analyzable, but these cases would seem to fall in the group of higher-order borderlines.
2. The extent of the ego-defect, the capacity for object relations, and the vulnerability to regression must be carefully assessed. Significant impediments in any of these areas would contraindicate analysis.
3. The capacity to form a meaningful therapeutic alliance and the quality of motivation are particularly important areas.
4. An adequate assessment cannot be made on an acute basis or in terms of the nature or intensity of symptoms. The assessment of analyzability requires enough time to evaluate the patient's usual level of characterological functioning . . . (Meisnner, pp. 296-297).

* * *

As I notice myself penning this review of reviews, I am haunted by the dark suspicion that the subject has gotten out of hand. The borderline literature has swollen to a size too vast to be digested by one anthologist. I hope I have made the developments in this field over the past century clearer to the reader than they were before. Much remains unclear even so—but, as for that, another century lies ahead.

18. A Study of the Separation-Individuation Process

Margaret S. Mahler

The question of the kind of inferences, if any, that can be drawn from preverbal material in and outside the psychoanalytic situation is a most controversial one. It is, I feel, a very interesting issue, yet quite difficult to deal with. Precisely because verbal means lend themselves only very poorly to the translation of such material, most researchers have seen fit to create a new language, often filled with metaphors, in order to communicate their findings to others.

EARLY DEVELOPMENT IN OBSERVATIONAL RESEARCH

Psychoanalytic observational research of the first years of life touches on the essence of reconstruction and on the problem of coenesthetic empathy, both so essential for the clinical efficiency of psychoanalysis.

At one end of the spectrum of opinion on these questions stand those who believe in innate, complex oedipal fantasies, those who, like Melanie Klein and her followers, assume and rely on earliest extrauterine (human) mental life. They believe in a quasi-phylogenetic memory, an inborn symbolic process. For them, no phenomenological, behavioral data can have sufficient validity to refute their *a priori* convictions about complex mental positions, such as the schizoid position in the fourth month of life, or the depressive position at 8 months.

At the other end of the spectrum stand those among us Freudian analysts who look with favor on stringent verbal and reconstructive evidence. We organize these on the basis of Freud's metapsychological constructs; yet some of us seem to accord preverbal material no right to serve as the basis for even the most cautious and tentative extension of our main body of hypotheses, unless these, too, be supported by reconstruction, that is to say, by clinical and, of course, predominantly verbal material.

Yet Freud's hope was that his fundamental body of theory—that truly monumental basis of clinical and theoretical work—would remain a *living heritage*. Even his genius could not work out every detail in one lifetime; these, added bit by bit, should eventually coalesce to form a general psychology.

Instead of entering into the controversy on whether or not preverbal infant observation has any validity for drawing inferences about the evolution of *intrapsychic* human life, I would like to present an account of one such effort. I do so in order to show what possible inferences were permitted from some of the repetitive, fairly regularly occurring clusterings of the data, which we accumulated around our tentative working hypotheses.

I will put aside the history of my work and descriptions of our methods and proceed to some observations made, and inferences drawn, from my more recent studies at the Masters Children's Center and in the psychoanalytic situation.

Beyond the conceptualization of the subphases of the separation-individuation[1] process, we have made additional observations relevant to substantive issues of the study. They are repetitive, if not ubiquitous, age-specific clusterings of behavioral sequences and affective reactions found in our children between 5 and 36 months of age. These were polarized by the mother-child interaction during their coenesthetic[2] period of life, and continued in individually more and more differentiated sequences and reactions into the period Spitz has called the "diacritic organization."[3]

First Substantive Issue. We observed the bridge function of mother-related parts of the familiar inanimate surroundings of our nursery of our infants—for example, the chair on which mother habitually sat or her handbag and so on. The infant, within a certain age span, turned to these objects as substitues for the mother when she left the room, rather than to another adult. This mechanism we recognized as a transitional

---

[1] I owe the term *separation-individuation* to Dr. Annemarie Weil's suggestion to point out clearly the two aspects of this intrapsychic process (personal communication, 1954).

[2] *Coenesthesia* is defined in Drever's *Dictionary of Psychology* as: common sensibility, the total undifferentiated mass of sensations derived from the body as a whole, but more particularly, the internal organs.

[3] *Diacritic*—from the Greek—is "to distinguish, to separate across" (cf. Spitz, 1945).

phenomenon between Kestenberg's (1971) organ-object bridges, Winnicott's (1953) transitional, and Greenacre's (1969, 1970) fetishlike objects.

Second Substantive Issue. We observed in life and on film a differential, truly coenesthetic response to the *warmth* and *turgor,* to the "feel" of the human body (molding phenomena [Mahler and La Perriere, 1965], tactile and visual exploration of the human face and similar behaviors) quite different from their handling of inanimate objects (Mahler and McDevitt, 1968). The inverted and grossly distorted response to the animate and inanimate object world in psychosis was described by Sechehaye (1947), Mahler (1960), Searles (1960), and others.

Third Substantive Issue. Our data have indicated the importance of the "carrying power," as it were, of the young child's "confident expectation" (Benedek, 1938) as contrasted with some children's "basic mistrust," to use Erikson's term (1950). This we saw in some children as early as 6 or 7 months. We observed children of the same mother at comparable ages, one of whom showed minimal stranger anxiety and optimal basic trust; the other, increased stranger anxiety and a lack of basic trust.

One tries to understand these variations by way of the siblings' different endownment on the one hand and, on the other, through the prevalent emotional climate of the particular mother-infant relationship, as observed in their interaction and through interviews with the mother (cf. Weil, 1970).

This phenomenon of "confident expectation," as well as its oppositve—more than optimal stranger anxiety and "basic mistrust"—contributes and relates to later attitudes in life, even though intervening drive and defense vicissitudes will, of course, greatly influence and may even change these patterns.

Fourth Substantive Issue. The basic mood, our study indicated, appeared to have its beginning as early as the last half of the second year. It seemed to derive substantially from this very "basic trust" or, in contrast, from "basic mistrust"; as I have described (1966), it also derived from a too sudden deflation of the obligatory infantile belief in the own and the borrowed magic omnipotence (Jacobson, 1953).

Our research design had built into it brief, passive separation experiences, experiments as it were. Once a week, a senior worker assigned to a particular mother-child pair interviewed the mother in a room outside the nursery.

From the infant's reactions to these brief separations I believe that we were able to judge fairly how the infant's "need" became a "wish" in Max Schur's sense (1966). Our data indicated the phenomenological concomitants of the development from an "unspecific craving" to the specific "object-bound" affect of "longing" (Mahler, 1961, 1963). This seemed to occur gradually and had, at first, a "waxing and waning" quality. It had its beginnings at the height of bodily differentiation from the love object and continued into the practicing period of 10 to 15 months. At the age "longing" is indicated by the phenomenon of *"low-keyedness"* during brief separations. This culminates—during the *rapprochement* period at 15 to 25 months—in impressive, individually different reactions to mother's absences, which are much more specific and readable.

The smoothly separating and individuating toddler easily finds solace in his rapidly developing ego functions. The child concentrates on practicing mastery of his own skills and autonomous capacities.

During this practicing subphase of separation-individuation, one can occasionally see with particular clarity that the intrapsychic process of separation and individuation runs on two intertwined, but not always synchronized developmental tracks: one is *individuation*—the evolution of intrapsychic autonomy; the other is the intrapsychic *separation* process, which runs along the track of differentiation, distancing, boundary-structuring, and disengagement from mother.

As I indicated elsewhere, in a study such as ours, one learns most when elements of the process are "out of kilter."

Brief Comparative Developmental Histories of Barney and Sammy

I shall illustrate this with two brief vignettes.

Barney, whose maturational process enabled him to achieve upright locomotion precociously at 9 months of age, had the opportunity, by endowment and by the nature of the mother-child relationship, to take into and integrate in his early ego structure certain patterns of the mother-child relationship, and eject, i.e., externalize, others. He also seemed to have ample opportunity to emulate and eventually to identify with his father, who was very much a hero for him by the last half of the second year. Barney's mother emphasized this again and again.

Barney's early darting away from his mother with the expectation of being chased by her had interesting components of the mother-child as well as of the father-child relationship.

The contrasting mother-child pair, *Sammy* and his mother, had a greatly prolonged symbiotic and—on the mother's part—parasitic relationship. His mother breast-fed Sammy for 1½ years. Both parents kept him in continual dependency. Confined to a small area by his own, partly constitutional, partly environmental, delay in locomotor capacity, Sammy made the most extensive use of his visibly emerging perceptive, cognitive, and prehensile faculties. He occupied and amused himself alone in our playpen for long periods of time when his mother was out of the room. This he did at an age when children of comparable age would vigorously protest against such confinement. He willingly engaged others and accepted their active comforting, which other children would not. He did not show any sign of low-keyedness or of specific longing at the age at which we observed such phenomena in other children. (Such behavior appeared delayed in Sammy.)

The normal child's early defensive struggle against interferences with his autonomy was, however, amply exemplified by Sammy. He valiantly struggled, from an early age, in fact, from the fifth month on and attempted to extricate himself from the smothering grip of his mother (cf. Spock, 1963).

Most of the time children in the practicing period appeared relatively elated and self-sufficient. They became low-keyed only when they became aware that mother was absent from the room. In those instances their gestural and performance motility slowed down, their interest in their surroundings diminished; they appeared to be preoccupied with inwardly concentrated attention, with what Rubinfine (1961) called "imaging." This we were permitted to assume from behavioral evidence: (1) when another person than the mother actively tried to comfort the child, he would lose his intrapsychic balance and burst into tears; and, of course, also from (2) the child's reaction to reunion with the briefly absent mother. The low-keyedness and apparent "imaging" of mother, I tend to interpret at the attempt to hold on to a state of mind that

Sandler et at. (1963) have termed "the ideal state of self." This seems to consist of a symbiotic closeness, completeness, a coenesthetically sensed dual unity with mother.

Separation Anxiety

Some children transiently appeared quite overwhelmed by fear of object loss, so that the "ego-filtered affect of longing was in danger of very abruptly turning into desperate crying. This was the case with Barney for a short time at a period when his "individuation" had not yet caught up with this maturational spurt of locomotion, serving separation. He was unable to cope emotionally, for a while, with the experience of the self-induced separations from mother in space. He was visibly bewildered when he hurt himself and noticed that his mother was not, automatically, close.

Our data, in their rich detail, have unmistakably shown regularly occurring combinations of factors from which we were permitted to conclude that there was a dawning awareness that the still-symbiotic mothering half of the self was missed. The ensuing behavior of low-keyedness had different shadings in individual children compared with each other and with themselves over time. In a paper written with McDevitt (1968) I likened this initial "low-keyedness" with the "conservation-withdrawal" of monkeys as described by Charles Kaufman and L. A. Rosenblum (1967).

This longing for the state of well-being and unity, or closeness, with mother we found peculiarly lacking in children whose symbiotic relationship had been an unduly prolonged or a disturbed one: in Sammy, who had an exaggeratedly close, parasitic symbiosis with his mother; in another child, a little girl (Harriet), in whom the mother-infant relationship was what Robert Fliess (1961) termed *a*-symbiotic. It seemed diminished and irregular in children in whom the symbiotic relationship with mother was marred by the unpredictability and impulsivity of a partly engulfing and partly rejecting mother.

In the course of the practicing period, we were impressed by the tremendously exhilarating, truly dramatic effect that upright locomotion had on the hitherto also very busy quadruped infant's general mood! I became aware of its importance for the achievement of the "psychological birth experience," the "hatching," through unexpected, regularly occurring observations of behavioral sequences, comparing them with Phyllis Greenacre's work (1957) on the childhood of the artist. It seemed to me that most practicing toddlers had a "love affair with the world" as well!

This exhilaration occurred later than usual in those cases where the ascendancy of the child's free locomotor capacity was delayed. Thus, this phenomenon seemed definitely connected with and dependent on the function of free locomotor activity of the ego.

With this acquisition of exhilarating upright, free locomotion and the closely following attainment of that stage of cognitive development that Piaget (1936) regards as the beginning of representational intelligence, the human being has emerged as a separate and autonomous being. These two powerful "organizers" (Spitz, 1959) seem to be the midwives of *psychological birth*. With this "hatching" process the toddler reaches the first level of identity, that of being a separate individual entity (Mahler, 1957).

Now that the child has come to be more aware of his separate self, he has once again an increased need to seek closeness with mother. This had been, so to speak, held in abeyance throughout the practicing period. That is why I gave this subphase the name *rapprochement*.

Importance of the Emotional Availability of Mother and Disengagement from Her in the Rapprochement Subphase

One cannot emphasize too strongly the importance of the optimal emotional availability of the mother during this subphase. The value of the father in this period has been stressed by Loewwald (1951), Greenacre (1966), and Abelin (1971).

The refueling type of bodily approach described by Furer,[4] which characterized the practicing infant, was now replaced in the period between 15 and 25 months by interaction of toddler and mother on a much higher level; symbolic language, vocal and other intercommunications, as well as play became increasingly prominent (Galenson, 1971.

We observed separation reactions in all our children during this rapprochement subphase. And I would venture the hypothesis that it is in those children whose separation reactions are characterized by mod-

---

[4] Personal communication.

erate and ego-filtered affects, in which the libidinal valence—love instead of aggression—predominated, that subsequent development is more likely to be favorable.

Through this rapprochement process, the sense of identity, the self representation as distinct from the object representation, begins to become consolidated.

Two characteristic patterns of behavior—the shadowing of mother and the darting away from her with the expectation of being chased and swept into her arms—indicate the toddler's wish for reunion with the love object, and, side-by-side with this, also a fear of re-engulfment. One can continually observe the warding-off pattern against impingement upon the toddler's recently achieved autonomy. Moreover, the incipient fear of loss of love represents an element of the conflict on the way to internalization. Some toddlers of rapprochement age already seem to be rather sensitive to disapproval. Autonomy is defended by the "no" as well as by the increased aggression and negativism of the anal phase. (One is reminded of Anna Freud's classic paper on negativism and emotional surrender [1951].)

In most mother-toddler pairs, these rapprochement conflicts, which McDevitt calls the *rapprochement crises*, do finally come to an end. This is helped by the developmental spurt of the conflict-free parts of the autonomous ego (Hartmann, 1939). These then, in the third year, help the child in his progress toward the attainment of libidinal object constancy, in Hartmann's sense (1952).

During the time of normal symbiosis, the narcissistically fused object is felt to be "good," i.e., in harmony with the symbiotic self, so that primary identification takes place under a positive valence of love. Later on, after separation, the child may have encountered "bad," frustrating, unpleasurable, even frightening experiences in his interaction with mother and "other," so that the image of the object may have assumed a "negative emotional valence" (Heimann, 1966).

The Role of Aggression and the Defense Mechanism of Splitting the Object World into "Good" and "Bad"

The less gradually the intrapsychic separation-individuation process takes place, and the less the modulating, negotiating function of the ego gains ascendancy, the greater the extent to which the object remains an unassimilated foreign body, a "bad" introject in the intrapsychic emotional economy. In the effort to eject this "bad" introject, derivatives of the aggressive drive come into play and there seems to develop an increased proclivity to identify with, or to confuse, the self representation with the "bad" introject. If this situation prevails during the rapprochement subphase, then aggression may be unleashed in such a way as to inundate or sweep away the "good" object, and with it the "good" self representation. This would be indicated by early, severe temper tantrums, for example, in children in whom the too sudden and painful realization of their helplessness results in the too abrupt deflation of their previous sense of their own and shared magic omnipotence (in Edith Jacobson's sense, 1964).

I observed many of our normal children recoil, or show signs that had to be interpreted as a kind of erotized fear, on being cornered by an adult who wanted to seek, often playfully, bodily contact with the child. This seemed to be felt as overwhelming by the toddler because of the adult's sheer bodily size and strength.

These behaviors remind us of the fear of re-engulfment by the by-then already somehow contaminated, dangerous "mother of separation" in whose omnipotence the child still believes, but who does not seem to let him share in her omnipotence anymore.

There were other early constellations of variables, which may represent fixation points for pathological regression, such as the precocious differentiation of a "false self" (Winnicott, 1965) by a little girl (Heather), who played peek-a-boo with herself when her mother rejected her because she was a late walker; or the narcissistic hypercathexis of the body ego in the case of Harriet, a child whose mother did not seem to have enough tender emotion for her children, but rather overstimulated them. All these constellations of factors are possible contributories to borderline features in personality development.

In incipient infantile neurosis, conflict is indicated by coercive behaviors directed toward the mother, designed to force her to function as the child's omnipotent extension. This alternates with signs of desperate clinging. In other words, in those children with less than optimal development, the ambivalence conflict is discernible during the rapprochement subphase in rapidly alternating clinging and increased negativistic behaviors. This may be in some cases a reflection of the fact that the chid has split the object world, more permanently than is optimal, into "good" and "bad." By means of this splitting, the "good" object is defended against the derivatives of the aggressive drive.

These mechanisms, coercion and splitting of the objet world, are characteristic in most cases of borderline transference. We were able to study these in the verbal, primary process material of a few children at the end of their second and during their third year of life. These mechanisms, along with the problem of finding what the late Maurice Bouvet (1958) described as the "optimal distance," may prevail as early as in the fourth subphase of separation-individuation at a time when "libidinal object constancy" should have been achieved and separation reactions be receding.

Disturbances during the rapprochement subphase are likely to reappear in much more definite and individually different forms during the final phase of that process in which a unified self representation should become demarcated from a blended and integrated object representation.

The clinical outcome of these rapprochement crises will be determined by: (1) the development toward libidinal object constancy; (2) the quantity and quality of later disappointments (stress traumata); (3) possible shock traumata; (4) the degree of castration anxiety; (5) the fate of the oedipus complex; and (6) the developmental crises of adolescence—all of which function within the context of the individual's constitutional endowment.

Two Important Findings

During the years of our data collection, we classified and sorted the material and ordered it into distinct categories that were relevant to our working hypotheses.

One interesting yield of our data processing was the finding that, from 16 or 17 months on, the data no longer "fit" comfortably into discrete categories. It began to appear increasingly arbitrary to describe any one item of behavior without referring to more and more of the total array of behaviors that were to be seen in the child at a particular period of time. It seemed that the behavior of the child was becoming increasingly integrated.

That also meant that early affectomotor and preverbal sensorimotor patterns had already been integrated by the middle of the second year, solidly enough, so that derivatives could not be reconstructively traced back, step-by-step, by means of deduction. In other words, we learned inductively that in most individuals the derivatives of the early, pre-verbal, sensorimotor period became integrated into character structure.

The second observation during data processing had to do with sex differences. Until this point, the children often seemed to us to fit into various subgroups from the separation-individuation point of view— subgroups containing both boys and girls. But now while, on the one hand, the complexity of the children made it difficult to group them, on the other hand, those common traits that existed were suggestive of a growing trend toward sexual differentiation and identity formation.

In average development, as I indicated in my Brill Memorial Lecture (1963), the progressive forces of the growing ego are astonishingly successful. Often they tend to even out most of the discrepancies and minor deviations.

It is precisely the deficiencies of integration and internalization which will leave residua and thus may manifest themselves in borderline mechanisms, which indicate a degree of failure of the synthetic function of the ego.

EARLY DEVELOPMENT RECONSTRUCTED

I should emphasize, however, as others and I myself have done before, that in terms of reconstruction in the psychoanalytic situation in general, none of the phenomena that can be reconstructed from unintegrated residua will be an equivalent repetition, a replica as it were, of early developmental sequences of the preverbal phase.

One must expect that reconstructions will always contain telescoped screen memories and defense formations that have been altered by subsequent progressive development, as well as by regressive changes in the instinctual drives, in the ego, and in the super-ego. These may, or may not, make their appearance in the verbal and nonverbal material.

For many borderline phenomena, one can apply what is learned from observation, not so much to content as to general behaviors and atti-tudes of the patient in the psychoanalytic situation, that is to say, to certain configurations, persistent transference or acting out-patterns which seem to be the outcome of unresolved conflicts of the separation-individuation process.

My intention, at first, was to establish in this paper a linking up, in neat detail, of the described substantive issues with specific aspects of borderline phenomena shown by child and adult patients in the psychoanalytic situation. But I have come to be more and more convinced that there is no "direct line" from the deductive use of borderline phenomena to one or another substantive finding of observational research.

It cannot be accidental, however, that in the literature it is the borderline pathology that authors single out as a paradigmatic of fixation or regression, traceable to certain aspects of the formative events of the separation and individuation process (Kohut, 1966; Tartakoff, 1966; Kernberg, 1967; Frijling-Schreuder, 1969).

The literature abounds in papers and symposia dealing with the sequelae of the failure of internalization, increased separation anxiety, and other clinical signs that indicate, for example, the following: that the blending and synthesis of "good" and "bad" self and object images have not been achieved; that ego-filtered affects have become inundated by surplus unneutralized aggression; that delusions of omnipotence alternate with utter dependency and self denigration; that the body image has become or remains suffused with unneutralized id-related erogeneity and aggressive, pent-up body feelings, and so on.

Before I proceed to my case illustration, I would like to single out two main additional propositions which seem to me relevant for the understanding of borderline phenomena in the psychoanalytic situation. One is the importance of reconciliation and thus of integration of the image of the erstwhile "good" symbiotic mother, whom we long for "from the cradle on to the grave," this image to become blended with the representation of the ambivalently loved—dangerous because potentially re-engulfing—"mother after separation."

I also wish to point out my impression—just an impression—gained of the importance of the preoedipal father's role in the sample that we have studied. We gained the impression that he was not only the "awakener from sleep" (Lewin, 1952), but also the protector from the by-then, in so many cases, contaminated (Kris, 1954), potentially overwhelming "mother of separation."

The second proposition refers to the erogeneity of the body image, its suffusion with narcissistic cathexis (Schur, 1955). This seems to be due to a disturbed cathectic balance of libido distribution between the self and the object. I found a group of borderline phenomena which seems to be related to heightened body narcissism, focal and diffuse erogeneity of the body image, prevalent in many borderline features of male and female patients alike.

If there was major failure of integration during the first three subphases of separation-individuation, particularly on the level of gender identity, the child might not have taken autonomous, representationally clearly separated possession of his or her own bodily self, this partly because he or she did not experience the mother's gradual relinquishment of her possession of the toddler's body (Anna Freud, 1952, 1953; Hoffer, 1950a, 1950b; Greenson, 1945). Such male and female patients alike will ever so often act out in the transference and in life, especially in marriage, the unconscious role of a cherished or rejected part of the parent's hypothetical body-self ideal, or treat the spouse's body as a cherished or rejected organ of their own self (Stein, 1956).

Let me cite only one example of borderline phenomena in the psychoanalytic situation.

Mr. A., an unmarried man in his late 20s, and an only child, was one of those patients who demonstrated as well as unconsciously acted out man's eternal search for the "good symbiotic mother," so as to latch on to her, to be united with her, to be "safe" with her. The basic importance of this archaic mechanism has been described by the Hungarian analyst Imre Hermann (1936). In many cases the so-called primordial transference (Stone, 1961) is found to contain this basic longing for reunion with the symbiotic mother—with the search for her in fantasy after intrapsychic separation had severed the tie with her.

My patient, Mr. A., after a period of analysis, during which he occasionally complained bitterly that he could not feel close to or relate to the analyst, or to anybody else, gave vent to his great resentment, and every so often his rage against his superiors, his contemporaries, his father, his mother, and of course also his analyst. They had all "let him down; they just expected too much of him." His mother, in particular, was impossible to please, she was unloving, undemonstrative, and so on. His anger was readily turned back upon the self.

In the midst of these "grievance sessions," in which self-accusations and self-denigration played just as prominent a role as his complaints about people, there were by contrast, but only on rare occasions, hours in which he saw the object world and himself in a rather rosy light. On those days his grandiose fantasies (Kohut, 1968) easily came through, and his transference feelings swung from despondency and self-denigration to childlike admiration for and unqualified overestimation of others—particularly his analyst (Greenacre, 1966). In real life he showed a more adequate evaluation of his real worth and of his truly excellent endowment, but in his transference neurosis his mood swings were extreme, as was his belief in his own magic omnipotence and that of analysis itself, although both collapsed from one day to another (We owe the description of this mechanism to Edith Jacobson, 1953, 1957, 1964, 1967).

During a long stretch of analysis, two screen memories stood out. I believe that these will be better conveyed if they are interwoven with and discussed in the light of the working-through process.

In one of these all-too-rare "good hours" (Kris, 1956), the patient brought out—this time with an amazing array of rather libidinally cathected strong affects dominated by muted anxiety and longing—the helplessness and misery of the episodes that we knew so well as screen memories: his helplessness and lonesome desperation when as a schoolboy he had been wheeled away from his parents into the operating room and another traumatic episode when he had been banished from the parental bed.

The impact of his upsurging affects was connected in the transference with his apprehension about being taken from and thus losing the analyst by the demands of his job.

He indicated that when he was lying on the couch, he would feel himself floating far away into space. He associated this feeling with those he had had when he was anaesthesized and also with man's flight into space away from his safe anchorage on earth. Both groups of associations shook him up considerably. At the end of the hour he seemed to be literally collapsed and miserable. In spite of his tall, imposing stature he became little more than a small heap of misery— an abandoned child. His body narcissism was greatly increased, and counterphobic mechanisms became prominent as a way of fending off his hypochondriacal preoccupations.

In one of the succeeding hours, the patient, in one of his characteristic mood swings, announced that he definitely wanted to sit up; he said this with what was for him unusual determination. "When I lie down, I get this floating feeling again, as if I am floating far away from you into space." The feeling he experienced during anaesthesia, of the stars and rockets overhead falling upon him, piercing his skin, was related to the prickly feeling in his limbs that he had felt before falling asleep at the onset of anesthesia. He considered man's ambition to land on another planet to be the culmination of his detachment from earth, a demonstration of the possibility that man would never achieve anchorage again.

These fantasies were associated with the other affect-laden screen memory as well; his mother, who had until then allowed him to snuggle up to her and occupy his father's bed, had told him one day that he was now too big a boy for such intimacy. He insisted that this had occurred when he was not yet 3 years old.

The predominant nightly fear of his early childhood had reappeared during his anesthesia. There was the little dark man of his early nightmares, sitting on his shoulder, grinning unmercifully and thus indicating that "he was about to kidnap me." He desperately wanted his father—not his mother—to come to his rescue with a flashlight, as he had indeed done during the patient's early childhood, so as to dispel his son's night terrors.

During the hour in which he sat up, the patient, with averted gaze, expressed his past longing to throw his arms around his mother's neck and to be told by her that everything will be all right! He now felt the same way about his analyst, and he dreaded, when lying down, the vivid sensation that he was about to float away into space. At times, he said, the distance between the analyst and himself became too threatening.

Fear of the grinning, dark little man, who had perched on his shoulder during anesthesia, seemed to have originated at the height of the phallic phase; it occurred coincidentally with or subsequently to the time when he had been banned by his mother from his snuggling position beside her. The fear of the little dark man was, of course, overdetermined. The homunculus symbolized his body as a whole, detached—banished—from his anchorage at his mother's body. It also symbolized many other elements.

Ever since that very early occurrence of being banished, the patient felt that he could not approach his mother; she was hard, forbidding, and critical of him. He could not share with her. He had had the urge to run away from home and search—but *for what* and *where?* Until his analysis during his adult life he used to wander aimlessly in the streets or take endless drives without any goal—away from people.

Fixation to the rapprochement subphase of development seemed to be quite obvious and convincing. His splitting of the object world was overdetermined; it consisted basically of searching for the good symbiotic mother as contrasted with the forbidding "bad" mother after separation. The bad castrated and castrating, yet phallic woman's forbidding quality was projected onto the "bad outside world," and his relationships with women were marred by a fear of being engulfed by them. The competitive, but admired, protective, "good" masculine world as represented by his father was pitted against this "bad mother of separation."

After this sequence of analysis he again brought out, but with attenuated guilt feelings, his death wishes concerning the "mother of separation." She was standing in the way of his pallike relationship to his father. This came to the fore with appropriate affective cathexis and could be connected by him with many of the subsequent vicissitudes of his instinctual drives, conflicts around the two levels of his identity, and the adverse fate of his originally quite adequate "basic trust" (Mahler, 1957).

His main primordial transference began to change when, after we had worked through his utter dependency needs, he exclaimed that, for the first time, he felt that the analyst was his friend!

I think these are the instances to which Winnicott (1969) was referring when he spoke of his patients' long-standing inability and then their final ability to use the object, the analyst, in the transference.

It was clear that the patient felt an intense longing for the symbiotic mother—not just the need-satisfying one—the symbiotic half of the self, the longing for the probably still coenesthetically remembered harmony of the dual-unity stage. Side by side with this there was the impotent rage, hatred that the patient felt toward the depreciated, castrated, and castrating "mother of separation." This was connected, of course, with the patient's feeling that sexuality was dirty and that because mother and father had indulged in it, the product would inevitably have to be an anal monster—the little dark homunculus—he himself.

It befits this Freud Anniversary Lecture that I conclude by quoting Freud himself, by citing from *Civilization and Its Discontents* (1930), which bears on his implicit recognition of the importance of the coenesthetic realm of human experiences.[5] He said:

> . . . through a deliberate direction of one's sensory activities and through suitable muscular action, one can differentiate between what is internal . . . and . . . what emanates from the outer world. In this way one makes the first step towards the introduction of the reality principle which is to dominate future development. This differentiation, of course, serves the practical purpose of enabling one to defend oneself against sensations of unpleasure which one actually feels or with which one is threatened. In order to fend off certain unpleasurable excitations arising from within, the ego can use no other methods than those which it uses against unpleasure coming from without. . . .
>
> In this way then, the ego detaches itself from the external world. Or, to put it more correctly, originally the ego includes everything, later it separates off an external world from itself. Our present ego-feeling is, therefore, only a shrunken residue of a much more inclusive—indeed, an all-embracing—feeling which corresponded to a more intimate bond between the ego and the world about it. If we may assume that there are many people in whose mental life this primary ego-feeling has persisted to a greater or less degree, it would exist in them side by side with the narrower and more sharply demarcated ego-feeling of maturity, like a kind of counterpart to it. In that case, the ideational contents appropriate to it would be precisely those of limitlessness and of a bond with the universe—the same ideas with which my friend [Romain Rolland] elucidated the 'oceanic' feeling [p. 67f.].

BIBLIOGRAHY

Abelin, E. L. (1971), The Role of the Father in the Separation-Individuation Process. In: *Separation-Individuation,* ed. J. B. McDevitt & C. F. Settlage. New York: International Universities Press, pp. 229–252.

Benedek, T. (1938), Adaptation to Reality in Early Infancy. *Psychoanal. Quart.,* 7:200–214.

Bouvet, M. (1958), Technical Variations and the Concept of Distance. *Int. J. Psycho-Anal.,* 39:211–221.

Erikson, E. H. (1950), *Childhood and Society.* New York: Norton.

Fliess, R. (1961), *Ego and Body Ego.* New York: Schulte Publishing Co.

Freud, A. (1951), Notes on a Connection between the States of Negativism and of

[5] I am grateful to Dr. Ketenberg (1971) for drawing my attention to this quotation.

Emotional Surrender *(Hörigkeit). The Writings of Anna Freud,* 4:256–259. New York: International Universities Press, 1968.

—— (1952), The Role of Bodily Illness in the Mental Life of Children. In *The Psychoanalytic Study of the Child,* 7:69–81.

—— (1953), Some Remarks on Infant Observation. In *The Psychoanalytic Study of the Child,* 8:9–19.

Freud, S. (1930), Civilization and its Discontents. *Standard Edition,* 21:59–145. London: Hogarth Press, 1961.

Frijling-Schreuder, E. C. M. (1969), Borderline States in Children. In *The Psychoanalytic Study of the Child,* 24:307–327.

Galenson, E. (1971), A Consideration of the Nature of Thought in Childhood Play. In: *Separation-Individuation,* ed. J. B. McDevitt & C. F. Settlage. New York: Internatinal Universities Press, pp. 41–59.

Greenacre, P. (1957), The Childhood of the Artist: Libidinal Phase Development and Giftedness. In *The Psychoanalytic Study of the Child,* 12:47–72.

—— (1966), Problems of Overidealization of the Analyst and of Analysis. In *The Psychoanalytic Study of the Child,* 21:193–212.

—— (1969), The Fetish and the Transitional Object. In *The Psychoanalytic Study of the Child,* 24:144–164.

—— (1970), The Transitional Object and the Fetish: With Special Reference to the Role of Illusion. *Int. J. Psycho-Anal.,* 51:447–456.

Greenson, R. R. (1954), The Struggle against Identification. *J. Amer. Psychoanal. Assn.,* 2:200–217.

Hartmann, H. (1939). *Ego Psychology and the Problem of Adaptation.* New York: International Universities Press, 1958.

—— (1952). The Mutual Influences in the Development of Ego and Id. In *The Psychoanalytic Study of the Child,* 7:9–30.

Heimann, P. (1966), Comment on Dr. Kernberg's Paper [Structural Derivatives of Object Relationships]. *Int. J. Psycho-Anal.,* 47:254–260.

Hermann, I. (1936), *Sich Anklammern, Auf-Suche-Gehen. Int. Z. Psychoanal.,* 20:553–555.

Hoffer W. (1950a), Oral Aggressiveness and Ego Development. *Int. J. Psycho-Anal.,* 31:156–160.

—— (1950b), Development of the Body Ego. In *The Psychoanalytic Study of the Child,* 5:18–24.

Jacobson, E. (1953), Contribution to the Metapsychology of Cyclothymic Depression. In: *Affective Disorders,* ed. P. Greenacre. New York: International Universities Press, pp. 49–83.

—— (1957), On Normal and Pathological Moods: Their Nature and Functions. In *The Psychoanalytic Study of the Child,* 12:73–113.

—— (1964), *The Self and the Object World.* New York: International Universities Press.

—— (1967), *Psychotic Conflict and Reality.* New York: International Universities Press.

Kaufman, I. C. & Rosenblum, L. A. (1967), The Reaction to Separation in Infant Monkeys: Anaclitic Depression and Conversation-Withdrawal. *Psychosom. Med.,* 29:648–675.

Kernberg, O. (1967), Borderline Personality Organization. *J. Amer. Psychoanal. Assn.,* 15:641–685.

Kestenberg, J. S. (1971), From Organ-Object Imagery to Self and Object Representation. In: *Separation-Individuation,* ed. J. B. McDevitt & C. F. Settlage. New York: International Universities Press, pp. 75–99.

Kohut, H. (1966), Forms and Transformations of Narcissism. *J. Amer. Psychoanal. Assn.,* 14:243–272.

—— (1968). The Psychoanalytic Treatment of Narcissistic Personality Disorders: Outline of a Systematic Approach. In *The Psychoanalytic Study of the Child,* 23:86–113.

Kris, E. (1954), Discussion of paper, On Symbiotic Child Psychosis, by M. S. Mahler & B. Gosliner, at the New York Psychoanalytic Society.

—— (1956), On Some Vicissitudes of Insight in Psycho-Analysis. *Int. J. Psycho-Anal.,* 37:445–455.

Lewin, B. D. (1952), Phobic Symptoms and Dream Interpretation. *Psycho-anal. Quart.,* 21:295–322.

Loewald, H. W. (1951), Ego and Reality. *Int. J. Psycho-Anal.,* 32:10–18.

Mahler, M. S. (1957), On Two Crucial Phases of Integration of the Sense of Identity: Separation-Individuation and Sexual Identity. Abstr. in: Panel on Problems of Identity, rep. D. L. Rubinfine. *J. Amer. Psychoanal. Assn.,* 6:131–142, 1958.

—— (1960), Symposium on Psychotic Object Relationships: III. Perceptual De-Differentiation and Psychotic 'Object Relationship.' *Int. J. Psycho-Anal.,* 41:548–553.

—— (1961), On Sadness and Grief in Infancy and Childhood: Loss and Restoration of the Symbiotic Love Object. In *The Psychoanalytic Study of the Child,* 16:332–351.

—— (1963), Thoughts about Development and Individuation. In *The Psychoanalytic Study of the Child,* 18:307–324.

—— (1966), Notes on the Development of Basic Moods: The Depressive Affect. In: *Psychoanalysis—A General Psychology,* ed. R. M. Loewenstein, L. M. Newman, M. Schur, & A. J. Solnit. New York: International Universities Press, pp. 152–168.

—— & La Perriere, K. (1965), Mother-Child Interaction during Separation-Individuation. *Psychoanal. Quart.,* 34: 483–498.

—— & McDevitt, J. B. (1968), Observations on Adaptation and Defense *in statu nascendi. Psychoanal. Quart.,* 37:1–21.

Piaget, J. (1936), *The Origins of Intelligence in Children.* New York: International Universities Press, 1952.

Rubinfine, D. L. (1961), Perception, Reality Testing, and Symbolism. In *The Psychoanalytic Study of the Child,* 16:73–89.

Sandler, J., Holder, A., & Meers, D. (1963), The Ego Ideal and the Ideal Self. In *The Psychoanalytic Study of the Child,* 18:139–158.

Schur, M. (1955), Comments on the Metapsychology of Somatization. In *The Psychoanalytic Study of the Child,* 10:119–164.

—— (1966), *The Id and the Regulatory Principles of Mental Functioning.* New York: International Universities Press.

Searles, H. F. (1960), *The Nonhuman Environment.* New York: International Universities Press.

Sechehaye, M. A. (1947), *Symbolic Realization: A New Method of Psycho-therapy Applied to a Case of Schizophrenia.* New York: International Universities Press, 1951.

Spitz, R. A. (1945), Diacritic and Coenesthetic Organizations. *Psychoanal. Rev.,* 32:146–162.

—— (1959), *A Genetic Field Theory of Ego Formation.* New York: International Universities Press.

Spock, B. (1963), The Striving for Autonomy and Regressive Object Relationships. In *The Psychoanalytic Study of the Child,* 18:361–364.

Stein, M. (1956), The Marriage Bond. *Psychoanal. Quart.,* 25:238–259.

Stone, L. (1961), *The Psychoanalytic Situation.* New York: International Universities Press.

Tartakoff, H. H. (1966), The Normal Personality in Our Culture and the Nobel Prize Complex. In: *Psychoanalysis—A General Psychology,* ed. R. M. Loewenstein, L. M. Newman, M. Schur, & A. J. Solnit. New York: International Universities Press, pp. 22–252.

Waelder, R. (1930), The Principle of Multiple Function. *Psychoanal. Quart.,* 5:45–62, 1936.

—— (1963). Psychic Determinism and the Possibility of Predictions. *Psychoanal. Quart.,* 32:15–42.

Weil, A. P. (1970), The Basic Core. In *The Psychoanalytic Study of the Child,* 25:442–460.

Winnicott, D. W. (1953), Transitional Objects and Transitional Phenomena. *Int. J. Psycho-Anal.,* 34:89–97.

—— (1965). *The Maturational Processes and the Facilitating Environment.* New York: International Universities Press.

—— (1969). The Use of an Object. *Int. J. Psycho-Anal.,* 50:711–716.

19. Defining Borderline Patients: An Overview

John G. Gunderson and Margaret T. Singer

In 1953 Knight noted that the term "borderline" was applied to patients who could not be classified in other ways, i.e., as psychotic or neurotic, hence making it something of a wastebasket diagnosis (1). No doubt much of the dissatisfaction with recognizing such a category, whether it is termed borderline or any of its alternative labels, stems from the wish to keep schizophrenia as a clearly distinct disorder. Yet despite this objection, its use has steadily expanded.

Stern (2) was the first to use the term borderline, but the real parentage for this unwanted category is traceable to the "as-if" personality described by Deutsch (3), the ambulatory schizophrenia of Zilboorg (4), and the latent schizophrenia as introduced and developed by Rorschach (5), Bleuler (6), and Federn (7). Latent schizophrenia was sanctioned by Bleuler in 1911 to classify persons whose conventional social behavior he felt concealed underlying schizophrenia. Ambulatory schizophrenia was subsequently offered by Zilboorg in 1941 to combat the therapeutic nihilism that clinicians felt the latent schizophrenia label implied. Deutsch's article on the "as if" personality described persons whose superficial social appropriateness masqueraded highly disturbed personal relationships.

Before and even after Knight's paper popularized the term borderline, many other names were suggested and then silently retired in favor of the ever-widening use of this term. Among these are preschizophrenia (8), schizophrenic character (9), abortive schizophrenia (10), pseudo-psychopathic schizophrenia (11), psychotic character (12), subclinical schizophrenia (13) borderland (14, 15), and occult schizophrenia (16).

The most serious competition in the nomenclature has come from the term pseudoneurotic schizophrenia. This term was particularly popular in New York because of the local influence of its originators, Hoch and

Polatin and associates (17, 18). Hoch urged replacing the term border-line with pseudoneurotic schizophrenia, which defined a specific psy-chopathological condition characterized by the combination of panneu-rosis, pananxiety, and pansexuality together with symptoms of schizophrenia. The broadening of the concept of schizophrenia which followed in New York may be responsible for a discrepancy in diag-nostic habits between New Yorkers and other American psychiatrists as well as the British (19). Yet this term, too, has given way in the most recent APA diagnostic manual (20).

Although the use of the term borderline has become more common, disagreement over its definition has not subsided but has merely been displaced and camouflaged. Many who accept this term now disagree about whether it refers to borderline patient (21), state (22), personality organization (23, 24), character (25), pattern (26), schizophrenia (27, 28), condition (29), or syndrome (30). The increasing frequency of "borderline" patients (31–36), the greatly expanding literature, and the existing confusion about diagnosis and treatment make it imperative that some method for defining the patient group be devised that is replicable and from which research can proceed and conclusions can be generalized. In this paper we will attempt to survey the major rele-vant descriptive accounts of the borderline and to chronicle the common and discriminating features of these accounts.

Before we expand on these descriptive accounts, certain features about the literature itself should be noted. Since Knight's pivotal article appeared, there has been a large and still expanding descriptive litera-ture on the borderline patient. There were approximately 25 articles on borderline patients up to 1955, and that number has doubled in the past 10 years. Nevertheless, there remains a confusing overlap and discrep-ancy among authors in their descriptive attempts to define borderline patients. While most authors pay lip service to the previous literature, they proceed to describe borderline patients anew without noting how their descriptions add to or simply repeat earlier contributions. It is not clear whether this provincialism stems from an unfamiliarity or an unspoken dissatisfaction with the existing literature.

In this article we will discuss the major descriptive accounts of the borderline syndrome. Clearly, not all of the writings are of equal im-portance. The work of some authors is extremely well known and widely quoted, while others' work is obscure and/or limited to a single publication. Certain writers attribute every imaginable trait to borderline patients, while others are quite selective in their descriptions. Furthermore, some authors expand or contract their definitions of borderline patients in later publications. In addition, some descriptive accounts are secondary or preliminary to a discussion of other issues, e.g., psychodynamics (37, 38), theory (27, 38), treatment (21, 31–33, 36, 37 39–42), testing technique (43, 44), and schizophrenia (45). Yet in many the descriptive accounts are the primary goal of the paper (12, 17, 23, 29, 30 46–49). Among the latter, only Grinker and associates (30) have undertaken a prospective and systematic collection of observations and data analysis.

Nevertheless, each of the authors cited has attempted to articulate his conceptualization of borderline patients and in so doing has implied either his agreement or disagreement with others. Taken in their entirety, these various views reflect the present clinical opinion about these patients. Any attempt by researchers to reliably define borderline patients should encompass these major clinical impressions. In this review, the most common and distinguishing characteristics will be identified, and a rational guide for standardizing clinical criteria for diagnosing borderline patients will be offered.

METHODOLOGICAL PROBLEMS

There are essentially three types of descriptive accounts: symptomatic and behavioral observations, psychodynamic formulations, and psychological test findings. Although these sources of descriptive data are parallel, they seldom seem touched or influenced by each other's proximity. This independence, or ignoring of other sources, arises in part from the different contexts in which the observations are made and reported. Symptom and behavior observations tend to be published in the psychiatric literature and are the purview of clinical researchers and of those involved in residential treatment. Psychodynamic formulations frequent the psychoanalytic literature and usually are developed within individual psychotherapeutic office practice. Finally, the psychological literature contains the accounts made of the borderline patient by psychologists who have administered controlled clinical testing procedures. In addition, the independence of these three groups no doubt grows out of a traditional suspicion each group holds for each other's methodologies. In any event, the psychologist tends to focus upon intrapsychic structure, the psychoanalyst upon theory and therapy, and the general psychiatrist upon diagnosis, prognosis, and outcome.

Clearly, the amount of structure provided by a setting in which the borderline phenomenology is observed will influence how these patients are described. For example, clinicians using psychoanalytic techniques and psychologists using the Rorschach test agree in emphasizing the major ego defects and primitive intrapsychic mechanisms and thinking found in these patients. Yet clinicians observing these patients in structured hospital settings or evaluating them with structured interview techniques emphasize their stable personality features and interpersonal patterns. Certainly the broad agreement among authors from all persuasions (4, 21, 22, 27, 29, 31–33, 35, 37, 39–41, 43, 50, 51) about the borderline patient's proclivity for regression in unstructured settings draws attention to the critical need to define the context in which the observations and descriptions of the borderline patient are being made. This propensity to regress when structure is low becomes an important and perhaps pathognomonic criterion for defining any sample of borderline persons.

The circumstances that lead the borderline person and his evaluator to meet are also important. For example, there appears to be a remarkable contrast between borderline outpatients voluntarily seeking treatment and borderline inpatients, who may be referred by others for treatment. A comparison of the observations made by Hoch and Cattell (17) with those made by Grinker and associates (30), the only authors whose descriptive data were collected in a systematic manner, sheds light on the influence of sample selection upon the conclusions reached about borderline patients.

Both research groups viewed schizophrenia as a distinct pathological condition and selected borderline patients who were free of overt schizophrenic symptomatology, such as clear-cut delusions and hallucinations, on the basis of their history and mental status examination. Hoch and Cattell further limited their sample to patients who presented mainly severe psychoneurotic symptoms, but who, on closer evaluation in psychoanalytic therapy and eventually in hospitals, revealed primary signs of schizophrenia in their thinking, feelings, and physiological functioning. Grinker and associates, on the other hand, selected patients on the basis of good functioning between hospitalizations and the presence of an ego-alien quality to any psychotic behavior. The diagnosis of borderline was made on outpatients, who were then hospitalized for participation in a prospective study. Thus Grinker and associates chose as their sample suspects with good premorbid features, and hospitalization was not a clinical necessity but rather for research purposes. It is not surprising, then, that their sample showed rare psychotic phenomena and developed virtually no schizophrenia during a five-year follow-up (52). In contrast, slightly more than one-fourth of Hoch and Cattell's hospitalized population later developed manifest schizophrenia (53).

It is clear that the initial selection of samples influenced the conclusion that Grinker and associates reached that borderlines and schizophrenics have separate and distinct disorders while Hoch and Cattell concluded that their patients were a subgroup of schizophrenics. It is somewhat like packing a suitcase and then being surprised later to find what is in it when it is opened.[1] Most authors choose to regard borderline patients as a group somewhere between, and perhaps including, both of these extremes. Thus the need for hospitalization is a critical variable in comparing samples. Borderline patients who are referred for hospitalization because of severe symptoms would be expected to be more disordered than those functioning as outpatients.

In summary, we have cited four major variables to be considered in any descriptive account of borderline patients: who is describing them, the methods used to collect descriptive data, the context in which the patients were observed, and how the sample was selected. Each has an important impact on the resulting description of borderline patients.

What follows is a selective review of the literature covering three major descriptive conceptualizations of the borderline: first, the literature on symptoms and behavior; second, the psychological test literature; and third; the analytic literature as it views ego functioning.

SYMPTOMS AND BEHAVIOR

In the descriptive behavioral and symptom literature for borderlines, a number of characteristics are repeatedly mentioned that can be grouped under the general headings of affect, behavior, and psychosis. Among

[1]Grinker and associates noted that Hoch and Cattell tended to include more clearly schizophrenic symptoms in their later definitions of pseudoneurotic patients. Dyrud (32) has commented that Grinker and associates may have too readily dismissed the relationship between borderline and schizophrenic patients.

the studies that have considered the behavior and symptoms of borderlines, the study by Grinker and associates (30) deserves special citation
as the only prospective, systematic one. Despite the slanted selection
of patients in that sample, the findings must be considered as the marker
against which all other reports should be measured. It is thus of special
value to compare the findings of Grinker and associates with those other
descriptions based on purely clinical impressions.

Affect

Of the four prevailing characteristics that Grinker and associates found
in their borderline patients, two were qualities of affect.

1. *Anger.* "Expressed more or less directly to a variety of targets,
anger seems to constitute the main or only affect that the borderline
patient experiences" (30, p. 90). The expression of this anger—or the
defenses against it—are a major discriminating feature used to identify
four separate subgroups of borderline patients.

2. *Depression.* "Not the typical guilt-laden, self-accusatory, remorseful 'end-of-the-rope' type, but more a loneliness as the subjects
realize their predicament of being unable to commit themselves in a
world of transacting individuals" (30, p. 91). Grinker and associates
pointed out that this depression was not present in their healthiest
borderline group, which suffered instead from a clinging, childlike,
anaclitic depression.

These conclusions by Grinker and associates are given substantial
albeit inconsistent support by others. Some authors have noted the
prevalence of anger but do not mention depression (21, 33), and vice
versa (17, 36, 54). It seems likely that the confusion over the qualities
of affect is traceable to at least two major sources. First, there is
confusion about whether one is describing affects the patient presents
with, affects that are covert, or affects that emerge in treatment. Second, as some authors have noted, the borderline patient's anger and
depression have peculiar qualities.

How these two sources of confusion influence the descriptions of
borderline affects becomes apparent when one examines some of the
statements about depression in the literature. For example, there are
frequent qualifying phrases used by those clinicians who note a predominance of depression. Cary (29) has noted that the borderline patient

is characterized by a "sense of futility and pervasive feelings of loneliness and isolation" that he says do not constitute a "true" depression.
Hoch and Cattell (17) stated that they found frequent secondary depressions due to the persistent illness in their pseudoneurotic patients, but
that primary depressions were infrequent. Kernberg (23) noted the
prevalence of depressive-masochistic character traits in some of his
borderline patients but differentiated these from depressive symptoms.
Further, he advised that depression "as a symptom should not be used
directly as an indicator of borderline personality organization" but
suggested that only severe depression approaching psychosis in the
form of "ego depersonalization" should be a presumptive indicator for
a diagnosis of borderline personality. Gruenewald (55) commented that
there is often a "covert" depression that emerges later. Chessick (56)
described a chronic "existential despair" in borderline patients.

Anger is less controversial than depression. Many authors have noted
a prevailing anger in borderline patients. This one feature seems to have
been used progressively to discriminate borderlines from the original
description of the "as if" personality (3, 30) and from "schizoid"
personalities (29), where withdrawal from frustration is considered
more characteristic. One author (57) felt that the borderline patient's
anger is so prominent that he suggested changing the name to "chol-
eric." Despite the apparent agreement about the prevalence of anger,
such a broad range of behaviors is cited as being "angry" that a high
degree of inference may be required. Some examples are hostility (50),
rage reactions (31, 49), acting out (3), self-destructiveness (23, 31, 33,
58), detachment (59), mutism (33, 57), and demandingness (29, 57).
Several authors have said that anger is not a presenting theme but one
that emerges in the course of treatment (42, 50, 59). Kernberg (23) and
Meza (57) speculated about excessive aggressive drive, while Modell
(38) saw the anger as "mostly defensive."

In contrast, several authors have regarded anxiety as the typical affect
shown by their patients. Hoch and Cattell (17) gave this anxiety the
status of a "defining secondary diagnostic symptom." Although others
(23, 32, 41, 47, 49) have also commented on anxiety in borderline
patients, it is difficult in most instances to know if they are describing
a symptomatic problem among borderlines or are making an inference
based on a theoretical role given anxiety in personality theories.

Finally, another term frequently applied to borderline patients is anhedonia (32). In fact, there is considerable agreement that they lack a capacity for pleasure and rarely experience truly satisfied feelings. Their anhedonia has been discussed in terms of borderline dysphoria, unhappiness (47, 60), anguish (56), and lack of tenderness (3,38).

In summary, the affective state of borderline patients is characterized by the prominence of anger and depression plus varying degrees of anxiety and anhedonia. If a generalization can be made, it is that these patients are not flat in their affect tone; they tend, in fact, to experience intense and variable affects, although this does not seem to include the experience of pleasure.

Behavior

Much of the literature on the treatment of borderline patients describes behavior during therapy, especially during hospitalization. Here we are interested in those behaviors which characterize borderline patients when they come for evaluation and that would therefore be used as criteria for making the diagnosis of borderline and in planning treatment. This is an important issue, since there may be a typical and highly distressing behavioral regression following hospitalization whose active prevention may be required from the start (21, 29, 31, 33, 35, 50, 61). Within the repertoire of hospital behaviors, such acts as window breaking, wrist slashing (31, 33, 58), and repeated overdosing (50, 62) emerge as quite specific to this kind of patient.

One historical factor, which led psychoanalysts to the conception of an interest in borderline patients as a distinct entity, was the discovery that many patients who by their histories and demeanors seemed relatively healthy underwent regressions on the couch. This disparity between good social behavior and poor intrapsychic structure has been mentioned repeatedly by both analysts (18, 48, 63, 64) and psychologists (28, 60, 65). What is meant by good social behavior seems to be good appearance and manners combined with superficial interpersonal relationships, and—more surprisingly—good functioning at work (12, 36, 42, 48, 60, 66, 67). The latter is surprising because this impression is noted almost in passing by many writers despite its apparent conflict with the behavioral record the patients have elsewhere in their lives. Schmideberg (47) took exception to this view. She described her borderline patients as marginal and transient in their work histories and cited their "sense of entitlement" as a source of their work problems. Grinker and associates summarized their follow-up data by saying, "Although gainfully employed and largely self-sufficient economically, the facts suggest that the group was occupationally and academically static at a fairly low level" (30, p. 132). Frosch (12, 66) noted that a borderline person may have a surprisingly stable work record when he is employed in a highly structured environment.

The characteristic most frequently and consistently ascribed to the behavior of borderline patients is that of impulsive and self-destructive acts. "Self-destructive" is used here to indicate a broad range of behaviors whose *result* is self-destructive although their intent or *purpose* is not. Examples include sexual promiscuity and perversions in search of affection (56, 68), self-mutilation with the goal of object manipulation (58, 61) or establishing self-identity (66), and addiction in search of escape (15, 32). Generally, borderline patients do not regard these behaviors as self-destructive, self-degradative, or guilt provoking. Although relatively little of the literature on borderline patients has dealt with actual suicide, repeated suicidal gestures and threats have been noted (50, 54, 57) and specific manipulative behavior attributed to such patients (69, 70).

Diverse sexual problems are attributed to borderline persons, but there is little agreement on their prevalence. Certain authors have noted a preoccupation with sex (17), and others have described polymorphous perverse sexuality (17, 23, 35, 46). Some authors (3, 12) have even included within the borderline category most persons with specific sexual deviances. Greenson (35) noted a "prominence of organ pleasures at the expense of object relations" among this group. Several authors (17, 41, 42) believe that these behaviors reflect a basic confusion in the sexual identity of the individuals.

The presence of obvious behavioral disturbances in a variety of spheres including drug use and sexual deviance often causes the borderline diagnosis to overlap with various character problem diagnoses in which chronic acting-out patterns such antisocial, addictive, alcoholic, and homosexual behavior are seen. Because of this, Kernberg (71) has argued for a new classification of character types based upon what he believes are more fundamental personality features than behavior. He and many others have included a number of specific character disorders within the broader diagnostic category of borderline syndrome (21, 38, 41, 46, 47, 54, 68). Jan Frank (35) has suggested that various acting-out behaviors provide outlets for many persons now diagnosed as borderline who previously would have become overtly schizophrenic. He and others (71, 72) believe that inadequate impulse control is the dominant ego defect in these persons.

One concludes that in considering the behavioral evidence for the diagnosis of borderline, a clinician should not be deterred by the presence of a stable work history or superficial social adequacy but should examine other areas, where he may often find evidence of impulsive sexual, drug-taking, or other activies whose results are self-destructive even though the patient's intent or purpose is not.

Psychosis

While there has been general agreement that borderline syndrome is a stable personality disorder (12, 23, 30, 33, 38, 39, 47), there is also widespread recognition that a number of these patients may develop psychotic symptoms (1, 17, 36, 39, 45, 46, 49, 51, 66, 73). Indeed, as indicated earlier, the borderline person's capacity to develop regressive psychotic symptoms may be a pathognomonic feature. Weiner would seem to concur with this conclusion in his review of literature (28). However, there is a consensus that when psychoses do occur, they have the following differential features: 1) stress related (21, 23, 36, 43, 49, 68), 2) reversible (21, 30, 41, 49), 3) transient (12, 15, 30, 49), 4) ego-alien (1, 12, 30), and 5) unsystematized (23, 29, 30, 43, 45, 60, 74). Numerous authors have used some or all of these features to differentiate borderline psychoses from the psychoses of schizophrenia and other disorders (21,23, 29, 30, 38, 45, 54, 66). Thus there is general agreement as to absence of stable or clear delusions or hallucinations, with only a few dissenting opinions (17, 33). Some authors have postulated that the borderline's psychoses occur in response to intolerable rage (29, 30, 41, 73).

Interestingly, despite the consensus about the vulnerability of certain borderline persons to psychotic-like episodes and regressions, only a few authors have viewed this as an essential feature of the borderline syndrome (1, 12, 45, 73, 75). Most authors have hastened to note that the occurrence of psychoses is the exception, not the rule (23, 29-31, 39, 46, 76). A few have taken a determined position that psychoses do not occur at all in borderline persons (33, 50, 63). At the opposite extreme, Hoch and Cattell (53) found that the psychoses in their sample of pseudoneurotic schizophrenic patients were not necessarily transient and reversible. A more recent report (77) suggested that the psychoses of this group cannot be differentiated from those of schizophrenics, and another (46) reported that they are brief and rare. This last report would thereby place pseudoneurotic schizophrenia within the mainstream of thought about psychoses among borderline persons.

There have also been widespread references to the similarity between the psychotic thought processes of borderline and schizophrenic persons. Some borderline persons demonstrate fears of being controlled (17), ideas of reference (38), externalization (1, 56), and other paranoid tendencies (12, 23, 56). Some writers have noted that they have vividly loose associations and other symptoms of formal thought disorder. For example, Kinght (1) stated that loose associations can be detected by use of the Rorschach test and free-associative interviews. On the other hand, Grinker and associates (30) emphasized that they found no looseness of associations. (However, they did not use projective tests or free-associative interviews in their assessment of their patients.) Hoch and Cattell (17) took an intermediate position, stating that "approximate" or "parallel" associations are frequent. Thus there is little agreement among clinicians about the presence of thought disturbances in borderline persons. Some say there are none (23, 30), while others say there are many (1, 47, 50, 65, 73). It is clear that these differences result from problems in defining and assessing thought disorder as well as from the methodological problems cited earlier.

Some authors have underscored the frequent occurrence of disturbed states of consciousness. These peculiar ego states, which were first described by Deutsch (3), have been variously categorizied as depersonalization, dissociation, and derealization (23, 29, 36, 45, 61, 66). They have been called borderline "states, " to be differentiated from borderline "personalities." These states are seen as responses to anxiety (66), depression (23), and rage (29) and as prepsychotic experiences (3).

Separate from the purely clinical literature already summarized, a literature grew in the 1960s that recognized a vulnerability among borderline persons to psychoses when exposed to pharmacological stress, namely, that produced by marijuana (78), LSD (68, 79), and mescaline (68). These reports suggest that the borderline person is unique in his sensitivity to pharmacological stress. This special sensitivity or vulnerability seems to support Schmideberg's often quoted characterization of the borderline personality as "stably unstable" (47).

From the many foregoing clinical reports, which vary in their positions on whether psychoses occur among the borderline group, a series of clinical questions arise: Do all borderline persons have a vulnerability to psychosis even if they are not psychotic when assessed? Are most borderline persons free from psychosis throughout their life despite such a vulnerability? Clinicians are uncertain and divided over these issues. Grinker and associates (30) contended that psychoses occur in only one subgroup of borderline persons. Equally important, they are the only authors who have attempted to identify subgroups of borderlines who they contend will *not* develop psychoses. Other authors have implied or hinted that many or even most borderline persons could develop psychoses, given properly stressful circumstances. Parallel issues concerning the extent and type of their reality testing and the nature and type of their cognitive style will be considered in a later section of this paper.

To conclude, reports in the clinical literature generally agree that an undetermined number of borderline persons do develop psychoses in stressful situations. Moreover, when such psychoses occur, they are characterized by their limited symptoms and limited duration. There are, however, few actuarial data on the prevalence of vulnerability to psychosis among borderline persons. Some authors have suggested that dissociative states may be quite marked in these patients.

INTRAPSYCHIC PHENOMENA

The psychological test literature devoted to characterizing borderline patients has generally been in agreement that they demonstrate ordinary reasoning and responses to structured tests such as the Wechsler Adult Intelligence Scale (WAIS), but that less structured tests such as the Rorschach reveal deviant thought and communication processes (27,

28, 43, 60, 74, 80–83). As in the clinical literature, most articles on which this conclusion is based are impressionistic. Their many methodological issues require attention before this broadly held viewpoint is accepted (6). The seminal contributions were made by Rorschach, Rapaport and associates, and Schafer, with subsequent authors generally being content to add confirmatory evidence.

Rorschach (5) and later Rapaport and associates (8) used the terms "fabulizing, combinatory, and confabulated" thinking to describe the propensities of borderline persons to overspecify secondary elaborations of their associations and to combine and reason oddly. They are prone to reason circumstantially rather than logically. Their separate perceptions tend to become intermingled and related simply because they occur close together in time or space. Borderline persons read more affective elaboration into their perceptions than others can validate, i.e., they tend to add too much and too specific affective material to simple perceptions. Other persons then have trouble accepting this affective meaning, although they might accept the same basic percept that the borderline person sees.

Rorschach, in 1921 (5), was the first to call attention to some seemingly adequately functioning persons whose responses to inkblot tests resembled those given by schizophrenic patients. He applied the term latent schizophrenic to those persons who had average surface behavior but Rorschach test features in common with schizophrenics, such as self-references, belief in the reality of the cards, scattered attention, variability in quality of ideas, and absurd and abstract associations.

It was Rapaport and associates (8) who first described the borderline person's intact performance on the WAIS and a pervasively odd Rorschach record; this has subsequently become an almost axiomatic diagnostic rule for later writers presenting single case studies. Although these authors defined two groups of what they called preschizophrenics, namely, the coarctated group and the overideational group, it has been largely the overideational borderline patient who is referred for psychological testing and upon whom subsequent literature has concentrated. Stone and Dellis (74) reiterated Rorschach's observation about the disparity between social functioning and thinking. They went on to confirm in a prospective study (74) Rapaport and associates' finding of a discrepancy between the Rorschach test and the WAIS in their evidence for pathology in borderline patients.

Schafer (82) introduced a third distinguishing feature about the disturbed thinking of borderline patients when he suggested that they are more comfortable about their bizarre and distorted thinking than are schizophrenics. Although Schafer's finding seems to differ from the general impression in the clinical literature that psychoses are ego-dystonic, it was later repeated in a report by Fisher (60).

In an interesting report DeSlullitel and Sorribas (84) compared the Rorschach test results of normal subjects, borderline persons, and creative artists. They found that the negative unpleasant content within "fabulized combination" responses by borderline persons distinguished them from the creative artists, who presented positive content within similar types of responses.

Gruenewald (55) reported on psychological test batteries given to 10 of Grinker and associates' original 51 borderlines five or more years after their discharge. She noted that based solely on test results, 2 would have been diagnosed as schizophrenic. However, when these data were combined with other information, the results were consistent with the borderline diagnosis and fit within the subgroups Grinker and associates had derived. She noted that "maladaptive primary process manifestations" were sometimes present in thought content and organization. Unfortunately, she made no mention of any discrepant functioning on individual tests.

In summary, borderline persons are believed to connect unrelated percepts illogically, overelaborate on the affective meaning of percepts, and give circumstantial and unpleasant associations to the Rorschach inkblots. This disturbed thinking may be more flamboyant and more ego-syntonic than that found among schizophrenic persons. Yet such borderline persons are reported to function adequately on the WAIS, showing few or none of the ideational deviances.

EGO FUNCTIONS

There are various ways to assess and classify ego functions. Thus it is difficult to select from the literature comparable descriptions of specific ego-function characteristics of borderline persons. However, two functions do emerge as particularly relevant to this group, namely, reality testing and interpersonal relationships. While the latter remains almost solely within the purview of clinical impressions, several approaches to evaluating reality testing have been made.

Reality Testing

Any discussion of psychosis is based upon the concept of reality testing. Frosch (12, 40) has stated that an intactness in reality testing differentiates borderline persons from schizophrenics. Distinguishing among reality testing, sense of reality, and relationship to reality, he concluded that borderline and psychotic persons share a poor sense of reality and relationship to reality, but that the borderline person can test out his experiences whereas the psychotic cannot. In a panel report on the "as if" personality, a similar conclusion was reached about this subgroup of borderline persons (85). This position is akin to the frequent comments of several authors that borderline persons, when compared to schizophrenics, have more distance from their psychotic experiences and regard the episodes as ego-alien or ego-dystonic. Zetzel (21) added a twist to Frosch's viewpoint by stating that it is the capacity to reverse impaired reality testing, given a good situation (in treatment), that distinguishes borderline persons from schizophrenics.

A number of authors seem to agree with Frosch that reality testing is generally maintained in borderline persons (23, 30, 85). Wolberg (85) has stated that the reality distortions that do occur are defensive in nature and that the borderline person's actual perception of reality is always extant. However, Kernberg (51) has noted that "under special circumstances—severe stress, regression induced by alcohol or drugs, or transference psychosis"—they may lose this capacity. Kernberg and others have noted that these patients are prone to develop psychotic transference reactions. Of course, unless this feature is cited in the patient's history, it would not be of use in an initial diagnostic evaluation. Authors using psychological tests have assigned relatively greater importance to the vulnerability of the borderline person's reality testing to stress (31, 43, 60). Knight (1) noted the borderline person's inability to distinguish between dreaming experiences and reality. Hoch and Cattell (53) later drew a similar conclusion about the impairment in reality testing in their group of pseudoneurotic schizophrenic patients.

A number of authors have emphasized that reality testing should not be viewed as a phenomenon that one has or does not have but, rather, that there is a spectrum of reality testing (1, 16, 38, 50). Modell (38) and others (21, 23) have discussed the borderline person's reality testing problems in the context of self-object differentiation. Modell noted,

The testing of reality depends upon the fact that in the ego's growth a distinction has been made between self and object . . . . there are degrees of alteration of this function of testing reality that correlate with the degree to which self and object can be differentiated . . . . the borderline transference is based on a transitional object relation where there is some self-object discrimination, but where this discrimination is imperfect (38, p. 228).[2]

Such a graded view of reality testing helps to reconcile certain discrepancies noted earlier among authors who have presented contradictory views of reality testing in borderline persons.

As Hurvich (86) has pointed out, there is a need for quantifiable measurements of this ego function, which could be used to evaluate whether and to what extent impairment exists. Although Grinker and associates (30) included "relation to reality" as one of the seven ego functions they intended to evaluate in their borderline patients, they did not include any instruments to measure this directly. Their evaluation was based on behavior that was generally labeled as "positive" or "negative" and upon ratings of perception devised from global judgments of the patient's awareness of self, others, time, events, and things. These assessments did not give any consideration to latent vulerability to disruptions in reality testing. Further, their validity as reflections of reality testing is not always obvious. Grinker and associates seemed aware of these problems and did not draw any definite conclusions about the relationship to reality and the capacity for reality testing in their sample. Until instruments or methods of measuring reality testing are developed, the literature on borderline persons will continue to reflect the ambiguity of the concept, and clinical impressions will be subject to the unstated and therefore unknown biases of the researchers.

Interpersonal Relationships

A number of authors have pointed to borderline patients' style of relatedness as the most distinguishing diagnostic feature of this group. Zetzel (21) said that for the borderline patient in particular, "the kind of doctor-

---

[2] Burnham (61) has suggested that borderline patients frequently have pets or toy animals.

patient relationship that is established may prove to be a crucial factor in reaching a definitive diagnostic evaluation.'' This relationship is best illustrated by the following observations.

A frequently cited feature of the borderline patient's object relationships is a predictable superficiality and transiency (30, 32, 60, 87). Fisher (60) suggested that ''superficiality in relationships'' distinguishes borderline patients as a group from neurotic patients. Knight alluded to this somewhat differently by noting, ''Other ego functions, such as conventional (but superficial) adaptation to the environment and superficial maintenance of object relationships, may exhibit varying degrees of intactness'' (1, p. 6). This echoes the observation made earlier about the borderline person's surprising capacity for adequate social functioning but adds that this apparent behavioral normality may depend on superficiality. Dyrud (32) commented that case material cited by Grinker and others demonstrates more than anything else the remarkably short sequences of interactive behavior that these patients are capable of maintaining.

This quality of superficiality and transiency is supported and explained in some measure by the original formulations of the ''as if'' personality by Deutsch (3). Deutsch described the borderline person's interpersonal relationships as ''plastic'' and ''mimicry.'' She stated that the ''essential characteristic is that outwardly he conducts his life as if he possessed a complete and sensitive emotional capacity.'' Eventually, the absence of real emotional responsiveness leads to repeated dissolution of relationships. This disparity between adequate superficial relatedness and inadequate internal relatedness has been used to characterize borderline patients more generally (29, 30, 48–50, 60, 80). It may be attributable to a lack of coherent self-identity, which Grinker and associates (30) found in their sample and which other authors have also noted (1, 21, 23, 45, 49, 56, 66).

In contrast to the recurrent theme that borderline persons' interpersonal relationships are superficial and transient is the claim that they are prone to form intense, clinging relationships. Adler (31) stated that their ''readiness to form rapid, intense, engulfing relationships'' is what differentiates them from schizoid and schizophrenic persons. Similarly, Modell (38) stated, ''My principal reason for considering this group homogeneous is that they develop a consistent and primitive form of object relationships in the transference.'' Grinker and associates (30) referred to this when they cited as one of the four identifying characteristics of borderlines "a defect in affectional relationships. These are anaclitic, dependent, or complementary, but rarely reciprocal." These accounts of borderline persons' intense relationships are underscored by the consensus that their initial relationships with therapists are dependent and demanding (12, 21, 23, 29, 31, 38, 50, 76). In addition, many authors have noted that the intense therapeutic relasionship is characteristically devaluative and manipulative (21, 31, 38, 50, 57). The emergence of such angry behaviors may in turn lead to the repeated disruption of such close relationships (49, 50, 57). These qualities of the borderline person's close relationships may not be immediately discernible. Houck (50) pointed out that this initial deception can lead to later problems for unsuspecting therapists.

Thus in their everyday relationships borderline persons relate in a fairly normal but superficial and transient manner, while in their close relationships they become intense, dependent, and manipulative. In any event, these individuals are actively involved with other people and are not particularly socially withdrawn.

SUMMARY

In this paper we have surveyed the large literature of descriptive accounts of borderline patients. Within the major variations in these accounts we have attempted to identify certain themes and prevailing clinical impressions. We have discussed the four methodoligical issues that significantly influence the resulting descriptive accounts. Taking these methodolgical issues into account, we have identified a number of features that most of the authors believe seem to characterize most borderline persons. These features are as follows:

1. *The presence of intense affect.* It is usually of a strongly hostile or depressed nature. The absence of flatness and pleasure and the presence of depersonalization may be useful in differential diagnosis.
2. *A history of impulsive behavior.* This may take many forms, including both episodic acts (e.g., self-multilation, overdose of drugs) and more chronic behavior patterns (e.g., drug dependency, promiscuity). Often the result of these behaviors is self-destructive although their purpose is not.
3. *Social adaptiveness.* This may be manifested as good achievement in school or work, appropriate appearance and manners, and strong social awareness. However, this apparent strength may reflect a disturbed identity masked by mimicry, a form of rapid and superficial identification with others.

4. *Brief psychotic experiences.* These are likely to have a paranoid quality. It is felt that this potential is present even in the absence of such experiences. The psychoses may become evident during drug use or in unstructured situations and relationships.
5. *Psychological testing performance.* Borderline persons give bizarre, dereistic, illogical, or primitive responses on unstructured tests such as the Rorschach, but not on more structured tests such as the WAIS.
6. *Interpersonal relationships.* Characteristically, these vacillate between transient, superficial relationships and intense, dependent relationships that are marred by devaluation, manipulation, and demandingness.

These six features provide a rational basis for diagnosing borderline patients. The criteria can be readily assessed during an initial evaluation. Further research is under way to evaluate the relative frequency and discriminating value of each of these features. From these studies a reliable system of diagnostic criteria can develop. It is hoped that such prestated and standardized means of identifying borderline patients will permit better treatment planning and clinical research on these patients to proceed.

REFERENCES

1. Knight R: Borderline states. Bull Menninger Clin 17:1–12, 1953.
2. Stern A: Psychoanalytic investigation of and therapy in the borderline group of neuroses. Psychoanal Q 7:467–489, 1938.
3. Deutsch H: Some forms of emotional disturbance and their relationship to schizophrenia. Psychoanal Q 11:301–321, 1942.
4. Zilboorg G: Ambulatory schizophrenia. Psychiatry 4:149–155, 1941.
5. Rorschach H: Psychodiagnostics (1921), 5th ed. Bern, Hans Huber, 1942, pp 120–121, 155–158.
6. Bleuler E: Dementia Praecox, or the Group of Schizophrenias (1911). Translated by Zinkin J. New York, International Universities Press, 1950, p 239.
7. Federn P: Ego Psychology and the Psychoses. New York, Basic Books, 1952, pp 166–183.
8. Rapaport D, Gill M, Schafer R: The Thematic Apperception Test, in Diagnostic Psychological Testing, vol 2. Chicago, Year Book Publishers, 1946, pp 395–459.
9. Schafer R: The Clinical Application of Psychological Tests. New York, International Universities Press, 1948, pp 218–223.
10. Mayer W: Remarks on abortive cases of schizophrenia. J Nerv Ment Dis 112:529–542, 1950.
11. Dunaif S, Hoch PH: Pseudopsychopathic schizophrenia, in Psychiatry and the Law. Edited by Hoch PH, Zubin J. New York, Grune & Stratton, 1955, pp 169–195.
12. Frosch J: The psychotic character: clinical psychiatric considerations. Psychiatr Q 38:81–96, 1964.

13. Peterson DR: The diagnosis of subclinical schizophrenia. J Consult Psychol 18:198–200, 1954.
14. Clark LP: Some practical remarks upon the use of modified psychoanalysis in the treatment of borderland neuroses and psychoses. Psychoanal Rev 6:306–308, 1919.
15. Chessick R: The psychotherapy of borderland patients. Am J Psychother 20:600–614, 1966.
16. Stern A: Psychoanalytic therapy in the borderline neuroses. Psychoanal Q 14:190–198, 1945.
17. Hoch P, Cattell J: The diagnosis of pseudoneurotic schizophrenia. Psychiatr Q 33:17–43, 1959.
18. Hoch P, Polatin P: Pseudoneurotic forms of schizophrenia. Psychiatr Q 23:248–276, 1949.
19. Kuriansky J, Deming W, Gurland G: On trends in the diagnosis of schizophrenia. Am J Psychiatry 131:402–408, 1974.
20. American Psychiatric Association: Diagnostic and Statistical Manual of Mental Disorders, 2nd ed. Washington, DC, APA, 1968.
21. Zetzel E: A developmental approach to the borderline patient. Am J Psychiatry 128:867–871, 1971.
22. Weinshel EM: Panel report: severe regressive states during analysis. J Am Psychoanal Assoc 14:538–568, 1966.
23. Kernberg O: Borderline personality organization. J Am Psychoanal Assoc 15:641–685, 1967.
24. Kernberg O: Prognostic considerations regarding borderline personality organization. J Am Psychoanal Assoc 19:595–635, 1971.
25. Giovacchini PL: Character disorders: with special reference to the borderline state. International Journal of Psychoanalytic Psychotherapy 2(1):7—20, 1973.
26. Millon T: Pathological personalities of moderate severity: borderline patterns, in Modern Psychopathology. Philadelphia, WB Saunders Co, 1969, pp 302–337.
27. McCully RS: Certain theoretical considerations in relation to borderline schizophrenia and the Rorschach. Journal of Projective Techniques 26:404–418, 1962.
28. Weiner IB: Borderline and pseudoneurotic schizophrenia, in Psychodiagnosis in Schizophrenia. New York, John Wiley & Sons, 1966, pp 398–430.
29. Cary GL: The borderline condition: a structural dynamic viewpoint. Psychoanal Rev 59:33–54, 1972.
30. Grinker RR, Werble B, Drye R: The Borderline Syndrome: A Behavioral Study of Ego Functions. New York, Basic Books, 1968.
31. Adler G: Hospital treatment of borderline patients. Am J Psychiatry 130:32–35, 1973.
32. Dyrud JE: The treatment of the borderline syndrome, in Modern Psychiatry and Clinical Research, Edited by Offer D, Freedman D. New York, Basic Books, 1972, pp 159–173.
33. Friedman HJ: Some problems of inpatient management with borderline patients. Am J Psychiatry 126:299–304, 1969.
34. Schimel JL, Salzman L, Chodoff P, et al: Changing styles in psychiatric syndromes: a symposium. Am J Psychiatry 130:146–155, 1973.
35. Rangell L: The borderline case (panel report). J Am Psychoanal Assoc 3:285–298, 1955.
36. Arnstein RL: The borderline patient in the college setting, in Psychosocial Problems of College Men. Edited By Wedge BM. New Haven, Conn, Yale University Press, 1958, pp 173–199.

37. Blum HP: Borderline regression. International Journal of Psychoanalytic Psychotherapy 1(1):46–59, 1972.
38. Modell A: Primitive object relationships and the predisposition to schizophrenia. Int J Psychoanal 44:282–292, 1963.
39. Chessick RD: Use of the couch in psychotherapy of borderlines. Arch Gen Psychiatry 25:306–313, 1971.
40. Frosch J: Technique in regard to some specific ego defects in the treatment of borderline patients. Psychiatr Q 45:216–220, 1971.
41. Wolberg A: The psychoanalytic treatment of the borderline patient in the individual and the group setting, in Topical Problems of Psychotherapy. Edited by Hulse J. New York, S Karger, 1960, pp 174–197.
42. Rosner S: Problems of working through with borderline patients. Psychotherapy: Therapy, Research, and Practice 6:43–45, 1969.
43. Shapiro D: Special problems in testing borderline psychotics. Journal of Projective Techniques 18:387–394, 1954.
44. Stern A: Transference in borderline neuroses. Psychoanal Q 17:527–528, 1948.
45. Kety SS, Rosenthal D, Wender PH, et al: The types and prevalence of mental illness in the biological and adoptive families of adopted schizophrenics. Edited by Rosenthal D, Kety SS. New York, Pergamon Press, 1968, pp 345–362.
46. Godbey AL, Guerra JR: Pseudoneurotic schizophrenia. Journal of the Florida Medical Association 57(4):17–20, 1970.
47. Schmideberg M: The borderline patient, in American Handbook of Psychiatry, vol 1, Edited by Arieti S. New York, Basic Books, 1959, pp 398–416.
48. Wolberg A: The Borderline Patient. New York, Intercontinental Medical Book Corp, 1973.
49. Pfeiffer E: Borderline states. Dis Nerv Syst 35:212–219, 1974.
50. Houck JH: The intractable female patient. Am J Psychiatry 129:27–31, 1972.
51. Kernberg O: The treatment of patients with borderline personality organization. Int J Psychoanal 49:600–619, 1968.
52. Werble B: Second follow-up study of borderline patients. Arch Gen Psychiatry 23:3–7, 1970.
53. Hoch P, Cattell J: The course and outcome of pseudoneurotic schizophrenias. Am J Psychiatry 119:106–115, 1962.
54. Chessick RD: The borderline patient, in How Psychotherapy Heals. New York, Science House, 1969, pp 144–160.
55. Gruenewald D: A psychologist's view of the borderline syndrome. Arch Gen Psychiatry 23:180–184, 1970.
56. Chessick RD: Externalization and existential anguish in the borderline patient. Arch Gen Psychiatry 27:764–770, 1972.
57. Meza C: El Colerico. Mexico City, Mortiz, 1970.
58. Grunebaum H, Klerman G: Wrist slashing. Am J Psychiatry 124:524–534, 1967.
59. Wolberg A: The "borderline patient." Am J Psychother 6:694–701, 1952.
60. Fisher S: Some observations suggested by the Rorschach test concerning "the ambulatory schizophrenic." Psychiatr Q 29 (suppl 1):81–89, 1955.
61. Burnham DL: The special-problem patient: victim or agent of splitting: Psychiatry 29:105–122, 1966.
62. Havens L: Some difficulties in giving schizophrenic and borderline patients medication. Psychiatry 31:44–50, 1968.
63. Bellak L (ed): Schizophrenia: A Review of the Syndrome. New York, Logos, 1958, pp 55–56.

64. Bychowski G: The problem of laten psychosis. J Am Psychoanal Assoc 1:484–503, 1953.
65. Weiner H: Diagnosis and symptomatology, in Schizophrenia: A Review of the Syndrome. Edited by Bellak L. New York, Logos, 1958, pp 107–173.
66. Frosch J: Psychoanalytic considerations of the psychotic character. J Am Psychoanal Assoc 18:24–50, 1970.
67. Little M: Transference in borderline states. Int J Psychoanal 47:476–495, 1966.
68. Denber H: Mescaline and LSD: therapeutic implications of the drug-induced state. Dis Nerv Syst 30(Feb suppl):23–27, 1969.
69. Jensen V, Petty T: The fantasy of being saved in suicide. Psychoanal Q 27:327–339, 1958.
70. Sifneos PE: Manipulative suicide. Psychiatr Q 40:525–537, 1966.
71. Kernberg O: A psychoanalytic classification of character pathology. J Am Psychoanal Assoc 18:800–822, 1970.
72. Eisenstein VW: Differential psythotherapy of borderline states. Psychiatr Q 25:379–401, 1951.
73. Willett AB, Jones FD, Morgan DW, et al: The borderline syndrome: an operational definition. Read at the 126th annual meeting of the American Psychiatric Association, Honolulu, Hawaii, May 7–11, 1973.
74. Stone HK, Dellis NP: An exploratory investigation into the levels hypothesis. Journal of Projective Techniques 24:33–44, 1960.
75. Miller MH: The borderline psychotic patient. Ann Intern Med 46:736–743, 1957.
76. Schmideberg M: The treatment of psychopaths and borderline patients. Am J Psychother 1:45–70, 1947.
77. Weingarten LL, Korn S: Psychological test findings on pseudoneurotic schizophrenics. Arch Gen Psychiatry 17:448–454, 1967.
78. Heiman E: Marijuana precipitated psychoses in patients evacuated to CONNUS. US Army Medical Bulletin 40(9):75–77, 1968.
79. Laurie P (ed): LSD applied in Drugs: Medical, Psychological and Social Facts. Baltimore, Penguin Books, 1967, pp 112–130,
80. Forer BR: The latency of latent schizophrenia. Journal of Projective Techniques 14:297–302, 1950.
81. Mercer M, Wright SC: Diagnostic testing in a case of latent schizophrenia. Journal of Projective Techniques 14:287–296, 1950.
82. Schafer R: Psychoanalytic Interpretation in Rorschach Testing. New York, Grune & Stratton, 1954, pp 66–67.
83. Zucker LJ: The psychology of latent schizophrenia: based on Rorschach studies. Am J Psychother 6:44–62, 1952.
84. DeSlullitel SI, Sorribas E: The Rorschach test in research on artists. Rosario, Argentina, 1973 (unpublished paper).
85. Weiss J: Clinical and theoretical aspects of "as if" characters (panel report). J Am Psychoanal Assoc 14:569–590, 1966.
86. Hurvich M: On the concept of reality testing. Int J Psychoanal 51:299–312, 1970.
87. Knight R: Management and psychotherapy of the borderline schizophrenic patient, in Psychoanalytic Psychiatry and Psychology, Edited by Knight R, Friedman CR. New York, International Universities Press, 1954, pp 110–122.

20. The Borderline Syndrome: Evolution of the Term, Genetic Aspects, and Prognosis

Michael H. Stone

If a man tells me that he is grievously disturbed, for that he *imagines* he sees a ruffian coming against him with a drawn sword, though at the same time he is *conscious* it is a delusion, I pronounce him to have a disordered imagination; but if a man tells me that he *sees* this, and in consternation calls me to look at it, I pronounce him to be *mad*.

Professor Gaubius of Leyden
18th Century

"Borderline" has been used to designate conditions intermediate between psychosis and neurosis, analyzability and nonanalyzability; also, for dilute or questionable schizophrenia. Contemporary usage inclines toward patients with manic-depressive heredity, although borderlines are still etiologically heterogeneous. Various subtypes are outlined, each responsive to a particular method of psychotherapy or pharmacotherapy. If drug-abuse or antisocial tendencies are absent, prognosis is often favorable.

Psychodiagnosis, for all its complexity and controversial issues, contains fundamentally but three universes of discourse: constitution, coping, and character. Abnormalities of constitution include the special group of disturbances in ego-boundary and integration that we subsume under the heading schizophrenia; another group of disturbances involves disorders of behavioral regulation such as the manic-depressive disorders, where the emotional thermostat seems innately set either too high or too low. Coping refers to levels of over-all adaptation; character, to the personal styles, both typical and exaggerated, within which one's constitution and adaptive capacity express themselves. The term "borderline" has been incorporated into two universes of discourse: constitution and coping. A condition that is neither obviously schizophrenic nor obviously manic or epileptic and so forth, will get spoken of as borderline. An adaptational level that is neither in keeping with the functional capacities of the ordinary man (neurotic) nor with the incapacities of the man who lost touch with reality (psychotic), is, again, borderline.

What follows is (1) a review of the various terms utilized since the turn of the century to designate borderline or intermediate-level psychiatric disorders; (2) material relating to the hereditary factor in these borderline conditions; (3) data regarding their prognosis; and (4) a method of demonstrating correspondences between the various popular terms and the more traditional diagnostic entities in psychiatric nomenclature.

EVOLUTION OF THE CONCEPT

When we have portrayed the history of the usages of the term "borderline" in psychiatry, we will have simultaneously defined the term. Its history is its meaning. The scant references to borderline conditions to be found in the 19th-century literature, reviewed by Mack[1] and later by Grinker,[2] are of less interest to us today, because most of the usages employed currently derive from psychoanalytic papers of the 1930s.

One can see the germ of a borderline concept in Bleuler's correction of Kraepelinian pessimism about dementia praecox, and in Freud's deemphasis of an organic etiology for what he preferred to call the narcissistic neuroses. As Freud's psychoanalytic method and Meyer's optimism began to spread, particularly in the United States, interest shifted away from the abstract categorization of the 19th-century German school of psychiatry, to the issue of analyzability. The world of mental disorders divided itself into the transference psychoneuroses— susceptible to amelioration by classical psychoanalysis—and the psychoses, which resisted improvement by this means. Interest in the ideational and psychodynamic aspects of schizophrenic conditions, especially the nondelusional cases, carried the analytic pioneers further away from their original organic moorings and from the traditional gloom in which these cases had earlier been enveloped. It soon became obvious there was a large number of patients who were not ill enough to warrant a clear-cut psychotic diagnosis, yet were too ill to benefit from, or even withstand, unmodified psychoanalysis. They were borderline between neurosis and psychosis (as those terms were then employed); also, between analyzability and nonanalyzability.

Wilhelm Reich's *The Impulsive Character* was based on his efforts to apply analysis to the patients of a Viennese clinic.[3] There he encountered severe characterologic disorders noteworthy for what he called "the grotesque quality of their symptoms. . . ." As he put it, "the compulsive thought of killing one's child, as conceived by the simple neurotic, appears trite and innocuous in comparison to the compulsive urge of an impulsive individual to roast his child slowly over a fire" (op. cit., pp. 16–17).

Reich's idea about the impulsive character's simultaneous involvement with two sharply contradictory feeling states (maintained without conscious discomfort, via *splitting*) has become central to all later theoreticians concerned with borderline cases, including Kohut[4] and Kernberg.[5]

In the late 1920s, early 1930s, there was considerable interest in patients who seemed just beyond the reaches of psychoanalysis amongst the followers of Melanie Klein in England. The Kleinians tended to adopt a linear model of causation, in which biologic-constitutional factors were ignored and only the psychologic factor was seriously acknowledged. The more severe disorders were seen as having earlier, pregenital fixation-points along a continuum of psychosexual development.

In 1933 Kasanin[6] described nine patients of the Boston State Hospital, diagnosed originally as dementia praecox, but whose premorbid personality, emotionality, and course were atypical. He coined the term "schizoaffective" to categorize them. Many were in between Kraepelinian schizophrenia and the manic-depressive disorders; also their course, while not deteriorating, was usually characterized by some residual disability. These patients enjoyed life, and had good work adjustments; they were more often sociable than shy; were introspective, sexually maladjusted, but not eccentric. Their intelligence was average to superior, and in their immediate past was some unusually difficult environment situation.

Five cases are presented in detail; a close reading of the material reveals that by contemporary diagnostic standards two were very near to bipolar-II manic-depressive illness; one, pure schizophrenic with thought insertion and no mood disturbance; and two with evenly divided schizophrenic and affective symptoms we would still tend to call "schizoaffective."

The first to give the term borderline formal status was Stern[7] who, in

1938, outlined the characteristics of a group of office patients "too ill for classical psychoanalysis."

The characteristics of Stern's cases included (1) narcissisim, (2) paralysis in the face of crises ("psychic bleeding"), (3) inordinate hypersensitivity, (4) bodily and psychical "rigidity," (5) negative therapeutic reaction, (6) constitutional feeling of inferiority, (7) masochism, (8) "organic insecurity." (9) projective mechanisms (usually short of frank delusions) and (10) difficulties in reality testing, especially in relation to interpersonal relations. Stern felt there was some hereditary or constitutional factor, "deeply embedded in the personality of the patient," fostering the borderline patient's ingrained self-esteem deficit. Some patients exhibited melancholia, others, an infantile personality. By organic insecurity Stern is referring to an apparently constitutional incapacity to tolerate much stress. No guess is hazarded as to the nature of these presumed constitutional deficits.

In 1941 Zilboorg[8] described a number of cases under the rubric "ambulatory schizophrenia." He regarded schizophrenia as the generic name for a psychopathologic *process:* what was essential was the "trait," not the "state." Therefore if one had the *trait,* and only mild clinical signs, one was just as schizophrenic as the patient on the back wards.

Within the population of schizophrenics was a group with outward normality, dereistic thinking, shallow human relationships (acquaintances, but no friends), and incapacity to settle upon one job or life-pursuit. Zilboorg called this group "ambulatory," owing to the fact that the social facade was fairly well preserved, and hospitalization not necessary. The "ambulatory schizophrenic" is, in any case, a sicker patient, with a poorer prognosis (though some had a good recovery) than Kasanin's schizoaffective patient, and in a different realm altogether than Stern's patients.

A year after Zilboorg's paper came that of Helene Deutsch,[9] in which she described an "as-if" group of patients, whose most striking features were (1) a curious kind of non-ego-alien depersonalization, (2) repeatedly acted-out narcissistic identifications with others, (3) a good grasp on reality testing, (4) impoverishment of object-relations, (5) repudiation of aggressive tendencies, and (6) feelings of inner emptiness. The tendency of these patients to adopt the qualities of others as a means of retaining their love gave a non-genuine ("as-if") cast to their personality.

Five patients were discussed in detail: four women, and one, a homosexual boy of 17. Because of the family history of psychosis in four or five, Deutsch was led to conclude that the as-if personality might represent a phase of the schizophrenic process, "before it built up to the delusional form" (p. 319).

The importance of her contribution lay in its emphasis on the pathology of internalized object-relations. Similar conclusions, as Kernberg has mentioned, were reached soon afterwards by Fairbairn[10] and Melanie Klein.[11]

One the analytic writers of the 1940s who did favor the term borderline was Melitta Schmideberg.[12] Characterologically, many of Schmideberg's borderlines were schizoid or narcissistic. She is describing a group with less depressive manifestations and worse functioning than Stern's. One reason she felt it justifiable to place this group in a separate category was because the patients tended to remain true to their type over long periods of time. As Schmideberg put it, they were "stable in their instability." Borderline for her meant in-between neurosis and frank psychosis. Some of her borderline patients she pictured, like her predecessors, as "early cases of schizophrenia." Characteristically these patients (1) were unable to tolerate routine and regularity, (2) tended to break many rules of social convention, (3) were often late for appointments and unreliable about payment, (4) were unable to free-associate during their sessions, (5) were poorly motivated for treatment, (6) failed to develop meaningful insight, (7) led chaotic lives where something dreadful was always happening, (8) would engage in petty criminal acts, unless they happened to be well-off, and (9) could not easily establish contact. They might, for example, appear deeply committed to their analyst one day—and precipitously quit, the next.

Much more systematic in their attempt to define the borders of the "in-between" patient were Hoch and Polatin.[13] They felt they had isolated a new syndrome within the larger realm of schizophrenia, to which they gave the label "pseudoneurotic schizophrenia." In their 1959 paper, Hoch and Cattell[14] were at pains to point out that theirs was not a borderline group of an ill-defined sort between neurosis and psychosis, but a genuine variant of schizophrenia. The best-known aspects of Hoch and Polantin's description are of course the widespread symptoms mimicking the classical neuroses: compulsions, phobias, depressions, and so forth, all occurring in a jumble and in such intensity as to cripple the patient's functioning. The caricature of all the neuroses they named "pan-neurosis," and it was apt to be accompanied by pervasive anxiety ("pan-anxiety") and chaotic sexuality combining promiscuity and perversions—"pan-sexuality." Instead of clear-cut delusions and hallucinations were what they called "overvalued ideas" (a term later incorporated by Kernberg[5] in his description of the borderline). These involved statements such as "it is as if I were to hear a voice." Psychologic tests revealed Rorschach responses characteristic of schizophrenia in general. Of the five hospitalized cases presented *in extenso* in their earlier paper, three have an unmistakeable schizophrenic ring (eccentricity, formal thought disorder, chronicity, etc.), and two had a mixture of schizophrenic and affective signs that we might regard as more in keeping with a schizoaffective label, or even a bipolar-II manic-depressive psychosis. Of these five cases, four were young women (21–38); all were of superior intelligence. Over the years pseudoneurotic schizophrenia has remained a kind of trademark for the bright, young and rather flamboyant schizophrenic patients, selected for intensive psychotherapy.

Robert Knight also worked with hospitalized young adults receiving intensive psychotherapy. Adopting a more ego-psychologic approach than some of his predecessors, Knight[15] emphasized the severe *weakening* in borderline cases of many ego functions, including (1) secondary process thinking, (2) realistic planning, (3) defenses against primitive impulses. During a *free-associational* interview, the borderline patient is "more likely to show in bolder relief the various microscopic and macroscopic signs of schizophrenic illness" (p. 104; ital. mine). Furthermore, the Rorschach responses are often suggestive of a schizophrenic disorder, just as the word-association test frequently reveals loosening of associations. So Knight is actually defining borderline in a manner that overlaps greatly with at least the less dramatic cases of *schizophrenia*. But is Knight merely describing a kind of subclinical or, if you can bear with me, "pseudopseudoneurotic" schizophrenia? Not quite. Although his theoretical model is much more a part of what we would call the spectrum concept of schizophrenia than Knight seems willing to admit, the four actual cases he outlines in the original article are somewhat mixed. By contemporary standards, two would be considered chronically schizophrenic, and it is clear he wished to utilize a term divorced from the central concept of schizophrenia.

During the late 1950s Frosch[16] made a number of contributions to psychoanalytic theory regarding impulsive and psychopathic character deformations. Frosch distinguished between symptomatic disturbances of impulse, as seen in the perversions, and diffuse, pervasively impulsive life styles expressing themselves as a character disorder. Some evidence for an organic factor was occasionally noted in the latter, suggested by abnormal EEG tracings, for example. The impulsive character is closely allied to what others were calling borderline at this time. Psychodynamic formulations of impulse disturbances dwelt on the incapacity to postpone gratification, supposedly stemming from traumata in very early childhood: an engulfing mother might minimize frustration in a child to the point where proper delay patterns do not develop; a frustrating mother might contribute to the fostering of ungovernable wishes and faulty impulse control. The as-if character was said to illustrate the former; the impulsive character, the latter.

In the 1960s Frosch[17] proposed the term "psychotic character" for patients others had begun calling borderline. As director of a large municipal hospital Frosch was particularly conversant with a group of highly impulsive patients from chaotic home environments. In their background there was often a history of perinatal minimal brain damage (M.B.D.) contributing to the schizophrenia-like picture described recently by Bellak[18] and Quitkin[19] in M.B.D. patients.

Also in the mid-1960s Easser and Lesser[20] introduced the term "hysteroid" to describe a group of histrionic female patients too ill for classical psychoanalysis, whose character structure was a "caricature" of the hysteric. Erratic work history, chaotic relationships, and primitive defenses were recurring features. The authors provided no information about mental illness in the families nor about possible premenstrual symptom aggravation, though abnormalities in both areas were probably frequent in "hysteroids."

In the early 1960s a group at the Chicago Psychoanalytic Institute sought to outline the characteristics most commonly encountered in patients accorded the borderline label. The following were singled out for special attention: (1) marked lowering of self-esteem, (2) hypersensitivity to criticisim and rejection, (3) suspiciousness, (4) extreme fearfulness, (5) fears of *aggression* (whether their own or of others), of *closeness,* of *responsibility,* and of *change,* (6) tenuousness in interpersonal relations, (7) deficiency in reality orientation and (8) heightened use of primitive defenses *denial* and *projection.* The Chicago group further noted that these borderline features were to be seen over a fairly broad band of psychopathology, spanning the narcissistic character disorders to conditions they described as "near the psychoses."

The Chicago outline was later used as guide in the diagnosis of the borderline patients studied extensively by Grinker, Werble and Drye.[2] These investigators pursued an ego-psychologic approach, studying 93 observable variables in some 60 hospitalized patients. Cluster-analysis of their data yielded for subgroups. Group I, called the "psychotic border," consisted of patients exhibiting inappropriate negative behavior, poor grooming, rage outbursts, and depression. Group II, the "core borderline" group, was comprised of individuals with pervasive negative affect, little involvement with others, a tendency to act impulsively and self-destructively, and an awareness of their own identity side by side with behavior that was inconsistent with this identity. Group III contained "as-if" patients, who tended to copy the identities of others. Group IV, rather near the psychoneuroses, consisted of patients with "anaclitic" depression.

Studying mental illness in the biological and adoptive families of adoptive schizophrenics, Kety[21] realized that "a system of classification with finer gradations would be needed . . . in making diagnostic evaluations of the relatives" (p. 352). Two varieties of borderline were eventually acknowledged: an *acute* (as proposed to chronic) schizophrenic reaction and a *borderline* state. The acute schizophrenic reactions, similar to Kasanin's schizoaffective cases, were usually preceded by clearcut precipitants in individuals with fairly good premorbid adjustment. By contrast, the *borderline schizophrenia* group exhibited (1) strange or atypical mentation, with faulty logic and ultimately a poor adaptation to life experience (even in the face of a normal I.Q.), (2) rapid onset with clear-cut precipitants, (3) a clinical picture in which productive symptoms are often present during brief psychotic episodes (ego-alien obsessive thoughts may remain *afterward*), (4) depersonalization, (5) anhedonia, (6) chaotic sexuality, which may include homosexual as well as heterosexual activity, and (7) multiple neurotic symptoms. The results of Kety's study showed that the ill biologic relatives of index cases who were diagnosed either as core schizophrenics or *borderline* schizophrenics, suffered one or the other disorder, suggesting that this type of borderline case was indeed affiliated with the less easily mistakable form of schizophrenia. On the other hand the acute reactive schizophrenia probands had no core or borderline schizophrenics among *their* biologic relatives. This inclined the authors toward the attitude of many European psychiatrists and geneticists who regard the reactive psychoses as a distinctive type.

Over the past decade Kernberg[5] has been influential both as advocate of the borderline concept and as theoretician, redefining the concept in a more circumscribed and manageable fashion. Kernberg's description of borderline is from the psychostructural vantage point, placing reliance more on the nature and vicissitudes of internalized representations of the self and of others. Hence his classification, strictly speaking, is one of personality organizations, of which borderline represents the intermediate variant between neurotic and psychotic organizations. The critical points in the diagnostic spectrum, psychostructurally viewed, are *reality testing* and *ego-integration*. Reality testing demarcates borderline from psychotic structure. The tradition for this distinction in psychiatry is of course well established. Ego-integration, which is present in neurotic structures but enfeebled in the borderline, is conceptually less easily defined. A crucial aspect of faulty ego-integration, is the presence of sharply contradictory attitudes permeating vital sectors of the personality and interfering with every day life, especially in the sector of interpersonal relations. Kernberg's "non-specific" signs include lowered anxiety tolerance, poor impulse control, and poor sublimatory capacity. Low anxiety tolerance overlaps considerably with the concept of vulnerability, used by the geneticist, but, like faulty ego-integration, is an abstraction derived from a specialized confrontational interview or from long acquaintance with the patient. Notice that Kernberg's use of *borderline, neurotic,* and *psychotic* to denote structural levels is divorced from the issue of distal etiology. Nevertheless the term *psychotic structure,* implying chronic impairment of reality testing, is seldom observed other that in clearly schizophrenic patients. Reality testing in manic-depressive disorders is much better preserved, apart from the acute psychotic episodes.

It is of interest that, in spite of the strong difference in Kernberg's versus Grinker's[2] theoretical orientations, patients diagnosed borderline according to Kernberg's criteria are regularly so diagnosed by those adhering to Grinker's. Gunderson's criteria, an outgrowth of Grinker's model, also select out a set of patients very nearly coextensive with Kernberg's. Thus far there appears to be good accord between the afore-mentioned systems and the check list for borderline personality currently being developed at the New York State Psychiatric Institute by the biometrician Robert Spitzer.

Spitzer and his group have attempted specifically to create a set of items which could serve to demarcate borderline from neurotic structures on the basis of the numerical scores achieved. The checklist is still in the process of revision, but it is of interest that of the 19 items in the current draft, patients considered neurotic by a number of independent raters usually have fewer than 5 items that are applicable. Patients judged borderline rarely have as few as 5; usually more than 6. Items found positive in the majority of the borderline group include (1) underachievement in work or at school, (2) impulsivity or unpredictability in at least two areas which are potentially self-damaging (namely, spending, sex, gambling, drug or alcohol use), (3) a pattern of unstable and intense interpersonal relationships, (4) identity disturbance in several important areas (namely, self-image, gender identity, long-term goals), (5) affective instability, (6) problems (especially depressive) tolerating being alone, (7) undue social anxiety or hypersensitivity to criticism, and (8) chronic feelings of emptiness or boredom. Preliminary results suggest that good discrimination can be achieved and that it makes sense to speak of a borderline group that is distinct from the neurotic with respect to this questionnaire.

All four systems will include some patients with mild schizophrenic stigmata, others with significant depressive of bipolar-II disorders, and still others (especially adolescents) with severe character disorders, whose affiliation to the classical heredofamilial psychoses—here in the sense of schizophrenia or the manic-depressive illnesses—is either nonexistent or still obscure.

Gunderson and Singer[22] recently reviewed the literature on borderline cases, from which they abstracted the following characteristics as discernable in the majority of the patients described:

1. *Intense affect* (usually hostile or depressed: sometimes accompanied by depersonalization),
2. *Impulsive behavior* (whether directed against the self as in addiction, self-mutilation etc., or against others),

3. *Social adaptiveness* (mostly a superficial adaptiveness, beneath which is a disturbed identity camouflaged by rapid and shifting identifications with others),
4. *Brief psychotic experiences* (often a paranoid quality, and often provoked by abuse of illicit drugs),
5. *Abnormal results on psychological testing* (viz., bizarre responses on the Rorschach, but with good performance on the structural tests),
6. *Disturbed interpersonal relationships* (either transient and superficial or excessively intense and extractive).

Another method that has been proposed, over the past ten years, for coming to grips with the diagnostic problems in the borderline area is that of D. Klein,[23] who has suggested a differential responsiveness to various neuroleptic and antidepressant drugs as a means of separating out cases hitherto not readily classifiable. Noting the difficulty clinicians have, especially in working with adults, in distinguishing fundamental phenomena of mental illness from the epiphenomena that accrue over the years, he has put forward a theoretical model calling for a new nosology more attentive to drug response. The justification for such a revision, he feels, rests on the close linkage between certain pharmacologic agents and the presumed basic biochemical defects underlying the major functional psychoses. Klein has done considerable work with a patient group that appears to respond favorably and rather specifically to M.A.O. inhibitors. This group has previously presented serious problems in taxonomy, to say nothing of treatment, because of co-existence of schizophrenia-like symptoms with severe affect storms, hysterical personality features (in the extreme), all in the absence of deterioration or serious premorbid deformations of the personality. Such patients have often been called schizophrenic on the past "because their marked lability and disorganized life are considered evidence of ego-defect" (op.cit., p. 149). At other times the labels borderline, and schizoaffective have been applied. Klein has suggested the term "hysteroid dysphoria," and has also noted the close affinity of this syndrome to the manic-depressive disorders. Premenstrual symptom aggravation is frequently seen in these as in more typical manic-depressive females.[24]

GENETIC ASPECTS

To achieve homogeneity of diagnosis and greater replicability of results, psychogenetic research customarily concentrates upon paradigmatic cases of the disorder under study. Only a few studies have been done working backwards from borderline cases to the paradigm cases to which they presumably belong. Kety's study[21] showed that the mentally ill relatives of borderline schizophrenics (as defined by the authors) were themselves either process or borderline schizophrenics. The earlier reports on borderline patients in the psychoanalytic literature provide only anecdotal and fragmentary information about the hereditary factor. Thus, one of Kasanin's schizoaffective patients had two manic-depressive relatives. Most of Deutsch's as-if patients had at least one psychotic relative, either schizophrenic or of an unspecified type.

Recent studies incline toward the impression that poor-outcome schizophrenics have a higher proportion of ill relatives with schizophrenia, whereas the ill relatives of good-outcome schizophrenics tend to have affective disorders.[25] Some have felt the good-outcome schizophrenia is therefore a misnomer, either for an affective disorder or an atypical, third type of functional psychosis. Still others envision a phenotypic, perhaps even a genotypic, spectrum of psychoses with the manic-depressive disorders at one end, the schizophrenias at the other, and schizoaffective illness in the center.[26,27] This is the hypothesis utilized in the present report.

Systematic analysis of families of patients considered borderline according to the currently most-accepted definitions had thus far not been done.

In an effort to rectify this deficiency, I have recently examined the pedigrees of borderline patients, using psychotic and psychoneurotic patients as reference groups on either side.

Patients were considered borderline if they met the criteria of Kernberg, and had at least six positive items of the 19 on the Spitzer checklist.

(1) Patient Evaluation

A. A group of 18 hospitalized borderline patients was studied where the psychostructural diagnosis had been made by consensus of three psychiatrists (Drs. Kernberg, Bauer, and myself). Several of these patients had been examined personally by Gunderson, who considered them borderline by his criteria. These inpatients were compared with 23 patients hospitalized on the same ward whose consensus psychostructural diagnosis was psychotic (the latter were usually schizophrenic from the standpoint of traditional nosology). These 41 patients were consecutive admissions selected for probable capacity to benefit from psychoanalytically oriented psychotherapy. While chronically ill "treatment failures," they had good intellectual assets and some degree of social relatedness and affect. Mental illness in first- and second-degree relatives was assessed by the hospital staff in accordance with a semistructured questionnaire, the Genetic Data Sheet, devised by the author. Personal interviews, usually with parents and siblings, were done where possible. Family members with a severe emotional illness were categorized as suffering from a schizophrenia-spectrum disorder, a manic-depressive disorder (including unipolar depression), or—if there were evenly divided schizophrenic and affective symptoms, using the rating scale of Cohen et al[28]—a schizoaffective disorder.

Results. The 23 patients with psychotic structure had 28 mentally ill first- and second-degree relatives. Of the latter, 9 had a schizophrenic-spectrum disorder; 3 were schizoaffective; and 16 had a manic-depressive disorder.

The 18 patients with a borderline structure had 27 ill relatives of which none were clearly schizophrenic, 3 were schizoaffective and 24 had a manic-depressive disorder.

The excess of schizophrenic relatives (whether or not one counted in the schizoaffectives) in the families of psychotic probands was at a level (p. < 0.01) suggesting significance.

B. The 41 patients were also assessed according to the weighted rating scale of Cohen et al., and were then placed along a phenotypic continuum ranging from classical schizophrenia (without affective symptoms) through schizoaffective to classical manic-depressive (free of schizophrenic signs). For purposes of analysis two intermediate regions wre recognized: (a) schizophrenia with minimum to moderate affective symptoms and (b) manic-depressive disorder with minimum to moderate schizophrenic symptoms (namely, ideas of reference, bizarre eccentric speech). Two patients were excluded as having no signs of either major psychosis. The remaining 39 consisted of (I) 9 schizophrenics, (II) 10 schizophrenics with some affective symptoms, (III) 4 schizoaffectives (evenly divided symptoms), (IV) 5 predominantly affective-disorder patients with some schizophrenic symptoms, and (V) 11 patients with a manic-depressive disorder (usually predominantly in the depressive range).

Results. The category I patients had 9 mentally ill first-and second-degree relatives: 5 with schizophrenia, 1 with a schizoaffective disorder, 3 with manic-depressive illness. The category II patients had 13 ill relatives: 4 schizophrenic, 1 schizoaffective, 8 manic-depressive. The category III patients had 1 schizoaffective and 3 manic-depressive relatives. The category IV patients had 7 manic-depressive relatives. Finally, the 11 category V patients had 3 schizoaffective and 17 manic-depressive relatives. Thus in this patient sample schizophrenic relatives were confined to probands with conditions which were either purely schizophrenic or schizophrenic with only modest admixture of affective symptoms. In contrast the mostly to pure manic-depressive probands had no purely schizophrenic relatives. The observed difference was significant at the p. < 0.01 level, if one grouped together the relatives of categories I and II probands and compared them with the relatives of categories IV and V. The schizoaffective group was too small to permit statistical analysis.

(2) Evaluation of Patients' Families

An effort was made to evaluate mental illness in the families of a somewhat healthier group of borderline patients who were ambulatory when first seen. 72 pedigrees were assessed by the author; probands, gathered during ten years of private practice, were divided into three groups: 25 neurotics, 28 borderlines, and 15 psychotics. A combination of Kernberg's and Spitzer's criteria were used, this resulted in exclusion of 4 patients as transitional, by virtue of being considered either neurotic, but with 5 or more positive Spitzer items, or borderline, but with less than 4 positive items.

Ill relatives of the 68 probands with the more secure structural diagnoses were assessed as with the inpatients' relatives.

Results. In the borderline group family pedigrees were more apt to include at least one ill relative (19 out of 28, as against only 7 in the 25 neurotic families).

In the borderline group there were approximately 4 times as many affected relatives per patient as in the neurotic group (1.19 compared to 0.32). Both sets of difference are significant at the p. < 0.01 level.

The borderline probands in this patient sample had 33 ill relatives of whom 16 were either schizophrenic or schizoaffective. The 15 patients with psychotic structure (most of whom were schizophrenic in the standard nomenclature) had 20 ill relatives, of whom 14 were schizophrenic. Here no significant difference was noted in the percentage of schizophrenic relatives of borderline versus psychotic probands.

Nine of the 28 borderline patients were ultimately hospitalized, usually briefly; admitting diagnoses were diverse: 3 schizoaffective, 2 bipolar-II manic-depressive, 1 unipolar depression, 2 drug abuse, and 1 premenstrual rage outbursts. *All 9 female,* an even more dramatic finding than the skewed sex-ratio in the borderline group as a whole (21 females, 7 males).

Comment. The term *borderline* in contemporary usage, whether defined psychostructurally (Kernberg) or phenomenologically (Grinker, Gunderson, Spitzer) applies to patients a great many of whom (two out of three in the author's series) appear to have strong genetic loading for a major functional psychosis, as impressive as that noted among patients with psychotic structure. Thus far this loading is inclined toward the manic-depressive end of the phenotypic spectrum. Different patient samples may, however, yield different results in this regard, which probably reflect variations in referral sources or other extrinsic factors.

PROGNOSIS

Partly as a reflection of their etiological diversity, no simple statement is possible regarding outcome in borderline states. Although outcomes intermediate between those for neurotic and chronically psychotic patients would be expected, borderline patients with antisocial tendencies will often do worse than certain schizophrenic psychotic individuals with high social or intellectual assets.

In the psychoanalytic literature before the 1960s there are only anecdotal references to outcome in borderlines; usually, the patient samples were quite small. Prognosis seemed poorer in those samples where the term borderline referred to nonparadigmatic cases of schizophrenia.[8,11] Where affective symptoms were present, the prognosis was often better.[2,6]

The more systematic study of Grinker showed an improvement rate in 51 hospitalized borderlines of 3/5, using stable employment 2 to 3 years after admission as a criterion.

The 42 outpatient borderlines (some of whom were later hospitalized) in the Menninger Psychotherapy Project[29] showed improvement with expressive psychotherapy, but (as with Grinker's cases) were not compared with matched psychotic controls.

Such a comparison was attempted by the author in a preliminary follow-up study of the 45 in patients admitted to the New York State Psychiatric Institute, General Clinical Service, during calendar 1974. Using Kernberg's structural criteria the patients, by consensus of three diagnosticians, were divided in two groups; one comprised of 27 borderline and the other of 18 psychotic patients. Both groups were homgeneous with respect to age (avg. age = 22), ethnic background, educational experience, intelligence (avg. I.Q. = 122), and socioeconomic status. Females exceeded males in a ratio of 1.3:1 in each group.

Outcome at two to three years was rated by various members of the hospital staff according to a nine-point scale ("4 + " for dramatic social and occupational recovery, through "0" for no change to "4 − " for completed suicide).

The 27 borderlines consisted of 4 with schizophrenic stigmata (without hallucinations and delusions) and 23 with predominantly affective disturbances. The psychotic group were schizophrenic in traditional nomenclature. 3 + improvement was seen in 6 and 4 + in 5 patients, all of them borderlines with affective (mostly depressive) disorders. Moderate of 2 + improvement was noted in 9 borderlines (including 3 with schizophrenic stigmata) and 4 psychotics. Two borderlines—both of whom abused illicit drugs—were much worse at 2 −, whereas 5 of the 18 psychotics were worse at "2 −," "3 −" and "4 −" levels.

If one arbitrarily considered "2 + " as the minimal level of *unequivocal* improvement, the two groups could be divided as follows: improvement (2 + to 4 +) was seen in 20 borderlines and 4 psychotics; no improvement or worsening in 7 borderlines and 14 psychotics. These figures are significant at the p. < 0.01 level.

Comment. In this patient sample borderline personality organization predicted favorable outcome; psychotic personality organization (chronically impaired reality testing) predicted modest improvement or actual worsening. This was true despite the etiological and syndromal heterogeneity of the borderline patients, among whom were *formes frustes* of manic-depressive illness and, to a lesser extent, schizophrenia, severe character disorders, and anorexia nervosa cases, and in whom a variety of treatment modalities were employed (chiefly intensive psychotherapy, pharmacotherapy, and behavior modification according to the merits of each case). The excellent prognosis in the borderlines must have been in part a reflexion of the strong manic-depressive component noted in the majority of this group. In contrast the psychotic group was essentially schizophrenic, and was characterized by chronicity and poorer socialization.

TOPOGRAPHIC REPRESENTATION

Because there are so many varieties of borderline syndromes, and so many terms proposed to label them—some widely used, others popular only in a certain locale—collectively they create an area of much semantic confusion within contemporary psychiatric taxonomy. Worse still, there are loose definitions (Stern, Easser), strict definitions (Kernberg, Gunderson), definitions relating to traditional categories (Kasanin, Kety, Hoch, D. Klein), and others relating to the issue of analyzability (Easser, Deutsch, Knight, Stern, Kernberg).

In attempting to clarify some of this confusion, I have found it useful to compare the various borderline usages with some broader concept, within which these usages can be located. Because most borderline patients (by whatever label) represent either mild versions or *formes frustes* of the major functional psychoses (and a few such patients would appear to have genetic loading for *both* schizophrenia, M.D.P. via dual but mixed mating), the realm of all patients with schizophrenia, M.D.P., and mixed psychoses seemed the most relevant, broader concept available. Nevertheless, the term borderline is often applied to patients' conditions whose distal etiology does not seem to contain such genetic predisposition. (Organic and unusually adverse environmental factors are seen instead.) For this reason it seemed advisable to map borderline conditions onto a universe encompassing all severe psychiatric conditions and containing two realms: one for conditions where hereditary predisposition to schizophrenia or M.D.P. plays a major role; another for conditions related to other factors. Figure 1. repesents such a universe: within it are mapped nine representative borderline concepts.

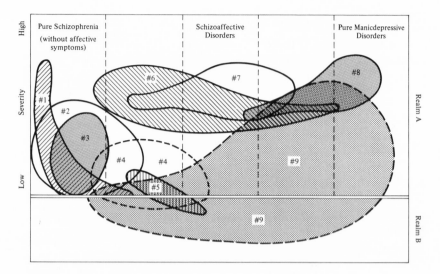

Figure 1.

EXPLANATORY NOTE TO FIGURE 1

The universe of severe emotional disorders has been divided into two realms: (A) the realm including the severe and mild forms of schizophrenia and manic-depressive disorders, arranged as a continuum of phenotypes from schizophrenia (without affective symptoms) through the evenly mixed schizoaffective disorders to the pure affective disorders; (B) the realm of disorders in which no hereditary predisposition to schizophrenia or M.D.P. is discernible.

Onto this universe are mapped a number of regions relating to various borderline types.

Region #1: Zilboorg's ambulatory schizophrenia.

Region #2: Schmideberg's borderine.

Region #3: borderline schizophrenia of Kety and Rosenthal.

Region #4: borderline of Robert Knight.

Region #5: Helene Deutsch's as-if personality.

Region #6: pseudoneurotic schizophrenia of Hoch and Polatin.

Region #7: schizoaffective as used by Kasanin.

Region #8: hysteroid dysphoria of Donald Klein.

Region #9: borderline in Kernberg's usage.

Note that Regions 4, 5 and 9 overlap with both realms, since they correspond to patient-groups some of whom have genetic loading for schizophrenia or M.D.P., and some of whom do not.

The etiological diversity of these concepts will be readily apparent: some are well within the pure schizophrenia end of the phenotypic continuum (namely, Kety's borderline schizophrenia); others are predominantly manic-depressive disorders (namely, Klein's hysteroid dysphoria); still others cover a much broader territory and spill over into the nonhereditary realm. All mappings were made from careful reading of individual case histories supplied in articles by proponents of the various borderline labels.

Other terms connoting borderline levels of psychopathology can be mapped onto such a universe in a similar fashion. This method is helpful in orienting the patient samples of the different investigators interested in borderline states. Borderline as used by Schmideberg, for example, is close to the usage of Knight, but substantially different from Kernberg's.

CONCLUSION

Many patients called borderline—by most of the popular definitions— appear to have a pronounced hereditary predisposition to mental illness. Often this factor is sufficiently striking to permit the clinician to make an educated guess about the patient's vulnerability, his eventual course, and the type of psychotherapy and medication that will prove most effective. The importance of a hereditary factor in these conditions is no new discovery;[30] it was taken for granted by the psychiatric and psychoanalytic communities until the second generation of psychoanalysts began to adopt a more linear and purely psychologic model of causation.

In Table 1, I have attempted to show the correspondence between the various terms for borderline conditions and the factor of genetic predisposition. The latter was evaluated in accordance with the more detailed case descriptions provided by the authors mentioned—in which comments about ill family members were included in the anamnesis.

It will be noted that the trend in usage, particularly since Knight's 1954 paper, has been to define borderline in such a way that it moves away from schizophrenia and into the penumbra of the manic-depressive disorders.

Table 1. Genetic Predisposition in Borderline Cases

Author	Term Proposed	Contributing Factors in Sample	
		Hereditary*	Other**
Clark, 1919[31]	Borderline Neuroses	Sz, MDP	
Moore, 1921	Borderline; Parataxes	MDP	
Reich, 1925	Impulsive Character	Sz	AEE
Oberndorf, 1930[32]	Borderline	MDP, Sz	
Glover, 1932[33]	Incipient Schizophrenia	Sz	
Kasanin, 1933	Schizoaffective	Sz, MDP	SSS
Stern, 1938	Borderline	MDP, (?)Sz	AEE
Zilboorg, 1941	Ambulatory Schizophrenia	Sz	
H. Deutsch, 1942	"As-If" Personality	Sz	AEE
Schmideberg, 1947	Borderline	Sz	
Federn, 1947[34]	Latent Psychosis	Sz	
Hoch & Polatin, 1949	Pseudoneurotic Schizophrenia	Sz, MDP	
Bychowski, 1953[35]	Latent Schizophrenia	Sz	
Knight, 1954	Borderline	Sz	AEE
Frosch, 1954	Psychotic Character	(?)MDP	AEE, MBD
Easser, 1965	Hysteroid	(?)MDP	
Mitsuda, 1965[36]	Atypical Psychosis	Sz MDP	
Kernberg, 1967	Borderline	MDP>Sz	AEE
Grinker, 1968	Borderline	MDP>Sz	AEE
Kety, 1968	Borderline Schizophrenia	Sz	
D. Klein, 1969[37]	Hysteroid Dysphoria	MDP	MBD
Mahler, 1971[38]	Borderline	??	DA
Aarkrog, 1973[39]	Borderline Psychosis	Sz	
Gunderson, 1975	Borderline	MDP>Sz	AEE
Spitzer, 1976	Borderline Personality	MDP, Sz	AEE, MBD

* Sz = Schizophrenia; MDP = Manic-Depressive Psychosis
**AEE = Adverse Early Environment (viz., death of a parent, chaotic home, parental neglect, parental brutality, etc.)
MBD = Minimal Brain Damage
SSS = Severe Situational Stress
DA = Developmental Arrest

SUMMARY

The various terms designating intermediate levels of psychopathology in use over the past sixty years have been reviewed by the author. The focus has been on the term "borderline." Earlier usage of borderline related to the region between psychosis and neurosis or analyzability and nonanalyzability. Mild or questionabale cases of schizophrenia were also given this label. Contemporary usage emphasizes borderline as a level of personality organization (between the psychotic and neurotic) with more precisely delineated features: poor ego-integration, preserved reality-testing, along with *lowered* anxiety tolerance, impulse control and sublimatory capacity (Kernberg). Other current usages define an attenuated form of schizophrenia where family history is often positive for schizophrenia (Kety), a combined hysteric-depressive state amenable to antidepressants (Klein), or a particular clinical picture characterized by intense negative affect, shallow relationships, impulsivity, good reality-testing (Gunderson). Apart from Kety's definition, contemporary usage inclines toward patients with manic-depressive heredity, although borderlines are still an etiologically heterogeneous group. Though a number of subtypes have been described, each responsive to a particular method of psychotherapy or pharmacotherapy, prognosis in the borderline group is often favorable, provided drug-abuse and antisocial features are minimal or absent. Patients meeting criteria for borderline personality organization have distinctively better 2- to 3-year outcomes than those with psychotic organization. A topographic method for comparing different borderline labels is described and illustrated.

REFERENCES

1. Mack, J. E. *Borderline States in Psychiatry*, Grune & Stratton, New York, 1975.
2. Grinker, R. R., Sr., Werble, B. and Drye, R. C. *The Borderline Syndrome*, Basic Books, New York, 1968.
3. Reich, W. *Der triebhafte Character*, Internationaler Psychoanalytischer Verlag, Leipzig, 1925.
4. Kohut, H. *The Analysis of the Self*, International Universities Press, New York, 1971.
5. Kernberg, O. F. Borderline Personality Organization. *J. Amer. Psychoanal. Assoc.* 15:641, 1967.
6. Kasanin, J. The Acute Schizo-affective Psychoses. *Amer. J. Psychiatry* 97:97, 1933.
7. Stern, A. Psychoanalytic Investigation and Therapy in the Borderline Group of Neuroses. *Psychoanal. Q.* 7:467, 1938.
8. Zilboorg, G. Ambulatory Schizophrenia. *Psychiatry* 4:149, 1941.
9. Deutsch, H. Some Forms of Emotional Disturbance and Their Relationship to Schizophrenia. *Psychoanal. Q.* 11:301, 1942.
10. Fairbairn, W. R. D. Endopsychic Structure Considered in Terms of Object-Re-

lationships (1944). In *An Object-Relations Theory of the Personality,* Basic Books, New York, 1952, pp. 82–136.

11. Klein, M. Notes on some Schizoid Mechanisms. In *Developments in Psychoanalysis,* Riviere, J. Ed. Hogarth Press, London, 1952, pp. 292–320.

12. Schmideberg, M. The Treatment of Psychopaths and Borderline Patients. *Amer. J. Psychother.* 1:45, 1947.

13. Hoch, P. and Polatin, P. Pseudoneurotic Forms of Schizophrenia. *Psychiatric Q.* 23:248, 1949.

14. Hoch, P. and Cattell, J. P. The Diagnosis of Pseudoneurotic Schizophrenia. *Psychiatric Q.* 33:17, 1959.

15. Knight, R. P. Borderline States. In *Psychoanalytic Psychiatry and Psychology,* Knight, R. P. and Friedmann, C. R., Eds. International Universities Press, New York, 1954, pp. 97–109.

16. Frosch, J. A Contribution to the Nosology of the Impulse Disorders. *Amer. J. Psychiatry* 111:132, 1954.

17. Frosch, J. The Psychotic Character. *Psychiatric Q.* 38:81, 1964.

18. Bellak, L. A Possible Subgroup of the Schizophrenic Syndrome and Implications for Treatment. *Amer. J. Psychother.* 30:194, 1976.

19. Quitkin, F., Rifkin, A. and Klein, D. Neurologic Soft Signs in Schizophrenia and Character Disorder. *Arch. Gen. Psychiatry* 33:845, 1976.

20. Easser, R. R. and Lesser, S. Hysterical Personality: A Reevaluation. *Psychoanal. Q.* 34:390, 1965.

21. Kety, S. S. Rosenthal, D., Wender, P. H. and Schulsinger, F. The Types and Prevalence of Mental Illness in the Biological and Adoptive Families of Adopted Szhizophrenics. In *The Transmission of Schizophrenia,* Rosenthal, D. and Kety, S. S., Eds. Pergamon Press, Oxford, pp. 345–362.

22. Gunderson, J. G. and Singer, M. T. Defining Borderline Patients: An Overview. *Amer. J. Psychiatry* 132:1, 1975.

23. Klein, D. F. Drug Therapy as a Means of Syndromal Identification and Nosological Revision. In *Psychopathology and Psychopharmacology,* Cole, J. O., Freedman, A. M. and Friedhoff, A. J., Eds. The Johns Hopkins University Press, Baltimore, 1973, pp. 143–160.

24. Diamond, S. B., Rubinstein, A. A., Dunner, D. L. and Fieve, R. R. Menstrual Problems in Women with Primary Affective Illness. *Comp. Psychiatry* 17:541, 1976.

25. Procci, W. R. Schizo-affective Psychosis: Fact or Fiction? *Arch. Gen. Psychiatry* 33:1167, 1976

26. Beck, A. T. *Depression: Causes and Treatment,* University of Philadelphia Press, Philadelphia, 1967.

27. Fish, F. The Cycloid Psychoses. *Compr. Psychiatry* 5:155, 1964.

28. Cohen, S. M., Allen, M. G., Pollin, W. and Hrubec, Z. Relationship of Schizo-affective Psychosis to Manic-Depessive Psychosis and Schizophrenia. *Arch. Gen. Psychiatry* 26:539, 1972.

29. Kernberg, O. F., Burstein, E. D., Coyne, L., Appelbaum, A., Horwitz, L. and Voth, H. Psychotherapy and Psychoanalysis. *Bull. Menninger Clin.* 36:1, 1972.

30. Moore, T. V. The Parataxes: A Study and Analysis of Certain Borderline Mental States. *Psychoanal. Rev.* 8:252, 1921.

31. Clark, L. P. Some Practical Remarks upon the Use of Modified Psychoanalysis in the Treatment of Borderland Neuroses and Psychoses. *Psychoanal. Rev.* 6:306, 1919.

32. Oberndorf, C. P. The Psychoanalysis of Borderline Cases. *N.Y.S.J. Med.* 30:648, 1930.

33. Glover, E. Psychoanalytic Approach to the Classification of Mental Disorders. *J. Mental Sci.* 78:819, 1932.
34. Federn, P. Principles of Psychotherapy in Latent Schizophrenia. *Amer. J. Psychother.* 1:129, 1947.
35. Bychowski, G. The Problem of Latent Psychosis. *J. Amer. Psychoanal. Assoc.* 4:484, 1953.
36. Mitsuda, H. The Concept of Atypical Psychoses from the Aspect of Clinical Genetics. *Acta Psychiat. Scand.* 41:372, 1965.
37. Klein, D. F. and Davis, J. *Drug Treatment and Psychodiagnosis.* William & Wilkins, Baltimore, 1969.
38. Mahler, M. S. A Study of the Separation Individuation Process and its Possible Application of the Borderline Phenomena in the Psychoanalytic Situation. *Psychoanal. Study of the Child* 26:403, 1971.
39. Aarkrog, T. Conditions in Adolescents who were Borderline Psychotics as Children. *Acta Psychiat. Scand.* 49:377, 1973.

21. The Countertransference with the Borderline Patient

Harold F. Searles

A working definition of what I mean by "countertransference" is provided by the first sentence of a lengthy definition in *A Glossary of Psychoanalytic Terms and Concepts,* edited by Moore and Fine, and published by the American Psychoanalytic Association in 1967: "Countertransference: Refers to the attitudes and feelings, only partly conscious, of the analyst towards the patient. . . ." The rest of their definition is one with which I largely concur, but is unnecessary to reproduce here.

For many years, I have found that the countertransference gives one the most reliable approach to understanding patients of whatever diagnosis. My monograph (Searles 1960) on the nonhuman environment and many of my previous papers have contained detailed data and discussions of the countertransference in my work with frankly psychotic patients; this contribution will not attempt to condense those earlier writings.

As an example of the usefulness of the countertransference, consider the question of whether it is well for the borderline patient to use the couch. For nearly thirty years now it has seemed to me that the patient is unlikely to be panicked by his experience if the analyst himself, sitting behind the couch, does not give way to panic.

Comparably, in my work with an ambulatory schizophrenic woman who had moved from sitting in a chair to sitting on the couch, I found that the next analytic-developmental step, her becoming able to lie down on the couch, involved not merely *her* ability to adapt to the isolation attendant upon no longer being able to see my face. I came to realize after she had started lying down, but sitting up from time to time to get a look at my face, that my relief at these "interruptions" was fully comparable with her own. I had been myself repressing the feelings of deprivation attendant upon no longer being able to watch her fascinating, mobile facial expressions while she was lying on the couch.

Recently, when a borderline patient who had been sitting in a chair for some months began lying on the couch, I found that, during the first session sitting behind it, I was speaking to her much more than had been my custom. My first thought was that I was supplying, empathically, sufficient verbal feedback to help her become accustomed to this new and, for her, much more emotionally isolated situation. Only some time later in this session did I realize that, again, I myself evidently was repressing abandonment anxiety, and struggling to keep such anxiety repressed and projected upon her.

In work with the borderline patient, there are several readily apparent reasons why the realm of the countertransference is so important. I intend to discuss in this paper additional, more subtle reasons; but first I shall make brief mention of some of the more obvious ones.

The intensity of the borderline patient's repressed emotions is so great as to make unusual demands upon the emotionality of the analyst. The demands are greatly accentuated because of the patient's wide gamut of ego developmental levels at work in his mode of relating with the analyst, such that the latter finds himself called upon to relate with the patient upon unpredictably shifting levels which vary from relatively mature, healthy-neurotic modes to extremely primitive modes essentially akin to those found in the transference psychoses of frankly schizophrenic patients. Not uncommonly, the analyst feels related with the patient upon two or more such levels simultaneously.

So much of the borderline patient's ego functioning is at a symbiotic, preindividuation level that very frequently it is the analyst who, through relatively ready access to his own unconscious experiences, is first able to feel in awareness, and conceptualize and verbally articulate, the patient's still-unconscious conflicts. Though these conflicts inherently "belong" to the patient, they can come to be known to and integrated by him only through his identification with the analyst into whom they have been able to flow, as it were, through the liquidly symbiotic transference.

Because the *borderline* patient does indeed seem, during much if not most of our work with him, to be walking a tightrope between neurosis and psychosis, he requires us to face our fear lest he become psychotic, our envy of him for his having this avenue so widely open to him, our hateful desire for him to become psychotic, as well as our ambivalent fear and wish to become psychotic ourselves.

Because the normal phase of mother-infant symbiosis in him never has been resolved into predominantly individuated ego functioning, we find that in the transference-symbiosis which naturally ensues over the course of the analysis, we are cast not only as the symbiotic mother in the transference but, equally often and by the same token, as the symbiotic infant. We must accustom ourselves, therefore, to experiencing symbiotic-dependency feelings toward the mother-patient such as are only relatively subtly present in our work with neurotic patients.

THE IMPACT UPON THE ANALYST OF THE PATIENT'S SPLIT EGO FUNCTIONING

Gunderson and Singer (1975) in an article entitled, "Defining Borderline Patients: An Overview," provide a helpful survey of the extensive literature of descriptive accounts of borderline patients. Among several features which they found that most authors believe to characterize most borderline patients, foremost is the presence of intense affect. Now in entering into more detailed discussion, I want first to highlight the impact upon the analyst of the patient's unintegrated ambivalence— or, perhaps better expressed, the impact of the unintegrated affects which the patient expresses toward him, referable to splits in the patient's ego functioning such that intensely hateful affects are not integrated with (and thus modified by) intensely loving affects, and vice versa.

I cannot fully convey here this impact, for the reason that I cannot achieve, at will, such a complete splitting of intense emotions as prevailed at the level of ego functioning in these patients on these occasions; I must elaborate upon the following comments, therefore, with some brief description. One woman patient said, "I can't tell you how much I love you or how much of a shit I think you are." In saying, "how much I love you," her affective tone was one of glowingly unambivalent love; but in saying only moments later, "how much of a shit I think you are," her affect was unambivalently one of hostile contempt. Another woman, reminiscing that her mother used to address her as "my darling rat," conveyed by her tone that the words "darling" and "rat" had been expressive of forcefully contrasting emotions without any acknowledgment, in the mother's ego functioning, of any conscious conflict between these two images of her daughter. A chronically schizophrenic woman once said to me, "You should have the Congressional Medal of Spit." The first seven words of that eight-word sentence conveyed heartfelt admiration; but the last one, said with no break at all in the rhythm of her speech, was uttered in unalloyed contempt.

The examples of patients' affective expressions which I have just cited are expressions which switch instantaneously from loving to hateful ones. Even more unsettling, oftentimes, are a patients' expression of highly incongruous emotions simultaneously. Such phenomena comprise a part of what is not only difficult but also fascinating in the work with borderline patients, for one discovers that there are combinations of intense emotions never before encountered within one's conscious memory.

For example, I have come to realize that two of the part-aspects of one of my patients comprise what I experience as an irresistibly funny homicidal maniac. I had long been aware of his quick-tempered fury at any perceived insult, and of his underlying murderousness; but as the work went on it became evident that he possessed also an enormous ability to be funny. At times I felt overwhelmed by the urge to laugh at some of his raging comments, and yet, simultaneously, felt that it was of life-and-death importance not to let him detect my amusement. On rare occasions with him and comparable patients, I have been seized with strangled, epileptic seizurelike laughter, and on some of these occasions have managed, apparently successfully, to disguise it as a cough or somatically-based fit of choking. My underlying terror of being detected in some instances is that I will be murderously attacked physically or—hardly less frightening—subjected to a demolishing verbal attack. More often, the terror is lest the outraged patient sever, instantly and irrevocably, the treatment relationship which he and I have built up so slowly and arduously.

In my work with one such patient after another, it becomes evident that the patient's largely unconscious sadism has had much to do with my finding myself in so tortured a position. Only somewhat milder forms of this same phenomenon are to be found in one's work with a supervisee who, with a simultaneous hawklike sensitivity to any increment of somnolence, is reporting clinical material in a soothing, boring, or some similar tone which drives one almost irresistibly toward sleep.

To return to borderline patients, a woman was reporting a dream in her usual overmodulated tone which was thoroughly enigmatic as regards emotions. She said that in her dream: "We were all under some kinda interstellar influence, some kinda unseen force that was controlling things . . . kinda malevolent force hovering around. . . . " As I was writing down the dream, I noticed that each time I wrote the word "force," I had a momentary thought, either that it was written "farce" or else that I had to be careful not to write "farce." I sensed there to be an unusual theme, here, of a murderous or sinister farce. The patient gave a brief chuckle at the beginning of her description of the parts of the dream which I have quoted; but in the main she sounded to be fending off an awed, whistling-in-the-graveyard feeling. Later in this session she commented, without identifiable emotion of any sort, that her former roommate, years ago in law school, had been electrocuted in a strange "accident." During the years of her analysis, her fear lest she possess an omnipotent destructiveness proved to be one of the major themes of our work together.

To simply mention other unusual affective combinations, I have been struck by the diabolical naïveté of one of my male patients, and by this same patient's ferocious idealizing of me—his idealizing me with ferocity. I have felt one patient to give me a slashing smile when she walked in from the waiting room, and another (far more ill than borderline) to give me a decapitatingly saccharine verbal greeting when I walked into the seclusion room for my usual session with her. Another female patient has often provided me gratification with the caustic warmth of her so ambivalent responses to me.

I have found this same phenomenon (of strange-seeming combinations of affects) at work in many teaching-interviews I have had with patients who were manifesting pathologic grief reactions. That is, I have found myself experiencing sadistic urges toward depressed patients who clearly were repressing intense grief; only gradually did my initial shock at finding these sadistic urges in myself, in that setting, give way to an understanding that I was experiencing something of the sadistic feelings at work on an unconscious level in the patients themselves, and which thus far had been preventing further accomplishment of their grieving.

Surely some of these instances of patients giving expression simultaneously to so intensely incongruous emotions are manifestations of incongruously nonfitting introjects, within the patient, derived from the two parents; the disharmoniously wedded parents halved counterparts (however exaggerated or otherwise distorted) in comparably poorly married parental introjects largely unintegrated in the patient's ego functioning. But even more pathogenically, neither parent was well-integrated within himself or herself. Thus the mother alone, or the father alone (or both), presumably presented to the child, as a model for identification, the embodiment of intensely incongruent emotionality such as we find in the patient himself. Hence either parent, taken alone, can have been the source (so to speak) of an abundance of nonfitting parental introjects within the patient.

AMUSEMENT

In relation to those occasions, which I mentioned earlier, when the analyst finds himself in the grip of amusement which he experiences as crazily incongruous with the more predominant and explicit aspects of his interaction with the patient, I wish to emphasize that, during the childhood of such a patient, some of the most traumatic effects of his family-relatedness derived from having to maintain under repression essentially healthy laughter. It is this healthy laughter which, more often than not, in the patient-therapist interaction is experienced first by the analyst, and only after much resistance of the latter's part. Laughter is, after all, precisely one of the most appropriate, healthiest kinds of response to the crazy things that have gone on in the childhood families of borderline patients, and that transpire not infrequently during their analytic sessions in adult life.

In the many teaching-interviews I have done, it is usual for there to emerge some occasion, during the interview, for the patient and I to laugh at least briefly together. Not rarely, this is the first time the therapist and other hospital staff members, for example, have seen such a capacity for humor in the patient. It is rare indeed for me to encounter a patient in whom I am unable, during a single interview, to perceive a sense of humor, no matter how straight-faced or laden with lugubrious-ness, or however sadistic or psychotically distorted its means of expression.

Our traditional training, as well as the mores of our culture, have so schooled us with the rigorous taboo against laughing *at* the poor victim of psychosis that it is difficult for us to realize that some of this most grievous warp, in childhood, derived from the family-wide taboo agaist healthy laughter, lest such laughter do violence to the so vulnerable sensibilities of the other family members. If we can dare to let our "own" healthy laughter come into the patient-therapist interaction, we can help him to find access to his "own" long-repressed healthy capacities in this regard. Parenthetically, in many years of work with a chronically schizophrenic woman, there have been many sessions in which I felt the only solidly healthy responses she manifested consisted in her occasional belly laughs, unaccompanied by any verbal communication. It is amusement which I have shared at such times, however uncomprehendingly in any secondary-process terms.

THE ANALYST'S EXPERIENCE OF TRANSFERENCE ROLES WHICH ARE BOTH STRANGE IN NATURE AND INIMICAL TO HIS SENSE OF REALITY AND TO HIS SENSE OF PERSONAL IDENTITY

Turning from the subject of the impact upon the analyst of the patient's emotions *per se,* I want briefly to delineate the integrally related topic of the analyst's experience of the strange transference roles in which he finds himself, by reason of the patient's developing transference, at times psychotic or near-psychotic in its reality value for the patient.

The major roots of the patient's transference reactions are traceable to a stage in ego development prior to any clear differentiation between inner and outer world, and prior to the child's coming to function as a whole person involved in interpersonal relationships with other persons experienced as whole objects. Hence the analyst finds that these transference reactions and attitudes of the adult borderline patient cast him, the analyst, in roles strangely different from those he commonly encounters in working with the neurotic patient whose transference casts him, say, as a domineering father or sexually seductive, masochistic mother. Instead, the analyst finds the patient reacting to him as being nonexistent, or a corpse, or a pervasive and sinister supernatural force, or as God, or as being the patient's mind, or some anatomical part-aspect of his mother (her vagina, for example, or her fantasized penis). My monograph concerning the nonhuman environment (Searles 1960) contains many examples of schizophrenic patients' transference reactions to the therapist as being one or another of a wide variety of nonhuman entities, and one finds an equally wide range in the work with borderline patients.

Not only the bizarre content or structure of the patient's transference images of him, but also their near-psychotic reality value for the patient, at times formidably threaten the analyst's own sense of reality and his own sense of identity. For example, I found that one of the sources for my persistent hatred of one such patient was his intense transference to me as being his highly obsessive mother, which exerted upon me a powerful pull toward my earlier, much more obsessive, only partially outgrown self. A woman reported, several years into our work together, that for the first time the thought had just occurred to her that perhaps I was *not* crazy, and went on to associate the craziness, which she now realized she had been attributing to me all along, with that which she had perceived in her father since early childhood. All along I had had to cope, alone, with the patient's persistent but unconscious transference image of me as being crazy. Another woman, whose childhood was lived in remarkable isolation from both parents, and who used to talk with insects and birds, manifested transference reactions to me as being one or another of these creatures, and I never was able fully to determine whether, even in childhood, the conversations she had were with real creatures of this sort, or fantasied ones.

The omnipotent creativity, for good or evil but predominantly for evil, which frankly psychotic patients attribute to their own and the therapist's thought processes, is only to a somewhat lesser degree true of the borderline patient. Whereas the borderline patient possesses, most of the time, sufficient observing ego to not fully misidentify the therapist as being someone, or a part-aspect of someone, or something, from the patient's real past, he nonetheless comes sufficiently close to doing so that the therapist may feel submergedly threatened lest his transference role become, indeed, his—the therapist's—only subjective reality.

In a session several years into her analysis, a middle-aged woman said during a brief interchange between us as to whom various persons in a just-reported dream personified or represented: "People are never to me who *they* think they are. They are who *I* think they are." She said this in a tone of small-childlike grandiosity and without appearing consciously disturbed or threatened. She said it by way of pointing out or reminding me of an obvious fact. The charming little child quality of this expressed recognition on her part was in marked contrast to the genuinely threatening effects upon me, many times in earlier years, when her negative transference had been much more intense and her ability to differentiate between mental images and flesh-and-blood outer reality had been much less well established. During those years I had felt anything but charmed by her reacting to me with the full conviction that I was (to give but one example) literally a stone-hearted witch.

To the extent that a patient is unable to distinguish between the analyst as, say, a mother in the transference situation, and the actual mother in the patient's early childhood, he is likewise unable to differentiate between *mental images of persons* (i.e., images within his own head) and the corresponding *persons in outer reality*. This is another way of understanding why the analyst reacts to the borderline patient's transference images of him as being such a threat to his sense of personal identity—that is, why the patient's transference *image* of him, which the patient experiences as being so fully and incontestably real, carries with it the threat to the analyst that it will indeed fully create or transform him into conformity with that image.

I shall turn again to my work with frankly and chronically schizophrenic patients for relatively unambiguous examples of this point. Each of the following two instances occurred relatively early in my work with such patients, at a time when more areas of my own identity existed at a repressed or dissociated level than I find to be the case in my work these days. One chronically and severely assaultive woman asked me, at a time when I was conscious of feeling toward her only a wish to help her and a physical fear of her, "Dr. Searles, *why* do you hate me?" She asked me this in a tone that assumed it to be an incontrovertible fact that I hated her, that hatred was the predominant—if not the only—feeling I experienced toward her, and that this was something we both had known all along. In response to her question I felt thorougly disconcerted and a loss to know what, if anything, to say. I thought that theoretically I must hate her, but was entirely unaware of hating her and—most pertinent for the point I am making here—I felt completely alone, without any ally in her, as regards any attempt on my part to question, with her, whether her view of me was not at all exaggerated, oversimplified, or otherwise distorted.

Another chronically ill woman, who for several years in our work perceived me most of the time as being, in flesh-and-blood reality, a woman, and who was herself the mother of several children, once said to me in very much the same tone as that used by the woman I have just mentioned, *"You're* a reasonable woman; what do *you* do with a daughter who . . ." She was speaking for all the world in terms of our being two women comparing notes, companionably, about the problems of rearing daughters.

In the neurotic patient it may be that an unconscious *personality aspect* such as hostile domineeringness, based upon an unconscious identification with the domineeringness, say, of the father, is projected during the course of treatment upon the analyst, who meanwhile is perceived by the patient as essentially the same person as before but with—so the patient now perceives—a hateful and perhaps intimidating, domineering aspect. The analyst may sense himself, in response to these developments, to have an uncomfortably domineering personality aspect, but does not feel his basic sense of his own identity to be appreciably disturbed.

Although such a state of things may be true in psychoanalytic work between a neurotic patient and the analyst, in the borderline patient there is insufficient ego integration for the unconscious domineeringness to exist as merely a repressed component of the patient's ego identity. It exists, instead, in a dissociated, split-off state as a largely unintegrated introject derived from experiences with the parent in question. It exists as a separate self, as it were, a component with its own separate identity. Now, when the analyst becomes involved in psychoanalytic psychotherapy with such a patient, he finds that the latter, through projecting this introject upon the analyst, comes not merely to perceive him as being the analyst with a newly-revealed hateful domineeringness. The analyst finds, instead, that the patient becomes more or less fully convinced that the analyst has been replaced by the hateful and intimidating, domineering father.

That is, in the work with the borderline or schizophrenic patient, the unconscious affect is encapsulated in, or pervades, an introject structure which has an identity value all its own. This affect-laden structure which the patient, to the extent that he is schizophrenic, is convinced *is* the real identity of the analyst has, by being projected forcibly and persistently upon the latter for many months or even years, an effect at times formidably shaking the analyst's own sense of identity.

But on the positive side the analyst, attentive to the resultant fluctuations in his sense of his "own" personal identity in the course of sessions with these patients, finds that he possesses a priceless (and, more often than not, previously unrecognized) source of analytic data. In a paper entitled, "The Sense of Identity as a Perceptual Organ" I mentioned that,

Somewhere midway through my own analysis, after I had undergone much change, I visualized the core of myself as being, none the less, like a steel ball bearing, with varicolored sectors on its surface. At least, I told myself, this would not change. I have long since lost any such image of the core of my identity. . . . In a succession of papers I have described the process whereby my sense of identity has become sufficiently alive to change . . . so that it is now my most reliable source of data as to what is transpiring between the patient and myself, and within the patient. I have described . . . the "use" of such fluctuations in one's sense of identity as being a prime source of discovering, in work with the patient, not only counter-transference processes but also transference processes, newly-developed facets of the patient's own self-image and so on; and in supervision, of discovering processes at work not only between the supervisee and oneself, but also between the supervisee and the patient. [Searles 1965b]

For a number of years during the analysis of a young woman, I felt, more often than not, somnolent during the session and much of the time indeed sensed that her transference to me was, even more, as being comatose, moribund. Many of the sessions felt endless to me. After several years, her transference to me began to emerge into her own awareness through such dreams as this:

I was at a dinner party. This woman seated across the table from me seemed to fluctuate between being dead and being alive. I was conversing with her and it was almost as though the more involved I became with her, the more dead she would become. That kind of thing went back and forth several times. From a distance she seemed vigorously alive, but up close she seemed lifeless and dull.

Associative connections between that woman in the dream and myself as a representative of a number of personality aspects of various persons from the patient's childhood, as well as connections to components of herself which were identified with those emotionally dead figures from her past, emerged in the subsequent analytic work.

A childless woman, after detailing how moved she had felt at the aliveness of a pair of twin babies she had seen the day before, became somberly philosophical and said, with an undertone of fear and awe in her voice, "There's always the death in the background." I heard this as a clear but unconscious reference to me, behind her, as being death;

I said nothing. She went on, " . . . I do have a lot more thoughts about the finiteness of my own life."

Other patients, of various diagnostic categories, have associated me—partly by reason of not feeling free to look at me during the session—with those parts of a parent's body which they had not been permitted to look at during their childhood, most frequently the parent's genital.

Parenthetically, it seems to me not coincidental that in those very frequent instances in which such transference responses as I am citing prevail in work with borderline patients for years, the analyst seldom indeed finds it feasible to make effective transference interpretations. The patient is largely deaf, unconsciously, to verbalized intelligence from an analyst who is powerfully assumed, again at an unconscious level in the patient, to be something quite other than a whole human being.

Further, in a number of patients with varying degrees of illness, I have found that *words*—from either patient or analyst—are equivalent to *father,* intruding unwanted into a nonverbal mother-infant symbiosis. This transference "father" is most significantly traceable to components of the biological mother herself, in these instances of split mother-transference, wherein intense jealousy permeates both the transference and the countertransference.

The borderline patient's impaired sense of reality is another typical factor which makes the development, and work of resolution, of the transference psychosis stressful for both participants. Helen Deutsch's classic paper on "as if" personalities (Deutsch 1942) is highly relevant here. One woman emphasized to me that "I am very different in person from the way I am here." This curious phrase, "in person," seemed to indicate that the analytic sessions possessed for her the reality value merely of a television show or a movie, for example. Later in the session she commented that her relationship with her father was so stormy that she sometimes felt an urge to write a novel about it; my own private impression was that, in that relationship, she was indeed living a novel. I have found it commonplace for these patients to emphasize that "in my *life*" or "in my *real* life" they are quite different persons from the way they are in the analysis. Admittedly, an analytic relationship commonly can be seen to be in many ways different from other areas of a patient's life; but these patients refer persistently to the analytic relationship and setting as being not really part of their lives at all. Many times, while reminiscing about events earlier in their lives, they will recall that, "In my *life.*" . . . ," saying this as though from the vantage point either of a very old person whose life is essentially *all* past now or—very often, in my experience—of one who has already died and can therefore look back upon his own life in its totality, as something now behind and quite apart from him.

THE ANALYST'S REACTIONS TO THE DEVELOPMENT OF THE TRANSFERENCE-BORDERLINE-PSYCHOSIS IN THE PATIENT

Now I shall discuss various of the emotions which the therapist comes to experience in consequence of the development of the transference-borderline-psychosis in the patient, and some of the sources of these emotions. While the literature is not in full and explicit agreement that a transference psychosis typically develops in psychoanalytic therapy with the borderline patient, it seems generally agreed that he brings into the treatment relationship a vulnerability (or, one might say, a treatment need) for this development, and that the emergence of so intense and primitive a constellation of transference reactions is at the least a standard hazard in the therapist's work with these patients. I think it fair and accurate to say that the borderline patient needs to develop and, if treatment proceeds well, will develop a transference-borderline-psychosis in the course of the work.

Certainly in my own work with borderline patients, and in my supervision of analytic candidates and psychiatric residents concerning their work with such patients, as well as in my study of the literature regarding psychoanalytic therapy with borderline patients, I find that a transference-borderline-psychosis commonly develops over the course of the work and needs, of course, to become resolved in order for the treatment to end relatively successfully.

My own clinical and supervisory experience strongly indicates to me that there are certain intense, and intensely difficult, feelings which the therapist can be expected to develop in response to the patient's development of the transference-borderline-psychosis. It may well be that, as the years go on, we shall become able to do psychoanalytic therapy with borderline and schizophrenic patients with increasing success in proportion to our ability to accept that, just as it is to be assumed an inherent part of the work that the *patient* will develop a transference-borderline-psychosis or transference-psychosis, it is also to be assumed no less integrally that the *therapist* will develop—hopefully, to a limited, self-analytically explorable degree, appreciably sharable with the patient—an area of countertransference-borderline-psychosis or even countertransference psychosis. It should be unnecessary to emphasize that going crazy, whole hog, along with the patient will do no good and great harm. But I believe that we psychoanalytic therapists collectively will become, through the years, less readily scared and better able to take up this work and pursue it as a job to be done relatively successfully, as we become proportionately able, forthrightly and unashamedly, to take the measure of feelings we can *expect* ourselves to come to experience, naturally, in the course of working with these patients.

Pao (1975) reports his project concerning a schema, devised at Chestnut Lodge by himself, Fort (1973), and presumably others on the staff there, for dividing schizophrenia into four subgroups. Pao, the Director of Psychotherapy at the Lodge, describes that in the course of this project he interviewed each new patient shortly after admission. It is of much interest to me that, evidently without having encountered my (1965b) paper concerning the sense of identity as a perceptual organ, his experience led him in what seems to me the same general direction: "My emphasis is that the diagnosis should begin with the study of the interviewer's own emotional reactions in the interaction between the patient and himself. . . . Such personal experience must be supplemented by a careful scrutiny of the patient's background, the course of illness, the patient's ability to tolerate anxiety, etc." I can believe that the time will come in our work with neurotic patients when, just as we now use as a criterion for analyzability the patient's capability for developing a transference neurosis, we may use as an additional criterion, of earlier predictive significance in our work with the patient, his capability to foster a counter-transference neurosis, so to speak, in the analyst.

Having said this much by way of preface, I shall detail some of the therapist's expectable feeling-experiences in the course of his work with the borderline patient.

The therapist comes to feel guilty and personally responsible for the patient who, appearing initially relatively well, becomes over the months or years of the transference evolution appreciably psychotic or borderline psychotic in the context of the treatment sessions. It is only in relatively recent years, after many years of tormented countertransference experiences of this sort, that I have come to realize how largely referable is the therapist's guilt and remorse, in this regard, to unconscious empathy with the patient's own child-self. That is, the patient in childhood tended to feel that only he possessed the guilty awareness of how deeply disturbed the mother is and that, moreover, he personally was totally responsible for driving her to the edge, of, or even into, madness. The father may have been the more central parent in this regard; but much more often it was, from what I have seen, the mother.

It is garden variety experience for children in our culture to hear reproaches from a parent, "You're driving me crazy!" and, of course, I do not mean that such words alone, even with more than a modicum of appropriately maddened demeanor, cause the child any serious and lasting trauma. But the parents of borderline patients have themselves more than a mere garden variety, neurotic degree of psychopathology. Hence it is a formidably serious degree of parental psychopathology for which the child is assigned, day after day, totally causative personal responsibility.

The therapist's guilt in this same regard stems partly from his finding, over the course of the work, that the patient's crazier aspects provide him (the therapist) covertly with much more of lively interest, and even fascination, than do the patient's relatively dull areas of neurotic ego functioning. Although the therapist's conscientious goal is to help the patient to become free from the borderline-schizophrenic modes of experience, privately and guiltily he feels fascinated by these very sickest aspects of the patient, and fears that his fascination with them has led him to foster, to deepen, these most grievously afflicted components of the patient's personality functioning.

Typically the treatment process itself, in work with these patients, becomes highly sexualized, such that the patient reveals newly-experienced and fascinating borderline symptoms in a basically coquettish, seductive manner, while the enthralled therapist struggles to match this priceless material with brilliantly penetrating interpretations. Typically, too, the treatment process becomes laden with acted-in aggression. For instance, as I have mentioned in a recent paper (Searles 1976b) the therapist who develops formidable quantities of hatred toward the patient comes to feel for a time that the only effective "outlet" for his hatred is to be found in seeing the patient suffer from persistent symptoms.

All these details of the therapist's countertransference have had, so my clinical experience indicates, prototypes in the patient's childhood experience with the parent in question. As one simple example, the child could not help deriving gratification, no matter how guilt-laden, from feeling himself capable of bringing mother out of her depressive deadness into a highly animated and vocal state verging upon madness.

My work with a patient far more ill than borderline had shown me another point relevant for this discussion. She is a chronically schizophrenic woman with whom I have worked for many years. After the first few years of our work she refused to acknowledge her name as her own and, although she has improved in many ways over subsequent years, it has become rare for her to be concious of bits of her own real, personal childhood history such as were relatively abundantly available to her, despite many already-present delusions, at the beginning of our work. For many years now, one of the harshest of my countertransference burdens is a guilty and remorseful feeling that I personally have long since destroyed her only real and sane identity—destroyed it out of, more than anything else, my hateful envy of her for her many and extraordinary capabilities, and for her childhood lived in a setting far different from my own small-town, middle-class one.

It is only as she has been improving, recently, to such an extent that some of her psychotic transference reactions have become clearly linked with newly remembered childhood experiences, that I have felt largely relieved of this burden of guilt and remorse. Specifically, I have come to see that my long-chafing feeling, often intensely threatening to the point of engendering in me fantasies of suicide, of having destroyed her sense of identity, has a precise counterpart in *her* having been given to feel, by her mother, that as a child she had destroyed the mother's so-called real and true identity–an identity based, in actuality, in the mother's ego-ideal as a woman of myriad magnificent accomplishments, above all in the field of dramatics. The mother had been given to maniac flights of fancy, and her fantasied accomplishments were not to her so much ambitions thwarted by the patient; rather, she reacted to the daughter as having destroyed these supposedly actual accomplishments and, in the process, destroyed the mother's supposedly real, true identity.

THE ANALYST AS UNWANTED CHILD

To return to the discussion of borderline patients *pers se,* I have indicated that the therapist is given to feel that he has had, and is having, a diabolically, malevolently, all-powerful influence in the development and maintenance of the patient's transference-borderline-psychosis. But I have found, in my work with a reliably long succession of patients, that such an experience of myself in the work comes in course of time to reveal, at its core, the experience of myself as being an unwanted little child in relation to the patient. It gradually dawns on me that this is who I am, in the patient's transference relationship with me, as I listen month after month and year after year to the patient's reproaches that all the rest of his or her life is going relatively well these days, with my being the only fly in the ointment. If only he were rid of me, he says more and more explicitly, his life would be a breeze. In case after case, I become impressed, inevitably, with how much the patient sounds like a mother reproaching and blaming her small child, giving him to feel that, had he only not been born, her life would be a paradise of personal fulfillment.

In the instance of my work with one patient after another, the awareness of my unwanted child countertransference comes to me as an exciting meaningful revelation and, although its appearance has been made possible only by my having come to realize, more fully than before, how deeply hurt and rejected I am feeling in response to the patient, this phase comes as a relief from my erstwhile grandiose and guilt-ridden countertransference identity as the diabolical inflictor of psychosis. In some instances, more specifically, I no longer hear the patient as reproaching me with diabolically *spoiling* his otherwise satisfactory life, but hear him saying, as the stronger, parental one of the two of us, that I, as the smaller one, the child, am not, and never was, loved or wanted.

All these processes in the patient's childhood regularly involved his becoming the object, beginning in early childhood or infancy or even before birth, of transference reactions on the mother's (and/or father's) part from her own mother and/or father (or sibling, or whomever) to the patient. Typically, the more ill the adult patient is, the more sure we can be that such transference responses on the parent's part were powerfully at work remarkably early in the patient's childhood. I have written a number of times of the schizophrenic patient's childhood in this regard, and I am aware that a number of other writers have done so. But I feel that we are only beginning to mine this rich lode of psychodynamics.

Here is, I believe, a prevailing atmosphere in the background of many borderline patients. Beginning when the patient was, say, two years of age (or even younger; I do not know just when), his mother had an unconscious transference image of him as being, all over again, her own mother and/or father, in relationship to whom she had felt herself to be an unwanted child, and whose love she had despaired of evoking. Now she blames and reproaches her little son (or daughter) for all sorts of events and situations which are far beyond his realistic powers to control, as if he were God Almighty; just as later on, in psychotherapy, the adult patient who was once this child comes to vituperate against his therapist as being a diabaolical god. During the patient's childhood the mother does this basically because she unconsciously experiences herself as being an unwanted child to this transference "parent" of hers, who is actually her little child. I sense that we come to understand more fully the poignancy of such mother-child relationships, we will discard the crude and cruel "schizophrenogenic mother" concept (to which I, among many others, devoted much attention in my early papers) once and for all.

THE ANALYST'S GUILTY SENSE OF LESS-THAN-FULL COMMITMENT TO HIS THERAPEUTIC ROLE

A countertransference experience which has been long-lasting in my work with one patient after another is a guilty sense of not being fully committed, inwardly, to my functional role as the patient's therapist, despite my maintenance of all the outward trappings of therapeutic devotion. Any thoroughgoing discussion of this aspect of the counter-transference would require a paper in itself, since it has, undoubtedly, so many connections to the patient's primitive defenses of fantasied omnipotence and of splitting, with powerfully idealized or diabolized transference images of the therapist. It is my impression, in essence, that it is only in proportion to a deflation of grandiosity, in the transference and countertransference, that the therapist can come to feel fully committed to his now human-sized functional role as the patient's therapist. My treatment records abound with data from earlier phases in work with, for example, schizophrenic patients who would talk adoringly and loyally of a delusional construct hallucinatorily conversed with as "my doctor," while shutting me out of any functional relatedness with them; but at those rare moments when I would feel he or she was giving me an opportunity, supposedly long sought by me, to step into the shoes of "my doctor," I would quail at doing so.

In this same vein, but in work with a much less ill female patient, she developed a headache during a course of a session, and in association to this headache reported conjectures about "rage at myself—*at you, maybe my mother*" [my italics]. I sensed that she was manifesting an unconscious transference to me as being her mother who was only "*maybe* my mother," which fit not only with my frequent countertransference reactions to her, but also with her childhood experience of a mother who persistently remained tangential to the mother role, rather than more fully committed to it. It fit also, needless to say, with her own unresolved, fantasied omnipotence, which allowed her to acknowledge only grudgingly, at best, any mother figure as being "*maybe* my mother."

THE ANALYST'S OWN FEELINGS AS COMPRISING LAYER UNDER LAYER OF COUNTERTRANSFERENCE ELEMENTS

I cannot overemphasize the enormously treatment-facilitating value, as well as the comforting and liberating value for the therapist personally, of locating where this or that tormenting or otherwise upsetting countertransference reaction links up with the patient's heretofore unconscious and unclarified *transference* reactions to him. In other words, the analyst's "own" personal torment needs to become translated into a fuller understanding of the patient's childhood family events and daily atmosphere. I find it particularly helpful when a "personal," "private" feeling-response within myself, a feeling which I have been experiencing as fully or at least predominantly my "own," becomes revealed as being a still deeper layer of reaction to a newly-revealed aspect of the patient's transference to me.

For a case in point, I shall turn briefly to my very long work with a previously mentioned chronically schizophrenic woman. I felt on many occasions over the years how seriously disadvantaged I was, as her therapist, in trying to function, since my role in her life precluded responding to her in the only manner appropriate to her behavior toward me, that is, by administering a brutal physical beating such as her mother frequently had given her. Only after many years did I come to realize that, in so reacting, I was being her transference-father; she had come by now to clearly portray me, in the transference, as a diabolical, omnipotent father who controlled from a distance both her and her mother, and who delegated to the mother the physical punishment of the child. His godlike, aloof role forebade, by the same token, that he dirty his hands with such matters.

A borderline man expressed, during a session after a number of years of work, the realization, at an unprecedentedly deep level, that "you are not my father." What I found fascinating about this was the attendant evidence of still-unresolved transference which revealed to me that, in saying this, although he was consciously expressing the realization that I was actually his therapist rather than his father, unconsciously he was expressing the realization that I was his uncle, who had provided most of his fathering following the death of his actual father, early in the patient's boyhood. Experiences such as this have led me, incidentally, to assume that any presumed "therapeutic alliance," supposedly involving relatively transference-free components of the patient's ego functioning in a workmanlike bond with the analyst, needs constantly to be scrutinized for subtle but pervasively powerful elements of unconscious transference.

SUSPENSE; CHOICE BETWEEN ILLNESS AND HEALTH; THE PATIENT'S ACTING OUT ON BASIS OF IDENTIFICATIONS WITH THE ANALYST

Suspense is prominent among the feelings of the analyst who is working with the borderline patient: suspense as to whether the patient will become frankly psychotic or will commit suicide, or both; whether he will leave treatment suddenly and irrevocably; or even, at times when the transference is particularly intense and disturbing to analyst as well as patient, whether the analyst himself will fall victim to one or another such outcome.

In the writings of Kernberg concerning borderline conditions I find much to admire and from which to learn. But one of the major differences between his views (in those writings of his which I have read) and mine is that he does not portray the suspenseful aspect which seems to me so highly characteristic of the analyst's feelings in working with the borderline patient. Kernberg (1975) says, for example, that patients with borderline personality organization "have in common a rather specific and remarkably stable form of pathological ego structure. . . . Their personality organization is not a transitory state fluctuating between neurosis and psychosis" (p. 3). In a similar vein, he (Kernberg 1972) comments: "Under severe stress or under the effect of alcohol or drugs, transient psychotic episodes may develop in these patients; these psychotic episodes usually improve with relatively brief but well-structured treatment approaches" (p. 255).

Kernberg's writings on borderline states are in part the product of his work in the Psychotherapy Research Project of the Menninger Foundation, and I do not doubt that his experience in that project helps to account for the widely-admired soundness, both theoretically and clinically, of his writings. But in those passages which I have quoted, in their tone typical of a recurrent emphasis in his work (and, incidentally, passages the validity of which I am not contesting here, as far as they go), Kernberg fails to convey how very far removed indeed the analyst feels, in his work, from any such statistician's or theoretician's cooly Olympian view. All too often, for example, the analyst feels desperately threatened lest his patient become frankly psychotic, and the analyst finds little or no reason for confidence that, in such an event, the psychosis will prove transitory.

Any in-depth discussion of this area of the countertransference would include an exploration of the analyst's envy of the patient for the latter's psychopathology, his hateful wishes to be rid of the patient by the latter's becoming frankly psychotic and hospitalized somewhere, and his own—the analyst's—fears of, and wishes for, becoming psychotic himself. I have discussed (Searles 1965a) various among these countertransference phenomena, as regards the work with frankly psychotic patients, in a number of earlier papers.

In several years of work with a woman who showed a borderline personality organization at the outset, I found that she recurrently held over my head, mockingly, year after year, the threat that she would become frankly and chronically schizophrenic. She did not say this in so many words; but her behavior conveyed, innumerable times, that implicit, sadomasochistic threat. In many of the sessions during those years, I felt a strong impulse to tell her that I had felt for years, and still did, that she could become chronically schizophrenic if she would just try a little harder. Essentially, I wanted at such times to somehow convey to her that this was a *choice* she had. I suppressed this urge each time; but had I given way to it, this would have been an attempt to deal with her infuriating, year-after-year expressions of defiance and mockery and of, above all, the highly sadistic, implicit threat of her becoming chronically psychotic.

The following comments of mine in a recent paper concerning psychoanalytic therapy with schizophrenic patients are also in my opinion fully applicable, in principle, to such work with borderline patients. I wrote there of

the crucial issue of *choice*—of the patient's coming to feel *in a position to choose* between continued insanity on the one hand, or healthy interpersonal and intrapersonal relatedness on the other hand. In order for the analyst to help the patient to become able to choose, the former must be able not only to experience, indeed, a passionately tenacious devotion to helping the latter to become free from psychosis, but also become able to tolerate, to clearly envision, the alternative "choice"—namely, that of psychosis for the remainder of the patient's life. I do not see how the patient's individuation can ever occur if the analyst dare not envision this latter possibility. The patient's previous life-experience presumably has proceeded in such a manner and his therapy at the hands of a too-compulsively "dedicated" analyst may proceed in such a manner likewise, that chronic psychosis may be the only subjectively *autonomous* mode of existence available to the patient.

An analyst who, for whatever unconscious reasons, cannot become able to live comfortably with the possibility that his patient may never become free from psychosis cannot, by the same token, foster the necessary emotional atmosphere in the sessions for the development of the contented, unthreatened emotional oneness to which I refer by the term therapeutic symbiosis (Searles 1961), a form of relatedness which is of the same quality as that which imbues the mother-infant relatedness in normal infancy and very early childhood. Any so-called individuation which occurs in the patient which is not founded upon a relatively clear phase of therapeutic symbiosis in the treatment is a pseudo-individuation, and only a seeming choice of sanity, with the urge toward psychosis, the yearning for psychosis, subjected to repression rather than faced at all fully in the light of conscious choice. Essentially, at the unconscious level, the patient chooses to remain psychotic [Searles 1976a, pp. 400–40].

Although these passages may be reminiscent of what I have termed the Olympian quality of the passages from Kernberg, most of my writings have emphasized—as I emphasized in the bulk of this recent paper—the struggles which even the experienced analyst must go through, as an inherent part of his countertransference work with one patient after another, to come to any such harmony with his own feelings, formerly so ambivalent, which have been at the basis of his experiencing so much of a threatened suspensefulness.

Along the way, it is especially threatening to the analyst to feel kept in suspense as to whether the patient is headed toward destruction precisely by reason of functioning loyally as being a chip off the old block—namely, the analyst as perceived by the patient in the transference. That is, the analyst finds much reason to fear that it is exactly the patient's identification with one of the analyst's qualities, no matter how exaggeratedly perceived because of the patient's mother- or father-transference to him, which is carrying the patient toward destruction. Thus the analyst feels responsible, in an essentially omnipotent fashion, for the patient's self-destructive acting out behavior outside the office. The analyst feels that the patient's behavior vicariously manifests his— the analyst's—own acting-out proclivities.

For example, although I seldom feel inordinately threatened lest any one of my psychiatrist analysands act out sexual fantasies toward one or another of his or her own patients. I had a more threatened time of it in my work with one analysand. This man was convinced, for years, that I had sexual intercourse with an occasional patient, casually and without subsequent remorse or other disturbed feelings. When he became strongly tempted to give way to his sexual impulses toward one or another of his own current patients, he reported these impulses during his analytic sessions with me as being in the spirit of his overall wishes to emulate me as an admired, virile father in the transference. Not to leave the reader in any unnecessary suspense, here I can report that this aspect of his transference became analyzed successfully.

Another example of this same principle is to be found in another recent paper of mine, "Violence in Schizophrenia" (Searles 1975), in which I describe my single teaching-interviews with a number of schizophrenic patients whose histories included seriously violent behavior. In the instance of one particularly frightening man, with whose therapist I worked subsequently in supervision, the role of a threatened suspensefulness, in both the therapist and me, was especially prominent. My paper describes the end of the therapy with this man, who had run away from the sanitarium previously:

He again ran away, was found and taken by his parents to another sanitarium, and ran away from there and joined the Marines without divulging his psychiatric background. Our last bit of information about him was a telephone call to the therapist from an official at an Army prison, stating that this man had stabbed a fellow marine three times, that his victim was barely surviving, and that an investigation was under way to determine whether Delaney was mentally competent to stand trial. The therapist and I agreed that he had finally committed the violent act which we both had known he eventually would. . . . I want to emphasize the aspect of relief, of certainty, which this clearly afforded me and, I felt, the therapist also. It was as though the distinction between the patient's actualized murderousness and your own murderous fantasies and feelings was now clear beyond anyone's questioning it. . . .

Both the therapist and I, in relating to him, evidently had mobilized in ourselves such intensely conflicting feelings of love and murderous hatred that a regressive de-differentiation occurred in our respective ego-functioning, such that we attributed to the patient our own murderous hatred, and unconsciously hoped that he would give vicarious expression to our own violence, so as to restore the wall between him and us. More broadly put, such a patient evokes in one such intensely conflicting feelings that, at an unconscious level, one's ego-functioning undergoes a pervasive de-differentiation: one loses the ability deeply to distinguish between one's self and the patient, and between the whole realms of fantasy and reality. Thus the patient's committing of a violent act serves not only to distinguish between one's own "fantasied" violence and his "real" violence but, more generally, serves to restore, in one, the distinction between the whole realms of fantasy and outer reality [pp. 14–16].

Still concerning the matter of the analyst's experiencing suspense, to consider it less globally (e.g., whether the patient will become psychotic or commit suicide), and more particularly as regards any symptom or personality trait or current transference reaction, I find pertinent the following note I made half a dozen years ago concerning my work with a man who manifested a predominantly narcissistic form of ego functioning.

Regarding the therapist's experiencing *suspense*. Thinking back on the hour yesterday with Cooper, it occurs to me that, in reacting to his projection upon me of his own sadistic unfeelingness, I tend to function as distinctly *more* so than I actually feel—partly for the reason, as I see it now, of trying to make this issue become clear enough so that he can see it and we can thrash it out, analyze it, resolve it.

In other words, one of the major reasons why it is so difficult to maintain a genuinely neutral position, not reacting in tune with the patient's transference, is because it is so very difficult to endure the tantalizing ambiguity, the suspense, of the unworked-through transference reactions which one can see in the patient, and to which one *does* react genuinely. That is, I do experience myself as uncomfortably sadistic, unfeeling, unlikable and unadmirable to my self in reaction to Cooper's transference.

In a paper subsequently, "The Function of the Patient's Realistic Perceptions of the Analyst in Delusional Transference" (Searles 1972), I describe some aspects of my work with a far more ill patient, in terms both of her delusional transference perceptions of me, and of my own subjective experience of what I was "really" feeling, and communicating to her, in the therapeutic sessions. That paper mainly emphasizes my discovery, over the course of years, that again and again seemingly purely delusional perceptions of me on her part proved to be well rooted in accurate and realistic perceptions of aspects of myself which heretofore had been out of my own awareness.

What was mentioned above, concerning my work with the narcissistic man, suggests something of why the analyst may introject (unconsciously, of course, for the most part) some of the patient's psychopathology, in an attempt to hasten its resolution and thereby end the feelings of suspense which permeate the treatment-atmosphere in one's work with so tantalizingly ambiguous a patient.

It has seemed to me that some of these same psychodynamics have applied in a considerable number of instances of my work with patients who have been involved in chronically troubled marital situations where there is a chronic, suspense-laden threat of divorce hanging over the marriage. In the course of my work with each of these patients, it has appeared to me no coincidence that, concurrent with especially stressful phases of the analytic work, my own marriage has felt uncharacteristically in jeopardy. My strong impression is that the analyst under these circumstances tends to regress to a level of primitively magical thinking, whereby if his own marriage were to dissolve, this would end the years-long suspenseful question as to whether the patient's verge-of-divorce marriage will or will not endure. Whether the analyst were thereby to bring about, vicariously, the disruption of the patient's marriage or, on the other hand to preserve the patient's marriage by sacrificing his own, the tormenting element of suspense in the analytic situation—so goes in my speculation, the analyst's primitively magical reasoning—would be brought to a merciful end.

DIFFERING KINDS (REPRESSIVE VERSUS NONREPRESSIVE) OF THE ANALYST'S SENSE OF IDENTITY AS AN ANALYST

Lastly, I want explicitly to discuss a point which has been implied throughout this paper—namely, that the analyst's sense of identity as an analyst must be founded in a *kind* of analyst-identity which in major ways is different from the analyst-identity traditionally striven for and consonant with classical analysis. For the sake of this discussion, at least, it is not an oversimplification to say that classical analysis enjoins the analyst to develop, and strive to maintain, a sense of identity as an analyst which constrains him to evenly hovering attentiveness to the analysand's productions, and to participating actively in the analytic session only to the extent of offering verbal interpretations of the material which the analysand has been conveying to him. Such a traditional analyst-identity is neither tenable for the analyst who is analyzing a borderline patient, nor adequate to meet the analytic needs of the patient.

Knight (1953) described that in a relatively highly structured interview, the borderline patient's basic difficulties in ego functioning tend not to become available for either the patient or the psychiatrist to see and work upon:

During the psychiatric interview the neurotic defenses and the relatively intact ego functions may enable the borderline patient to present a deceptive, superficially conventional, although neurotic, front, depending on how thoroughgoing and comprehensive the psychiatric investigation is with respect to the patient's *total* ego functioning. The face-to-face psychiatric interview provides a relatively structured situation in which the conventional protective devices of avoidance, evasion, denial, minimization, changing the subject, and other cover-up methods can be used—even by patients who are genuinely seeking help but who dare not yet communicate their awareness of lost affect, reality misinterpretations, autistic preoccupations, and the like. [pp. 102–103]

To be sure, Knight's comments suggest that a relatively free form of analytic-interview participation on the part of the patient most facilitates the emergence of the latter's borderline difficulties, and with this I am in full agreement. But his comments suggest, too, that such a patient is unlikely to be helped much by an analyst who himself is clinging, in a threatened fashion, to some rigidly-constructed analyst-identity. I hope that this present paper, when considered with my previous writings concerning countertransference matters, will serve forcefully to convey my conviction that the analyst must far outgrow the traditional, classical analyst-identity in order to be able to work with a reasonable degree of success with the borderline patient—to be able, for example, to utilize his sense of identity as a perceptual organ in the manner I have described here; to enter to the requisite degree into (while maintaining under analytic scrutiny) the so necessary therapeutic symbiosis; and to be able to preserve his analyst-identity in face of the extremely intense, persistent, and oftentimes strange transference images which, coming from (largely unconscious) processes at work in the patient, tend so powerfully to dominate the analyst's sense of his actual identity.

I have seen that various psychiatric residents and analytic candidates who, partly because of a relative lack of accumulated experience, have not yet established a strong sense of identity-as-therapist, are particularly threatened by the intense and tenacious negative transference images wherein the patient is endeavoring, as it were, to impose upon the therapist a highly unpalatable sense of identity. By the same token, it should be seen that an analyst who is struggling to maintain, in his work with such a patient, a professional identity untainted by such emotions as jealousy, infantile-dependent feelings, sexual lust, and so on, is undoubtedly imposing, by projection, such largely unconscious personality components upon the already overburdened patient. In essence, I am suggesting here that, in the analyst's work with the borderline patient, he needs to have or, insofar as possible, to develop a kind of professional identity which will not work on the side of the forces of repression but will, rather, facilitate the emergence from repression of those feelings, fantasies, and so on which the borderline patient needs for his analyst to be able to experience, on the way to his own becoming able, partly through identification with his analyst, to integrate comparable experiences within his—the patient's—own ego functioning.

SUMMARY

The countertransference provides the analyst with his most reliable approach to understanding borderline (as well as other) patients. The impact upon him of the patient's split ego functioning is discussed. His experience of transference roles which are both strange in nature, and inimical to his sense of reality and to his sense of personal identity, is explored; in the latter regard, the value of his sense of identity as a perceptual organ is highlighted.

There are detailed some of the analyst's reactions—his guilt, envy, and so on—to the development of the transference-borderline-psychosis in the patient. The analyst finds that, underneath the patient's transference to him as being an omnipotent, diabolical inflictor of psychosis, is the patient's transference to him as being an unwanted child.

The analyst's guilty sense of less than full commitment to his therapeutic role is described briefly, as is the general principle of his finding, time and again, that what have felt to be his "own" feelings toward the patient include layer under layer of responses which are natural and inherent counterparts to the patient's transference responses and attitudes toward him.

The prominent role of suspense is discussed at some length, as is the related issue of choice between illness and health. The phenomenon of the patient's acting out on the (partial) basis of unconscious identifications with the analyst, and the impact of this phenomenon upon the countertransference, is mentioned.

Lastly, the significant role, in the countertransference, of the analyst's sense of identity as an analyst is discussed, and it is suggested that the borderline patient needs for the analyst to have, or, insofar as possible, to develop, a sense of identity as analyst which will predominantly enhance derepression rather than repression of countertransference attitudes and feelings.

REFERENCES

Deutsch, H. (1942). Some forms of emotional disturbance and their relationship to schizophrenia. *Psychoanalytic Quarterly* 11:301–321.

Fort, J. (1973). The importance of being diagnostic. Read at the annual Chestnut Lodge Symposium, October 5, 1973.

Gunderson, J.G., and Singer, M.T. (1975). Defining borderline patients: an overview. *American Journal of Psychiatry* 132:1–10.

Kernberg, O. (1972). Treatment of borderline patients. In *Tactics and Techniques in Psychoanalytic Therapy*, ed. P. Giovacchini, pp. 254–290. New York: Jason Aronson.

—— (1975). *Borderline Conditions and Pathological Narcissism*. New York: Jason Aronson.

Knight, R.P. (1953). Borderine states. In *Psychoanalytic Psychiatry and Psychology*, eds. R.P. Knight and C.R. Friedman. New York: International Universities Press, 1954.

Moore, B.E. & Fine, B.D., eds. (1967). *A Glossary of Psychoanalytic Terms and Concepts.* New York: American Psychoanalytic Association.

Pao, P-N. (1975). On the diagnostic term, "schizophrenia." *Annual of Psychoanalysis* 3:221–238.

Searles, H.F. (1960). *The Nonhuman Environment in Normal Development and in Schizophrenia.* New York: International Universities Press.

—— (1961). Phases of patient-therapist interaction in the psychotherapy of chronic schizophrenia. In *Collected Papers on Schizophrenia and Related Subjects,* pp. 521–559. New York: International Universities Press, 1965.

—— (1965a). *Collected Papers on Schizophrenia and Related Subjects.* New York: International Universities Press.

—— (1965b). The sense of identity as a perceptual organ. Presented at Sheppard and Enoch Pratt Hospital Scientific Day Program, Towson, Maryland, May 29, 1965. Reprinted in "Concerning the Development of an Identity" *Psychoanalytic Review* 53:507–530, Winter 1966–67.

—— (1972). The function of the patient's realistic perceptions of the analyst in delusional transference. *British Journal of Medical Psychology* 45:1–18.

—— (1976a). Psychoanalytic therapy with schizophrenic patients in a private-practice context. *Contemporary Psychoanalysis* 12:387–406.

—— (1976b). Transitional phenomena and therapeutic symbiosis. International Journal of Psychoanalytic Psychotherapy 5:145–204.

—— (1977). Dual- and multiple-identity processes in borderline ego functioning. In *Borderline Personality Disorders,* ed. P. Hartocollis. New York: International Universities Press.

Searles, H.F., Bisco, J.M., Coutu, G., and Scibetta, R.C. (1975). Violence in schizophrenia. *Psychoanalytic Forum* 5:1–89.

22. Crossing the Border Into Borderline Personality and Borderline Schizophrenia: The Development of Criteria

Robert L. Spitzer, Jean Endicott, and
Miriam Gibbon

There is large psychiatric literature on various "borderline" conditions, including articles that review the different contradictory and often obscure ways in which the concept has been used.[1-10] However, the official classifications of mental disorders, such as the first and second editions of the American Psychiatric Association's *Diagnostic and Statistical Manual,* and the eighth and ninth editions of the *International Classification of Diseases,* have omitted any reference to the concept. The single exception is a reference in DSM-II to the inclusion of patients designated as "borderline schizophrenia" within the official category of schizophrenia, latent type.[11]

One of the guiding principles in the development of DSM-III has been an attempt to include in the classfication all conditions that a significantly large group of clinicians believe are of clinical importance, providing that the condition can be readily defined so that it can be distinguished from other conditions.[12] Therefore, the APA Task Force on Nomenclature and Statistics decided that an effort should be made to develop criteria for one or more of the borderline conditions frequently referred to in the literature. This was a decision not easily reached, since members of the Task Force were divided as to the value of any such attempt. Their attitudes reflect the divided opinions within our profession. Some believed that the borderline concept represents everything that is wrong with American psychiatry because of the confused way in which the term has been used, the heavy reliance in the borderline literature on metapsychological concepts, and the relative paucity of hard data regarding the usefulness (validity) of the concept. Others believed that there is sufficient evidence of the utility of one or more of these concepts to warrant their inclusion in the classification if reliable criteria could be developed.

Although the term "borderline" has been used in the literature as an adjective to modify a large number of terms (condition, syndrome, personality, state, character, pattern, organization, schizophrenia), it appeared to us, from a review of the literature as well as from personal contact with current investigators interested in this area, that there are two major ways in which "borderline" is currently used that covers the range of uses. The first refers to a constellation of relatively enduring personality features of instability and vulnerability that have important treatment and outcome correlates. Examples of this use of the concept are reflected in the writings of Gunderson and Singer[1] on the "borderline patient" and Kernberg[6] on "borderline personality organization."

The second major use of the term is to describe certain psychopathological characteristics that are usually stable over time and are assumed to be genetically related to a spectrum of disorders including chronic schizophrenia. This usage is exemplified by the term "borderline schizophrenia" as used by Wender, Kety, Rosenthal, and their colleagues[13],[14] in their adoptive studies of the contribution of nature and nurture to the development of schizophrenia.

There are two major problems with these two concepts as they are currently being used. First of all, there is no commonly accepted phenomenological criteria for defining either concept. Kety, Wender, and Rosenthal have acknowledged that although they are able to agree with each other in categorizing patients as having borderline schizophrenia, they are not confident that they could convey to others the clinical cues to which they are responding. They have only given rather general clinical descriptions of some of the attributes of patients they call borderline schizophrenic. Gunderson and Singer[1] have reviewed the descriptive literature on borderline patients and have proposed a set of criteria that in their judgment most authors would use in characterizing most borderline persons. However, in yet another review article, Perry and Klerman[11] compared the clinical criteria proposed by Gunderson and Singer with those proposed by Knight,[5] Kernberg,[6] and Grinker et al,[7] and noted the lack of overlap in the four sets of specific criteria. Second, it is not at all clear whether borderline is a unitary concept or whether it is best conceptualized as two or even more types. It is of interest in this regard to note that some of the features in Gunderson

and Singer's proposed criteria, namely the presence of paranoid ideation and other mild but definite impairment in reality testing, are also
noted in Wender, Kety, and Rosenthal's description of borderline
schizophrenia.

Our goal has been to define operationally each of these two major
ways in which the borderline concept has been used, and to study the
relationship between them in order to determine whether a single category is sufficient or whether two or more are warranted. Finally, what
proportion of patients called borderline by clinicians is covered by the
proposed criteria? As we began our work, we found it useful to avoid
the term "borderline" and instead to coin new terms for the two major
uses of the borderline concept. Schizotypal personality was chosen to
represent the concept of borderline schizophrenia, since the term means
"like schizophrenia." We chose the term "unstable personality" to
represent the concept of borderline personality, since most descriptions
for such patients referred to unstable affect, interpersonal relationships,
job functioning, and sense of identity.

DEVELOPMENT OF SCHIZOTYPAL PERSONALITY ITEM SET

There were several stages in the development of criteria, for schizotypal
personality. We began by consulting with Wender, Kety, and Rosenthal
(henceforth referred to as WKR). In discussions with them, we derived
a list of 24 behavioral items that seemed to them to capture the cues
that they were using in making their borderline schizophrenia diagnoses.
It should be noted that the items are considered applicable only if the
behavior is characteristic of long-term functioning and not limited to
discrete episodes of psychiatric illness, or accounted for by a more
pervasive disorder, such as schizophrenia.

These items were then applied by research assistants to 36 cases from
their family study diagnosed by WKR as borderline schizophrenia. (The
term "borderline schizophrenia" is being used by us here as a succinct
way of referring to patients diagnosed by WKR in their studies under a
variety of terms, including uncertain schizophrenia, which refers to
conditions within the schizophrenia spectrum other than acute or
chronic schizophrenia.) Although most of these cases had many of these
items, it was apparent that many important clinical features were not
included in the initial list of 24 items, such as signs of odd communi-

cation short of gross formal thought disorder. In addition, many of the 24 items proposed by WKR described behaviors that were not seen at all in this group of patients. We therefore employed a different strategy. Instead of asking WKR to tell us what cues they thought they were attending to, we systematically reviewed the 36 case records, noting any clinical feature we believed might have served as a cue to them. By eliminating rare behaviors and combining behaviors that appeared to be related to the same clinical concept, we developed 17 items. This item set was then applied to the same 36 cases. Using eight of the most frequently observed items, a cutoff of at least three items correctly identified 30 of the 36 cases. When the eight items were applied to 43 cases considered by WKR to be outside of the schizophrenia spectrum, only two cases had three items, and none had more than three.

Two technical terms are useful in indexing the success with which a procedure is able to correctly identify "cases" within a group that contains both cases and noncases. Sensitivity is the proportion of the total number of cases that are correctly identified as cases by the procedure. Specificity is the proportion of the total number of noncases that are correctly identified as noncases by the procedure. Thus, the sensitivity (cases correctly identified) of at least three of the eight items applied to the 36 cases is 30/36 (86%). The specificity (noncases correctly identified) when applied to the 43 noncases is 41/43 (95%). In the absense of knowledge regarding the cost-benefit ratio of misidentification of either a case or a noncase, one would prefer a procedure that is high in both sensitivity and specificity.

The procedure was cross-validated by applying the eight-item set to 61 cases from an adoptee study in which 30 cases were judged by WKR to be within the spectrum, and 31 to be outside of the spectrum. Here, the sensitivity dropped to 63%, whereas the specificity was 100%. The reasons for the change in the sensitivity of the procedure in the two samples are not clear. It may be, in part, a function of an apparent lowering of the threshold with which the spectrum diagnoses were made by WKR in the second study.

Despite the drop in the sensitivity of the eight items using a cutoff of three items, we decided to use them in further studies with patients rather than relatives. The schizotypal items are given in Table 1. As can be seen, they tap the concepts of deviations in communication,

Table 1. Results of Questionnaire Study of Schizotypal Personality Items*

	Frequency		Factor Loading				Discriminant Function	
	Border-line (B) (N=808)	Control (C) (N=808)	B Only (N=808)		B + C (N=1,616)		B vs C (N=808 vs 808)	Schizotypal vs Unstable (N=222 vs 234)
			1	2	1	2		
Odd communication (*not* gross formal thought disorder), e.g., speech that is tangential, digressive, vague, over-elaborate, circumstantial, metaphorical	58	11	08	**33**†	23	**56**	**.35**	**−55**
Ideas of reference, self-referential thinking	58	16	−07	**58**	11	**66**	**.23**	⋯
Suspiciousness or paranoid ideation	59	17	−04	**50**	15	**62**	**.21**	**−28**
Recurrent illusions, sensing the presence of a force or person not actually present (e.g., "I felt as if my dead mother were in the room with me"), depersonalization or derealization, not associated with panic attacks	33	5	02	39	12	49	.17	⋯
Magical thinking e.g., superstitiousness, clairvoyance, telepathy, "sixth sense," "others can feel my feelings"	47	10	01	**49**	11	**58**	.24	**−1.04**
Inadequate rapport in face-to-face interaction due to constricted or inappropriate affect e.g., aloof, distant, cold, superficial, histrionic, effusive	66	23	05	**20**	26	**43**	**.24**	⋯
Undue social anxiety or hypersensitivity to real or imagined criticism	85	60	18	**25**	35	**25**	⋯	⋯
Social isolation, e.g., no close friends or confidants, social contacts limited to essential everyday tasks	58	29	−04	**17**	16	**33**	**.12**	⋯

* Judged applicable only if characteristic of long-term functioning and not limited to discrete episodes of illness.
† Highest loading is indicated by boldface type.

referential or paranoid ideation, odd perceptual experiences, and social isolation and anxiety.

DEVELOPMENT OF UNSTABLE PERSONALITY ITEM SET

The development of the items for the unstable personality concept began with a review of the literature and consultation with a number of investigators working in this area, including Gunderson, Sheehy, Stone, Rinsley, and Kernberg. This resulted in nine items, which we believed would be adequate to tap the key features that seemed to be most frequently described in the literature. Several of the items are elaborations of variables noted by Gunderson[15] as useful in discriminating "borderline patients" from other diagnostic groups. As with the schizotypal item set, the items were considered applicable only if characteristic of long-term functioning and not limited to discrete episodes of illness, or accounted for by a more pervasive disorder, such as schizophrenia.

The set of nine items is given in Table 2. As can be seen, they tap the concepts of identity disturbance, unstable and intense interpersonal relationships, impulsive and self-damaging behavior, anger dyscontrol and affective instability, problems tolerating being alone, chronic feelings of emptiness, and poor work or school achievement.

The item set was applied to patients undergoing therapy on the General Clinical Service of the New York State Psychiatric Institute. At that time, Kernberg was director of the Service and was conducting a study of patients with borderline personality organization. Each therapist on the Service (second-year psychiatric residents) was asked to use the nine-item set with any of his patients that Kernberg or the other two attending psychiatrists judged to have a borderline personality organization. The therapist was also asked to apply the same item set to a control patient whom he knew well who did not have either schizophrenia or a borderline personality organization. This resulted in 18 borderline cases and 15 control cases. (A few of the therapists claimed not to know well any nonborderline, nonschizophrenic patients!) Using a cutoff of at least three items, the sensitivity of the item set was 100% and the specificity was 80%.

Stone, an attending psychiatrist on the General Clinical Service, then applied the item set to 19 borderline patients whom he had treated and on whom he had detailed case notes. He also applied the item set to 18 controls defined as above. Using the same cutoff of three or more items, the sensitivity was 89% and the specificity was 94%. (It should be noted that although Stone's ratings were not blind, he had no investment in this particular item set for defining the borderline group.)

CROSS-VALIDATION OF SCHIZOTYPAL AND UNSTABLE PERSONALITY ITEM SETS

The results of these developmental studies with the two sets of items suggested that each procedure seemed able to identify individuals characterized as belonging to either of the two major types of "borderline" categories. Still unresolved were three major questions: (1) What is the concurrent validity of using each item set applied to a large sample of patients diagnosed by a large sample of psychiatrists? That is, how well will the item sets correctly identify patients diagnosed as borderline by psychiatrists as distinguised from patients diagnosed as nonborderline? (2) Do the two item sets describe two relatively independent dimensions that characterize patients diagnosed as borderline? (3) If there are two independent dimensions that characterize patients diagnosed as borderline, are they mutually exclusive?

In searching for an appropriate method to resolve these three questions, we believed it was important to have a large sample of psychiatrists that would be, as far as possible, representative of American psychiatrists. In addition, we believed it was important that the patients not be limited to a particular type of facility, such as inpatients, as has been done in many previous studies of borderline patients. Finally, since many of the items described behaviors that are difficult to assess in an initial evaluation, we believed that it was important to limit the data collection to patients that the psychiatrist knew well.

A questionnaire was developed that contained the two sets of items as well as five additional items thought to be related to the borderline concept. The 22 items were intermingled and all were in a true-false format. In addition, there were questions on the type of borderline or control, age and sex, type of patient, and the theoretical orientation of the psychiatrist. Finally, they were asked to describe any borderline features not covered in the 22 items.

Table 2. Results of Questionnaire Study of Unstable Personality Items*

	Frequency		Factor Loading				Discriminant Function	
	Border-line (B) (N=808)	Control (C) (N=808)	B Only (N=808) 1	2	B + C (N=1,616) 1	2	B vs C (N=808 vs 808)	Schizotypal vs Unstable (N=222 vs 234)
Identity disturbance manifested by uncertainty about several issues relating to identity, such as self-image, gender identity, long-term goals or career choice, friendship patterns, values, and loyalties, e.g., "Who am I?," "I feel like I am my sister when I am good"	80	33	23†	13	43	.34	.36	...
A pattern of unstable and intense interpersonal relationships, e.g., marked shifts of attitude, idealization, devaluation, manipulation (consistently using others for his own ends)	80	30	45	−01	61	26	.36	1.39
Impulsivity or unpredictability in at least 2 areas which are potentially self-damaging, e.g., spending, sex, gambling, drug or alcohol use, shoplifting, overeating, physically self-damaging acts	78	34	44	−01	52	22	.24	...

Inappropriate intense anger or lack of control of anger, e.g., frequently loses temper, always angry	**68**	27	**39**	07	**47**	27	.19	...
Physically self-damaging acts, e.g., suicidal gestures, self-mutilation, recurrent accidents, or physical fights	**53**	16	**44**	−02	**48**	19	.16	−.28
Work history or school achievement unstable or below expected on basis of intelligence, training, or opportunity	**75**	38	**22**	−00	**41**	21	...	−.47
Affective instability, marked shifts from normal mood to depression, irritability, or anxiety, usually lasting hours and only rarely for more than a few days, with a return to normal mood	**77**	43	**45**	03	**52**	15	.12	...
Chronic feelings of emptiness or boredom	**74**	38	**26**	04	**44**	24	.13	...
Problems tolerating being alone, e.g., frantic efforts to avoid being alone, depressed when alone	**58**	38	**38**	−03	**42**	04	...	.47

* Judged applicable only if characteristic of long-term functioning and not limited to discrete episodes of illness.
† Highest loading is indicated by boldface.
‡ Not included in final list.

In January 1977, four thousand members of the American Psychiatric Association, randomly selected from the membership, were sent the questionnaire with the following letter of explanation, signed by the senior author as chairman of the APA Task Force on Nomenclature and Statistics:

Dear APA Member:

We would like your help in developing criteria for the DSM-III category of borderline personality disorder. As you know, although there is considerable interest in this diagnostic category, there is as yet no consensus as to how it should be defined.

After reviewing the literature and consulting with various investigators with a special interest in this area, we have identified a group of behavioral descriptions which frequently are applied to patients designated as either borderline personality, borderline personality organization, or borderline schizophrenia. Pilot work indicates that a clinical diagnosis of borderline is extrememly likely for patients who over long periods of time exhibit a large number of these behaviors.

In order to determine which of these items are most useful for defining borderline personality disorder in DSM-III, we are asking you to make ratings of these items on two adolescent or adult patients that you know well. (We have added to the list a few items that are *not* specific for borderline patients.) The first patient should be one that in your judgment warrants a diagnosis of borderline personality, borderline personality organization, or borderline schizophrenia. We would assume that such a patient has never had any of the chronic forms of schizophrenia and that the borderline designation refers to behavior that is relatively persistent and characteristic of the patient's functioning over time and is not limited to discrete episodes of illness. The second patient will act as a control, and should be moderately to severely ill but not have a diagnosis of a psychosis nor any of the borderline categories.

To avoid any bias in the selection of your two patients, it would be best if you chose them prior to looking at the questionnaire which is in the return envelope.

Please return the questionnaire within the next two weeks so that we may begin data analysis. If you wish to receive a copy of the report of this study, please enclose a note to that effect. We appreciate your help.

Eight hundred eight usable sets of questionnaires were received in time for data analysis. A small number of questionnaires were rejected because they were incomplete. A few psychiatrists returned blank questionnaires with such statements as: "I don't have any borderline patients," or "I don't believe in the concept."

Table 3. Demographic Characteristics of Borderline and Control Patients

	% of Patients	
	Borderline (N = 808)	Control (N = 808)
Sex		
Male	32	41
Female	68	59
Age, yr		
16–25	33	19
26–35	45	46
≥36	22	35
Sources of patients		
Private outpatient	73	77
Clinic outpatient	14	13
Inpatient	11	7
Other	2	3

CHARACTERISTICS OF SUBJECTS

The diagnostic distribution of the borderline patients was as follows: borderline personality, 39%; borderline personality organization, 29%; borderline schizophrenia, 27%; and other, 4%. The diagnostic distribution for the controls was as follows: personality disorders, 40%; neurosis, 55%; affective disorder; 18%, alcoholism or drug abuse, 6% and other, 4%. (The total percent exceeds 100 because multiple diagnoses were permitted.) Various demographic characteristics of the two groups are shown in Table 3. There were more females, particularly in the borderline group. Both groups were relatively young, particularly the borderline group. As might be expected, approximately three quarters of the patients in both groups were private outpatients. Few of the patients were inpatients, approximately one in ten.

Fifty-six percent of the psychiatrists identified their theoretical orientation as "psychological, psychoanalytic," while 34% called themselves "eclectic." Very few used the other available categories: organic, behaviorist, social/community, other psychological, or other. This distribution of orientation is somewhat different from that obtained in response to a questionnaire sent to a large sample of the membership regarding their attitude toward electroconvulsive therapy. Thirty-seven percent of those respondents categorized themselves as psychological, psychoanalytic, and 49% called themselves eclectic. It is not surprising that a larger percentage of the respondents to the borderline questionnaire would have a psychological or psychoanalytic orientation. On the other hand, the two distributions are not markedly different, suggesting that the respondents to the borderline questionnaire are fairly representative of American psychiatrists who are treating patients whom they consider diagnostically as some variety of borderline.

Only 138 of the clinicians noted borderline features of the specific patient that were not covered in any of the items. The most common features noted related to dependency, individuation, and brief psychotic episodes. Examination of the 138 patients disclosed that there were very few of these patients who failed to meet the criteria for either schizotypal or unstable personality on the basis of the item sets that were included in the questionnaire. This indicates that additional items would not have significantly improved the sensitivity, and might have decreased specificity.

FREQUENCY DISTRIBUTION OF ITEMS

The first two columns in Tables 1 and 2 present the frequency of each item in the borderline and control group. In each instance, the relative frequency was far greater in the borderline group. The ordering of the items in these two tables is by decreasing magnitude of the odds ratio, which measures the ratio of relative frequencies controlling for the pairing of borderlines and controls resulting from each psychiatrist contributing one borderline and one control.[16]

As can be seen, all of the items describe behaviors that are also seen in the controls. Therefore, none of the items are pathognomonic. Although the schizotypal items are seen less frequently than the unstable items in both the borderline and control patients, the contrast between the two groups is greater for schizotypal items.

FACTOR ANALYSES

Two factor analyses were performed, using principle factor and varimax rotation. The first involved the 808 borderline patients only. The second involved the combined sample of 1,616 borderline and control patients.

Whereas the first deals with the structure of the variability within the borderline group, the second deals with variability within a more heterogeneous group. In each case, two factors were rotated to test the hypothesis that the schizotypal and unstable item sets each described two separate and relatively independent dimensions.

The results of the two factor analyses are given in columns three through six in Tables 1 and 2. The highest loading is boldfaced. With only a single exception, in both factor analyses, the schizotypal items load highest on factor 2, and the unstable items load highest on factor 1. The exception is the schizotypal item, "undue social anxiety or hypersensitivity to real or imagined criticism," which loads highest on factor 2 in the borderline-only factor analysis, and highest on factor 1 in the combined factor analysis. This item was extremely common in each of the borderline categories as specified by the clinicians. It therefore does not have a strong and consistent loading on either factor.

Although the schizotypal and unstable items describe two separate dimensions of borderline characteristics, it should be acknowledged that the two factors account for only a relatively small proportion of the total variance (22% of the borderline-only analysis and 33% of the combined analysis.)

When the combined factor analysis was rotated for five factors, the first two factors continued to largely describe the schizotypal and unstable dimensions. Thus, the first factor retained items describing unstable and intense interpersonal relationships, impulsivity or unpredictability, anger dyscontrol, physically self-damaging acts, and poor work or school achievement. The second factor retained items describing odd communication, ideas of reference, odd perceptual experiences, and magical thinking. The additional three factors reflected the dimensions of affective dysphoria and instability; social isolation, inadequate rapport, and boredom; and suspiciousness or paranoid ideation (a single item), which had its second highest loading on the second factor. The five factor solution does not clearly correspond to either the four types described by Grinker et al[7] or Klein's [17] hypothesized five groups.

DISCRIMINANT FUNCTION ANALYSES

A discriminant function analysis was performed to determine the degree to which the combined item set could discriminate the borderline from the control patients. Column 7 of Tables 1 and 2 give the beta weights, which reflect the discriminant power of the individual items. The sensitivity of the discriminant function for discriminating borderline vs control was 88%. The specificity was 87%. This shows that a high degree of separation is possible using this combined item pool.

Next, we performed a discriminant function analysis to determine the degree to which the combined item set could discriminate between those 222 patients given a clinical diagnosis of borderline schizophrenia and those 234 patients given a clinical diagnosis of borderline personality organization. The beta weights for this analysis are given in the last column of Tables 1 and 2. Minus weights indicate items predictive of borderline schizophrenia. Positive weights predict borderline personality organization. This discriminant analysis was less successful, as indicated by correct classification of only 64%.

SELECTION OF FINAL ITEM SETS

As a result of this series of analyses, it was decided to eliminate from the unstable item set the item, "Work history or school achievement unstable or below expected on basis of intelligence, training, or opportunities," because in the discriminant function analysis it predicted borderline schizophrenia even though it was listed in the unstable item set. Furthermore, the odds ratio was relatively low, the relative loadings on the two factors were not markedly different, and it had no power in the discriminant analysis contrasting borderline with control patients.

INTERNAL CONSISTENCY OF FINAL ITEM SETS

The internal consistency coefficient for each item set was determined by using the Kuder-Richardson procedure. This is a measure that reflects the degree to which a set of items measures a unitary dimension. The internal consistency for the schizotypal items was .54, and that for the unstable items was .58. These values indicate only modest support for measurement of the two unitary dimensions. However, the internal consistency of the combined item set was only .57. Ordinarily, one expects an increase in internal consistency as a function of increase in the number of items if all of the items are indexing a single dimension. Thus, the lack of an increase for the combined item set is further support

Table 4. Sensitivity and Specificity of Two-item Sets at Differing Cutoff Levels

	Schizotypal Item Sets	
Cutoff Level	Sensitivity, % (N = 222)*	Specificity, % (N = 808)†
3+	92	76
4+	80	89
5+	66	94
	Unstable Item Sets	
Cutoff Level	Sensitivity, % (N = 234)‡	Specificity, % (N = 808)
3+	96	53
4+	90	70
5+	77	82
6+	59	91

*Patients given a clinical diagnosis of borderline schizophrenia.
†Control patients.
‡Patients given a clinical diagnosis of borderline personality organization.

for the appropriateness of two measures of the borderline concept, rather than a single measure.

SENSITIVITY AND SPECIFICITY OF FINAL ITEM SETS

The sensitivity of the schizotypal items was determined for the 222 patients given a clinical diagnosis of borderline schizophrenia. In a similar fashion, the sensitivity of the unstable items was determined for the 234 patients given a clinical diagnosis of borderline personality organization. The specificity for both the schizotypal and the unstable items was determined for the 808 control patients. Table 4 presents the sensitivity and specificity for the two item sets at different cutoff levels. Very good sensitivity and specificity for the schizotypal item set was obtained using a cutoff of at least four items. For the unstable item set, a cutoff of at least five items was almost as good. This is represented visually in Fig. 1 and 2. In the control patients, a lower cutoff results in inadequate specificity (ie, too many nonborderline patients called borderline).

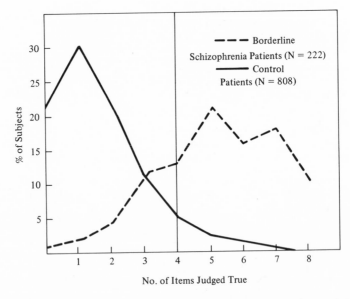

Fig. 1. Frequency distribution of number of schizotypal items judged true for borderline schizophrenia patients and control patients.

RELATIONSHIP BETWEEN THE TWO ITEM SETS

The relationship between the two item sets was determined by several procedures. Table 5 presents the distribution of schizotypal and unstable scale scores within the 808 borderline patients. Using the at-least-four and at-least-five-item cutoff scores, 54% of the patients meet the criteria for both schizotypal and unstable personality. Only 7% are neither. Eighteen percent are schizotypal only and 21% are unstable only. Although more than half of the borderline patients meet the criteria for both sets, the correlation between the two item sets is actually .06, indicating that within a group of borderline patients, the two item sets are independent but not mutually exclusive. However, if the control patients are added to the sample, so that the proportion of borderline to control patients is equal the correlation rises to .52. This indicates that although the two item sets are independent in a group of borderline patients, there is a substantial correlation between the two item sets in a heterogeneous group that includes nonborderline patients. This is a mathematical necessity because of the different frequencies with which

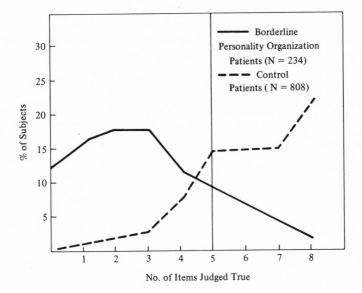

Fig. 2. Frequency distribution of unstable items judged true for borderline personality organization patients and control patients.

Table 5. Distribution of Schizotypal and Unstable Scale Scores Within 808 Borderline Patients*

Unstable Score	Schizotypal Score							
	1	2	3	4	5	6	7	8
1			X	X				
2			X	X		X		
3		X	X	XX	X	X	X	
4		X	XX	XX	XX	XX	XX	
					X	X		
5	X	X	XX	XX	XX	XX	X	
			X	X	X			
6	X	XX	XX	XX	XX	XX	X	X
			XX	XX	XX	XX		
7	X	X	XX	XX	XXX	XX	XX	XX
			X	X	XX	XX	X	
8	X	X	XX	XX	XX	XX	XX	XX
			X	XX	X			

*Each X represents 1% rounded up.

both items sets occur in the borderline and control groups. However, it may explain the perception of some investigators that the borderline phenomenon is unitary. It appears to be unitary only when borderline patients are contrasted with nonborderline patients.

SEX DIFFERENCES

The factor structure found for the total borderline sample was replicated when the analysis was done for males and females separately. The factor loadings were practically the same with each sex as with the total group.

The total sample of borderline patients was 32% male, 68% female. Using the operational criteria, 81% of the females met the criteria for unstable personality as compared to 64% of the males, whereas 70% of the females and 75% of the males met the criteria for schizotypal personality. Therefore, there is a greater tendency for females to meet the criteria for unstable personality whereas there is no difference with regard to schizotypal personality.

Since the sample of borderline patients was limited to individuals in treatment, it is not known whether or not these sex differences would be replicated in community surveys that include outpatients.

COMMENT

We believe we have demonstrated that it is possible to operationally define the two major concepts used in discussions of "borderline patients." Furthermore, we have provided consensual validity that these item sets identify patients diagnosed as borderline by clinicians without misidentifying a large group of patients diagnosed as nonborderline. Only 7% of the borderline group failed to be categorized as either schizotypal or unstable, resulting in an overall sensitivity of 93%. On the other hand, 25% of the nonborderline group met the criteria for one of the two borderline groups, resulting in a specificity of 75%. Most of the misidentification of the control group consisted of incorrectly identifying them as unstable.

Given the ambiguities of the borderline concept and the likelihood that the different clinicians had different criteria and thresholds, the sensitivity and specificity obtained in these studies is quite high, and certainly satisfactory for clinical purposes. In fact, it may well exceed that obtained for several of the personality disorders that have traditionally been included in psychiatric classification systems.

One may question the strength of the cross-validation evidence presented here because it is based on questionnaire data from clinicians of unknown reliability. Although it is possible that the clinicians were simply describing stereotyped patients, it should be remembered that they were asked to describe a specific patient that they knew well, and they were unfamiliar with the composition of the two item sets or with our question as to whether these two independent specific dimensions would emerge. In fact, they were presented with three possible types of borderline when they were asked to provide a clinical subtype diagnosis.

The adequacy of the two item sets is attested to by the sensitivity of each procedure, as well as the relative rarity with which clinicians noted additional behaviors that they thought were of diagnostic significance for making the borderline diagnosis.

We believe we have presented strong evidence that the borderline concept is not unitary, and is best conceptualized as consisting of at least two major dimensions that are relatively independent *within* a borderline group.

If one is primarily interested in contrasting borderline with nonborderline patients, it is possible to use the combined item sets presented here with a high degree of sensitivity and specificity. However, if one is looking for divisions within the borderline group that might be differentially related to important external correlates, such as treatment response and familial psychopathology, then the two item sets are best treated separately. Some borderline patients will undoubtedly meet the criteria for both sets, whereas others will not. This is somewhat analogous to the situation with regard to depressive disorders and anxiety disorders. Whereas most patients with a disturbance of mood experience both anxiety and depression, the separation of depressive disorders from anxiety disorders have proved useful clinically. Although the apparent genetic relationship of schizotypal personality to chronic schizophrenia is still controversial, no such relationship for what we have called unstable personality has been demonstrated. (We applied the unstable item set to the WKR cases and found that they were rarely present. However, it is possible that the interviewers were not asking for or noting such behaviors because they were focusing on mild schizohrenic-like symptoms.) Stone[18] has argued that there is some evidence relating the unstable personality to affective disorder and not schizophrenia. Combining both the schizotypal and the unstable into a single borderline category would interfere with the clarification of these issues, and possibly treatment issues as well.

By asserting that there are two dimensions of the borderline concept, we are not asserting that there are two mutually exclusive borderline types. In fact, the evidence is quite clear that approximately half of the patients considered borderline will meet our criteria for both unstable and schizotyal personality. This may, in part, explain some of the reasons why different lists of borderline features have contained items that are represented in both of our item sets. For example, Gunderson[15] has included both brief paranoid experiences (in our schizotypal item set) and problems tolerating being alone (in our unstable item set) in his proposed operational criteria for diagnosing borderline patients. In using DSM-III, if the patient meets the criteria for both categories, both personality diagnoses should be made. In fact, some patients will, in addition, meet the criteria for other specific personality diagnoses, such as histrionic personality or antisocial personality.

Our impression from having presented the results of this study to various investigators and clinicians is that there is far more agreement about the content of the item lists than there is about the two names that we have suggested. Although the proponents of the borderline schizophrenia concept appear to be satisfied with the term "schizotypal," the investigators and clinicians who have used the borderline personality concept are far from satisfied with the term "unstable personality disorder." They argue that the term "unstable" is a misnomer because the personality is in fact quite stably unstable. They assert that clinicians will never abandon the term "borderline" in favor of the term "unstable."

Schizophrenia and conversion are both examples of terms whose original meaning has little to do with the current conception of the conditions which they name. Similarly, the term "borderline" has been a useful metaphor, indicating that the patient had some features that were sometimes seen in patients with psychoses. It would now appear that the term "schizotypal personality disorder" can be applied to cases that previously have been called borderline schizophrenia, and that the term "borderline personality disorder" can be applied to the other patients previously referred to as borderline. There would thus be no need for the term "unstable personality disorder," even though that term was helpful to us in developing the item set. Thus, the current plan is for the Task Force on Nomenclature and Statistics to recommend that DSM-III contain both schizotypal personality disorder and borderline personality disorder, using the criteria described here.

What needs to be done? Future studies using both item sets and well-trained observers should clarify some of the validity issues that now are unresolved. Genetic studies and treatment response studies with long-term follow-up will help determine if the division made here has practical clinical significance.

REFERENCES

1. Gunderson JG, Singer M.T: Defining borderline patients: An overview. *Am J. Psychiatry* 132:1–9, 1975.
2. Pfeiffer E: Borderline states. *Dis Nerv Sys* 32:212–219,1974.
3. Deutsch H: Some forms of emotional disturbance and their relationship to schizophrenia. *Psychoanal Q* 11:30–321, 1942.
4. Hoch P, Polatin P: Pseudoneurotic forms of schizophrenia. *Psychiatr Q* 23:248–276, 1949.
5. Knight R: Borderline states. *Bull Menninger Clin* 17:1–12, 1953.
6. Kernberg O.: Borderline personality organization. *J. Psychoanal Assoc* 15:641–685, 1967.
7. Grinker RR, Werble B, Drye R.: *The Borderline Syndrome*. New York, Basic Books Inc, 1968.
8. Schmideberg M.: The borderline patient, in Arieti S. (ed): *American Handbook of Psychiatry*. New York, Basic Books Inc, 1959. vol 1, pp 398–416.
9. Perry JC, Klerman GL: The borderline patient: A comparative analysis of four sets of diagnostic criteria. *Arch Gen Psychiatry* 35:141–152, 1978.
10. Mack JE: Borderline states: An historical perspective, in Mack JE (ed): *Borderline States in Psychiatry*. New York, Grune & Stratton Inc, 1975.
11. American Psychiatric Association: *Diagnostic and Statistical Manual of Mental Disorders,* ed 2. Washington, DC. American Psychiatric Association, 1968.
12. Spitzer RL, Sheehy M, Endicott J: DSM-III: Guiding principles, in Rakoff V (ed): *Psychiatric Diagnosis*. New York, Brunner/Mazel Inc, 1977.
13. Kety SS. Rosenthal D, Wender PH, et al: Mental illness in the biological and adoptive families of adopted schizophrenics. *Am J Psychiatry* 128:302–306, 1971.
14. Rosenthal D, Wender PH, Kety SS. et al: The adopted-away offspring of schizophrenics. *Am J Psychiatry* 128:307–311, 1971.
15. Gunderson JG.: Discriminating characteristics of borderlines. Read before the International Conference on Borderline Disorders, Topeka, Kan, March 1976.
16. Fleiss JL: *Statistical Methods for Rates and Proportions*. New York, John Wiley & Sons Inc, 1973.

17. Klein D: Psychopharmacology and the borderline patients, in Mack JE (ed): *Borderline States in Psychiatry*. New York, Grune & Stratton Inc, 1975, pp 75–91.
18. Stone MH: *The Borderline Syndrome: Constitution, Coping and Character*. New York, McGraw-Hill, 1980.

This investigation was supported in part by the American Psychiatric Association's Task Force on Nomenclature and Statistics, by grant 23864 from the National Institute of Mental Health, and by the New York State Department of Mental Hygiene.

Joseph Fleiss, PHD, Jacob Cohen, PhD, and John Nee, PhD, offered statistical consultation. Seymour Kety, MD, Paul Wender MD, David Rosenthal, PhD, Donald Klein, MD, Michael Sheehy, MD, John Gunderson, MD, Lawrence Sharpe, MD, and Michael Stone, MD, as well as Janet Forman, MSW, and Robert Simon, MA assisted in the development of the item pool. Lee Gurel, PhD, director of Membership Services and Studies, American Psychiatric Association, assisted in the distribution of the questionnaire.

23. Borderline: An Adjective in Search of a Noun

Hagop S. Akiskal, Shen E. Chen,
Glenn C. Davis, Vahe R. Puzantian,
Mark Kashgarian, John M. Bolinger

One hundred borderline outpatients prospectively followed over a 6–36 month period were examined from phenomenologic, developmental, and family history perspectives. At index evaluation, 66 met criteria for recurrent depressive, dysthymic, cyclothymic, or bipolar-II disorders, but only 16 for those of schizotypal personality. Other subgroups included sociopathic, somatization, panic-agoraphobic, attention deficit, epileptic and identity disorders. Compared with nonborderline personality controls, borderlines had a significantly elevated risk for major affective but not for schizophrenic breakdowns during follow-up. Prominent substance abuse history, tempestuous biographies and unstable early home environment were common to all diagnostic subgroups. As for family history, borderlines were most like bipolar controls, and significantly different from schizophrenic, unipolar and personality controls. We conclude that despite considerable overlap with subaffective disorders, the current adjectival use of this rubric does not identify a specific psychopathologic syndrome.

The diagnosis of borderline conditions enjoys great clinical popularity in North American psychiatry today. The most prevalent opinion is that they are primitive disorders of developmental origin characterized by an unstable sense of self and low level defensive operations.[1] It is also thought that borderline patients have an unusually high liabilty for transient breaks with reality.[2] Despite criticism by phenomenologically oriented clinical investigators, [3-5] the concept has been introduced into DSM-III. DSM-II had recognized such conditions only as "dilute" or "latent" forms of schizophrenia. In restricting the operational territory of schizophrenia to process or Kraepelinian schizophrenia, DSM-III has now pushed the borderline concept into the domain of personality disorders, where they are listed under two overlapping rubrics: 1) *borderline personality disorder* proper, manifested by such unstable characterologic attributes as impulsivity, drug-seeking, polymorphous sexuality, extreme affective lability, boredom, anhedonia, and bizarre attempts at self-harm; and 2) *schizotypal personality disorder,* the hallmark of which are oddities of communication or perception, and other soft signs of "micropsychosis" typically, though not exclusively, associated with a schizoid existence.

Despite efforts to identify a distinct schizotypal disorder, [6-9] considerable overlap exists between schizotypal, schizoid, and avoidant types. Likewise, borderline patients are not easily discriminable from antisocial and histrionic personality disorders. One is reminded of Mack's suggestion that borderline refers to a personality disorder without a characterologic specialty.[10] Implicit in the DSM-III position is that schizotypal disorders, believed to be on the border of schizophrenia, should be split off from the more nebulous mélange of unstable characterologic attributes constituting borderlines. In line with these developments, recent research exemplified by Stone's work[11] has suggested a shift of the borderline concept from a subschizophrenic to a subaffective disorder. Gunderson, however, who was among the first to attempt to bring operational clarity to this murky psychopathologic area, in recent collaborative work seems to espouse the view that the characterologic pathology of borderline patients is distinct from any concurrent affective episodes.[12] Monroe, who subscribes to the existence of a third (neither schizophrenic nor affective) psychosis related to epilepsy, has postulated "episodic dyscontrol" manisfested by unmodulated affects to be at the core of borderline psychopathology.[13] Kernberg's concept, probably the broadest of all, embraces a wide spectrum of subpsychotic temperamental and polysymptomatic neurotic disorders tied together by identity diffusion and common, primitive defensive operations like splitting, projective identification, while maintaining grossly intact reality testing.[1]

Despite considerable amount of empirical work in the past few years, controversies regarding the nosologic status of borderline conditions have not been resolved: 1) Is borderline a personality disorder? 2) Does it refer to *formes frustes* or interepisodic manifestations of affective, schizophrenic, or epileptic psychoses? 3) Or is it a mode of functioning intermediate between neurosis and psychosis. Several interview sched-ules for a descriptive identification of borderline and schizotypal per-sonality disorders have been developed. Khouri et al, in their attempt to focus on subschizophrenic disorders, have excluded affective symp-toms from their inventory.[7] By contrast, Gunderson et al's diagnostic interview for borderlines (DIB) throws a wider net, which includes circumscribed psychotic, affective, acting out, interpersonal and social areas.[14] Pope et al attempted to validate DIB borderlines by using the Washington University approach to validating psychiatric entities.[12] Soloff and Millward[15] and Loranger et al,[16] who also used the same instrument, focused on the familial aspects of the disorder. Perry and Klerman, using a related instrument, examined the phenomenological features of the disorder.[17] The data from these studies indicate: 1) lack of relationship of the disorder to schizophrenia, 2) failure of discrimi-nation from antisocial and histrionic character disorders; and 3) at least some degree of overlap with primary affective disorder.

Considering the generally confused state of the art in this area, the substantive findings of these studies are quite impressive. Nevertheless, one must bear in mind the following limitations: 1) they are not generally conducted in outpatient settings where the largest number of borderlines are encountered clinically; 2) proband axis I diagnoses and family his-tory were often based on chart review; 3) a control group of bipolar affective disorder was not specifically provided; 4) failure to institute repeated evaluations at follow-up, which minimizes the chances of detecting hypomanic episodes; and 5) the degree of overlap of border-lines with antisocial and histrionic personality disorders could not be estimated in the absence of a control group consisting of such personalities.

We have elsewhere reported preliminary family history and follow-up data suggesting substantial overlap of borderline personality disor-ders with dysthymic and cyclothymic temperaments and atypical bi-polar-II disorder.[18] Our findings were tentative because data collection on control groups had not been completed when our report was pub-lished. In the present article, we attempt to address the methodologic issues raised above and provide comparisons with schizophrenic, bi-polar, unipolar, and personality disorder controls. Furthermore, we explore the possibility that childhood object loss and unstable home environment due to assortative parental psychopathology may form the developmental background of borderline conditions. The overall aim of this exercise is to delineate prospectively the range of psychopathologic conditions for which the adjective "borderline" is currently applicable.

METHODS

Selection of Borderline Probands

One hundred borderline patients were selected from a large pool of *general* psychiatric outpatients by examining *consecutive* admissions in two urban mental health centers. These subjects met at least 5 of the 6 Gunderson-Singer criteria.[2] (This study was conducted prior to the availability of the DIB[14] and, therefore, inclusion of patients into our study was based on the narrative criteria enunciated by Gunderson and Singer). Most probands had extensive psychiatric histories dating back to adolescence or early adulthood. They had been considered complex diagnostic problems by referring clinicians—having been often presented at teaching diagnostic staff conferences—and having received, at various times such dignoses as "borderline" and "mixed" personality disorder, as well as "latent" and "pseudoneurotic" schizophrenia. Although 40% had had one or more psychiatric hospitalizations prior to the index outpatient interview, none had received the diagnosis of a definite affective or schizophrenic disorder.

Control Subjects

Four control groups were selected from consecutive admission in the same outpatient settings: 57 schizophrenic subjects, 50 nonaffective personalities (definite or probable somatization and antisocial), 50 classical (bipolar-I) manic depressives, and 40 episodic major (unipolar) depressives.

Diagnostic Procedures

All probands and control subjects were evaluated in semi-structured diagnostic interviews based on the Washington University Criteria.[19] Because at this writing *DSM-III* is more widely known to practicing psychiatrists, we have translated diagnoses to the corresponding *DSM-III* terms.

All Gunderson-Singer borderline probands also met the DSM-III criteria for borderline personality, but only 16 fully met those for schizotypal personality. Borderline, schizotypal and antisocial personalities were the only Axis II diagnoses used in this study. All other diagnoses were based on Axis I. Since DSM-III does not specifically distinguish hypomania from mania, we found it useful to set the following threshold for hypomania: 1) meeting the symptomatic criteria for mania for at least 2 days; 2) absence of belligerence; 3) no psychotic symptoms; and 4) no hospitalization.

Each proband received principal and, when applicable, concurrent diagnoses. Principal diagnosis refers to the chronologically "primary" or most incapacitating disorder which usually brought the patient to clinical attention. Concurrent diagnoses include all additional diagnoses, which often followed the principal disorder chronologically.

Substance (including ethanol) use disorders were so prevalent in our borderline probands (unsurprisingly, because they are part of the Gunderson-Singer and *DSM-III* defining criteria) that it was more meaningful to consider them independently from descriptive diagnoses. They were classified into three categories: 1) sedative-hypnotic abuse or dependence; 2) alcohol abuse or dependence; and 3) psychedelic (hallucinogen-cannabis-psychostimulant) abuse or dependence.

Follow-up

Patients were seen at 1-8 week intervals (as warranted clinically) and followed over a 6-36 month prospective observation period. Mean duration of follow-up was comparable for study and control groups. Pharmacologic, psychotherapeutic, and sociotherapeutic interventions were provided as deemed clinically appropriate. Schizophreniform, hypomanic, manic, and major depressive episodes, as well as mixed states, were carefully noted during follow-up. Hypomanic responses to antidepressants were considered pharmacologically occasioned if they occurred within 6 weeks after administration of tricylic antidepressants or monoamine oxidase inhibitors.

Criteria for Familial and Developmental Factors

One-third of affected family members were patients in our mental health clinics, one-third were directly interviewed to ascertain their diagnoses and, in the remaining third, diagnostic information was obtained from family members who knew them well based on the Research Diagnostic Criteria—Family History version.[20] Except for familial schizophrenia (which included both first and second-degree relatives), all other family history items refer to *first*-degree biologic relatives. Assortative mating, i.e., where both parents suffered from psychiatric disorders, was noted in particular. Because 3 borderlines were adopted, family history was available for 97 probands only.

Developmental object loss was assessed by the following criteria, modified from Amark:[21] 1) proband born out of wedlock, and parents did not subsequently marry or live together; 2) one or both parents lost by death prior to age 15 years; 3) parents separated or divorced before proband turned 15; 4) proband adopted, or lived in foster homes or orphanages.

Hypotheses

Our main hypotheses is that borderlines are heterogeneous groups of patients who meet specific criteria for more explicit Axis I psychiatric diagnoses. Based on prior work, we also hypothesized that borderlines will show high rates of familial affective (but not of schizophrenic) disorders, and will develop full-blown affective (rather that schizophrenic) breakdowns during prospective follow-up similar to affective but unlike nonaffective controls. Because borderline patients are often considered to have complicated biographies, we wished to test the possibility that increased rates of early separations and broken homes—associated with assortative parental psychopathology—might underlie their character pathlogy.

Statistical Techniques

Except for age distribution which was analyzed by ANOVA, comparisons between groups were made by chi-square analysis, with Yates' correction when appropriate.

RESULTS

Demographic Characteristics

Borderline and control probands were preponderantly fom Hollingshead-Redlich classes III and IV. The mean age at index evaluation was 29 years for borderline probands, 34 for schizophrenics, 30 for nonaf-

Table 1. Family History in Borderlines Compared with
Process Schizophrenic Controls

Family History	Borderline Group (N = 97)		Schizophrenic Controls (N = 57)		χ^2 (df = 1)	P
	N	%	N	%		
Schizophrenia*	3	3	12	21	11.21	<.001
Affective Disorder†	34	35	5	9	11.76	<.001

* Includes first- and second-degree relatives.
† Combines major depressive and bipolar disorders in first-degree relatives.

fective personalities, 38 for the bipolar controls, and 47 for recurrent major depressive controls; these differences in age were not statistically significant. About two-thirds of the subjects in each group were women.

Family History for Schizophrenic and Affective Disorders

As shown in Table 1, borderline probands, when compared with schizophrenic controls, had a significant excess of familial affective disorders and a significantly lower rate of schizophrenia.

Borderlines and control groups did not differ in family history for major depression (Table 2). However, with respect to familial bipolar disorder, borderlines were similar to bipolar controls but significantly different from personality disorder and unipolar controls.

Table 2. Family History for Major Depression and Bipolar
Disorders in Borderline and Control Groups

Family History	Borderline Group (BG) n = 97		Personality Controls (PC) n = 50		Bipolar Controls (BC) n = 50		Unipolar Controls (UC) n = 40	
	N	%	N	%	N	%	N	%
Major depression	17	17.5	5	10	11	22	8	20
Bipolar disorder	17	17.5	1*	2	13	26	1†	3

* BG vs PC, χ^2 (df = 1) = 6.03, p < .02.
† BG vs UC, χ^2 (df = 1) = 4.36, p < .05.

Diagnoses at Index Evaluation

Table 3 provides diagnostic information on the 100 borderline probands at index evaluation. These probands can be categorized into five groups based on principal diagnosis. The largest group (N = 45) is comprised by *affective disorders*, most of which were other than "classic" disorders, i.e., cyclothymic or dysthymic, and atypical (bipolar-II). The next large group is *personality disorders* (N = 21), consisting of probable or definite somatization disorder and antisocial personalities. An almost equal category is the *polysymptomatic neurosis group* (N = 18), consisting of panic, agoraphobic, and obsessive-compulsive disorders. There were 9 patients with *schizotypal personality* and no concurrent disorders. The *organic group* is represented by 2 epileptic patients and 1 with adult (residual) attention deficit disorder. The remaining 4 probands were considered *undiagnosed* at index evaluation; they had some affinity to adolescent identity disorder as defined in *DSM-III*, except that their condition had persisted beyond adolescence, was chronic, and had its basis in a physical factor that could be expected to produce an irreconcilable identity conflict. For example, one subject was an albino girl born to black parents and another was a very intelligent college educated woman with multiple congenital abnormalities and short stature. The profound identity disturbance in these patients was based or realistic anatomic factors.

Also displayed in Table 3, are the concurrent diagnoses given to 37 cases. Of these, secondary or superimposed dysthymia with chronic fluctuating course was the most common (N = 21). Of the remaining patients with multiple diagnoses, 7 met the criteria for schizotypal personality disorder, 2 for epilepsy, 2 for adult (residual) attention deficit disorder, and 5 for somatization, sociopathic, and panic disorders. Patients with multiple concurrent diagnoses were not uncommon, e.g., an agoraphobic woman who suffered from pre-existing somatization disorder and superimposed (secondary) dysthymic disorder.

Substance Use Disorders

Substance abuse/dependence occurred in 55% and was equally distributed across all diagnostic groups (Table 3). Sedative-hypnotics were most frequent (46%), followed by alcohol (21%) and psychedelics (19%).

The sum total exceeds 55%, because many patients abused multiple drugs.

Follow-up Course

As shown in Table 4, major depressive episodes with melancholic features developed in 29 patients; 11 others had brief hypomanic excursions (6 on tricyclic challenge), 4 had manic episodes (1 of which was on tricyclic administration), 8 evolved into mixed affective states (co-existing manic and depressive features). Four patients were known to have committed suicide after dropping out of treatment; their diagnoses ranged from obsessive-compulsive to somatization, schizotypal and epileptic disorders.

Schizophreniform episodes (nonaffective psychotic symptoms that cleared within weeks) occurred in 4 borderlines and 1 personality disorder control. One borderline proband developed full-fledged paranoid schizophrenia, and 2 others (who at follow-up satisfied the Hoch and Polatin description of pseydoneurotic schizophrenia[22]) were classified as chronic undifferentiated type. Thus, 8% of the borderline group developed "schizophrenia-related" disorders (assuming schizopreniform illness is related to schizophrenia) compared with 2% of personality disorder controls (df $= 1$, $X^2 = 1.19$, $.05 < p < .1$). This nonsignificant trend for borderlines to develop schizophrenia-related outcomes should be contrasted with their highly significant liability for affective breakdowns (df $= 1$, $X^2 = 19.18$, $p < .001$).

The link of borderline personality to affective disorder was further strengthened when we examined rates for pharmacologically-occasioned hypomanic switches. Twenty percent of the affective subgroup of borderlines (9 out of 45) and 35% of bipolar controls had such switches as compared with 0% of personality and 2.5% of unipolar controls (df $= 3$, $X^2 = 29.02$, $p < .001$).

As expected, most of the affective episodes occured in those given primary affective diagnoses at index evaluation (26 of 45). It is also noteworthy that 20% of those without primary affective diagnoses developed major affective episodes, including *all* of the 4 completed suicides in this cohort. Schizophreniform episodes were equally distributed in the nonaffective groups, but a chronic schizophrenic

Table 3. Axis I Diagnoses in 100 Borderline Patients at Index Evaluation*

Principal Diagnosis	Concurrent Diagnosis	Substance Use Disorders†
Affective Group (N = 45)		
Recurrent major depression (6)		SH (2)
Dysthymic disorder (14)	Schizotypal disorder (3)	SH (2) A (1) P (1)
Cyclothymic disorder (7)	Somatization disorder (1)	SH (4) P (2) A (1)
(Atypical) bipolar-II disorder (17)	Sociopathy (1) Somatization disorder (1) Residual (adult) attention deficit disorder (1)	SH (4) A (1) P (2)
Personality (N = 21)		
Sociopathy (9)	Residual (adult) attention deficit disorder (1) Schizotypal disorder (1) Temporal lobe epilepsy (1) Dysthymia (3)	SH (8) P (6) A (5)
Somatization disorder (12)	Panic disorder (2) Sociopathy (2) Temporal lobe epilepsy (1) Schizotypal disorder (1) Dysthymia (7)	SH (12) A (2) P (2)

Group	Disorder	Condition†
Polysymptomatic Neurosis Group (N = 18)	Panic and agoraphobic disorders (10)	SH (8)
	Dysthymia (6)	A (2)
	Sociopathy (1)	P (1)
	Somatization disorder (1)	
	Schizotypal disorder (1)	
	Obsessive-Compulsive disorder (8)	SH (1)
	Dysthymia (5)	
	Schizotypal disorder (1)	
Schizotypal Group (N = 9)	Schizotypal disorder (9)	SH (2)
		A (1)
		P (2)
Organic Group (N = 3)	Grand mal epilepsy (1)	A (1)
	Temporal lobe epilepsy (1)	SH (1)
	Residual (adult) attention deficit disorder (1)	P (1)
		A (1)
Undiagnosed Group (N = 4)	"Chronic identity disorder" (4)	A (3)
		P (2)
		SH (2)

* Numbers in parentheses refer to the number of patients with given disorder or condition.
† SH = sedative-hypnotic, A = alcohol, and P = psychedelic abuse or dependence.

Table 4. Prospective Follow-up Outcome in Borderlines and
Nonaffective Personality Disorder Controls

Outcome	Borderline Group (N = 100)		Personality Controls (N = 50)		χ^2 (df = q)	P
	N	%	N	%		
Affective Episodes						
Major Depression	29	29	2	4	11.22	<.001
Hypomania or mania*	15	15	0	0	6.75	<.01
Mixed States*	8	8	0	0	2.79	NS
Suicide	4	4	0	0	0.80	NS
Schizophrenia-related outcome						
Schizophreniform psychosis	5	5	1	2	0.20	NS
Pseudoneurotic schizophrenia	2	2	0	0	0.06	NS
Paranoid Schizophrenia	1	1	0	0	0.13	NS

*Includes full episodes during antidepressant drug administration which did not remit upon reduction of drug dosage and required lithium administration.

denouement was strictly limited to the pure schizotypal group (3 out of 9).

Developmental Object Loss and Parental Assortative Mating

With respect to childhood object loss, borderlines were intermediate between affective and personality controls (Table 5). Borderlines were not different from personality controls on parental assortative mating, but differed significantly from affective controls. Parental units with alcoholism-affective disorder were the most common, followed by alcoholism-sociopathy disorder. These data suggest that many borderlines had "stormy" home environments due to psychiatric disorder in both parents (roughly two-thirds of patients with early breaks in attachment bonds had assortative parental psychopathology) that led to frequent separations, orphanage, or adoption experience.

DISCUSSION

The major finding of the present study is that the borderline rubric encompasses a heterogeneous group of psychopathologic conditions lying predominantly on the border of affective, anxiety, and somatiza-

Table 5. Developmental Factors in Bordeline and Control Groups

History	Borderline Group (BG) N = 100		Primary Affective Controls (PAC) N = 40		Personality Controls (PC) N = 30†		Three Way Comparison		Pairwise Comparisons	
	N	%	N	%	N	%	χ^2	P	Groups	P
Parental Assortative Mating*	40	41*	5	13	14	47	12.29	<.005	BG vs PAC	<.01
									PC vs PAC	<.01
									BG vs PC	NS
Developmental Object Loss	36	37	7	18	18	60	13.46	<.005	BG vs PAC	<.05
									PC vs PAC	<.01
									BG vs PC	<.05

*The computation is based on the biologic parents of 97 probands because of early adoption in 3 borderlines.
† Reliable history available in only 30 of the 50 subjects.

tion-antisocial disorders, and, to a minimal extent that of schizophrenic and organic disorders.

The Affective Border

Our data favor the notion that borderline disorders are located predominantly on the border of affective rather than schizophrenic psychoses. At index evaluation, nearly half the sample met criteria for subaffective disorders, and two-thirds had a strong affective component if concurrent or follow-up episodes are taken into account. The relationship to affective disorder is also supported by high rates of familial affective disorder, especially bipolar illness, and those for pharmacologic hypomania. This latter finding is in line with earlier reports by our group regarding a lowered threshold for pharmacologic hypomania in cyclothymic[23] and dysthymic disorders,[24] and suggests a common neuropharmacologic substrate for subaffective and borderline disorders. The relatively young age of the borderline group is also in keeping with the insidious onset of bipolar disorders in adolescence or early adulthood. Many seem to suffer from life-long affective temperamental disorders—cyclothymia and dysthymia—and make transient shifts into melancholic, hypomanic, manic, and mixed affective episodes, with rapid return to their habitual temperaments. Hence, their diagnosis is best described as borderline *manic-depressive* psychosis. The 20% rate of depressive episodes with melancholic depth—including 4 suicides on follow-up in the 55 borderline probands who were placed into nonaffective subgroups at index evaluation—suggests that the *entire* cohort of borderlines suffers from intense affective arousal. This is not surprising in that 6 of the 8 *DSM-III* criteria for borderline personality are affectively loaded! In brief, the clinical data on the close link between borderline and affective conditions reported here support other findings that have emerged from the application of neuroendocrine[25–27] and sleep electroencelphalographic [18,28,29] techniques to borderlines.

The Border with Anxiety Disorders

This conforms to what in the British literature is described as atypical depression[30] or phobic-anxiety-depersonalization syndrome.[31] Intermittent depression occurs in the context of a chronically anxious multiphobic, usually agoraphobic, illness with spontaneous panic attacks characterized by fears of cardiac catastrophe or total mental collapse and associated helplessness and dependency. The highly idiosyncratic manner in which depersonalization and derealization (as part of a panic attack) are experienced, coupled with strong histrionic or obsessional elements, may *stimulate* bizarre but sort-lived reactive or schizophreniform psychotic episodes. Work by Klein's group suggests that some of these patients may represent affective variants with history of childhood school phobia, dependent and histrionic features in adulthood, and positive response to imipramine or monoamine oxidase inhibitors.[32]

The Schizophrenia Border

Nine percent of our sample appears to lie on a schizophrenia spectrum as identified in the Danish Adoption studies.[7,8] This modest affinity to schizophrenia is evidenced by clinical schizotypal features with familial background for schizophrenia, and progression to "soft" schizophrenic illnesses (schizophreniform and "pseudoneurotic") and even to process schizophrenia in 3 instances. All three patients with chronic schizophrenic denouement on follow-up belonged to this schizotypal group. Seven additional patients, who had other principal diagnoses, also met the criteria for schizotypal disorder. None of these patients had family history for schizophrenia, suggesting that many of the schizotypal features defined in *DSM-III* may be nonspecific accompaniments of chronic psychiatric or affective disorders, and that they have diagnostic value in suggesting a subschizophrenic disorder only when they occur in the *absence* of validated psychiatric disorders.

The Personality Border

This subgroup consists of a spectrum of histrionic and socipathic individuals[4] who have parents with similar or related disorders, who have sustained the tempestuous developmental vicissitudes of unstable parental marriages, and who complain of lifelong intermittent dysphoria. Brief dysphoric psychotic episodes are often precipitated by substance abuse, but may also result from other organic factors described next.

The Organic Border

This very small subgroup in our study is similar to patients described by Androlunis et al in their larger impatient sample of borderline males.[33] These authors suggested that subtle temporal lobe pathology underlies the impulsivity, affective lability, and anger outbursts of some of these patients. Until the nature of this pathology is defined in a more rigorous fashion, it may be preferable to limit the concept of episodic dyscontrol to those who evidence electroencephalographic findings of a seizure disorder or show unequivocal response to anti-convulsant medication such as carbamazepine.

The Nature of Micropsychotic Episodes

Our data suggest that schizophreniform episodes are the exception in borderline patients. Grandiose or irritable forms of hypomania—which are sometimes mobilized by antidepressant treatment—as well as depressive delusions are more common. Drug-induced psychoses (i.e., secondary to ethanol, sedative-hypnotic, psychedelic and stimulant abuse, or withdrawal states) represent another plausible explanation for micropsychotic episodes. Finally, depersonalization, derealization, and brief reactive psychoses, which are not uncommon in panic, sociopathic and somatization disorders, could easily simulate schizophreniform symptomatology.

The Origin of Character Pathology

Borderline patients appear to suffer from early breaks in attachment bonds largely because of assortative parental psychopathology. In this respect they seem intermediate between nonaffective personality disorder and unipolar affective controls. There is some evidence that among the affective disorders, history of assortative parental psychopathology is most common in bipolar II disorders.[34] Such findings strengthen the link between borderline and atypical bipolar disorders. More importantly, our findings suggest that borderline probands are at a double disadvantage: they may inherit the illnesses of one or both parents, and may develop exquisite vulnerability to adult object loss as a result of the tempestuous early home environment. As stated in

Bowlby's latest formulations,[35] childhood object loss may not predispose to affective disorder *per se*, but to character-based affective expressions. Since loss of parents is not an uncommon experience in the early life history of affective probands,[36] their adult affective illnesses can be complicated by separation-related characterologic disturbances, similar to the hysteroid dysphoric women described by Liebowitz and Klein.[37] It is also likely that when one parent has affective disorder, the other a sociopathic or somatization disorder, the progeny may inherit both illnesses and thereby exhibit manifestations of both disorders—affective and characterologic. Another possible source of characterologic pathology in "borderline" disorders like cyclothymia or bipolar-II is in the hinderance to optimal ego maturation due to the high-frequency episodes beginning in early adolescence.[18] Indeed, in an adolescent sample studied at Cornell, borderline personality disturbances generally *followed* affective episodes.[38] Thymoleptic therapy or long-term lithium stabilization can bring many such patients to a level of ego stability that had not been achieved in years of psychotherapy and nonspecific pharmacotherapy.[39] However, this outcome is not universal, suggesting that maladaptive personality patterns may become irreversible after many years of inadequately treated affective disorders. The reversibility of "conduct disorders" in depressed children treated with thymoleptics illustrates the importance of early energetic and specific pharmacologic therapies in preventing post-depressive personality disturbances.[40] In brief, the characterologic disturbances of borderline patients sometimes represent *primary* character pathology but more often are *secondary* to an affective disorder or concurrent to such a disorder (i.e., to be coded on an axis orthogonal to the phenomenologic diagnosis).

Lack of Predictive Utility

Borderline conditions emerge as an enormously heterogeneous group of disorders that embrace the entire gamut of psychopathology. Proportions of specific subtypes in different studies are probably a function of the different populations sampled. Borderline conditions do not seem to represent a definable personality type, and, therefore, they don't belong on DSM-III's axis II. We suggest that the potential utility of the concept might be explored on a distinct psychodynamic axis. Despite an unwieldy degree of diagnostic heterogeneity, the concept may still prove useful in setting the stage for a psychotherapeutic intervention geared to the common developmental vicissitudes and ego functioning of patients with certain low level defenses best described in Kernberg's work.[1]

Yet it would seem that the very heterogeneity of disorders within the borderline realm argues against a unitary therapeutic modality. For instance, if the clinician were to consider pharmacologic approaches, one could make the case for tricyclics, MAO inhibitors. lithium carbonate, neuroleptics, stimulants, anticonvulsants—as well as avoidance of pharmacotherapy for the various subtypes.

In summary, the current nosologic use of the concept of borderline seems to map a large universe of chronically and seriously ill "difficult" patients outside the area of the "classical" psychoses and neuroses.[41] It is necessary to look beyond the characterologic "masks" in order to appreciate the phenomenologic diversity of these conditions. A specific personality type or psychopathologic entity as the proper noun for the borderline adjective has not been found yet. Not is it likely to be found because, similar to the imprecise adjectival use of terms like "neurotic" and "psychotic," it has no place in modern descriptive psychopathology; there are simply too many neurotic and psychotic conditions which render futile all descriptive efforts to identify a specific "border."[5,41] In a very literal sense then borderline personality can be considered to be a borderline diagnosis.

REFERENCES

1. Kernberg OF: Structural interviewing. Psychiatr Clin North Am 4:169–195, 1981.
2. Gunderson JG and Singer MT: Defining borderline patients: An overview. Am J Psychiatry 132:1–10, 1975.
3. Klein D: Psychopharmacology and the borderline patient. In Mack J (ed): Borderline States in Psychiatry. New York, Grune & Stratton, 1975.
4. Guze SB: Differential diagnosis of the borderline patient, in Mack JE (ed): Borderline States in Psychiatry. New York, Grune & Stratton, Inc, 1975.
5. Rich CL: Borderline diagnoses. AM J Psychiatry 135:1399–1401, 1978.
6. Spitzer R, Endicott J, Gibbon M: Crossing the border into borderline personality and borderline schizophrenia: The development of criteria. Arch Gen Psychiatry 36:17–24, 1979.
7. Khouri PJ, Haier RJ, Rieder RO et al: A symptom schedule for the diagnosis of borderline schizophrenia: A first report. Br J Psychiatry 137:140–147, 1980.
8. Kendler KS, Gruenberg AM, Strauss JS: An independent analysis of the Copen-

hagen sample of the Danish adoption study of schizophrenia: II. The relationship between schizotypal personality disorder and schizophrenia. Arch Gen Psychiatry 38:928–987, 1981.

9. Siever LJ and Gunderson JG: The search for a schizotypal personality: Historical origins and current status. Compr Psychiatry 24:199–212, 1983.

10. Mack JE: Borderline states: An historical perspective, in Mack JE (ed): Borderline States in Psychiatry. New York, Grune & Stratton Inc, 1975.

11. Stone MH: The Borderline Syndrome: Constitution, Personality, and Adaptation. New York, McGraw-Hill Book Co, 1980.

12. Pope HG, Jones JM, Hudson JI, Cohen MB, Gunderson GJ: The validity of DSM-III Borderline personality disorder. Arch Gen Psychiatry 40:23–30, 1983.

13. Monroe RR: Episodic Behavioral Disorders. Cambridge, Harvard University Press, 1970.

14. Gunderson JG, Kolb JE and Austin V: The diagnostic interview for borderline patients. Am J Psychiatry 138:896–903, 1981.

15. Soloff PH, Millward JW: Psychiatric disorders in the families of borderline patients. Arch Gen Psychiatry 40:37–44, 1983.

16. Loranger AW, Oldham JM, Tulis EH: Familial transmission of DSM-III borderline personality disorder. Arch Gen Psychiatry 39:795–799, 1982.

17. Perry JC, Klerman GL: Clinical features of the borderline personality disorder. Am J Psychiatry 137:167–173, 1980.

18. Akiskal HS: Subaffective disorders: Dysthymic cyclothymic, and bipolar II disorders in the "borderline" realm. Psychiatr Clin North Am 4:25–46, 1981.

19. Feighner JP, Robins E, Guze SB, et al: Diagnostic criteria for use in psychiatric research. Arch Gen Psychiatry 26:57–63, 1972.

20. Andreasen NC, Endicott J, Spitzer RL, et al: The family history method using diagnostic criteria—Reliability and validity. Arch Gen Psychiatry 34:1229–1235, 1977.

21. Amark C: A study in alcoholism. Acta Psychiatr Neurol Scand 70 (Suppl), 1951.

22. Hoch P and Polatin P: Pseudoneurotic forms of schizophrenia. Psychiatr Q 23:248–276, 1949.

23. Akiskal HS, Djenderedjian AH, Rosenthal RH, Khani MK: Cyclothymic disorder: Validating criteria for inclusion in the bipolar affective group. Am J Psychiatry 134:1227–1233, 1977.

24. Akiskal HS: Dysthymic disorder: Psychopathology of proposed chronic depressive subtypes. Am J Psychiatry 140:11–20, 1983.

25. Carroll BJ, Greden JF, Feinberg M, et al: Neuroendocrine evaluation of depression in borderline patients. Psychiatr Clin North Am 4:89–99, 1981.

26. Garbutt JC, Loosen PT, Tipermas A, Prange AJ: The TRH test in patients with borderline personality disorders. Psychiatry Res 9:107–113, 1983.

27. Baxter L, Edell W, Gerner R and Fairbanks L: Dexamethasone suppression test and axis I diagnoses of inpatients with DSM-III borderline personality disorder. J Clin Psychiatry 45:150–153, 1984.

28. Bell J. Lycaki H, Jones D, Kelwala S, Sitaram N: Effect of preexisting borderline personality disorder on clinical and EEG sleep correlates of depression. Psychiatry Res 9:115–123, 1983.

29. McNamara ME, Reynolds CF, Soloff FH, Mathias R, Rossi A, Spiker D, Cobles PA and Kupfer DJ: EEG sleep evaluation of depression in borderline patients. Am J Psychiatry 141:182–186, 1984.

30. West ED and Dally PJ: Effect of Iproniazid in depressive syndromes. Br Med J 1:2491–2494, 1959.

31. Roth M: The phobic-anxiety-depersonalization syndrome. Proc Roy Soc Med 52:587–595, 1959.
32. Klein DF, Gittleman R, Quitkin F and Rifkin A: Diagnosis and Drug Treatment of Psychiatric Disorder: Adult and children, 2nd ed. Baltimore, Williams & Wilkins.
33. Andrulonis PA, Glueck BC, Stroebel CF, et al: Borderline personality subcategories. J Nerv Ment Dis 170:670–679, 1982.
34. Dunner DL, Fleiss JL, Addonizio G, and Fieve RR: Assortative mating in primary affective disorder. Biol Psychiatry 11:43–51, 1976.
35. Bowlby J: The making and breaking of affectional bonds: L. Aetiology and psychopathology in the light of attachment theory. Br J Psychiatry 130:201–210, 1977.
36. Akiskal HS, Tashjian R: Affective disorders: Part II. Recent advances in laboratory and pathogenetic approaches. Hosp Community Psychiatry 34:822–830, 1983.
37. Liebowitz MR, Klein DF: Hysteroid dysphoria. Psychiatr Clin North Am 2:555–575, 1979.
38. Friedman RC, Clarkin JF, Corn R, et al: DSM-III and affective pathology in hospitalized adolescents. J Nerv Ment Dis 170:511–521, 1982.
39. Akiskal HS, Khani MK, Scott-Strauss A: Cyclothymic temperamental disorders. Psychiatr Clin North AM 2:527–554, 1979.
40. Kroll J, Sines L, Martin K, et al: Borderline personality disorder. Construct validity of the concept. Arch Gen Psychiatry 38:1021–1026, 1981.
41. Dickes R: The concept of borderline states: An alternative proposal. Int J Psychoanal Psychother 3:1–27, 1974.

References

Aarkrog, T., (1981). "The Borderline Concept in Childhood, Adolescence and Adulthood." *Acta Psych. Scand.*, Suppl. 293, Vol. 64.

Abrahamson, D. (1980). The borderline syndrome and affective disorders: A comment on the Wolf-Man. *Schiz. Bull.* 6:549–551.

Andrulonis, P.A., et al. (1981). Organic brain dysfunction and the borderline syndrome. *Psy. Clin. N. Am.* 4:47–66.

Battegay, R. (1981). *Grenzsituationen*. Bern: Verlag Hans Huber.

Bergeret, J. (1975). *La Depression et les Etats Limites*. Paris: Payot.

Bourgeois, M. (1980). Les états-limites borderlines. *Bordeaux Méd.* 13:1295–1304.

Buie, D.H. and Adler, G. (1982). Definitive treatment of the borderline personality. *Internat. J. Psychoan. Psychother.* 9:51–87.

Bychowski, G. (1928). Ueber Psychotherapie der Schizophrenie. *Nervenarzt.* 1:478–487.

Carpenter, W.T., Jr., Gunderson, J.G., and Strauss, J.S. (1977). Considerations of the borderline syndrome: a longitudinal and comparative study of borderline and schizophrenic patients. In Hartocollis, P. (ed.). *Borderline Personality Disorders*. NY: Int. Univ. Press, pp. 231–253.

Clark, L.P. (1919). Some remarks upon the use of modified psychoanalysis in the treatment of borderland neuroses and psychoses. *Psychoanal. Rev.* 6:306–308.

Collum, J.L. (1972). Identity diffusion and the borderline manuever. *Comprehen. Psychiat.* 13:179–184.

Diagnostic and Statistical Manual (DSM)-III. Washington, D.C.: Amer. Psychiat. Assoc. 1980.

Easser, R.R., and Lesser, S. (1965). Hysterical personality: a reevaluation. *Psychoan. Q.* 34:390–402.

Falret, J. (1890). Etudes Cliniques sur les Maladies Mentales. Paris: Baillière.

Fard, K., Hudgens, R.W., and Welner, A. (1978). Undiagnosed psychiatric illness in adolescents. *Arch. Gen. Psychiat.* 35:279–282.

Gidro-Frank, L., Peretz, D., Spitzer, R.L., and Winikus, W., (1967). A five-year follow up of male patients hospitalized at Psychiatric Institute. *Psychiat. Q.* 41:1–34.

Giovacchini, P.L., and Bryce Boyer, L. (eds.). (1982). *Technical Factors in the Treatment of the Severely Disturbed Patient*. NY: Aronson.

Greenacre, P. (1941). The predisposition to anxiety. Part II. *Psychoan. Q.* 10:610–638.

Gunderson, J.G. (1985). Borderline personality disorder and affective disorder. *Am. J. Psychiat.* 142:277–288.

Hartmann, E. (1982). From the biology of dreaming to the biology of the mind. *Psychoan. Study of the Child* 37:303–335.

Kernberg, O.F. (1982). The theory of psychoanalytic psychotherapy. In Slipp, S.C. (ed.). *Curative Factors in Dynamic Psychotherapy* N.Y.: McGraw-Hill, pp. 21–43.

Klein, D. (1977). Psychopharmacological treatment and delineation of borderline disorders. In Hartocollis, P. (ed.). *Borderline Personality Disorders*. NY: Int. Univ. Press, pp. 365–383.

Kwawer, J.S., Lerner, H.D., Lerner, P.M. and Sugarman, A. (1980). *Borderline Phenomena and the Rorschach Test*. NY: Int. Univ. Press.

LeBoit, J., and Capponi, A. (eds.) (1979). *Advances in Psychotherapy of the Borderline Patient*. NY: Aronson.

Liebowitz, M., and Klein, D. (1981). Interrelationship of hysteroid dysphoric and borderline personality. *Psy. Clin. N. Am.* 4:67–88.

Little, M. (1966). Transference in borderline states. *Internat. J. Psychoanal.* 47:476–485.

Mack, J.E. (1975). *Borderline States in Psychiatry*. NY: Grune & Stratton.

Mavissakalian, M.R. (1984). Agoraphobia: behavioral therapy and pharmacotherapy. In Beitman, B.D., and Klerman, G.L. (eds). *Combining Psychotherapy and Drug Therapy in Clinical Practice*. Englewood Cliffs, N.J.: Prentice-Hall, Inc. Spectrum Publ., pp. 187–211.

McGlashan, T.H. (1984). The Chestnut-Lodge follow-up study. Parts I and II. *Arch. Gen. Psychiat.* 41:573–585; 586–601.

Meissner, W.W. (1984). *The Borderline Spectrum*. NY: Aronson.

Moore, T.V. (1921). The parataxes. A study and analysis of certain borderline mental states. *Psychoanalytic Review* 8:252–275.

Ostwald, P., (1985). *Schumann: The Inner Voices of a Musical Genius*. Boston: Northeastern Univ. Press.

Paykel, E.S. (1982). *Handbook of Affective Disorders*. NY: Guilford.

Perry, J.C., and Klerman, G.L. (1978). The borderline patient. *Arch. Gen. Psychiat.* 35:141–150.

Pope, H.G. et al. (1983). The validity of DSM-III borderline personality disorder. *Arch. Gen. Psychiat.* 40:23–30.

Rado, S. (1956). *The Psychoanalysis of Behavior*. N.Y.: Grune & Stratton.

Robson, K.S. (ed.) (1983). *The Borderline Child*. N.Y.: McGraw-Hill.

Sass, H., and Koehler, K. (1983). Borderline-Syndrome: Grenzgebiet oder Niemansland? *Nervenarzt*. 53:221–230.

Searles, H.F. (1979). *Countertransference*. NY: Internat. Univ. Press.

Serban, G., and Siegel, S. (1984). Response of borderline and schizotypal patients to small doses of thiothixene and haloperidol. *Amer. J. Psychiat.* 141:1455–1458.

Snyder, S., et al. (1982). MMPI Profile of DSM-III borderline personality disorder. *Amer. J. Psychiat.* 139:1046–1048.

Stone, M.H. (1979/80). Dreams of fragmentation and of the death of the dreamer. *Psychopharm. Bulletin.* 15:12–14.

Stone, M.H. (1980). *The Borderline Syndromes* NY:McGraw-Hill

Stone, M.H. (1981). *Borderline Disorders*. Vol. 4. *Psych. Clin. N. Am.* Philadelphia: Saunders.

Stone, M. (1981). Borderline syndromes. *Psych. Clin. N. Am.* 4:3–24.

Timsit, M. (1971). Les états-limites: évolution des concepts. *Evolution Psychiatrique*. 36:679–724.

Vaillant, G.E. (1963). The natural history of remitting schizophrenia. *Amer. J. Psychiat.* 120:367–375.

Vanggaard, T. (1979). *Borderlands of Sanity*. Copenhagen: Munksgaard

Name Index

Subject Index

feeling of, 265, 268
relationships with 265, 268, 271
Reality principle, 190
Reality testing capacity, 49, 266, 269, 467
  in "as-if" patients, 88
  in interpersonal relations, 55, 64 ff.
  in pseudoneurotic schizophrenia, 124
Regression, 174
  in pseudoneurotic schizophrenia, 125
  strong tendency toward, in border-
    lines, 456
  therapeutic, 396
Relationships, interpersonal, 468
Religion,
  preoccupation with, 38
R.E.M. (Rapid Eye Movement) latency,
  425
Resiliency,
  lowered, in borderline cases, 57
Reversibility of psychosis, 266, 274
Reviews of the borderline literature, 430
"Rigid personality," 55, 58 ff.
Rorschach test, 465
  in pseudoneurotic schizophrenia, 125

Sadomasochism, 124
Sadomasochistic character, 293
Schizo-adaptation, decompensated,
  equivalent of "pseudoneurotic schizo-
    phrenia," 261
Schizoaffective illness, 46
Schizoid patients, 282, 386
Schizoid personality, 90
  in a borderline patient, 93, 94
"Schizoid position" (Guntrip), 151
Schizophrenia, 176
  absence of relationship to, of DSM-III
    borderlines, 551
  ambulatory, 160
  and "as-if" personality, 74 ff., 89
  borderline, 9
  and borderline states, 160
  chronic, diagnosis of, 369
  hereditary factor, 357 ff.
  incipient (as borderline state), 170
  low incidence in borderlines, at follow-
    ups, 352
  pseudoneurotic, 51, 119–147
  pseudopsychopathic, 263

relationship to borderline conditions,
  50, 92, 149, 457, 482 ff.
similarity to, during free association, in
  borderlines, 167
Schizophrenia spectrum, 371
Schizotypal,
  item set, 529
Schizotypal disorders, 245, 249–261
Schizotypal personality, 9, 48, 287
  on continuum with schizophrenia, 126
Schizotype
  as schizophrenic phenotype, 250
Schumann, R.,
  as "borderline case," 10
"Secondary" process,
  development of, 190
Self-destructiveness, 294, 461
Self-images, 188
Self-mutilation, 470
Self-object differentiation, 300
Self-representation, 174 ff.
  blurring in borderline states, 180
Sensation-seeking, 83, 422
Separation,
  fear of, 194
Separation anxiety, 438
Separation-individuation, 433–452
  phase of, 412
Sex differences,
  in populations of borderline patients,
    544
Sexual inhibition, 290
Sexual overstimulation,
  as etiological factor, 412
Sexual provocativeness, 290
Sexuality,
  infantile, normal development, 190
  polymorphous-perverse, 286
Shallowness, 224
  in "as-if," 75
Shoplifting, 422
Sleep abnormalities, 425
Socialization,
  superficial, 460
Sociopathy
  as borderline case, 6
Soothing,
  need for in borderlines, 422
Splitting, 282, 440, 500